FAMILY DELUXE EDITION

THE NEW TESTAMENT MADE EASIER

VOLUME 1

MATTHEW, MARK, LUKE, & JOHN

FAMILY DELUXE EDITION

— THE NEW — TESTAMENT MADE EASIER

VOLUME 1

MATTHEW, MARK, LUKE, & JOHN

DAVID J. RIDGES

CFI

SPRINGVILLE, UTAH

PRESENTED TO

NAME

DATE

Vol. 1 ISBN: 978-1-4621-1474-0

Set ISBN: 978-1-4621-1476-4

Published by CFI, an imprint of Cedar Fort, Inc., 2373 W. 700 S., Springville, UT 84663
Distributed by Cedar Fort, Inc., www.cedarfort.com

THE LIBRARY OF CONGRESS HAS CATALOGUED VOLUME 1 OF THE PAPERBACK EDITION AS FOLLOWS:

Bible. N.T. English. Authorized. 2007.
The New Testament made easier / by David J. Ridges.—Rev. 2nd ed.
p. cm.
ISBN-13: 978-1-59955-000-8
1. Bible. N.T.—Criticism, interpretation, etc. I. Ridges, David J. II. Title.

BS1852003 .S6 2007
225.5'2034--dc22

2006034116

Designed and typeset by Shawnda T. Craig

Edited by Kevin Haws

Printed in China

10 9 8 7 6 5 4 3 2 1

Printed on acid-free paper

Contents

BOOKS BY DAVID J. RIDGES

The Gospel Study Series:

- *Your Study of The Book of Isaiah Made Easier, Second Edition*
- *The New Testament Made Easier, Part 1 (Second Edition)*
- *The New Testament Made Easier, Part 2 (Second Edition)*
- *Your Study of The Book of Mormon Made Easier, Part 1*
- *Your Study of The Book of Mormon Made Easier, Part 2*
- *Your Study of The Book of Mormon Made Easier, Part 3*
- *Book of Mormon Made Easier, Family Deluxe Edition, Vols. 1 and 2*
- *Your Study of The Doctrine and Covenants Made Easier, Part 1*
- *Your Study of The Doctrine and Covenants Made Easier, Part 2*
- *Your Study of The Doctrine and Covenants Made Easier, Part 3*
- *The Old Testament Made Easier—Selections from the Old Testament, Part 1, Second Edition*
- *The Old Testament Made Easier—Selections from the Old Testament, Part 2, Second Edition*
- *The Old Testament Made Easier—Selections from the Old Testament, Part 3, Second Edition*
- *Your Study of the Pearl of Great Price Made Easier*
- *Your Study of Jeremiah Made Easier*
- *Your Study of The Book of Revelation Made Easier, Second Edition*

- *Our Savior, Jesus Christ: His Life and Mission to Cleanse and Heal*
- *Mormon Beliefs and Doctrines Made Easier*
- *The Proclamation on the Family: The Word of the Lord on More Than 30 Current Issues*
- *65 Signs of the Times and the Second Coming*
- *Doctrinal Details of the Plan of Salvation: From Premortality to Exaltation*
- *Using the Signs of the Times to Strengthen Your Testimony*

FOREWORD

IN OVER 45 years of teaching in the Church and for the Church Educational System, I have found that members of the Church encounter some common problems when it comes to understanding the scriptures. One problem is understanding the language of the scriptures themselves. Another is understanding symbolism. Another common concern is how best to mark their own scriptures and perhaps make brief notes in them. Yet another concern is how to understand what the scriptures are actually teaching. In other words, what are the major messages being taught by the Lord through His prophets?

This book is designed to address each of the concerns mentioned above. One of my objectives in these "Teacher in Your Hand" Gospel Studies Series books is to teach the language of the scriptures. Many Latter-day Saints struggle with the beautiful language of the scriptures. There is a special Spirit that attends it. The Brethren use it often to bring us the word of God, matched to our exact needs by the Holy Ghost. Therefore, I add brackets on occasion within the verses, for the purpose of defining difficult scriptural terms. I hope that as you read and study this work, you will get to the point that you do not need these definitions in brackets anymore. When that happens, please be patient because others may still need them.

The format is intentionally simple, with some license taken with respect to capitalization and punctuation in order to minimize interruption of the flow. It is intended to help readers to

- Quickly gain a basic understanding of these scriptures as they read, through the use of brief explanatory notes in brackets within the verses as well as occasional notes between verses. This paves the way for even deeper testimony and understanding later.
- Better understand the beautiful language of the scriptures. This is accomplished in this book with in-the-verse notes that define difficult terms.
- Mark their scriptures and put brief notes in the margins that will help them understand now and remember later what particular passages of scripture teach.
- Better understand symbolism.

Over the years, one of the most common expressions of gratitude from my students has been "Thanks for the notes you had us put in our scriptures." This book is dedicated to that purpose. Sources for the notes given in this work are as follows:

- The standard works of The Church of Jesus Christ of Latter-day Saints.
- Footnotes in the Latter-day Saint version of the King James Bible.
- The Joseph Smith Translation of the Bible.
- The Bible Dictionary in the back of our Bible.
- Various dictionaries.
- Various student manuals provided for our institutes of religion.
- Other sources as noted in the text and in the "Sources" section.

I hope that this study guide will serve effectively for members of the Church, as well as others, as they seek to increase their understanding of the writings and teachings contained in these portions of the Bible, specifically the New Testament. Above all, if this work serves to bring increased understanding and testimony of the Atonement of Christ, all the efforts to put it together will have been far more than worth it. A special thanks goes to my wife, Janette, and to my daughters and sons, who have encouraged me every step of the way.

DAVID J. RIDGES

COLOR CODE USED IN THIS BOOK

- (black) New Testament Text
- (brown) Background Commentary
- (dark blue) Commentary Within Verses
- (green) Commentary Between Verses
- (purple) Text from Other Sources

THE JST

(The Joseph Smith Translation of the Bible)

References Used in Study Guides by David J. Ridges

Be aware that some of the JST references I use in my study guides are not found in the footnotes nor in the JST section at the back of our LDS edition of the King James Bible (the one we use in the English-speaking part of the Church). The reason for this, as explained to me some years ago while writing curriculum materials for the Church, is simply that there is not enough room, for practical purposes, to include all of the JST additions and changes. As you can imagine, as was likewise explained to me, there were difficult decisions that had to be made by the Scriptures Committee and Church leaders as to which JST contributions were included and which were not.

The Joseph Smith Translation of the Bible in its entirety can generally be found in LDS bookstores or ordered through them. It was originally published under the auspices of the Reorganized Church of Jesus Christ of Latter Day Saints in Independence, Missouri. The version of the JST that I prefer to use is a parallel column version, entitled, Joseph Smith's "New Translation" of the Bible, published by Herald Publishing House, Independence, Missouri, in 1970. This parallel column version compares the King James Bible with the JST side by side and includes only the verses that have changes, additions, or deletions made by the Prophet Joseph Smith.

By the way, some members of the Church have wondered whether we can trust the JST since it was published by a breakaway faction from our church who retained the original manuscripts after the martyrdom of the Prophet Joseph Smith. They worry that some changes to the Prophet's original manuscript might have been made to support doctrinal differences between the RLDS Church (the Reorganized Church of Jesus Christ of Latter Day Saints) and us. This is not the case. Many years ago, Robert J. Matthews of the Brigham Young University Religion Department was teaching a summer school class I attended. He told us that he was given permission by leaders of the RLDS Church to come to their Independence, Missouri, headquarters to see their publication of the JST. Brother Matthews was thus able to verify that they had been meticulously true to the Prophet's original work.

THE GOSPEL ACCORDING TO ST MATTHEW

THE JST (JOSEPH Smith Translation of the Bible) calls this "The Testimony of St. Matthew." The Gospel of Matthew was written by the Apostle Matthew. He was sometimes called Levi (Mark 2:14; Luke 5:27). He lived in Capernaum, in Galilee, and worked as a tax collector, or "publican" until he was called by the Savior to follow Him. Matthew wrote primarily to a Jewish audience. In order to appeal to the Jews, who placed great emphasis on the Old Testament, he placed particular emphasis on how the Savior's life fulfilled Old Testament prophecy. For more information about Matthew, see Bible Dictionary (in the back section of your Bible), under "Matthew."

You will often see words in italics in the King James Version of the Bible. King James, of England, assembled a group of scholars to make a new translation of the Bible. It was completed in A.D. 1611. We will quote from the Bible Dictionary as it explains this use of italics:

Bible Dictionary—Italics

"In the KJV, italics identify words that are necessary in English to round out and complete the sense of a phrase, but were not present in the Hebrew or Greek text of the manuscript used. Such additions were necessary because in some instances the manuscript was inadequate, and the translators felt obliged to clarify it in the translation. In other instances italics were necessary in cases where the grammatical construction of English called for the use of words that were not needed to make the same thought in Hebrew or Greek. Italics thus represent the willingness of the translators to identify these areas. It appears that generally, though not always, their judgment was justified in their choice of italicized words."

As we study this portion of the New Testament, we will use bold to emphasize certain things for teaching purposes. They are generally the kinds of things I emphasized to my students during my thirty-five plus years of teaching in the Church Educational System. You may wish to underline or otherwise mark some of these bolded words and phrases in your own scriptures.

We will include several changes made in the JST (the Joseph Smith Translation of the Bible). You will find many of them in your English edition of the LDS Scriptures by way of footnotes. However, since all JST changes and additions are not included in our Bible, because of space limitations, you will see that we have included some which are not in your Bible. If you would like to, you could purchase a copy of the complete JST at almost any LDS bookstore. One other thing that you will notice is that the verse numbers of the JST are often different than those of the King James Version of the Bible. This is because the Prophet Joseph Smith often added missing information and corrected things as needed.

MATTHEW 1

1 **The book of the generation** [*genealogy*] **of Jesus Christ**, the son of [*descendant of*] David, the son of [*who was a descendant of*] Abraham.

The genealogy of Christ, given by Matthew, is the legal successors to the throne of David, not a strict father-to-son genealogy. It includes living successors such as grandson, nephew, etc. Luke's genealogy of the Savior, as given in Luke 3:23–38, is a strict father-to-son genealogy. Since Joseph and Mary were cousins (see *New Testament Student Manual*, p. 22), Joseph's genealogy is essentially Mary's genealogy and thus, the Savior's.

We will use **bold** to point out the genealogy as given by Matthew.

2 **Abraham** begat [*was the father of*] **Isaac**; and Isaac begat **Jacob**; and Jacob begat **Judas** [*Judah—see Genesis 29:35*] and his brethren;

3 And Judas begat **Phares** and Zara of Thamar; and Phares begat **Esrom**; and Esrom begat **Aram**;

4 And Aram begat **Aminadab**; and Aminadab begat **Naasson**; and Naasson begat **Salmon**;

5 And Salmon begat **Booz** [*Boaz, Ruth's husband—see Ruth 4:13*] of Rachab; and Booz begat **Obed** of Ruth; and Obed begat **Jesse** [*King David's father*];

You've no doubt noticed that some of the names here are spelled differently than you are used to from the Old Testament. What is happening here is that the New Testament is using Greek forms of the names, which sometimes differ from the Hebrew. Thus, Ruth's husband, Boaz, is listed here (in verse 5, above) as "Booz," and Judah was listed as "Judas" (in verses 2 and 3, above).

6 And Jesse begat **David** the king; and David the king begat **Solomon** of her [*Bathsheba*] that had been the wife of Urias;

7 And Solomon begat **Roboam**; and Roboam begat **Abia**; and Abia begat **Asa**;

8 And Asa begat **Josaphat**; and Josaphat begat **Joram**; and Joram begat **Ozias**;

9 And Ozias begat **Joatham**; and Joatham begat **Achaz**; and Achaz begat **Ezekias**;

10 And Ezekias begat **Manasses**; and Manasses begat **Amon**; and Amon begat **Josias**;

11 And Josias begat **Jechonias** and his brethren, about the time they were carried away to Babylon:

12 And after they were brought to Babylon, Jechonias begat **Salathiel**; and Salathiel begat **Zorobabel**;

13 And Zorobabel begat **Abiud**; and Abiud begat **Eliakim**; and Eliakim begat **Azor**;

14 And Azor begat **Sadoc**; and Sadoc begat **Achim**; and Achim begat **Eliud**;

15 And Eliud begat **Eleazar**; and Eleazar begat **Matthan**; and Matthan begat **Jacob**;

16 And Jacob begat **Joseph the husband of Mary**, of whom was born **Jesus**, who is called Christ [*Greek: the "Anointed One"*].

The JST adds "as the prophets have written, who is called Christ" to verse 16, above. We know, of course, that Jesus was literally the Son of God, not the son of Joseph. In tracing this genealogy, Matthew points out that Joseph, the Savior's wonderful stepfather, would have been the political king of the Jewish nation at this time if the Romans had not been in power. And Joseph's legal successor to the crown would have been Jesus. See *Jesus the Christ*, p. 87.

17 So all the generations from Abraham to David are fourteen generations; and from David until the carrying away into Babylon are fourteen generations; and from the carrying away into Babylon unto Christ are fourteen generations.

Next, Matthew summarizes the birth of the Savior. Many people use the word "engaged" to explain "espoused," as used in verse 18, next. Among the Jews, being espoused was a much more serious obligation than our "engagement." During the espousal period, the bride-to-be lived with her family or friends, and communication between her and her husband-to-be was carried on by a friend.

18 ¶ **Now the birth of Jesus Christ was on this wise** [*happened this way*]: When as his mother **Mary was espoused to Joseph**, before they came together [*before they married and had intimate relations*], **she was found with child of the Holy Ghost.**

In Jewish culture at this time, an unmarried woman found to be expecting a child was subject to being stoned to death.

19 **Then Joseph her husband, being a just** [*righteous; fair; strict in truly living the gospel*] **man**, and not willing to make her a publick example [*which would protect his own reputation, but could subject Mary to humiliation and even execution by stoning*], **was minded to put her away privily** [*privately, so as to avoid embarrassing her, and to avoid putting her life in danger*].

20 **But while he thought on these things,** behold, **the angel of the Lord appeared unto him** in a dream, saying, Joseph, thou son of David [*descendant of David*], **fear not to take unto thee Mary thy wife** [*don't be afraid to marry her*]: **for that** [*the child*] **which is conceived in her is of the Holy Ghost.**

Luke clarifies what is meant at the end of verse 20, above, where it says that Mary's child was "of the Holy Ghost." He says, in effect, that the Holy Ghost came upon Mary so that the divine conception could be accomplished. Luke wrote:

LUKE 1:35

35 And the angel answered and said unto her, The Holy Ghost shall come upon thee, and the power of the Highest [*the Father*] shall overshadow thee: therefore also that holy thing [*the Christ child*] which shall be born of thee shall be called the Son of God.

Elder James E. Talmage, of the Quorum of the Twelve, further explained: "That Child to be born of Mary was begotten of Elohim, the Eternal Father, not in violation of natural law but in accordance with a higher manifestation thereof; and, the offspring from that association of supreme sanctity, celestial Sireship, and pure though mortal maternity, was of right to be called the 'Son of the Highest.' In His nature would be combined the powers of Godhood with the capacity and possibilities of mortality; and this through the ordinary operation of the fundamental law of heredity declared of God, demonstrated by science, and admitted by philosophy, that living beings shall propagate—after their kind. The Child Jesus was to inherit the physical, mental and spiritual traits, tendencies, and powers that characterized His parents—one immortal and glorified—God, the other human—woman" (*Jesus the Christ*, p. 81).

21 And **she shall bring forth a son, and thou shalt call his name JESUS: for he shall save his people from their sins** [*in other words, Mary is expecting the promised Messiah*].

It is interesting to note that the angel came and put Joseph's mind at ease *after* he made the decision to be merciful to Mary.

22 Now all this was done, that it might be fulfilled [*that Isaiah's prophecy would be fulfilled—see Isaiah 7:14*] which was spoken of the Lord by the prophet, saying,

23 Behold, **a virgin shall be with child, and shall bring forth a son,** and they shall call his name Emmanuel, which being interpreted is, God with us.

24 **Then Joseph** being raised from sleep did as the angel of the Lord had bidden him, and **took unto him his wife** [*Joseph obeyed the angel immediately, no doubt with great relief and joy, and married Mary*]:

25 And **knew her not** [*had no sexual relationship, so that Jesus was born to a virgin, as prophesied*] **till she had brought forth her firstborn son:** and he called his name JESUS.

Joseph and Mary went on to have at least six children of their own. See Mark 6:3. In fact, the Greek text of that verse indicates that there were at least three sisters plus the four brothers mentioned.

MATTHEW 2

The Wise Men Come

1 Now **when Jesus was born in Bethlehem** of Judæa in the days of Herod the king [*see Bible Dictionary, p. 700–701, for background information on Herod the Great*], behold, **there came wise men** [*no doubt inspired men of God; perhaps prophets*] from the east to Jerusalem,

2 **Saying, Where is he that is born King of the Jews?** for **we have seen his star** in the east, and are come to worship him..

JST MATTHEW 3:2

2 Saying, Where is the child that is born, **the Messiah of the Jews**? for we have seen his star in the east, and have come to worship him.

3 When **Herod the king** had heard these things, he **was troubled,** and **all Jerusalem with him** [*this stirred up much discussion in Jerusalem*].

4 And when **he** had **gathered all the chief priests and scribes** [*the Jewish religious leaders*

and scholars] of the people **together, he demanded of them where Christ should be born.**

5 **And they said** unto him, **In Bethlehem** of Judæa: **for thus it is written** by the prophet [*Micah 5:2*],

6 And thou Bethlehem, in the land of Juda, art not the least among the princes of Juda: for **out of thee shall come a Governor** [*Christ*], **that shall rule my people Israel.**

JST MATTHEW 3:4–6

4 And when he had gathered all the chief priests, and scribes of the people together, he demanded of them, saying, **Where is the place that is written of by the prophets, in which Christ should be born? For he greatly feared, yet he believed not the prophets.**

5 And they said unto him, **It is written by the prophets, that he should be born in Bethlehem of Judea**, for thus have they said,

6 **The word of the Lord came unto us**, saying, And thou Bethlehem, which lieth in the land of Judea, in thee shall be born a prince, which art not the least among the princes of Judea; for out of thee shall come the Messiah, who shall save my people Israel.

7 **Then Herod**, when he had privily [*privately*] **called the wise men**, enquired of them diligently what time the star appeared.

8 And he **sent them to Bethlehem, and said,** Go and search diligently for the young child; and **when ye have found him, bring me word again, that I may come and worship him also** [*Herod is lying. He secretly wants to kill the child*].

9 When they had heard the king, **they departed**; and, lo, **the star**, which they saw in the east, **went before them, till it came and stood over where the young child was.**

By the time the wise men arrived in Jerusalem, enquiring about the birth of Christ, Jesus was already a young child. Joseph and Mary had apparently decided to stay in Bethlehem for a while, after the Savior's birth, and had settled in a house there. You can see that this is implied in verse 11, which informs us that He was now living in a house in Bethlehem. Thus, the pictures we see of the wise men and shepherds visiting baby Jesus in a stable are a composite of two separate events.

10 When they saw the star, they rejoiced with exceeding great joy.

11 **And when they were come into the house, they saw the young child with Mary his mother**, and fell down, **and worshipped him**: and when they had opened their treasures, **they presented unto him gifts; gold**, and **frankincense**, and **myrrh** [*frankincense and myrrh were costly gifts, as was gold, and were highly prized for their use as incense in this culture where sanitation was a concern and incense helped mask unpleasant odors; it may well be that these gifts from the wise men helped pay expenses for the trip to Egypt, mentioned in verse 13*].

Remember that the wise men had been requested by King Herod to report back to him when they found Jesus, so that he also could worship Him. They are warned not to do so.

12 And **being warned of God in a dream that they should not return to Herod, they departed into their own country** another way.

Righteous Joseph is also warned by an angel. He is told to take Mary and Jesus to Egypt, where the child will be out of reach of Herod.

13 And when they were departed, behold, **the angel of the Lord appeareth to Joseph** in a dream, **saying, Arise, and take the young child and his mother, and flee into Egypt**, and be thou there until I bring thee word: **for Herod will seek the young child to destroy him.**

14 When he arose, **he took the young child and his mother by night, and departed into Egypt** [*this would be a long and difficult journey, of about 200–300 miles, depending on where they stayed in Egypt, but Joseph and Mary were obedient*]:

15 **And was there until the death of Herod**: that it might be fulfilled which was spoken of the Lord by the prophet [*Hosea 11:1*], saying, Out of Egypt have I called my son.

By way of information, the paragraph mark (¶) you see in your Bible (if it is the King James

SHE SHALL BRING FORTH A SON, AND THOU SHALT CALL HIS NAME JESUS: FOR HE SHALL SAVE HIS PEOPLE FROM THEIR SINS.

MATTHEW 1:21

version, published through the Church) indicates a change in topic.

16 ¶ **Then Herod**, when he saw that he was mocked of the wise men, **was exceeding wroth** [*very angry*], **and sent forth, and slew all the children** [*Greek: male babies*] **that were in Bethlehem, and in all the coasts thereof** [*the area surrounding Bethlehem*], **from two years old and under**, according to the time which he had diligently enquired of the wise men.

John the Baptist was also a small child at this time, just six months older than Jesus (Elizabeth was six months along with John—see Luke 1, verses 26 and 36—when Mary visited her, right after Gabriel told her she would be the mother of Jesus). He lived in the vicinity of Bethlehem when Herod gave his murderous order to kill all the male babies two years old and younger in the Bethlehem area. John the Baptist's father, Zacharias, was killed—see Matthew 23:35—because he would not tell where he had sent John and his mother to hide. The Prophet Joseph Smith gives us more information about this. "When Herod's edict went forth to destroy the young children, John was about six months older than Jesus, and came under this hellish edict, and Zacharias caused his mother to take him into the mountains, where he was raised on locusts and wild honey. When his father refused to disclose his hiding place, and being the officiating high priest at the Temple that year, was slain by Herod's order, between the porch and the altar, as Jesus said" (*Teachings of the Prophet Joseph Smith*, p. 261).

In verse 17, next, we see another example of Matthew emphasizing that Jesus was the fulfillment of numerous Old Testament prophecies.

17 **Then was fulfilled that** [*the prophecy given in Jeremiah 31:15*] **which was spoken by Jeremy** [*Jeremiah*] the prophet, saying,

18 **In Rama** [*a place northwest of Jerusalem where the Jewish captives were assembled prior to being taken to Babylon—see Bible Dictionary, under "Rachel"*] was there a voice heard, **lamentation**, and **weeping**, and great **mourning**, **Rachel** [*Jacob's wife, the mother of Joseph and Benjamin; she died giving birth to Benjamin—see Genesis 35:16–20*] **weeping for her children**, and would not be comforted, because they are not.

Thus, according to Matthew, the deaths of the male children in the Bethlehem area, because of Herod's edict, were yet another fulfillment of the prophecy given by Jeremiah. Rachel's tomb is located near the northern entrance to old Bethlehem, and we can picture her in our minds weeping for the slain children in the Bethlehem area.

After Herod died, an angel appeared in a dream to Joseph, who was still living with his little family in Egypt, and told him to bring Mary and Jesus back to Israel. Their stay in Egypt may have been relatively short, since Herod died just a few months after he issued the order to slay the male infants in Bethlehem—see Bible Dictionary, under "Herod."

19 But **when Herod was dead**, behold, **an angel** of the Lord **appeareth** in a dream **to Joseph in Egypt**,

20 Saying, **Arise, and take the young child and his mother, and go into the land of Israel**: for they are dead which sought the young child's life.

21 And **he arose, and took the young child and his mother, and came into the land of Israel.**

It is likely that Joseph and Mary had determined to return to their home in Bethlehem at this time, but fear of Herod's son, Archelaus, who now ruled Judea, caused them to be afraid. An angel confirmed Joseph's concerns and instructed him to take his family back to Nazareth, where they had been living prior to coming to Bethlehem where Jesus was born—see Luke 2:4–5.

22 **But when he heard that Archelaus did reign in Judæa in the room of** [*in place of*] **his father Herod, he was afraid** to go thither [*there*]: notwithstanding, **being warned of God in a dream, he turned aside into the parts of Galilee**:

23 **And he came and dwelt in a city called Nazareth**: that it might be fulfilled which was spoken by the prophets, He shall be called a Nazarene [*we don't know where this prophecy is; it is one of the lost scriptures*].

The JST adds three verses that fit here.

JST MATTHEW 3:24–26

24 And it came to pass that Jesus grew up with his brethren, and waxed strong, and waited upon the Lord for the time of his ministry to come.

25 And he served under his father, and he spake not as other men, neither could he be taught; for he needed not that any man should teach him.

26 And after many years, the hour of his ministry drew nigh.

MATTHEW 3

John the Baptist Comes Preaching

1 **In those days came John the Baptist, preaching in the wilderness** of Judæa [*a desert area, west of the Dead Sea*],

2 And **saying, Repent ye: for the kingdom of heaven is at hand** [*is near; the gospel of Jesus Christ is now available to you*].

3 For **this is he that was spoken of by the prophet Esaias** [*Isaiah*], **saying,** The voice of one crying in the wilderness, Prepare ye the way of the Lord, make his paths straight.

As you will see, the Prophet Joseph Smith made a change in verse 3 which changes the whole meaning:

JST Matthew 3:29

29 For **I am he** who was spoken of by the prophet Esaias, saying, The voice of one crying in the wilderness, Prepare ye the way of the Lord and make his paths straight.

4 And the same **John had** his **raiment** [*clothing*] **of camel's hair** [*coarse cloth woven from camel's hair*], and a leathern girdle about his loins; **and his meat** [*food*] **was locusts and wild honey.**

The Bible generally uses the word "meat" to mean any kind of food. The word "flesh" is used when referring to meat, such as beef, chicken, lamb, etc.

Elder Bruce R. McConkie explained the importance of John the Baptist and his mission. He said: "This miraculously born son of Zacharias was the last legal administrator of the old dispensation, the first of the new; he was the last of the old prophets, the first of the new. With him ended the old law, and with him began the new era of promise. He is the one man who stood, literally, at the crossroads of history; with him the past died and the future was born. He was the herald of the Messianic age, the messenger, fore-runner, and Elias who began the great restoration in the meridian of time and on whose secure foundation the Son of Man himself built the eternal gospel structure. His ministry ended the preparatory gospel; Messiah's commenced again the era of gospel fulness" (*Doctrinal New Testament Commentary*, p. 113).

Next, we see that there was great excitement about John the Baptist throughout the region.

5 **Then went out to him Jerusalem, and all Judæa, and all the region round about Jordan** [*i.e., people from all over came to the Jordan River to see John the Baptist*],

6 **And were baptized of** [*by*] **him** in Jordan [*the Jordan River*], confessing their sins.

Verses 5 and 6, above, remind us that John the Baptist was baptizing by immersion. It was necessary for people to come over twenty miles from Jerusalem to a place where there was "much water" (John 3:23). The word "baptize" itself comes "from a Greek word, meaning to dip or immerse" (see Bible Dictionary, under "Baptism").

Have you noticed in reading these verses that no one was bothered by the idea of baptism? That is because baptism itself was a familiar ordinance. It had been practiced in Old Testament times, in fact, since the time of Adam (Moses 6:64–66), whenever the gospel of Jesus Christ was available. We will quote from the Bible Dictionary:

Bible Dictionary—Baptism

"Baptism has always been practiced whenever the gospel of Jesus Christ has been on the earth and has been taught by men holding the holy priesthood who could administer the ordinances. Although there is some obscurity in the Bible as to the antiquity of baptism before the time of Jesus, from latter-day revelation it is clear that Adam was baptized (Moses 6:64–68) and that the patriarchs and prophets since his time have taught the gospel and administered the ordinances that pertain to the gospel. This includes both water baptism and the laying on of hands for the Holy Ghost (Moses 8:23–24). The Book of Mormon shows also that baptism was taught and practiced long before the coming of Jesus Christ (2 Ne. 31; Mosiah 18:8–17)."

Verse 7, next, mentions Pharisees and Sadducees. These were religious groups among the Jews of the day, and many of them were hypocrites. Pharisees believed in the resurrection. Sadducees did not. Consequently, there was much arguing and disagreement between the two groups.

7 **But when he saw many of the Pharisees and Sadducees** come to his baptism, **he said unto them, O generation of vipers, who hath warned you to flee from the wrath to come?**

8 **Bring forth therefore fruits meet** [*necessary*] **for repentance:**

9 **And think not to say within yourselves, We have Abraham to our father** [*as our ancestor*]: for I say unto you, that God is able of these stones to raise up children [*descendants*] unto Abraham.

The JST adds to and makes changes in verses 8–9, above. The verse numbering is different because Joseph Smith combined Matthew chapters 2 and 3 together as chapter 3 in the JST. You will see that he added an entire verse before verse 8 in the King James version (the one we use) of the Bible. (By the way, as previously mentioned in this study guide, all of the changes made by the Prophet Joseph Smith are not contained in our Bible. There is simply not room enough for them. Thus, some of the changes mentioned in this study guide are only found in the complete text of the JST, which is available at most LDS book stores.)

JST Matthew 3:34–36

34 **Why is it that ye receive not the preaching of him whom God hath sent? If ye receive not this in your hearts, ye receive not me; and if ye receive not me, ye receive not him of whom I am sent to bear record; and for your sins ye have no cloak.**

35 **Repent**, therefore, and bring forth fruits meet for repentance;

36 And think not to say within yourselves, We are the children of Abraham, and **we only have power to bring seed unto our father Abraham** [*in effect, saying we are the only ones who can be saved*]; for I say unto you that God is able of these stones to raise up children into Abraham.

It helps to understand the above verses if you are aware that the Jews had a belief that, since they were direct descendants of Abraham, they were automatically entitled to the highest position in heaven in the afterlife, and, that all other people, no matter how good they were, could attain only second class status in heaven. As you noticed, John spoke strongly against this false belief in verse 9, above, and will continue to do so in verse 10, next.

10 And now also the axe is laid unto the root of the trees [*trees often represent people in the scriptures*]: therefore **every tree which bringeth not forth good fruit** [*every person who does not live righteously*] **is hewn** [*cut*] **down, and cast into the fire** [*in other words, the wicked, no matter who they are, will be destroyed, punished according to the law of justice, if they do not repent when given a fair chance to do so*].

Next, in verse 11, John humbly directs the people's attention to the Master.

11 I indeed baptize you with water unto repentance: but **he** [*Christ*] **that cometh after me is mightier than I, whose shoes I am not worthy to bear**: he shall baptize you with the Holy Ghost, and with fire:

Note: In the scriptures, the Holy Ghost is often compared to fire. The symbolism comes from the use of fire to purify gold. The gold ore is put in a container (a crucible) and fire is used to heat it. The ore melts, the impurities float to the top, and the pure gold settles to the bottom. The impurities are then discarded and pure gold remains. Thus, the gold is purified by fire. Similarly, the Holy Ghost purifies us, if we allow it. Example: We commit sin. The Holy Ghost points it out and causes our conscience to burn within us. We respond by repenting. The Atonement of Christ cleanses us. Thus we are purified, bit by bit.

12 **Whose fan** [*used to blow the chaff away from the kernels of wheat on the threshing floor*] **is in his hand**, and he will throughly purge [*cleanse*] his floor [*the earth*], and gather his wheat [*the righteous*] into the garner [*the barn*]; but he will burn up the chaff [*the wicked*] with unquenchable fire.

The JST makes changes in verses 11–12, above.

JST Matthew 3:38–40

38 I indeed baptize you with water, **upon your repentance**; and when he of whom I bear record cometh, who is mightier than I, whose shoes I am not worthy to bear **(or whose place I am not able to fill), as I said, I indeed baptize you before he cometh, that when he cometh he may baptize you with the Holy Ghost and fire**.

39 **And it is he of whom I shall bear record,** whose fan shall be in his hand, and he will thoroughly purge his floor, and gather his wheat into the garner; but **in the fulness of his own time** will burn up the chaff with unquenchable fire.

40 **Thus came John, preaching and baptizing in the river of Jordan; bearing record, that he who was coming after him had power to baptize with the Holy Ghost and fire.**

The Baptism of Jesus

13 ¶ **Then cometh Jesus from Galilee to Jordan unto John, to be baptized of** *[by]* **him.**

14 **But John forbad him,** saying, I have need to be baptized of thee, and comest thou to me?

15 **And Jesus** answering **said unto him, Suffer** *[allow]* **it to be so now:** for thus it becometh us to fulfil all righteousness *[to do the will of the Father]*. Then he suffered him.

The JST makes changes to verses 14–15, above.

JST MATTHEW 3:42–44

42 But John **refused** him, saying, I have need to be baptized of thee, and **why comest thou to me?**

43 And Jesus, answering, said unto him, **Suffer me to be baptized of thee,** for thus it becometh us to fulfill all righteousness. Then he suffered him.

44 **And John went down into the water and baptized him.**

16 And Jesus, when he was baptized, went up straightway **out of the water** *[evidence that He was baptized by immersion]*: **and, lo, the heavens were opened unto him, and he** *[John the Baptist]* **saw the Spirit of God** *[the Holy Ghost]* **descending like a dove, and lighting upon him** *[the Savior—see JST quoted below]*:

17 And lo **a voice from heaven, saying, This is my beloved Son, in whom I am well pleased.**

The Joseph Smith Translation (JST) gives verses 16–17 as follows (remember, the numbering is sometimes different in the JST):

JST MATTHEW 3:45–46

45 And Jesus when he was baptized, went up straightway out of the water; and **John saw,** and lo, the heavens were opened unto him, and he saw the Spirit of God descending like a dove and lighting upon **Jesus.**

46 And lo, **he heard** a voice from heaven, saying, This is my beloved Son, in whom I am well pleased. **Hear ye him.**

Because of these and other verses in the scriptures, some people have come to believe that the Holy Ghost occasionally turns into a dove. Such is not the case. The Prophet Joseph Smith taught that the Holy Ghost does not transform himself into a dove. He said:

"The Holy Ghost is a personage, and is in the form of a personage. It does not confine itself to the *form* of the dove, but in *sign* of the dove. The Holy Ghost cannot be transformed into a dove; but the sign of a dove was given to John to signify the truth of the deed, as the dove is an emblem or token of truth and innocence" (*Teachings of the Prophet Joseph Smith*, pp. 275–76).

MATTHEW 4

THE JST (THE Joseph Smith Translation of the Bible) makes many changes to this chapter. You will see a number of them referenced in footnotes in your LDS edition of the Bible. (Remember, as we mentioned previously, several JST changes are not contained in our Bible simply because they would take up too much space. Therefore, some JST changes that we give in this study guide are not found in your Bible.)

We see a very significant change to verse 1, next. We will quote the JST after we read verse 1 as it stands in our Bible. We will use **bold** to help you see the difference.

1 Then was Jesus led up of the Spirit into the wilderness **to be tempted of the devil.**

JST MATTHEW 4:1

1 Then Jesus was led up of the Spirit, into the wilderness, **to be with God.**

As you can see, in the JST verse quoted above, the Prophet Joseph Smith teaches us that the Savior went into the wilderness to be with His Father. From this we learn that He did not go specifically to confront the devil nor to be tempted by him.

Perhaps one of the things we can learn from this is that we should not deliberately put ourselves in a position to be tempted. In fact, the Savior

JESUS, WHEN HE WAS
BAPTIZED, WENT
UP STRAIGHTWAY OUT
OF THE WATER: AND, LO,
THE HEAVENS WERE
OPENED UNTO HIM,
AND HE SAW THE SPIRIT
OF GOD DESCENDING
LIKE A DOVE.

MATTHEW 3:16

THE BAPTISM OF CHRIST, by Robert T. Barrett

said, "lead us not into temptation" (Matthew 6:13). And if you look at Matthew 6:13, footnote b, in your Bible, you will see that "do not let us enter into temptation" is given as another translation of this phrase.

Thus we understand that temptation will come to us as a result of being here on earth, but we should not deliberately place ourselves in tempting circumstances.

As we move ahead now in this chapter, we note that the Savior was subjected to temptation by the devil. Likewise, God does not constantly protect us from the temptations of the devil and his evil followers because we need opposition in order to grow and exercise our agency. This principle is taught in the Book of Mormon as follows:

2 NEPHI 2:11
For it must needs be, that there is an opposition in all things.

The Devil Tempts Jesus

The JST provides important additions to verse 2, next.

2 And **when he had fasted forty days and forty nights, he was** afterward an **hungred.**

JST MATTHEW 4:2
2 And when he had fasted forty days and forty nights, **and had communed with God**, he was afterwards an hungered, **and was left to be tempted of the devil**.

Paul taught us why the Savior was tempted. He said:

HEBREWS 2:18, 4:15
18 For in that he himself hath suffered being tempted, **he is able to succour** [*help, nourish*] **them that are tempted**.

15 For we have not an high priest [*Jesus is sometimes referred to as the "Great High Priest"*] which cannot be touched with the feeling of our infirmities [*in other words, we do not have a Savior who is unable to sympathize with our weaknesses*]; but **was in all points tempted like as *we are*,** *yet* without sin.

As we continue, we will see that the devil tempted the Savior in three major areas in which he likewise tempts us.

1. Physical appetites (verse 3).
2. Vanity and pride (verse 6).
3. Materialism and power (verse 9).

But you will see another form of temptation associated with the above temptations. It is the word "if" in verses 3 and 6. The devil challenged Jesus to prove that He was indeed the Son of God. This "if" challenge can be a very effective tool for Satan as he likewise challenges us to "prove it." People often find themselves committing sin or taking foolish chances in order to respond to someone who is suggesting that they are not what they claim to be.

3 And when the tempter [*Satan*] came to him, he said, **If** thou be the Son of God, command that these stones be made bread [*temptation to yield to physical appetite*].

4 **But he answered** and said, It is written [*in Deuteronomy 8:3*], **Man shall not live by bread alone, but by every word that proceedeth out of the mouth of God.**

5 Then the devil taketh him up into the holy city [*Jerusalem*], and setteth him on a pinnacle of the temple,

JST MATTHEW 4:5
Then Jesus was taken up into the holy city and **the Spirit setteth him on the pinnacle of the temple**.

6 And saith unto him, **If** thou be the Son of God, cast thyself down: for it is written [*in Psalm 91:11–12*], He shall give his angels charge concerning thee: and in their hands they shall bear thee up, lest at any time thou dash thy foot against a stone [*temptation to yield to vanity, pride*].

JST MATTHEW 4:6
6 **Then the devil came unto him** and said, If thou be the Son of God, cast thyself down, for it is written, He shall give his angels charge concerning thee, and in their hands they shall bear thee up, lest at any time thou dash thy foot against a stone.

7 Jesus said unto him, It is written again [*in Deuteronomy 6:16*], **Thou shalt not tempt the Lord thy God.** [*Note that Jesus answers each temptation with a scriptural quote. This is a reminder of the power of the scriptures to safeguard us against successful temptation.*]

8 Again, **the devil taketh him up into an exceeding high mountain, and sheweth him** all the kingdoms of the world, and the glory of them;

JST MATTHEW 4:8
8 And again, **Jesus was in the Spirit, and it taketh him up into an exceeding high mountain, and showeth him** all the kingdoms of the world and the glory of them.

9 And saith unto him, All these things will I give thee, if thou wilt fall down and worship me [*temptation to yield to materialism and power*].

JST MATTHEW 4:9
9 **And the devil came unto him again**, and said, All these things will I give unto thee, if thou wilt fall down and worship me.

10 Then saith Jesus unto him, **Get thee hence** [*leave me*], **Satan:** for it is written [*in Deuteronomy 6:13*], **Thou shalt worship the Lord thy God, and him only shalt thou serve.**

11 **Then the devil leaveth him,** and, behold, angels came and ministered unto him.

The topic now changes to John the Baptist, who has been imprisoned by Herod (see Mark 6:17).

John the Baptist in Prison

12 Now when Jesus had heard that John [*the Baptist*] was cast into prison, he departed into Galilee;

The JST makes some changes in verses 10–12, above. Among other things, we learn that the angels spoken of in verse 11 were actually sent by the Savior to minister to John the Baptist, who had been put in prison.

JST MATTHEW 4:10–12
10 Then said Jesus unto him, Get thee hence, Satan; for it is written, Thou shalt worship the Lord thy God, and him only shalt thou serve. Then the devil leaveth him.

11 And now Jesus knew that John was cast into prison, and he sent angels, and, behold, they came and ministered unto him.

12 And Jesus departed into Galilee, and leaving Nazareth, in Zebulun, he came and dwelt in Capernaum, which is upon the seacoast, in the borders of Nephthalim,

13 And leaving Nazareth, he came and dwelt in Capernaum, which is upon the sea [*Sea of Galilee*] coast, in the borders of Zabulon and Nephthalim [*the area where Zebulon and Naphtali, two of the twelve tribes, settled when Joshua brought the children of Israel into the promised land*]:

You will see yet another example, beginning with verse 14, next, of the emphasis by Matthew that Jesus was the fulfillment of Old Testament prophecies concerning the Messiah.

14 **That it might be fulfilled** which was spoken by Esaias [*Isaiah*] the prophet [*in Isaiah 9:1–2*], saying,

15 The land of Zabulon, and the land of Nephthalim, by the way of the sea, beyond Jordan, Galilee of the Gentiles;

16 **The people which sat in darkness** [*spiritual darkness*] **saw great light** [*the Savior and His gospel*]; and to them which sat in the region and shadow of death [*spiritual darkness*] light is sprung up.

17 **From that time Jesus began to preach** [*Jesus now begins His formal ministry*], and to say, **Repent: for the kingdom of heaven is at hand** [*salvation is now being made available to you*].

Watch, now, as the Savior begins calling the men who will later become Apostles. Note how humbly and quickly they left their worldly pursuits in order to follow Him.

Jesus Calls Men Who Will Become Apostles

18 **And Jesus,** walking by the sea of Galilee, **saw two brethren** [*brothers*], Simon called **Peter, and Andrew** his brother, casting a net into the sea: for they were fishers [*fishermen; they earned their living by fishing*].

19 **And** he **saith** unto them, **Follow me, and I will make you fishers of men.**

20 **And they straightway** [*immediately*] **left their nets, and followed him.**

JST MATTHEW 4:18–19

18 And he said unto them, **I am he of whom it is written by the prophets**; follow me, and I will make you fishers of men.

19 And they, **believing on his words**, left their net, and straightway followed him.

From the JST changes given above, we can glean that Peter and Andrew knew the scriptures and the prophecies about the coming Messiah. They recognized what He was saying because they knew the scriptures. This can remind us, among other things, of the great value of reading and studying the scriptures ourselves.

21 And going on from thence [*from that place*], **he saw other two brethren, James** the son of Zebedee, **and John** his brother, in a ship with Zebedee their father, mending their nets; **and he called them.**

22 **And they immediately left the ship and their father, and followed him.**

Luke gives more detail about the calling of these humble fishermen. You may wish to put a cross reference in your scriptures by Matthew 4:18, which sends you to Luke 5:1–11.

23 **And Jesus went about all Galilee, teaching** in their synagogues [*church buildings*], and **preaching** the gospel of the kingdom, and **healing** all manner of [*all kinds of*] sickness and all manner of disease among the people.

The JST adds an important lesson to the end of verse 23, above, about the necessity of believing. (Also, just a reminder that the verse numbering in the JST is sometimes different than in the King James Version of the Bible, which we use as a Church for English speaking areas of the world.)

JST MATTHEW 4:22

22 And Jesus went about all Galilee teaching in their synagogues, and preaching the gospel of the kingdom; and healing all manner of sickness, and all manner of diseases among the people **which believed on his name**.

In a significant way, the Savior's healing of physical illnesses is symbolic of His power and desire to heal our spiritual illnesses. For example, when He healed the blind, literally, it was symbolic of His ability to heal our spiritual blindness. When He healed the lame, it can be considered symbolic of His ability to heal our inability to walk along the strait and narrow path toward salvation in celestial glory.

24 **And his fame went throughout all Syria: and they brought unto him all sick people** that were taken with [*who had*] divers [*various*] diseases and torments, and those which were possessed with devils, and those which were lunatick, and those that had the palsy; **and he healed them.**

It would have taken a significant amount of time for Jesus to travel and preach and heal throughout "all Galilee" (verse 23, above). Thus, at this point in time, the first year of the Savior's three year formal mortal mission is drawing to a close. He has become tremendously popular by this time and crowds from all over the area are constantly following Him around.

25 And **there followed him great multitudes of people** from Galilee, and from Decapolis, and from Jerusalem, and from Judæa, and from beyond Jordan.

MATTHEW 5

The Sermon on the Mount

AT THIS POINT in Matthew, we are with the Savior in Galilee and are at the beginning of the second year of His formal three-year ministry. Matthew chapters 5, 6, and 7 are known as "The Sermon on the Mount." Many Christians consider these chapters to contain a series of desirable ethical behaviors, and indeed they do. But they are much more than this. As explained in 3 Nephi as well as in the JST (the Joseph Smith Translation of the Bible), the righteous behaviors stressed here by the Master are among those which enable baptized members of the Church to obtain celestial glory and exaltation. You may wish to make a cross reference in the heading to Matthew, chapter 5, in your Bible, which sends you to 3 Nephi 12:1–2, wherein we are told that the sermon which follows in 3 Nephi (basically, the Sermon on the Mount as given to the Nephites) is addressed to baptized members of the Church, and is a series of instructions for continuing after baptism to the point of qualifying for celestial glory.

Likewise, the JST teaches this fact, as you will see when we quote it after Matthew 5:2, below.

We will now begin Matthew, chapter 5, joining the multitude which has gathered on a hillside in Galilee to listen to the Savior.

1 And **seeing the multitudes, he went up into a mountain**: and **when he was set**, his disciples came unto him:

2 And **he opened his mouth, and taught them, saying,**

The JST adds two complete verses to Matthew 5:1–2 which are not found in the Bible.

JST MATTHEW 5:1–4

1 And Jesus, seeing the multitudes, went up into a mountain; and **when he was set down**, his disciples came unto him;

2 And he opened his mouth, and taught them, saying,

3 Blessed are they who shall believe on me; and again, more blessed are they who shall believe on your words, when ye shall testify that ye have seen me and that I am.

4 Yea, blessed are they who shall believe on your words, and come down into the depth of humility, and be **baptized** in my name; for they shall be visited with fire and the **Holy Ghost**, and shall receive a **remission of their sins** [*which leads to celestial glory—see D&C 76:52, which is talking about the celestial kingdom*].

The Beatitudes

(How to continue to exaltation after baptism)

Verses 3–12 are often referred to as the "Beatitudes," meaning "to be happy or blessed" (see Matthew 5, footnote 3a, in your Bible). Notice that verses 3, 5, 8, 9, 10, and 12 all refer to heaven (celestial glory) in one way or another.

3 **Blessed are the poor in spirit** [*who come unto me. 3 Nephi 12:3*]: **for theirs is the kingdom of heaven** [*celestial glory*].

JST MATTHEW 5:5

5 Yea, blessed are the poor in spirit, **who come unto me**; for theirs is the kingdom of heaven.

From the JST addition to verse 3, above, we are taught, among other things, that those who recognize that they are "poor in spirit," (in other words, who recognize that they are poor in spirituality) who repent and come to Christ, can obtain celestial glory.

Verse 4, next, can have several meanings, including mourning for the loss of a loved one and being comforted by the Holy Ghost. But in the context of verse 3, above, dealing with repenting of sins, one possible interpretation is that verse 4 is continuing the theme of repenting, and the necessity of being truly sorry for sins committed.

4 **Blessed are they that mourn** [*for their sins; in other words, those who repent*]: **for they shall be comforted** [*by the Holy Ghost*].

5 Blessed are the meek: for they shall inherit the earth [*this earth will become the celestial kingdom; see D&C 130:8–9*].

6 **Blessed are they which do hunger and thirst after righteousness: for they shall be filled** [*with the Holy Ghost; 3 Nephi 12:6*].

JST MATTHEW 5:8

8 And blessed are all they that do hunger and thirst after righteousness; for they shall be filled **with the Holy Ghost**.

Have you noticed that when you truly "hunger and thirst after righteousness" the commandments are a joy rather than a burden?

Verse 7, next, is, in effect, a "formula." Based on how we treat others, the script is basically being written for the day when we appear before God to be judged ourselves.

7 **Blessed are the merciful: for they shall obtain mercy.**

8 **Blessed are the pure in heart: for they shall see God** [*including when they are in the celestial kingdom*].

9 **Blessed are the peacemakers: for they shall be called the children of God** [*another term for those who inherit the celestial kingdom*].

The phrase "children of God," in verse 9, above, can also refer to faithful followers of Christ right here on earth—see Mosiah 5:7, which, of course, is another way of saying that they ultimately attain celestial glory.

10 **Blessed are they which are persecuted for righteousness' sake: for theirs is the kingdom of heaven** [*celestial glory*].

11 **Blessed are ye, when men shall revile you** [*mock you, ridicule you for your righteous beliefs*

and lifestyle], and **persecute you**, and shall **say all manner of evil against you falsely, for my sake** [*because you follow the Savior*].

12 **Rejoice**, and be exceeding glad: **for great is your reward in heaven** [*celestial glory*]: for so persecuted they the prophets which were before you [*who lived before you came to earth*].

JST MATTHEW 5:14
14 **For ye shall have great joy**, and be exceeding glad; for great **shall be** your reward in heaven; for so persecuted they the prophets which were before you.

13 **Ye are the salt of the earth**: but if the salt have lost his savour [*its ability to improve flavor, symbolic of the good the righteous can do to improve the lives of others*], wherewith shall it be salted [*how will others here on earth be helped*]? it is thenceforth good for nothing, but to be cast out, and to be trodden under foot of men.

JST MATTHEW 5:15
15 **Verily, verily, I say unto you, I give unto you to be the salt of earth**; but if the salt shall lose its savor, **wherewith shall the earth be salted?** the salt shall thenceforth be good for nothing, but to be cast out, and to be trodden under foot of men.

14 Ye are the light of the world. A city that is set on an hill cannot be hid.

JST MATTHEW 5:16
16 **Verily, verily, I say unto you, I give unto you to be the light of the world**; a city that is set on a hill cannot be hid.

It is helpful to know that in the Holy Land, cities were built upon the hills, saving valuable land in the valleys for agricultural and pasture use.

The wording in JST Matthew 5:16, above, reminds us of the responsibility of those who are given the blessings of Abraham, Isaac, and Jacob (as often stated in patriarchal blessings) to take the gospel and accompanying blessings of the priesthood to all the world—see Abraham 2:9–11.

15 **Neither do men light a candle, and put it under a bushel** [*a bushel basket*], **but on a candlestick; and it giveth light unto all** that are in the house.

JST MATTHEW 5:17
17 **Behold, do men light a candle and put it under a bushel? Nay**, but on a candlestick; and it giveth light to all that are in the house.

16 **Let your light so shine before men, that they may see your good works, and glorify your Father which is in heaven.**

JST MATTHEW 5:18
18 Therefore, let your light so shine before **this world**, that they may see your good works, and glorify your Father who is in heaven.

The topic now changes, starting with verse 17, next, to the Savior's role with respect to the Law of Moses. Misunderstanding of this issue, or deliberate refusal to accept Jesus as the fulfillment of Old Testament prophecies about the Messiah, led the Jewish religious leaders to demand that the Master be crucified.

17 **Think not that I am come to destroy the law** [*of Moses*], **or the prophets** [*the Old Testament*]: I am not come to destroy, but to fulfil.

Old Testament Atonement Symbolism

The Savior was accused by the Jews of trying to destroy all the laws and teachings of the Law of Moses. In fact, the rituals, teachings, and animal sacrifices taught by the Law of Moses all were designed by God to point people's minds toward the Savior and His Atonement. A good example of this Old Testament Atonement symbolism is found in Leviticus 14:1–9. We will take the time here to examine these verses and make notes about such symbolism in them. Keep in mind that symbolism allows for many meanings and interpretations. What we present is one possible approach to these verses in Leviticus.

The message and symbolism here is the power of the Atonement of Christ to cleanse and heal people from very serious sins. Leprosy is described in Webster's New World Dictionary, Second College Edition, as follows: "a chronic infectious disease . . . that attacks the skin, flesh, nerves, etc.; it is characterized by nodules, ulcers, white scaly scabs, deformities, and wasting of body parts."

LEVITICUS 14:1–9
1 And the LORD spake unto Moses, saying,
2 This shall be **the law of the leper** [*the rules*

LET YOUR LIGHT
SO SHINE BEFORE
MEN, THAT THEY MAY
SEE YOUR GOOD
WORKS, AND GLORIFY
YOUR FATHER WHICH
IS IN HEAVEN.

MATTHEW 5:16

for being made clean; symbolic of serious sin and great need for help and cleansing] **in the day of his cleansing** [*symbolic of the desire to be made spiritually clean and pure*]: **He shall be brought unto the priest** [*authorized servant of God; bishop, stake president, who holds the keys of authority and judgment to act for God*]:

3 And **the priest shall go forth out of the camp** [*the person with leprosy did not have fellowship with the Lord's people and was required to live outside the main camp of the children of Israel; the bishop, symbolically, goes out of the way to help sinners who want to repent and return to good standing in the Church*]; and **the priest shall look, and, behold, *if* the plague of leprosy be healed in the leper** [*the bishop serves as a judge to see if the repentant sinner is ready to return to full membership privileges*];

4 Then shall the priest command to take for him that is to be cleansed [*the person who has repented*] **two birds** [*one represents the Savior during His mortal mission, the other represents the person who has repented*] alive *and* clean, and **cedar wood** [*symbolic of the cross*], and **scarlet** [*associated with mocking Christ before his crucifixion, Mark 15:17*], and **hyssop** [*associated with Christ on the cross, John 19:29*]:

5 And the priest shall command that **one of the birds** [*symbolic of the Savior*] be **killed in an earthen vessel** [*Christ was sent to earth to die for us*] **over running water** [*Christ offers "living water," the gospel of Jesus Christ—John 7:37–38, which cleanses us when we come unto Him*]:

6 **As for the living bird** [*representing the person who has repented*], **he** [*the priest; symbolic of the bishop, stake president, one who holds the keys of judging*] **shall take it** [*the living bird*], **and the cedar wood**, and the **scarle**t, and the **hyssop** [*all associated with the Atonement*], **and shall dip them and the living bird in the blood of the bird *that was* killed over the running water** [*representing the cleansing power of the Savior's blood which was shed for us*]:

7 And he shall **sprinkle upon him that is to be cleansed from the leprosy** [*symbolically, being cleansed from sin*] **seven times** [*seven is the number which, in Biblical numeric symbolism, represents completeness, perfection*], **and shall pronounce him clean** [*he has been forgiven*], **and shall let the living bird** [*the person who has repented*] **loose into the open field** [*representing the wide open opportunities again available in the kingdom of God for the person who truly repents*].

8 And **he that is to be cleansed shall wash his clothes** [*symbolic of cleaning up your life from sinful ways and pursuits—compare with Isaiah 1:16*], and **shave off all his hair** [*symbolic of becoming like a newborn baby; fresh start*], and **wash himself in water** [*symbolic of baptism*], **that he may be clean** [*cleansed from sin*]: and **after that he shall come into the camp** [*rejoin the Lord's covenant people*], and shall tarry abroad out of his tent seven days.

9 But it shall be on the seventh day, that he shall shave all his hair off his head and his beard and his eyebrows, even all his hair he shall shave off [*symbolic of being "born again"*]: and he shall wash his clothes [*clean up his life—clothing is often used in scripture to symbolize our lives; thus, cleansing our clothing or garments from sin is a way of saying that our lives are made clean through the blood of Christ—see 1 Nephi 12:10*], also he shall wash his flesh in water [*symbolic of baptism*], and he shall be clean [*a simple fact, namely that we can truly be cleansed and healed by the Savior's Atonement*].

Such Atonement symbolism and teaching is found much in the Old Testament. We will now return to Matthew, chapter 5, and continue with verse 18 as the Savior continues to explain how His coming fulfills the Law of Moses.

Jesus Fulfills the Law of Moses

18 For verily I say unto you, Till heaven and earth pass, **one jot or one tittle** [*tiny bit*] **shall in no wise pass from the law** [*Law of Moses*], **till all be fulfilled.**

JST 5:20
20 For verily I say unto you, **Heaven and earth must pass away**, but one jot or one tittle shall in no wise pass from the law, until all be fulfilled.

19 **Whosoever** therefore **shall break one of these least commandments, and shall teach men so, he shall be called the least in the kingdom of heaven** [*will not receive a great reward on Judgment Day; in other words, will be punished*]: **but whosoever shall do and teach them, the same shall be called great in the kingdom of heaven** [*will gain a great reward in the celestial kingdom*].

JST MATTHEW 5:21
21 Whosoever, therefore, shall break one of these least commandments, and shall teach men so to do, he shall in no wise be saved in the kingdom of heaven; **but whosoever shall do and teach these commandments of the law until it**

be fulfilled, the same shall be called great, and shall be saved in the kingdom of heaven.

In verse 20, next, the Master points out that the religious leaders of the Jews at the time claim to be living the laws of God, as embodied in the Law of Moses, but are actually wicked men.

20 For I say unto you, That **except your righteousness shall exceed the righteousness of the scribes** [*Jewish religious leaders who explain and interpret the scriptures*] **and Pharisees** [*a particular group of Jews who adhered very strictly to the Law of Moses*], **ye shall in no case enter into the kingdom of heaven.** [*This was a direct blow to the hypocritical scribes and Pharisees*]

The Law of Moses had been given as a "schoolmaster" (see Galatians 3:24) to bring the people to the point where they could accept Christ and His higher gospel. Beginning with verse 21, next, we see the Savior teaching to help the people make this transition.

The Law of Moses Was a "Schoolmaster"

21 **Ye have heard that it was said by them of old time, Thou shalt not kill**; and whosoever shall kill shall be in danger of the judgment [*punishments of God*]:

22 **But I say unto you, That whosoever is angry with his brother** without a cause [*both the JST and 3 Nephi 12:22 omit the phrase "without a cause"*] **shall be in danger of the judgment**: and **whosoever shall say to his brother, Raca** [*a term of derision, such as "You stupid idiot!" See Matthew 5, footnote 22d, in your Bible*], shall be in danger of the council: but **whosoever shall say, Thou fool, shall be in danger of hell fire.** [*In other words, don't put others down, as if you didn't have any imperfections yourself.*]

JST MATTHEW 5:24

24 But I say unto you that whosoever is angry with his brother, shall be in danger of his judgment; and whosoever shall say to his brother, Raca, or Rabcha, shall be in danger of the council; and whosoever shall say to his brother, Thou fool, shall be in danger of hell fire.

Some people believe that the word "fool" should never be used, because of the warning in verse 22, above. However, it appears from the scriptures that it is the behavior of demeaning people as if we had no faults or imperfections ourselves, that is referred to here, since the Savior uses the word in Matthew 23:17 and Luke 24:25. Also, the Apostle Paul uses it in Romans 1:22 as well as in other places, and Nephi, son of Helaman, uses it in Helaman 9:21.

23 **Therefore if thou bring thy gift to the altar, and there rememberest that thy brother hath ought against thee** [*you have contention with someone close to you*];

JST MATTHEW 5:25

Therefore, if ye shall come unto me, or shall desire to come unto me,

24 Leave there thy gift before the altar, and go thy way; **first be reconciled to** [*make peace with*] **thy brother**, and then come and offer thy gift.

25 **Agree with thine adversary** [*make peace with the person you have contention with*] **quickly**, whiles thou art in the way with him [*while you have the opportunity*]; **lest** at any time the adversary deliver thee to the judge, and the judge deliver thee to the officer, and **thou be cast into prison.** [*If you don't try to make peace, it does a lot of damage to you, yourself.*]

26 Verily I say unto thee, **Thou shalt by no means come out** thence [*from the prison you put yourself into*], **till thou hast paid the uttermost farthing.** [*You pay dearly for holding grudges etc. in terms of lack of peace for yourself.*]

27 **Ye have heard that** it was said by them of old time [*in the Law of Moses*], **Thou shalt not commit adultery:**

28 **But I say unto you, That whosoever looketh on a woman to lust after her hath committed adultery with her already in his heart.**

29 And **if thy right eye** [*symbolic of specific temptation, bad environment, friends, bad habit, specific sin, etc.*] **offend thee** [*puts you in spiritual danger*], **pluck it out, and cast it from thee**: for it is profitable for thee that one of thy members should

perish, and not that thy whole body should be cast into hell.

Body parts in verses 29 and 30 are symbolic of choices, behaviors, associations with friends, etc., which could cause you to lose salvation.

30 And **if thy right hand offend thee, cut it off,** and cast it from thee: for it is profitable for thee that one of thy members should perish, and not that thy whole body should be cast into hell.

JST Matthew 5:34
And now this I speak, a parable concerning your sins; wherefore, cast them from you, that ye may not be hewn down and cast into the fire.

31 **It hath been said, Whosoever shall put away** [*divorce*] **his wife, let him give her a writing of divorcement** [*a legal divorce*]:

Verses 31 and 32 deal with divorce. Clearly, marriage and family involve sacred promises which are very serious. In an ideal society, there would seldom if ever be a divorce. In cases where divorce has taken place, verse 32 can sometimes be misunderstood to teach that anyone who gets a divorce and then remarries is now living in adultery, except where fornication was involved in leading up to the divorce.

Follow the Brethren

A very important principle about following the Brethren, our First Presidency and Quorum of the Twelve, can be taught here. The principle is: The current practice of the Brethren, under the direction of the Lord, constitutes the correct interpretation of the scriptures. Even if you don't completely understand verse 32, you can understand the Brethren. The principle is: What do the Brethren do? Do they ever allow a worthy divorced person to be sealed to another spouse, in the temple? Answer: Yes. Would they allow such a thing if such sealing led automatically to adultery? Answer: No. It would be a mockery of most sacred ordinances. Conclusion: There must be some things we don't understand about verse 32.

With this in mind, we might wonder at the meaning of specific words in verse 32. For instance, the word "fornication" is usually used with respect to sexual sin between unmarried individuals. Why, then, is it used in this verse where married people are involved? One possibility is that the word "fornication" is often used in the scriptures to mean total disloyalty, breaking covenants, etc. See, for example, Revelation 14:8, 17:2, 19:2.

The word "adultery" is likewise often used in the sense of total disloyalty to God, apostasy, etc. This is mentioned in the Bible Dictionary, in the back of your LDS Bible, under the topic "Adultery," where it says: "While adultery is usually spoken of in the individual sense, it is sometimes used to illustrate the apostasy of a nation or a whole people from the ways of the Lord, such as Israel forsaking her God and going after strange gods and strange practices" (Exodus 20:14; Jeremiah 3:7–10; Matthew 5:27–32; Luke 18:11).

32 **But I say unto you, That whosoever shall put away** [*divorce*] **his wife, saving for** [*except for*] **the cause of fornication,** causeth her to commit adultery: and whosoever shall marry her that is divorced committeth adultery. [*See notes above.*]

33 Again, ye have heard that it hath been said by them of old time, **Thou shalt not forswear thyself** [*commit perjury; make false or insincere promises*], **but shalt perform unto the Lord thine oaths** [*keep your word*]:

34 **But I say unto you, Swear** [*make contracts, promises, etc.*] **not at all**; neither **by heaven**; for it is God's throne:

35 **Nor by the earth**; for it is his footstool: **neither by Jerusalem**; for it is the city of the great King.

36 **Neither** shalt thou swear **by thy head,** because thou canst not make one hair white or black.

It was common among the Jews to make agreements, contracts, and such, so complex that they were easy to get out of, legally. For instance, if one promised "by the full moon" that a chariot for sale was in top shape, and it wasn't, one could later say to the irate customer that the moon wasn't actually a full moon on the day of the contract; rather, was a day or two away from its full phase. Thus, the one giving his word was legally exempt from keeping it.

37 But **let your communication be, Yea, yea; Nay, nay**: for whatsoever is more than these cometh of evil. [*In other words, if you make a promise, keep it.*]

38 Ye have heard that it hath been said, An **eye for an eye, and a tooth for a tooth:**

This could be considered a rather high law, as given in Exodus 21:24–25, Leviticus 24:20, etc. In effect, it meant "Only one eye for an eye, only one tooth for a tooth, only one cow for a cow, only one sheep for a sheep." Many people tended to get revenge, kill off a whole village in retaliation for the death of a sheep or other wrong against themselves. Now, the Savior will give a much higher law, a law requiring even more self-control and forgiving. Keeping such higher laws develops Christlike qualities in us. These higher laws are designed by the Lord to lead us along the path toward exaltation, as stated in verse 45, "That ye may be the children of (successful followers of) your Father which is in heaven." In other words, this is a vital part of our education toward becoming gods.

39 But I say unto you, That ye resist not evil: but **whosoever shall smite thee on thy right cheek, turn to him the other also.**

40 And **if any man will sue thee at the law, and take away thy coat, let him have thy cloke also.**

41 And **whosoever shall compel thee to go a mile, go with him twain.**

Note: Often, we tend to look at these verses and think in terms of extremes. For instance, if attacked by a mob, intent on severely harming or killing us, we might be hesitant to give them a head start by "turning the other cheek." In fact, D&C 98:31 seems to give different instructions for situations where life is in immediate danger. If we look at the Savior's words in terms of daily living, we see and experience that exercising self-control on our part, returning good for evil, does much good in our relationships with others.

42 **Give to him that asketh thee, and from him that would borrow of thee turn not thou away.**

43 **Ye have heard** that it hath been said, Thou shalt **love thy neighbour, and hate thine enemy.**

44 **But I say unto you, Love your enemies, bless them** that curse you, **do good to them** that hate you, and **pray for them** which despitefully use you, and persecute you;

45 **That ye may be the children of your Father** which is in heaven [*that you may be received into celestial glory and become gods*]: for he maketh his sun to rise on the evil and on the good, and sendeth rain on the just [*the righteous*] and on the unjust [*the wicked*]. [*He shows love and kindness for all.*]

46 For **if ye love them which love you, what reward have ye?** do not even the publicans the same? [*Publicans were Jews who worked for the Roman government as tax collectors. They were hated by the Jews and were excommunicated when they accepted such employment. See Bible Dictionary, under "Publicans."*]

47 And **if ye salute your brethren only, what do ye more than others?** do not even the publicans so?

As we become more successful in developing the Christlike qualities given in the above commandments, we draw closer to fulfilling the startling yet wonderful commandment given next in verse 48.

48 **Be ye therefore perfect, even as your Father which is in heaven is perfect.** [*The word "perfect," as used here, means complete, finished, fully developed, as stated in Matthew 5:48, footnote b. This denotes our actively pursuing the path leading to exaltation, eventually becoming "fully developed," and thus makes this commandment attainable for us.*]

JST MATTHEW 5:50

Ye are therefore commanded to be perfect, even as your Father who is in heaven is perfect.

MATTHEW 6

The Sermon on the Mount (continued)

Proper Motives

1 **Take heed that ye do not your alms** [*righteous deeds; contributions to the poor, etc.*] **before men, to be seen of them** [*your main motive for doing them*]: otherwise ye have no reward of your Father which is in heaven.

2 Therefore **when thou doest thine alms, do not sound a trumpet before thee, as the hypocrites** [*people who want to look righteous but do not want to be righteous*] **do** in the synagogues and in the streets, that they may have glory of men. Verily I say unto you, They have their reward [*the reward of having people think they are righteous*].

3 **But when thou doest alms** [*give offerings for the poor, etc.*], **let not thy left hand know what thy right hand doeth**:

4 **That thine alms may be in secret**: and thy Father which seeth in secret himself shall reward thee openly.

5 And **when thou prayest, thou shalt not be as the hypocrites are**: for they love to pray standing in the synagogues [*church buildings where the Jews worshipped*] and in the corners of the streets, that they may be seen of men. Verily I say unto you, They have their reward.

6 **But thou**, when thou prayest, enter into thy closet, and when thou hast shut thy door, **pray to thy Father which is in secret**; and thy Father which seeth in secret shall reward thee openly.

7 But **when ye pray, use not vain** [*useless, meaningless, ineffective*] **repetitions**, as the heathen [*non-Jews, non-Christians*] do: for they think that they shall be heard for their much speaking.

8 **Be not ye therefore like unto them**: for your Father knoweth what things ye have need of, before ye ask him.

The Savior now gives us what is commonly known as "The Lord's Prayer." It is a beautiful example of prayer and may be considered to be one example of appropriate prayer, rather than a rigid form to be followed without deviation.

The Lord's Prayer

9 **After this manner therefore pray ye: Our Father which art in heaven, Hallowed** [*sacred, holy*] **be thy name.**

10 **Thy kingdom come. Thy will be done in earth, as it is in heaven.**

11 **Give us this day our daily bread.**

12 **And forgive us our debts** [*sins, faults, offenses—see Matthew 6:12, footnote a*], **as we forgive our debtors.** [*This is an important formula for our obtaining forgiveness for our own sins.*]

13 And lead us not into temptation [*we should avoid purposely putting ourselves into temptation*], but deliver us from evil: For thine is the kingdom, and the power, and the glory, for ever. Amen.

Forgiving Others

14 For **if ye forgive men their trespasses** [*their sins against you*], **your heavenly Father will also forgive you:**

15 **But if ye forgive not men their trespasses, neither will your Father forgive your trespasses.** [*This is a very simple guide to obtaining forgiveness ourselves.*]

The Savior now reminds us again that our internal motives are what really count in pursuing the path to exaltation.

16 Moreover **when ye fast, be not, as the hypocrites** [*people who want to look righteous but don't*

LEAD US NOT INTO TEMPTATION, BUT DELIVER US FROM EVIL.

MATTHEW 6:13

want to be righteous], **of a sad countenance: for they disfigure their faces, that they may appear unto men to fast.** Verily I say unto you, They have their reward [*their reward is that people look at them and think that they are righteous*].

17 **But thou, when thou fastest, anoint thine head, and wash thy face;**

18 **That thou appear not unto men to fast, but unto thy Father which is in secret:** and thy Father, which seeth in secret, shall reward thee openly.

Another reminder about priorities is presented now.

Priorities

19 **Lay not up for yourselves treasures upon earth,** where moth and rust doth corrupt, and where thieves break through and steal:

20 **But lay up for yourselves treasures in heaven,** where neither moth nor rust doth corrupt, and where thieves do not break through nor steal:

In the Book of Mormon, Jacob 2:17–19, we find the following counsel about obtaining personal wealth which can go along with these teachings of the Savior in the Sermon on the Mount:

JACOB 2:17–19

17 Think of your brethren like unto yourselves, and be familiar with all and free with your substance, that they may be rich like unto you.

18 But before ye seek for riches, seek ye for the kingdom of God.

19 And after ye have obtained a hope in Christ ye shall obtain riches, if ye seek them; and ye will seek them for the intent to do good—to clothe the naked, and to feed the hungry, and to liberate the captive, and administer relief to the sick and the afflicted.

21 For **where your treasure is, there will your heart be also.**

22 **The light of the body is the eye: if therefore thine eye be single** [*Matthew 6:22, footnote b, healthy, sincere, without improper motives*], **thy whole body shall be full of light.** [*What you watch, read, intentionally look at, etc., strongly affects your spiritual well-being.*]

JST MATTHEW 6:22

...single to the glory of God...

23 **But if thine eye be evil** [*intentionally takes in evil things*], **thy whole body shall be full of darkness.** If therefore the light that is in thee be darkness, how great is that darkness [*spiritual darkness*]!

24 ¶ **No man can serve two masters:** for either he will hate the one, and love the other; or else he will hold to the one, and despise the other. **Ye cannot serve God and mammon** [*worldly sins, pleasures, desires*].

We learn from the wording in the JST that the Savior now turns from the multitude, and addresses verses 25–34 specifically to His Apostles and some disciples, telling them how they will be taken care of by the Father while on their missions. If you do not understand this, you might mistakenly consider some of the counsel in verses 25 to 34 to apply to all people. For instance, you might quit working and trust the Lord to take care of you, thinking that if you have sufficient faith all your needs will be taken care of. Some people and groups have misapplied these verses with sad results.

JST MATTHEW 6:25–27

25 And, again, I say unto you, Go ye into the world, and care not for the world; for the world will hate you, and will persecute you, and will turn you out of their synagogues.

26 Nevertheless, ye shall go forth from house to house, teaching the people; and I will go before you.

27 And your heavenly Father will provide for you, whatsoever things ye need for food, what ye shall eat; and for raiment, what ye shall wear or put on.

Instructions to the Apostles

25 **Therefore I say unto you** [*the Savior's Apostles and disciples, who are now being given*

instructions to take the gospel to all the world], **Take no thought for your life, what ye shall eat, or what ye shall drink; nor yet for your body, what ye shall put on.** Is not the life more than meat [*food (in our Bible's language, "meat") means food in general, "flesh" means meat as we use the word*], and the body than raiment [*clothing*]?

26 **Behold the fowls of the air**: for they **sow not** [*don't plant crops*], **neither do they reap** [*harvest crops*], nor gather into barns [*nor store grain in barns*]; **yet your heavenly Father feedeth them. Are ye** [*the Savior's Apostles and disciples*] **not much better than they?**

27 Which of you by taking thought can add one cubit [*about 18 inches*] unto his stature [*physical height*]?

28 And why take ye thought for raiment [*clothing*]? **Consider the lilies of the field**, how they grow; they toil not, neither do they spin [*weave cloth*]:

29 And yet I say unto you, That **even Solomon in all his glory was not arrayed** [*dressed*] **like one of these.**

30 Wherefore, **if God so clothe the grass of the field**, which to day is, and to morrow is cast into the oven, **shall he not much more clothe you**, O ye of little faith?

31 **Therefore take no thought** [*don't worry about your physical needs while on missions, etc.*], **saying, What shall we eat?** or, What shall we **drink?** or, **Wherewithal shall we be clothed?**

32 (For after all these things do the Gentiles seek:) for **your heavenly Father knoweth that ye have need of all these things.**

33 But **seek ye first the kingdom of God, and his righteousness**; and all these things shall be added unto you. [*Cross-reference this with Jacob 2:17–19 as given between verses 20 and 21 above.*]

34 **Take therefore no thought for the morrow: for the morrow shall take thought for the things of itself** [*in other words, the Lord will take care of the Apostles' physical needs while they are on missions*]. **Sufficient unto the day is the evil thereof** [*The New International Version of the Bible translates this sentence to read, "Each day has enough trouble of its own." In other words, the Apostles and disciples are being told that they will have enough daily troubles in preaching the gospel, without the distraction of worrying about their physical needs.*]

MATTHEW 7

The Sermon on the Mount (continued)

Judging

1 **Judge not, that ye be not judged** [*judged harshly on Judgment Day, etc.*].

Obviously, there are situations in which we must judge, or we would constantly be victims of foolishness and deceit. The JST adds important clarity to this verse, as follows:

JST MATTHEW 7:1–2

1 Now these are the words which Jesus taught his disciples that they should say unto the people.

2 **Judge not unrighteously**, that ye be not judged; **but judge righteous judgment**.

2 **For with what judgment ye judge, ye shall be judged**: and with what measure ye mete [*give out to others*], it shall be measured to you again.

3 And **why beholdest thou the mote** [*tiny speck; imperfection*] **that is in thy brother's eye, but considerest not the beam** [*large wooden beam; symbolic of shortcomings, faults*] **that is in thine own eye?**

4 **Or how wilt thou say to thy brother, Let me pull out the mote out of thine eye; and, behold, a beam is in thine own eye?**

5 **Thou hypocrite**, first cast out the beam out of thine own eye; and then shalt thou see clearly to

cast out the mote out of thy brother's eye.

JST MATTHEW 7:4–8

And again, ye shall say unto them, Why is it that thou beholdest the mote that is in thy brother's eye, but considerest not the beam that is in thine own eye?

5 Or how wilt thou say to thy brother, Let me pull out the mote out of thine eye; and canst not behold a beam in thine own eye?

6 And Jesus said unto his disciples, Beholdest thou the scribes, and the Pharisees, and the priests, and the Levites? They teach in their synagogues, but do not observe the law, nor the commandments; and all have gone out of the way, and are under sin.

7 Go thou and say unto them, Why teach ye men the law and the commandments, when ye yourselves are the children of corruption?

8 Say unto them, Ye hypocrites, first cast out the beam out of thine own eye; and then shalt thou see clearly to cast out the mote out of thy brother's eye.

Cautions about Sharing Sacred Things

6 **Give not that which is holy unto the dogs, neither cast ye your pearls before swine** [*be careful with whom you share sacred things*], lest they trample them under their feet, and turn again and rend you [*they may turn on you and try to destroy your testimony*].

The Lord next invites us to feel free to ask for help from Him.

Ask, Seek, Knock

7 **Ask, and it shall be given you; seek, and ye shall find; knock, and it shall be opened unto you:**

The words "ask," "seek," and "knock" remind us that work is required on our part.

8 For **every one that asketh receiveth; and he that seeketh findeth; and to him that knocketh it shall be opened.**

9 Or **what man is there of you, whom if his son ask bread, will he give him a stone?**

10 **Or if he ask a fish, will he give him a serpent?**

11 If ye then, being evil, know how to give good gifts unto your children, **how much more shall your Father which is in heaven give good things to them that ask him?**

The Savior gives what is known as "The Golden Rule" in the next verse.

The Golden Rule

12 Therefore **all things whatsoever ye would that men should do to you, do ye even so to them:** for this is the law and the prophets [*the "law" means the first five books of the Old Testament, and the "prophets" means the inspired writings of Old Testament prophets; the meaning of the phrase "for this is the law and the prophets" is that a major focus of the law and the prophets was to teach us to be good to each other*].

13 **Enter ye in at the strait** [*spelled this way, the word "strait" means narrow, reminding us that this gate has limited access, and requires focus, faith, repentance, baptism, and personal righteousness for entrance*] **gate:** for wide is the gate, and broad is the way [*there are many ways to be wicked*], **that leadeth to destruction,** and many there be which go in thereat:

In the next verse we find the words "strait" and "narrow" used together. This is often referred to as "the strait and narrow path," meaning, in effect, the "narrow and narrowing path." The message here is that the more righteous you become, the more you restrict your behaviors away from evil and toward personal righteousness. The imagery is that the less you wander back and forth toward the outer edges of the path, seeing how close you can get to temptation and evil, the "narrower" your chosen path becomes. There is a bit of a caution here: As you become more righteous, you discover inappropriate personal behaviors which you didn't even notice before. Sometimes, faithful Saints become discouraged and think, "It's no use. I'll never be perfect!" as these so-called "smaller" imperfections come to light. Actually, you might want to rejoice in the fact that your path has become sufficiently "narrow" that you notice these imperfections. Then, go ahead and work on overcoming them.

14 Because **strait is the gate, and narrow is the way, which leadeth unto life** [*eternal life, exaltation*], and few there be that find it.

"By Their Fruits Shall Ye Know Them"

15 **Beware of false prophets** [*anyone who teaches false philosophies, behaviors, etc., by word, example, deed, or whatever*], **which come to you in sheep's clothing** [*they seem harmless*], **but inwardly they are ravening** [*very dangerous*] **wolves.**

16 **Ye shall know them by their fruits** [*what they ultimately produce*]. Do men gather grapes of thorns, or figs of thistles [*can you harvest good food from weeds*]?

17 Even so **every good tree bringeth forth good fruit; but a corrupt tree bringeth forth evil fruit.**

"Tree" is used here to symbolize people.

18 **A good tree cannot bring forth evil fruit, neither can a corrupt tree bring forth good fruit.**

19 **Every tree that bringeth not forth good fruit is hewn down, and cast into the fire** [*symbolic of the burning of the wicked at the Second Coming; also symbolic of the final judgment*].

20 Wherefore [*therefore*] **by their fruits ye shall know them.**

The Master now emphasizes again that the gate is "strait" (narrow). In other words, we must keep the commandments in order to enter celestial glory.

21 **Not every one that saith unto me, Lord, Lord, shall enter into the kingdom of heaven** [*celestial glory*]; **but he that doeth the will of my Father which is in heaven.**

22 **Many will say to me** in that day [*judgment day*], Lord, Lord, **have we not** prophesied in thy name? and in thy name have cast out devils? and in thy name **done many wonderful works?**

23 And then will I profess unto them, **I never knew you:** depart from me, ye that work iniquity [*commit sin; disobey the laws of God*].

JST Matthew 7:33

And then will I say, **Ye never knew me.**

House Built on the Rock

24 Therefore whosoever heareth these sayings of mine, and doeth them, I will liken him unto a wise man, which built his house [*symbolic of his life*] **upon a rock** [*symbolic of Christ, who is the "rock" of our salvation. See, for example, Hymn #258*]:

25 **And the rain descended, and the floods came, and the winds blew** [*trials and difficulties of life*], **and beat upon that house** [*his life*]; **and it fell not: for it was founded upon a rock** [*Christ*].

House Built on Sand

26 And **every one that heareth these sayings of mine** [*in other words, who is accountable*], **and doeth them not, shall be likened unto a foolish man, which built his house upon the sand** [*worldly ways, priorities etc.*]:

27 **And the rain descended, and the floods came, and the winds blew, and beat upon that house** [*his life*]; **and it fell: and great was the fall of it.**

Did you notice that the "rain descended, and the floods came, and the winds blew and beat upon" both houses? In other words, trials and tribulation are a part of mortality for the righteous as well as the wicked. The outcome for us is determined by the foundation upon which we build.

28 And it came to pass, **when Jesus had ended these sayings, the people were astonished at his doctrine:**

JST Matthew 7:36

36 And it came to pass when Jesus had ended these sayings **with his disciples**, the people were astonished at his doctrine;

29 **For he taught them as one having authority,** and not as the scribes [*the main teachers and interpreters of the law among the Jews who rose in*

great opposition to the Savior. See Bible Dictionary, under "Scribes"].

JST MATTHEW 7:37
37 For he taught them as one having authority from God, and **not as having authority from the scribes**.

MATTHEW 8

THE MASTER NOW continues His ministry and teaching in Galilee. His popularity has resulted in large crowds following Him.

1 **When he was come down from the mountain** [*after giving the Sermon on the Mount*], **great multitudes followed him.**

The Healing of a Leper

2 And, behold, **there came a leper** and worshipped him, **saying, Lord, if thou wilt, thou canst make me clean** [*heal me*].

Leprosy is described in Webster's New World Dictionary, Second College Edition, 1980, as follows: "A chronic infectious disease . . . that attacks the skin, flesh, nerves, etc.; it is characterized by nodules, ulcers, white scaly scabs, deformities, and wasting of body parts."

3 **And Jesus put forth his hand, and touched him, saying, I will; be thou clean. And immediately his leprosy was cleansed.**

Every time you read of a physical healing of the sick, performed by the Savior, you can consider it symbolic of His ability to heal us spiritually, through His Atonement. Thus, every healing will remind you of the Master's power to heal you spiritually, through your repentance and His forgiving you. In this case of the healing of a leper, leprosy could be symbolic of very serious sin which can gradually destroy us spiritually.

4 **And Jesus saith unto him** [*the leper who had been healed*], **See thou tell no man** [*keep this spiritual experience very private*]; but go thy way, **shew thyself to the priest, and offer the gift that Moses commanded, for a testimony unto them** [*keep the requirements of the Law of Moses with respect to the cleansing of lepers*].

Healing of the Centurion's Servant

5 And when Jesus was entered into Capernaum, **there came unto him a centurion** [*a Roman soldier in charge of 100 soldiers*], **beseeching him,**

The Romans were Gentiles, and thus were considered by the Jews to be inferior in the eyes of God, compared to the Jews, who considered themselves to be God's only chosen people. All others, despite their best efforts, were considered to be second class citizens in the Kingdom of God.

6 And **saying, Lord, my servant lieth at home sick of the palsy**, grievously tormented.

7 And **Jesus saith** unto him, **I will come and heal him.**

8 The **centurion** answered and said, Lord**, I am not worthy that thou shouldest come under my roof:** but **speak** the word only, **and my servant shall be healed.**

9 For I am a man under authority, having soldiers under me: and I say to this man, Go, and he goeth; and to another, Come, and he cometh; and to my servant, Do this, and he doeth it.

10 When **Jesus** heard it, he marvelled, and **said** to them that followed, **Verily I say unto you, I have not found so great faith, no, not in Israel.**

JST MATTHEW 8:9
9 And when they that followed him, heard this, **they marveled**. And **when Jesus heard this**, he said unto them that followed,

11 And I say unto you, That **many shall come from the east and west** [*many foreigners, including Gentiles*], **and shall sit down with Abraham, and Isaac, and Jacob, in the kingdom of heaven** [*will be saved along with Abraham, Isaac, and Jacob in celestial glory*].

12 **But the children of the kingdom** [*those Jews who considered themselves to be elite, above all other people*] **shall be cast out into outer darkness** [*probably not meaning into perdition, with Satan, rather, in the spirit world prison, as explained in*

Alma 40:11–13]: there shall be weeping and gnashing of teeth.

13 **And Jesus said unto the centurion, Go thy way; and as thou hast believed, so be it done unto thee.** And his servant was healed in the selfsame hour.

Peter's Mother-in-law Healed

14 And **when Jesus was come into Peter's house, he saw his wife's mother laid, and sick of a fever** [*Peter's mother-in-law was very ill*].

15 **And he touched her hand, and the fever left her**: and she arose, and ministered unto them [*attended to their needs*].

Many Others Healed

16 When the even [*evening*] was come, they brought unto him many that were possessed with devils: and **he** cast out the spirits with his word, and **healed all that were sick** [*symbolic of the Atonement's power to cleanse and heal*]:

17 **That it might be fulfilled which was spoken by Esaias** [*Isaiah*] the prophet, saying, Himself [*Christ*] took our infirmities, and bare our sicknesses [*see Isaiah 53:5, Alma 7:12*].

From the above verse and cross-references, we learn that the Savior's Atonement works not only for our sins, but also for our infirmities, meaning our shortcomings, imperfections, etc., as we strive to live righteously.

18 Now **when Jesus saw great multitudes about him, he gave commandment to depart unto the other side** [*of the Sea of Galilee*].

19 And **a certain scribe** [*a leader among the Jews*] **came, and said** unto him, **Master, I will follow thee whithersoever thou goest.**

20 **And Jesus saith unto him, The foxes have holes**, and the **birds** of the air **have nests; but the Son of man hath not where to lay his head** [*in other words, following the Savior can require difficult personal sacrifices*].

21 And **another of his disciples** [*followers*] **said** unto him, Lord, **suffer me** [*allow me*] **first to go and bury my father.**

22 **But Jesus said unto him, Follow me; and let the dead bury their dead** [*there is probably more to the story here, but the message is clear, that following the Savior requires real commitment to Him and His instructions*].

"Master, the Tempest Is Raging"

23 And when **he** was **entered into a ship**, his disciples followed him.

We now read of the experience during the storm which was the inspiration for Hymn #105, *Master the Tempest Is Raging*. In these next verses we will again be clearly taught that Christ has power over the elements.

24 And, behold, **there arose a great tempest** [*storm*] in the sea, insomuch that the ship was covered with the waves: but he [*the Savior*] was asleep.

One can imagine the stress on the disciples in the ship, being in such danger while the Master slept. Also, we are reminded that the Savior could get very, very tired and weary. In Mosiah 3:7, we read: "And lo, he shall suffer temptations, and pain of body, hunger, thirst, and fatigue, even more than man can suffer, except it be unto death." We might also imagine the dilemma faced by the frightened disciples, knowing how tired the Savior was, in deciding which one of them should attempt to awaken the sleeping Master.

25 **And his disciples** came to him, and **awoke him, saying, Lord, save us: we perish.**

26 And he saith unto them, Why are ye fearful, O ye of little faith? **Then he arose, and rebuked the winds and the sea; and there was a great calm.**

27 But **the men marvelled, saying, What**

manner of man is this, that even the winds and the sea obey him [*the disciples are still learning about the Savior and who He really is*]!

Two Possessed by Devils

28 And **when he was come to the other side** into the country of the Gergesenes [*an area on the eastern side of the Sea of Galilee; see* Talmage, *Jesus the Christ, pp. 323–24*], **there met him two possessed with devils,** coming out of the tombs, exceeding fierce, so that no man might pass by that way.

29 And, behold, **they** [*the evil spirits*] cried out, saying, What have we to do with thee, Jesus, thou Son of God? art thou come hither to torment us before the time?

There are many things that can be learned about evil spirits, based on this incident. Apostle Bruce R. McConkie summarized these things as follows:

"(1) That evil spirits, actual beings from Lucifer's realm, gain literal entrance into mortal bodies;

"(2)That they then have such power over those bodies as to control the physical acts performed, even to the framing of the very words spoken by the mouth of those so possessed;

"(3)That persons possessed by evil spirits are subjected to the severest mental and physical sufferings and to the basest sort of degradation—all symbolical of the eternal torment to be imposed upon those who fall under Satan's control in the world to come;

"(4) That devils remember Jesus from pre-existence, recognize him as the One who was then foreordained to be the Redeemer, and know that he came into mortality as the Son of God;

"(5) That the desire to gain bodies is so great among Lucifer's minions as to cause them, not only to steal the mortal tabernacles of men, but to enter the bodies of animals;

"(6) That the devils know their eventual destiny is to be cast out into an eternal hell from whence there is no return;

"(7) That rebellious and worldly people are not converted to the truth by observing miracles; and

"(8) That those cleansed from evil spirits can then be used on the Lord's errand to testify of his grace and goodness so that receptive persons may be led to believe in him." (*Doctrinal New Testament Commentary*, p. 311)

2,000 Swine Drown

30 And **there was a good way off from them** an herd of **many swine** [*pigs*] feeding.

31 So **the devils besought** [*asked*] him, saying, If thou cast us out, suffer [*allow*] **us to go away into the herd of swine.**

32 And **he said unto them, Go.** And when they were come out, **they went into the herd of swine**: and, behold, **the whole herd of swine ran violently down a steep place into the sea,** and perished in the waters.

33 **And they** [*the herdsmen*] **that kept them** [*the pigs*] **fled,** and went their ways into the city, **and told every thing,** and what was befallen to the possessed of the devils.

34 And, behold, **the whole city came out to meet Jesus**: and when they saw him, **they besought** [*asked*] **him that he would depart out of their coasts** [*they asked Jesus to leave*].

It is sad that the people of the city asked the Savior to leave, rather than inviting Him to stay and teach them His gospel. Perhaps they didn't want another economic disaster—Mark 5:13 tells us there were 2,000 swine.

MATTHEW 9

IN THIS CHAPTER, Matthew tells us that the Savior now went to His own home town of Nazareth. Watch how He is treated by those who knew Him as He was growing up.

1 And **he entered into a ship,** and passed over [*went back over to the west side of the Sea of Galilee*], **and came into his own city** [*Nazareth*].

Healing of the Man with Palsy

2 And, behold, **they brought to him a man sick of the palsy**, lying on a bed: and **Jesus seeing their faith said** unto the sick of the palsy; Son, **be of good cheer** [*cheer up*]**; thy sins be forgiven thee.**

3 And, behold, certain of **the scribes** [*religious leaders among the Jews who claimed the right to interpret the scriptures and had great power in the Jewish culture*] **said within themselves, This man blasphemeth** [*is acting with total disrespect for God and sacred things; a crime punishable by death in the Jewish society*].

4 And **Jesus knowing their thoughts** [*the scribes' thoughts*] **said, Wherefore** [*why*] **think ye evil in your hearts?**

5 For **whether** [*which*] **is easier, to say, Thy sins be forgiven thee; or to say, Arise, and walk?** [*Any person could say, "Your sins are forgiven," because there is no immediate proof as to whether or not he speaks with authority. But, if a person says, "Arise and walk," there will be immediate evidence as to whether or not he is a fake.*]

6 **But that ye may know that the Son of man** [*the "Son of "Man of Holiness." Man of Holiness is Heavenly Father's name in Adam's language—see Moses 6:57. In other words, Jesus is telling these scribes that He is the Son of God*] **hath power on earth to forgive sins,** (then saith he to the sick of the palsy,) **Arise, take up thy bed, and go unto thine house.**

7 **And he** [*the man healed of palsy*] **arose, and departed to his house.**

> JST MATTHEW 9:5–7
>
> 5 For **is it not easier to say**, Thy sins be forgiven thee, than to say, Arise and walk?
>
> 6 But **I said this that ye may know that the Son of man hath power on earth to forgive sins.**
>
> 7 Then Jesus said unto the sick of the palsy, Arise, take up thy bed, and go unto thy house.

8 But **when the multitudes saw it, they marvelled, and glorified God**, which had given such power unto men.

9 And **as Jesus passed forth from thence, he saw a man, named Matthew**, sitting at the receipt of custom [*Matthew was a tax collector*]: **and he saith unto him, Follow me. And he arose, and followed him.**

10 And it came to pass, **as Jesus sat at meat** [*eating a meal*] in the house, behold, **many publicans** [*Jews who worked for the Romans as tax collectors; see Bible Dictionary, under "Publicans"*] **and sinners came and sat down with him and his disciples.**

11 **And when the Pharisees** [*religious leaders among the Jews; see Bible Dictionary, under "Pharisees"*] **saw it, they said unto his disciples, Why eateth your Master with publicans and sinners?**

12 But **when Jesus heard that, he said unto them** [*the Pharisees*], **They that be whole need not a physician, but they that are sick.**

13 But **go ye and learn what that meaneth** [*what it means in the scriptures when it says*], **I will have mercy, and not sacrifice** [*quoting Hosea 6:6; the Pharisees were very strict in living the letter of the Law of Moses, including proper animal sacrifice, but did not often show mercy*]: **for I am not come to call the righteous, but sinners to repentance.**

14 **Then came to him the disciples of John** [*followers of John the Baptist, who was in prison by this time and soon to be beheaded by Herod*], **saying, Why do we and the Pharisees fast oft, but thy disciples fast not?**

15 And **Jesus said unto them, Can the children of the bridechamber mourn, as long as the bridegroom is with them?** but the days will **come, when the bridegroom shall be taken** from them, and then shall they fast.

Understanding a bit of Jewish culture will help with the last verse. Wedding imagery is involved.

Jesus is the bridegroom, or groom, as we would say it. Faithful followers are the bride. "Bridechamber" would be the place where the wedding feast is held and, symbolically, would be the land of Israel where the Savior was performing His mortal mission. While the groom and the bride are together, much celebrating and feasting—hearing and understanding the Savior's teachings—would take place. It would not make sense to mourn and fast at this time. But, when the Savior is crucified and taken from them, the "children of the bridechamber," the faithful Saints, will mourn and fast.

The JST adds four verses here.

MATTHEW

JST MATTHEW 9:18–21

18 Then said the Pharisees unto him, Why will ye not receive us with our baptism, seeing we keep the whole law?

19 But Jesus said unto them, Ye keep not the law. If ye had kept the law, ye would have received me, for I am he who gave the law.

20 I receive not you with your baptism, because it profiteth you nothing.

21 For when that which is new is come, the old is ready to be put away.

Next, Jesus will teach that people who are set in their ways do not usually accept new ideas, in this case, the true gospel.

16 **No man putteth** [*sews*] **a piece of new cloth** [*the true gospel*] **unto an old garment** [*piece of clothing; symbolic of people set in their ways with false religions and philosophies*], for that which is put in to fill it up taketh from the garment, and the rent [*rip, tear*] is made worse.

New Wine, Old Bottles

17 **Neither do men put new wine** [*symbolic of the newly restored gospel which the Savior was bringing to the people*] **into old bottles** [*symbolic of people who are steeped in tradition*]: else the bottles break, and the wine runneth out, and the bottles perish: but they put new wine into new bottles, and both are preserved.

Healing of Jairus' Daughter

18 While he spake these things unto them, behold, **there came a certain ruler** [*Luke 8:41 tells us his name was Jairus and that he was a ruler in a synagogue*], and worshipped him, **saying, My daughter is even now dead: but come and lay thy hand upon her, and she shall live.**

19 And **Jesus arose, and followed him, and so did his disciples.**

A Woman Touches Christ's Garment

20 And, behold, **a woman**, which was diseased **with an issue of blood** twelve years [*who had been hemorrhaging for twelve years; see Matthew 9:20, footnote a*], **came behind him, and touched the hem of his garment** [*robe*]:

21 **For she said within herself, If I may but touch his garment, I shall be whole** [*healed*].

22 But **Jesus turned him about, and when he saw her, he said, Daughter, be of good comfort; thy faith hath made thee whole.** And the woman was made whole from that hour.

23 And **when Jesus came into the ruler's house,** and saw the minstrels [*musicians*] and the people [*mourners–often paid*] making a noise,

24 **He said** unto them, Give place: for **the maid** [*the ruler's daughter*] **is not dead, but sleepeth. And they laughed him to scorn** [*ridiculed Jesus*].

25 But when the people were put forth [*had been sent out of the house*], **he went in, and took her by the hand, and the maid arose.**

26 And the fame hereof went abroad into all that land.

Two Blind Men Healed

27 And when Jesus departed thence [*from that*

place], **two blind men followed him**, crying, and saying, Thou Son of David [*it was widely taught among the Jews that the Messiah would be a descendant of King David; thus, these blind men were acknowledging Jesus as the promised Messiah*], have mercy on us.

28 And when he was come into the house, the blind men came to him: and **Jesus saith unto them, Believe ye that I am able to do this? They said unto him, Yea, Lord.**

29 **Then touched he their eyes, saying, According to your faith be it unto you.**

30 **And their eyes were opened** [*they were healed*]; and **Jesus straitly charged them** [*strictly instructed them*], **saying, See that no man know it.**

31 **But they**, when they were departed, **spread abroad his fame** in all that country.

Man Possessed with a Devil

32 As they went out, behold, **they brought to him a dumb man** [*one who could not speak*] possessed **with a devil** [*an evil spirit*].

33 And **when the devil was cast out**, the dumb spake: and **the multitudes marvelled, saying, It was never so seen in Israel.**

Jesus Is Accused of Healing by Satan's Power

34 **But the Pharisees** [*religious leaders among the Jews*] **said, He casteth out devils through the prince of the devils** [*the Pharisees, who seem good at missing the point, miss it again, and accuse Jesus of working for Satan and using the devil's power to cast out other devils*].

35 And **Jesus went about all the cities and villages, teaching in their synagogues, and preaching the gospel of the kingdom, and healing every sickness and every disease among the people** [*symbolic of the power of the Atonement to cleanse and heal all our spiritual ills*].

36 But **when he saw the multitudes, he was moved with compassion on them**, because they fainted, and were scattered abroad, as sheep having no shepherd [*they didn't really know where they were going*].

37 **Then saith he unto his disciples, The harvest truly is plenteous** [*there are so many people who need the true gospel*], **but the labourers** [*missionaries, etc.*] **are few;**

38 **Pray ye therefore the Lord of the harvest, that he will send forth labourers into his harvest.**

MATTHEW 10

THIS CHAPTER CONTAINS much specific instruction and training for the newly called Apostles. This could be thought of as the first "Handbook of Instructions" for the Twelve.

The Twelve Are Called and Instructed

1 **And when he had called unto him his twelve disciples** [*the Twelve Apostles*], **he gave them power** against unclean spirits, to cast them out, and to heal all manner of sickness and all manner of disease.

2 Now **the names of the twelve apostles** are these; The first, Simon, who is called **Peter**, and **Andrew** his brother; **James** the son of Zebedee, and **John** his brother;

3 **Philip**, and **Bartholomew**; **Thomas**, and **Matthew** the publican [*tax collector*]; **James** the son of Alphaeus, and Lebbaeus, whose surname [*last name; family name*] was **Thaddaeus;**

4 **Simon** the Canaanite, and **Judas Iscariot**, who also betrayed him.

5 **These twelve Jesus sent forth**, and commanded them, **saying, Go not into the way of the**

Gentiles, and into any city of the Samaritans enter ye not [*in other words, don't go to the Gentiles yet*]:

6 **But go rather to the lost sheep of the house of Israel.**

7 And as ye go, **preach, saying, The kingdom of heaven is at hand** [*the saving gospel of Jesus Christ is available to you now*].

8 **Heal the sick, cleanse the lepers, raise the dead, cast out devils: freely ye have received, freely give.**

9 **Provide neither gold, nor silver, nor brass in your purses,**

10 **Nor scrip** [*a bag containing food and provisions*] for your journey, **neither two coats**, neither **shoes**, nor yet **staves**: for the workman is worthy of his meat [*the Lord will take care of you*].

11 And **into whatsoever city or town ye shall enter, enquire who in it is worthy; and there abide** till ye go thence [*stay with a worthy person while there*].

12 And **when ye come into an house, salute it** [*Luke 10:5 helps with this; it says "Into whatsoever house ye enter, first say, Peace be to this house"*].

13 And if the house be worthy, let your peace come upon it: but if it be not worthy, let your peace return to you.

14 And **whosoever shall not receive you**, nor hear your words, when ye depart out of that house or city, **shake off the dust of your feet** [*as a witness that they have had an opportunity to accept the gospel*].

15 Verily I say unto you, It shall be more tolerable for the land of Sodom and Gomorrha [*Old Testament cities which were destroyed completely because of wickedness*] in the day of judgment, than for that city. [*It is a very serious thing to reject the Lord's servants.*]

16 Behold, **I send you forth as sheep in the midst of wolves: be ye therefore wise as serpents** [*use honest cunning and common sense*], **and harmless as doves** [*be without guile*].

17 **But beware of men** [*worldly and wicked people*]: for they will deliver you up to the councils [*arrest you and turn you over to local courts*], and they will scourge [*flog, whip*] you in their synagogues;

18 And **ye shall be brought before governors and kings for my sake** [*because of me and my work*], for a testimony against them and the Gentiles.

19 But when they deliver you up [*arrest you*], **take no thought how or what ye shall speak: for it shall be given you** [*by the Spirit*] **in that same hour what ye shall speak.**

20 For **it is not ye that speak, but the Spirit of your Father which speaketh in you.**

21 And the brother shall deliver up the brother to death, and the father the child: and the children shall rise up against their parents, and cause them to be put to death [*you will see much wickedness during your missions*].

22 And **ye shall be hated of all men for my name's sake** [*because of the work you do for me*]: **but he that endureth** [*remains faithful*] **to the end** [*can mean "goal" or "purpose," as well as "to the end of mortal life"*] **shall be saved.**

23 But **when they persecute you in this city, flee ye into another**: for verily I say unto you, **Ye shall not have gone over the cities of Israel, till the Son of man** [*Christ, Son of Man of Holiness—see Moses 6:57*] **be come** [*there is so much missionary work to be done that it will not all be finished before the Second Coming—see McConkie,* Doctrinal New Testament Commentary, Vol. 1, *p. 332*].

24 The disciple is not above his master, nor the servant above his lord [*just as the Savior will go*

through much of persecution, so also His servants will go through much].

25 **It is enough for the disciple that he be** [*become; see Matthew 10:25, footnote a*] **as his master, and the servant as his lord** [*the reward of faithful servants of the Savior is to be joint heirs with Christ, exalted like He is*]. If they have called the master of the house [*Christ*] Beelzebub, how much more shall they call them of his household [*if they call me the devil, don't you think you can expect similar treatment*]?

26 **Fear them not therefore** [*they can't take away your exaltation*]: for there is nothing covered [*evil that is hidden, done in secret*], that shall not be revealed; and hid, that shall not be known [*see 2 Nephi 9:14*].

27 What I tell you in darkness [*private*], that speak ye in light [*in public*]: and what ye hear in the ear [*what I whisper to you*], that preach ye upon the housetops [*preach to everybody*].

28 And **fear not them which kill the body, but are not able to kill the soul** [*don't fear those who may kill you but can't take your salvation from you*]: **but rather fear** [*respect*] **him** [*God, see McConkie, Doctrinal New Testament Commentary, Vol. 1, p. 334*] **which is able to destroy both soul and body in hell.**

The Savior now reminds the Twelve (and us) that the Father is aware of all things and is always aware of our concerns, needs, and desires.

29 Are not two sparrows sold for a farthing? and **one of them shall not fall on the ground without your Father** [*being aware of it*].

30 But **the very hairs of your head are all numbered** [*the Father literally knows everything about you and can bless you as needed*].

31 **Fear ye not therefore, ye are of more value than many sparrows.**

32 **Whosoever therefore shall confess me** [*make covenants with Christ; see Matthew 10:32, footnote a*] **before men, him will I confess** [*acknowledge, accept*] **also before my Father which is in heaven.**

33 **But whosoever shall deny me before men, him will I also deny before my Father which is in heaven.**

In the next verses, the Savior tells the Twelve that, on some occasions, the gospel will divide and separate people from others, even loved ones sometimes.

34 **Think not that I am come to send peace on earth: I came not to send peace, but a sword.**

35 For I am come to set a man at variance against [*in opposition to*] his father, and the daughter against her mother, and the daughter in law against her mother in law.

36 And a man's foes shall be they of his own household [*will be family members*].

37 **He that loveth father or mother more than me is not worthy of me: and he that loveth son or daughter more than me is not worthy of me** [*we must follow Christ no matter what the cost*].

38 And **he that taketh not his cross** [*whatever sacrifices are necessary*], **and followeth after me, is not worthy of me.**

39 **He that findeth his life** [*follows priorities less important than the gospel*] **shall lose it** [*shall not gain exaltation*]: **and he that loseth his life for my sake** [*prioritizes on the gospel above all else*] **shall find it** [*will gain exaltation*].

JST MATTHEW 10:34

34 **He who seeketh to save his life shall lose it**; and he who loseth his life for my sake shall find it.

40 **He that receiveth you re-ceiveth me, and he that receiveth me receiveth him that sent me** [*Heavenly Father*].

41 **He that receiveth a prophet** [*accepts and sustains Church leaders*] in the name of a prophet **shall receive a prophet's reward** [*exaltation*]; and he that receiveth a righteous man in the name of a righteous man shall receive a righteous

man's reward.

Finally, the Savior reminds His Apostles and us, as His disciples (followers), that charity and service must accompany the above-mentioned attributes, if we want to attain exaltation.

42 And **whosoever shall give to drink unto one of these little ones a cup of cold water** only in the name of a disciple, verily I say unto you, **he shall in no wise lose his reward.**

MATTHEW 11

1 And it came to pass, **when Jesus had made an end of commanding his twelve disciples, he departed thence** [*from that place*] **to teach and to preach in their cities.**

2 **Now when John** [*John the Baptist, who was in prison at this time*] **had heard** in the prison **the works of Christ, he sent two of his disciples** [*John's faithful followers*],

3 And said unto him [*John the Baptist's disciples asked Jesus*], **Art thou he that should come** [*are you the promised Messiah?*], **or do we look for another?**

JST MATTHEW 11:3
3 And said unto him, **Art thou he of whom it is written in the prophets** [*in other words, in Old Testament prophecies*] that he should come, or do we look for another?

4 **Jesus answered** and said unto them, **Go and shew John again those things which ye do hear and see:**

5 The **blind receive their sight, and the lame walk, the lepers are cleansed, and the deaf hear, the dead are raised up, and the poor have the gospel preached to them.** [*John the Baptist will recognize that this is the prophesied Savior, when he hears what He has been doing.*]

6 And **blessed is he, whosoever shall not be offended in me.**

7 **And as they** [*John's disciples*] **departed, Jesus began to say unto the multitudes concerning John** [*the Baptist*], **What went ye out into the wilderness to see? A reed shaken with the wind** [*a man who was timid and afraid of opposition*]?

8 But **what went ye out for to see? A man clothed in soft raiment** [*luxurious clothing; in other words, a man pampered by easy living*]? behold, they that wear soft clothing are in kings' houses.

9 But **what went ye out for to see? A prophet? yea, I say unto you, and more than a prophet.** [*Jesus has tender feelings for John the Baptist, and bears witness of John's divine calling and mission.*]

10 **For this is he, of whom it is written** [*prophesied*], Behold, I send my messenger [*John the Baptist*] before thy [*the Savior*] face, which shall prepare thy way before thee [*John is the messenger sent by God to prepare the way before Me*].

11 Verily **I say unto you, Among them that are born of women there hath not risen a greater than John the Baptist:** notwithstanding he that is least in the kingdom of heaven is greater than he.

Verse 11, above, can be a bit confusing, but the Prophet Joseph Smith explains it to us. He tells us that John the Baptist is the greatest prophet born of woman, but that He, Christ, who is considered by the Jews to be the least in the kingdom, is above John the Baptist. See *Teachings of the Prophet Joseph Smith*, pp. 275–76.

12 And **from the days of John the Baptist until now the kingdom of heaven suffereth violence,** and the violent take it by force [*violent people have done much to harm the work of the Lord; see Matthew 11:12, footnote a*].

13 For **all the prophets** [*the Old Testament prophets*] **and the law** [*the first five books of the Old Testament*] **prophesied until John** [*prophesied of things leading up to this time*].

14 **And if ye will receive it** [*accept my word about who John is*], **this is Elias, which was for**

to come [*John is the "Elias," the preparer-of-the-way, who was prophesied to prepare the way for the Savior*].

JST MATTHEW 11:13–15

13 But **the days will come, when the violent shall have no power**; for all the prophets and the law prophesied that it should be thus until John.

14 Yea, as many as have prophesied have foretold of these days.

15 And if ye will receive it, verily, **he was the Elias**, who was for to come and prepare all things.

15 **He that hath ears to hear, let him hear** [*he who is in tune with the Spirit will understand what has just been taught*].

16 But **whereunto shall I liken this generation** [*unto what shall I compare the present generation of people*]? It is like unto children sitting in the markets, and calling unto their fellows,

17 And saying, We have piped unto you, and ye have not danced; we have mourned unto you, and ye have not lamented [*the current generation is ignoring the messengers of God*].

Jesus now tells them that the righteous can never win in the eyes of the wicked. No matter what the righteous do, the wicked still criticize them.

18 For **John** [*the Baptist*] **came neither eating nor drinking, and they say, He hath a devil.**

19 **The Son of man** [*the Son of God, Christ; see Moses 6:57*] **came eating and drinking, and they say, Behold a man gluttonous, and a winebibber, a friend of publicans and sinners.** But wisdom is justified of her children [*actions, deeds; in other words, wise people will see through this constant criticism*].

Some people ask whether or not the Savior ever did come right out and say that He is the Son of God. As you study Matthew, Mark, Luke, and John, you will find many instances, including in verse 19 above, wherein He openly told people that He was the Son of God, the promised Messiah.

20 **Then began he to upbraid** [*scold*] the cities wherein most of his mighty works were done, because they repented not:

21 **Woe unto** thee, **Chorazin**! woe unto thee, **Bethsaida**! for if the mighty works, which were done in you, had been done in Tyre and Sidon, they would have repented long ago in sackcloth and ashes [*"sackcloth and ashes" means in deep humility and mourning for their sins*].

22 But I say unto you, It shall be more tolerable for Tyre and Sidon at the day of judgment, than for you [*because you have the true gospel available and they don't, yet*].

23 And thou, **Capernaum**, which art exalted unto heaven [*full of pride*], shalt be brought down to hell: for if the mighty works, which have been done in thee, had been done in Sodom, it would have remained until this day [*would not have been destroyed*].

24 But I say unto you, That it shall be more tolerable for the land of Sodom in the day of judgment, than for thee.

That Jesus kept in close touch with the Father is evidenced again in these next verses.

25 At that time Jesus answered and said, **I thank thee, O Father**, Lord of heaven and earth, **because thou hast hid these things from the wise and prudent** [*"old bottles" who won't accept "new wine"*], **and hast revealed them unto babes** [*humble people who are willing to accept truth*].

26 Even so [*let it be so*], Father: **for so it seemed good in thy sight.**

27 **All things are delivered unto me of my Father**: and no man knoweth the Son, but the Father; neither knoweth any man the Father, save the Son, and he to whomsoever the Son will reveal him.

The Joseph Smith Translation (JST), helps us understand verses 25–27, above:

JST MATTHEW 11:27–28

27 And at that time, **there came a voice out of heaven, and Jesus answered** and said, I thank thee, O Father, Lord of heaven and earth, because thou hast hid these things from the wise and prudent, and hast revealed them unto babes.

BLESSED IS
HE, WHOSOEVER
SHALL NOT BE
OFFENDED
IN ME.

MATTHEW 11:6

Even so, Father, for so it seemed good in thy sight!

28 All things are delivered unto me of my Father; and no man knoweth the Son, but the Father; neither knoweth any man the Father, save the Son, and they to whom the Son will reveal himself; they shall see the Father also.

28 **Come unto me, all ye that labour and are heavy laden, and I will give you rest.**

29 **Take my yoke** *[make covenants through which you, in effect, put yourselves in the harness with the Savior]* **upon you, and learn of me**; for **I am meek and lowly in heart** *[I am humble and love to help you]*: **and ye shall find rest unto your souls.**

30 For **my yoke is easy, and my burden is light.**

Above, the Savior teaches us that the path to exaltation is actually the easiest way as well as the happiest. The "burdens" one carries as a devout follower of the Master are nothing compared to the burdens of guilt and shame carried by those who choose wickedness as a lifestyle.

MATTHEW 12

THIS CHAPTER BEGINS with a lesson about the proper use of the Sabbath day.

1 At that time **Jesus went on the sabbath day through the corn** *[grain; perhaps wheat]*; **and his disciples were an hungred, and began to pluck the ears of corn** *[the heads of the grain]*, and **to eat.**

2 **But when the Pharisees** *[religious leaders among the Jews]* **saw it, they said** unto him, Behold, **thy disciples do that which is not lawful to do upon the sabbath day.**

3 **But he said unto them, Have ye not read what David** *[David, the one who killed Goliath and later became king]* **did**, when he was an hungred, and they that were with him;

4 How **he entered into the house of God, and did eat the shewbread** *[holy bread used for worship services; see 1 Samuel 21:6]*, which was not lawful for him to eat, neither for them which were with him, but only for the priests?

5 **Or have ye not read in the law, how that on the sabbath days the priests in the temple profane the sabbath** *[break some of the sabbath rules]*, **and are blameless?** *[In other words, you allow it in some cases, but won't allow my disciples to do it; you are hypocrites.]*

JST MATTHEW 12:4
4 Or have ye not read in the law, how that on the Sabbath days the priests in the temple profane the Sabbath, and **ye say they are blameless**?

6 **But I say unto you, That in this place is one greater than the temple** *[I am here among you and I am greater than the temple]*.

Here, again (verse 6, above), Jesus has told them who He is.

7 **But if ye had known what this** *[the following quote]* **meaneth**, I will have mercy, and not sacrifice *[quoting Hosea 6:6]*, **ye would not have condemned the guiltless.** *[In other words, if you are not merciful to others, all the animal sacrifices you can possibly do are of no value and are just empty ritual. You claim to know the scriptures, but you sure don't understand Hosea 6:6!]*

The Pharisees and scribes are becoming quite alarmed and puzzled that Jesus knows the Old Testament so well. Of course, as the God of the Old Testament, Christ was the very one who gave the revelations to the Old Testament prophets.

8 **For the Son of man** *[Son of Man, Son of God; Jesus; see Moses 6:57]* **is Lord even of the sabbath day** *[I am the one who gave the commandments concerning the Sabbath day]*.

9 And when he was departed thence, **he went into their synagogue:**

10 And, behold, **there was a man which had his hand withered.** And **they** *[the Jewish religious leaders]* **asked him** *[Jesus]*, saying, **Is it lawful to heal on the sabbath days?** that they might accuse him *[that they might trap Him and have grounds to have Him arrested]*.

As you will see, the Savior is a master at answering questions with questions.

11 **And he said** unto them, **What man shall there be among you, that shall have one sheep, and if it fall into a pit on the sabbath day, will he not lay hold on it, and lift it out?** [*In other words, you yourselves rescue your animals that fall into trouble on the Sabbath.*]

12 **How much then is a man better than a sheep** [*how much more important are people than sheep*]? **Wherefore it is lawful to do well on the sabbath days.** [*This direct statement, that it is proper to do good on the Sabbath, must have been quite frustrating to these hypocritical religious leaders. To them, it appeared that Jesus was speaking as if He had authority to make the laws, which, of course, He did.*]

13 **Then saith he to the man** [*with the withered hand*], **Stretch forth thine hand.** And he stretched it forth; **and it was restored** whole, like as the other. [*The man's hand was healed, and it was done on the Sabbath in front of many witnesses, in defiance of these Pharisees, these Jewish religious leaders.*]

14 **Then the Pharisees went out, and held a council against him, how they might destroy him.**

15 But when Jesus knew it [*that they were plotting against Him*], **he withdrew himself from thence: and great multitudes followed him, and he healed them all** [*symbolic of His power to heal all of us spiritually*];

16 **And charged them that they should not make him known** [*He asked them to keep these personal experiences with Him private*]:

JST Matthew 12:13

13 But **Jesus knew when they took counsel, and he withdrew himself** from thence; and great multitudes followed him, and he healed their sick, and charged them that they should not make him known;

The next four verses remind us that one of Matthew's main purposes in writing his gospel was to prove that Jesus fulfilled Old Testament prophecies foretelling the coming of the Savior. In other words, Matthew wanted his audience to realize that Jesus was the promised Messiah.

17 **That it might be fulfilled which was spoken by Esaias** [*Isaiah*] the prophet, saying [*in Isaiah 42:1–3*],

Isaiah's Description of the Messiah

18 Behold my servant [*Christ*], whom I have chosen; my beloved, in whom my soul is well pleased: **I will put my spirit upon him**, and **he shall shew judgment** [*justice, fairness, mercy*] to the Gentiles.

19 He shall **not strive** [*fight, quarrel*], **nor cry** [*shout*]; neither shall any man hear his voice [*shouting*] in the streets [*Jesus will be peaceable and low key as He goes forth in His mortal ministry*].

20 **A bruised** [*bent, crushed*] **reed shall he not break** [*He is not here to hurt the weak, the already bruised and broken, but rather to heal and help them and save them if they will*], and **smoking flax** [*literally a tiny spark smoldering in a bit of fire starter material*] **shall he not quench** [*symbolic of the fact that Christ will come to gently fan the tiny spark of spirituality into a flame, rather than snuffing it out*], till he send forth judgment unto victory.

21 And **in his name shall the Gentiles trust** [*a prophecy that many Gentiles will take Christ's name upon them*].

22 **Then was brought unto him one possessed with a devil, blind, and dumb** [*could not talk*]: **and he healed him**, insomuch that the blind and dumb both spake and saw.

23 And **all the people were amazed**, and said, **Is not this the son of David** [*isn't this the Messiah who was prophesied to come*]?

24 **But when the Pharisees** [*corrupt Jewish religious leaders*] **heard it, they said, This fellow doth not cast out devils, but by Beelzebub the prince of the devils** [*in other words, Satan—see Bible Dictionary, under "Beelzebub;" in other words, the Pharisees claim that Jesus is in partnership with the devil and uses that power to cast out devils*].

25 **And Jesus knew their thoughts, and said** unto them, **Every kingdom divided against itself is brought to desolation** [*destruction*]; and every city or house divided against itself shall not stand [*will not survive*]:

26 And **if Satan cast out Satan, he is divided against himself; how shall then his kingdom stand?**

27 **And if I by Beelzebub** [*using Satan's power*] **cast out devils, by whom do your children cast them out?** therefore they shall be your judges.

28 **But if I cast out devils by the Spirit of God, then the kingdom of God is come unto you** [*then you know that I am the promised Messiah and am making the kingdom of God available to you*].

From JST Matthew 12:22–23, we learn the correct interpretation of verses 27–28, above:

JST MATTHEW 12:22–23

22 And if I by Beelzebub cast out devils, by whom do your children cast out devils? Therefore they shall be your judges.

23 But if I cast out devils by the Spirit of God, then the kingdom of God is come unto you. **For they** [*righteous priesthood holders among the Jews at this time*] **also cast out devils by the Spirit of God, for unto them is given power over devils, that they may cast them out.**

From the words in bold italics, in JST, verse 23, above, we find that there were righteous Jews, obviously baptized and faithful, who were enabled by the Spirit of God to cast out evil spirits. See McConkie, *Doctrinal New Testament Commentary, Vol. 1*, p. 269.

29 **Or else how can one enter into a strong man's house, and spoil** [*plunder, rob*] **his goods, except he first bind the strong man?** and then he will spoil his house [*in other words, one must truly have the power of God over devils in order to cast them out*].

30 **He that is not with me is against me**; and he that gathereth not with me [*does not join with me*] scattereth abroad [*works against me*].

31 Wherefore I say unto you, **All manner of sin and blasphemy** [*evil speaking of and evil behavior toward sacred things*] **shall be forgiven unto men:** but the blasphemy against the Holy Ghost [*denying the Holy Ghost*] shall not be forgiven unto men.

JST MATTHEW 12:26

26 Wherefore I say unto you, All manner of sin and blasphemy shall be forgiven unto men **who receive me and repent**; but the blasphemy against the Holy Ghost, it shall not be forgiven unto men.

Simply put, denying the Holy Ghost means knowing full well, by the power of the Holy Ghost, that God exists, that the Church is true, etc., then going completely against that sure knowledge, trying to destroy the Church and knowledge of God. In other words, it means becoming like Satan, thinking like he does and acting like he does. See D&C 76:31–35. See also Teachings of the Prophet Joseph Smith, p. 358.

32 **And whosoever speaketh a word against the Son of man** [*Jesus; Son of Man of Holiness (Heavenly Father); see Moses 6:57*], **it shall be forgiven him: but whosoever speaketh against the Holy Ghost** [*denies the Holy Ghost—see note between verses 31 and 32, above*], **it shall not be forgiven him, neither in this world, neither in the world to come.**

33 **Either make the tree good, and his fruit good; or else make the tree corrupt, and his fruit corrupt: for the tree is known by his fruit.** [*Jesus is rebuking the Pharisees for accusing Him of being evil, yet doing good in the healing of the man in verse 22. He is saying to them to make up their minds. Anybody knows that a bad tree doesn't give good fruit. If I'm doing good, I must be a "good tree."*]

34 **O generation of vipers** *[you poisonous serpents! This is exactly what John the Baptist called them in Matthew 3:7.]*, **how can ye, being evil, speak good things? for out of the abundance of the heart the mouth speaketh** *[you can tell what is in your hearts by the evil which comes out of your mouths]*.

35 A good man out of the good treasure of the heart bringeth forth good things: and an evil man out of the evil treasure bringeth forth evil things.

36 But I say unto you, That **every idle word** *[gossip; unjust criticism, profanity, etc.; see Matthew 12:36, footnotes b and c]* **that men shall speak, they shall give account thereof in the day of judgment.**

37 **For by thy words** *[righteous words]* **thou shalt be justified** *[saved; approved by God on judgment day]*, **and by thy words** *[idle words, wicked words]* **thou shalt be condemned** *[stopped; cast out on judgment day]*.

38 **Then certain of the scribes** *[lawyers, interpreters of the religious laws among the Jews, usually Pharisees]* **and of the Pharisees** *[religious leaders among the Jews]* **answered** *[responded]*, saying, Master, **we would see a sign from thee** *[show us a sign which proves that you are the Messiah, the Christ]*.

39 **But he answered** and said unto them, **An evil and adulterous generation seeketh after a sign**; and there shall no sign be given to it, but the sign of the prophet Jonas *[if I do give you a sign, it will not be what you want, as in the case when Jonah was swallowed by the whale]*:

40 **For as Jonas** *[Jonah]* **was three days and three nights in the whale's belly; so shall the Son of man** *[I, Christ; Son of man means Son of Man of Holiness, meaning Son of Heavenly Father—see Moses 6:57]* **be three days and three nights in the heart of the earth** *[I will be in the tomb for three days and three nights]*.

41 **The men of Nineveh** *[the city to which Jonah finally went and preached]* **shall rise in judgment with this generation, and shall condemn it: because they repent-ed at the preaching of Jonas** *[Jonah]*; and, behold, **a greater than Jonas is here** *[the Son of God is here among you right now; you have no excuse for not repenting!]*.

These scribes and Pharisees do indeed understand that Jesus is telling them that He is the Son of God. The Joseph Smith Translation of the Bible confirms this fact in JST Mark 3:21 as follows: "And then came certain men unto him, accusing him, saying, **Why do ye receive sinners, seeing thou makest thyself the Son of God.**"

42 **The queen of the south** *[the Queen of Sheba, a famous queen who visited Solomon to learn from him; see 1 Kings 10:1–13]* **shall rise up in the judgment with this generation, and shall condemn it: for she came from the uttermost parts of the earth to hear the wisdom of Solomon; and, behold** *[JST "ye behold," i.e., before your very eyes you are seeing]*, **a greater than Solomon is here** *[the Son of God is greater than Solomon and you are seeing me here right now, and if you had the good sense the Queen of Sheba had, you would be seeking my help rather than trying to destroy me]*.

Verses 43–45, which come next, may seem at first to be a bit out of context with the foregoing verses. However, in verses 31 and 32 above, the Savior taught that the sin against the Holy Ghost cannot be forgiven in this life or in the life to come. In verses 33 to 42, Jesus is warning these wicked Jewish leaders that they are seeing things which make them very accountable! They are actually seeing the Savior in person, among them, witnessing His teachings and miracles, perhaps feeling His Spirit, and yet denying it and seeking to destroy Him and His work among them. Next, in verses 43–45, He continues His warning to them by giving an illustration which explains why a person who denies the Holy Ghost can't be forgiven. In effect, a person who denies the Holy Ghost (see the note between verses 31 and 32 above) deliberately invites Satan and his evil spirits into his soul (his "house"), and associates with them until he thinks, acts, and becomes like Satan, having absolutely no desire to be anything other than like the devil, and thus qualifies to live with him and his evil spirits forever as a son of perdition. We will use the JST for clarification, after we have read verses 43–45.

43 **When the unclean spirit is gone out of a man**, he walketh through dry places, seeking rest, and findeth none.

44 Then he saith, I will return into my house from whence I came out; and when he is come, he findeth it empty, swept, and garnished.

45 Then goeth he, and taketh with himself seven other spirits more wicked than himself, and they enter in and dwell there: and the last state of that man is worse than the first. **Even so shall it be also unto this wicked generation.**

As stated previously, we will now use the JST to help us understand verses 43–45, above.

JST MATTHEW 12:37–39

37 [*Note: This verse is entirely missing from the Bible.*] Then came some of the scribes [*Jewish religious leaders who specialized in interpreting the gospel doctrines and laws*] and said unto him, Master, it is written that, Every sin shall be forgiven; but ye say, Whosoever speaketh against the Holy Ghost shall not be forgiven. And they asked him, saying, How can these things be? [*In other words, what you, Jesus, are teaching contradicts our traditional written doctrines.*]

38 And he said unto them, When the unclean spirit is gone out of a man, he [*the evil spirit*] walketh through dry places, seeking rest and findeth none; but when a man speaketh against the Holy Ghost [*when a man reverts back to his evil ways to the extent of denying the Holy Ghost*], then he [*the evil spirit*] saith, I will return into my house [*the man in whom the evil spirit used to reside*] from whence I came out; and when he [*the evil spirit*] is come, he findeth him [*the man in whom the evil spirit formerly resided*] empty, swept and garnished [*was cleansed from sin, with a sure testimony given him by the Holy Ghost, but who is now speaking against that testimony*]; for the good spirit [*the Holy Ghost*] leaveth him unto himself.

39 Then goeth the evil spirit, and taketh with himself seven other spirits more wicked than himself; and they enter in and dwell there [*with the man who has denied the Holy Ghost*]; and the last end of that man is worse than the first [*the man is worse off now than he was before he gained a sure testimony from the Holy Ghost*]. Even so shall it be also unto this wicked generation.

Elder Bruce R. McConkie helps us understand the above three verses as follows: "JST Matthew 12:37–39. Having already taught that every sin shall be forgiven except the sin against the Holy Ghost, Jesus now illustrates why. In effect he says: 'If you gain a perfect knowledge of me and my mission, it must come by revelation from the Holy Ghost; that Holy Spirit must speak to the spirit within you; and then you shall know, nothing doubting. But to receive this knowledge and revelation, you must cleanse and perfect your own soul; that is, your house must be clean, swept, and garnished. Then if you deny me by speaking against the Holy Ghost who gave you your revelation of the truth, that is if you come out in open rebellion against the perfect light you have received, the Holy Ghost will depart, leaving you to yourself. Your house will now be available for other tenancy, and so the evil spirits and influences you had once conquered will return to plague you. Having completely lost the preserving power of the Spirit, you will then be worse off than if you had never received the truth; and many in this generation shall be so condemned'" (*Doctrinal New Testament Commentary*, Volume 1, p. 276).

46 **While he yet talked to the people, behold, his mother and his brethren** [*Mary and some family members; see Matthew 12, footnote 46a, in your Bible*] **stood without** [*outside*], **desiring to speak with him.**

47 **Then one** [*someone*] **said unto him,** Behold [*look*], **thy mother and thy brethren stand without, desiring to speak with thee.**

48 **But he** answered and **said** unto him that told him, **Who is my mother? and who are my brethren?** [*In other words, who is my family? This is a teaching moment.*]

49 **And he stretched forth his hand toward his disciples** [*followers*], **and said, Behold** [*you are seeing*] **my mother and my brethren!** [*My followers are my family. This answers the question Christ posed in verse 48. See also the answer in verse 50.*]

50 **For whosoever shall do the will of my Father which is in heaven, the same is my brother, and sister, and mother.**

JST MATTHEW 12:44

44 **And he gave them charge concerning her** *[asked them to take good care of His mother]*, **saying, I go my way, for my Father hath sent me.** And whosoever shall do the will of my Father which is in heaven, the same is my brother, and sister, and mother.

MATTHEW 13

THE SAVIOR WILL now use a number of parables to illustrate his teachings. A parable is a story which is used to teach us about real life situations. The Prophet Joseph Smith said: "I have a key by which I understand the scriptures. I enquire, what was the question which drew out the answer, or caused Jesus to utter the parable?" (*Teachings of the Prophet Joseph Smith*, pp. 276–77).

1 **THE same day went Jesus out of the house, and sat by the sea side.**

2 And **great multitudes** were **gathered** together unto him, **so** that **he went into a ship, and sat**; and the whole multitude stood on the shore.

The Parable of the Sower

3 **And he spake many things unto them in parables**, saying, Behold, a **sower** *[a farmer]* went forth to sow *[plant seeds]*;

4 And when he sowed, **some seeds fell by the way side**, and the fowls *[birds]* came and devoured them up:

5 **Some fell upon stony places** *[where there was only a thin layer of soil; see Matthew 13:5a]*, where they had not much earth: and forthwith *[immediately]* they sprung up, because they had no deepness of earth:

6 And when the sun was up, they were scorched; and because they had no root, they withered away *[dried up and died]*.

7 And **some fell among thorns**; and the thorns sprung up, and choked them:

8 But **other fell into good ground**, and brought forth fruit, some an hundredfold, *[a hundred times what was planted]* some sixtyfold, some thirtyfold. *[The Savior will explain this parable starting with verse 18.]*

9 **Who hath ears to hear, let him hear** *[those who are spiritually mature and in tune will understand what I am saying]*.

Why Parables?

10 And **the disciples came, and said** unto him, **Why speakest thou unto them** *[the multitude in verse 2]* **in parables?**

11 He answered and said unto them, Because it is given unto you to know the mysteries of the kingdom of heaven *[because you want to learn spiritual things]*, but to them it is not given *[because they do not want to learn of spiritual things]*.

12 For **whosoever hath, to him shall be given**, and he shall have more abundance: **but whosoever hath not, from him shall be taken away even that he hath.**

The JST helps us understand verse 12, above:

JST MATTHEW13:10–11

10 For **whosoever receiveth, to him shall be given, and he shall have more abundance**;

11. **But whosoever continueth not to receive, from him shall be taken away even that he hath.**

The point is that these people don't want to understand the Savior's teachings.

13 **Therefore** *[for this reason]* **speak I to them in parables**: because they seeing see not; and hearing they hear not, neither do they understand *[they don't understand spiritual things because they don't want to]*.

14 And **in them is fulfilled the prophecy of Esaias** *[Isaiah]*, which saith, By hearing ye shall hear, and shall not understand; and seeing ye shall see, and shall not perceive *[you are so far gone spiritually that you can't understand spiritual things]*:

15 For **this people's heart is waxed gross** [*they have become hard-hearted*], **and their ears are dull of hearing** [*they are deaf to spiritual things*], **and their eyes they have closed** [*they don't want to see spiritual things*]; lest at any time they should see with their eyes, and hear with their ears, and should understand with their heart, and should be converted, and I should heal them [*these people are intentionally avoiding conversion to Christ*].

16 **But blessed are your eyes, for they see: and your ears, for they hear.**

JST Matthew 13:15

15 But blessed are your eyes, for they see; and your ears, for they hear. **And blessed are you because these things are come unto you, that you might understand them.**

17 For verily I say unto you, That **many prophets and righteous men have desired to see those things which ye see, and have not seen them; and to hear those things which ye hear, and have not heard them.**

Explanation of the Parable of the Sower

18 **Hear ye therefore the parable of the sower** [*I will explain the parable of the sower to you*].

19 **When any one heareth the word of the kingdom** [*the gospel*], **and understandeth it not**, then cometh **the wicked one**, and **catcheth away that which was sown in his heart**. This is he which received seed by the way side.

20 But he that received the seed into **stony places**, the same is he that heareth the word, and anon [*immediately*] with joy receiveth it;

21 Yet hath he not root in himself, but dureth [*lasts*] for a while: for when tribulation or persecution ariseth because of the word [*the gospel*], by and by he is offended.

22 He also that received seed **among the thorns** is he that heareth the word [*the gospel*]; and the care of this world, and the deceitfulness of riches, choke the word, and he becometh unfruitful [*does not remain faithful*].

23 But he that received seed into the **good ground** is he that heareth the word, and understandeth it; [*this takes work and commitment*] which also beareth fruit [*lives the gospel, remains faithful*], and bringeth forth, some an hundredfold, some sixty, some thirty.

JST Matthew 13:21

21 But he that received seed into the good ground, is he that heareth the word and understandeth **and endureth**; which also beareth fruit, and bringeth forth, some an hundred-fold, some sixty, and some thirty.

Joseph Smith gives additional insights about the parable of the sower as follows: "But listen to the explanation of the parable of the Sower: 'When any one heareth the word of the Kingdom, and understandeth it not, then cometh the wicked one, and catcheth away that which was sown in his heart.' Now mark the expression—that which was sown in his heart. This is he which receiveth seed by the way side. Men who have no principle of righteousness in themselves, and whose hearts are full of iniquity, and have no desire for the principles of truth, do not understand the word of truth when they hear it. The devil taketh away the word of truth out of their hearts, because there is no desire for righteousness in them. 'But he that receiveth seed in stony places, the same is he that heareth the word, and anon, with joy receiveth it; yet hath he not root in himself, but dureth for a while; for when tribulation or persecution ariseth because of the word, by and by, he is offended. He also that receiveth seed among the thorns, is he that heareth the word; and the care of this world, and the deceitfulness of riches choke the word, and he becometh unfruitful. But he that received seed into the good ground, is he that heareth the word, and understandeth it, which also beareth fruit, and bringeth forth, some an hundred fold, some sixty, some thirty.' Thus the Savior Himself explains unto His disciples the parable which He put forth, and left no mystery or darkness upon the minds of those who firmly believe on His words.

"We draw the conclusion, then, that the very reason why the multitude, or the world, as they were designated by the Savior, did not receive an explanation upon His parables, was because of unbelief. To you, He says [*speaking to His disciples*] it is given to know the mysteries of the Kingdom of God. And why? Because of the faith and confidence they had in Him" (*Teachings of the Prophet Joseph Smith*, 1976, p. 97).

The Parable of the Wheat and the Tares

24 **Another parable** put he forth unto them, saying, **The kingdom of heaven is likened unto a man** [*Christ, see verse 37*] **which sowed** [*planted*] **good seed** [*faithful followers of Christ, verse 38*] **in his field** [*the world, verse 38*]:

25 But while men slept, his enemy [*the devil, verse 39*] came and sowed tares [*wicked people, verse 38*] among the wheat [*faithful members of the Church*], and went his way.

A tare is a weed that looks very much like wheat while it is growing. Often, the roots of tares intertwine with the roots of the wheat while both are growing.

26 But when the blade was sprung up, and brought forth fruit, then appeared the tares also.

27 **So the servants of the householder** [*Christ*] **came and said** unto him, Sir, didst not thou sow [*plant*] good seed [*wheat*] in thy field? from whence then hath it tares [*where did the tares come from*]?

28 He said unto them, An enemy hath done this. The servants said unto him, **Wilt thou then that we go and gather them up** [*would you like us to weed out the tares now*]?

29 But **he said, Nay** [*No*]; lest [*for fear that*] while ye gather up the tares, ye root up also the wheat with them.

There are several messages here in verse 29. One message might be that there are usually insincere and unrighteous members living among the righteous members of wards and branches of the Church. Another message could be that each of us has some "tares" in our own lives and personalities and we would be wise to weed them out as our righteous attributes mature. Jacob 5:65–66 in the Book of Mormon reminds us that as the good in people grows, the bad can gradually be cleared away. See also D&C 86:6.

30 **Let both grow together until the harvest:** and in the time of harvest I will say to the reapers [*harvesters, angels in verse 39*], Gather ye together **first the tares** [*the wicked*], and bind them in bundles to burn them: but gather the wheat [*the righteous*] into my barn [*my kingdom*].

JST 13:29

29 Let both grow together until the harvest, and in the time of harvest, I will say to the reapers, Gather ye together **first the wheat** into my barn; and the tares are bound in bundles to be burned.

Both the JST, quoted above, and D&C 86:7 change the order of the harvesting. The correct order is that the wheat is gathered first. Then the tares are gathered, bundled [bound] and burned. This is significant doctrinally, because it indicates that, at the Second Coming, the righteous will be taken up first [D&C 88:96], and then the wicked will be burned.

The Parable of the Mustard Seed

31 **Another parable** put he forth unto them, saying, **The kingdom of heaven is like to a grain of mustard seed**, which a man took, and sowed in his field:

32 Which indeed is **the least** [*smallest*] **of all seeds:** but when it is grown, it is the greatest among herbs, and becometh a tree, so that the birds of the air [*symbolic of angels; see* Teachings of the Prophet Joseph Smith, *p. 159*] come and lodge in the branches thereof.

Joseph Smith explained this parable: "And again, another parable put He forth unto them, having an allusion to the Kingdom that should be set up, just previous to or at the time of the harvest, which reads as follows—'The Kingdom of Heaven is like a grain of mustard seed, which a man took and sowed in his field: which indeed is the least of all seeds: but, when it is grown, it is the greatest among herbs, and becometh a tree, so that the birds of the air come and lodge in the branches thereof.' Now we can discover plainly that this figure is given to represent the Church as it shall come forth in the last days." For more of the Prophet's explanation, see *Teachings of the Prophet Joseph Smith*, pp. 98–99 and p. 159.

The Parable of the Leaven

33 **Another parable** spake he unto them; **The kingdom of heaven is like unto leaven** [*an ingredient such as yeast, which, when mixed into bread dough, causes the whole loaf to rise*], which a woman took, and hid in three measures of meal, till the whole was leavened.

Joseph Smith explained that the "leaven" in verse 33 could be compared to the true Church as it expands into the whole world. See *Teachings of the Prophet Joseph Smith*, pp. 100–102.

34 **All these things spake Jesus unto the multitude in parables; and without a parable spake he not unto them:**

35 **That it might be fulfilled which was spoken by the prophet**, saying [*in Psalm 78:2*], I will open my mouth in parables; I will utter things which have been kept secret from the foundation of the world.

The Parable of Wheat and Tares Explained

36 Then Jesus sent the multitude away, and went into the house: and **his disciples came unto him, saying, Declare** [*explain*] **unto us the parable of the tares of the field** [*verses 24–30*].

37 **He answered** and said unto them, **He that soweth** [*plants*] **the good seed** [*wheat; righteousness*] **is the Son of man** [*Christ; Son of Man of Holiness—see Moses 6:57*];

38 The **field is the world**; the **good seed are the children of the kingdom** [*faithful members of the Church; the righteous*]; but the **tares are the children of the wicked one** [*followers of Satan; the wicked*];

39 **The** enemy that sowed them is the devil; the **harvest is the end of the world**; and the **reapers** [*harvesters*] **are the angels.**

40 As therefore **the tares** [*the wicked*] **are gathered and burned in the fire; so shall it be in the end of this world** [*the wicked will be burned at the Second Coming*].

People often ask how the wicked will be burned. D&C 5:19 along with 2 Nephi 12:10, 19, and 21, explain that the wicked will be burned by the brightness of the glory of Christ, who comes in full glory at the time of the Second Coming.

41 **The Son of man** [*Christ*] **shall send forth his angels, and they shall gather out of his kingdom all things that offend, and them which do iniquity** [*the wicked*];

42 **And shall cast them into a furnace of fire** [*the burning at the Second Coming—see note above*]: there shall be wailing [*bitter crying*] and gnashing [*grinding*] of teeth.

JST MATTHEW 13:39–44

39 The harvest is the end of the world, **or the destruction of the wicked**.

40 The reapers are the angels, **or the messengers sent of heaven**.

41 As, therefore, the tares are gathered and burned in the fire, so shall it be in the end of this world, **or the destruction of the wicked**.

42 **For in that day, before the Son of man shall come**, he shall send forth his angels **and messengers of heaven**.

43 And they shall gather out of his kingdom all things that offend, and them which do iniquity, and **shall cast them out among the wicked**; and there shall be wailing and gnashing of teeth.

44 **For the world shall be burned with fire**.

43 **Then shall the righteous shine forth as the sun** [*symbolic of celestial glory for the righteous Saints*] **in the kingdom of their Father.** Who hath ears to hear, let him hear [*those who are spiritually in tune will understand what I am saying*].

The Parable of the Treasure Hid in a Field

44 Again [*another parable*], **the kingdom of heaven is like un-to treasure hid in a field**; the which when a man hath found, he hideth, and for joy thereof goeth and selleth all that he hath, and buyeth that field. [*It is worth the sacrificing of whatever it takes to join the Church and to remain faithful.*]

The Parable of the Pearl of Great Price

45 Again, **the kingdom of heaven is like unto a merchant man, seeking goodly pearls:**

46 Who, when he had found one **pearl of great price** [*this is where the name for the Pearl of Great Price comes from*], went and sold all that he had, and bought it.

The Parable of the Net

47 Again, **the kingdom of heaven is like unto a net**, that was cast into the sea, and gathered of every kind [*the missionary work of the Church gathers all kinds of converts, some sincere who remain faithful, others who are not sincere etc.*]: [*This verse also exemplifies that all people will get a chance to join with the Savior's church, whether in this life or in the spirit world.*]

48 Which, when it was full, they drew to shore, and sat down, and gathered the good into vessels, but cast the bad away.

49 **So shall it be at the end of the world: the angels shall come forth, and sever the wicked from among the just** [*the righteous*],

50 And **shall cast them** [*the wicked*] **into the furnace of fire** [*the burning of the wicked*]: there shall be wailing [*bitter anguish*] and gnashing [*grinding*] of teeth [*symbolic of the extreme suffering of the wicked as they face the consequences of their evil choices*].

JST MATTHEW 13:50–51

50 **And the world is the children of the wicked.**

51 **The angels shall come forth, and sever the wicked from among the just, and shall cast them out into the world to be burned**. There shall be wailing and gnashing of teeth.

51 **Jesus saith unto them, Have ye understood all these things?** They say unto him, Yea, Lord.

The Parable of the Scribe Who Is Converted to the Gospel of Christ

52 **Then said he unto them**, Therefore **every scribe** [*scribes were Jewish leaders, generally enemies of Christ; who determined correct interpretation of the scriptures among their people*] **which is instructed unto the kingdom of heaven** [*who has been converted and become a true follower of Christ, see Matthew 13:52, footnote b*] **is like unto a man that is an householder, which bringeth forth** [*throws out*] **out of his treasure things new and old** [*has to throw out many previously held beliefs; see* Sperry Symposium, *1983, p. 101*].

53 And it came to pass, that when **Jesus** had **finished these parables,** he departed thence.

The Master Goes to Nazareth

54 And **when he was come into his own country** [*Nazareth*], **he taught them in their synagogue**, insomuch that they were astonished, and said, Whence hath this man this wisdom, and these mighty works?

55 **Is not this the carpenter's son? is not his mother called Mary?** and his **brethren** [*brothers (actually half-brothers)*], **James**, and **Joses**, and **Simon**, and **Judas**?

56 And his **sisters** *[the Greek form of this word means three or more]*, are they not all with us? **Whence then hath this man all these things?** *[Isn't this Joseph and Mary's son? We know the family. How could He possibly be saying and doing such incredible things?]*

57 **And they were offended in him** *[embarrassed and offended by what He was doing]*. **But Jesus said** unto them, **A prophet is not without honour, save** *[except]* **in his own country, and in his own house.**

58 And **he did not many mighty works there because of their unbelief.**

MATTHEW 14

IN VERSE 1, we meet "Herod the tetrarch," also known as Herod Antipas. His father, Herod the Great, was the ruler who commanded that all the infant boys at Bethlehem be killed, in an unsuccessful attempt to kill the Christ child. See Matthew 2:16. Upon the death of Herod the Great, his kingdom was divided among three of his sons, Antipas, Archelaus, and Philip. Herod the tetrarch was the wicked ruler who ordered the death of John the Baptist (about two years ago at this point in Matthew). Herod has heard of Jesus' fame and is afraid that John the Baptist has come back from the dead.

1 AT that time **Herod the tetrarch heard of the fame of Jesus,**

2 **And said unto his servants, This is John the Baptist**; he is risen from the dead *[he has come back from the dead]*; and therefore mighty works do shew forth themselves in him.

Herod Beheaded John the Baptist

3 **For Herod had laid hold on** *[arrested]* **John**, and bound him, **and put him in prison** for Herodias' sake *[because of Herodias]*, his brother Philip's wife. *[Herod was an immoral man who had married Herodias, his own brother's wife]*.

4 **For John** *[the Baptist]* **said unto him** *[Herod the tetrarch]*, **It is not lawful for thee to have her** *[it was wrong for you to marry her]*.

5 And **when he** *[Herod]* **would have put him** *[John the Baptist]* **to death, he feared the multitude**, because they counted him as a prophet *[considered John the Baptist to be a prophet]*.

6 **But when Herod's birthday was kept** *[when they were celebrating Herod's birthday]*, **the daughter of Herodias** *[the daughter's name was Salome; see Bible Dictionary, under "Salome"]* **danced** before them, **and pleased Herod.**

7 **Whereupon he promised with an oath to give her whatsoever she would ask.**

8 **And she, being before instructed of her mother** *[Salome had already been given instructions by her mother, Herodias, who hated John the Baptist, because he boldly told her she was living in adultery with Herod]*, **said, Give me** here **John Baptist's head in a charger** *[on a platter]*.

9 And **the king was sorry: nevertheless** for the oath's sake, and them which sat with him at meat *[because he had promised to her in front of all those at his birthday party]*, **he commanded it** *[John's head]* **to be given her.**

10 And **he sent, and beheaded John in the prison.**

11 And **his head was brought in a charger, and given to the damsel: and she brought it to her mother.**

12 And his disciples *[John's followers]* came, and took up the body, and buried it, and went and told Jesus.

13 **When Jesus heard of it, he departed thence** *[from there]* by ship into a desert place apart: **and** when **the people** had heard thereof, they **followed him** on foot out of the cities.

14 And **Jesus** went forth, and **saw a great multitude**, and was moved with compassion toward them, and he **healed their sick.**

The Feeding of the 5,000

15 And **when it was evening, his disciples came to him, saying,** This is a desert place, and the time is now past; **send the multitude away, that they may** go into the villages, and **buy themselves victuals** [*food*].

Watch now as the Master startles his disciples.

16 But **Jesus said** unto them, **They need not depart; give ye them to eat.**

17 And **they say** unto him, **We have here but five loaves** [*of bread*], and **two fishes.**

18 **He said, Bring them** hither **to me.**

19 And **he commanded the multitude to sit down on the grass,** and **took the** five **loaves,** and the two **fishes,** and looking up to heaven, he **blessed,** and **brake,** and **gave the loaves to his disciples, and the disciples to the multitude.**

20 And **they did all eat, and were filled:** and they took up of the fragments that **remained twelve baskets full.**

21 And they that had eaten were about **five thousand men, beside** [*in addition to*] **women and children.**

22 And **straightway Jesus constrained** [*instructed*] **his disciples to get into a ship, and to go before him** [*go on ahead of him*] unto the other side [*of the Sea of Galilee*], while he sent the multitudes away.

23 And when he had sent the multitudes away, **he went up into a mountain** apart [*to be alone*] **to pray:** and when the evening was come, he was there alone.

24 **But the ship was** now in the midst of the sea, **tossed with waves:** for the wind was contrary.

Jesus Walks on the Water

25 And in the fourth watch of the night [*between 3 AM and 6 AM*] **Jesus went unto them, walking on the sea.**

26 And **when the disciples saw him walking on the sea, they were troubled, saying, It is a spirit;** and they cried out for fear [*they thought they were seeing a ghost*].

27 But straightway [*immediately*] **Jesus spake** unto them, saying, **Be of good cheer; it is I; be not afraid.**

Peter Walks on Water

28 And **Peter answered** him and said, Lord, if it be thou, **bid** [*ask*] **me come unto thee on the water.**

29 And he said, Come. And when **Peter** was come down out of the ship, he **walked on the water,** to go to Jesus.

30 **But** when he saw the wind boisterous, **he was afraid; and beginning to sink,** he cried, saying, Lord, save me.

31 And **immediately Jesus stretched forth his hand, and caught him,** and said unto him, O thou of little faith, wherefore [*why*] didst thou doubt?

32 And when they were come into the ship, **the wind ceased.** [*Once again, the Lord's power over the elements is displayed.*]

33 **Then they** that were in the ship came and **worshipped him,** saying, Of a truth [*for sure*] **thou art the Son of God.**

34 And when they were gone over [*had crossed the Sea of Galilee from east to west*], **they came into the land of Gennesaret** [*on the northwestern side of the Sea of Galilee*].

35 And when the men of that place had knowledge of him [*found out that it was Jesus*], **they** sent out [*spread the word*] into all that country round about, and **brought unto him all that were diseased;**

36 And besought him that they might only touch the hem of his garment: and **as many as touched were made perfectly whole.**

As mentioned previously, every physical healing performed by the Savior is symbolic of his power and desire to heal us spiritually, in order that we might come to the Father through him and his Atonement.

MATTHEW 15

THE SAVIOR BEGAN his three-year formal ministry at age 30. With the feeding of the 5000 in chapter 14, we begin our study of the last year of His earthly ministry. By this time, the hatred and jealousy of the Jewish religious leaders had grown to the point that they sent a delegation all the way from Jerusalem to Galilee to challenge Jesus and to try to discredit Him. The scribes were the most powerful and influential of these leaders. Perhaps it would be helpful for you at this point to read a description of the scribes, given by a noted Biblical scholar. Here it is:

A DESCRIPTION OF THE SCRIBES

"A foremost actor in a New Testament list of characters is the scribe. He is found in Jerusalem, Judea, and Galilee and is not new to Jewish life and culture. Present in Babylon and also throughout the dispersion, he is spokesman of the people; he is the sage; he is the man of wisdom, the rabbi who received his ordination by the laying on of hands. His ability to cross-examine and to question is renowned. Dignified and important, he is an aristocrat among the common people who have no knowledge of the law. Regarding faith and religious practice, he is the authority and the last word; and as a teacher of the law, as a judge in ecclesiastical courts, is the learned one who must be respected, whose judgment is infallible. He travels in the company of the Pharisees, yet he is not necessarily a member of this religious party. He holds office and has status. His worth is beyond that of all the common folk and they must honor him, for he is to be praised by God and by angels in heaven. In fact, so revered are his words regarding law and practice that he must be believed though his statements contradict all common sense, or though he pronounce that the sun does not shine at noon day when in fact it is visible to the naked eye" (Edersheim, *The Life and Times of Jesus the Messiah, 1:93–94*).

1 **THEN came to Jesus scribes and Pharisees** [*wicked religious leaders of the Jews*], which were of Jerusalem, **saying,**

2 **Why do thy disciples transgress** [*sin against*] **the tradition of the elders** [*laws and customs established over the centuries by Jewish religious leaders, not necessarily the laws of God*]? for **they wash not their hands when they eat bread** [*before eating a meal*].

The Savior will now teach a major lesson, namely, that inner cleanliness of mind and spirit are far more important than outward physical cleanliness.

3 But **he answered** and said unto them, **Why do ye also transgress the commandment of God by your tradition?**

4 For **God commanded**, saying, **Honour thy father and mother:** and, He that curseth father or mother, let him die the death [*the penalty, given by Moses for failing to honor one's father and mother, was death*].

5 **But ye say, Whosoever shall say to his father or his mother, It is a gift**, by whatsoever thou [*the parents*] mightest be profited [*helped*] by me;

6 **And honour not his father or his mother, he shall be free** [*of obligation to help his parents*]. Thus have ye made the commandment of God [*"Honor thy father and thy mother," Exodus 20:12*] of none effect by your tradition.

The Savior here challenges the wicked practice, approved by the Jewish leaders, of gaining freedom from taking care of their aging parents by saying, "It is a gift" (verse 5, above), meaning that it is a gift to God—see Bible Dictionary, under "Corban." By formally saying this, they could make their material means, time, etc., off limits to their elderly parents who needed their help. This practice is called "Corban" in Mark 7:11.

7 **Ye hypocrites** [*people who want to appear righteous but like to do evil*], **well did Esaias** [*Isaiah*] **prophesy of you, saying** [*in Isaiah 29:13*],

AND WHEN PETER WAS COME DOWN OUT OF THE SHIP, HE WALKED ON THE WATER TO GO TO JESUS.

MATTHEW 14:29

CHRIST AND PETER, by Robert T. Barrett

8 This people draweth nigh unto me with their mouth, and honoureth me with their lips; but their heart is far from me.

9 But **in vain** [*it does no good*] **they do worship me** [*as illustrated in Isaiah 1:13*], teaching for doctrines the commandments of men.

10 And **he called the multitude, and said** unto them, **Hear, and understand:**

11 **Not that which goeth into the mouth defileth a man; but that which cometh out of the mouth, this defileth a man.**

This is a stinging rebuke to these wicked Jewish leaders. Jesus said to the multitudes who have gathered around, within the hearing of the scribes and Pharisees, that the teachings which come out of the scribes' mouths and influence daily behavior of their people defile, or, in other words, make filthy. His disciples are worried about His bold scolding of the scribes as evidenced by the next verse.

12 **Then came his disciples, and said** unto him, **Knowest thou that the Pharisees were offended**, after they heard this saying?

13 **But he answered and said, Every plant, which my heavenly Father hath not planted, shall be rooted up** [*everything which is false will ultimately be exposed and destroyed*].

14 **Let them alone**: they be blind leaders of the blind. And if the blind lead the blind, both shall fall into the ditch [*ultimately, they and their followers will get caught up with*].

15 **Then answered** [*responded*] **Peter** and said unto him, **Declare unto us this parable** [*please explain what You just said*].

16 And **Jesus said, Are ye also yet without understanding?**

17 Do not ye yet understand, that **whatsoever entereth in at the mouth goeth into the belly, and is cast out into the draught** [*eventually leaves the body*]?

18 **But those things which proceed out of the mouth come forth from the heart**; and they defile [*make filthy*] the man [*because they show what he is really like*].

19 **For out of the heart proceed evil thoughts,** murders, adulteries, fornications, thefts, false witness, blasphemies:

20 **These are the things which defile a man:** but to eat with unwashen hands [*verse 2*] defileth not a man.

21 **Then Jesus went** thence, and departed **into** the coasts [*borders*] of **Tyre and Sidon** [*a bit north and then west of the Sea of Galilee*].

22 And, behold, **a woman of Canaan** [*a Gentile, non-Israelite, probably a descendant of Ham; see Bible Dictionary, under "Canaan"*] came out of the same coasts [*from the same area*], and **cried unto him, saying, Have mercy on me, O Lord, thou Son of David** [*thou Messiah, who was prophesied to be a descendant of King David*]; **my daughter is grievously vexed** [*is very sick*] **with a devil.**

23 **But he answered her not a word.** And his disciples came and besought him, saying, Send her away; for she crieth after us.

24 But he answered and said, **I am not sent but unto the lost sheep of the house of Israel.**

As he states here, Jesus' mortal mission was limited to the house of Israel, specifically, the Jews. This limitation will be done away with later, as exemplified by Mark 16:15 and Peter's dream in Acts 10:9–48.

25 **Then came she** and worshipped him, **saying, Lord, help me.**

26 But **he answered** and said, **It is not meet** [*appropriate, necessary*] **to take the children's bread** [*the gospel nourishment designated at this time for the Jews—see note above*], **and to cast it to dogs.**

27 And **she said,** Truth, Lord: yet **the dogs eat**

of the crumbs which fall from their masters' table.

The word "dogs" in this context means "little dogs" or household pets (a term of endearment). A Bible scholar named Dummelow explains as follows:

"The rabbis often spoke of the Gentiles as dogs . . . (Jesus) says not 'dogs,' but 'little dogs,' i.e. house-hold, favourite dogs, and the woman cleverly catches at the expression, arguing that if the Gentiles are household dogs, then it is only right that they should be fed with the crumbs that fall from their master's table." (Dummelow, *Commentary*, pp. 678–79)

28 **Then Jesus** answered and **said** unto her, **O woman, great is thy faith: be it unto thee even as thou wilt. And her daughter was made whole** from that very hour.

29 **And Jesus** departed from thence, and **came nigh unto the sea of Galilee; and went up into a mountain, and sat down there.**

30 And **great multitudes came unto him, having with them those that were lame, blind, dumb** *[not able to speak]*, **maimed**, and many others, and cast them down at Jesus' feet; **and he healed them**:

31 Insomuch that **the multitude wondered** *[marveled]*, when they saw the dumb to speak, the maimed to be whole, the lame to walk, and the blind to see: **and they glorified the God of Israel.**

The Feeding of the 4,000

32 **Then Jesus called his disciples unto him, and said, I have compassion on the multitude, because they continue with me now three days** *[they have been following me for three days]*, **and have nothing to eat**: and I will not send them away fasting *[hungry]*, lest they faint in the way *[collapse on the way home]*.

33 **And his disciples say** unto him, **Whence should we have so much bread** in the wilderness, as **to fill so great a multitude** *[where can we get enough bread to feed such a large group]*?

34 **And Jesus saith** unto them, **How many loaves have ye?** And they said, **Seven, and a few little fishes.**

35 And he commanded the multitude to sit down on the ground.

36 And **he took the seven loaves and the fishes, and gave thanks, and brake them, and gave to his disciples, and the disciples to the multitude.**

37 **And they did all eat, and were filled**: and they took up of the broken meat *[food]* that was **left seven baskets full.**

38 And they that did eat were **four thousand men, beside** *[plus]* **women and children.**

39 And **he** sent away the multitude, and took ship, and **came into** the coasts *[borders]* of **Magdala** *[near the northwestern shore of the Sea of Galilee]*.

MATTHEW 16

THE PHARISEES AND Sadducees, traditionally bitter enemies of each other, have now joined forces to stop Jesus, and have come all the way to Galilee to confront Him.

1 **THE Pharisees** *[Jewish religious leaders who believed in resurrection]* also **with the Sadducees** *[Jewish religious leaders who did not believe in resurrection]* **came**, and tempting **desired** him that he would shew them **a sign from heaven.**

The Pharisees and the Sadducees were usually enemies, but here we see them teamed up together against the Savior.

2 **He answered** and said unto them, **When it is evening, ye say, It will be fair weather: for the sky is red.**

3 And **in the morning, It will be foul weather to day: for the sky is** red and lowring *[threatening]*, **O ye hypocrites** *[people who want to appear*

righteous but inwardly like to be evil], **ye can discern the face of the sky** *[you can predict the weather by looking at the sky]*; **but can ye not discern** *[JST tell]* **the signs of the times** *[the obvious fulfillment of prophecies about Christ's mortal ministry, which, if paid attention to, would present these hypocrites with sure evidence that this Jesus, against whom they were fighting, is the promised Messiah]*?

4 **A wicked and adulterous generation seeketh after a sign**; and there shall no sign be given unto it, but the sign of the prophet Jonas *[just as Jonah spent three days and three nights in the whale's belly, so also will Christ spend three days and three nights in the tomb; see JST Mark 8:12]*. And **he left them, and departed.**

5 And **when his disciples were come to the other side, they had forgotten to take bread.**

6 **Then Jesus said** unto them, Take heed and **beware of the leaven of the Pharisees and of the Sadducees.**

Here the Master Teacher uses the setting to teach and warn his disciples against the evil doctrines (verse 12) of the Pharisees and Sadducees. He compares these doctrines to leaven (yeast) which is put in bread dough to make it rise. As the leaven works its way through the entire lump of dough, it influences everything. So also with these hypocritical Jewish leaders, who are influencing everything in Jewish society. At first, the disciples did not understand what Jesus was saying.

7 And **they reasoned among themselves, saying, It is because we have taken no bread.**

8 Which **when Jesus perceived, he said** unto them, **O ye of little faith, why reason ye among yourselves, because ye have brought no bread** *[you are missing the point]*?

JST MATTHEW 16:9

9 And when they reasoned among themselves, Jesus perceived it; and he said unto them, O ye of little faith! why reason ye among yourselves, because ye have brought no bread?

9 **Do ye not yet understand, neither remember the five loaves of the five thousand, and how many baskets ye took up** *[Matthew 14:20]*?

10 **Neither the seven loaves** of the four thousand, **and how many baskets ye took up** *[Matthew 15:37]*?

11 **How is it that ye do not understand that I spake it** *[what I said about leaven, yeast]* **not to you concerning bread**, *[but, rather]* that ye should **beware of** *[watch out for]* **the leaven** *[influence]* **of the Pharisees and of the Sadducees?**

12 **Then understood they** *[the Apostles]* how **that he bade them** *[warned them]* not *[to]* **beware** of the leaven *[yeast]* of bread, but **of the doctrine of the Pharisees and of the Sadducees.**

In other words, just as a little bit of yeast can spread itself throughout the whole lump of bread dough, and thus influence it all, so also can the evil influence of corrupt religious leaders, such as the Pharisees and Sadducees, spread throughout the whole nation.

13 When **Jesus came into** the coasts of *[area around]* **Caesarea Philippi** *[about 15 to 20 miles north of the Sea of Galilee]*, **he asked his disciples**, saying, **Whom do men say that I the Son of man** *["Son of God," "Son of Man of Holiness;" see Moses 6:57]* **am?**

14 And **they said**, Some say that thou art John the Baptist: some, Elias *[Elijah]*; and others, Jeremias *[Jeremiah]*, or one of the prophets.

15 **He saith** unto them, **But whom say ye that I am?**

Peter Bears His Testimony of Christ

16 And Simon **Peter answered** and said, **Thou art the Christ, the Son of the living God.**

17 **And Jesus answered** and said unto him,

Blessed art thou, Simon Bar-jona [*son of a man named Jona*]: **for flesh and blood** [*man*] **hath not revealed it unto thee, but my Father which is in heaven** [*you have received your testimony of me through revelation*].

18 And I say also unto thee, That **thou art Peter, and upon this rock** [*the "rock" of revelation, see* TPJS, *p. 274; also, Christ is the "rock" upon which the Church is based; see Matthew 16:18, footnote a*] **I will build my church**; and the gates of hell shall not prevail [*win*] against it. [*Satan's kingdom absolutely will not ultimately win against Christ's kingdom, a very comforting fact!*]

19 And **I will give unto thee the keys** [*including the sealing power*] **of the kingdom of heaven** [*Peter is authorized to serve as the president of the Church after the Savior leaves*]: **and whatsoever thou shalt bind** [*seal*] **on earth shall be bound in heaven: and whatsoever thou shalt loose** [*unseal*] **on earth shall be loosed in heaven.**

20 Then charged he his disciples that they should **tell no man that he was Jesus the Christ.**

Apostle Bruce R. McConkie explained verse 20, above, as follows: "For the time being, to avoid persecution and because the available hearers were not prepared to heed their witness, the apostles were restrained from bearing witness of the divine Sonship of their Master" (*Doctrinal New Testament Commentary*, Vol. 1, p. 390).

21 **From that time forth began Jesus to shew unto his disciples**, how that **he must go unto Jerusalem**, and suffer many things of the elders and chief priests and scribes, **and be killed, and be raised again the third day.**

22 Then **Peter took him, and began to rebuke** [*scold*] **him**, saying, Be it far from thee, Lord: this shall not be unto thee [*this can't happen to You!*].

23 **But he turned, and said unto Peter, Get thee behind me, Satan**: thou art an offence unto me: for thou savourest [*you cherish*] not the things that be of God, but those that be of men. [*You must not try to stop me from following through with the Atonement.*]

24 Then said Jesus unto his disciples, **If any man will come after me, let him deny himself** [*put off worldly concerns*], **and take up his cross** [*sacrifice whatever is necessary*], **and follow me.**

The JST adds a verse after verse 24, above.

JST MATTHEW 16:26

26 And now for a man to take up his cross, is to deny himself of all ungodliness, and every worldly lust, and keep my commandments.

25 For whosoever will save his life shall lose it: and whosoever will lose his life [*sacrifice his own comforts and desires*] for my sake shall find it.

JST MATTHEW 16:27–28

27 **Break not my commandments for to save your lives**; for whosoever will save his life in this world, shall lose it in the world to come.

28 And whosoever will lose his **life in this world**, for my sake, shall find it **in the world to come.**

26 **For what is a man profited, if he shall gain the whole world, and lose his own soul?** or what shall a man give in exchange for his soul?

JST MATTHEW 16:29

29 **Therefore, forsake the world, and save your souls**; for what is a man profited, if he shall gain the whole world, and lose his own soul? Or what shall a man give in exchange for his soul?

27 **For the Son of man shall come in the glory of his Father with his angels** [*the Second Coming—see Matthew 16:27, footnote b*]; and **then he shall reward every man according to his works.** [*Those who sacrifice whatever is necessary to truly follow me will find the reward more than worth it.*]

28 Verily I say unto you, **There be some standing here, which shall not taste of death, till they see the Son of man coming in his kingdom.** [*Some will be translated and will continue living on earth, doing the work of the Lord until He comes again. The Apostle John is the only one of these men whom we know by name as having been translated. See D&C 7. For more information about translated beings, see 3 Nephi 28.*]

MATTHEW 17

IT IS NOW near October, and the Savior will be crucified the following April, thus ending His mortal ministry. Three of His Apostles, Peter, James, and John are already taking on the role of First Presidency. They will experience tremendous additional training now as the Master takes them with Him up on the mountain which is referred to as the Mount of Transfiguration. There, they will see Christ transfigured before their eyes, will hear the Father's voice, and will see, among others, the great prophets Moses and Elijah, from whom they will receive additional priesthood keys. From JST Mark 9:3, we learn that John the Baptist was also there.

The Transfiguration of Christ

1 AND after six days **Jesus taketh Peter, James, and John** his brother, and bringeth them up **into an high mountain** apart,

2 **And was transfigured** before them: and his face did shine as the sun, and his raiment [*clothing*] was white as the light.

3 And, behold, **there appeared** unto them Moses and Elias [*Elijah*] talking with him.

4 **Then answered Peter** [*Peter responded*], and said unto Jesus, **Lord, it is good for us to be here**: if thou wilt, let us make here three tabernacles [*small booths, typically used among the Jews for private worship during the annual Feast of Tabernacles*]; one for thee, and one for Moses, and one for Elias [*Elijah*].

5 While he yet spake, behold, **a bright cloud overshadowed them**: and behold **a voice out of the cloud**, which **said, This is my beloved Son, in whom I am well pleased; hear ye him.**

6 **And** when **the disciples** heard it, they **fell on their** face [*a show of humility*], **and were sore** [*very*] **afraid.**

7 And **Jesus came and touched them, and said, Arise, and be not afraid.**

8 **And when they had lifted up their eyes, they saw no man, save** [*except*] **Jesus** only.

Apostle Bruce R. McConkie summarizes what took place on the Mount of Transfiguration in the following quote: "From the New Testament accounts and from the added light revealed through Joseph Smith it appears evident that:

(1) Jesus singled out Peter, James, and John from the rest of the Twelve; took them upon an unnamed mountain; there He was transfigured before them, and they beheld His glory. Testifying later, John said, "We beheld his glory, the glory as of the only begotten of the Father" (John 1:14); and Peter, speaking of the same event, said they "were eyewitnesses of his majesty" (2 Peter 1:16).

(2) Peter, James, and John, were themselves "transfigured before him" (*Teachings*, p. 158), even as Moses, the Three Nephites, Joseph Smith, and many prophets of all ages have been transfigured, thus enabling them to entertain angels, see visions and comprehend the things of God (*Mormon Doctrine*, pp. 725–26).

(3) Moses and Elijah—two ancient prophets who were translated and taken to heaven without tasting death, so they could return with tangible bodies on this very occasion, an occasion preceding the day of resurrection—appeared on the mountain; and they and Jesus gave the keys of the kingdom to Peter, James, and John (*Teachings*, p. 158).

(4) John the Baptist, previously beheaded by Herod, apparently was also present. It may well be that other unnamed prophets, either coming as translated beings or as spirits from paradise, were also present.

(5) Peter, James, and John saw in vision the transfiguration of the earth, that is, they saw it renewed and returned to its paradisiacal state—an event that is to take place at the Second Coming when the millennial era is ushered in (D&C 63:20–21; *Mormon Doctrine*, pp. 718–19).

(6) It appears that Peter, James, and John received their own endowments while on the mountain (*Doctrines of Salvation*, vol. 2, p. 165). Peter says that while there, they "received from God the Father honour and glory," seemingly bearing out this conclusion. It also appears that it was while on the mount that they received the more sure word of prophecy, it then being revealed to them that they were sealed up unto eternal life (2 Peter 1:16–19; D&C 131:5).

(7) Apparently Jesus himself was strengthened and encouraged by Moses and Elijah so as to be prepared for the infinite sufferings and agony ahead of him in connection with working out the

infinite and eternal atonement. (*Jesus the Christ,* p. 373.) Similar comfort had been given him by angelic visitants following his forty-day fast and its attendant temptations (Matthew 4:11), and an angel from heaven was yet to strengthen him when he would sweat great drops of blood in the Garden of Gethsemane (Luke 22:42–44).

(8) Certainly the three chosen apostles were taught in plainness "of his death and also his resurrection" (JST Luke 9:31), teachings which would be of inestimable value to them in the trying days ahead.

(9) It should also have been apparent to them that the old dispensations of the past had faded away, that the law (of which Moses was the symbol) and the prophets (of whom Elijah was the typifying representative) were subject to Him whom they were now commanded to hear.

(10) Apparently God the Father, overshadowed and hidden by a cloud, was present on the mountain, although our Lord's three associates, as far as the record stipulates, heard only his voice and did not see his form" (*Doctrinal New Testament Commentary,* Vol. 1, p. 399).

9 And **as they came down from the mountain, Jesus charged** [*instructed*] **them, saying, Tell the vision to no man, until the Son of man be risen again from the dead.**

10 And **his disciples asked** him, saying, **Why then say the scribes that Elias must first come?**

Here, Peter, James, and John seem to be asking the Savior to clear up some doctrinal confusion in their own minds about Elias. They had been taught by their scriptures that Elias would come and prepare the way for the Lord. Yet, they had just seen Elias (Elijah) on the Mount and this was after the Savior had come. In fact, this was near the end of the Master's mortal ministry. It is helpful for us, as we study these scriptures, to be aware that the name "Elias" has many meanings. See Bible Dictionary, p. 663. Thus, here, in this setting as explained by the Savior, Elias can mean John the Baptist who came before Jesus and prepared the way for Him. It can also mean Elijah who ministered on the Mount of Transfiguration and would yet appear in the Kirtland Temple (D&C 110:13–15). It is also helpful to read JST Matthew 17:10–14 in the back of our Bible, concerning Elias.

11 And **Jesus answered** and said unto them, **Elias truly shall first come, and restore all things.**

12 **But** I say unto you, **That Elias is come already**, and they knew him not, but have done unto him whatsoever they listed. Likewise shall also the Son of man suffer of them.

13 Then the disciples understood that **he spake unto them of John the Baptist.**

JST MATTHEW 17:10–14

10 And Jesus answered and said unto them, Elias truly shall first come, and restore all things, **as the prophets have written**.

11 And again I say unto you that Elias has come already, **concerning whom it is written, Behold, I will send my messenger, and he shall prepare the way before me**; and they knew him not, and have done unto him, whatsoever they listed.

12 Likewise shall also the Son of man suffer of them.

13 **But I say unto you, Who is Elias? Behold, this is Elias, whom I send to prepare the way before me.**

14 Then the disciples understood that he spake unto them of John the Baptist, **and also of another who should come and restore all things, as it is written by the prophets.**

The Healing of a Lunatick Son

14 And **when they were come to the multitude, there came to him a certain man, kneeling down to him, and saying,**

15 Lord, have mercy on **my son**: for he **is lunatick**, and sore vexed [*very sick and troubled*]: for ofttimes he falleth into the fire, and oft into the water.

16 And **I brought him to thy disciples, and they could not cure him.**

17 **Then Jesus answered and said, O faithless and perverse generation**, how long shall I be with you? how long shall I suffer you [*put up with you*]? bring him hither to me.

18 And Jesus rebuked the devil; and he departed out of him: and **the child was cured** from that very hour.

This is yet another reminder that Christ has power over Satan and his kingdom. Also, we are reminded here, as elsewhere, that the Savior has power to heal whatever ails us, symbolic of His power to save all who will follow Him.

19 Then came **the disciples** to Jesus apart [*privately*], and **said, Why could not we cast him out?**

20 **And Jesus said** unto them, **Because of your unbelief**: for verily I say unto you, If ye have faith as a grain of mustard seed, ye shall say unto this mountain, Remove hence to yonder place; and it shall remove; and nothing shall be impossible unto you.

21 **Howbeit** [*however*] **this kind goeth not out but by prayer and fasting.**

Jesus Tells His Apostles of His Coming Death and Resurrection

22 And while they abode **in Galilee, Jesus said** unto them, **The Son of man** [*Christ; Son of Man of Holiness; see Moses 6:57*] **shall be betrayed into the hands of men:**

23 And **they shall kill him**, and **the third day he shall be raised again**. And they were exceeding sorry.

Temple Tax Money Miraculously Comes from the Mouth of a Fish

24 And **when they were come to Capernaum** [*Peter's home town on the northern edge of the Sea of Galilee*], **they** [*temple tax collectors*] **that received tribute money** [*annual temple tax of a half shekel, required from every male, twenty years old and older*] **came to Peter, and said, Doth not your master pay tribute** [*the temple tax*]?

25 **He saith, Yes.** And **when he** [*Peter*] **was come into the house, Jesus prevented him** [*spoke to him first, before he had a chance to mention the temple tax to Jesus—see Matthew 17:25, footnote a, in your Bible*], **saying, What thinkest thou, Simon** [*here's a question for you, Peter*]? of whom [*from whom*] do the kings of the earth take custom [*collect taxes*] or tribute? of their own children, or of strangers [*others*]?

26 Peter saith unto him, Of strangers. Jesus saith unto him, Then are the children [*of kings*] free [*exempt*].

There is a subtle play on words at work here. Jesus is the Son of the King (Heavenly Father). He is also the King, the Messiah. He is even the rightful political King of the Jews if the Romans had not been in political power at the time, because Joseph, Mary's husband, was the rightful heir to the political throne of the Jews. Thus, Jesus, as King and as the Son of the King (Elohim) should not have to pay this tax. Approaching it from another angle, since Jesus is a King in many ways, His children (His followers, the apostles, etc.) including Peter, should not have to pay this tribute either.

27 **Notwithstanding** [*nevertheless*], **lest we should offend them** [*in order to keep the peace*], **go thou to the sea** [*Sea of Galilee, which is probably just a few hundred feet or less away*], and **cast an hook** [*go fishing*], and **take up the fish that first cometh up** [*the first one you catch*]; **and when thou hast opened his mouth, thou shalt find a piece of money** [*a one shekel (four-drachma) coin, the exact amount to pay the temple tax for Christ and Peter; see NIV Bible, Matthew 17:27*]: **that take, and give unto them** [*the temple tax collectors*] **for me and thee.**

MATTHEW 18

1 AT the same time came the disciples unto Jesus, saying, **Who is the greatest in the kingdom of heaven?**

2 And **Jesus called a little child unto him, and set him in the midst of them,**

3 And said, Verily I say unto you, **Except ye be converted, and become as little children, ye**

shall not enter into the kingdom of heaven *[celestial glory]*.

4 **Whosoever therefore shall humble himself as this little child, the same is greatest in the kingdom of heaven.**

5 And **whoso shall receive one such little child in my name receiveth me.**

6 **But whoso shall offend** *[lead astray, cause to commit sin]* **one of these little ones which believe in me, it were better for him that a millstone** *[a large, heavy stone used to grind grain in a flour mill]* **were hanged about his neck, and that he were drowned in the depth of the sea.**

7 Woe unto the world because of offences! for **it must needs be that offences come; but woe to that man by whom the offence cometh!**

Sometimes people think that, since there needs to be opposition in all things [*2 Nephi 2:11*], they are helping the Lord's plan by being wicked, tempting others to sin, etc. Verse 7, above, shows such thinking to be very wrong!

8 Wherefore **if thy hand** *[friend; see JST explanation after verse 9, below]* **or** thy **foot** *[friend]* **offend thee, cut them off**, and **cast them from thee**: it is better for thee to enter into life halt or maimed, rather than having two hands or two feet to be cast into everlasting fire.

9 And **if thine eye** *[your own family members; see* **offend thee, pluck it out, and cast it from thee** *JST explanation below]*: it is better for thee to enter into life with one eye, rather than having two eyes to be cast into hell fire.

The JST explains the symbolism of "hand," "foot," and "eye" in verses 8 and 9 above as follows:

JST MATTHEW 18:9
And a man's hand is his friend, and his foot, also; and a man's eye, are they of his own household.

10 Take heed that ye **despise not one of these little ones**; for I say unto you, That in heaven their angels do always behold the face of my Father which is in heaven *[they will be saved in the celestial kingdom; see D&C 137:10]*.

11 For **the Son of man** *[the Savior]* **is come to save that which was lost.**

JST MATTHEW 18:11
11 For the Son of man is come to save that which was lost, **and to call sinners to repentance; but these little ones have no need of repentance, and I will save them.**

12 **How think ye** *[what do you think]*? **if a man have an hundred sheep, and one of them be gone astray, doth he not leave the ninety and nine, and goeth into the mountains, and seeketh that which is gone astray** *[God does everything he can to bring back the strays (symbolic of sinners)]*?

13 **And if** so be that **he find it**, verily I say unto you, **he rejoiceth** more of that sheep, than of the ninety and nine which went not astray. *[There is much joy when a stray returns to the fold.]*

14 Even so **it is not the will of your Father which is in heaven, that one of these little ones should perish.**

15 Moreover **if thy brother shall trespass against thee**, go and **tell him his fault between thee and him alone** *[keep it private; don't gossip about it; see D&C 20:80]*: if he shall hear thee *[responds positively]*, thou hast gained thy brother.

Gossip (implied in verse 15, above) can actually be a type of emotional terrorism, because it often claims innocent victims.

16 But **if he will not hear thee** *[will not accept your efforts to make peace]*, then **take** with thee **one or two** more *[as witnesses that you have tried to work the matter out with him]*, that **in the mouth of two or three witnesses every word may be established** *[this is known as the law of witnesses]*.

17 And **if he shall neglect to hear them** *[if he won't respond favorably to that effort on your part]*, **tell it unto the church** *[go to the authorities of the church]*: but **if he neglect to hear the church, let him be unto thee as an heathen man and a publican** *[go ahead and excommunicate him]*.

Remember that the Savior is speaking primarily to His Apostles here whom He called, as recorded in Matthew, chapter 10. In verse 18, next, He instructs them concerning the sealing power of priesthood keys which they will exercise as part of their calling.

Priesthood Keys and Sealing Power

18 Verily I say unto you, **Whatsoever ye** [*the Apostles*] **shall bind on earth shall be bound in heaven**: and **whatsoever ye shall loose on earth shall be loosed in heaven.**

19 Again I say unto you, That if two of you shall agree on earth as touching any thing that they shall ask, it shall be done for them of my Father which is in heaven.

20 For **where two or three are gathered together in my name, there am I in the midst of them.**

How Often Should We Forgive?

21 Then came Peter to him, and said, Lord, **how oft shall my brother sin against me, and I forgive him?** till seven times?

22 Jesus saith unto him, I say not unto thee, Until seven times: but, **Until seventy times seven.** [*In other words, forgive him every time he repents. See D&C 98:40.*]

This doctrine of forgiving is a most important one for our own salvation. When we forgive others, we free ourselves of the heavy burdens of hatred, grudges, bitterness, pity parties, etc. Nephi is a great example to us in 1 Nephi 7:21 where he "frankly forgave" his brothers. The Savior goes on now to teach Peter and all of us the importance of our forgiving others if we want the Lord to forgive us.

The Parable of the Unmerciful Servant

23 Therefore is **the kingdom of heaven likened unto a certain king**, which would take account of his servants [*see who is in debt to him etc.*].

24 And when he had begun to reckon [*check the accounting records*], **one was brought unto him, which owed him ten thousand talents.**

One calculation of this amount, based on an average day's wage, yields a debt which would require 60,000,000 work days to pay off, which, of course, is an impossible debt to repay. A person who starts full-time work at age 15 and works six days a week for 55 years, would have 17,160 days of work in his or her lifetime.

25 **But forasmuch as he had not to pay, his lord commanded him to be sold, and his wife, and children, and all that he had, and payment to be made.** [*This can be symbolic of the fact that we would lose family and all that counts (see 2 Nephi 9:8–9) without the Atonement and its power to free us and cleanse us so that we can enter exaltation and dwell in family units forever.*]

26 The servant therefore fell down, and worshipped him, saying, Lord, **have patience with me, and I will pay thee all.**

27 Then **the lord** of that servant **was moved with compassion**, and loosed him, and **forgave him the debt** [*symbolic of the Atonement*].

28 **But the same servant** went out, and **found one of his fellowservants, which owed him an hundred pence** [*an amount equivalent to about 100 days' wages; see Matthew 20:2*]: and **he** laid hands on him, and **took him by the throat, saying, Pay me that thou owest.**

29 And his fellowservant fell down at his feet, and besought him, saying, **Have patience with me, and I will pay thee all** [*the exact words he himself had used as he begged for mercy in verse 26, above*].

30 **And he would not** [*he refused to be merciful to the person who owed him and couldn't pay*]: but went and cast him into prison, till he should pay the debt.

31 So **when his fellowservants saw what was done, they were very sorry, and came and told** unto **their lord** [*the king in verse 23*] **all that was done.**

32 Then his lord, after that he had called him [*the man who refused to forgive the relatively small debt of 100 days' wages*], said unto him, **O thou wicked servant, I forgave thee all that debt, because thou desiredst me:**

33 **Shouldest not thou also have had compassion on thy fellowservant, even as I had pity on thee?**

34 **And his lord** was wroth [*angry; righteous indignation*], and **delivered him to the tormentors, till he should pay all that was due unto him** [*symbolic of the law of justice*].

> Symbolically, "tormentors" would represent the punishment of the wicked who are eventually turned over to the buffetings of Satan (D&C 82:21) to pay for their own sins. Even after they have paid the penalty for their own sins, the highest degree of glory they can enter is the Telestial (D&C 76:84–85). Also, this parable teaches the interplay between the Law of Justice and the Law of Mercy. The Law of Mercy allows us to be forgiven of unfathomable debt to God, through obedience to the gospel, including forgiving others. However, if we, through our actions, refuse the Law of Mercy, then the Law of Justice takes over, and we bear the burden of our sins as explained in D&C 19:15–18].

35 **So likewise shall my heavenly Father do also unto you, if ye from your hearts forgive not every one his brother their trespasses.** [*This is fair warning to us about forgiving others and quite an answer to Peter's question in verse 21, wherein he asked how often he should forgive others.*]

MATTHEW 19

HAVING RECENTLY PROPHESIED to His apostles that He will be arrested, tried, and crucified in Jerusalem and then resurrected three days afterward, the Savior now leaves Galilee and travels toward Jerusalem. Can you imagine how His Apostles felt about this? He continues to instruct them in their duties and teach them how to apply the gospel in their lives. The religious leaders of the Jews continue their attempts to trap Him.

1 AND it came to pass, that when **Jesus** had finished these sayings, he **departed from Galilee, and came into** the coasts [*borders*] of **Judæa** beyond Jordan [*getting close to Jerusalem but still east of the Jordan River*];

2 And **great multitudes followed him; and he healed them there.**

3 **The Pharisees** [*religious leaders of the Jews*] also **came unto him, tempting him** [*trying to trap him so they could arrest Him*], and **saying** unto him, **Is it lawful for a man to put away** [*divorce*] **his wife for every cause?**

4 And **he answered** and said unto them, **Have ye not read**, that he [*Heavenly Father*] which made them at the beginning made them male and female,

5 And said, **For this cause** [*marriage and family*] **shall a man leave father and mother, and shall cleave to** [*stick to; be faithful to*] **his wife: and they twain** [*two*] **shall be one flesh?**

6 Wherefore they are no more twain [*two people*], but one flesh [*one family unit*]. **What therefore God hath joined together, let not man put asunder** [*take apart*].

> As you can see, they are trying to pit the Master against the great lawgiver and prophet, Moses, who is very highly esteemed among the Jews at this time in the New Testament.

7 **They say** unto him, **Why did Moses then command to give a writing of divorcement** [*a legal certificate of divorce*], **and to put her away** [*divorce her*]?

8 **He saith** unto them, **Moses because of the hardness of your hearts suffered** [*allowed*] **you to put away** [*divorce*] **your wives: but from the beginning it was not so.**

9 And **I say unto you, Whosoever shall put away his wife, except it be for fornication**, and

shall marry another, committeth adultery: and whoso marrieth her which is put away doth commit adultery.

Refer to the note between Matthew, chapter five, verses 31 and 32, in this study guide, for help with verse 9, above.

10 **His disciples say** unto him, **If the case of the man be so with his wife, it is not good to marry** [*if this is such a serious matter, it would be better not to risk getting married*].

11 But **he said** unto them, **All men cannot receive this saying, save they to whom it is given.**

12 For there are some eunuchs [*men who are physically unable to have children*], which were so born from their mother's womb: and there are some eunuchs, which were made eunuchs of men [*men who have been surgically rendered incapable of having children; see Bible Dictionary, under "Eunuch"*]: and there be eunuchs, which have made themselves eunuchs for the kingdom of heaven's sake. He that is able to receive it, let him receive it.

Verse 12 above seems incomplete and fragmentary. We don't know what it really means. Concerning this verse, Apostle Bruce R. McConkie said, "Some added background and additional information is needed to understand fully what is meant by this teaching about eunuchs" (*Doctrinal New Testament Commentary*, Vol. 1, p. 549).

13 **Then were there brought unto him little children**, that he should put his hands on them, and pray: **and the disciples rebuked them** [*rebuked those who brought the little children to Jesus*].

14 But Jesus said, **Suffer** [*allow*] **little children, and forbid them not, to come unto me: for of such is the kingdom of heaven.**

15 **And he laid his hands on them**, and departed thence.

16 And, behold, **one** [*the rich young man in verse 22*] **came and said unto him, Good Master** [*"Teacher"; see NIV Bible*], **what good thing shall I do, that I may have eternal life?**

This rich young man seems to believe that doing one "good thing" will secure his place in heaven. We see this thinking on his part again in verse 18 when he asks which commandment he should keep in order to attain heaven.

17 And **he said** unto him, **Why callest thou me good? there is none good but one, that is, God** [*Jesus wants no glory for Himself, rather, gives all credit and glory to the Father*]: but if thou wilt enter into life [*exaltation*], keep the commandments.

18 **He saith unto him, Which?** [*The young man still hasn't got the point.*] **Jesus said**, Thou shalt do **no murder**, Thou shalt **not commit adultery**, Thou shalt **not steal**, Thou shalt **not bear false witness**,

19 **Honour thy father and thy mother**: and, Thou shalt **love thy neighbour as thyself.**

20 **The young man saith** unto him, **All these things have I kept from my youth up: what lack I yet?**

From what the Savior says to him next, in verse 21, it seems that the young man lacks true charity. Also, notice that the Master also kindly invites him to come and follow Him, a reminder that qualifying for exaltation is a process, not an event.

21 **Jesus said** unto him, **If thou wilt be perfect, go and sell that thou hast, and give to the poor**, and thou shalt have treasure in heaven: and **come and follow me.**

22 **But** when **the young man** heard that saying, he **went away sorrowful: for he had great possessions** [*was very rich*].

Verse 23, next, reminds us that Jesus is still giving His Apostles some intense training.

23 **Then said Jesus unto his disciples**, Verily [*"Listen carefully, this is an important point."*] I say unto you, **That a rich man shall hardly** [*it is "hard" for him, not "almost impossible"*] **enter into the kingdom of heaven** [*celestial kingdom*].

24 And again I say unto you, **It is easier for a camel to go through the eye of a needle, than for a rich man to enter into the kingdom of God.**

There is a rumor going around that the "eye of a needle" (verse 24, above) was a small gate in the walls of Jerusalem, used for entry into the city by night, after the main gates were closed. The rumor states that it was very difficult for a camel to get down and scrunch through the gate. Bible scholars indicate that this rumor has no truth to it. They indicate that the word "needle," as used in verse 24, refers to an ordinary sewing needle in the original Bible languages. Therefore, what the Savior is doing with this comparison is the use of exaggeration in order to make a point.

25 When **his disciples** heard it, they **were** exceedingly **amazed, saying, Who then can be saved?**

26 But **Jesus** beheld them, and **said** unto them, **With men this** [*being saved*] **is impossible; but with God** [*with the help of God, through the Atonement*] **all things are possible.**

JST MATTHEW 19:2
But Jesus beheld their thoughts, and said unto them, With men this is impossible; **but if they will forsake all things for my sake**, with God **whatsoever things I speak are possible**.

27 **Then answered Peter** [*this is old English and means that Peter asked a question*] and said unto him, Behold, **we have forsaken all, and followed thee; what shall we have therefore** [*what will our reward be? The answer to Peter's question is given in verses 28 and 29*].

28 And **Jesus said** unto them, Verily [*listen very carefully, this is an important point*] I say unto you, That **ye which have followed me, in the regeneration** [*JST resurrection*] **when the Son of man** [*Christ; Son of Man of Holiness—see Moses 6:57*] **shall sit in the throne of his glory** [*in exaltation*], **ye also shall sit upon twelve thrones** [*you, too, will be exalted*], **judging the twelve tribes of Israel.**

Apostle Bruce R. McConkie explains the judging referred to in verse 28 above in the following quote:

"Christ is the great judge of all the earth. 'The Father judgeth no man, but hath committed all judgment unto the Son' (John 5:22). In due course, every living soul shall stand before his judgment bar, be judged according to his own works, and awarded a place in the mansions that are prepared (Mormon 3:20).

"Under Christ a great hierarchy of judges will operate, each functioning in his assigned sphere. John saw many judges sitting upon thrones (Revelation 20:4). Paul said the Saints would judge both the world and angels (1 Corrinthians 6:2–3). The elders are to sit in judgment on those who reject them (D&C 75:21–22; Matthew 10:14–15). Daniel saw that judgment would be given to the Saints (Daniel 7:22). The Nephite Twelve will be judged by the Twelve from Jerusalem and then in turn will judge the Nephite nation (1 Nephi 12:9–10; 3 Nephi 27:27; Mormon 3:19). And the Twelve who served with our Lord in his ministry shall judge the whole house of Israel (D&C 29:12). No doubt there will be many others of many dispensations who will sit in judgment upon the peoples of their days and generations—all judging according to the judgment which Christ shall give them, "which shall be just" (3 Nephi 27:27) (*Doctrinal New Testament Commentary*, Vol. 1, pp. 558–59).

29 [*This is a continuation of the answer to Peter's question in verse 27.*] **And every one that hath forsaken** [*given up*] houses, or brethren, or sisters, or father, or mother, or wife, or children, or lands, **for my name's sake**, shall receive an hundredfold, and **shall inherit everlasting life** [*exaltation*].

30 **But many** that are first [*JST Mark 10:30–31 "**who make themselves first**"*] **shall be last; and the last** [*those who consider themselves least, and who are humbly obedient*] **shall be first** [*highest up in the celestial kingdom*].

MATTHEW 20

The Parable of the Laborers (The Eleventh Hour Parable)

1 FOR **the kingdom of heaven is like unto a man that is an householder**, which **went out early in the morning to hire labourers** into his vineyard.

2 And **when he had agreed with the labourers for a penny a day** [*a day's wages*], **he sent them into his vineyard.**

When we see the word "penny," we think of a coin of very little worth. This misunderstanding can distract us as we read this parable. The King James Bible (the version we use) translators consistently used the word "penny" for "denarius." A denarius is a Roman silver coin (see Bible Dictionary, under "Money"). It was worth a day's wages and thus was a significant amount of money.

3 And **he went out about the third hour, and saw others** standing idle in the marketplace,

4 **And said** unto them; **Go ye also into the vineyard, and whatsoever is right I will give you.** And they went their way.

5 Again he went out about **the sixth and ninth hour**, and did **likewise.**

6 And about **the eleventh hour** he went out, and **found others** standing idle, and saith unto them, Why stand ye here all the day idle?

7 They say unto him, Because no man hath hired us. **He saith unto them, Go ye also into the vineyard**; and whatsoever is right, that shall ye receive.

8 **So when even** [*the end of the day*] **was come, the lord of the vineyard saith unto his steward,** Call the labourers, and **give them their hire** [*wages*], beginning from the last unto the first.

9 **And** when they came that were hired about the eleventh hour, **they received every man a penny** [*a full day's wages*].

10 But when **the first** [*those who began working at the beginning of the day, verse 2*] came, they supposed that they should have received more [*than those who hadn't worked all day*]; and they likewise received every man a penny [*a full day's wages; see note by verse 2 above*].

11 And when they had received it, they **murmured** [*complained*] against the goodman of the house [*the householder who hired them, verse 1*],

12 **Saying, These last have wrought** [*worked*] **but one hour, and thou hast made them equal unto us,** which have borne [*had to put up with*] the burden and heat of the day.

13 But **he answered** one of them, and said, **Friend, I do thee no wrong:** didst not thou agree with me for a penny? [*I kept my part of the agreement and gave you full payment as we agreed upon.*]

14 Take that thine is, and go thy way: **I will give unto this last** [*the workers who started at the eleventh hour, verses 6 and 7*], **even as unto thee.**

15 Is it not lawful for me to do what I will with mine own? **Is thine eye evil, because I am good** [*are you jealous because I am generous to others; NIV Bible*]?

16 So **the last shall be first, and the first last:** for many be called, but few chosen [*all are "called" or invited to come to exaltation, but few are chosen to receive it because they don't overcome sins*].

The Parable of the Laborers, as Matthew 20:1–16 is called, is very rich in symbolism and presents an opportunity for you to improve your skill in recognizing symbolism in the scriptures as you read and study them. We will repeat verses 1–16 here and call your attention to some of the symbolism with notes in parentheses. As is the case with symbolism, there are many ways it can be interpreted, so the following is just one possibility for your consideration:

MATTHEW 20:1–16 (REPEATED)

1 FOR the **kingdom of heaven** [*celestial glory*] is like unto **a man** [*Heavenly Father*] that is an householder, which went out early in the morning to hire **labourers** [*faithful Saints who have been active in the Church all their lives*] into his **vineyard** [*the earth*].

2 And when he had agreed with the labourers for **a penny a day** [*full pay for a righteous mortal life; symbolic of exaltation*], he sent them into his **vineyard** [*the earth*].

3 And he went out **about the third hour**, and saw **others standing idle** [*people who had not yet joined the Church or become active*] in the marketplace,

4 And said unto them; **Go ye also into the vineyard** [*"Join the church, get active, go to work."*], and **whatsoever is right I will give you** [*"I will be fair with you."*]. And **they went their way** [*they joined the Church and remained faithful to the end of their lives*].

5 Again he went out **about the sixth and ninth hour**, and did **likewise** [*others joined the Church or became active later in their lives and remained faithful in the work*].

6 And about **the eleventh hour** [*representing people who find the truth and join the Church or get active near the end of their lives and remain faithful and work hard to the end*] he went out, and found others standing idle, and saith unto them, Why stand ye here all the day idle?

7 They say unto him, Because no man hath hired us. He saith unto them, **Go ye also into the vineyard** [*join the Church and remain faithful*]; and whatsoever is right, that shall ye receive.

8 So when **even** [*"evening," in other words, life is over and judgment day has arrived*] was come, the **lord of the vineyard** [*Heavenly Father*] saith unto **his steward** [*Christ, who is the final judge—see John 5:22*], **Call the labourers, and give them their hire** [*give them their reward*], beginning from the last unto the first.

9 And when they came that were hired about the **eleventh hour**, they **received every man a penny** [*those who became faithful Saints much later in life—not "deathbed" repentance—were* given exaltation].

Note: In these next verses, lifelong Saints are cautioned not to become jealous or feel unfairly treated since they have "bourne the burden and heat of the day" (verse 12), i.e., sacrificed and worked hard all their lives to be obedient, when they see converts or reactivated Saints get the same reward they have worked longer to achieve.

10 But when **the first** [*those who had been active all their lives*] came, they **supposed that they should have received more**; and they likewise received every man a penny.

11 And when they had received it, **they murmured against the goodman of the house** [*the Father*],

12 **Saying**, These last have wrought [*worked*] but one hour [*haven't worked nearly as long as we have to gain exaltation*], and **thou hast made them equal unto us**, which have borne the burden and heat of the day.

13 But he answered one of them, and said, Friend, I do thee no wrong: didst not thou agree with me for **a penny** [*exaltation*]?

14 **Take that thine is** [*take your exaltation—by the way, the Lord is being very patient with these complainers at this point; if they don't repent of this bad attitude, they will obviously lose their exaltation as indicated in verse 16*], and go thy way: I will give unto this last, even as unto thee.

15 Is it not lawful for me to do what I will with mine own? **Is thine eye evil, because I am good** [*are you jealous and sinning in your heart because I am forgiving and generous*]?

16 So **the last shall be first, and the first last** [*it is possible to lose exaltation because of a bad attitude such as that demonstrated by the workers in verses 10–15*]: for **many be called, but few chosen** [*all are in fact called or invited to become exalted, but not all make it*].

17 And **Jesus going up to Jerusalem took the twelve disciples apart** [*aside where they could be alone*] in the way, **and said** unto them,

18 Behold, **we go up to Jerusalem; and the Son of man** [*Christ, "Son of Man of Holiness" (Heavenly Father)*; see Moses 6:57] **shall be betrayed unto the chief priests and unto the scribes, and they** [*religious leaders of the Jews*] **shall condemn him to death,**

19 And shall **deliver him to the Gentiles** [*the Romans*] to **mock**, and to **scourge**, and to **crucify** him: **and the third day he shall rise again** [*be resurrected*].

20 **Then came to him the mother of Zebedee's children** [*James and John's mother*] **with her sons**, worshipping him, and **desiring a certain thing of him.**

21 And **he said** unto her, **What wilt thou? She saith** unto him, **Grant that these my two sons** [*James and John*] **may sit, the one on thy right hand, and the other on the left, in thy kingdom.**

22 **But Jesus** answered and **said, Ye know not what ye ask.** Are ye able to drink of the cup that I shall drink of, and to be baptized with the baptism that I am baptized with [*can you remain*

MATTHEW

faithful at all costs]? They [*James and John*] say unto him, We are able.

23 And he saith unto them, **Ye shall drink indeed of my cup**, and be baptized with the baptism that I am baptized with [*in other words, you will go through much persecution also*]: **but to sit on my right hand, and on my left, is not mine to give, but it shall be given to them for whom it is prepared of my Father** [*it is not to be given as a matter of favoritism or mere request, rather it will be given to those who earn it according to the laws established by the Father*].

24 And **when the ten** [*the other ten in the Quorum of Twelve*] **heard it, they were moved with indignation** [*angry*] **against the two** brethren [*the Apostles, James and John*].

This is a reminder that these Apostles are still learning and maturing in their work and callings, just as each of us is. It is also a view of the Savior's tenderness and patience, as He teaches them yet another lesson.

25 **But Jesus called them unto him**, and said, **Ye know that the princes** [*kings, leaders, etc.*] **of the Gentiles** [*non-Israelites*] **exercise dominion** [*power and authority*] **over them**, and they that are great [*those leaders*] exercise authority upon them [*the Gentiles*].

26 **But it shall not be so among you**: but **whosoever will be great among you, let him be your minister;**

27 And **whosoever will be chief among you, let him be your servant:**

28 **Even as the Son of man** [*Christ*] **came not to be ministered unto, but to minister**, and to give his life a ransom for many [*to redeem many*].

29 And **as they departed from Jericho** [*about 25 miles from Jerusalem*], **a great multitude followed him.**

30 And, behold, **two blind men** sitting by the way side, when they heard that Jesus passed by, **cried out**, saying, Have mercy on us, O Lord, thou Son of David [*in other words, You, the Messiah, who are, as prophesied, a descendant of King David*].

31 And **the multitude rebuked** [*scolded*] **them**, because they should hold their peace [*keep quiet*]: **but they cried the more, saying, Have mercy on us**, O Lord, thou Son of David.

32 **And Jesus stood still** [*stopped walking*], **and called them**, and said, **What will ye that I shall do** unto you?

33 They say unto him, Lord, that our eyes may be opened.

34 So **Jesus had compassion** on them, and **touched their eyes**: and immediately their eyes received sight, and **they followed him.**

MATTHEW 21

THESE NEXT VERSES lead up to what is known as "the Triumphal Entry," the day when Jesus rode into Jerusalem accompanied by throngs of people shouting "Hosanna to the Son of David." In other words, celebrating and cheering Jesus as the promised Messiah who would save them and free them from their enemies. The Passover was underway and throngs of Jewish pilgrims had arrived in Jerusalem from many lands to join in Passover celebration and worship. This begins the last week of the Savior's mortal life.

The Triumphal Entry

1 AND when **they drew nigh** [*near*] **unto Jerusalem**, and were come to Bethphage [*on the east side of the Mount of Olives*], unto the mount of Olives, **then sent Jesus two disciples,**

2 **Saying** unto them, **Go into the village** over against you [*ahead of you*], and straightway [*immediately*] **ye shall find an ass** [*donkey*] **tied, and a colt** [*a young male donkey*] **with her: loose**

[*untie*] **them, and bring them unto me.**

3 And **if any man say ought** unto you [*questions you about what you are doing*], ye shall **say, The Lord hath need of them**; and straightway [*immediately*] **he will send them.**

4 **All this was done, that it might be fulfilled** which was **spoken by the prophet** [*Zechariah; see Zechariah 9:9*], saying,

5 Tell ye the daughter of Sion, **Behold, thy King cometh unto thee, meek, and sitting upon an ass**, and a colt the foal [*offspring*] of an ass.

In Hebrew symbolism, a donkey represents humility and submission. Thus, the Savior's riding into Jerusalem on a donkey is symbolic of his humility and submission to the coming suffering and crucifixion.

6 And **the disciples went, and did as Jesus commanded** them,

7 And brought the ass, and the colt, **and put on them their clothes**, and they set him thereon.

JST MATTHEW 21:5

. . . brought the colt, and **put on it their clothes**; and Jesus took the colt and sat thereon; and they followed him" (see also Luke 19:30).

Have you ever noticed the miracle that just happened here? Luke 19:30 informs us that the colt had never been ridden before. Yet, the Master sat on it with no trouble from the colt, reminding us that Jesus has power over the animal kingdom too.

8 And **a very great multitude spread their garments in the way** [*along the path where Jesus rode*]; **others cut down branches from the trees** [*from palm trees—John 12:13*], **and strawed** [*spread*] **them in the way.**

In Jewish symbolism, palm branches symbolized triumph and victory. Thus, in cutting palm branches and excitedly waving them and spreading them on the ground in front of the Savior, the crowd was enthusiastically expressing their belief that Jesus would bring them military triumph and victory over their Roman enemies.

9 And **the multitudes** that went before, and that followed, **cried**, saying, **Hosanna to the Son of David: Blessed is he that cometh in the name of the Lord; Hosanna in the highest.**

The word "Hosanna" means "Lord, save us, now!" (see Bible Dictionary, under "Hosanna") and ties in with the symbolism of palm branches mentioned above.

10 And **when he was come into Jerusalem, all the city was moved** [*everyone in the city was excited about him*], **saying, Who is this?**

11 **And the multitude said, This is Jesus the prophet of Nazareth** of Galilee.

Jesus Cleanses the Temple

12 **And Jesus went into the temple** of God, **and cast out all them that sold and bought in the temple**, and overthrew the tables of the moneychangers, and the seats of them that sold doves,

John tells us (John 2:14–17) that Jesus cleansed the temple at the beginning of his ministry. Now, three years later, Jesus cleanses the temple again. This is the second time. The temple crowd obviously didn't learn their lesson the first time.

13 **And said** unto them, **It is written** [*in Isaiah 56:7*], **My house shall be called the house of prayer; but ye have made it a den of thieves.**

14 And the blind and the lame came to him **in the temple**; and he healed them.

Did you notice that Jesus didn't immediately leave the temple, after having cleansed it? No doubt there was potential danger to him from the authorities. Nevertheless, he remained for a considerable time to heal people who came to him. This must have been extremely frustrating to the Jewish religious leaders who "were sore displeased" (verse 15).

15 And when **the chief priests and scribes** [*Jewish religious leaders*] **saw the wonderful things that he did**, and the **children crying in the temple, and saying, Hosanna** [*"Save now;" see Bible Dictionary, under "Hosanna"*] to the Son of David; **they were sore** [*very*] **displeased,**

JST MATTHEW 21:13

children of the kingdom, [*in other words, faithful members of the Church*]

JESUS WENT INTO THE TEMPLE OF GOD, AND CAST OUT ALL THEM THAT SOLD AND BOUGHT IN THE TEMPLE.

MATTHEW 21:12

16 **And said unto him**, Hearest thou what these *[the "children of the kingdom" in verse 15]* say? *[In other words, do you realize how dangerous it is to you for them to be calling you the Messiah?]* **And Jesus saith unto them**, Yea; have ye never read, Out of the mouth of babes and sucklings thou hast perfected praise? *[In other words, among other possible interpretations, Jesus is saying, "You are supposed to know the scriptures. Haven't you ever read that from child-like faithful members come true praises of God?"]*

17 **And he left them, and went** out of the city **into Bethany**; and he **lodged there.**

The Fig Tree Is Cursed and Withers

18 Now **in the morning as he returned into the city** *[Jerusalem]*, **he hungered** *[was hungry]*.

19 **And when he saw a fig tree** in the way *[by the roadside]*, **he came to it, and found nothing thereon**, but leaves only, **and said unto it, Let no fruit grow on thee henceforward for ever. And presently** *[immediately]* **the fig tree withered away.**

The fig tree is symbolic of the hypocritical Jewish religious leaders who pretend to look official but do not produce the fruit of the gospel. It is also symbolic of the Jewish nation, the covenant people, who are "barren" as far as the gospel is concerned. See *Jesus the Christ*, p. 443.

20 And **when the disciples saw it, they marvelled**, saying, How soon is the fig tree withered away!

21 **Jesus answered** *[responded]* and said unto them, Verily I say unto you, **If ye have faith**, and doubt not, **ye shall not only do this** which is done to the fig tree, **but** also **if ye shall say unto this mountain, Be thou removed**, and be thou cast into the sea; **it shall be done.**

22 And **all things, whatsoever ye shall ask in prayer, believing, ye shall receive.** *[See also D&C 46:30, 50:30.]*

23 **And when he was come into the temple, the chief priests and the elders** of the people *[the Jewish religious leaders who are trying to trap Him]* **came** unto him as he was teaching, **and said, By what authority doest thou these things?** and who gave thee this authority?

24 And **Jesus answered** and said unto them, **I also will ask you one thing, which if ye tell me, I in like wise will tell you by what authority I do these things.**

25 **The baptism of John** *[the Baptist]*, **whence was it?** from heaven, or of men *[did John the Baptist have authority from heaven, or was he just another man]*? **And they reasoned with themselves, saying, If we shall say, From heaven;** he *[Jesus]* will say unto us, Why did ye not then believe him?

26 **But if we shall say, Of men**; we fear the people; for all hold John as a prophet. *[If we say John the Baptist was just an ordinary man, the people will mob us, because they consider him to be sent from God.]*

27 **And they answered** Jesus, and said, **We cannot tell.** And **he said unto them, Neither tell I you** by what authority I do these things.

The following parable is known as The Parable of the Two Sons. The second son in the parable represents the hypocritical Jewish religious leaders who claim to agree to do the work of the Lord, but do not do it.

The Parable of the Two Sons

28 **But what think ye?** A certain man had **two sons**; and he came to **the first**, and said, Son, go work to day in my vineyard.

29 He answered and **said, I will not: but afterward he repented, and went.**

30 And he came to **the second**, and said likewise. And he answered and **said, I go, sir: and went not.**

31 **Whether of them twain** *[which of the two]*

did the will of his father? They say unto him, **The first. Jesus saith** unto them, Verily I say unto you, **That the publicans** [*hated Jewish tax collectors*] **and the harlots** [*prostitutes*] **go into the kingdom of God before you** [*are more likely to get to heaven than you are*].

32 **For John** [*the Baptist*] **came unto you** in the way of righteousness, **and ye believed him not: but the publicans and the harlots** [*sinners*] **believed him** [*repented*]: **and ye,** when ye had seen it, **repented not** afterward [*like the first son in the above parable*], that ye might believe him.

JST MATTHEW 21:32–34

32 For John came unto you in the way of righteousness, **and bore record of me**, and ye believed him not; but the publicans and the harlots believed him; and **ye, afterward, when ye had seen me, repented not, that ye might believe him**.

33 **For he that believed not John concerning me, cannot believe me, except he first repent**.

34 **And except ye repent, the preaching of John shall condemn you at the day of judgment.** And, again, hear another parable; for **unto you that believe not, I speak in parables; that your unrighteousness may be rewarded unto you.**

In this next parable, known as the Parable of the Wicked Husbandmen, the Savior clearly compares the wicked Jewish religious leaders to the wicked husbandmen who kill the owner's son in an attempt to take the kingdom from him. The notes in parentheses in the parable represent one possible interpretation of it.

The Parable of the Wicked Husbandmen

33 Hear another parable: There was **a certain householder** [*Heavenly Father*], which **planted a vineyard** [*had the earth created and put people on it*], and **hedged it round about** [*set up protections for it*], and **digged a winepress in it** [*planned on a good harvest*], and **built a tower** [*so people could watch for enemies*], and **let it out to husbandmen** [*stewards who were supposed to take good care of it*], **and went into a far country** [*heaven*]:

JST MATTHEW 21:34

34 **And except ye repent, the preaching of John shall condemn you at the day of judgment.** And, again, hear another parable; for **unto you that believe not, I speak in parables; that your unrighteousness may be rewarded unto you.**

34 And **when the time of the fruit** [*harvest time*] **drew near, he sent his servants** [*prophets*] to the **husbandmen** [*the Jewish religious leaders*], that they might receive the fruits of it.

35 And **the husbandmen took his servants** [*prophets*], and **beat** one, and **killed** another, and **stoned** another.

36 Again, **he sent other servants** [*prophets*] more than the first: **and they** [*the wicked husbandmen*] **did unto them likewise.**

37 But **last of all he sent unto them his son** [*Christ*], saying, They will reverence my son.

38 **But when the husbandmen saw the son, they said among themselves, This is the heir; come, let us kill him, and let us seize on his inheritance.**

39 **And they** caught him, and cast him out of the vineyard, and **slew him** [*crucified Him*].

Now, the question, to which this parable has been leading:

40 **When the lord** [*Christ*] **therefore of the vineyard cometh, what will he do unto those husbandmen?**

The answer:

41 They [*the chief priests and elders in verse 23*] say unto him [*Jesus*], **He will miserably destroy those wicked men, and will let out his vineyard unto other husbandmen** [*righteous religious leaders*], **which shall render him the fruits in their seasons** [*will bring righteous souls to Him at the time of harvest.*

42 **Jesus saith** unto them, **Did ye never read in**

the scriptures [*in Psalm 118:22–23*], **The stone** [*Christ*] **which the builders rejected, the same is become the head of the corner** [*the capstone or cornerstone*]: **this is the Lord's doing, and it is marvellous in our eyes?**

43 **Therefore say I unto you** [*Jewish religious leaders*], **The kingdom of God shall be taken from you, and given to a nation** [*Gentiles*] **bringing forth the fruits thereof** [*who will bring the desired harvest of righteous souls to Me*].

44 And **whosoever shall fall on this stone** [*Christ*] **shall be broken: but on whomsoever it shall fall, it will grind him to powder** [*no one can ultimately stop the Lord's work*].

Next, the Jewish religious leaders finally get the message.

45 And when the chief priests and Pharisees had heard his parables, **they perceived that he spake of them.**

"They perceived that he spake of them" in verse 45 above is very important to our understanding of what is going on here. Some people think that the Jewish religious leaders did not really understand who Jesus was. That is not true. They did indeed understand who Jesus was and set out to kill Him. On the cross, when Christ said "Father, forgive them for they know not what they do" (Luke 23:34), He was obviously referring to the Roman soldiers and perhaps others, but not the Jewish religious leaders. This fact is confirmed again in JST Matthew 21:47, quoted after verse 46, below, where it says the same thing, "they perceived that he spake of them."

46 **But when they sought to lay hands on him, they feared the multitude,** because they took him for a prophet. [*They were afraid the people would mob them if they arrested Jesus.*]

The JST contains over two hundred added words of explanation for this parable. They are included here:

JST Matthew 47–56

47 And when the chief priests and Pharisees had heard his parables, they perceived that he spake of them.

48 And they said among themselves, Shall this man think that he alone can spoil this great kingdom [*the religious kingdom set up by these Jewish religious leaders for their own advantage*]? And they were angry with him.

49 But when they sought to lay hands on him, they feared the multitude, because they learned that the multitude took him for a prophet.

50 And now his disciples came to him, and Jesus said unto them, Marvel ye at the words of the parable which I spake unto them?

51 Verily, I say unto you, **I am the stone, and those wicked ones reject me**.

52 I am the head of the corner. **These Jews shall fall upon me, and shall be broken**.

53 And the kingdom of God shall be taken from them, and shall be given to a nation bringing forth the fruits thereof; [*meaning the Gentiles.*]

54 Wherefore, on whomsoever this stone shall fall, it shall grind him to powder.

55 And when the Lord therefore of the vineyard cometh, **he will destroy those miserable, wicked men, and will let again his vineyard unto other husbandmen, even in the last days** [*the restoration through the Prophet Joseph Smith*], who shall render him the fruits in their seasons.

56 And **then understood they the parable which he spake unto them, that the Gentiles** [*the wicked Gentiles in the last days*] **should be destroyed also, when the Lord should descend out of heaven** [*the Second Coming*] **to reign in his vineyard, which is the earth and the inhabitants thereof**.

MATTHEW 22

1 AND **Jesus** answered and **spake unto them again by parables,** and said,

Jesus will give more parables, but this next one, the Parable of the Marriage of the King's Son, will be the last one directed specifically to the Jewish religious leaders and rulers who have been aggressively trying to trap Him all day (see chapter 21 above). The parable is a direct warning to the murderous Jewish rulers who have killed past prophets and now seek to arrest and kill Jesus. Notes in brackets provide one possible interpretation of the parable.

The Parable of the Marriage of the King's Son

2 **The kingdom of heaven is like** unto **a certain king** [*Heavenly Father*], which **made a marriage**

[marriage symbolizes an opportunity to make covenants; the "bride" for this marriage would be those who are willing to become righteous Saints by making and keeping covenants] **for his son** [*Christ*],

3 And **sent forth his servants** [*prophets, missionaries, members, etc.*] **to call them** that were bidden [*invited; Israelites*] **to the wedding**: and **they would not come.**

4 Again, **he sent forth other servants** [*prophets*], saying, Tell them which are bidden, Behold, **I have prepared my dinner** [*gospel feast*]: my oxen and my **fatlings** [*the very best; symbolic of the gospel of Jesus Christ*] are killed, and all things are ready: **come unto the marriage.** [*In other words, I have a great gospel feast prepared for you. Come make covenants with me in order to partake.*]

5 **But they made light of it** [*made fun of it, ridiculed it*], **and went their ways**, one to his farm, another to his merchandise: [*Some ignored the invitation.*]

6 **And the remnant** [*the wicked Jewish religious leaders and rulers in Matthew 21:23*] **took his servants, and entreated them spitefully** [*treated them cruelly*], **and slew them.** [*Some violently opposed the Lord's servants who brought the invitation to come to the feast.*]

7 **But when the king heard thereof, he was wroth** [*angry*]: **and he sent forth his armies, and destroyed those murderers, and burned up their city.** [*This was partially fulfilled when the Roman armies devastated the Jews, especially about 70 to A.D. 73.*]

8 **Then saith he to his servants, The wedding** [*the gospel, the true Church*] **is ready, but they which were bidden** [*the covenant people who were in a state of wickedness and apostasy at the time of Christ*] **were not worthy.**

9 **Go ye therefore into the highways**, and **as many as ye shall find, bid to the marriage.** [*Go to all the world and invite everyone.*]

10 **So those servants** went out into the highways, and **gathered** together all **as many as they found, both bad and good** [*note that in this gathering, some unrighteous join the Church, along with the righteous converts*]: **and the wedding was furnished with guests.**

11 And **when the king came** in to see the guests, **he saw there a man which had not on a wedding garment** [*"robes of righteousness"—see* N.T. Student Manual, *Rel. 211, p. 146; symbolic of one who had had time and opportunity to properly prepare for meeting the Savior, but had not*]:

12 **And he saith** unto him, Friend, **how camest thou in hither not having a wedding garment** [*not having made and kept covenants; personal righteousness—see Revelation 19:8*]? **And he was speechless** [*was without excuse—see 2 Nephi 9:14*].

13 **Then said the king** to the servants, **Bind** him hand and foot, and take him away, and **cast him into outer darkness** [*in this context, "outer darkness" would mean the spirit prison—see Alma 40:13—and also could mean telestial glory—see D&C 76:103*]; there shall be weeping and gnashing of teeth. [*The wicked cannot remain in the presence of God and must be punished for their sins.*]

14 **For many are called** [*to make and keep covenants with God*], **but few are chosen** [*to receive exaltation*]. [*In fact, all are "called" to come unto Christ, but few are "chosen" to remain with him forever, because they do not make themselves worthy.*]

JST MATTHEW 22:14

14 For many are called, but few chosen; **wherefore all do not have on the wedding garment** [*symbolic of having made and kept covenants with God*].

The "few" in verse 14, above, must be considered in context of the wicked Jewish kingdom at this time in the history of the world. Few of them will be ultimately chosen for exaltation because they deliberately reject the Savior.

Elsewhere in the scriptures, we find that there will ultimately be "innumerable" who will make it to exaltation (see D&C 76:67, Revelation 7:9). Also, taking into account that "all children who die before they arrive at the years of accountability are saved in the celestial kingdom of heaven" (D&C 137:10), and recognizing that statistics show that between 50% and 80% of all children born have died in infancy throughout the history of the world, we come to the conclusion that well over half of the people ever born will inherit celestial glory. Furthermore, President Joseph F. Smith taught that these children not only gain celestial glory, but they "will inherit their exaltation" (*Gospel Doctrine*, pp. 453–55).

As we continue, we see that the leaders of the Jews are now getting desperate.

15 **Then went the Pharisees** [*Jewish religious leaders*], **and took counsel how they might entangle** [*trap*] **him in his talk.**

16 **And they sent out unto him** [*Christ*] **their disciples** [*their loyal, wicked followers*] **with the Herodians** [*a political party among the Jews (see Bible Dictionary, under "Herodians") who normally opposed the Pharisees, but now joined with them in opposing Christ*], **saying, Master, we know that thou art true, and teachest the way of God in truth, neither carest thou for any man: for thou regardest not the person of men.**

Verse 16, above, is dripping with sarcasm and false flattery. These men are going to try to get Jesus to say something against the Roman government so they can get him arrested and executed for treason. Watch as they attempt to lure Him into their trap, in verse 17, next.

Paying Taxes

17 Tell us therefore, **What thinkest thou? Is it lawful to give tribute** [*pay taxes*] **unto Cæsar** [*the Roman emperor*], **or not?**

18 **But Jesus perceived their wickedness, and said, Why tempt ye me, ye hypocrites?**

19 **Shew** [*pronounced "show"*] **me the tribute money.** And **they brought unto him a penny** [*a Roman denarius, about the equivalent of a day's pay*].

20 And he saith unto them, **Whose is this image** [*picture*] **and superscription** [*the writing on the coin*]?

21 **They say** unto him, **Cæsar's. Then saith he** unto them, **Render** [*give*] **therefore unto Cæsar the things which are Cæsar's; and unto God the things that are God's.**

22 **When they had heard these words, they marvelled** [*were amazed*], and left him, **and went their way.**

23 **The same day came to him the Sadducees,** which say that there is no resurrection [*who do not believe in the resurrection*], **and asked him,**

The Sadducees were another influential group of religious leaders among the Jews. They did not believe in the resurrection, and were normally enemies of the Pharisees who did believe in resurrection. The Sadducees have now joined forces with the Pharisees in attempting to do away with Jesus.

24 Saying, **Master, Moses said, If a man die, having no children, his brother shall marry his wife, and raise up seed unto his brother** [*have children for his dead brother; plural marriage was in practice at this time in the Old and New Testament*].

One Wife, Seven Brothers

25 Now **there were with us seven brethren** [*brothers*]: and **the first, when he had married a wife, deceased** [*died*], **and, having no issue** [*children*], **left his wife unto his brother** [*as required by the Law of Moses—see Deuteronomy 25:5*]:

26 **Likewise the second also, and the third, unto the seventh.** [*Each of the six brothers likewise married her, but died, without her having any children.*]

27 And **last of all the woman died also.**

And now, the question designed by the Sadducees to entrap the Master.

28 **Therefore in the resurrection whose wife shall she be of the seven?** for they all had her [*had her as a wife*].

Eternal Marriage Is Preached Here in These Verses.

Here is a major doctrinal point. Many religions use these next two verses to prove that there is no such thing as eternal marriage and family in the next life. On the contrary, the simple fact that the Sadducees asked the Savior (in verse 28) whose wife she will be when they are all resurrected is proof that the Savior had indeed preached marriage in the resurrection, in other words, eternal marriage. Otherwise, their question would not make any sense at all!

29 **Jesus answered** and said unto them, **Ye do err, not knowing the scriptures**, nor the power of God.

30 For **in the resurrection they neither marry, nor are given in marriage, but are as the angels of God in heaven** [*refers to those who do not qualify for eternal marriage either in this life or in the postmortal spirit world or during the Millennium—see D&C 132:15–17*].

Here again, correct doctrine needs to be understood. After everyone from this earth is resurrected, there will be no more eternal marriages performed for them, because such marriages have to be done by mortals for themselves, or by mortals who serve as proxies for those who have died—see D&C 128:15 & 18. Brigham Young said: "And **when the Millennium is over, ...all the sons and daughters of Adam and Eve**, down to the last of their posterity (bold added for emphasis), **who come within the reach of the clemency of the Gospel, [will] have been redeemed in hundreds of temples through the administration of their children as proxies for them**." *Discourses of Brigham Young*, p. 395. Since there will be no mortals left on earth after the resurrection is completed, there would be no one left to serve as proxies for eternal marriages.

31 **But as touching the resurrection of the dead, have ye not read** that which was spoken unto you by God, saying,

32 I am the God of Abraham, and the God of Isaac, and the God of Jacob [*quoting Exodus 3:6*]? **God is not the God of the dead, but of the living.** [*In other words, you Sadducees should believe in resurrection.*]

33 And **when the multitude heard this, they were astonished at his doctrine.**

34 But **when the Pharisees had heard that he had put the Sadducees to silence, they were gathered together.** [*The Pharisees now take over again, since the Sadducees were unsuccessful.*]

35 Then **one of them, which was a lawyer, asked him a question**, tempting him [*trying to trap Jesus*], and saying,

36 **Master, which is the great commandment in the law?** [*"The law," as used here, means the Law of Moses, in other words, the first five books of the Old Testament: Genesis, Exodus, Leviticus, Numbers, Deuteronomy.*]

37 **Jesus said** unto him, **Thou shalt love the Lord thy God with all thy heart, and with all thy soul, and with all thy mind** [*Deuteronomy 6:5*].

38 **This is the first and great commandment.**

39 And **the second is like unto it, Thou shalt love thy neighbour as thyself** [*Leviticus 19:18*].

40 **On these two commandments hang all the law and the prophets.** [*All the other commandments are based on these two commandments. As stated above, the "law" meant Genesis, Exodus, Leviticus, Numbers, and Deuteronomy. The "prophets" meant writings of Old Testament prophets such as Isaiah, Jeremiah, etc.*]

41 While the Pharisees were gathered together, **Jesus asked them,**

42 Saying, **What think ye of Christ? whose son is he? They say unto him, The Son of David** [*a descendant of King David*].

43 **He saith** unto them, **How then doth David in spirit call him Lord** [*why would David, speaking under inspiration, refer to Him as "Lord?"*], **saying,**

44 **The LORD** [*Heavenly Father*] **said unto my Lord** [*Christ*], **Sit thou on my right hand, till I make thine enemies thy footstool?** [*See Hebrews 1:3 for the interpretations given in brackets above; also see Bruce R. McConkie, Doctrinal New Testament Commentary, Vol. 1, p. 612.*]

45 **If David then call him Lord, how is he his son?**

46 And **no man was able to answer** him a word, **neither durst** [*dared*] **any man from that day forth ask him any more questions.** [*It was getting pretty embarrassing trying to trap Jesus with questions because He outsmarted them every time!*]

MATTHEW 23

IN THIS CHAPTER, the scribes and Pharisees get a scathing rebuke from the Savior because of their wickedness and hypocrisy. Perhaps you have noticed that hypocrites were the only category of people who incurred such scathing righteous indignation of the Savior. It is obviously wise to avoid hypocrisy, since it is one of the most spiritually debilitating sins.

Imagine the rapt attention given to the Master as He delivered the following words to the scribes and Pharisees within the hearing of the multitudes as well as His loyal followers.

1 **THEN spake Jesus to the multitude, and to his disciples,**

2 Saying, **The scribes and the Pharisees sit in Moses' seat** [*have offices of high authority among you*]:

3 **All therefore whatsoever they bid you observe, that observe and do** [*go ahead and do everything they ask you to do; in other words, respect the office they hold*]; **but do not ye after their works** [*don't behave like they do*]: **for they say, and do not** [*they are hypocrites*].

4 For **they bind heavy burdens** and grievous to be borne, and lay them **on men's shoulders** [*they give you all kinds of very difficult tasks to accomplish*]; **but they themselves will not move them with one of their fingers** [*but they won't lift a finger to help*].

5 **But all their works they do for to be seen of men** [*everything they do is for show*]: **they make broad their phylacteries, and enlarge the borders of their garments,**

Phylacteries were small leather boxes, beautifully crafted, which faithful Jews tied to their forehead ("forehead" was symbolic of loyalty to God in their culture) and left arm (to be near the heart). Inside these small leather boxes were four tiny scrolls containing Exodus 13:2–10, Exodus 13:11–17, Deuteronomy 6:4–9, and Deuteronomy 11:13–21. The scribes and Pharisees had made their phylacteries larger than normal so people could see how "righteous" they were. Likewise, they had enlarged the blue fringes on their clothing (see Numbers 15:38–39) which symbolized keeping the commandments of God.

6 **And love the uppermost rooms at feasts** [*want to be seen and recognized publicly as very important people*], **and the chief seats in the synagogues** [*Jewish church buildings*],

7 **And greetings in the markets, and to be called of** [*by*] **men, Rabbi, Rabbi** [*"my master"—see Bible Dictionary, under "Rabbi"*].

8 **But be not ye** [*Jesus is addressing the multitude and His disciples—see verse 1*] **called Rabbi: for one is your Master, even Christ;** and all ye are brethren [*you should not consider yourselves better than each other*].

9 And **call no man your father upon the earth:** for one is your Father, which is in heaven.

JST MATTHEW 23:6
6 And **call no one your creator upon the earth, or your heavenly Father; for one is your creator and heavenly Father, even he who is in heaven**.

10 **Neither be ye called masters: for one is your Master, even Christ.**

JST MATTHEW 23:7

7 Neither be ye called masters; for one is your master, **even he whom your heavenly Father sent, which is Christ; for he hath sent him among you that ye might have life**.

11 But **he that is greatest among you shall be your servant.** [*This is a major message that Christ is teaching the multitude and His disciples.*]

12 **And whosoever shall exalt himself** [*pridefully set himself up as an example*] **shall be abased** [*humbled, put down*]; **and he that shall humble himself shall be exalted.**

JST MATTHEW 23:9

9 And whosoever shall exalt himself shall be abased **of him**; and he that shall humble himself shall be exalted **of him**.

13 **But woe unto you, scribes and Pharisees, hypocrites!** for **ye shut up the kingdom of heaven against men** [*you make so many nitpicky rules that nobody could get into heaven*]: **for ye neither go in yourselves** [*you won't get to heaven yourselves*], **neither suffer** [*allow*] **ye them that are entering to go in** [*and you won't let anyone else in either!*].

14 **Woe unto you, scribes and Pharisees, hypocrites!** for **ye devour widows' houses** [*foreclose on widows' mortgages and take their houses from them via technicalities of the law*], **and for a pretence** [*for show*] **make long prayer: therefore ye shall receive the greater damnation.**

15 **Woe unto you, scribes and Pharisees, hypocrites!** for **ye compass sea and land to make one proselyte** [*you travel far and wide to get one convert*], **and when he is made** [*when he joins your church*], **ye make him twofold more the child of hell than yourselves.**

JST MATTHEW 23:12

12 Woe unto you, scribes and Pharisees, hypocrites! For ye compass sea and land to make one proselyte; and when he is made, ye make him **twofold more the child of hell than he was before, like unto yourselves**.

In verses 16–24, next, Jesus points out several examples of the hypocritical, nitpicky, laden-with-details rules which these religious leaders have forced upon their people. They have made so many rules that nobody can figure them out and follow them all properly, which puts these leaders in a position of constant power over the people.

16 **Woe unto you,** ye **blind guides, which say, Whosoever shall swear** [*make vows, promises, covenants*] **by the temple, it is nothing; but whosoever shall swear by the gold of the temple, he is a debtor!**

17 **Ye fools and blind:** for **whether is greater** [*which is more important*], **the gold, or the temple that sanctifieth the gold** [*makes the gold holy*]?

18 **And** [*according to the rules you have made*], **Whosoever shall swear by the altar, it is nothing; but whosoever sweareth by the gift that is upon it, he is guilty** [*of sin*].

19 **Ye fools and blind:** for **whether is greater** [*which is more important*], **the gift, or the altar that sanctifieth the gift?**

20 **Whoso therefore shall swear by the altar, sweareth by it, and by all things thereon.**

21 **And whoso shall swear by the temple, sweareth by it, and by him that dwelleth therein.**

22 **And he that shall swear by heaven, sweareth by the throne of God, and by him that sitteth thereon.** [*More of their impossible rules.*]

23 **Woe unto you, scribes and Pharisees, hypocrites!** for **ye pay tithe of mint and anise** [*dill*] **and cummin** [*you weigh out the tiniest amounts of seeds and spices with exactness to see how much tithing you should pay on them*], **and have omitted** the weightier [*more important*] **matters of the law, judgment** [*fairness; integrity*], **mercy,** and **faith: these ought ye to have done, and not to leave the other undone.**

24 **Ye blind guides, which strain at a gnat**

[*Greek: "strain out a gnat"*], **and swallow a camel.**

JST MATTHEW 23:21

21 Ye blind guides, who strain at a gnat, and swallow a camel; **who make yourselves appear unto men that ye would not commit the least sin, and yet ye yourselves, transgress the whole law.**

The Savior's use of gnats and camels in verse 24, above, carries an extra dimension of meaning for these hypocrites, since both gnats (Leviticus 11:23) and camels (Leviticus 11:4) were "unclean" and thus forbidden as food for the Jews.

25 **Woe unto you, scribes and Pharisees, hypocrites!** for **ye make clean the outside of the cup and of the platter, but within they are full of extortion** [*greed*] **and excess** [*self-indulgence—see Matthew 23:25, footnotes a and b*].

26 Thou blind Pharisee, **cleanse first that which is within the cup and platter, that the outside of them may be clean also.**

27 **Woe unto you, scribes and Pharisees, hypocrites!** for **ye are like unto whited sepulchres** [*whitewashed graves, tombs*], **which indeed appear beautiful outward, but are within** [*inside*] **full of dead men's bones, and of all uncleanness.**

28 Even so **ye also outwardly appear righteous unto men, but within ye are full of hypocrisy and iniquity** [*wickedness*].

29 **Woe unto you, scribes and Pharisees, hypocrites!** because **ye build the tombs of the prophets, and garnish** [*decorate*] **the sepulchres** [*graves, tombs*] **of the righteous** [*you appear to honor ancient prophets, such as Abraham, Moses, Isaiah, Jeremiah, etc.*],

30 **And say, If we had been** [*lived*] **in the days of our fathers** [*ancestors*], **we would not have been partakers with them in the blood of the prophets** [*we wouldn't have killed prophets like they did*].

31 Wherefore **ye be witnesses unto yourselves,** that ye are the children of them which killed the prophets. [*You are just like your ancestors!*]

JST MATTHEW 23:28

28 Wherefore, ye are witnesses unto yourselves of your own wickedness, and ye are the children of them who killed the prophets;

32 **Fill ye up then the measure of your fathers** [*go ahead and fill your lives with sin just like your ancestors did*].

JST MATTHEW 23:29

29 **And will fill up the measure then of your fathers** [*will become as wicked as your ancestors*]; **for ye, yourselves, kill the prophets like unto your fathers.**

33 **Ye serpents** [*you are like Satan—see Revelation 12:9*], **ye generation of vipers** [*poisonous snakes*], **how can ye escape the damnation of hell?**

Some people claim that Jesus never did come right out and claim that He was the promised Messiah, the Son of God or the God of the Old Testament. Such is clearly not the case, as evidenced in verse 34, next.

34 Wherefore, **behold, I send unto you prophets, and wise men, and scribes:** and some of them ye shall kill and crucify; and some of them shall ye scourge [*whip, beat*] in your synagogues [*churches*], and persecute them from city to city:

35 **That upon you may come all the righteous blood shed upon the earth** [*you have murderous hearts and deserve to be punished with others who have likewise persecuted and killed the righteous in the past*], from the blood of righteous **Abel** unto the blood of **Zacharias** [*John the Baptist's father*] son of Barachias, **whom ye slew between the temple and the altar.**

Zacharias was the father of John the Baptist. Joseph Smith tells us that when King Herod ordered all the babies two years old and younger killed in Bethlehem and surrounding area (see Matthew 2:16), Zacharias sent Elizabeth and John "into the mountains" to hide. "When his father refused to disclose his hiding place (he) was slain by Herod's order, between the porch and the altar." of the temple. See *Teachings of the Prophet Joseph Smith*, p. 261. Apparently, from what Jesus is saying to the scribes and Pharisees in verse 35, these evil leaders must have had a hand in getting Zacharias killed.

36 Verily I say unto you, **All these things shall come upon this generation.**

The JST adds three verses here:

JST MATTHEW 23:34–36

34 Ye bear testimony against your fathers, when ye, yourselves, are partakers of the same wickedness.

35 Behold your fathers did it through ignorance, but ye do not; wherefore, their sins shall be upon your heads.

36 Then Jesus began to weep over Jerusalem, saying,

37 **O Jerusalem, Jerusalem, thou that killest the prophets, and stonest them which are sent unto thee, how often would I have gathered thy children together, even as a hen gathereth her chickens under her wings, and ye would not!** [*You wouldn't let me gather and protect you.*]

38 Behold, **your house is left unto you desolate** [*your nation will be destroyed and scattered*].

39 For **I say unto you, Ye shall not see me henceforth, till ye shall say, Blessed is he that cometh in the name of the Lord.** [*You won't see me until the Second Coming.*]

JST MATTHEW 23:39–41

39 For I say unto you, that ye shall not see me henceforth, **and know that I am he of whom it is written by the prophets**, until ye shall say,

40 Blessed is he who cometh in the name of the Lord, **in the clouds of heaven, and all the holy angels with him** [*the Second Coming*].

41 **Then understood his disciples that he should come again on the earth, after that he was glorified and crowned on the right hand of God.**

MATTHEW 24

AT THIS POINT in history, it is still the third day of the last week of the Savior's mortal life (see *New Testament Student Manual*, Religion 211, pp. 136 and 150). The most common thinking is that this is Tuesday. He will be crucified on Friday. After His severe scolding of the hypocritical Jewish leaders in chapter 23, Jesus has left the temple. He will not teach the public any more, rather He will spend the rest of the last week of His mortal life teaching the Twelve. They will approach Him now and look back at the temple, and He will teach them many things that will occur before His Second Coming.

Matthew 24 is very well known among Christians because it contains so many prophecies which will be fulfilled before the Second Coming. These prophecies are known as "the signs of the times." Many of them are being fulfilled in our day and bear witness to us that the gospel is true and that the Second Coming is near. However, since we do not know how close it is, we should plan on living a full lifetime and keeping our lives in order, so that when we meet the Savior, whether at our death, or at His coming, we will be prepared.

Because Joseph Smith added about 450 words to this chapter, as well as rearranged the verse order in some cases in JS—Matthew in the Pearl of Great Price, we will include it in this study guide after we have gone through Matthew 24 as it stands in our Bible.

1 AND **Jesus went out, and departed from the temple** [*in Jerusalem*]: **and his disciples came to him for to shew** [*show*] **him the buildings of the temple.**

2 **And Jesus said** unto them, See ye not all these things? verily I say unto you, **There shall not be left here one stone upon another, that shall not be thrown down.** [*The temple will be destroyed. The Romans destroyed much, culminating with the final conquering of Jerusalem about* A.D. *70.*]

3 And **as he sat upon the mount of Olives** [*located just outside of Jerusalem*], **the disciples came unto him privately, saying, Tell us, when shall these things be** [*the things Jesus had just prophesied*]? and **what shall be the sign of thy coming, and of the end of the world?**

The disciples asked Jesus two questions: 1. "When shall these things be?" (meaning the things which will happen to Jerusalem, the Jews, and the early Christians following the crucifixion), and 2. "What shall be the sign of thy coming, and of the end of the world?" (meaning the "signs of the times" preceding his Second Coming).

4 And **Jesus answered** and said unto them, **Take heed** [*be careful*] **that no man deceive you.**

5 For **many shall come in my name**, saying, I am Christ; and **shall deceive many.**

6 And ye shall hear of **wars and rumours of wars:** see that ye be not troubled [*don't let the signs of the times cause undue fear or panic in you*]: for all these things must come to pass, but the end is not yet.

7 For **nation shall rise against nation**, and kingdom against kingdom: and there shall be **famines**, and **pestilences**, and **earthquakes**, in divers [*various*] places.

8 All these are the beginning of sorrows.

9 **Then shall they deliver you up to be afflicted**, and shall **kill you**: and **ye shall be hated of all nations for my name's sake.**

10 And then shall **many** be **offended** [*many will leave the Church*], and shall **betray one another**, and shall **hate one another.**

11 And many **false prophets** shall rise, and shall deceive many.

Many people, when they read "false prophets," think only of false ministers and preachers of false doctrines and philosophies. They would be wise not to limit their understanding to these types, rather to include any famous, influential individuals and groups who gather followers and lead them astray. This can include politicians, movie stars, singers, gang leaders, and so forth.

12 And because **iniquity** [*wickedness*] **shall abound** [*will be everywhere*], the **love of many shall wax** [*grow*] **cold.**

13 **But he that shall endure unto the end, the same shall be saved.**

14 And **this gospel of the kingdom shall be preached in all the world for a witness unto all nations** [*one of the last major signs which will happen before the Savior's Second Coming*]; **and then shall the end** [*of wickedness*] **come.** [*The Millennium will then begin*].

15 When ye therefore shall see **the abomination of desolation**, spoken of by Daniel the prophet [*in Dan. 11:31; 12:11*], **stand in the holy place**, (whoso readeth, let him understand):

"Abomination of desolation" means terrible things which will cause much destruction and misery. The abomination of desolation spoken of by Daniel was to have two fulfillments. The first occurred in A.D. 70 when Titus, with his Roman legions, surrounded Jerusalem and laid siege to conquer the Jews. This siege resulted in much destruction and terrible human misery and loss of life. In the last days, the abomination of desolation will occur again (see Joseph Smith–Matthew 1:31–32), meaning that Jerusalem will again be under siege. (See also Bible Dictionary, under "Abomination of Desolation).

16 **Then let them which be in Judæa flee into the mountains:** [*Many faithful Saints heeded this warning and fled to Pella, east of Samaria, and thus escaped the Romans.*]

17 **Let him which is on the housetop not come down to take any thing out of his house:**

18 **Neither let him which is in the field return back to take his clothes.**

19 And **woe unto them that are with child, and to them that give suck in those days!**

20 But **pray ye that your flight be not in the winter, neither on the sabbath day** [*when city gates are closed*]:

21 For then shall be **great tribulation**, such as was not since the beginning of the world to this time, no, nor ever shall be.

22 And **except those days should be shortened, there should no flesh be saved:** but for the elect's sake those days shall be shortened [*the Lord will stop the destructions in time so that some covenant people will remain*].

23 [*Now, Jesus answers their second question—see note, verse 4.*] **Then if any man shall say unto you, Lo, here is Christ, or there; believe it not.**

24 For there shall arise **false Christs, and false prophets**, and shall shew [*show*] great signs

and wonders; insomuch that, **if it were possible, they shall deceive the very elect** *[meaning those who have made covenants with God—see JS–Matthew 1:22]*.

25 **Behold, I have told you before.**

26 Wherefore **if they** *[false prophets, "gatherers," teachers, leaders, etc.]* **shall say unto you, Behold, he** *[Christ]* **is in the desert; go not forth** *[don't go to see him]*: **behold, he is in the secret chambers; believe it not.**

27 For **as the lightning** *["lightning" is a mistake in the translation of the Bible, since lightning can come in any direction; it should be "as the light of the morning cometh out of the east"; see JS–Matthew 1:26]* **cometh out of the east, and shineth even unto the west; so shall also the coming of the Son of man be.** *[In other words, when He comes for the actual Second Coming, everyone will see Him. It will not be a low-key, quiet, secret coming as some false gatherers will suggest—see verse 26.]*

28 **For wheresoever the carcase** *[carcass]* **is, there will the eagles be gathered together.**

This is an unusual use of the word "carcase." Symbolically, in this context, it means "the body of the Church." In other words, the true Church with the true gospel. The "eagles" are converts, faithful members of the Church who will be gathered to the Church for nourishment in all parts of the world. See JS–Matthew 1:27. In short, this verse prophecies of the gathering of Israel in the last days prior to the Second Coming. See also *Doctrinal New Testament Commentary*, Vol. 1, pp. 648–49.

29 Immediately after the tribulation of those days shall the **sun** be **darkened**, and the **moon shall not give her light** *[can refer to spiritual darkness as well as actual things in nature]*, and the **stars shall fall from heaven**, and the **powers of the heavens shall be shaken**:

30 And **then shall appear the sign of the Son of man in heaven** *[we don't yet know what this means]*: and **then shall all the tribes of the earth mourn** *[the wicked will mourn, but the righteous will rejoice—see 2 Nephi 9:14, D&C 88:96]*, **and they shall see the Son of man coming in the clouds of heaven with power and great glory.**

Even those who caused the Savior's crucifixion will see Him at this time. See Revelation 1:7.

31 *[As you can see, these verses are not all in chronological order.]* And he shall send his angels with a great sound of a trumpet, and **they shall gather together his elect from the four winds, from one end of heaven to the other.** *[This is the final gathering of the righteous.]*

The Parable of the Fig Tree

32 Now learn a parable of the fig tree; **When his branch is yet tender, and putteth forth leaves, ye know that summer is nigh** *[when a fruit tree starts putting on leaves, you know that summer is near]*:

33 **So likewise ye, when ye shall see all these things** *[signs of the times being fulfilled]*, **know that it** *[the Second Coming]* **is near, even at the doors.**

34 Verily I say unto you, **This generation** *["generation" can sometimes mean "dispensation"]* **shall not pass, till all these things be fulfilled.**

35 **Heaven and earth shall pass away, but my words shall not pass away** *[you can rely on my words completely!]*.

36 **But of that day and hour knoweth no man, no, not the angels of heaven, but my Father only.**

On occasion we hear of people who claim to know when the Second Coming will be. Sometimes they gather others around them to await the exact day they have predicted He will come. Some say they don't know the hour and day, but they do know the month and year. Some say that the Brethren know but are not allowed to tell us. Elder M. Russell Ballard, of the Quorum of the Twelve, taught the following:

"I do not know when He is going to come again. As far as I know, none of my brethren in the Council of the Twelve or even in the First Presidency knows. And I would humbly suggest to you, my young brothers and sisters, that if we do not know, then nobody knows" (Talk given March 12, 1996 at a BYU Devotional).

37 **But as the days of Noe** *[Noah]* **were, so shall also the coming of the Son of man** *[Jesus]* **be.** *[Just as the wicked in the days of Noah did not believe the Flood would come, so also the wicked in the last days will not believe the Savior will come and thus they will be caught unprepared.]*

38 For as **in the days** that were **before the flood** they were **eating** and **drinking, marrying** and giving in marriage, **until the day that Noe** *[Noah]* **entered into the ark,**

39 And knew not until **the flood came, and took them all away** *[destroyed them]*; **so shall also the coming of the Son of man** *[Jesus]* **be.**

40 Then shall two be in the field; the **one shall be taken, and the other left.** *[One who is worthy will be taken up to meet Christ (see D&C 88:96), and the other who is not worthy will be left on earth to be destroyed at His coming.]*

41 Two women shall be grinding at the mill; the **one shall be taken, and the other left.**

42 **Watch therefore: for ye know not what hour your Lord doth come.**

43 But **know this,** that **if the goodman** *[symbolic of people who will be caught off guard by the Second Coming]* **of the house had known in what watch** *[the Jews divided the night into "watches" of about four hours each; see Bible Dictionary, under "Watches"]* **the thief would come, he would have watched** *[would have been ready]*, and would not have suffered *[allowed]* his house to be broken up.

44 **Therefore be** ye also **ready: for in such an hour as ye think not the Son of man cometh.**

In the next verses, the Savior, in effect, asks the disciples who they think the people are who will be saved at the Second Coming. He answers His own question and basically says that it will be those who are faithful to the gospel and who, as servants in the gospel, serve others with kindness and wisdom.

45 **Who then is a faithful and wise servant,** whom his lord hath made ruler over his household, **to give them** *[people under his jurisdiction]* **meat** *[food, nourishment]* **in due season** *[according to their needs]*?

46 **Blessed is that servant, whom his lord when he cometh shall find so doing.**

47 Verily I say unto you, That **he shall make him ruler over all his goods.** *[They will be exalted and will become gods. See D&C 84:38, D&C 132:20.]*

48 But and **if that evil servant** *[symbolic of the wicked in the last days]* **shall say in his heart, My lord** *[Christ]* **delayeth his coming** *[similar to the wicked in 3 Nephi 1]*;

49 **And shall begin to smite his fellowservants** *[be mean and cruel to others]*, and to **eat and drink with the drunken** *[participate in riotous living]*;

50 **The lord** *[Christ]* of that servant **shall come in a day when he looketh not for him,** and in an hour that he is not aware of,

51 **And shall cut him asunder** *[destroy him]*, **and appoint him his portion** *[put him in hell]* **with the hypocrites** *[people who want to appear righteous but like to do evil]*: there shall be weeping and gnashing of teeth *[grinding of teeth together in agony and misery]*.

As stated in the notes at the beginning of Matthew 24, in this study guide, the Prophet Joseph Smith added about 450 words to the Bible version of Matthew 24, and rearranged the order of some verses. Thus, we are in a much better position to understand this chapter. The Prophet's revision of this chapter appears as Joseph Smith–Matthew in the Pearl of Great Price. It is included next in this book in a parallel column format so that you can compare at-a-glance the inspired contributions of the Prophet Joseph Smith with Matthew, chapter 24, as it stands in the King James version of the Bible. Remember, as stated above, that Joseph Smith rearranged the order of some of the verses as they stand in the Bible here.

JOSEPH SMITH—MATTHEW AND MATTHEW 24
PARALLEL COLUMN COMPARISON

Prepared by David J. Ridges

Joseph Smith—Matthew	King James Version
(With Joseph Smith's changes in bold)	**Matthew 24**
1 For I say unto you, that ye shall not see me henceforth **and know that I am he of whom it is written by the prophets,** until ye shall say: Blessed is he who cometh in the name of the Lord, **in the clouds of heaven, and all the holy angels with him. Then understood his disciples that he should come again on the earth, after that he was glorified and crowned on the right hand of God.**	Matthew 23:39 For I say unto you, Ye shall not see me henceforth, till ye shall say, Blessed *is* he that cometh in the name of the Lord.
2 And Jesus went out, and departed from the temple; and his disciples came to him, for to **hear him, saying: Master,** show **us concerning** the buildings of the temple, **as thou hast said—They shall be thrown down, and left unto you desolate.**	1 And Jesus went out, and departed from the temple: and his disciples came to *him* for to shew him the buildings of the temple.
3 And Jesus said unto them: See ye not all these things, **and do ye not understand them?** Verily I say unto you, there shall not be left here, **upon this temple,** one stone upon another that shall not be thrown down.	2 And Jesus said unto them, See ye not all these things? verily I say unto you, There shall not be left here one stone upon another, that shall not be thrown down.

Joseph Smith—Matthew	Matthew 24
4 **And Jesus left them, and went upon the Mount of Olives.** And as he sat upon the Mount of Olives, the disciples came unto him privately, saying: Tell us when shall these things be **which thou hast said concerning the destruction of the temple, and the Jews;** and what **is** the sign of thy coming, and of the end of the world, **or the destruction of the wicked, which is the end of the world?**	3 And as he sat upon the mount of Olives, the disciples came unto him privately, saying, Tell us, when shall these things be? and what *shall be* the sign of thy coming, and of the end of the world?
5 And Jesus answered, and said unto them: Take heed that no man deceive you;	4 And Jesus answered and said unto them, Take heed that no man deceive you.
6 For many shall come in my name, saying—I am Christ—and shall deceive many;	5 For many shall come in my name, saying, I am Christ; and shall deceive many.
7 Then shall they deliver you up to be afflicted, and shall kill you, and ye shall be hated of all nations, for my name's sake;	9 Then shall they deliver you up to be afflicted, and shall kill you: and ye shall be hated of all nations for my name's sake.
8 And then shall many be offended, and shall betray one another, and shall hate one another;	10 And then shall many be offended, and shall betray one another, and shall hate one another.
9 And many false prophets shall arise, and shall deceive many;	11 And many false prophets shall rise, and shall deceive many.
10 And because iniquity shall abound, the love of many shall wax cold;	12 And because iniquity shall abound, the love of many shall wax cold.
11 But he that **remaineth steadfast and is not overcome,** the same shall be saved.	13 But he that shall endure unto the end, the same shall be saved.
	14 And this gospel of the kingdom shall be preached in all the world for a witness unto all nations; and then shall the end come.

Joseph Smith—Matthew

12 When you, therefore, shall see the abomination of desolation, spoken of by Daniel the prophet, **concerning the destruction of Jerusalem, then** you shall stand in the holy place; whoso readeth let him understand.

13 Then let them **who are** in Judea flee into the mountains;

14 Let him who is on the housetop **flee, and not return** to take anything out of his house;

15 Neither let him who is in the field return back to take his clothes;

16 And wo unto them that are with child, and unto them that give suck in those days;

17 **Therefore,** pray ye **the Lord** that your flight be not in the winter, neither on the **S**abbath day;

18 For then, **in those days,** shall be great tribulation **on the Jews, and upon the inhabitants of Jerusalem,** such as was not **before sent upon Israel, of God,** since the beginning of **their kingdom until** this time; no, nor ever shall be **sent again upon Israel.**

19 **All things which have befallen them** are **only** the beginning of **the** sorrows **which shall come upon them.**

20 And except those days should be shortened, there should none of their flesh be saved; but for the elect's sake, **according to the covenant,** those days shall be shortened.

Matthew 24

15 When ye therefore shall see the abomination of desolation, spoken of by Daniel the prophet, stand in the holy place, (whoso readeth, let him understand:)

16 Then let them which be in Judæa flee into the mountains:

17 Let him which is on the housetop not come down to take any thing out of his house:

18 Neither let him which is in the field return back to take his clothes.

19 And woe unto them that are with child, and to them that give suck in those days!

20 But pray ye that your flight be not in the winter, neither on the sabbath day:

21 For then shall be great tribulation, such as was not since the beginning of the world to this time, no, nor ever shall be.

8 All these *are* the beginning of sorrows.

22 And except those days should be shortened, there should no flesh be saved: but for the elect's sake those days shall be shortened.

Joseph Smith—Matthew	Matthew 24
21 **Behold, these things I have spoken unto you concerning the Jews; and again, after the tribulation of those days which shall come upon Jerusalem,** if any man shall say unto you, Lo, here is Christ, or there, believe him not;	23 Then if any man shall say unto you, Lo, here is Christ, or there; believe *it* not.
22 For **in those days** there shall **also** arise false Christs, and false prophets, and shall show great signs and wonders, insomuch, that, if possible, they shall deceive the very elect, **who are the elect according to the covenant.**	24 For there shall arise false Christs, and false prophets, and shall shew great signs and wonders; insomuch that, if it *were* possible, they shall deceive the very elect.
23 **Behold, I speak these things unto you for the elect's sake;** and you also shall hear of wars, and rumors of wars; see that ye be not troubled, for all **I have told you** must come to pass; but the end is not yet.	6 And ye shall hear of wars and rumours of wars: see that ye be not troubled: for all *these things* must come to pass, but the end is not yet.
24 Behold, I have told you before;	25 Behold, I have told you before.
25 Wherefore, if they shall say unto you: Behold, he is in the desert; go not forth: Behold, he is in the secret chambers; believe it not;	26 Wherefore if they shall say unto you, Behold, he is in the desert; go not forth: behold, *he is* in the secret chambers; believe *it* not.
26 For as the **light of the morning** cometh out of the east, and shineth even unto the west, **and covereth the whole earth,** so shall also the coming of the Son of Man be.	27 For as the lightning cometh out of the east, and shineth even unto the west; so shall also the coming of the Son of man be.
27 **And now I show unto you a parable. Behold,** wheresoever the carcass is, there will the eagles be gathered together; **so likewise shall mine elect be gathered from the four quarters of the earth.**	28 For wheresoever the carcase is, there will the eagles be gathered together.

Joseph Smith—Matthew	Matthew 24
28 **And they shall hear of wars and rumors of wars.**	
29 **Behold I speak for mine elect's sake;** for nation shall rise against nation, and kingdom against kingdom; there shall be famines, and pestilences, and earthquakes, in divers places.	7 For nation shall rise against nation, and kingdom against kingdom: and there shall be famines, and pestilences, and earthquakes, in divers places.
30 **And again, because iniquity shall abound, the love of men shall wax cold; but he that shall not be overcome, the same shall be saved.**	
31 And **again,** this Gospel of the Kingdom shall be preached in all the world, for a witness unto all nations, and then shall the end come, **or the destruction of the wicked;**	14 And this gospel of the kingdom shall be preached in all the world for a witness unto all nations; and then shall the end come.
32 (This is not the same as verse 15 in Matthew 24.) **And again shall the abomination of desolation, spoken of by Daniel the prophet, be fulfilled.**	
33 **And** immediately after the tribulation of those days, **the sun shall be darkened,** and the moon shall not give her light, and the stars shall fall from heaven, and the powers of heaven shall be shaken.	29 Immediately after the tribulation of those days shall the sun be darkened, and the moon shall not give her light, and the stars shall fall from heaven, and the powers of the heavens shall be shaken:
34 Verily, I say unto you, this generation, **in which these things shall be shown forth,** shall not pass away **until** all **I have told you shall** be fulfilled.	34 Verily I say unto you, This generation shall not pass, till all these things be fulfilled.

Joseph Smith—Matthew	Matthew 24
35 **Although, the days will come, that** heaven and earth shall pass away; yet my words shall not pass away, **but all shall be fulfilled.**	35 Heaven and earth shall pass away, but my words shall not pass away.
36 And, **as I said before, after the tribulation of those days, and the powers of the heavens shall be shaken,** then shall appear the sign of the Son of Man in heaven, and then shall all the tribes of the earth mourn; and they shall see the Son of Man coming in the clouds of heaven, with power and great glory;	30 And then shall appear the sign of the Son of man in heaven: and then shall all the tribes of the earth mourn, and they shall see the Son of man coming in the clouds of heaven with power and great glory.
37 **And whoso treasureth up my word, shall not be deceived, for the Son of Man shall come,** and he shall send his angels **before him** with **the** great sound of a trumpet, and they shall gather together **the remainder of** his elect **from the four winds,** from one end of heaven to the other.	31 And he shall send his angels with a great sound of a trumpet, and they shall gather together his elect from the four winds, from one end of heaven to the other.
38 Now learn a parable of the fig-tree—When **its** branch**es are** yet tender, and **it begins to** put forth leaves, **you** know that summer is nigh **at hand;**	32 Now learn a parable of the fig tree; When his branch is yet tender, and putteth forth leaves, ye know that summer *is* nigh:
39 So likewise, **mine elect**, when **they** shall see all these things, **they** shall know that **he** is near, even at the doors;	33 So likewise ye, when ye shall see all these things, know that it is near, *even* at the doors
40 But of that day, and hour, no **one** knoweth; no, not the angels of **God in** heaven, but my Father only.	36 But of that day and hour knoweth no *man*, no, not the angels of heaven, but my Father only.

Joseph Smith—Matthew	Matthew 24
41 But as **it was in** the days of Noah, so **it** shall **be** also **at** the coming of the Son of Man;	37 But as the days of Noe *were*, so shall also the coming of the Son of man be.
42 For **it shall be with them,** as **it was** in the days **which** were before the flood; **for until the day that Noah entered into the ark** they were eating and drinking, marrying and giving in marriage;	38 For as in the days that were before the flood they were eating and drinking, marrying and giving in marriage, until the day that Noe entered into the ark,
43 And knew not until the flood came, and took them all away; so shall also the coming of the Son of Man be.	39 And knew not until the flood came, and took them all away; so shall also the coming of the Son of man be.
44 Then **shall be fulfilled that which is written, that in the last days,** two shall be in the field, the one shall be taken, and the other left;	40 Then shall two be in the field; the one shall be taken, and the other left.
45 Two shall be grinding at the mill, the one shall be taken, and the other left;	41 Two *women shall* be grinding at the mill; the one shall be taken, and the other left
46 **And what I say unto one, I say unto all men;** watch, therefore, for **you** know not at what hour your Lord doth come.	42 Watch therefore: for ye know not what hour your Lord doth come.
47 But know this, if the good man of the house had known in what watch the thief would come, he would have watched, and would not have suffered his house to have been broken up, **but would have been ready.**	43 But know this, that if the goodman of the house had known in what watch the thief would come, he would have watched, and would not have suffered his house to be broken up.
48 Therefore be ye also ready, for in such an hour as ye think not, the Son of Man cometh.	44 Therefore be ye also ready: for in such an hour as ye think not the Son of man cometh.

Joseph Smith—Matthew

49 Who, then, is a faithful and wise servant, whom his lord hath made ruler over his household, to give them meat in due season?

50 Blessed is that servant whom his lord, when he cometh, shall find so doing; **and** verily I say unto you, he shall make him ruler over all his goods.

51 But if that evil servant shall say in his heart: My lord delayeth his coming,

52 And shall begin to smite his fellow-servants, and to eat and drink with the drunken,

53 The lord of that servant shall come in a day when he looketh not for him, and in an hour that he is not aware of,

54 And shall cut him asunder, and **shall** appoint him his portion with the hypocrites; there shall be weeping and gnashing of teeth.

55 And thus cometh the end of the wicked, according to the prophecy of Moses, saying: They shall be cut off from among the people; but the end of the earth is not yet, but by and by.

Matthew 24

45 Who then is a faithful and wise servant, whom his lord hath made ruler over his household, to give them meat in due season?

46 Blessed *is* that servant, whom his lord when he cometh shall find so doing.

47 Verily I say unto you, That he shall make him ruler over all his goods.

48 But and if that evil servant shall say in his heart, My lord delayeth his coming;

49 And shall begin to smite *his* fellowservants, and to eat and drink with the drunken;

50 The lord of that servant shall come in a day when he looketh not for *him*, and in an hour that he is not aware of,

51 And shall cut him asunder, and appoint *him* his portion with the hypocrites: there shall be weeping and gnashing of teeth.

LEARN A PARABLE OF
THE FIG TREE;
WHEN HIS BRANCH
IS YET TENDER, AND
PUTTETH FORTH
LEAVES, YE KNOW THAT
SUMMER IS NIGH.

MATTHEW 24:32

NO MAN KNOWETH THE HOUR,

by Liz Lemon Swindle

MATTHEW 25

IN CHAPTER 24, many prophecies were given that will be fulfilled as the time of the Second Coming approaches, and counsel was given to be prepared by living faithfully and serving others. Chapter 25 continues with instructions on how to prepare personally for the Second Coming. The Savior uses the parable of the ten virgins to teach us how to prepare.

The Parable of the Ten Virgins

1 **THEN** [*the last days leading up to the time of the Second Coming*] **shall the kingdom of heaven be likened unto ten virgins** [*symbolic of members of the Church; see McConkie, Doctrinal New Testament Commentary, Vol. 1, pp. 684–85*], **which took their lamps, and went forth to meet the bridegroom** [*"groom;" symbolic of Christ—see Talmage, Jesus the Christ, p. 578*].

JST MATTHEW 25:1
1 And then, **at that day, before the Son of man comes**, the kingdom of heaven shall be likened unto ten virgins, who took their lamps, and went forth to meet the bridegroom.

2 And **five** of them were **wise**, and **five** were **foolish**.

3 They that were **foolish** took their lamps, and **took no oil with them:**

4 But the **wise took oil in their vessels with their lamps.**

Did you notice that all ten virgins had lamps with oil in them to begin with? But the five wise virgins carried flasks with extra oil and thus were able to "endure to the end" until the bridegroom (groom) finally arrived.

5 **While the bridegroom tarried, they all slumbered and slept.**

6 And **at midnight** [*ties in with the "eleventh hour" parable, in Matthew 20:6 (verses 1–16)*] there was a cry made, Behold, **the bridegroom cometh** [*symbolic of the Second Coming*]; go ye out to meet him.

7 Then **all those virgins arose, and trimmed their lamps.**

8 And **the foolish said unto the wise, Give us of your oil; for our lamps are gone out.**

9 But **the wise answered**, saying, **Not so; lest there be not enough for us and you:** but **go ye rather to them that sell, and buy for yourselves.**

To some, it may seem that the five wise virgins were not living the gospel because they would not share their supplies of oil with the five foolish virgins. The point is that their extra oil is symbolic of personal worthiness and preparedness which the righteous cannot share or give to others, such as personal righteousness, church attendance, tithe paying, moral cleanliness, Sabbath observance, keeping the commandments, and so forth.

10 **And while they** [*the foolish virgins*] **went to buy, the bridegroom came** [*sadly, they were unprepared and unworthy, and could not get ready in time*]; and **they that were ready went in with him to the marriage** [*"marriage" generally symbolizes making and keeping covenants with God; here, the marriage represents the Second Coming, see Talmage, Jesus the Christ, p. 578*]: **and the door was shut.**

11 **Afterward came also the other virgins, saying, Lord, Lord, open to us.**

12 But he answered and said, Verily I say unto you, **I know you not.** [*"I know you not" is another way of saying "You do not know me." See Talmage, Jesus the Christ, p. 579. See also JST quoted next.*]

JST MATTHEW 25:11
11 But he answered and said, Verily I say unto you, **Ye know me not**.

13 **Watch** therefore, **for ye know neither the day nor the hour wherein the Son of man** [*Christ*] **cometh.**

As the Savior continues to teach His Apostles, we are given additional advice as to how to prepare ourselves for the Second Coming.

The Parable of the Talents

14 For **the kingdom of heaven is as a man** [*symbolic of Christ (who will be crucified within three days)*] travelling into a far country [*symbolic of heaven*], who called his own servants [*disciples, apostles*], and delivered unto them his goods.

15 And unto one he gave five talents, to another two, and to another one; to every man according to his several ability [*in other words, each is an individual and is given a stewardship according to personal capacities, talents and abilities*]; and straightway took his journey.

Some biblical scholars suggest that a talent was a substantial sum of money in New Testament times. See Bible Dictionary, under "Money," wherein it says a talent is a sum of money.

16 Then **he that had received the five** talents went and traded with the same, and **made them other five talents.** [*He developed and increased his God-given talents.*]

17 And likewise **he that had received two,** he also **gained other two.** [*He developed and increased his talents.*]

18 **But he that had received one** went and digged in the earth, and **hid his lord's money.** [*He did not develop and increase his talent.*]

19 After a long time **the lord** [*symbolic of Christ*] of those servants **cometh, and reckoneth with them** [*had them account for how they had used that which He gave them; symbolic of Judgment Day*].

20 And so **he that had received five** talents came and **brought other five talents,** saying, Lord, thou deliveredst unto me five talents: behold, I have gained beside them five talents more.

21 **His lord said** unto him, **Well done, thou good and faithful servant: thou hast been faithful over a few things, I will make thee ruler over many things** [*symbolic of exaltation*]: **enter thou into the joy of thy lord.**

22 He also **that had received two talents** came and said, Lord, thou deliveredst unto me two talents: behold, I have **gained two other talents** beside them.

23 **His lord said** unto him, **Well done, good and faithful servant; thou hast been faithful over a few things, I will make thee ruler over many things** [*symbolic of exaltation*]: **enter thou into the joy of thy lord.**

Did you notice that the reward for both the servant who had received five talents and the servant who was given two talents, was exactly the same? Note wording of the rewards in verses 21 and 23. It is comforting that those with fewer talents and abilities, who do their best, will receive the same reward, exaltation, as those who currently have higher abilities.

24 **Then he which had received the one talent came and said** [*made excuses for his lack of performance*], **Lord, I knew thee that thou art an hard man** [*that You expect a lot from Your employees*], reaping [*harvesting*] where thou hast not sown [*planted*], and gathering [*harvesting*] where thou hast not strawed [*thrown or scattered seeds*]:

25 And **I was afraid**, and went and hid thy talent in the earth: **lo, there thou hast that is thine.**

26 **His lord answered** and said unto him, **Thou wicked and slothful** [*lazy*] **servant**, thou knewest that I reap [*harvest*] where I sowed [*planted*] not, and gather [*harvest*] where I have not strawed [*planted; in other words, you knew that you would someday have to account to Me*]:

27 **Thou oughtest therefore to have put my money to the ex-changers, and then at my com-ing I should have received mine own with usury** [*interest*].

28 **Take therefore the talent from him, and give it unto him which hath ten talents.**

Next, the Master explains the important message He had in mind for us as He gave the parable of the talents.

THEN SHALL THE KINGDOM OF HEAVEN BE LIKENED UNTO TEN VIRGINS, WHICH TOOK THEIR LAMPS, AND WENT FORTH TO MEET THE BRIDEGROOM.

MATTHEW 25:1

GO FORTH TO MEET THE BRIDEGROOM,

by Elspeth Young

29 For **unto every one that hath** *[symbolizing those who have done the best they can with what they were given]* **shall be given, and he shall have abundance** *[symbolic of exaltation]*: **but from him that hath not** *[symbolizing those who have not done their best with what the Lord gave them]* **shall be taken away even that which he hath.**

30 And **cast ye the unprofitable servant** *[symbolic of the wicked]* **into outer darkness** *[see Alma 40:13]*: there shall be weeping and gnashing of teeth *[among other things, symbolic of the fact that the wicked will have to suffer for their own sins since they were unwilling to repent and take advantage of the Atonement; see D&C 19:15–16]*.

31 **When the Son of man** *[Jesus]* **shall come in his glory** *[the Second Coming]*, and all the holy angels with him, **then shall he sit upon the throne of his glory** *[He will be our King during the Millennium]*:

The Parable of the Sheep and the Goats

32 And before him shall be gathered all nations: **and he shall separate** them one from another, as a shepherd divideth his **sheep from the goats:**

33 And **he shall set the sheep on his right hand, but the goats on the left.**

Here, in this context, sheep symbolize the righteous and goats symbolize the wicked. The right hand, in Jewish symbolism, is the covenant hand. Thus, being on the Lord's right hand symbolizes those who have made and kept covenants.

34 **Then shall the King say unto them on his right hand,** Come, ye blessed of my Father, inherit the kingdom *[celestial kingdom]* prepared for you from the foundation of the world *[as planned in the premortal council]*:

In the next verses, the Savior will beautifully detail more ways to be righteous and prepared for the Second Coming, as was the case with the five wise virgins. In other words, He is showing us how to have extra oil for our lamps.

35 For **I was an hungred** *[hungry]*, **and ye gave me meat** *[food]*: **I was thirsty, and ye gave me drink**: I was **a stranger, and ye took me in:**

36 **Naked, and ye clothed me**: I was **sick, and ye visited me**: I was **in prison, and ye came unto me.**

37 Then shall the righteous answer him, saying, **Lord, when saw we thee** an **hungred**, and fed thee? or **thirsty**, and gave thee drink?

38 When saw we thee **a stranger**, and took thee in? **or naked**, and clothed thee?

39 Or when saw we thee **sick**, or in **prison**, and came unto thee?

40 **And the King** *[Christ]* **shall answer** and say unto them, **Verily** *[listen carefully, this is the main point]* I say unto you, **Inasmuch as ye have done it unto one of the least of these my brethren, ye have done it unto me.** *[King Benjamin talked about this kind of service to others in Mosiah 2:17.]*

41 **Then shall he say also unto them on the left hand** *[in this context, being on the left hand of God symbolizes the wicked]*, **Depart from me**, ye cursed, into everlasting fire *[hell]*, prepared for the devil and his angels:

42 For I was an hungred, and **ye gave me no meat** *[food]*: I was thirsty, and ye gave me **no drink:**

43 I was a stranger, and **ye took me not in:** naked, and ye **clothed me not:** sick, and in prison, and ye **visited me not.**

44 **Then shall they also answer him, saying, Lord, when saw we thee** an hungred, or athirst, or a stranger, or naked, or sick, or in prison, and did not minister unto thee *[take care of your needs]*?

45 **Then shall he answer** them, saying, Verily *[when He says "verily," it means "listen very*

carefully because this is the point I am trying to teach you."] I say unto you, **Inasmuch as ye did it not to one of the least of these, ye did it not to me.**

46 And **these shall go away into everlasting punishment: but the righteous into life eternal** [*celestial glory and exaltation*].

MATTHEW 26

IN THIS CHAPTER, the Savior will again prophesy of His coming crucifixion. As the Jewish religious leaders continue to plot His death, He will institute the sacrament, then go to Gethsemane, be betrayed by Judas, be arrested, and be subjected to an illegal trial. Peter will deny that he knows Jesus three times.

1 AND it came to pass, **when Jesus had finished all these sayings, he said unto his disciples,**

2 Ye know that **after two days is the feast of the passover, and the Son of man is betrayed to be crucified.**

The Feast of the Passover was celebrated in the springtime at about the same time as we celebrate Easter. It commemorated the time when the destroying angel passed over the houses of the children of Israel in Egypt, when the firstborn of the Egyptians were killed. The Israelites in Egypt at the time were instructed by Moses to sacrifice a lamb without blemish and to put blood from the lamb which was sacrificed on the doorposts of their houses. See Bible Dictionary, under "Feasts." Thus, through the blood of a lamb, the Israelites were protected from the anguish and punishment brought to the Egyptians by the destroying angel. The symbolism is clear. It is by the "blood of the Lamb" (the sacrifice of the Savior) that we are saved, after all we can do (2 Nephi 25:23). Now, at the time of Passover in Jerusalem, the "Lamb of God," Christ, will present Himself to be sacrificed, that we might be saved. The Feast of the Passover brought large numbers of Jews from near and far to Jerusalem to join in the worship and celebration.

As we continue, verse 3 informs us that the Jewish leaders have gathered together to plot the death of Jesus.

3 **Then assembled together the chief priests,** and the **scribes**, and the **elders** of the people [*the Jewish religious leaders*], **unto the palace of the high priest**, who was called Caiaphas,

4 **And consulted that they might take Jesus by subtilty, and kill him.** [*In other words, they plotted how they might arrest Jesus as quietly as possible so that they would not stir up the people and perhaps get mobbed themselves.*]

5 But **they said, Not on the feast day**, [*not on Thursday, the day of Passover*] **lest there be an uproar** among the people.

6 Now when **Jesus was in Bethany** [*about two or three miles east and south of Jerusalem*], in the house of Simon the leper,

In verses 7–13, a woman (Mary—see John 12:3) anoints Jesus with costly ointment. Jesus is the Messiah. "Messiah" means "the Anointed One" (Bible Dictionary, under "Messiah"). It would seem that this woman understood what the disciples did not yet fully understand, and symbolically "anointed" the Savior in preparation for His Atoning sacrifice. This sheds light on the divine nature and spiritual sensitivity of women.

7 **There came unto him a woman having** an alabaster box of **very precious ointment**, and **poured it on his head**, as he sat at meat [*at dinner*].

8 But **when his disciples saw it, they had indignation**, saying, To what purpose is this waste [*why are you wasting this expensive ointment*]?

9 For **this ointment might have been sold for much, and given to the poor.**

10 When **Jesus** understood it, he **said** unto them, **Why trouble ye the woman?** for **she hath wrought** [*done*] **a good work upon me.**

11 For **ye have the poor always with you; but me ye have not always.** [*You need to keep things in perspective.*]

12 For in that she hath poured this ointment on my body, **she did it for my burial.** [*In other words, she understands that I will be crucified and buried now.*]

Next, the Master gives a prophecy about what this woman did.

13 Verily I say unto you, **Wheresoever this gospel shall be preached** in the whole world, there **shall also this, that this woman hath done, be told for a memorial of her.**

The Betrayal by Judas Iscariot

14 **Then** one of the twelve, called **Judas Iscariot, went unto the chief priests** [*the Jewish religious leaders, Christ's enemies*],

15 **And said** unto them, **What will ye give me, and I will deliver him unto you?** And they covenanted with him for **thirty pieces of silver.**

Thirty pieces of silver was an insult to Judas and demeaned Jesus, since it was the going price for a common slave.

16 **And from that time he** [*Judas*] **sought opportunity to betray him** [*Christ*].

17 Now **the first day** [*Thursday*] of the feast of unleavened bread [*part of the Passover*] **the disciples came to Jesus**, saying unto him, **Where wilt thou that we prepare for thee to eat the passover?**

18 And **he said, Go into the city to such a man, and say unto him, The Master saith, My time is at hand** [*it is time for me to be sacrificed*]; **I will keep the passover at thy house** with my disciples.

19 And **the disciples** did as Jesus had appointed them; and they **made ready the Passover** [*the Passover meal*].

20 Now **when the even** [*evening*] **was come, he sat down with the twelve.**

21 And as they did eat, he said, Verily I say unto you, that **one of you shall betray me.**

22 And they were exceeding sorrowful, and began every one of them to say unto him, **Lord, is it I?**

23 And he answered and said, **He that dippeth his hand with me in the dish**, the same shall betray me.

24 **The Son of man goeth as it is written of him** [*I will perform the Atonement and be crucified as prophesied in the scriptures*]: **but woe unto that man by whom the Son of man is betrayed!** it had been good for that man if he had not been born. [*It would have been better for Judas Iscariot not to have been born.*]

25 **Then Judas**, which betrayed him, **answered** [*responded*] and said, **Master, is it I? He said** unto him, **Thou hast said.**

Many versions of the Bible give "Thou hast said" as "Yes." in one form or another, which fits with JST Mark 14:30 which says, "And he said unto Judas Iscariot, What thou doest, do quickly; but beware of innocent blood." It is likely that this was a whispered conversation between Jesus and Judas because Matthew, Mark, Luke, and John do not indicate that the other Apostles were aware of it.

In the next verses, Jesus introduces the sacrament to His Apostles. This is known as the "Last Supper."

The Savior Introduces the Sacrament

26 And as they were eating, **Jesus took bread, and blessed it, and brake it, and gave it to the disciples**, and said, **Take, eat; this is my body** [*this bread is symbolic of the Savior's body; when we partake of the sacrament bread, we are symbolically "internalizing" His gospel and making it a part of us*].

27 And **he took the cup** [*representing the blood which the Savior shed for our sins*], **and gave thanks, and gave it to them, saying, Drink ye all of it** [*not "part" of it, rather, "all" of it, symbolizing that we must fully accept Christ and His gospel and apply it in our lives*];

28 For **this is my blood** of the new testament [*"testament" means "covenant;" in other words, the*

new covenants associated with the full gospel which Christ had restored], **which is shed for many for the remission of sins.**

29 But I say unto you, **I will not drink henceforth of this fruit of the vine, until that day when I drink it new with you in my Father's kingdom.** [*This is the last time the Master will partake of the sacrament with His disciples during His mortal life.*]

30 And when **they** had **sung an hymn,** they **went out into the mount of Olives** [*just a few minutes walk from the city wall of Jerusalem*].

31 Then saith Jesus unto them, **All ye shall be offended because of me this night** [*meaning they will desert Him—see verses 33–34, 56*]: for it is written [*in Zechariah 13:7*], I will smite the shepherd [*Christ*], and the sheep of the flock [*disciples*] shall be scattered abroad.

32 **But after I am risen** again [*resurrected*], **I will go before you** [*ahead of you*] **into Galilee.**

33 **Peter** answered and **said** unto him, **Though all men shall be offended because of thee, yet will I never be offended.**

34 **Jesus said** unto him, Verily I say unto thee, That this night, **before the cock crow** [*before the rooster crows in the early morning*], **thou shalt deny me thrice** [*three times*].

Verse 34 presents a difficult dilemma to the student of the scriptures with respect to Peter. We need clarification on this situation and until we get it from a reliable source, we are left to wonder about his denying knowing the Savior three times. Some think he denied his testimony and thus denied the Holy Ghost, which is an unpardonable sin. He did not. He denied knowing the Savior. It is out of character for Peter to be afraid of people and what they think. In fact, before this most difficult night is over, he will draw a sword and cut off an ear of one of those who arrested Christ (see verse 51). Perhaps the Savior was prophetically commanding Peter to deny knowing Him on the three upcoming occasions during the night when it will be claimed that he is an associate of Jesus, in order to prevent Peter's death at this time. Perhaps it is to remind Peter that he is not as strong and committed as he thinks he is. Whatever the case, we need more information before we draw any final conclusion on this matter.

35 **Peter said** unto him, **Though I should die with thee, yet will I not deny thee. Likewise also said all the disciples.**

The Garden of Gethsemane

36 **Then cometh Jesus with them unto a place called Gethsemane** [*the Garden of Gethsemane, just a few minutes walk from Jerusalem*], **and saith** unto the disciples, **Sit ye here, while I go and pray yonder.**

"Gethsemane" means "oil press." There is significant symbolism here. The Jews put olives into bags made of mesh fabric and placed them in a press to squeeze olive oil out of them. The first pressings yielded pure olive oil which was prized for many uses, including healing and giving light in lanterns. In fact, we consecrate it and use it to administer to the sick. The last pressing of the olives, under the tremendous pressure of additional weights added to the press, yielded a bitter, red liquid which can remind us of blood and the "bitter cup" which the Savior partook of. Symbolically, the Savior is going into the "oil press" (Gethsemane) to submit to the "pressure" of all our sins which will "squeeze" His blood out in order that we might have the healing "oil" of the Atonement to heal us from our sins.

37 And **he took** with him **Peter and the two sons of Zebedee** [*James and John*], and **began to be sorrowful and very heavy.**

38 Then saith he unto them, **My soul is exceeding sorrowful, even unto death:** tarry [*wait*] ye here, and watch with me.

39 And he went a little further, and fell on his face [*showing submission and humility, in Jewish culture*], and prayed, saying, **O my Father, if it be possible, let this cup pass from me: nevertheless not as I will, but as thou wilt.**

40 And **he cometh unto the disciples, and findeth them asleep,** and saith unto Peter, What, could ye not watch with me one hour?

41 **Watch and pray, that ye enter not into temptation: the spirit indeed is willing, but the flesh is weak.**

42 He went away again the second time, and prayed, saying, **O my Father, if this cup may not pass away from me, except I drink it, thy will be done.**

43 And he came and **found them asleep again:** for their eyes were heavy [*they were very sleepy; it had been a very difficult and sleepless week for the Apostles, worrying about the Savior's safety*].

44 And he left them, and went away again, and **prayed the third time, saying the same words.**

45 Then cometh he to his disciples, and saith unto them, Sleep on now, and take your rest: behold, **the hour is at hand** [*the time has come*], **and the Son of man** [*Christ; in other words, "Son of Man of Holiness" (Heavenly Father), see Moses 6:57*] **is betrayed into the hands of sinners.**

46 Rise, let us be going: behold, he [*Judas*] is at hand that doth betray me.

47 And while he yet spake, lo, **Judas**, one of the twelve, **came**, and **with** him **a great multitude with swords and staves** [*NIV "clubs"*], from the chief priests and elders of the people [*the religious leaders of the Jews*].

48 **Now he** [*Judas*] **that betrayed him gave them** [*the soldiers*] **a sign, saying, Whomsoever I shall kiss, that same is he: hold him fast.** [*I will kiss Jesus so you know which one He is, then arrest Him and hold on to Him securely.*]

49 And forthwith **he came to Jesus, and said, Hail, master; and kissed him.**

50 And Jesus said unto him, Friend, wherefore [*why*] art thou come? **Then came they, and laid hands on Jesus, and took him.**

51 And, behold, **one of them** [*Peter*] which were with Jesus stretched out his hand, and **drew his sword, and struck a servant of the high priest's, and smote off his ear.** [*Jesus healed this man's ear; see Luke 22:51.*]

52 **Then said Jesus unto** him, **Put up** again **thy sword** into his place: for all they that take the sword shall perish with the sword.

53 **Thinkest thou that I cannot now pray to my Father, and he shall presently** [*immediately*] **give me more than twelve legions** [*a "legion" was about six thousand infantry plus some cavalry—see Bible Dictionary, under "Legion"*] **of angels?** [*In other words, don't you realize that if I wanted to stop this, I could?*]

54 But how then shall the scriptures be fulfilled, that **thus it must be?** [*I must be crucified.*]

55 In that same hour said Jesus to the multitudes, **Are ye come out as against a thief** with swords and staves for to take me? **I sat daily with you teaching in the temple, and ye laid no hold on me.**

56 But all this was done, that the scriptures of the prophets might be fulfilled. **Then all the disciples forsook him, and fled** [*as prophesied in verse 31*].

57 And **they** that had laid hold on [*arrested*] Jesus **led him away to Caiaphas the high priest,** where the scribes and the elders were assembled.

This trial during the night time was completely illegal according to the Jews' own laws.

58 But **Peter followed him** afar off unto the high priest's palace, and went in, and sat with the servants, to see the end.

59 Now **the chief priests, and elders, and all the council, sought false witness against Jesus,** to put him to death;

60 **But found none**: yea, though many false witnesses came, yet found they none [*whose false witness would work for their purposes*]. **At the last came two false witnesses,**

61 **And said,** This fellow said, I am able to destroy the temple of God, and to build it in three days.

62 And **the high priest arose, and said unto him** [*Jesus*], **Answerest thou nothing** [*why don't you say something*]? what is it which these witness against thee?

63 **But Jesus held his peace** [*said nothing*]. And **the high priest** answered and **said** unto him, I adjure thee [*I place you under oath*] by the living God, that thou **tell us whether thou be the Christ, the Son of God.**

64 **Jesus saith unto him, Thou hast said** [*NIV "Yes, it is as you say." In other words, Jesus is saying that He is God's Son*]: nevertheless I say unto you, **Hereafter shall ye see the Son of man** [*me*] **sitting on the right hand of power** [*God*], **and coming in the clouds of heaven** [*you will see me at my second coming*].

In addition to what the Savior told these men, in verse 64, above, Revelation 1:7 also informs us that those who crucified Christ will indeed see His Second Coming.

65 **Then the high priest rent his clothes** [*tore his clothes, a sign of extreme emotion*], **saying, He hath spoken blasphemy** [*great disrespect for God and our religious beliefs; blasphemy was punishable by death*]; **what further need have we of witnesses? behold, now ye have heard his blasphemy.**

66 **What think ye?** They answered and said, **He is guilty of death.**

JST MATTHEW 26:67

67 They answered and said, He is guilty, and worthy of death.

67 Then did **they spit in his face, and buffeted** [*hit*] **him**; and others smote [*hit*] him with the palms of their hands,

68 **Saying, Prophesy unto us, thou Christ, Who is he that smote thee?** [*Luke 22:54 tells us that they had put a blindfold on Him before hitting Him; thus they were mocking Him and asking Him to use His "great powers" to tell them which of them were hitting Him.*]

69 Now **Peter sat without** [*outside of the trial room*] in the palace: **and a damsel** [*young lady*] **came unto him, saying, Thou also wast with Jesus of Galilee.**

70 **But he denied** before them all, saying, I know not what thou sayest.

71 And when he was gone out into the porch, **another maid saw him**, and said unto them that were there, **This fellow was also with Jesus of Nazareth.**

72 And **again he denied** with an oath [*strongly*], I do not know the man [*Christ*].

73 And **after a while came unto him they that stood by, and said** to Peter, **Surely thou also art one of them** [*one of Christ's followers*]; for thy speech bewrayeth thee [*your Galilean accent gives you away*].

74 Then began he to curse and to swear, saying, **I know not the man** [*Jesus*]. And **immediately the cock crew** [*the rooster crowed*].

75 **And Peter remembered the word of Jesus** [*in verse 34*], which said unto him, Before the cock crow, thou shalt deny me thrice. **And he went out, and wept bitterly.**

As mentioned previously (after verse 34, above), we will someday know more about Peter's denial of knowing Christ, at the time of His trial. One thing is certain. He did not "deny" Christ in the sense of denying that He was the Christ. Rather, he denied knowing Him. Apostle James E. Talmage taught the following about this scene:

"When Jesus was taken into custody in the Garden of Gethsemane, all the Eleven forsook Him and fled. This is not to be accounted as certain evidence of cowardice, for the Lord had indicated that they should go. Peter and at least one other disciple followed afar off; and, after the armed guard had entered the palace of the high priest with their Prisoner, Peter "went in, and sat with the servants to see the end." He was

FOR THIS IS MY
BLOOD OF THE NEW
TESTAMENT, WHICH
IS SHED FOR MANY
FOR THE REMISSION
OF SINS.

MATTHEW 26:26

assisted in securing admittance by the unnamed disciple, who was on terms of acquaintanceship with the high priest. That other disciple was in all probability John, as may be inferred from the fact that he is mentioned only in the fourth Gospel, the author of which characteristically refers to himself anonymously.

"While Jesus was before the Sanhedrists, Peter remained below with the servants. The attendant at the door was a young woman; her feminine suspicions had been aroused when she admitted Peter, and as he sat with a crowd in the palace court she came up, and having intently observed him, said: 'Thou also wast with Jesus of Galilee.' But Peter denied, averring he did not know Jesus. Peter was restless; his conscience and the fear of identification as one of the Lord's disciples troubled him. He left the crowd and sought partial seclusion in the porch; but there another maid spied him out, and said to those nearby: 'This fellow was also with Jesus of Nazareth'; to which accusation Peter replied with an oath: "I do not know the man."

"The April night was chilly, and an open fire had been made in the hall or court of the palace. Peter sat with others at the fire, thinking, perhaps, that brazen openness was better than skulking caution as a possible safeguard against detection. About an hour after his former denials, some of the men around the fire charged him with being a disciple of Jesus, and referred to his Galilean dialect as evidence that he was at least a fellow countryman with the high priest's Prisoner; but, most threatening of all, a kinsman of Malthus [Malchus—see John 18:10], whose ear Peter had slashed with the sword, asked peremptorily: 'Did not I see thee in the garden with him?' Then Peter went so far in the course of falsehood upon which he had entered as to curse and swear, and to vehemently declare for the third time, 'I know not the man.' As the last profane falsehood left his lips, the clear notes of a crowing cock broke upon his ears, and the remembrance of his Lord's prediction welled up in his mind. Trembling in wretched realization of his perfidious cowardice, he turned from the crowd and met the gaze of the suffering Christ, who from the midst of the insolent mob looked into the face of His boastful, yet loving but weak apostle. Hastening from the palace, Peter went out into the night, weeping bitterly. As his later life attests, his tears were those of real contrition and true repentance." (*Jesus the Christ*, pp. 629–31)

MATTHEW 27

THIS IS THE day of the Savior's crucifixion. Pilate will yield to the cunning plot of the Jewish religious leaders and the illegal clamor of the masses to crucify Jesus, and will wash his hands of the whole thing. The Master will be mocked, crucified, and hastily buried in a new tomb donated by Joseph of Arimathaea.

1 **WHEN** the **morning was come** [*Friday morning, the day of the Savior's crucifixion*], all the **chief priests** and **elders** of the people **took counsel** [*plotted*] **against Jesus to put him to death:**

2 And when they had **bound him**, they **led him away**, and delivered him **to Pontius Pilate** the governor [*the Roman governor over that part of the Holy Land*].

3 **Then Judas**, which had betrayed him, when he saw that he was condemned, **repented himself** [*changed his mind*], **and brought again** [*returned*] **the thirty pieces of silver** [*which he had been paid to betray Jesus*] **to the chief priests and elders,**

4 **Saying**, I have sinned in that **I have betrayed the innocent blood**. And **they said, What is that to us? see thou to that** [*that is your problem!*].

JST MATTHEW 27:5

5 And **they said unto him, What is that to us? See thou to it; thy sins be upon thee.**

5 And he cast down [*threw down*] the pieces of silver in the temple, and departed, and went and **hanged himself.**

JST MATTHEW 27:6

6 And he cast down the pieces of silver in the temple, and departed, and went, and hanged himself **on a tree. And straightway he fell down, and his bowels gushed out, and he died**.

6 And **the chief priests took the silver** pieces, and said, It is not lawful [*legal*] for to put them into the treasury, because it is the price of blood [*it is blood money, the price paid to have someone killed*].

7 And they took counsel [*talked it over*], **and bought** with them [*the thirty pieces of silver*] **the potter's field, to bury strangers** [*foreigners*] **in.**

8 Wherefore that field was called, **The field of blood**, unto this day.

9 **Then was fulfilled that which was spoken by Jeremy** [*Jeremiah—we don't have this quote from Jeremiah in our Bible; it is apparently one of the missing scriptures—but we do have a related quote in Zechariah 11:12–13*] the prophet, saying, And **they took the thirty pieces of silver, the price of him that was valued, whom they of the children of Israel did value;**

10 **And gave them for the potter's field**, as the Lord appointed me.

The Trial Before Pontius Pilate

11 And **Jesus stood before the governor** [*Pontius Pilate*]: and **the governor asked** him, saying, **Art thou the King of the Jews?** And **Jesus said** unto him, **Thou sayest** [*in other words, it is as you say, yes, I am; see John 18:37*].

We learn more about Pontius Pilate from our Bible Dictionary: "Roman procurator in Judaea, A.D. 26–36 (Luke 3:1). His headquarters were at Caesarea, but he was generally present in Jerusalem at feast time. He had a great contempt for the Jewish people and for their religion. During his term of office there was much disorder, mainly in consequence of an attempt he made to introduce into the city silver busts of the emperor on the Roman ensigns. In Luke 13:1 there is a reference to an outbreak during one of the feasts, when Pilate sent soldiers into the temple courts and certain Galileans were slain. He is prominent in the story of our Lord's Passion (Matthew 27:2–26; 27:58–66; Mark 15:1–15, 42–47; Luke 23:1–25, 50–53; John 18:28–19:22, 31, 38). As the Sanhedrin had no power to carry out their sentence of death, Pilate's consent had to be obtained. The Lord was therefore charged before him with stirring up sedition, making himself a king, and forbidding to give tribute to Caesar. Pilate saw that there was no evidence to support the charge, and, having received a warning from his wife, he wished to dismiss the case. He also tried to avoid all responsibility in the matter by sending our Lord for trial to Herod Antipas, tetrarch of Galilee, but Herod sent him back without any formal decision on the case. It was not until the Jews threatened to send a report to the Emperor Tiberius, whose suspicious nature Pilate well knew, that he passed a death sentence, knowing it to be unjust. The sentence was carried out under his directions by Roman soldiers. Pilate was removed from office a few years later in consequence of a disturbance in Samaria."

12 And **when he was accused of the chief priests and elders** [*when the leaders of the Jews accused him in front of Pilate*], **he answered nothing.**

13 **Then said Pilate** unto him, **Hearest thou not how many things they witness against thee** [*don't you hear what they are accusing you of*]?

14 And **he answered him** to **never a word** [*Jesus did not reply*]; insomuch that the governor marvelled greatly [*was very surprised*].

15 Now **at that feast the governor was wont to release** [*was accustomed to releasing*] unto the people **a prisoner**, whom they would. [*It was a tradition for the governor to release a prisoner of the people's choice each year during the feast of the Passover.*]

16 And **they had then a notable** [*famous*] **prisoner, called Barabbas.**

The name "Barabbas" means "son of the father" (see Bible Dictionary, under "Barabbas"). This may be symbolic in that the "imposter," Satan, stirred up the multitude to demand the release of an "imposter," Barabbas, while the true "Son of the Father" is punished for crimes which He did not commit.

17 Therefore when they were gathered together, Pilate said unto them [*the multitude which had gathered*], **Whom will ye that I release unto you? Barabbas, or Jesus** which is called Christ?

18 For **he knew that for envy** [*because of hatred*] **they had delivered him** [*turned Christ over to Pilot*].

19 When he [*Pilate*] was set down on the judgment seat, **his wife sent unto him, saying, Have thou nothing to do with that just** [*NIV "innocent"*] **man** [*Jesus*]: for I have suffered many things this day in a dream because of him. [*Pilate's wife had been warned in a dream that her husband should not allow any injustice to happen to Jesus.*]

20 But the **chief priests and elders persuaded the multitude that they should ask** [*ask for*] **Barabbas, and destroy Jesus.**

21 **The governor** answered and **said** unto them [*the multitude*], **Whether of the twain** [*which of the two*] **will ye that I release unto you? They said, Barabbas.**

22 Pilate saith unto them, **What shall I do** then **with Jesus** which is called Christ? **They all say unto him, Let him be crucified.**

23 And the governor said, **Why, what evil hath he done?** But they cried out the more [*all the louder*], saying, **Let him be crucified.**

24 When **Pilate** saw that he could prevail nothing [*that he could not get the multitude to change their minds*], but that rather a tumult was made [*an uprising was in the making*], he took water, and **washed his hands** before the multitude, **saying, I am innocent of the blood of this just** [*innocent*] **person**: see ye to it [*it is on your heads now*].

25 **Then answered all the people**, and said, **His blood be on us, and on our children.** [*We and our children will take responsibility for killing Jesus.*]

26 Then **released** he **Barabbas** unto them: and when he had **scourged** [*whipped*] **Jesus**, he **delivered him to be crucified.**

"Scourging" was a very severe punishment and many prisoners did not live through it. It consisted of being whipped with a whip which was composed of leather thongs with bits of metal, bone, etc., secured to the ends of the thongs.

The Soldiers Mock Jesus

27 **Then the soldiers** of the governor **took Jesus** into the common hall [*the governor's house*], and gathered unto him the whole band of soldiers. [*The soldiers brought Jesus in front of all the soldiers to mock him.*]

28 And they **stripped him, and put on him a scarlet** [*JST: purple*] **robe** [*symbolic of royalty, mocking him for his claim to be king of the Jews*].

29 And when they had platted [*made, woven*] **a crown of thorns**, they put it upon his head, and **a reed** [*a stick, in mockery of a king's scepter*] in his right hand: and they bowed the knee before him, and **mocked him**, saying, Hail, King of the Jews!

30 And they **spit upon him**, and took the reed, and **smote** [*hit*] **him on the head.**

The Crucifixion

31 And **after that they** had mocked him, they took the robe off from him, and put his own raiment [*clothing*] on him, and **led him away to crucify him.**

32 And as they came out, they found a man of Cyrene [*a city in northern Africa*], **Simon** by name: him they **compelled** [*forced*] **to bear his cross** [*Jesus was too weak to carry His cross, because of His suffering in the Garden of Gethsemane as well as the scourging.*].

33 And **when they were come unto** a place called **Golgotha**, that is to say, a place of a skull,

JST MATTHEW 27:35
And when they were come unto a place called Golgotha (that is to say, **a place of burial**),

34 **They gave him vinegar to drink mingled with gall** [*designed to drug the victim of crucifixion to lessen the pain somewhat—see Jesus the Christ, pp. 654–55*]: and when he had tasted thereof, **he would not drink.**

35 And **they crucified him**, and parted his garments *[divided his clothing up among themselves]*, casting lots: that it might be fulfilled which was spoken by the prophet *[Psalm 22:18]*, They parted my garments among them, and upon my vesture *[clothing]* did they cast lots.

36 And sitting down they watched him there;

37 And set up over his head his accusation written *[they placed a sign over his head which said]*, **THIS IS JESUS THE KING OF THE JEWS.**

JST Matthew 27:39–42

39 And Pilate wrote a title, and put it on the cross, and the writing was,

40 JESUS OF NAZARETH, THE KING OF THE JEWS, in letters of Greek, and Latin, and Hebrew.

41 And the chief priests said unto Pilate, It should be written and set up over his head, his accusation, This is he that said he was Jesus, the King of the Jews.

42 But Pilate answered and said, What I have written, I have written; let it alone.

38 Then were there **two thieves** crucified with him, one on the right hand, and another on the left.

39 And **they that passed by reviled** *[made fun of Him]* **him**, wagging their heads *[shaking their heads]*,

40 And saying, Thou that destroyest the temple, and buildest it in three days, save thyself. **If thou be the Son of God, come down from the cross.**

These people obviously misunderstood what Jesus said regarding the temple. What he said is in John 2:19–21. He said that if they destroyed His body (the "temple of His body"), He would raise it up in three days (be resurrected in three days). By the time Jesus is on the cross, His statement has been misquoted and spread so that the mockers claim that He said He would destroy their massive temple in Jerusalem and rebuild it in three days.

41 Likewise **also the chief priests mocking him, with the scribes and elders**, said,

42 He saved others; himself he cannot save. If he be the King of Israel, let him now come down from the cross, and we will believe him.

43 He trusted in God; let him deliver him now, if he will have him: for he said, I am the Son of God.

44 **The thieves also**, which were crucified with him, **cast the same in his teeth** *[threw similar statements at Him]*.

The JST informs us that only one of the thieves railed against the Master.

JST Matthew 27:47–48

47 **One of the thieves** also, which were crucified with him, **cast the same in his teeth. But the other rebuked him**, saying, Dost thou not fear God, seeing thou art under the same condemnation; and this man is just, and hath not sinned; and he cried unto the Lord that he would save him.

48 And the Lord said unto him, This day thou shalt be with me in Paradise.

45 Now **from the sixth hour** *[about noon]* there was **darkness over all the land** unto the ninth hour.

In the Jewish time system, the "sixth hour" would be about noon, the "ninth hour" would be about 3 P.M. in our time system. We understand that Jesus was nailed onto the cross at the "third hour" which would be about 9 A.M.

46 And **about the ninth hour Jesus cried with a loud voice**, saying, Eli, Eli, lama sabachthani? that is to say, **My God, my God, why hast thou forsaken me?**

This was a very difficult time for the Savior, incomprehensibly difficult for us to understand. Apparently, as part of the Atonement, Jesus had to experience what sinners do when they sin so much that the Spirit leaves them. At this point on the cross, we understand that all available help from the Father withdrew in order that the Savior might experience all things, including the withdrawal of the Spirit which sinners experience.

Statements from the Cross

There are seven recorded statements made by the Savior from the cross. The references for these statements and the statements themselves follow, and are in chronological order:

1. Luke 23:34 "Father, forgive them; for they know not what they do."

2. Luke 23:43 "Today shalt thou be with me in paradise."

3. John 19:26–27 "Woman, behold thy son!" Behold thy mother!"

4. Matthew 27:46 "My God, my God, why hast thou forsaken me?"

5. John 19:28 "I thirst."

6. John 19:30 "It is finished."

7. Luke 23:46 "Father, into thy hands I commend my spirit."

47 **Some** of them that stood there, when they heard that, **said, This man calleth for Elias** [*Elijah—see footnote 47a, in your Bible*].

48 And **straightway** [*immediately*] **one** of them ran, and **took a spunge, and filled it with vinegar, and put it on a reed, and gave him to drink.**

49 **The rest said, Let be, let us see whether Elias** [*Elijah*] **will come to save him** [*don't help him; let's see if Elijah comes to help Him*].

50 **Jesus, when he had cried again with a loud voice, yielded up the ghost** [*left His body, died*].

JST MATTHEW 27:54

54 Jesus when he had cried again with a loud voice, **saying, Father, it is finished, thy will is done**, yielded up the ghost.

It startled some of the onlookers that Jesus had so much strength that He could speak so loudly. It was to them as if He had power to leave His body when He so chose, which indeed He did! We see this doctrine taught in John:

JOHN 10:17–18

17 Therefore doth my Father love me, because **I lay down my life, that I might take it again**.

18 **No man taketh it from me**, but **I lay it down of myself. I have power to lay it down, and I have power to take it again**. This commandment have I received of my Father.

51 And, behold, **the veil of the temple** [*in Jerusalem*] **was rent in twain** [*torn in two*] from the top to the bottom; and **the earth did quake**, and the rocks rent [*were torn apart*];

52 And **the graves were opened**; and **many** bodies of the **saints** [*those worthy of celestial glory*] **which slept** [*were dead*] **arose** [*were resurrected (three days later when Jesus was resurrected)*],

53 **And came out of the graves after his resurrection**, and went into the holy city [*Jerusalem*], **and appeared unto many.**

Verses 52 and 53 are out of chronological order. The resurrection of these Saints did not occur until Christ's resurrection. The resurrection of the Saints referred to here is mentioned in D&C 133:54–55. We understand this first resurrection to have included all those worthy of celestial resurrection from Adam and Eve up to the time of Christ's resurrection. This would include John the Baptist. Nobody worthy of terrestrial or telestial resurrection has yet been resurrected. The next major resurrection will be at the beginning of the Millennium when those who have died since Christ's resurrection and who are worthy of celestial glory will be resurrected at the Second Coming (see D&C 88:97–98). This is often referred to as "the morning of the first resurrection."

54 Now when **the centurion, and they that were with him**, watching Jesus, saw the earthquake, and those things that were done, they **feared greatly, saying, Truly this was the Son of God.**

55 And **many women were there** beholding [*watching*] afar off, which followed Jesus from Galilee, ministering unto him:

56 Among which was **Mary Magdalene**, and **Mary the mother of James and Joses** [*possibly the Savior's mother—see Mark 6:3*], **and the mother** [*named Salome, Mark 15:40*] **of Zebedee's children** [*James and John—see Mark 1:19*].

Joseph of Arimathaea Provides a Tomb for the Savior

57 When the even [*evening*] was come, there came **a rich man of Arimathæa, named Joseph**, who also himself was Jesus' disciple [*follower*]:

58 He **went to Pilate** [*the Roman governor of the area*], and **begged** [*requested*] **the body of Jesus.** Then Pilate commanded the body to be delivered [*given to Joseph of Arimathaea*].

59 And when Joseph had taken the body, **he wrapped it in a clean linen cloth,**

> We understand from John 19:38–40 that Nicodemus assisted Joseph of Arimathaea and in fact brought a very costly "hundredweight" of spices for anointing the Savior's body.

60 **And laid it in his own new tomb,** which he had hewn out in the rock: and he **rolled a great** [*large*] **stone to the door of the sepulchre** [*tomb*], and departed.

> There was an urgency to quickly get Christ's body in the tomb and close the tomb, because it was evening and the Jewish Sabbath [*Saturday*] was about to begin.

61 And there was **Mary Magdalene, and the other Mary, sitting over against** [*in front of*] **the sepulchre** [*tomb*].

> Because of the approaching Sabbath, which began in the evening in the Jewish system of days, there was no time for these women to do their part in the customary preparation of a body for final burial. Luke 23:55–56 tells us that they watched as the Savior's body was laid in the tomb and then left to prepare spices for Sunday morning (Sunday was the first day of the week among the Jews; Saturday was their Sabbath) when they would return to the tomb to finish anointing the body—see Luke 24:1.

62 Now **the next day** [*Saturday, the Jewish Sabbath*], that followed the day of the preparation [*part of Passover*], **the chief priests and Pharisees came** together **unto Pilate,**

63 **Saying, Sir,** we remember that **that deceiver** [*imposter, referring to Jesus, who they claimed was a deceiver*] **said, while he was yet alive, After three days I will rise again** [*in John 2:19–21, Jesus said that if they destroyed His body, He would raise it up again in three days*].

64 **Command therefore that the sepulchre** [*tomb*] **be made sure** [*secure*] **until the third day, lest his disciples** [*followers*] **come by night, and steal him away, and say unto the people, He is risen from the dead:** so the last error [*attempted deception*] shall be worse than the first. [*In other words, these wicked Jewish leaders feared that if Christ's disciples were to succeed in stealing the body and pretending that Jesus had resurrected, it would be harder for them to deal with than Christ's claim to come back to life if they killed him (John 2:19).*]

65 **Pilate said** unto them, **Ye have a watch** [*a group of soldiers of your own*]: **go your way, make it as sure as ye can** [*take your own soldiers and guard the tomb*].

66 **So they went, and made the sepulchre** [*tomb*] **sure, sealing the stone, and setting a watch.** [*They put a wax seal between the stone door and the wall of the tomb so they could tell if someone moved the stone, plus they set guards to watch the tomb for three days.*]

MATTHEW 28

THE MOST GLORIOUS of all mornings is recorded by Matthew in this chapter. The Savior has been resurrected! In sorrow the faithful women come to finish the preparation of the Master's crucified body, since there was not enough time for them to complete their tender ministering and preparing of the Lord's mortal remains after His body was removed from the cross on Friday. Picture them as their deep sorrow gradually turns to joy as first the angels (two witnesses) announce the Lord's resurrection, and then the Savior Himself personally meets them (verse 9) as they hurry to tell the disciples.

Imagine also the Joy in the Savior's heart as He appears to them, and later to others, having finished the Atonement and sharing His joy with them. Isaiah prophesied of this joy when he wrote, "He shall see of the travail of his soul, and shall be satisfied" (Isaiah 53:11).

The Resurrection of Christ

1 **IN the end of the sabbath** [*after the Sabbath was over*], **as it began to dawn** toward the

first day of the week [*Sunday*], **came Mary Magdalene and the other Mary to see the sepulchre** [*tomb*].

Up to now, Saturday was the Sabbath or holy day for the Jews. But Acts 20:7 shows us that, among the followers of Christ (the Christians), Sunday became the holy day or Sabbath, after the resurrection of the Savior.

2 And, behold, there was **a great earthquake**: for **the angel** of the Lord descended from heaven, and came and **rolled back the stone** from the door [*from the opening into the tomb*], and sat upon it.

JST MATTHEW 28:2

2 And behold, there **had been** a great earthquake; for **two angels** of the Lord descended from heaven, and came and rolled back the stone from the door, and sat upon it.

3 **His countenance** [*face*] was like lightning, and **his raiment** [*clothing*] white as snow:

4 And for fear of **him** the keepers [*guards*] did shake, and became **as dead men**.

5 And the **angel** answered and **said** unto the women, Fear not ye: for **I know that ye seek Jesus, which was crucified**.

JST MATTHEW 28:3–4

3 And **their countenance** was like lightning, and **their raiment** white as snow; and for fear of **them** the keepers did shake, and became **as though they were dead**.

4 And the **angels** answered and **said** unto the women, Fear not ye; for **we know that ye seek Jesus who was crucified**.

6 **He is not here: for he is risen** [*resurrected*], as he said. **Come, see the place where the Lord lay.**

7 And **go quickly, and tell his disciples that he is risen from the dead**; and, behold, **he goeth** before you [*ahead of you*] **into Galilee; there shall ye see him**: lo, I have told you.

Jesus told his disciples He would meet them in Galilee after His crucifixion—see Matthew 26:32. A description of His meeting them there is found in John, chapter 21.

8 And **they** [*the women in verse one*] **departed quickly** from the sepulchre [*tomb*] **with fear and great joy; and did run to bring his disciples word.**

9 And **as they went** to tell his disciples, behold, **Jesus met them**, saying, All hail [*a greeting*]. **And they came and held him by the feet, and worshipped him.**

10 **Then said Jesus** unto them, Be not afraid: **go tell my brethren** [*the Apostles*] **that they** [*should*] **go into Galilee** [*as Jesus told them in Matthew 26:32*], and **there shall they see me.**

The next verses describe the dilemma faced by the soldiers who had been on duty when the angels rolled back the stone from the entrance to the tomb, revealing that the body of the Savior was no longer there. Watch what the chief priests and elders conspire to do to attempt to cover up the resurrection of Christ.

11 **Now when they were going** [*while the women were going to tell the Apostles*], behold, **some of the watch** [*soldiers who had been assigned to guard the tomb*] came into the city, and **shewed** [*told*] **unto the chief priests all the things that were done.**

12 And **when they** [*the chief priests*] were assembled with the elders, and **had taken counsel** [*had plotted together*], **they gave large money** [*bribes*] **unto the soldiers,**

13 **Saying, Say ye, His disciples came by night, and stole him away while we slept.** [*In other words, lie about what happened.*]

14 **And if this** [*news of Jesus' body being gone from the tomb and angels saying that he is resurrected*] **come to the governor's ears, we will persuade him** [*we will handle him*], **and secure you** [*protect you from being executed for sleeping on guard duty*].

15 **So they** [*the soldiers*] **took the money** [*the bribes*], **and did as they were taught**: and this saying [*story*] is commonly reported among the Jews until this day.

The Remaining Eleven Apostles Go to Galilee as Instructed

16 **Then the eleven disciples** [*Apostles*] **went away into Galilee**, into a mountain where Jesus had appointed them.

17 And when **they saw him**, they **worshipped him**: but some doubted.

The statement "but some doubted" in verse 17, above, undoubtedly refers to people other than these Apostles who met the Savior as described in verses 18–20 and detailed in John 21. Some might think that this could refer to Thomas who is sometimes referred to as "doubting Thomas," but his doubt was done away with (see John 20:27–28) before they went to Galilee. Thus, "some doubted" is most likely a general comment of Matthew, contrasting the witness of the Apostles who "worshipped him" (verse 17) as opposed to some members who still doubted that He had been resurrected.

As you will recall, up to now, the Savior had limited His mortal ministry to the Jews. Now, though, He instructs His Apostles to take the gospel to all nations. Not only is this a major change in policy, but it is a strong statement that all must have the opportunity to hear and understand the gospel of Jesus Christ.

Remember that the Jews considered themselves to be superior in status to all other people, in the sight of God, because they were direct descendants of Abraham (Matthew 3:9). What Jesus now instructs is a clear reminder to these Apostles that their cultural background must be discarded in favor of the true doctrine that all souls are of equal worth in the sight of God (D&C 18:10).

18 And **Jesus came** and spake unto them, **saying, All power is given unto me in heaven and in earth.**

19 **Go** ye therefore, **and teach all nations, baptizing them in the name of the Father, and of the Son, and of the Holy Ghost:**

20 **Teaching them to observe all things whatsoever I have commanded you:** and, lo, I am with you always [*always*], even unto the end of the world. Amen.

AND THERE CAME A VOICE FROM HEAVEN, SAYING, THOU ART MY BELOVED SON, IN WHOM I AM WELL PLEASED.

MARK 1:11

THE GOSPEL ACCORDING TO ST MARK

THE JST (JOSEPH Smith Translation of the Bible) calls this book "The Testimony of St. Mark." The Gospel of Mark was written by John Mark, a missionary companion of the Apostle Paul (see Acts 12:25). Tradition has it that Mark also associated much with Peter, the Apostle, and that Mark got most of his material from Peter and wrote the book of Mark from Rome. His main emphasis, as he bears witness of the Savior, seems to be the miracles performed by Jesus. Mark is the shortest of the "Four Gospels" (Matthew, Mark, Luke and John) and has many of the same things as Matthew and Luke.

MARK 1

1 **THE beginning of the gospel of Jesus Christ, the Son of God;**

First, Mark introduces his readers to the coming of John the Baptist, who, according to the prophecies, was to come and prepare the way for the Messiah's mortal mission.

The Coming of John the Baptist

2 **As it is written in the prophets** [*the Old Testament*], **Behold, I send my messenger before thy face, which shall prepare thy way before thee.** [*Old Testament prophets prophesied that John the Baptist would come and prepare the way for Christ's earthly ministry.*]

3 **The voice of one** [*John the Baptist, as prophesied in Isaiah 40:3*] **crying** [*preaching*] in the wilderness, **Prepare ye the way of the Lord,** make his paths straight [*clear the way; symbolizing making a straight path into your heart for the Savior*].

4 **John** [*the Baptist*] **did baptize** in the wilderness, **and preach the baptism of repentance for the remission of sins.**

5 And **there went out unto him all** the land **of Judea, and** they of **Jerusalem** [*many people came out to listen to John the Baptist, including people from Jerusalem*], and **were all baptized of him** in the river of Jordan, confessing their sins.

As you can see, in the JST quoted next, the Prophet Joseph Smith made a correction for verse 5, above. Instead of everyone being baptized, the correct rendering of this verse is that "many" were baptized.

JST MARK 1:4

4 And there went out unto him all the land of Judea, and they of Jerusalem, and **many were baptized of him** in the river Jordan, confessing their sins.

The fact that they came all the way out to the Jordan River which was several miles from major population centers, is a reminder that baptism was performed by immersion. In fact the word "baptize" means "to immerse." See Bible Dictionary, under "Baptism."

6 And **John was clothed with camel's hair** [*wore clothing made from camel's hair*], and **with a girdle of a skin about his loins** [*wore a leather belt around his waist*]; and he did eat locusts and wild honey;

Perhaps this rough desert clothing worn by John the Baptist might have reminded people of Elijah the Prophet in the Old Testament who wore similar clothing (see 2 Kings 1:8).

As you can see, in verses 7–8, next, John is very careful to prevent people from thinking that he, himself, might be the Messiah. He humbly proclaims the difference between him and the coming Savior.

7 And **preached**, saying, **There cometh one** [*Christ*] **mightier than I after me, the latchet of whose shoes I am not worthy to stoop down and unloose** [*I am not even worthy to take off His shoes for Him*].

8 **I** indeed **have baptized you with water: but he** [*Christ*] **shall baptize you with the Holy Ghost.**

JST MARK 1:6

6 I indeed have baptized you with water; but **he shall not only baptize you with water, but with fire, and the Holy Ghost**.

The Baptism of Jesus

9 And it came to pass in those days, that **Jesus came from Nazareth** of Galilee, **and was baptized of** [*by*] **John** in Jordan [*in the Jordan River, about 25 miles from Jerusalem*].

The Holy Ghost Bears Witness

10 And straightway [*immediately*] coming up out of the water, **he** [*John*] **saw the heavens opened, and the Spirit** [*the Holy Ghost*] like a dove **descending upon him** [*the Savior*]:

Joseph Smith explained that the Holy Ghost does not turn into a dove and further explained that the Holy Ghost was present to testify to John of the truthfulness of what he was doing for the Savior (*Teachings of the Prophet Joseph Smith*, pp. 275–76).

The Father Bears Witness of the Son

11 And **there came a voice** [*the Father's voice*] **from heaven, saying, Thou art my beloved Son, in whom I am well pleased.**

12 And immediately **the Spirit driveth him into the wilderness.**

13 And he was there in the wilderness forty days, **tempted of Satan** [*see JST quoted below for clarification*]; and was with the wild beasts; and the angels ministered unto him.

JST MATTHEW 4:1

1 Then Jesus was led up of the Spirit, into the wilderness, to be with God.

JST MARK 1:10–11

10 And immediately **the Spirit took him into the wilderness**.

11 And he was there in the wilderness forty days, **Satan seeking to tempt him**; and was with the wild beasts; and the angels ministered unto him.

14 Now **after** that **John was put in prison** [*for criticizing Herod's marriage to Herodias—see Mark 6:16–29*], **Jesus came into Galilee,** preaching the gospel of the kingdom of God,

15 And **saying**, The time is fulfilled, and **the kingdom of God is at hand** [*is now being made available to you*]: **repent ye, and believe the gospel.**

The Calling of Peter, Andrew, James, and John

16 Now **as he walked by the sea of Galilee, he saw Simon** [*Peter*] **and Andrew** his brother casting a net into the sea: for they were fishers [*they fished for a living*].

17 And **Jesus said** unto them, **Come ye after me,** and I will make you to become fishers of men.

18 And **straightway** [*immediately*] **they** forsook [*left*] their nets, and **followed him.** [*They immediately gave up their professional fishing business and followed Jesus.*]

19 And **when he had gone a little further** thence, **he saw James** the son of Zebedee, **and John** his brother, who also were in the ship mending their nets.

20 And straightway *[immediately]* **he called them: and they** left their father Zebedee in the ship with the hired servants, and **went after him** *[followed Jesus]*.

The Master Teaches in a Synagogue on the Jewish Sabbath (Saturday)

21 And **they went into Capernaum** *[a city on the north end of the Sea of Galilee]*; **and** straightway *[first thing]* **on the sabbath day he entered into the synagogue** *[Jewish church building]*, **and taught.**

22 And **they were astonished at his doctrine: for he taught them as one that had authority,** and not as the scribes *[religious leaders and teachers who interpreted the gospel for the Jews]*.

Jesus Casts Out an Evil Spirit

23 And **there was in their synagogue a man with an unclean spirit** *[possessed by an evil spirit]*; **and he** *[the evil spirit]* **cried out,**

> From the wording in verses 23 and 24 here, it appears that this evil spirit is speaking for several of his colleague evil spirits as he questions Christ about what He is doing.

24 Saying, **Let us alone; what have we to do with thee** *[what business is it of Yours what we do?]*, **thou Jesus** of Nazareth? **art thou come to destroy us** *[to ruin our opportunity to possess people]*? **I know thee who thou art, the Holy One of God.**

> Here we learn an important thing, namely that evil spirits (the one third who were cast out of heaven—see Revelation 12:4—and are here on earth tempting us) do not have the veil over their memory of premortal life. Thus, they recognize Christ and know what He is doing.

25 And **Jesus rebuked him, saying, Hold thy peace** *[Jesus doesn't want evil spirits bearing witness of Him]*, **and come out of him.**

26 And **when the unclean spirit had torn him** *[severely shaken him]*, **and cried with a loud voice, he came out** of him.

27 And **they were all amazed**, insomuch that they questioned among themselves, saying, What thing is this? what new doctrine is this? for with authority commandeth he even the unclean spirits, and they do obey him.

28 And immediately **his fame spread** abroad throughout all the region round about Galilee.

29 And forthwith *[immediately]*, when they were come out of the synagogue *[church]*, **they entered into the house of Simon and Andrew,** with James and John *[the newly-called disciples—see verses 16–20]*.

Jesus Heals Peter's Mother-in-law

30 But **Simon's wife's mother** *[Peter's mother-in-law]* **lay sick** of a fever, and anon *[immediately]* they tell him *[Christ]* of her.

> This verse (30), which mentions Peter's wife's mother, is a good reminder that the early Apostles were married and that celibacy (deliberately remaining single as a sign of loyalty to God) was not part of the gospel taught by Jesus.

31 And **he came and took her by the hand, and lifted her up**; and immediately **the fever left her,** and she ministered unto them *[served them, probably including giving them something to eat]*.

Many Are Healed

32 And at even *[evening]*, when the sun did set, **they brought unto him all that were diseased, and** them that were **possessed with devils.**

> There is beautiful symbolism in the Savior's healing of the people. While Christ's miracles of healing all kinds of sickness were literal, the symbolism is that Jesus can heal all kinds of spiritual illness, through his Atonement. Therefore, each time you read of a healing performed by the Savior, you can consider it to be a reminder that he can heal us spiritually also, through the cleansing and healing power of the Atonement.

33 And all the city was gathered together at the door.

34 And **he healed many** that were sick of divers [*various*] diseases, and cast out many devils; and suffered not [*did not allow*] the devils to speak, because they knew him [*did not allow the evil spirits to acknowledge Him in public*].

Perhaps the Savior's not allowing evil spirits to bear witness of Him (see also verse 25) involves a principle similar to that seen when Satan commanded Cain to offer sacrifice to the Lord (Moses 5:18). Righteous testimony, accompanied by the witness of the Holy Ghost, cannot come from an unrighteous source.

35 And **in the morning**, rising up **a great while before day, he** [*Jesus*] went out, and **departed into a solitary place** [*a place where He could be alone*], **and** there **prayed.**

36 And **Simon** [*Peter*] **and they that were with him followed after him.**

37 And when they had found him, they said unto him, **All men seek for thee** [*everyone is looking for you*].

38 And he said unto them, Let us go into the next towns, that I may preach there also: for **therefore came I forth** [*that is the reason I came*].

39 And **he preached** in their synagogues [*Jewish churches*] **throughout all Galilee, and cast out devils.**

Healing of a Leper

40 And **there came a leper** [*a man with leprosy, a very painful and serious disease which caused the ends of fingers, toes, ears, nose, etc., to rot away; see note by Matthew 8:2 in this study guide*] to him, beseeching him, and kneeling down to him, and saying unto him, **If thou wilt** [*if it is Thy will*], **thou canst make me clean** [*heal me*].

41 And **Jesus, moved with compassion**, put forth his hand, and **touched him, and saith unto him, I will; be thou clean.**

42 And as soon as he had spoken, **immediately the leprosy departed from him**, and he was cleansed.

Here, again, is beautiful Atonement symbolism. The symbolism is that Christ can heal us not only physically but also from very serious sin and make us whole. See additional help with symbolism and leprosy in the note accompanying Matthew 5:17 in this study guide.

43 And **he straitly charged him** [*very firmly told him not to tell anyone but the priest—see verse 44*], and forthwith [*immediately*] **sent him away;**

44 And saith unto him, See thou **say nothing to any man: but go thy way, shew thyself to the priest**, and offer for thy cleansing those things which Moses commanded [*see Leviticus, chapter 14*], for a testimony unto them.

45 **But he** [*the leper*] **went out, and began to publish it much, and to blaze abroad the matter** [*the leper went out and told everyone he could about his being healed*], insomuch that **Jesus could no more openly enter into the city** [*because so many people were crowding to see Him*], **but was without** [*outside of the city*] **in desert places: and they came to him from every quarter.**

MARK 2

AS THIS CHAPTER begins, Mark tells us that after some time, Jesus came back to Capernaum, where Peter and Andrew lived—see chapter 1, verses 21 and 29. Jesus made Capernaum His home base for the majority of His Galilean ministry.

1 AND again **he entered into Capernaum after some days**; and it was noised [*made known*] that he was in the house.

2 And **straightway** [*immediately*] **many** were **gathered** together, insomuch that there was **no room to receive them**, no, not so much as about the door: and he preached the word unto them.

The Palsied Man Is Healed

3 And **they come unto him, bringing one sick of the palsy**, which was borne of four [*carried by four people*].

4 And when they could not come nigh *[near]* unto him for the press *[because of the crowd]*, **they uncovered the roof** *[climbed up onto the housetop and took part of the roof off]* where he *[Jesus]* was: and when they had broken it *[the roof]* up, they **let down** *[lowered]* **the bed wherein the sick of the palsy lay.**

Jesus Forgives Sins

5 When Jesus saw their faith, **he said** unto the sick of the palsy, **Son, thy sins be forgiven thee** *[a reminder to all of us that it is through the Atonement of Christ that our sins are forgiven, through repentance]*.

6 But there were certain of the **scribes** *[Jewish religious leaders whose position was threatened by Christ's popularity]* **sitting there**, and reasoning in their hearts,

7 **Why doth this man** *[Jesus]* thus **speak blasphemies** *[disrespectful speaking of God; mocking sacred things]*? **who can forgive sins but God only?** *[Only God can forgive sins, so why is Jesus pretending to forgive sins? This is terrible!]*

8 And immediately when **Jesus** perceived in his spirit that they so reasoned within themselves *[when Jesus read their minds]*, he **said** unto them, **Why reason ye these things in your hearts** *[why are you thinking such thoughts]*?

9 **Whether is** it **easier to say** *[which is easier to say]* to the sick of the palsy, **Thy sins be forgiven thee; or** to say, **Arise, and take up thy bed, and walk?** *[In other words, which would be safer for a fake, which you think I am, to say, without being exposed as an imposter: "Your sins are forgiven." or "Be healed, pick up your bed and walk away."?]*

10 **But that ye may know that the Son of man** *[Christ; see Moses 6:57 where we see that "Son of Man of Holiness" (Heavenly Father) is another name for Jesus]* **hath power on earth to forgive sins**, (he saith to the sick of the palsy,)

11 I say unto thee, **Arise, and take up thy bed, and go thy way into thine house.**

12 And **immediately he arose, took up the bed**, and went forth before *[in front of]* them all; insomuch that they were all amazed, and glorified God, saying, We never saw it on this fashion *[we've never seen anything like this before!]*.

13 And **he went forth again by the sea side** *[the Sea of Galilee]*; **and all the multitude resorted** *[came]* **unto him, and he taught them.**

Matthew (Levi) Is Called

14 And as he passed by, **he saw Levi** *[Matthew, who will become an Apostle]* the son of Alphæus sitting at the receipt of custom *[collecting taxes—Matthew worked as a tax collector]*, **and said unto him, Follow me.** And **he arose and followed him.**

Have you noticed how quickly these great men, who are being called to follow the Savior, obey? Certainly, there is a lesson for us in this. The simple faith which enabled them to follow the Master so completely is the key also to our exaltation.

15 And it came to pass, that, **as Jesus sat at meat** *[at dinner]* **in his house** *[Levi's house]*, **many publicans** *[much-hated and despised tax collectors—see Bible Dictionary, under "Publicans"]* **and sinners sat** also together **with Jesus and his disciples:** for there were many, and they followed him *[Jesus]*.

If you read the reference in the Bible Dictionary, under "Publicans," you will see that Matthew (Levi) had no doubt been excommunicated from the Jewish religion because he was a tax collector. Such was the case with all Jews who chose to work for the Roman government as tax collectors. This is helpful background for verses 16–17, next.

16 And **when the scribes and Pharisees** *[Jewish religious leaders]* **saw him eat with publicans and sinners, they said** unto his disciples, **How is it** *[why is it]* **that he** *[Jesus]* **eateth and**

drinketh with publicans and sinners [*something the scribes and Pharisees would never lower themselves to do*]?

The Whole Need No Physician

17 When Jesus heard it, he saith unto them, **They that are whole** [*are well, not sick*] **have no need of the physician, but they that are sick:** I came not to call the righteous, but sinners to repentance. [*In other words, how can I help those who need my help if I refuse to ever associate with them?*]

Mark gives us a bit of background in the first part of verse 18, next, which helps us understand the question asked by the scribes and Pharisees in the last part.

18 And **the disciples** [*followers*] **of John** [*the Baptist*] **and of the Pharisees used to fast** [*go without food and drink for religious purposes*]: and **they** [*the scribes and Pharisees*] **come** [*came*] **and say** [*said*] **unto him** [*Jesus*], **Why do the disciples of John and of the Pharisees fast, but thy disciples fast not?**

19 **And Jesus said** unto them, **Can the children of the bridechamber fast, while the bridegroom is with them?** as long as they have the bridegroom with them, they cannot fast.

20 **But the days will come, when the bridegroom shall be taken away from them**, and **then shall they fast** in those days.

Understanding a bit of Jewish culture will help with verses 19–20, above. Wedding imagery is involved. Jesus is the "bridegroom," or groom, as we would say it. Faithful followers are the "bride." "Bridechamber" would be the place where the wedding feast is held and, symbolically, would be the land of Israel where the Savior was performing His mortal mission. While the groom and the bride are together, much celebrating and feasting–hearing and understanding the Savior's teachings–would take place. It would not make sense to mourn and fast at this time. But, when the Savior is crucified and taken from them, the "children of the bridechamber," the faithful Saints, will mourn and fast, including in the sense that they are "fasting" from His direct presence with them.

Next, Jesus will teach that people who are set in their ways do not usually accept new ideas, in this case, the true gospel.

21 **No man also seweth a piece of new cloth on an old garment**: else the new piece that filled it up taketh away [*tears away*] from the old, and the rent [*tear*] is made worse.

New Wine in Old Bottles

22 And **no man putteth new wine into old bottles** [*old, brittle leather wineskins*]: else the new wine doth burst the bottles [*the old, hardened leather containers*], and the wine is spilled, and the bottles will be marred [*damaged*]: but new wine must be put into new bottles [*new leather containers which are flexible*].

Jesus' Disciples Pluck Grain on the Sabbath

23 And it came to pass, that **he** [*Jesus*] **went through the corn** [*grain*] **fields on the sabbath** day; and **his disciples began**, as they went, **to pluck the ears of corn** [*to pick some heads of grain to eat*].

24 And **the Pharisees** [*very prominent Jewish religious leaders*] **said** unto him, Behold, **why do they** [*your disciples*] on the sabbath day **that which is not lawful** [*not legal according to Jewish law*]?

25 And **he said** unto them, **Have ye never read** [*haven't you read in the scriptures*] **what David did**, when he had need, and was an hungred [*was hungry*], he, and they that were with him?

26 **How he went into the house of God** [*the temple*] in the days of Abiathar the high priest, **and did eat the shewbread** [*the holy bread in the house of God*], which is not lawful [*legal*] to eat but for the priests, **and gave also to them** [*his soldiers*] **which were with him?**

The Sabbath Was Made for Man, Not Man for the Sabbath

27 And he [*Jesus*] said unto them [*the Pharisees*], **The sabbath was made for man, and not man for the sabbath:**

28 Therefore **the Son of man is Lord also of the Sabbath** [*in other words, I am Lord of the Sabbath*].

JST Mark 2:26–27

26 **Wherefore the Sabbath was given unto man for a day of rest; and also that man should glorify God, and not that man should not eat;**

27 For **the Son of Man made the Sabbath day** therefore the Son of Man is Lord also of the Sabbath.

In JST, verse 27, given above, it becomes clear that Jesus was telling these Pharisees that He, Himself made the Sabbath, as the Son of God, the promised Messiah, and thus is in charge of the Sabbath and makes the rules for it.

MARK 3

YOU HAVE PROBABLY noticed already that Mark's account is moving along rather quickly through the mortal ministry of the Savior. In this chapter, we are already into the second year of the three-year formal earthly ministry of the Master. Because Mark moves so rapidly, some members like to read it occasionally for the purpose of quickly refreshing their memory about the earthly ministry of Christ.

Healing of the Man with the Withered Hand on the Sabbath

1 AND **he** [*Christ*] **entered again into the synagogue** [*Jewish church building*]; and there was **a man there which had a withered hand.**

Perhaps you can envision the scowls on the faces of these Jewish religious leaders as they look to see if Jesus will dare to violate the Sabbath by healing someone on this holy day.

2 And **they** [*the Pharisees*] **watched him, whether he would heal him on the sabbath day**; that they might accuse him. [*The Pharisees were looking for reasons to have Jesus arrested.*]

3 And **he saith unto the man which had the withered hand, Stand forth** [*stand up*].

4 And **he saith unto them** [*the Pharisees, who were trying to trap him*], **Is it lawful** [*legal*] **to do good on the sabbath days**, or to do evil? **to save life**, or to kill? **But they held their peace** [*they didn't answer His question*].

Imagine the tenseness among the people in the synagogue at this point!

5 And **when he had looked round about on them** [*Pharisees*] **with anger** [*this is often referred to as "righteous indignation"*], being grieved for the hardness of their hearts, **he saith unto the man, Stretch forth thine hand.** And he stretched it out: **and his hand was restored whole** as the other [*healed, as good as his other hand*].

6 And **the Pharisees went forth** [*left*], **and straightway** [*immediately*] **took counsel** [*plotted*] **with the Herodians against him, how they might destroy him.**

The Herodians were a political party among the Jews and were normally enemies of the Pharisees. (See Bible Dictionary, under "Herodians.") So here we have a situation where two groups who are normally enemies have joined together to destroy Jesus.

Next, Mark tells us that people came from several day's journeys in all directions to join the multitudes that were following the Master.

7 But **Jesus withdrew himself with his disciples to the sea**: and a great **multitude** from Galilee [*in northern Israel*] **followed him**, and from Judæa [*southern Israel, including Jerusalem*],

8 And **from Jerusalem**, and from **Idumæa** [*an area west of the southern end of the Dead Sea*], and **from beyond Jordan** [*east of the Jordan River*]; and they about **Tyre** [*on the Mediterranean Sea, northwest of the Sea of Galilee*] and **Sidon** [*north of Tyre*], a great multitude, when they had

heard what great things he did, **came unto him.** *[Multitudes of people from all over the country are now following Jesus around.]*

9 And **he spake to his disciples, that a small ship should wait on him** *[ask them to get a small boat for Him]* **because of the multitude**, lest they should throng him *[press in on Him too much]*.

10 For he had healed many; insomuch that **they pressed upon him for to touch him**, as many as had plagues *[diseases]*.

11 And **unclean** *[evil]* **spirits**, when they saw him, **fell down before him**, and cried, **saying, Thou art the Son of God.**

12 And **he straitly charged them** *[gave the evil spirits strict orders]* **that they should not make him known** *[that they should not bear witness of Him]*.

An important message for us in verse 12, above, is that righteous testimony, accompanied by the witness of the Holy Ghost, cannot come from an unrighteous source.

The Calling and Ordaining of the Twelve Apostles

13 And **he goeth up into a mountain**, and **calleth unto him whom he would** *[those whom he wanted to come]*: and they came unto him.

14 And **he ordained twelve** *[Apostles]*, that they should be with him, and that he might send them forth **to preach,**

15 And to have power **to heal sicknesses**, and to **cast out devils:**

16 And Simon he surnamed **Peter;**

17 And **James** the son of Zebedee, and **John** the brother of James; and he surnamed them Boanerges, which is, The sons of thunder:

18 And **Andrew**, and **Philip**, and **Bartholomew**, and **Matthew**, and **Thomas**, and **James** the son of Alphæus, and **Thaddæus**, and **Simon** the Canaanite,

19 And **Judas Iscariot**, which also betrayed him: and they went into an house.

Next, we see that the Savior continued to minister to the crowds to the point that the Apostles became worried that He would ruin His health.

20 And **the multitude cometh together again, so that they could not so much as eat bread** *[didn't even have time to eat]*.

21 And when **his friends** heard of it, they **went out to lay hold on him** *[to take Him away from the crowds so He could eat and get some rest; see McConkie,* Doctrinal New Testament Commentary, *Vol. 1, p. 211]*: for they **said, He is beside himself** *[not being reasonable, working too hard, not taking care of Himself]*.

Next, Mark informs us that the hypocritical Jewish religious leaders have journeyed all the way from Jerusalem to discredit Jesus, and now preach that His miracles and preaching are done through the power of the devil.

22 And **the scribes** *[Jewish religious leaders, interpreters of the religious laws and rules for daily living]* which **came down from Jerusalem** *[they came all the way from Jerusalem to Galilee to try to trap Jesus]* **said, He hath Beelzebub** *[Satan; see Bible Dictionary, under "Beelzebub"]*, **and by the prince of the devils** *[by the power of Satan]* **casteth he out devils.**

Watch now as the Savior responds to their accusations with clear logic.

23 And **he called them** *[the scribes]* **unto him, and said** unto them in parables, **How can Satan cast out Satan?**

24 And **if a kingdom be divided against itself, that kingdom cannot stand.**

25 And **if a house be divided against itself, that house cannot stand.**

26 And **if Satan rise up against himself** *[fights against his own evil spirits]*, **and be divided, he**

cannot stand [*will not continue as a powerful force*], but hath an end.

27 **No man can enter into a strong man's house, and spoil his goods, except he will first bind the strong man; and then he will spoil his house.**

In other words, Satan can't fight against himself and still maintain a strong force for evil.

Without the help of the JST, we are confused as we go from verse 27, above, to verse 28, next. But with the JST, we see that a verse has been left out here in the Bible. We will add it here, plus the one that follows it in the JST.

JST Mark 3:21–22

21 And then came certain men unto him, accusing him, saying, Why do ye receive sinners, seeing thou makest thyself the Son of God [*since You claim to be the Son of God*].

22 But he answered them and said, Verily I say unto you, All sins which men have committed, when they repent, shall be forgiven them; for I came to preach repentance unto the sons of men.

As you can see from JST verse 22, above, Jesus answers their question, telling them that He came to earth to teach sinners and invite them to repent, and that is why He associates with them.

Beginning with verse 28, next, the Savior continues by explaining that denying the Holy Ghost is not forgivable.

28 Verily I say unto you, All sins shall be forgiven unto the sons of men [*people*], and blasphemies [*speaking against God and holy things*] wherewith soever they shall blaspheme:

29 But **he that shall blaspheme against the Holy Ghost hath never forgiveness**, but is in danger of eternal damnation:

30 Because they said, He hath an unclean spirit. [*Christ's teachings in the above verses were in response to the claims of the scribes that Jesus was doing miracles by the power of Satan, including casting out evil spirits.*]

The JST adds much clarification for verses 28–30. Remember, as stated earlier in this study guide, the verses in the JST (Joseph Smith Translation of the Bible) often have different numbers than their counterparts in the King James Version of the Bible (the one we use for English speaking Latter-day Saints).

JST Mark 3:22–25

23 And blasphemies, wherewith soever they shall blaspheme, shall be forgiven them that come unto me, and do the works which they see me do.

24 But there is a sin which shall not be forgiven. He that shall blaspheme against the Holy Ghost, hath never forgiveness; but is in danger of being cut down out of the world. And they shall inherit eternal damnation.

25 And this he said unto them because they said, He hath an unclean spirit.

Simply put, denying the Holy Ghost means knowing full well, by the power of the Holy Ghost, that God exists, that the Church is true, etc., then going completely against that sure knowledge, trying to destroy the Church and knowledge of God. In other words, it means becoming like Satan, thinking like he does and acting like he does. See D&C 76:31–35. See also *Teachings of the Prophet Joseph Smith*, p. 358.

31 There came then his brethren and his mother, and, standing without [*outside*], sent unto him, calling him.

JST Mark 3:26

26 **While he was yet with them, and while he was yet speaking, there came then some** of his brethren, and his mother; and standing without, sent unto him, calling unto him.

32 And the multitude sat about him, and they said unto him, **Behold, thy mother and thy brethren without** [*on the outside of the crowd*] **seek for thee.**

33 **And he answered** them, saying, **Who is my mother, or my brethren?**

34 And **he looked round about on them which sat about him, and said, Behold my mother and my brethren!** [*In other words, all of you are my family.*]

Verse 35, next, teaches us a major lesson.

35 For **whosoever shall do the will of God, the same is my brother, and my sister, and mother.**

JST Matthew 12:44, adds understanding to verse

35. "And he gave them charge concerning her [*asked them to take good care of His mother while He continued on His mission*], saying, I go my way, for my Father hath sent me. For whosoever shall do the will of my Father which is in heaven, the same is my brother, and sister, and mother."

MARK 4

JESUS IS STILL in Galilee at this point. He will use many parables to teach the crowds that gather to Him now by the Sea of Galilee.

1 AND **he began again to teach by the sea side**: and there was gathered unto him a great multitude [*a large crowd of people had gathered*], so that **he entered into a ship**, and sat in the sea [*the ship in which He sat was just a little way off shore*]; and the whole multitude was by the sea on the land.

2 And **he taught them** many things **by parables**, and said unto them in his doctrine,

The Parable of the Sower

3 Hearken; Behold, **there went out a sower to sow** [*a farmer went out to plant seeds*]:

4 And it came to pass, as he sowed [*planted seeds*], **some fell by the way side** [*the footpath*], and the fowls [*birds*] of the air came and devoured it up [*ate the seeds*].

5 And **some fell on stony ground**, where it had not much earth [*the soil was very shallow*]; and immediately it sprang up [*started to grow*], because it had no depth of earth:

6 But when the sun was up, it was scorched; and because it had no root, it withered away [*dried up and died*].

7 And **some fell among thorns**, and the thorns grew up, and choked it, and it yielded no fruit [*did not produce food*].

Sometimes in the scriptures, the word "thorns" is symbolic of wicked behaviors, false doctrines, wicked people, bad habits, and so forth.

8 And **other fell on good ground**, and did yield fruit that sprang up and increased; and brought forth, some thirty, and some sixty, and some an hundred.

The Savior will explain this parable, starting in verse 13.

9 And he said unto them, **He that hath ears to hear, let him hear** [*people who are spiritually in tune should pay close attention to what I am teaching*].

10 And when he was alone, they that were about him with the twelve asked of him the parable [*asked Him to explain the parable*].

JST MARK 4:9

9 And when he was alone with the twelve, and **they that believed in him**, they that were about him with the twelve asked of him the parable.

As you saw in JST Mark 4:9, above, those who were asking Jesus for help in understanding the parable, were believers. This is an important fact as we move on to verse 11, next, where the Master explains why He teaches in parables to these people.

11 And he said unto them, **Unto you it is given to know the mystery** [*the basic teachings*] of the kingdom of God [*because you have a desire to learn spiritual things, you will be given understanding of the gospel*]: **but unto them that are without** [*those who are outside the Church and don't want to learn about these things*], **all these things are done in parables**:

12 That seeing they may see, and not perceive [*not understand*]; and hearing they may hear, and not understand; lest at any time they should be converted, and their sins should be forgiven them.

Verse 12 is a rather strong statement by Jesus indicating that there is truth all around us but if people don't want to pay attention to it, they won't understand it and won't be forgiven of their sins. The word "may," as used in the context of verse 12, above, seems to be saying that they have their agency.

13 **And he said unto them** [*the believers who asked the question in JST, verse 9, above*], **Know ye not this parable** [*don't you understand this parable*]**?** and how then will ye know [*understand*] all parables?

The Interpretation of the Parable of the Sower

14 **The sower** [*symbolic of the Savior, prophets, missionaries, members*] **soweth** [*plants*] **the word** [*teaches the gospel*].

15 And these [*this first group of people*] are **they by the way side**, where the word is sown [*where the gospel is taught*]; but **when they have heard, Satan cometh immediately, and taketh away the word that was sown in their hearts** [*Satan gets them to quickly disregard what they have heard of the true gospel; thus, the "seeds" don't even start to grow in their hearts*].

16 And these [*the second group of people*] are they likewise which are sown [*planted*] on **stony ground**; who, when they have heard the word [*the true gospel*], **immediately receive it with gladness;**

17 And **have no root** in themselves [*but don't do what is necessary for the gospel to take root in their hearts*], and so endure but for a time: afterward, **when affliction or persecution ariseth** for the word's [*gospel's*] sake, immediately **they are offended.** [*Peer pressure, social, family pressure, and so forth, causes them to reject the gospel and the beginning testimony which they had.*]

18 And these [*the third group of people*] are they which are **sown among thorns**; such as hear the word,

19 And **the cares of this world, and the deceitfulness of riches, and the lusts of other things entering in, choke the word**, and it becometh unfruitful. [*Worldliness, materialism, lustfulness etc. choke the gospel out of their lives so that it doesn't make righteous Saints out of them.*]

20 And these [*the fourth group*] are they which are sown on **good ground**; such as **hear the word** [*the gospel*], and **receive it** [*accept it and apply it in their lives*], and **bring forth fruit**, some thirtyfold, some sixty, and some an hundred [*the gospel is very productive in their lives, and they are very productive in blessing the lives of others*].

The symbolism of a seed growing in one's heart and life reminds us that it takes time for the gospel to grow in our lives (as taught in Alma 32) and that we must nourish it by being faithful to the teachings of the gospel.

The Parable of the Candle under the Bushel

21 ¶ And he said unto them, **Is a candle** brought **to be put under a bushel**, or under a bed? and not to be set on a candlestick? [*In other words, should the light of the gospel be hidden from people? Answer: No!*]

The paragraph mark, ¶, at the beginning of verse 21 in our Bible indicates that there is now a change to a new topic.

22 For **there is nothing hid, which shall not be manifested**; neither was any thing kept secret, but that it should come abroad. [*All things will eventually be revealed to the righteous, who allow the "seed" to continue growing in their hearts and lives. See* Doctrinal New Testament Commentary, *Vol. 1, page 291.*]

23 **If any man have ears to hear, let him hear** [*you who are spiritually in tune, listen carefully to what I say*].

The Law of the Harvest

24 And he said unto them, Take heed what ye hear [*pay close attention to what I am teaching*]: **with what measure ye mete** [*the attention and obedience you give to what I am teaching*], **it shall be measured to you** [*will determine how much more truth you get—compare with Alma 12:10*]: and **unto you that hear** [*hear and apply it in your lives*] **shall more be given.**

THE SOWER, by Liz Lemon Swindle

The Doctrine of "Receiving"

25 For he that hath, to him shall be given: and he that hath not, from him shall be taken even that which he hath.

JST Mark 4:20

20 And he said unto them, Take heed what ye hear; for with what measure ye mete, it shall be measured to you; and **unto you that continue to receive, shall more be given**; for **he that receiveth, to him shall be given**; but **he that continueth not to receive**, from him shall be taken even that which he hath.

Alma summarizes what the Savior taught in verses 24–25 and JST verse 20, above:

Alma 12:9-11

9 And now Alma began to expound these things unto him, saying: **It is given unto many to know the mysteries** [*"mysteries" are the basics of the gospel, which are mysteries to the unbelievers*] **of God**; nevertheless they are laid under a strict command that they shall not impart only according to the portion of his word which he doth grant unto the children of men, **according to the heed and diligence which they give unto him**.

10 And therefore, **he that will harden his heart, the same receiveth the lesser** portion of the word; and **he that will not harden his heart, to him is given the greater** portion of the word, until it is given unto him to know the mysteries of God **until he know them in full**.

11 And **they that will harden their hearts, to them is given the lesser portion of the word until they know nothing concerning his mysteries**; and then they are taken captive by the devil, and led by his will down to destruction. Now this is what is meant by the chains of hell.

The Parable of the Growing Seed

26 And he said, **So is the kingdom of God** [*this is like the Kingdom of God*], **as if a man should cast seed into the ground;**

27 And should sleep, and rise night and day, **and the seed should spring and grow up, he knoweth not how.**

28 For the earth bringeth forth fruit of herself; first the blade, then the ear, after that the full corn in the ear.

29 But **when the fruit is brought forth, immediately he putteth in the sickle, because the harvest is come.**

Interpretation of the Parable of the Growing Seed

This parable (verses 26–29) is only recorded in Mark. Apostle James E. Talmage interpreted it in his book *Jesus the Christ*, as follows:

"The sower in this story is the authorized preacher of the word of God; he implants the seed of the gospel in the hearts of men, knowing not what the issue shall be. Passing on to similar or other ministry elsewhere, attending to his appointed duties in other fields, he, with faith and hope, leaves with God the result of his planting. In the harvest of souls converted through his labor, he is enriched and made to rejoice. This parable was probably directed more particularly to the apostles and the most devoted of the other disciples, rather than to the multitude at large; the lesson is one for teachers, for workers in the Lord's fields, for the chosen sowers and reapers. It is of perennial value, as truly applicable today as when first spoken. Let the seed be sown, even though the sower be straightway called to other fields or other duties; in the gladsome harvest he shall find his recompense." (*Jesus the Christ*, pp. 289–290.)

The Parable of the Mustard Seed

30 And he said, **Whereunto shall we liken the kingdom of God?** or with what comparison shall we compare it?

31 **It is like a grain of mustard seed**, which, when it is sown in the earth, is less [*smaller*] than all the seeds that be in the earth:

32 But **when it is sown** [*planted*], **it groweth** up, **and becometh greater** [*larger*] **than all herbs**, and shooteth out great [*big*] branches; so that the fowls [*birds*] of the air may lodge under the shadow of it.

Interpretation of the Parable of the Mustard Seed
Joseph Smith explained this parable. "And again, another parable put He forth unto them, having an allusion to the Kingdom that should be set up, just previous to or at the time of the harvest, which reads as follows—'The Kingdom of Heaven is like a grain of mustard seed, which a man took and sowed in his field: which indeed is the least of all seeds: but, when it is grown, it is the greatest among herbs, and becometh a tree, so that the birds of the air come and lodge in the branches thereof.' Now we can discover plainly that this figure is given to represent the Church as it shall come forth in the last days."

For more of the Prophet's explanation, see *Teachings of the Prophet Joseph Smith*, pp. 98-99 and page 159.

MARK

33 And with many such parables [*stories that teach*] spake [*spoke*] he the word [*gospel*] unto them, **as they were able to hear it.**

JST Mark 4:26

26 And with many such parables spake he the word unto them, **as they were able to bear**; but without a parable spake he not unto them.

34 But without a parable spake he not unto them [*the people*]: and when they were alone, he expounded [*explained*] all things to his disciples.

The Tempest Rages and the Sea Is Calmed

35 And the same day, when the even was come [*in the evening*], he saith unto them [*the disciples*], **Let us pass over unto the other side** [*of the Sea of Galilee*].

36 And when they had sent away the multitude, **they took him** even as he was **in the ship**. And there were also with him other little ships.

37 And **there arose a great storm** of wind, and **the waves beat into the ship**, so that it was now full [*of water*].

38 And **he was** in the hinder [*back*] part of the ship, **asleep on a pillow**: and **they awake him, and say** unto him, **Master, carest thou not that we perish** [*don't You care if we drown*]?

39 And **he arose, and rebuked the wind** [*commanded the wind to stop*], **and said unto the sea, Peace, be still.** And the wind ceased, **and there was a great calm.**

40 **And he said unto them**, Why are ye so fearful? **how is it that ye have no faith?**

41 And they feared exceedingly, and said one to another, **What manner of man is this, that even the wind and the sea obey him?**

MARK 5

WE ARE STILL studying the second year of the Savior's earthly mission, and are still in Galilee, as this chapter of Mark begins.

1 AND **they came over unto the other side of the sea** [*of Galilee*], **into the country of the Gadarenes.**

Healing a Man Possessed with Evil Spirits

2 And when he was come out of the ship, **immediately there met him out of the tombs a man with an unclean spirit** [*who was possessed by evil spirits*],

3 Who had his dwelling among the tombs [*who lived among the tombs*]; and **no man could bind him**, no, not with chains:

4 Because that he had been often bound with fetters [*leg irons*] and chains, and the chains had been plucked asunder [*torn apart*] by him, and the fetters broken in pieces: **neither could any man tame him.**

5 And always, night and day, he was in the mountains, and in the tombs, crying, and cutting himself with stones.

6 **But when he saw Jesus afar off, he ran and worshipped him** [*bowed down in front of him*],

7 And cried with a loud voice, **and said, What have I** [*the evil spirit*] **to do with thee, Jesus**, thou

Son of the most high God? I adjure [*beg*] thee by God, that thou torment me not.

8 **For he said** [*Jesus had said*] unto him, **Come out of the man, thou unclean spirit.**

9 And he [*Jesus*] asked him, **What is thy name?** And he [*the evil spirit who was speaking for all the evil spirits who possessed the man*] answered, saying, **My name is Legion: for we are many.**

10 **And he** [*the evil spirit spokesman*] **besought** him much [*pleaded*] **that he would not send them** [*the evil spirits*] **away out of the country.**

Evil Spirits Enter about 2,000 Swine and They Drown

11 Now there was there nigh [*near*] unto the mountains **a great** [*large*] **herd of swine** [*pigs*] feeding.

12 And **all the devils besought him, saying, Send us into the swine**, that we may enter into them.

13 And forthwith [*immediately*] **Jesus gave them leave** [*permission*]. **And the unclean spirits went out, and entered into the swine**: and the herd **ran** violently down a steep place **into the sea**, (they were about two thousand;) **and were choked** [*drowned*] in the sea.

One might wonder why Jesus allowed the evil spirits He cast out of the man to enter into the pigs. We don't know. We do wonder what the people of that area were doing raising pigs, since pork was forbidden under the Law of Moses (see Leviticus 11:7). However, it also appears that most of the citizens of the area were not Israelites, so we will have to wait until another day for an authoritative answer on this issue.

14 And **they that fed the swine** [*those in charge of the herd of pigs*] **fled** [*ran away*], **and told it** [*what happened to the herd*] **in the city**, and in the country. And they [*the people who owned the swine*] went out to see what it was that was done.

15 **And they come to Jesus, and see him** [*the man*] **that** was possessed with the devil, and **had the legion** [*of evil spirits in him before Jesus cast them out*], **sitting, and clothed, and in his right mind:** and they [*the owners of the herd*] were afraid.

16 And they that saw it [*the people who had seen the whole thing as it happened*] told them [*the owners of the pigs*] how it befell [*what happened*] to him that was possessed with the devil, and also concerning the swine.

17 **And they began to pray** [*request*] **him** [*Jesus*] **to depart** out of their coasts [*area*].

It would be nice if these people who owned the herd of swine had been spiritually sensitive enough to recognize the great miracle which had been performed by the Savior and had been converted. However, sadly, such was not the case. It seems that they were so set on material things that, rather than asking the Master to teach them, they simply requested that he leave their area so that they would not risk suffering another economic disaster.

Next, beginning with verse 18, we see that the man who had been healed from the evil spirits wanted to go with Jesus. But the Master asked him to stay home as a witness of the healing that had taken place so that others in that region would have a better chance to hear and accept the gospel.

18 And **when he was come into the ship, he that had been possessed with the devil** [*evil spirits*] **prayed** [*requested*] him **that he might be with him.** [*The man healed of the evil spirits wanted to go with Jesus.*]

19 Howbeit [*however*] **Jesus suffered** [*allowed*] **him not, but saith unto him, Go home to thy friends, and tell them how great things the Lord hath done for thee,** and hath had compassion on thee. [*In other words, Jesus asked him to go home and be a witness of the healing so that others in that area could know of Christ.*]

20 **And he** [*the man who had been healed*] departed, and **began to publish** [*tell*] in Decapolis [*the country south and southeast of the Sea of Galilee*] **how** [*what*] **great things Jesus had done for him: and all men did marvel.**

21 And when **Jesus** was **passed over again by ship unto the other side** [*of the Sea of Galilee*], much people gathered unto him: and he was nigh [*near*] unto the sea.

The Healing of Jairus' Daughter

22 And, behold, there cometh one of the rulers of the synagogue [*Jewish church building*], **Jairus** by name; and when he **saw him**, he **fell at his feet**,

23 And **besought him** [*pleaded*] greatly, saying, **My little daughter lieth at the point of death**: I pray thee, **come and lay thy hands on her, that she may be healed**; and she shall live.

24 And **Jesus went with him**; and much people followed him, and thronged [*crowded, pushed against*] him.

A Woman Who Had Been Bleeding for Twelve Years Is Healed by Touching the Savior's Clothing

25 And **a certain woman, which had an issue of blood** [*had been bleeding for*] twelve years,

26 And had suffered many things of [*had suffered through treatments by*] many physicians, and had spent all that she had [*to pay the medical bills*], and was nothing bettered, but rather grew worse,

27 When she had heard of Jesus, **came in the press behind** [*pushed her way through the crowd and came up behind Jesus*], **and touched his garment.**

Next, we see the beautiful, simple faith of this woman.

28 For she said, **If I may touch but his clothes, I shall be whole** [*healed*].

29 And **straightway** [*immediately*] the fountain [*source*] of her blood was dried up; and **she felt in her body that she was healed of that plague.**

Next, the Savior, who is being crowded and pushed from every side by people in the huge crowd, startles His Apostles by asking who had just touched Him.

30 And **Jesus**, immediately knowing in himself that virtue [*strength*] had gone out of him, turned him about in the press [*crowd*], and **said, Who touched my clothes?**

31 And **his disciples said** unto him, **Thou seest the multitude thronging** [*pressing against*] **thee, and sayest thou, Who touched me?**

32 **And he looked round about to see** her that had done this thing.

33 But **the woman** fearing and trembling, knowing what was done in her [*knowing that she had been healed*], came and **fell down before him, and told him all the truth** [*that she was the one who touched Him*].

Notice how tenderly and quickly the Savior puts this worried woman's mind and heart at ease. Perhaps you've noticed that He is anxious to do the same for you and me.

34 **And he said** unto her**, Daughter, thy faith hath made thee whole; go in peace** [*don't be afraid of me*]**, and be whole** [*healed*] of thy plague.

Remember that Jesus was on His way to Jairus' home when He stopped to comfort the woman who had been hemorrhaging for twelve years and had touched His clothes. Now, as He comforts the woman, word comes that Jairus' daughter has died.

35 **While he yet spake, there came** from the ruler [*Jairus, verse 22*] of the synagogue's house **certain** [*people*] **which said, Thy daughter is dead:** why troublest thou the Master any further?

36 **As soon as Jesus heard** the word that was spoken, **he saith unto the ruler** of the synagogue [*Jairus*], **Be not afraid, only believe.**

Have you noticed that we are being taught lessons about the power of faith here?

37 And he suffered [*allowed*] no man to follow him, save [*except*] Peter, and James, and John the brother of James.

38 And **he cometh to the house** of the ruler of the synagogue, **and seeth the tumult** [*commotion*], and them that wept and wailed greatly [*the mourners, who, according to Jewish custom, were to make a big scene of noise and crying when someone had died*].

39 And **when he was come in, he saith** unto them [*the mourners*], Why make ye this ado [*fuss*], and weep? **the damsel** [*girl*] **is not dead, but sleepeth.**

Notice that the Savior now arranges for this to be a sacred, private miracle.

40 **And they laughed him** [*Jesus*] **to scorn** [*made fun of him*]. But when **he** had **put them all out,** he **taketh the father** and the **mother** of the damsel, **and them that were with him** [*Peter, James, and John—see verse 37*], and entereth in where the damsel was lying.

41 And he **took the damsel by the hand**, and said unto her, Talitha cumi; which is, being interpreted, **Damsel, I say unto thee, arise.**

42 And straightway [*immediately*] **the damsel arose, and walked**; for she was of the age of twelve years. And they were astonished with a great astonishment [*an understatement, no doubt*].

43 **And he charged them straitly** [*instructed them firmly*] **that no man should know it** [*that he had raised her from the dead, which he did—see heading to Mark, chapter 5 in our Bible*]; and commanded that something should be given her to eat.

We have not been told why Jesus instructed them not to tell anyone that he had actually raised her from the dead. Perhaps, as is often the case, it was a private, sacred matter for the parents and the three Apostles and was to be kept extra sacred by keeping it private.

MARK 6

JESUS WILL NOW return to His hometown of Nazareth, in Galilee, and be rejected there for the second time during His three-year ministry.

The Second Rejection at Nazareth

1 AND **he** went out from thence [*from there*], and **came into his own country** [*his hometown, Nazareth*]; and his disciples follow him.

2 And when **the sabbath day** was come, **he began to teach in the synagogue** [*the local Jewish church building*]: and **many hearing him were astonished**, saying, From whence hath this man these things [*where does this man get all these teachings*]? and what wisdom is this which is given unto him, that even such mighty works are wrought [*done*] by his hands?

3 **Is not this the carpenter**, the son of Mary, the brother of James, and Joses, and of Juda, and Simon? and are not his sisters here with us? And **they were offended at him** [*felt that Jesus was an embarrassment to them and their community*].

Jesus had been trained as a carpenter by Joseph, Mary's husband. The citizens of Nazareth knew the family, including Jesus, and could not accept that Jesus was anything but a common man. They were disturbed that one of their own citizens was causing such an uproar in the country.

Verse three, above, gives us information about the size of Joseph and Mary's own family, which they had after Jesus was born. They had four sons, whose names are mentioned in this verse, and at least three daughters. The Greek plural form for the word "sisters" in verse three means three or more. It is also interesting to note that it is generally believed that James, one of Christ's half-brothers mentioned in this verse, was the writer of the book of James in the New Testament. See Bible Dictionary, under "James, Epistle of."

4 **But Jesus said unto them, A prophet is not without honour, but in his own country**, and among his own kin, and in his own house.

5 And **he could there** *[in Nazareth]* **do no mighty work**, save *[except]* that he laid his hands upon a few sick folk, and healed them.

One of the important messages we can learn from verses 4–5, above, is that faith or lack thereof has a direct bearing on whether or not the work of the Lord goes forth.

6 And he marvelled *[NIV was amazed]* because of their unbelief. And he went round about the villages, teaching.

The Twelve Called and Instructed

7 And **he called unto him the twelve** *[the twelve Apostles]*, and **began to send them forth by two and two**; and **gave them power over unclean** *[evil]* **spirits**;

MARK

This is a time of training for these twelve men. They will be sent out to serve, will run into some situations and problems they are not able to understand or solve, will return with an intense desire to learn more, and will be even more ready to be taught.

8 And commanded them that they should **take nothing** for their journey, **save** *[except]* **a staff** *[walking stick]* only; **no scrip** *[a bag, usually made of leather and used for carrying food—see Bible Dictionary, under "Scrip"]*, **no bread, no money** in their purse:

9 But **be shod with sandals** *[wear sandals]*; and **not** put on **two coats**.

Sandals were worn by the common people in the days of the Savior and his Apostles. Shoes were very expensive and were worn only by the very wealthy.

It is apparent that He is teaching them to have faith in and be dependent on God. They will need this after He is gone.

10 And he said unto them, In what place soever ye enter into an house, there abide *[stay]* till ye depart from that place *[town or city]*.

The Purpose of Shaking the Dust off their Feet When Rejected

11 And whosoever shall not receive you, nor hear you, when ye depart thence, **shake off the dust under your feet for a testimony against them** *[as a witness that you tried to teach them the gospel but they rejected you]*. Verily I say unto you, It shall be more tolerable for Sodom and Gomorrha in the day of judgment, than for that city.

We understand from the scriptures that those who have a fair set of chances to hear, understand, and accept the gospel here in mortality, but reject it, will be in a worse position in spirit prison than those who did not have a chance here. Apostle Bruce R. McConkie explains this as follows: "It shall be more tolerable in the day of judgment, for heathen nations who had no opportunity to accept the gospel in this life, than for the more enlightened races who rejected the truths of salvation when such were offered to them" (*Doctrinal New Testament Commentary*, Vol. 1, page 327).

12 And **they went out, and preached** that men should repent.

13 And they **cast out many devils**, and **anointed with oil** *[part of the ordinance of administering to the sick—see James 5:14–15 for instructions on administering to the sick]* **many that were sick, and healed them.**

King Herod Fears that Jesus Is John the Baptist Returned from the Dead

14 And **king Herod heard of him**; (for his name was spread abroad:) *[Jesus had become famous]* and **he** *[Herod]* **said, That John the Baptist was risen from the dead**, and therefore mighty works do shew forth themselves in him *[King Herod had beheaded John the Baptist and was now worried that Jesus was actually John the Baptist come back alive]*.

15 Others said, That it *[Jesus]* is Elias *[Elijah the prophet]*. And others said, That it is a prophet, or as one of the prophets.

16 But when **Herod** heard thereof, he **said, It is John, whom I beheaded: he is risen from the dead.**

Next, in verses 17–28, Mark tells us why Herod was so afraid that John the Baptist had returned from the dead.

17 For **Herod himself had sent forth and laid hold upon** [*arrested*] **John, and bound him in prison for Herodias' sake** [*as requested by Herodias*], **his brother Philip's wife: for he had married her** [*Herod had married his own brother's wife, Herodias*].

18 **For John had said unto Herod, It is not lawful** [*legal*] **for thee to have thy brother's wife.**

19 Therefore **Herodias had a quarrel against him** [*was very angry at John the Baptist*], **and would have killed him; but she could not** [*could not talk her husband, King Herod, into having John killed*]:

20 For **Herod feared John, knowing that he was a just** [*righteous*] **man and an holy**, and observed [*protected; see Mark 6:20, footnote c*] him; and when he [*Herod*] heard him [*John*], he did many things, and heard him gladly [*Herod felt that John the Baptist was a prophet and gladly listened to his teaching*].

JST Mark 6:21

21 For Herod feared John, knowing that he was a just man, and **a holy man, and one who feared God and observed to worship him**; and when he heard him he **did many things for him**, and heard him gladly.

21 And when a convenient day was come, that **Herod on his birthday made a supper** to his lords, high captains, and chief estates of Galilee;

22 And **when the daughter of the said Herodias** [*her name was Salome; see Bible Dictionary, under "Salome"*] **came in, and danced**, and pleased Herod and them that sat with him, **the king said** unto the damsel, **Ask of me whatsoever thou wilt, and I will give it thee.**

23 **And he sware** unto [*promised*] her, **Whatsoever thou shalt ask of me, I will give it thee, unto the half of my kingdom.**

24 **And she went forth, and said unto her mother** [*Herodias*], **What shall I ask? And she** [*Herodias*] **said, The head of John the Baptist.**

25 **And she** [*Salome*] **came** in straightway [*immediately*] with haste **unto the king, and asked**, saying, I will that thou **give me** by and by [*immediately ("by and by" has changed in our day to mean "eventually")*] in a charger [*on a platter*] **the head of John the Baptist.**

26 And **the king was exceeding** [*very*] **sorry**; yet for his oath's sake [*because he had promised*], and for their sakes which sat with him [*because of peer pressure*], he would not reject her [*refuse granting her request*].

27 And **immediately the king sent an executioner, and commanded his** [*John the Baptist's*] **head to be brought**: and he [*the executioner*] went and beheaded him in the prison,

28 And **brought his head** in a charger, **and gave it to the damsel** [*Salome*]: and **the damsel gave it to her mother** [*Herodias*].

29 And when **his disciples** [*John's followers*] heard of it, they came and **took up his corpse** [*body*], **and laid it in a tomb.**

Next, having given us an account of the death of John the Baptist, Mark returns to his account of the Apostles who have been out preaching and healing the sick (as instructed by the Savior—see verses 12 and 13), as they return and report what they have been doing to the Savior.

30 **And the apostles gathered themselves together unto Jesus, and told him all things**, both what **they had done, and** what they had **taught.**

Even though it may sound like an obvious and simple thing, the message in verse 31, next, that members in busy Church callings need time out to rest, is an important matter.

31 **And he said unto them, Come ye yourselves apart into a desert place** *[a quiet place where we can be alone]*, **and rest a while**: for there were many *[crowds of people]* coming and going, and they had no leisure *[time to themselves]* so much as to eat.

32 And they departed into a desert place by ship privately.

Watch the Savior's response now, in verses 33–34, as the people run in order to arrive in advance at the anticipated arrival point of Jesus and His weary Apostles when their ship comes to shore.

33 And the people saw them departing, and **many** knew him *[had heard of Jesus]*, and **ran afoot** *[on foot]* thither *[to where they figured Jesus and his Apostles were going in the ship]* out of all cities, **and outwent them** *[beat them to their destination]*, **and came together unto him.**

34 **And Jesus, when he came out** *[of the ship]*, saw much people *[the large crowd]*, and **was moved with compassion toward them,** because they were as sheep not having a shepherd: and he began to teach them many things.

Feeding the 5,000

35 And **when the day was** now **far spent, his disciples came unto him, and said,** This is a desert place, and now the time is far passed *[the day is about over]*:

36 **Send them away, that they may go** into the country round about, and **into the villages, and buy themselves bread: for they have nothing to eat.**

Watch now as the Savior startles His Apostles-in-training by requesting that they feed the multitude (5,000 men plus women and children—see Matthew 14:21).

37 He answered and said unto them, **Give ye them to eat.** And **they say** unto him, **Shall we go and buy two hundred pennyworth of bread, and give them to eat?**

As you can see in verse 37, above, in reply, they told Him that enough bread to feed such a crowd would cost two hundred pennies. A penny, or Greek denarius, was an average days wage for a workman—see Mark 6:37, footnote a. In our day, assuming an average day's wage to be about $150, the cost of feeding the crowd, which had gathered to hear the Savior, would be about $30,000 and would be somewhat overwhelming to the Apostles.

38 **He saith** unto them, **How many loaves** *[of bread]* **have ye?** go and see. And when they knew, they say, **Five, and two fishes.**

Perhaps there is a subtle message that might easily be missed in verses 39–40, next. It is that in order to receive nourishment (spiritual "bread") from the Savior, we must become part of His kingdom, which is well-organized here on earth. Notice how He has His Apostles organize these people by hundreds and by fifties. This can remind us of the fact that He organizes us in wards and branches, in order that the blessings of the gospel be made available to us.

39 **And he commanded them to make all** *[the people]* **sit down by companies** *[groups]* upon the green grass.

40 And they sat down **in ranks, by hundreds, and by fifties.**

41 And **when he had taken the five loaves and the two fishes, he looked up to heaven, and blessed, and brake** *[broke]* the loaves, **and gave** them to his disciples to set before them *[the people]*; and the two fishes divided he among them all.

42 And **they did all eat, and were filled.**

Among other possible messages, verse 42, above, can certainly be symbolic of the fact that when we come unto Christ and partake of His nourishment for us, our spiritual need can be completely filled (exaltation).

43 **And they took up** *[picked up the leftovers]* **twelve baskets full** of the fragments *[pieces of bread]*, and of the fishes.

44 And they that did eat of the loaves were **about five thousand** men *[plus women and children; see Matthew 14:21]*.

45 **And** straightway *[immediately]* **he** *[Jesus]* **constrained** *[asked]* **his disciples to get into**

the ship, and to go to the other side [*of the Sea of Galilee*] before [*ahead of him*] unto Bethsaida, **while he sent away the people** [*while He dismissed the 5,000*].

It is helpful to remember that this is a time of training, learning faith, obedience, etc., for these Apostles. It was probably somewhat frustrating for them to get into the ship and leave for Bethsaida, on the northeastern side of the Sea of Galilee, leaving Jesus on the land with the multitudes who had just been fed. They may well have wondered how and when Jesus would catch up with them.

46 And **when he** [*Jesus*] **had sent them away** [*dismissed the crowd to go home*], **he departed** [*went*] **into a mountain to pray.**

Jesus Walks on the Water

47 And **when even** [*evening*] **was come, the ship** [*that his Apostles were on*] **was in the midst of the sea, and he alone on the land.**

48 And **he saw them toiling in rowing;** for the wind was contrary unto them [*they were struggling to row against the wind and waves, still trying to get to their destination*]: **and about the fourth watch of the night** [*between about 3 a.m. and 6 a.m.*] **he cometh unto them, walking upon the sea,** and would have passed by them.

The JST makes a rather helpful clarification to the last phrase of verse 48, above. From it we discover that Jesus intentionally acted as if He were going to walk on past them. He was the Master Teacher, and this certainly did get their attention and prepared them to be taught more about His power over the elements.

JST MARK 6:50

50 And about the fourth watch of the night he cometh unto them, walking upon the sea, **as if he** would have passed by them.

49 But **when they saw him walking upon the sea, they supposed it had been a spirit** [*ghost*], **and cried out** [*in fear*]:

The message given to these exhausted men in verse 50, next, is the same message the merciful Savior gives to all who are doing everything they can to come unto Him (these Apostles have been doing all in their power to row the boat against adversity in order to meet Him as instructed).

50 For [*because*] they all saw him, and were troubled [*very worried*]. And immediately he talked with them, and saith unto them, **Be of good cheer** [*be happy, rejoice, cheer up*]: **it is I; be not afraid.**

There is symbolism and comfort for us in these verses. We all go through "storms" of life and it is comforting to know that God is there to help and comfort us. He invites us to trust Him, cheer up, and stop being afraid.

Jesus Calms the Sea

51 And he went up unto them into the ship [*got into the ship*]; and **the wind ceased:** and they were sore [*very*] amazed in themselves beyond measure, and wondered. [*The Apostles were very surprised at the power Christ had over the wind and sea.*]

52 **For they considered not the miracle of the loaves: for their heart was hardened.**

The miracle of feeding the 5,000 hadn't yet sunk into their hearts as far as their understanding of the Savior's power was concerned. Again, we would do well not to criticize them for taking time to learn about the Master's power; rather, we ought to realize that these great men are in intense training now and are learning rapidly. The "learning curve" is steep!

53 And when they had passed over [*completed the journey*], **they came into the land of Gennesaret** [*the fertile plain on the northwestern shore of the Sea of Galilee*], and drew to the shore.

54 And when they [*Jesus and His Apostles*] were [*had*] come out of the ship, **straightway** [*immediately*] **they** [*the people of that area*] **knew him** [*recognized Him*],

55 **And ran through that whole region** round about, **and began to carry about** in beds **those that were sick,** where they heard he was [*to where Jesus was*].

56 And whithersoever [*wherever*] he entered, into villages, or cities, or country, **they laid the sick in the streets, and besought** [*asked*] **him that they might touch if it were but the border of his garment** [*cloak, robe*]: and **as many as touched him were made whole** [*healed*].

MARK 7

AT THIS POINT, the Jewish religious leaders are so worried about the popularity of Jesus and what He is teaching that they have traveled all the way from Jerusalem to Galilee to try to trap Him and get Him arrested.

1 **THEN came together** [*working and plotting together*] **unto him the Pharisees, and certain of the scribes, which came from Jerusalem.**

The Pharisees and scribes were very influential religious leaders among the Jews. They are desperately trying to find ways to discredit Him and His disciples in front of the people. Watch what they choose to complain about, in verse 2, next.

2 And **when they saw some of his disciples** [*followers*] **eat bread** with defiled, that is to say, **with unwashen** [*unwashed*], **hands, they found fault** [*criticized Jesus for letting his followers eat without washing their hands first*].

Recognizing that some of his readers will not understand why the Pharisees and scribes criticized the Savior's disciples for not washing their hands before eating, he explains the situation to us in verses 3–4, next.

3 **For the Pharisees, and all the Jews, except** [*unless*] **they wash their hands oft, eat not, holding** [*following*] **the tradition of the elders.**

4 **And when they** [*the Jews*] **come from the market, except they wash, they eat not** [*if they don't perform the ritual washing of their hands, they don't eat*]. **And many other things** [*rules and laws*] **there be, which they have received to hold** [*to do, to obey*], as the washing of cups, and pots, brasen vessels, and of tables.

The "tradition of the elders" (end of verse 3, above) consisted of thousands of rules and regulations which had developed among the Jews over the centuries. Most of these rules were not in harmony with the Law of Moses, and were, in fact, opposite to God's will. They killed the spirit of the gospel. The scribes were generally the ones who interpreted these rules and prescribed penalties for those who violated them. As an example, they had so many specific rules for Sabbath day observance that it was virtually impossible for anyone to keep them all. A few of the things the Jews were forbidden to do on the Sabbath, according to the "tradition of the elders", are summarized in the following list:

The Tradition of the Elders

According to these laws and rules, which had been falsely added to the Law of Moses over the years, the Jews were forbidden on the Sabbath to:

- Sweep or break a single clod (it was planting)
- Pluck one blade of grass (it was harvesting)
- Cut a mushroom (a double sin-harvesting and planting because a new mushroom would grow in its place)
- Rub the ends of wheat stalks (guilty of threshing)
- Dip a radish in salt too long (guilty of pickling)
- Rub mud off a dress (might bruise the cloth; however, if they let the mud dry and then carefully picked it off the dress so as to not bruise the fabric, it was ok).
- Spit on the ground, then rub it with the foot (guilty of farming, watering the ground; however, it was ok to spit on a stone, because nothing would grow as a result)
- Carry a legal burden more than 2000 cubits from home
- Replace wadding if it fell out of the ear
- Wear false teeth or wear a gold plug in a tooth
- Eat an egg that was laid on the Sabbath (unless the hen had been kept for eating rather than laying eggs, in which case the egg could be eaten because it was considered to be a part of the hen that had fallen off)

See *Mortal Messiah*, Vol. 1, pages 199–212 for many more examples of the laws and rules for the Sabbath that were a part of the "tradition of the elders."

5 Then **the Pharisees and scribes asked him, Why walk not thy disciples according to the tradition of the elders** [*why don't Your disciples keep the rules of the tradition of the elders*], **but eat bread with unwashen hands?**

Watch now as the Master (who gave the Law of Moses as Jehovah, the God of the Old Testament) responds to their charges, in verses 6–13.

6 **He answered** and said unto them, **Well hath Esaias** [*Isaiah*] **prophesied of you hypocrites** [*people who like to do evil, but want to look righteous*], as it is written [*you are fulfilling the prophecy which said (in Isaiah 29:13)*], **This people honoureth me with their lips, but their heart is far from me.**

7 Howbeit [*however*] **in vain** [*useless*] **do they worship me, teaching for doctrines the commandments of men.**

8 For **laying aside the commandment of God, ye hold the tradition of men,** as the washing of pots and cups: and many other such like things ye do. [*Your religious worship is useless. You don't keep God's commandments. You have replaced them with your own rules and laws.*]

9 And he said unto them, **Full well** [*absolutely*] **ye reject the commandment of God, that ye may keep your own tradition** [*tradition of the elders rules, and so forth*].

10 For **Moses said, Honour thy father and thy mother; and, Whoso curseth father or mother, let him die the death** [*death was the penalty given by Moses for being disrespectful or disobedient to parents; see Exodus 20:12*]:

JST Mark 7:10-12

10 **Full well is it written of you, by the prophets whom ye have rejected.**

11 **They testified these things of a truth, and their blood shall be upon you** [*you are just as guilty as those who killed the ancient prophets who prophesied about you*].

12 **Ye have kept not the ordinances of God**; for Moses said, Honor thy father and thy mother; and whoso curseth father or mother, let him die the death **of the transgressor**, as it is written in your law; **but ye keep not the law.**

11 **But ye say, If a man shall say to his father or mother, It is Corban,** that is to say, a gift, by whatsoever thou mightest be profited by me; **he shall be free** [*of obligation to care for his parents; see note in this study guide after Matthew 15:6*].

12 **And ye suffer** [*allow*] **him no more to do ought** [*anything*] **for his father or his mother;**

13 **Making the word of God of none effect** [*destroying God's commandment to honor parents*] through your tradition, which ye have delivered [*require people to obey*]: and many such like things do ye [*you are guilty of doing all kinds of things like this*].

Now, Jesus turns from the Pharisees and scribes whom He has severely chastised, to the people who have gathered to watch and listen and addresses them.

14 And **when he had called all the people unto him, he said** unto them, Hearken [*listen and obey*] unto me every one of you, and understand:

15 **There is nothing from without** [*outside*] **a man, that entering into him can defile him** [*can make him unclean, unworthy*]: **but the things which come out of him** [*his thoughts, his words, etc.*], **those are they that defile the man.**

JST Mark 7:15

15 There is nothing from without, that entering into a man, can defile him, **which is food**; but the things which come out of him; those are they that defile the man, **that proceedeth forth out of the heart.**

16 **If any man have ears to hear, let him hear** [*the spiritually in tune will understand and obey*].

17 And when he was entered into the house from the people [*away from the crowds*], **his disciples asked him concerning the parable** [*asked Him to explain the parable in verse 15*].

18 And **he saith** unto them, **Are ye so without understanding also** [*don't you understand either*]? Do ye not perceive [*recognize*], that **whatsoever** [*whatever*] **thing from without** [*outside of us*] entereth into the man, it **cannot defile him** [*make him unworthy*];

19 **Because it entereth not into his heart,** but into the belly, and goeth out into the draught

[*eventually passes out of the body*], purging all meats [*cleansing him from all food he has eaten*]?

In Bible language, "meat" means food. "Flesh" means "meat" as we now use the word.

20 And he said, **That which cometh out of the man, that defileth the man** [*your thoughts, words, actions, etc., are what can make you unclean, unworthy*].

21 For from within, **out of the heart of men, proceed evil thoughts, adulteries, fornications, murders,**

22 **Thefts, covetousness, wickedness, deceit** [*fraud, dishonesty*], **lasciviousness** [*pornography, lustful thinking, speaking, etc.*], **an evil eye** [*envy*], **blasphemy** [*speaking crudely, rudely, disrespectfully about God and sacred things*], **pride, foolishness:**

23 **All these evil things come from within, and defile the man** [*make him unclean and unworthy*].

24 And from thence [*there*] **he arose, and went into the borders of Tyre and Sidon** [*several miles north of the Sea of Galilee, on the coast of the Mediterranean Sea*], **and entered into an house, and would have no man know it** [*wanted to have some privacy*]: but he **could not be hid.**

JST MARK 7:22–23

22 And from thence he arose, and went into the borders of Tyre and Sidon, and entered into a house, and **would that no man should come unto him**.

23 **But he could not deny them; for he had compassion upon all men.**

A Gentile Woman Asks Jesus to Heal Her Daughter

25 For **a certain woman, whose young daughter had an unclean** [*evil*] **spirit**, heard of him, and **came** and fell at his feet:

We would understand the "young" daughter to be over age eight, because D&C 29:46–47 tells us that Satan does not have power over children until they begin to become accountable, which we know to be age eight—see D&C 68:25–27.

Mark points out now that the woman is a Gentile, by way of background for what the Savior says to her.

26 **The woman was a Greek, a Syrophenician** by nation; and she besought him that he would [*asked Him to*] cast forth the devil out of her daughter.

27 But Jesus said unto her, **Let the children** [*the Jews, the covenant people, Israel—see JST quoted next*] **first be filled: for it is not meet** [*appropriate*] to **take the children's bread** [*the gospel, intended for the Jews only at this time in God's plan*], **and to cast it unto the dogs** [*give it to the Gentiles*].

JST MARK 7:26

26 But Jesus said unto her, Let **the children of the kingdom** first be filled; for it is not meet to take the children's bread, and to cast it unto the dogs.

As He states here, Jesus' mortal mission was limited to the house of Israel, specifically, the Jews. This limitation will be done away with later, as exemplified by Mark 16:15 and Peter's dream in Acts 10:9–48.

The word "dogs" in this context means "little dogs" or household pets (a term of endearment). A Bible scholar named Dummelow explains as follows:

"The rabbis often spoke of the Gentiles as dogs . . . [Jesus] says not 'dogs,' but 'little dogs,' i.e. house-hold, favourite dogs, and the woman cleverly catches at the expression, arguing that if the Gentiles are household dogs, then it is only right that they should be fed with the crumbs that fall from their master's table" (Dummelow, Commentary, pp. 678–79).

28 And **she answered** and said unto him, **Yes, Lord: yet the dogs under the table eat of the children's crumbs.**

29 **And he said** unto her, **For this saying** [*you have talked me into it (He probably said this with a twinkle in His eye)*] go thy way; **the devil** [*evil spirit*] **is gone out of thy daughter.**

30 And **when she was come to her house, she found the devil gone out**, and her daughter laid upon the bed.

31 And again, departing from the coasts of Tyre and Sidon, **he came unto the sea of Galilee**, through the midst of the coasts [*borders*] of Decapolis [*an area south and east of the Sea of Galilee*].

The Healing of the Deaf and Speech-Impaired Man

32 And they bring [*brought*] unto him **one that was deaf**, and had an **impediment in his speech**; and they beseech him [*asked Jesus*] to put his hand upon him [*to heal the man*].

33 And **he took him aside** from the multitude, and **put his fingers into his ears** [*perhaps as a signal to the deaf man that He was going to heal his deafness*], and he **spit** [*the Jews believed that saliva had healing properties*], **and touched his tongue**;

34 And **looking up to heaven, he sighed, and saith unto him, Ephphatha**, that is, Be opened.

35 And straightway [*immediately*] **his ears were opened** [*he could hear*], and the string of his tongue was loosed, **and he spake plain** [*he could speak plainly*].

36 And he charged them that they should **tell no man** [*Jesus gave them strict instructions not to tell anyone*]: but the more he charged them, so much the more a great deal they published it [*told others about it*];

37 And were **beyond measure astonished** [*completely surprised*], saying, He hath done all things well: he maketh both the deaf to hear, and the dumb [*someone who can't talk*] to speak.

MARK 8

WITH THE FEEDING of the 5,000, in Mark 6:41, the Savior was in the third year of His mortal ministry. In this chapter He is still ministering and teaching in Galilee as this third year of His earthly formal mission continues. Mark begins chapter 8 by reporting the feeding of the 4,000.

Feeding the 4,000

1 IN those days **the multitude** being very great [*large*], and **having nothing to eat, Jesus called his disciples** unto him, and saith unto them,

2 **I have compassion on the multitude**, because **they** have now been with me three days, and **have nothing to eat**:

3 And **if I send them away** fasting to their own houses, **they will faint** by the way: for divers [*some*] of them came from far.

4 And **his disciples answered him, From whence can a man satisfy these men with bread here in the wilderness** [*where could we get bread since there are no markets here in the wilderness*]?

5 And **he asked** them, **How many loaves** [*of bread*] **have ye?** And they said, Seven.

6 And he commanded the people to sit down on the ground: **and he took the seven loaves, and gave thanks, and brake** [*broke the loaves of bread into pieces*], **and gave to his disciples to set before them** [*to give to the people*]; and they did set them [*the pieces of bread*] before the people.

7 And **they had a few small fishes: and he blessed, and commanded to set them also before them.**

8 So **they did eat, and were filled**: and they took up of the broken meat [*food*] that was **left seven baskets** [*seven basketfuls of food were left over*].

One of the major messages for us in the above verses is that when we give the Savior what little we have, whether physical or spiritual efforts, He can make them into much more than we can alone. The left over food in verse 8, above, could symbolize the infinite blessings of exaltation for those who accept nourishment from the Master.

9 And they that had eaten were **about four thousand** [*in addition to women and children—see Matthew 15:38*]: and he sent them away [*dismissed them to go home*].

10 And straightway [*immediately*] **he entered into a ship with his disciples, and came into the parts of Dalmanutha.** [*Bible scholars' best*

guess is that Dalmanutha is in Galilee, on the west shore of the Sea of Galilee.]

Next, we see that the Pharisees have come to attempt to trap Jesus. By the way, they have come all the way up to Galilee from Jerusalem, a journey of several days, which shows how desperate they are becoming.

11 And **the Pharisees** [*Jewish religious leaders*] **came** forth, and **began to question with him** [*Jesus*], seeking of him a sign from heaven, tempting him [*to prove that he was from God*].

12 And **he sighed deeply** in his spirit, and saith, **Why doth this generation** [*the wicked people living in Israel at that time*] **seek after a sign?** verily I say unto you, **There shall no sign be given unto this generation.**

JST MARK 8:12

12 Verily I say unto you, There shall no sign be given unto this generation, **save the sign of the prophet Jonah; for as Jonah was three days and three nights in the whale's belly, so likewise shall the Son of man be buried in the bowels of the earth.**

13 And **he left them**, and entering into the ship again departed to the other side [*of the Sea of Galilee*].

14 Now **the disciples had forgotten to take bread, neither had they in the ship with them more than one loaf.**

Remember that the Apostles are undergoing a period of intense training in preparation for taking over the leadership of the Church after the Savior finishes His mortal ministry and is resurrected. Watch now as the Master Teacher creates the desire to learn more in the hearts and minds of the Twelve.

The Leaven of the Pharisees

15 And he charged [*instructed*] them, saying, Take heed, **beware of the leaven** [*the yeast that causes bread to rise*] **of the Pharisees, and** of the leaven of **Herod.**

The Savior's "students" are now at full attention, trying to figure out the meaning of what He just said to them.

16 And **they reasoned** [*talked*] **among themselves**, saying, **It is because we have no bread** [*He is saying this because we haven't enough bread with us*].

JST MARK 8:16

16 And they reasoned among themselves, saying, **He hath said this**, because we have no bread.

17 And **when Jesus knew it, he saith** unto them, **Why reason ye, because ye have no bread?** [*You are missing the point.*] perceive ye not yet, neither understand? **have ye your heart yet hardened?** [*Are you still so spiritually insensitive that you can't understand the symbolism of what I say?*]

JST MARK 8:17

17 And **when they said this among themselves, Jesus knew it**, and he said unto them,

18 **Having eyes, see ye not** [*can't you see with spiritual eyes and understanding*]? and **having ears, hear ye not** [*can't you hear with spiritual ears and understanding*]? and **do ye not remember** [*can't you remember previous lessons I've taught you*]?

The Savior now reviews previous lessons with these Apostles.

19 **When I brake** [*broke*] **the five loaves among five thousand, how many baskets full of fragments took ye up** [*did you gather up*]? They say unto [*answered*] him, **Twelve.**

20 And when **the seven** [*loaves of bread*] **among four thousand, how many baskets full of fragments** took ye up? And they said, **Seven.**

21 And he said unto them, **How is it that ye do not understand** [*what I said regarding "leaven" in verse 15*]?

Matthew 16:11–12 finishes this account as follows:

11 How is it that ye do not understand that I spake it [*what I said about leaven, yeast*] not to you concerning bread, [*but, rather*] that ye should beware of [*watch out for*] the leaven [*influence*] of the Pharisees and of the Sadducees?

12 Then understood they [*the Apostles*] how that he bade them not [*was not warning them to*] beware of the leaven [*yeast*] of bread, but of the

doctrine [*teachings*] of the Pharisees and of the Sadducees [*hypocritical Jewish religious leaders*].

In other words, just as a little bit of yeast can spread itself throughout the whole lump of bread dough, and thus influence it all, so also can the evil influence of corrupt religious leaders, such as the Pharisees and Sadducees, spread throughout the whole nation.

A Blind Man Is Healed

22 And he cometh to Bethsaida [*just north of the Sea of Galilee*]; and they bring **a blind man** unto him, and besought [*asked*] him to touch him.

You are about to see a rather rare physical healing by the Master, because it will be done in increments.

23 And **he took the blind man** by the hand, and **led him out of the town**; and when he had **spit** [*the Jews had a belief that saliva had healing properties*] **on his eyes, and put his hands upon him**, he **asked him if he saw ought** [*anything*].

24 And he looked up, and said, **I see men as trees, walking** [*I can see, but not clearly*].

25 **After that he put his hands again upon his eyes**, and made him look up: **and he was restored, and saw every man clearly.**

Perhaps this healing of the blind man in stages is symbolic of the fact that, usually, we are healed in stages. We grow "line upon line." We are gradually healed from our spiritual sicknesses such as lack of faith, meanness, inactivity, lack of charity, lustful thinking, and so on, until we see "clearly" as did the blind man.

26 And he sent him away to his house, saying, **Neither go into the town, nor tell it** [*that I healed you*] to any in the town.

Peter Bears Strong Testimony of Christ

27 And Jesus went out, and his disciples, into the towns of Cæsarea Philippi [*an area north and a bit to the east of the Sea of Galilee*]: and by the way [*as they were traveling*] he asked his disciples, saying unto them, **Whom do men say that I am?**

28 And they answered, John the Baptist: but some say, Elias [*Elijah*]; and others, One of the prophets.

29 And he saith unto them, **But whom say ye that I am?** And **Peter answereth and saith unto him, Thou art the Christ.**

30 And he charged [*instructed*] them that they should tell no man of him.

It would seem that this instruction to the Apostles was temporary and for that particular time and circumstance. Perhaps they needed a bit of quiet time together for the Master to teach His disciples about His upcoming death (in about six months) and resurrection. Some manuscripts say "Don't go and tell anyone in the village."

Jesus Teaches His Coming Crucifixion and Resurrection

31 And **he began to teach them, that the Son of man** [*Christ; the "Son of Man." "Man" is "Man of Holiness" or Heavenly Father—see Moses 6:57*] **must suffer** many things, and **be rejected** of the elders, and of the chief priests, and scribes [*Jewish religious leaders*], and **be killed**, and after three days **rise again.**

32 And he spake that saying openly. And **Peter** took him, and **began to rebuke him** [*scold Him for saying such things*].

33 But when he had turned about and looked on his disciples [*implying that all the disciples shared Peter's expressed feelings*], **he rebuked Peter**, saying, Get thee behind me, Satan [*don't stand in my way like Satan does*]: for **thou savourest not** [*you are not considering*] **the things that be of God,** but the things that be of men.

Just a reminder that when you see a ¶ sign in your King James Version of the Bible, it means that there is now a change of topic.

Jesus Teaches What It Means to Truly Follow Him

34 And when he had called the people unto him with his disciples also, he said unto them, **Whosoever will come after me, let him deny himself** *[put aside his personal interests]*, **and take up his cross** *[sacrifice whatever is necessary]*, **and follow me.**

35 For **whosoever will save his life** *[pursue his own selfish interests]* **shall lose it** *[shall lose the real richness of eternal exaltation]*; **but whosoever shall lose his life** *[use his life]* **for my sake and the gospel's, the same shall save it.**

JST Mark 8:37–38 adds to verse 35 as follows:

JST MARK 8:37–38

37 For whosoever will save his life, shall lose it; **or whosoever will save his life, shall be willing to lay it down for my sake; and if he is not willing to lay it down for my sake, he shall lose it.**

38 But whosoever **shall be willing** to lose his life for my sake, and the gospel, the same shall save it.

36 For **what shall it profit a man, if he shall gain the whole world, and lose his own soul?**

37 Or **what shall a man give in exchange for his soul?**

JST adds a verse here:

JST MARK 8:40

40 Therefore deny yourselves of these, and be not ashamed of me.

38 **Whosoever** *[whoever]* therefore **shall be ashamed of me and of my words** *[will not accept me and my teachings]* in this adulterous and sinful generation; **of him also shall the Son of man** *[Christ]* **be ashamed** *[Christ will not accept them into His kingdom]*, **when he cometh in** the **glory** of his Father with the holy angels *[the Second Coming]*.

The JST adds two verses here: (Remember that the verse numbers in the JST are sometimes different than in the King James Bible—the version that we use in English speaking areas of the Church.)

JST MARK 8:42–43

42 And they shall not have part in that resurrection when he cometh.

43 For verily I say unto you, That he shall come; and he that layeth down his life for my sake and the gospel's, shall come with him, and shall be clothed with his glory in the cloud, on the right hand of the Son of man.

MARK 9

1 AND he said unto them, Verily I say unto you, That there be some of them that stand here, which shall not taste of death, till they have seen the kingdom of God come with power *[they will be alive until the Second Coming]*.

The JST (Joseph Smith Translation of the Bible) places Mark 9:1 as the last verse of Mark, chapter 8. The Apostle John would be one of those to whom the Savior referred. We know that he was translated (see D&C 7:3) and is still alive.

Next, Mark records the transfiguration of Christ, which occurred about six months before His crucifixion. For more detail about what happened upon the mountain, see the note after Matthew 17:8 in this study guide.

The Transfiguration of Christ

2 And after six days **Jesus taketh** with him **Peter**, and **James**, and **John** *[the "First Presidency"]*, and leadeth them **up into an high mountain** apart by themselves: and **he was transfigured** *[radiated tremendous light and glory]* **before them.**

3 And **his raiment** *[clothing]* **became shining, exceeding white as snow**; so as no fuller *[washer of clothes]* on earth can white *[bleach]* them.

4 And **there appeared** unto them **Elias** *[John the Baptist—see JST Mark 9:3, quoted below]* with **Moses**: and they were **talking with Jesus.**

JST MARK 9:3

3 And there appeared unto them Elias with Moses, **or in other words, John the Baptist and Moses**; and they were talking with Jesus.

As you can see, the JST Mark 9:3 informs us that John the Baptist, who had been killed (beheaded) by King Herod, also appeared on the Mount of Transfiguration. The "Elias" spoken of in Mark 9:3 was John the Baptist. The "Elias" spoken of in Matthew 17:3 was Elijah (see Matthew 17:3, footnote 3b). "Elias" is a title for one who is a forerunner, and can refer to any of several different prophets. See Bible Dictionary, under "Elias."

5 And **Peter** answered and **said** to Jesus, Master, **it is good for us to be here** [*we are grateful to be here*]: and let us make three tabernacles [*shelters*]; one for thee, and one for Moses, and one for Elias.

6 For he wist [*knew*] not what to say; for they were sore afraid [*very frightened*].

The Father's Voice Is Heard, Bearing Witness of the Son

7 And there was a cloud that overshadowed them: and **a voice** [*Heavenly Father's voice*] came out of the cloud, **saying, This is my beloved Son: hear him.**

8 And suddenly, when they had looked round about, they saw no man any more, save [*except*] Jesus only with themselves.

JST Mark 9:6

6 And suddenly, when they had looked round about **with great astonishment**, they saw no man any more, save Jesus only, with themselves. **And immediately they departed**.

The enormous impact of this experience for these three Apostles may be difficult for us to entirely comprehend. In the Jewish culture, Moses was the Prophet. You may have already noticed that the corrupt religious leaders of the Jews have been constantly quoting the teachings of Moses against the Savior's doings and teachings. It was a great and impactful teaching moment for Peter, James, and John to see Moses, as well as Elijah and John the Baptist, ministering to the Savior and acknowledging Him as the Messiah.

Both Moses and Elijah had been translated (taken up into heaven without dying) and still had their physical, mortal, translated bodies when they appeared on the Mount of Transfiguration and ministered to Jesus. John the Baptist would have appeared there as a spirit. All three, Moses, Elijah and John the Baptist were resurrected with Christ (see D&C 133:54–55).

Next, in verse 9, the Savior gives these three Apostles strict instructions not to tell anyone about the transfiguration until after His resurrection. This is perhaps a reminder to us that there are some sacred things that are best kept private.

9 And **as they came down from the mountain**, he charged them that they should **tell no man what things they had seen, till the Son of man** [*Christ; Son of Man*] **were risen** [*resurrected*] **from the dead**.

10 And **they kept that saying with themselves**, questioning one with another what the rising from the dead should mean. [*They didn't yet understand what resurrection meant or involved.*]

Next, these humble men ask the Master to teach them about a subject that has been confusing to them. The JST will help us understand the Savior's response to their question.

11 And they asked him, saying, **Why say the scribes that Elias must first come** [*what do the scribes mean when they say that Elias must come first*]?

12 And **he answered** and told them, **Elias** verily **cometh first** [*before Jesus*], and restoreth all things; and how it is written of the Son of man [*Christ; Son of Man*], that he must suffer many things, and be set at nought [*ignored, set aside, crucified*].

13 But I say unto you, That **Elias** [*John the Baptist*] **is indeed come, and they have done unto him whatsoever they listed** [*whatever they wanted to do*], as it is written [*prophesied*] of him.

JST Mark 9:10–11

10 And he answered and told them saying, Elias verily cometh first, and **prepareth** all things; **and teacheth you of the prophets** [*teaches about the prophecies of Old Testament prophets about the coming of the Messiah*]; how it is written of the Son of man, that he must suffer many things, and be set at naught.

11 Again I say unto you, That Elias is indeed come, but they have done unto him whatsoever they listed; and even as it is written of him; and **he bore record of me, and they received him not. Verily this was Elias**.

Matthew 17:13 tells us that the "Elias" referred to here was John the Baptist.

As the Savior, Peter, James, and John return from being up in the mountain, they come upon the scribes causing trouble for some of His disciples.

14 And when he came to his disciples, he saw a great multitude *[big crowd]* about them, and **the scribes** *[Jewish religious leaders]* **questioning** with **them.**

15 And straightway *[immediately]* all the people, when they beheld him *[Jesus]*, were greatly amazed *[surprised]* and, running to him saluted *[greeted]* him.

16 And **he asked the scribes, What question ye with them** *[what are you debating with my disciples about]*?

An Evil Spirit Is Cast Out

17 And **one of the multitude answered** *[responded]* and said, **Master, I have brought unto thee my son, which hath a dumb spirit** *[JST a devil]*;

18 And wheresoever he *[the evil spirit]* taketh him, he teareth him *[throws him on the ground, and he gets cut up]*: and he foameth, and gnasheth with his teeth, and pineth away: and I spake to *[asked]* thy disciples that they should cast him out; and they could not.

JST Mark 9:15

15 And one of the multitude answered, and said, Master, I have brought unto thee my son, who hath **a dumb spirit that is a devil**; and **when he seizeth him**, he teareth him; and he foameth and gnasheth with his teeth, and pineth away; and I spake to thy disciples **that they might cast him out**, and they could not.

19 **He answereth** him, and saith, **O faithless generation, how long shall I be with you?** how long shall I suffer you? **bring him unto me.**

20 And **they brought him unto him**: and when he *[the son possessed by the evil spirit]* saw him *[Jesus]*, straightway *[immediately]* **the spirit tare him** *[caused him to fall and get cut more]*; and he fell on the ground, and wallowed foaming *[at the mouth]*.

21 And he *[Jesus]* asked his father, How long is it ago since this came unto him? And he said, Of a child *[when he was a child]*.

22 And ofttimes it hath cast him into the fire, and into the waters, to destroy him: but **if thou canst do any thing, have compassion** *[mercy]* **on us, and help us.**

23 Jesus said unto him, If thou canst believe, all things are possible to him that believeth.

JST Mark 9:20

20 Jesus said unto him, If thou **wilt believe all things I shall say unto you, this is possible** to him that believeth.

24 And straightway *[immediately]* **the father** of the child **cried out**, and said with tears, Lord, **I believe; help thou mine unbelief.**

Verse 24, above, has a major message for us. Each of us, no doubt, at times have said or will say, "I believe; help thou mine unbelief." It is a beautiful, humble acknowledgment of our faith and yet our inadequacy to have as much faith as we would like to have.

25 When **Jesus** saw that the people came running together, he **rebuked the foul** *[evil]* **spirit,** saying unto him, Thou dumb and deaf spirit, I charge *[command]* thee, **come out of him**, and enter no more into him.

26 And **the spirit cried** *[shrieked]*, **and rent him sore** *[caused the son to flop around and get cut up more]*, **and came out of him:** and he *[the son]* was as one dead; insomuch *[to the extent]* that many said, He is dead.

27 But Jesus took him by the hand, and lifted him up; and he arose.

Next, when they have privacy, the disciples ask the Lord why they couldn't cast the evil spirit out.

28 And when he was come into the house, his disciples asked him privately, **Why could not we cast him** *[the evil spirit]* **out?**

29 And he said unto them, **This kind can come forth by nothing, but by prayer and fasting.**

The Prophet Joseph Smith mentioned something that might apply here. He said that there are times when people do not have sufficient faith for the desired miracle to be performed. Said he (**bold** added for emphasis):

"**If a man has not faith enough to do one thing, he may have faith to do another**: if he cannot remove a mountain, he may heal the sick. Where faith is there will be some of the fruits: all gifts and power which were sent from heaven, were poured out on the heads of those who had faith" (*History of The Church*, Vol. 5, page 355).

Next, the Savior teaches His Apostles privately of His approaching crucifixion and resurrection

The Savior Prophecies His Crucifixion and Resurrection

30 And **they departed** thence [*left that place*], **and passed through** Galilee; and he would not that any man should know it [*wanted to have time alone with His Apostles*].

31 For he taught his disciples, and said unto them, **The Son of man** [*Jesus; Son of Man; "Man" means "the Father"—see Moses 6:57*] **is delivered into the hands of men, and they shall kill him**; and after that he is killed, **he shall rise** [*be resurrected*] **the third day.**

32 **But they** [*the disciples*] **understood not** that saying [*what Jesus had said about His death and resurrection*], **and were afraid to ask him.**

Next, Mark informs us about a debate among these disciples which caused them some embarrassment. Remember that Jesus is training them for when He leaves and they take over the leadership of His church on earth.

33 And **he came to Capernaum** [*on the north end of the Sea of Galilee*]: and being in the house [*very likely Peter's home, since he lived in Capernaum*] **he asked them, What was it that ye disputed among yourselves by the way** [*what were you debating among yourselves as we were traveling*]?

34 But **they held their peace** [*didn't answer; obviously, they were embarrassed about it*]: **for** by the way [*while traveling*] **they had disputed** [*argued*] among themselves, **who should be the greatest.**

JST Mark 9:31

31 But they held their peace, being afraid, for by the way they had disputed among themselves, **who was the greatest among them.**

Watch as the Savior gently answers their question with a simple lesson.

35 And he sat down, and called the twelve, and saith unto them, **If any man desire to be first** [*the greatest in God's kingdom*], **the same** [*he*] **shall be last of all** [*should consider himself to be least important of all*], **and servant of all.**

36 And **he took a child, and set him in the midst of them**: and when he had taken him in his arms [*perhaps meaning hugging the child as it sat on His lap*], he said unto them,

37 Whosoever shall receive one of such children in my name, receiveth me: and whosoever shall receive me, receiveth not me, but him that sent me.

JST Mark 9:34–35

34 Whosoever shall **humble himself like one of these children**, and receiveth me, **ye shall receive in my name.**

35 And **whosoever shall receive me, receiveth not me only**, but him that sent me, **even the Father.**

Next, John brings up an issue that perhaps you have also wondered about.

38 And John answered him, saying, Master, **we saw one casting out devils in thy name**, and **he followeth not us** [*perhaps meaning that he is not one of the Twelve*]: and **we forbad him** [*told him not to do it*], because he followeth not us [*perhaps meaning that he is not traveling with us*].

39 But **Jesus said, Forbid him not**: for there is no man which shall do a miracle in my name, that can lightly speak evil of me.

40 For **he that is not against us is on our part** [*is on our side*].

Apostle Bruce R. McConkie explained verses 38–40, above, as follows:

"On a previous occasion, Jesus taught that neither Satan nor his false ministers can cast out devils, for 'Every kingdom divided against itself is brought to desolation; . . . And if Satan cast out Satan, he is divided against himself' (Matthew 12:25–30). Now he adds in plainness what was necessarily implied in his previous discourse that only those who follow him and are legal administrators in his kingdom can perform the miracle of casting out devils in his name.

"He was not one of the Twelve to whom the express power had been given to cast out devils (Matthew 10:8); he was not one of the inner circle of disciples who traveled, ate, slept, and communed continually with the Master. Luke has it: "He followeth not with us"; that is, he is not one of our traveling companions. But from our Lord's reply it is evident that he was a member of the kingdom, a legal administrator who was acting in the authority of the priesthood and the power of faith. Either he was unknown to John who therefore erroneously supposed him to be without authority or else John falsely supposed that the power to cast out devils was limited to the Twelve and did not extend to all faithful priesthood holders. It is quite possible that the one casting out devils was a seventy. There is no New Testament record of the calling of the first quorum of seventy, but when Jesus (at a later day) called a second quorum of seventy into the ministry, he expressly gave them the power to cast out devils (Luke 10:1–20).

"Only righteous men who are members of the Church, who hold the priesthood, and who are keeping the commandments, have power to perform miracles. 'There was not any man who could do a miracle in the name of Jesus save he were cleansed every whit from his iniquity' (3 Nephi 8:1).

"Our Lord had many faithful followers who had power by faith to cast out devils" (*Doctrinal New Testament Commentary*, Vol. 1, page 417).

41 For **whosoever shall give you a cup of water to drink in my name, because ye belong to Christ,** verily I say unto you, he **shall not lose his reward.**

Did you wonder how verse 41, above, fits in with what is being discussed here? It might be that the Master is dealing with the problem that often comes up among us and among many other groups. If we are not careful, we get to thinking that what others do can't be as valuable as what we do. It may be that the Savior is gently reminding these men that anyone, whether members of the Church or not, can do good, and that it is looked upon with favor by heaven, and such persons will be rewarded accordingly.

Next, Jesus refers to the little child on His lap and teaches another lesson.

42 And **whosoever shall offend** [*cause to stumble in their faithfulness—see Matthew 18:6, footnote 6a; many translations use "cause to commit sin" in place of "offend"*] **one of these little ones** that believe in me, **it is better for him that a millstone** [*a large grinding stone*] **were hanged about his neck, and he were cast into the sea.**

In the next verses, there is much symbolism where parts of the body represent people. The JST is very helpful in understanding verses 43–50. We will include the JST verses at the end of this chapter. It tells us that people are represented by hand, foot, and eye. JST Matthew 18:9 gives additional interpretation which is represented in many of the brackets below.

43 And **if thy hand** [*your brother; friend*] **offend thee** [*causes you to sin*], **cut it off** [*stay away from him*]: it is better for thee to enter into life maimed [*crippled*], than having two hands to go into hell [*than following the sinful example of family members and going to hell with them*], into the fire that never shall be quenched:

44 Where their worm dieth not [*where they do not cease to exist*], and the fire [*their suffering*] is not quenched [*does not stop*].

45 And **if thy foot** [*friend; the person who is leading you*] **offend thee** [*leads you into sin*], **cut it off** [*stop associating with that person*]: it is better for thee to enter halt [*crippled*] into life, than having two feet [*sticking with the friend*] to be cast into hell, into the fire that never shall be quenched:

46 Where their worm dieth not [*where they do not cease to exist*], and the fire is not quenched [*the suffering never ends*].

47 And **if thine eye** [*parents, family members who lead you*] **offend thee** [*cause you to stumble in the faith, commit sin, etc.*], **pluck it out** [*leave them*]: it is better for thee to enter into the kingdom of God with one eye [*alone*], than having two eyes [*following parents' sinful example*] to be cast into hell fire:

48 Where their worm dieth not, and the fire is not quenched.

49 For **every one shall be salted** [*tested*] with fire, and **every sacrifice shall be salted** with salt [*every sacrifice we make for the gospel is part of our test*].

Apostle Bruce R. McConkie ex-plains the phrase "salted with fire" as follows: "Every member of the Church shall be tested and tried in all things, to see whether he will abide in the covenant 'even unto death' (D&C 98:14), regardless of the course taken by the other members of his family or of the Church. To gain salvation men must stand on their own feet in the gospel cause and be independent of the spiritual support of others. If some of the Saints, who are themselves the salt of the earth, shall fall away, still all who inherit eternal life must remain true, having salt in themselves and enjoying peace one with another" (*Doctrinal New Testament Commentary*, Vol. 1, p. 421).

50 Salt is good: but **if the salt have lost his saltness,** wherewith will ye season it? Have salt in yourselves, and have peace one with another.

JST MARK 9:40–50

40 Therefore, if thy hand offend thee, cut it off; or if thy brother offend thee and confess not and forsake not, he shall be cut off. It is better for thee to enter into life maimed, than having two hands, to go into hell.

41 For it is better for thee to enter into life without thy brother, than for thee and thy brother to be cast into hell; into the fire that never shall be quenched, where their worm dieth not, and the fire is not quenched.

42 And again, if thy foot offend thee, cut it off; for he that is thy standard, by whom thou walkest, if he become a transgressor, he shall be cut off.

43 It is better for thee, to enter halt into life, than having two feet to be cast into hell; into the fire that never shall be quenched.

44 Therefore, let every man stand or fall, by himself, and not for another; or not trusting another.

45 Seek unto my Father, and it shall be done in that very moment what ye shall ask, if ye ask in faith, believing that ye shall receive.

46 And if thine eye which seeth for thee, him that is appointed to watch over thee to show thee light, become a transgressor and offend thee, pluck him out.

47 It is better for thee to enter into the kingdom of God, with one eye, than having two eyes to be cast into hell fire.

48 For it is better that thyself should be saved, than to be cast into hell with thy brother, where their worm dieth not, and where the fire is not quenched.

49 For every one shall be salted with fire; and every sacrifice shall be salted with salt; but the salt must be good.

50 For if the salt have lost his saltness, wherewith will ye season it? (the sacrifice:) therefore it must needs be that ye have salt in yourselves, and have peace one with another.

MARK 10

BY NOW THERE are less than six months remaining in the third year of the Savior's formal mission. As you can see, in verse 1, next, He now leaves Galilee, where He has spent the majority of His mortal ministry, and journeys toward Judea, in the southern region of the Holy Land.

1 AND **he arose from thence** [*from where he was in Galilee*], **and cometh into** the coasts [*borders*] of **Judæa** [*the southern part of Israel*] by the farther [*eastern*] side of Jordan [*river*]: and **the people resort** [*came*] **unto him** again; and, as he was wont [*accustomed to doing*], **he taught them** again.

Concerning Divorce

2 And **the Pharisees** [*Jewish religious leaders*] came to him, and asked him, **Is it lawful** [*legal*] **for a man to put away** [*divorce*] **his wife?** tempting him [*trying to trap Him so they would have an excuse to have Him arrested*].

3 And **he answered** and said unto them, **What did Moses command you?**

4 And **they said, Moses suffered** [*allowed*] **to write a bill of divorcement** [*a legal divorce document*], **and to put her away** [*divorce her*].

5 And **Jesus answered** and said unto them, **For the** [*because of the*] **hardness of your heart he wrote you this precept** [*gave you this teaching*].

6 **But from the beginning of the creation God** *[Heavenly Father]* **made them male and female.**

7 **For this cause** *[for marriage]* **shall a man leave his father and mother, and cleave** *[be loyal]* to his wife;

8 And **they twain** *[the two of them]* **shall be one flesh** *[a family unit]*: so then they are no more twain *[two]*, but one flesh.

9 **What therefore God hath joined together, let not man put asunder** *[destroy]*.

10 And in the house his disciples asked him again of the same matter *[to explain more of what he had said about divorce]*.

11 And he saith unto them, **Whosoever shall put away** *[divorce]* **his wife, and marry another, committeth adultery against her.**

12 And **if a woman shall put away her husband, and be married to another, she committeth adultery.**

For a discussion about the content of verses 11 and 12, above, regarding divorce, refer to the note after Matthew 5:31 in this study guide.

Little Children Welcomed

13 And **they** *[the people]* **brought young children to him, that he should touch them**: and his **disciples rebuked those** *[scolded them]* **that brought them.**

14 But when Jesus saw it, he was much displeased, and said unto them *[His disciples, who are still learning]*, **Suffer** *[allow]* **the little children to come unto me, and forbid them not: for of such is the kingdom of God.**

15 Verily I say unto you, Whosoever *[whoever]* shall not receive the kingdom of God *[accept the teachings of the gospel]* as *[like]* a little child, he shall not enter therein.

16 And **he** took them *[the children]* up in his arms, put his hands upon them, and **blessed them.**

The Rich Young Man

17 And when he was gone forth into the way *[when he had gone on down the road]*, there came one *[the rich young man in verse 22]* running, and kneeled to him, and asked him, Good Master, **what shall I do that I may inherit eternal life** *[exaltation]*?

18 And Jesus said unto him, Why callest thou me good? there is none good but one, that is, God. *[Jesus wants no glory for Himself, rather gives all glory and credit to the Father.]*

19 Thou knowest the commandments, **Do not commit adultery, Do not kill, Do not steal, Do not bear false witness** *[lie; accuse someone falsely]*, **Defraud** *[cheat]* not, **Honour thy father and mother.**

20 And he answered and said unto him, Master, **all these have I observed** *[done]* **from my youth.**

21 Then Jesus beholding him loved him *[looked at him with kind, loving eyes]*, and said unto him, **One thing thou lackest** *[there is one thing you haven't done yet]*: go thy way, **sell whatsoever** *[everything]* **thou hast, and give to the poor**, and thou shalt have treasure in heaven: and come, take up the cross *[take up my cause]*, **and follow me.**

22 **And he** *[the rich young man]* **was sad at that saying** *[counsel]*, **and went away grieved** *[troubled]*: for he had great possessions *[he was very rich]*.

23 And **Jesus** looked round about, and **saith unto his disciples, How hardly shall they that have riches enter into the kingdom of God** *[how hard it is for rich people to enter the kingdom of God]*!

24 And **the disciples were astonished** *[surprised, startled]* at his words. But Jesus answereth again *[continued]*, and saith unto them *[explained what He meant]*, Children, **how hard is it** *[it is very difficult]* **for them that trust in riches to enter into the kingdom of God!**

This is a very important point. Some people believe that to be rich is somehow evil and against the Savior's teachings. That is not what the Master taught here. To trust in wealth rather than God and to let wealth corrupt one's values and standards is the problem pointed out here by Jesus. See Jacob 2:16–20.

The Eye of a Needle

25 It is **easier for a camel to go through the eye of a needle, than for a rich man to enter into the kingdom of God.**

There is a common rumor that the "eye of a needle" was a small gate in the walls of Jerusalem, used for entry into the city by night, after the main gates were closed. The rumor states that it was very difficult for a camel to get down and scrunch through the gate. Scholars indicate that this rumor has no truth to it. They indicate that the word "needle," as used in verse 25, refers to an ordinary sewing needle in the original Bible languages.

The picture created in a person's mind of a large camel trying to get through the eye of a needle effectively demonstrates the impossibility of one entering heaven whose top priority is wealth. See JST Mark 10:26, quoted below.

26 And they were astonished out of measure [*could hardly believe what they had just heard*], saying among themselves, **Who then can be saved?**

27 And Jesus looking upon them saith, **With men it is impossible, but not with God**: for with God all things are possible

Watch what a difference the JST makes with verse 27, above!

JST Mark 10:26

26 And Jesus, looking upon them, said, **With men that trust in riches, it is impossible; but not impossible with men who trust in God and leave all for my sake, for with such all these things are possible.**

28 Then **Peter** began to say unto him, Lo, **we have left all, and have followed thee.**

Every Worthy Person Will Receive a Just Reward

29 And **Jesus answered** and said, Verily [*listen very carefully*] I say unto you, There is no man that hath left house, or brethren, or sisters, or father, or mother, or wife, or children, or lands, for my sake, and the gospel's,

30 But **he shall receive an hundredfold** [*a hundred times more*] now **in this time**, houses, and brethren, and sisters, and mothers, and children, and lands, with persecutions; **and in the world to come eternal life** [*eternal life*].

31 But many that are **first shall be last; and the last first.**

JST Mark 10:30–31

30 But there are **many who make themselves first, that shall be last**, and the last first.

The Savior Prophecies His Crucifixion and Resurrection Again

32 And **they were** in the way [*on the road*] **going up to Jerusalem**; and Jesus went before [*ahead of*] them: and they were amazed; and as they followed, they were afraid. And **he** took again the twelve, and **began to tell them what things should happen unto him,**

33 Saying, Behold, we go up to Jerusalem; and **the Son of man** [*Jesus, Son of Man*] **shall be delivered unto the chief priests** [*religious leaders of the Jews*], and **unto the scribes** [*Jewish religious leaders*]; and **they shall condemn him to death, and shall deliver him to the Gentiles** [*the Romans*]:

34 And they [*the Romans*] shall **mock** him, and shall **scourge** [*whip*] him, and shall **spit upon him**, and shall **kill him**: and **the third day he shall rise again** [*will be resurrected*].

James and John Ask a Favor

35 And **James and John**, the sons of Zebedee, come [*came*] unto him, saying, Master, **we would that thou shouldest do for us whatsoever we shall desire**.

36 And **he said** unto them, **What would ye that I should do for you?**

37 They said unto him, **Grant unto us that we may sit, one on thy right hand, and the other on thy left hand, in thy glory** [*in heaven*].

38 **But Jesus said** unto them, **Ye know not what ye ask**: can ye drink of the cup that I drink of [*can you really follow me in everything*]? and be baptized with the baptism that I am baptized with [*go through what I have to go through*]?

39 And **they said** unto him, **We can**. And **Jesus said** unto them, Ye shall indeed drink of the cup that I drink of; and with the baptism that I am baptized withal shall ye be baptized:

40 **But to sit on my right hand and on my left hand is not mine to give; but it shall be given to them for whom it is prepared.** [*In other words, it is not to be given as a matter of favoritism or mere request; rather it will be given to those who earn it according to the laws established by the Father.*]

41 And when **the ten** [*other Apostles*] heard it, they began to be much **displeased with James and John.**

Watch now as the Savior, with kindness and skill calms the feelings of contention which have arisen among the twelve Apostles here and uses the occasion to teach the principle of "servant leadership," which is that those who want to be greatest among the people of God must be those who humbly and sincerely serve the others.

A Lesson about Serving

42 But **Jesus** called them to him, and **saith** unto them, Ye know that they which are accounted to rule over the Gentiles [*leaders among the gentiles*] exercise lordship over them; and their great ones [*most important leaders*] exercise authority upon them.

43 But so shall it not be among you: but **whosoever will be great among you, shall be your minister:**

44 And **whosoever of you will be the chiefest, shall be servant of all.**

45 For **even the Son of man** [*Jesus*] **came not to be ministered unto, but to minister**, and to give his life a ransom [*payment*] for many.

Blind Bartimaeus Is Healed

46 And they came to Jericho [*east and down the mountain from Jerusalem, about 25 miles*]: and as he went out of Jericho with his disciples and a great number of people, **blind Bartimæus**, the son of Timæus, **sat by the highway side begging.**

47 And when he heard that it was Jesus of Nazareth, **he began to cry out** [*yell*], and say, Jesus, thou Son of David [*the promised Messiah, prophesied to come through David*], have mercy on me.

48 And **many charged him that he should hold his peace** [*told him to be quiet*]: **but he cried** [*shouted*] **the more** a great deal, Thou Son of David, have mercy on me.

49 And **Jesus stood still**, and **commanded him to be called.** And they call the blind man, saying unto him, Be of good comfort, rise; he calleth thee.

50 And **he**, casting away his garment [*throwing down his cloak, wasting no time*], **rose, and came to Jesus.**

51 And **Jesus** answered and **said** unto him, **What wilt thou** that I should do unto thee? **The blind man said** unto him, **Lord, that I might receive my sight.**

52 And Jesus said unto him, Go thy way; **thy faith hath made thee whole** [*healed*]. And **immediately he received his sight, and followed Jesus** in the way [*along the road*].

MARK 11

THESE NEXT VERSES lead up to what is known as "the Triumphal Entry," the day when Jesus rode into Jerusalem accompanied by throngs of people shouting "Hosanna to the Son of David;" in other words, celebrating and cheering Jesus as the promised Messiah who would save them and free them from their enemies. Most Bible chronologies suggest that this day was Sunday, in our calendar system. The Passover was underway and throngs of Jewish pilgrims had arrived in Jerusalem from many lands to join in the Passover celebration and worship. This begins the last week of the Savior's mortal life.

The Triumphal Entry

1 AND when **they came nigh** [*near*] to **Jerusalem,** unto Bethphage and Bethany, at the mount of Olives [*a few minutes' walk east of Jerusalem*], **he sendeth forth two of his disciples,**

2 And saith unto them, **Go** your way **into the village** over against you [*just ahead of you*]: and as soon as ye be entered into it, **ye shall find a colt** [*a young male donkey*] tied, whereon never man sat [*that has never been ridden*]; **loose** [*untie*] **him, and bring him.**

3 And **if any man say** unto you, **Why do ye this?** say ye that the Lord hath need of him; and straightway [*immediately*] he will send him hither [*here*].

Here is another miracle which is sometimes missed by people as they read. The young male donkey has never been ridden, yet when Jesus gets on him to ride into Jerusalem, the donkey does not object, rather, allows the Master to ride. This is another testimony of the Savior's power over all things.

4 **And they** [*the two disciples*] went their way, and **found the colt** tied by the door without [*outside*] in a place where two ways [*roads*] met; and they loose [*untied*] him.

5 And **certain of them that stood there** [*some people standing around*] **said** unto them, **What do ye, loosing the colt?**

6 And they said [*replied*] unto them even as Jesus had commanded: and they let them go.

7 And **they brought the colt to Jesus,** and cast their garments [*cloaks, robes*] on him [*the colt*]; **and he** [*Jesus*] **sat upon him.**

In Jewish culture and symbolism of that day, a donkey symbolized humility and submission. A horse, on the other hand, symbolized triumph and victory over enemies, in other words, military might and victory, in their culture.

Thus, the Savior's riding into Jerusalem on a donkey represents that He came in meekness and submission to carry out the Father's will in carrying out the Atonement, including being crucified. At His Second Coming, He is prophetically represented as riding on a white horse (Revelation 19:11), which symbolizes His triumph and victory over all enemies of righteousness, including Satan and his evil kingdom. White, by the way, symbolizes purity and righteousness, as well as celestial glory, in Biblical symbolism.

8 And **many spread their garments in the way** [*on the road*]: and **others cut down branches off the trees, and strawed** [*spread*] **them in the way** [*on the road in front of Jesus*].

9 And they that went before [*the people who went ahead*], and they that followed, cried [*shouted*], **saying, Hosanna** [*"Save us now." See Bible Dictionary, under "Hosanna"*]; Blessed is he that cometh in the name of the Lord:

10 Blessed be the kingdom of our father David, that cometh in the name of the Lord: Hosanna in the highest.

JST MARK 11:10–12

10 Hosanna! Blessed is he that cometh in the name of the Lord;

11 **That bringeth the kingdom of our father David** [*in other words, in effect, the prophesied Messiah is here, and will re-establish the kingdom of David and free us from Roman rule*];

12 Blessed is he that cometh in the name of the Lord; Hosanna in the highest.

11 And **Jesus entered into Jerusalem, and into the temple**: and when he had looked round about upon all things, and now the eventide was come, he **went out unto Bethany with the twelve.**

The Fig Tree Is Cursed

12 And **on the morrow** *[the next day]*, when they were come from Bethany, **he was hungry:**

13 And **seeing a fig tree afar** off having leaves *[in other words, appearing as if it was a productive tree with figs on it]*, **he came, if haply** *[to see if]* **he might find any thing thereon:** and when he came to it, he found nothing but leaves; for the time of figs was not yet.

14 And **Jesus** answered *[spoke]* and **said unto it** *[the fig tree]*, **No man eat fruit of thee hereafter for ever.** And his disciples heard it. *[See more about this in verses 20–21.]*

JST MARK 11:14–16

14 And on the morrow, when they came from Bethany he was hungry; and seeing a fig tree afar off having leaves, **he came to it with his disciples; and as they supposed**, he came to it to see if he might find anything thereon.

15 And when he came to it, there was nothing but leaves; **for as yet the figs were not ripe**.

16 And Jesus spake and said unto it, No man eat fruit of thee hereafter, forever. And the disciples heard him.

Jesus Cleanses the Temple for the Second Time

15 And **they come to** *[arrived at]* **Jerusalem**: and **Jesus went into the temple**, and began to **cast out them that sold and bought** in the temple, and overthrew the tables of the moneychangers, and the seats of them that sold doves;

The temple had become a major marketplace for buying and selling birds and animals to be used for sacrifices. There was much of yelling and cheating, and so forth, which typically go along with such dealings; therefore, Jesus cleansed the temple from these moneychangers and their merchandise. John tells us (John 2:14–17) that Jesus cleansed the temple at the beginning of His ministry. Now, three years later, Jesus cleanses the temple again. This is the second time and the temple crowd obviously hadn't learned their lesson the first time.

16 And would not suffer *[allow]* that any man should carry any vessel *[container]* through the temple.

17 And **he taught**, saying unto them, Is it not written *[in the scriptures, in Jeremiah 7:11]*, **My house shall be called of all nations the house of prayer? but ye have made it a den of thieves.**

18 And **the scribes and chief priests** *[Jewish religious leaders, who wanted desperately to arrest Jesus and have him executed]* **heard** it, and **sought how they might destroy him:** for they feared him, because all the people was astonished at his doctrine *[Jesus had become famous for His teachings]*.

19 And when even *[evening]* was come, he went out of the city.

The Fig Tree Has Dried Up and Died, Overnight

20 And **in the morning**, as they passed by, **they saw the fig tree dried up from the roots.**

The fig tree is symbolic of the hypocritical Jewish religious leaders who pretend to look official but do not produce the fruit of the gospel. It is also symbolic of the Jewish nation, the covenant people, who are "barren" as far as the gospel is concerned. See *Jesus the Christ*, p. 443.

21 And **Peter** calling to remembrance **saith** unto him, Master, behold, **the fig tree which thou cursedst is withered away** *[has dried up and died]*.

Jesus will now use the fig tree incident to teach His disciples about the power of faith.

A Lesson on the Power of Faith

22 And Jesus answering saith unto them, **Have faith in God.**

23 For verily I say unto you, That whosoever shall say unto this mountain, Be thou removed, and be thou cast into the sea; and shall not doubt in his heart, but shall believe that those things which he saith shall come to pass; he shall have whatsoever he saith.

24 Therefore I say unto you, **What things soever ye desire, when ye pray, believe that ye receive them, and ye shall have them.**

D&C 46:30 and 50:29–30 add to our understanding of this use of faith. In these Doctrine and Covenants verses we are instructed that, in order to have this kind of faith, the Holy Ghost must inspire us as to what is permissible for us to ask.

Next, beginning in verse 25, we are taught that in order to have the kind of faith spoken of in the above verses, we must forgive others. If we carry grudges in our heart, we cannot have this type of faith. One of the major messages here is that, since we need the constant forgiveness of God in our lives, if we ask for it and do not forgive others, we are hypocrites and cannot have the help of the Holy Ghost to sufficiently strengthen our own faith.

25 And **when ye stand praying** [*when you are asking God for blessings and help*], **forgive, if ye have ought** [*anything*] **against any: that your Father also which is in heaven may forgive you your trespasses.** [*In other words, another message here is that if you want God to forgive your sins, you must forgive others.*]

26 But **if ye do not forgive, neither will your Father which is in heaven forgive your trespasses.**

Jewish Religious Leader Make Another Attempt to Trap the Savior

27 And they come [*came*] again to Jerusalem: and as he was walking in the temple, **there come to him the chief priests, and the scribes, and the elders,**

These Jewish religious leaders are now working closely together to do away with Jesus. Keep in mind that there are large crowds of people standing near who are listening carefully to what now goes on.

28 And say [*and the Jewish leaders said*] unto him, **By what authority doest thou these things? and who gave thee this authority to do these things?**

29 And **Jesus answered** and said unto them, **I will also ask of you one question,** and answer me, and I will tell you by what authority I do these things. [*If you will answer one question I ask you, then I will answer your question.*]

30 [*Here is my question to you:*] **The baptism of John, was it from heaven, or of men?** answer me. [*Was John the Baptist sent by heaven, or was he just a man who falsely claimed authority?*]

31 And **they reasoned with** [*talked it over among*] **themselves,** saying, If we shall say, From heaven; he will say, Why then did ye not believe him?

32 But if we shall say, Of men; they feared the people [*feared that the people would mob them*]: for all men counted John, that he was a prophet indeed.

33 And **they answered and said unto Jesus, We cannot tell** [*we cannot answer Your question*]. And Jesus answering saith unto them, **Neither do I tell you by what authority I do these things** [*then I will not answer your question either*].

MARK 12

IN THIS NEXT parable, known as the Parable of the Wicked Husbandmen, the Savior clearly compares the wicked Jewish religious leaders to the wicked husbandmen [supervisors, foremen, stewards, those who run the business while the owner is away] who kill the owner's son in an attempt to take the kingdom from him. The notes in brackets in the parable suggest possible interpretations of symbolism found in the parable.

The Parable of the Wicked Husbandmen

1 AND **he began to speak unto them** [*the Jewish leaders mentioned in Mark 11:27, who are trying to trap Jesus*] **by parables** [*stories which teach a lesson*]. **A certain man** [*Heavenly Father*] planted a **vineyard** [*grape vines, symbolic of creating this earth and putting people on it*], and set an **hedge** [*protection from danger (Satan, temptation, etc.)*] about it, and **digged a place for the winefat** [*built a place to harvest the grape juice, in other words, planned for a good harvest of righteous people*], and built a **tower** [*so people could see enemies coming from far off and thus avoid being conquered; symbolic of prophets who see dangers and warn their people*], and **let it out to husbandmen** [*placed supervisors over it*], and went into a **far country** [*heaven*].

2 And **at the season** [*at harvest time*] **he sent to the husbandmen** [*supervisors, stewards*] **a servant** [*prophets*], that he might receive from the husbandmen of the **fruit of the vineyard** [*the harvest*].

3 And **they caught him**, [*the prophets*] and **beat him**, and **sent him away empty** [*wouldn't listen to the prophets*].

4 And again he sent unto them **another servant** [*more prophets*]; and **at him they cast stones**, and **wounded him** in the head, and **sent him away** shamefully handled [*reject them and badly abused them*].

5 And again **he sent another** [*more prophets*]; and **him they killed**, and **many others**; beating some, and killing some.

6 Having yet therefore one **son, his wellbeloved** [*Christ*], **he** [*the Father*] **sent him also** last unto them, saying, They will reverence my son.

7 But **those husbandmen said among themselves, This is the heir** [*the owner's son to whom all this will belong*]; **come, let us kill him**, and the inheritance shall be ours [*let's kill Jesus so we can keep our positions of power and leadership over the people*].

8 And **they took him** [*Jesus*], **and killed** [*crucified*] **him**, and cast him out of the vineyard [*got rid of Him from the earth*].

The Question and the Answer

9 **What shall therefore the lord of the vineyard** [*Christ*] **do? he will come and destroy the husbandmen** [*at the Second Coming*], and **will give the vineyard unto others** [*to the righteous, who will inherit the earth*].

10 And **have ye not read this scripture** [*in Psalm 118:22–23*]; The stone [*Christ*] which the builders [*the wicked husbandmen in verse two, and their people*] rejected is become the head of the corner [*the main part of the building*]:

11 This was the Lord's doing, and it is marvellous in our eyes?

12 And **they** [*the wicked Jewish religious leaders*] **sought to lay hold on him** [*tried to figure out a way to arrest Him*], but feared the people: **for they knew that he had spoken the parable against them**: and they left him, and went their way.

Having failed to stop Jesus themselves, these wicked chief priests, scribes, and elders now recruit others to help them trap Jesus and get Him arrested. It is interesting to note that the Pharisees and Herodians (verse 13) normally are enemies. Now they have joined together to trap the Master. The Herodians were a political party among the Jews who supported the Herodian family as rulers (see Bible Dictionary, under "Herodians") which was very distasteful to the Pharisees.

13 And **they send** [*sent*] unto him **certain of the Pharisees and of the Herodians, to catch him in his words** [*to get Him to say something for which He could be arrested*].

Watch now as these leaders, oozing with hypocrisy, foolishly attempt to trap the Jehovah of the Old Testament, who is among them in the flesh, with cunning words.

14 And **when they were come** [*had arrived*], **they say** [*said*] **unto him**, Master, we know that thou art true [*honest*], and carest for no man [*You are not afraid to say what You think*]: for thou regardest not the person of men [*You don't*

care who You are talking to], but teacheth the way of God in truth: [*This is dripping with false flattery!*] **Is it lawful to give tribute** [*pay taxes*] **to Cæsar, or not?**

15 **Shall we give** [*pay*], **or shall we not give?** But he, knowing their hypocrisy [*trying to look righteous, but enjoying being evil*], said unto them, **Why tempt ye me? bring me a penny,** [*a Roman coin equal to a normal day's pay—see Bible Dictionary, under "Money"*] that I may see it.

16 And **they brought it**. And he saith unto them, **Whose is this image and superscription** [*whose face and title are on the coin*]? And they said unto him, **Cæsar's.**

"Render to Cæsar the Things That Are Cæsar's"

17 And Jesus answering said unto them, **Render** [*pay to*] **to Cæsar the things that are Cæsar's, and to God the things that are God's.** And they marvelled at him [*were surprised at how skillfully He got out of their trap*].

Next, the Sadducees come along to try their hand at trapping the Master. The Sadducees were another somewhat influential group of religious leaders among the Jews. They did not believe in the resurrection and were normally enemies of the Pharisees who did believe in resurrection. The Sadducees have now joined forces with the Pharisees in attempting to do away with Jesus. They will try to trap Him by posing a question about marriage in the next life.

18 **Then come** [*came*] unto him **the Sadducees,** which say there is no resurrection [*who didn't believe in resurrection*]; and **they asked him,** saying,

19 Master, **Moses wrote** unto us [*gave us a law, saying*], If a man's brother die, and leave his wife behind him, and leave no children, that his brother should take [*marry*] his wife, and raise up seed [*children*] unto [*for*] his brother.

20 Now there were **seven brethren** [*brothers*]: and **the first took a wife, and dying left no seed** [*had no children before he died*].

21 And **the second took her** [*married her*], **and died, neither left he any seed:** and **the third likewise.**

22 And **the seven had her** [*all seven brothers eventually married her*], and **left no seed** [*children*]: last of all **the woman died also.**

The Question

23 **In the resurrection therefore, when they shall rise, whose wife shall she be of them? for the seven had her to wife.**

24 And **Jesus** answering **said** unto them, Do ye not therefore err, because ye know not the scriptures, neither the power of God?

JST MARK 12:28

28 And Jesus answering said unto them, **Ye do err therefore, because ye know not, and understand not the scriptures**, neither the power of God.

25 For **when they shall rise from the dead, they neither marry, nor are given in marriage; but are as the angels which are in heaven.** [*After everyone on this earth has been resurrected, there will be no more marrying for them.*]

Here is a major doctrinal point. Many religions use verse 25 to prove that there is no such thing as eternal marriage and family in the next life. On the contrary, the simple fact that the Sadducees asked the Savior the question "Whose wife shall she be of them?" (when they are all resurrected), is proof that the Savior had indeed preached marriage in the resurrection, in other words, eternal marriage. Otherwise, their question would not make any sense at all! The next point of correct doctrine which needs to be understood here is that after everyone from this earth is resurrected, there will be no more eternal marriages performed for them, because such marriages have to be done by mortals for themselves, or by mortals who serve as proxies for those who have died—see D&C 128:15 and 18. Brigham Young said: "And when the Millennium is over, . . . all the sons and daughters of Adam and Eve, down to the last of their posterity (**bold** added for emphasis), who come within the reach of the clemency of the Gospel, [will] have been redeemed in hundreds of temples **through the administration of their children**

MARK

as proxies for them" (Discourses of Brigham Young, p. 395). Since there will be no mortals left on earth after the resurrection is completed, there would be no one left to serve as proxies for eternal marriages.

The next point emphasized by the Savior here is particularly disturbing to the Sadducees, since, as previously mentioned, they do not believe in the resurrection of the dead.

26 And as touching **the dead**, that they **rise** [*get resurrected*]: **have ye not read** in the book of Moses, how in the bush [*the burning bush*] God spake unto him, saying, I am the God of Abraham, and the God of Isaac, and the God of Jacob [*Exodus 3:6*]?

27 **He is not the God of the dead, but the God of the living**: ye therefore do greatly err [*you Sadducees are making a big mistake in not believing in resurrection*].

JST MARK 12:32
32 He is not therefore the God of the dead, but the God of the living; **for he raiseth them up out of their graves**. Ye therefore do greatly err.

The Two Greatest Commandments

28 And **one of the scribes** [*prominent Jewish religious leaders*] **came**, and having heard them [*the Sadducees*] reasoning together, and perceiving that he [*Christ*] had answered them well [*had answered their question about the seven brothers skillfully*], **asked** him, **Which is the first commandment of all?**

29 And Jesus answered him, The first of all the commandments is, Hear, O Israel; The Lord our God is one Lord:

30 And **thou shalt love the Lord thy God with all thy heart, and with all thy soul, and with all thy mind, and with all thy strength**: this is the first commandment.

31 And **the second is like**, namely this, **Thou shalt love thy neighbour as thyself.** There is none other commandment greater than these.

32 And the scribe said unto him, Well, Master, thou hast said the truth: for there is one God; and there is none other but he:

33 And to love him with all the heart, and with all the understanding, and with all the soul, and with all the strength, and to love his neighbour as himself, is more than all whole burnt offerings and sacrifices [*is more important than all the laws of animal sacrifice*].

34 And when **Jesus** saw that he answered discreetly [*carefully and wisely*], he **said** unto him, **Thou art not far from the kingdom of God.** And no man after that durst [*dared*] ask him any question.

Jesus Teaches in the Temple

It must have been frustrating and even infuriating to the Jewish religious leaders at this point that Jesus boldly went back into the temple, which He had cleansed earlier in the week. It would have been an easy matter for them to have Him arrested there, but they did not dare.

Watch now as He poses a question to the people who have gathered in the courtyard of the temple, and then goes on to warn them about their religious leaders.

35 And **Jesus** answered [*spoke*] and said, while he **taught in the temple, How say the scribes** [*the Jewish religious leaders who interpreted the scriptures for the people*] **that Christ is the Son of David** [*what do the scribes mean when they say that Christ is the Son of David*]?

36 For David himself said [*Psalm 110:1*] by the Holy Ghost [*by inspiration*], The LORD [*Heavenly Father*] said to my Lord [*Christ*], Sit thou on my right hand, till I make thine enemies thy footstool [*until You conquer all Your enemies, including Satan*].

37 **David** therefore himself **calleth him Lord; and whence is he then his son** [*how can Christ be David's son if David himself calls him Lord*]? And **the common people heard him gladly**

[were pleased that Jesus was outsmarting their arrogant religious leaders].

38 And **he said unto them** *[the people]* in his doctrine, **Beware of** *[watch out for]* **the scribes,** which love to go in long clothing, and love salutations *[to be greeted by the common people]* in the marketplaces,

39 And the chief *[the most important]* seats in the synagogues, and the uppermost rooms at feasts:

40 Which devour widows' houses *[take widow's houses away from them]*, and for a pretence *[for show]* make long prayers: these *[wicked religious leaders]* shall receive greater damnation *[punishment]*.

The Widow's Mite

41 And **Jesus sat over against the treasury** *[across from where people contributed money in the temple]*, **and beheld** *[watched]* **how the people cast money into the treasury**: and many that were rich cast in much.

42 And there came **a certain poor widow**, and she **threw in two mites**, which make a farthing. *[Bible Dictionary, under "Money," tells us that one mite is equal to 1/64th of a day's pay.]*

43 And he called unto him his disciples, and saith unto them, Verily I say unto you, That **this poor widow hath cast more in, than all they which have cast into the treasury**:

44 For all **they did cast in of their abundance** *[they had plenty of money left over after they gave their contribution]*; **but she of her want** *[in her poverty]* **did cast in all that she had**, even all her living.

MARK 13

THIS CHAPTER DEALS with many of the signs of the times (prophecies that will be fulfilled before the Savior's Second Coming). In the JST, the Prophet made many corrections and changes to this chapter. JST Mark 13, JST Matthew 24, and JS—Matthew in the Pearl of Great Price cover the same material. Joseph Smith made many changes, added many words and phrases (about 450 additional words), and rearranged some of the verses. See Matthew 24 in this study guide for these changes and additions.

1 AND as he went out of the temple, **one of his disciples saith** unto him, Master, see what manner of stones and what buildings are here *[look at these magnificent temple buildings made of stones]*!

Temple Destruction Prophecy

2 **And Jesus** answering *[responding]* **said** unto him, Seest thou these great buildings *[of the temple]*? there shall not be left one stone upon another, that shall not be thrown down.

The Savior's prophecy that the buildings of the temple would be torn down was fulfilled by about A.D. 70 to 73 as the Romans finally conquered the Jews and destroyed many of their cities.

As you will see, four of the Master's Apostles came to Him privately and asked Him two specific questions.

3 And as he sat upon the mount of Olives over against *[across from]* the temple, **Peter** and **James** and **John** and **Andrew asked** him privately,

Two Questions

4 Tell us, [1] **when shall these things be** *[the things you have just prophesied]*? and [2] **what shall be the sign** when all these things shall be fulfilled *[what are the signs to be fulfilled before the Second Coming]*?

5 And **Jesus answering** them began to say, Take heed *[be careful]* lest any man deceive you:

Signs of the Times for Members of the Early Church at the Time of Christ

Verses 6–20 basically deal with prophecies of the future which will be fulfilled during the lifetimes of the early Apostles and members of the Church. Beginning with verse 21, we see things that will happen in our day, prior to the Second Coming.

6 For **many shall come in my name**, saying, I am Christ; **and shall deceive** [*fool*] **many**.

7 And when ye shall hear of **wars and rumours of wars**, be ye not troubled [*don't be too concerned*]: for such things must needs be; but the end [*of the world*] shall not be yet.

8 For **nation shall rise against nation**, and **kingdom against kingdom** [*there will be widespread, numerous wars*]: and there shall be **earthquakes** in divers [*various*] places, and there shall be **famines** and **troubles**: these are the beginnings of **sorrows**.

9 But take heed to yourselves: for **they shall deliver you up to councils** [*you will be arrested*]; and in the synagogues [*Jewish church buildings*] ye shall be beaten: and ye shall be brought before rulers and kings for my sake, for a testimony against them.

10 And the **gospel must first be published among all nations**.

11 But when they [*your enemies*] shall lead you, and deliver you up [*arrest you*], take no thought beforehand what ye shall speak, neither do ye premeditate: but whatsoever shall be given you in that hour, that speak ye: for it is not ye that speak, but the Holy Ghost [*the Holy Ghost will help you know what to say*].

12 Now the **brother shall betray** the **brother** to death, and the **father** the **son**; and **children shall rise up against their parents**, and shall cause them to be put to death [*families will come apart and treat each other terribly*].

13 And ye [*disciples*] shall be hated of all men for my name's sake [*because of your loyalty to me*]: but he that shall endure unto the end, the same shall be saved.

14 But when ye shall see the **abomination of desolation**, spoken of by Daniel the prophet [*Daniel 11:31 and 12:11*], standing where it ought not, (let him that readeth understand,) then let them that be in Judæa flee to the mountains [*to escape*]:

"Abomination of desolation" means terrible things which will cause much destruction and misery. The abomination of desolation spoken of by Daniel was to have two fulfillments. The first occurred in a.d. 70 when Titus, with his Roman legions, surrounded Jerusalem and laid siege to conquer the Jews. This siege resulted in much destruction and terrible human misery and loss of life. In the last days, the abomination of desolation will occur again (see Joseph Smith–Matthew 1:31–32), meaning that Jerusalem will again be under siege. See Bible Dictionary, under "Abomination of Desolation."

15 And let him that is on the housetop not go down into the house, neither enter therein, to take any thing out of his house [*just get away fast!*]:

16 And let him that is in the field not turn back again for to take up his garment [*robe, cloak*].

17 But woe to them that are with child [*pregnant*], and to them that give suck [*are nursing babies and small children*] in those days [*when these things happen to Jerusalem*]!

18 And pray ye that your flight be not in the winter [*when it is more difficult to flee*].

19 For in those days shall be affliction, such as was not from the beginning of the creation which God created unto this time, neither shall be.

20 And except that the Lord had shortened those days, no flesh should be saved [*the Lord will intervene so that some Jews will be left*]: but for the elect's sake, whom he hath chosen, he hath shortened the days.

Signs of the Times for Our Day

Now the topic changes from the days when the Romans conquered and destroyed the Jewish nation, culminating in about A.D. 70 to 73, to the last days and signs preceding the Savior's Second Coming.

21 And then **if any man shall say to you, Lo, here is Christ; or, lo, he is there; believe him not** [*Christ will not come secretly or in just one place at the actual Second Coming; rather He will come and everyone will see Him at once*]:

22 For **false Christs and false prophets** shall rise, and shall shew signs and wonders, to seduce [*fool*], if it were possible, even the elect.

23 But take ye heed: behold, I have foretold you all things.

24 But in those days, after that tribulation, the **sun shall be darkened**, and the **moon shall not give her light**,

25 And the **stars** of heaven **shall fall**, and the powers that are in heaven shall be shaken. [*There will be many signs of the times, that is, prophecies fulfilled in the last days showing that the Second Coming is near.*]

Verse 26 jumps ahead to the Second Coming; then verse 27 goes back to the gathering of Israel in the last days.

26 And then shall they **see the Son of man** [*Jesus, the Son of Man—see Moses 6:57*] **coming** in the clouds with great power and glory.

27 And then shall he send his angels, and shall **gather** together **his elect** from the four winds, from the uttermost part of the earth to the uttermost part of heaven [*the righteous will be gathered*].

The Parable of the Fig Tree

28 Now learn a parable [*a story that teaches*] of the fig tree; **When her branch is yet tender** [*has new growth*], and **putteth forth leaves**, ye **know that summer is near**:

29 So ye in like manner, **when ye shall see these things** [*signs of the times*] come to pass, **know that it** [*the Second Coming*] **is nigh** [*near*], even at the doors.

30 Verily I say unto you, that **this generation** [*the dispensation of the fulness of times, the last dispensation*] **shall not pass, till all these things be done.**

31 Heaven and earth shall pass away: but my words shall not pass away.

No One Knows Exactly When the Savior Will Come

32 But **of that day and that hour knoweth no man, no, not the angels which are in heaven, neither the Son, but the Father.**

Verse 32, above, is similar to Matthew 24:36, but adds that the Son, Jesus, won't know when the Second Coming will be, but only the Father.

33 Take ye heed [*pay attention*], watch and pray: for **ye know not when the time is** [*when the Savior will come*].

A Parable of the Coming

34 For **the Son of man** [*the Savior*] **is as a man taking a far journey**, who left his house [*went to heaven*], and gave authority to his servants [*the Apostles, leaders of the Church*], and to every man his work [*to all members their responsibilities*], and commanded the porter to watch.

35 **Watch ye therefore: for ye know not when the master of the house cometh** [*symbolic of the Savior at his Second Coming*], at even [*evening*], or at midnight, or at the cockcrowing, or in the morning:

36 **Lest coming suddenly he find you sleeping** [*not living righteously*].

37 And what I say unto you I say unto all, **Watch.**

MARK 14

THE FEAST OF the Passover, mentioned in verse 1, was celebrated in the springtime at about the same time as we celebrate Easter. It commemorated the destroying angel's passing over the houses of the children of Israel in Egypt, when the firstborn of the Egyptians were killed. The Israelites in Egypt at the time were instructed by Moses to sacrifice a lamb without blemish and to put blood from the lamb which was sacrificed on the doorposts and lintels of their houses. See Bible Dictionary, under "Feasts." Thus, through the blood of a lamb, the Israelites were protected from the anguish and punishment brought to the Egyptians by the destroying angel. The symbolism is clear. It is by the "blood of the Lamb" (the sacrifice of the Savior) that we are saved, "after all we can do" (2 Nephi 25:23). Now, at the time of Passover in Jerusalem, the "Lamb of God," Christ, will present Himself to be sacrificed, that we might be saved. The Feast of the Passover brought large numbers of Jews from near and far to Jerusalem to join in the worship and celebration.

As you can see in verse 1, the religious leaders of the Jews are frantically plotting to get the Master executed. It is interesting to note that even though the Roman government had given the Jewish religious leaders many powers, they had not given them power to carry out capital punishment.

1 AFTER two days was the **feast of the passover**, and of unleavened bread: and **the chief priests and the scribes** [*religious leaders of the Jews*] **sought how they might take him** [*Jesus*] by craft [*quietly*], **and put him to death.**

2 **But** they said, **Not on the feast day** [*not on Thursday, the day of the Feast of the Passover*], **lest there be an uproar** of the people [*for fear that the people will riot*].

A Woman Anoints Jesus with Costly Spikenard

3 And being **in Bethany** [*a village a short distance from Jerusalem, just over the Mount of Olives*] **in the house of Simon the leper, as he sat at meat** [*as Jesus ate dinner*], **there came a woman** [*Mary—see John 12:3*] **having an alabaster box of ointment of spikenard** very precious [*expensive*]; and she brake [*broke*] the box, and **poured it on his head.**

The anointing of Jesus by Mary, in verse 3, contains much significant symbolism. Jesus is the Messiah. "Messiah" means "the Anointed One" (see Bible Dictionary, under "Messiah"). It would seem that this Mary understood what the disciples did not yet fully understand and symbolically "anointed" the Savior in preparation for His Atoning sacrifice. This sheds light on the divine nature and spiritual sensitivity of women.

As you can see, in verse 4, next, some in attendance were angry because of what they perceived to be a terrible waste of expensive ointment.

4 And there were **some** that **had indignation** within themselves [*who were angry*], and said, **Why was this waste of the ointment made?**

5 For **it might have been sold for more than three hundred pence** [*about a year's wages*], **and** have **been given to the poor.** And they murmured against her.

A Lesson in Perspective

6 And **Jesus said, Let her alone**; why trouble ye her? she hath wrought [*done*] a good work on me.

7 For **ye have the poor with you always**, and whensoever ye will ye may do them good: **but me ye have not always.**

8 She hath done what she could: she is come aforehand **to anoint my body to the burying.**

JST Mark 14:8

8 She has done what she could, **and this which she has done unto me, shall be had in remembrance in generations to come, wheresoever my gospel shall be preached**; for verily she has come beforehand to anoint my body to the burying.

9 Verily I say unto you, Wheresoever this gospel shall be preached throughout the whole world, this also that she hath done shall be spoken of for a memorial of her.

Judas Iscariot Betrays Christ to the Chief Priests

10 And **Judas Iscariot**, one of the twelve, **went unto the chief priests** [*main religious leaders of the Jews*], **to betray him unto them.**

11 And when they heard it, **they** were glad, and **promised to give him money.** And **he sought how he might conveniently** [*watched for an opportunity to*] **betray him.**

Matthew 26:15 says they agreed to pay Judas thirty pieces of silver, which was the going price for a common slave. This devalued the Savior and was an insult to Judas.

The Savior Celebrates Passover with His Disciples

12 And the first day of unleavened bread [*Thursday*], when they killed the passover [*sacrificed the Passover lamb*], **his disciples said** unto him, **Where wilt thou** that we go and prepare that thou mayest **eat the passover** [*the Passover meal*]?

Watch as Jesus prophecies exactly what will happen as He sends two Apostles to make arrangements for them to celebrate the Passover meal together.

13 And **he sendeth forth two** of his disciples, and saith unto them, **Go ye into the city, and there shall meet you a man bearing** [*carrying*] **a pitcher** of water: **follow him.**

14 And **wheresoever he shall go in** [*whichever house he enters*], **say ye to the goodman** [*owner*] of the house, **The Master saith, Where is the guestchamber, where I shall eat the passover with my disciples?**

15 And **he will shew** [*pronounced "show"*] **you a large upper room furnished and prepared:** there make ready for us.

16 And **his disciples went forth**, and came into the city, **and found as he had said** unto them: and they made ready the passover.

17 And **in the evening he cometh** [*came*] **with the twelve.**

Imagine the concern among the Twelve as Jesus made the statement in verse 18.

18 And as they sat and did eat, Jesus said, Verily I say unto you, **One of you** which eateth with me **shall betray me.**

19 And they began to be sorrowful, and to say unto him one by one, **Is it I?** and another said, **Is it I?**

20 And **he answered** and said unto them, **It is one of the twelve, that dippeth** [*that dips his bread*] **with me in the dish.**

21 The Son of man [*Jesus*] indeed goeth [*will be arrested, tried and crucified*], as it is written of him [*as it is prophesied in the scriptures*]: but **woe to that man by whom the Son of man is betrayed!** good were it for that man if he had never been born.

The Last Supper and Sacrament

The Savior now introduces the sacrament to his Apostles. This meal for the Lord and His Apostles is known as the "Last Supper." Jesus introduces the sacrament as a "new testament" (verse 24) The word "testament" often means "covenant" (see Bible Dictionary, under "Covenant.) Thus, the sacrament becomes a "new covenant" and replaces the "old covenant" of animal sacrifice as a means of making covenants and pointing our minds and hearts toward Christ and our commitments to Him.

The Bread

22 And as they did eat, **Jesus took bread, and blessed, and brake it**, and gave to them, and said, Take, eat: **this is my body** [*this represents my body*].

The Wine

23 And **he took the cup, and when he had given thanks, he gave it to them**: and they all drank of it.

24 And he said unto them, **This is my blood** [*this represents my blood*] of the new testament [*the new covenant, associated with the full gospel which Christ had restored*], which is shed for many.

As you know, we now use water instead of wine for the sacrament. You may wish to read the heading for Doctrine and Covenants, Section 27, as well as D&C 27:2, for information regarding this change, as directed by the Lord.

Next, in verse 25, the Master informs His disciples that the next time He will partake of the sacrament with them will be in the kingdom of God. You may wish to read D&C 27, beginning with verse 5, in which the Saviors speaks of a great sacrament meeting to be held in the future. Note that Mark 14:25 is footnoted in the Doctrine and Covenants as a cross-reference for D&C 27:5.

25 Verily I say unto you, **I will drink no more of the fruit of the vine, until that day that I drink it new in the kingdom of God** [*this is the last time the Savior will partake of the sacrament with them during His mortal life*].

A Hymn Is Sung

26 And **when they had sung an hymn,** they went out into the mount of Olives.

27 And **Jesus saith** unto them, **All ye shall be offended** [*stumble, leave, scatter, desert; see Strong's* Concordance, *#4624*] **because of me this night** [*all of you will scatter, desert me tonight because of what happens*]: for it is written [*in Zachariah 13:7*], I will smite the shepherd, and the sheep shall be scattered.

28 But **after** that **I am risen** [*resurrected*], **I will go before you** [*ahead of you*] **into Galilee.**

29 **But Peter said** unto him, Although all shall be offended [*even if everyone else scatters and deserts you*], yet will not I.

30 And **Jesus saith unto him**, Verily I say unto thee, That this day, even in this night, before the cock crow [*a rooster crows*] twice, thou shalt deny me thrice [*you will deny knowing me three times before morning*].

Denying knowing Christ is forgivable and is not the same as denying the Holy Ghost. Peter was very disappointed by his behavior, as recorded in verses 66–72, but he went on to become a powerful Apostle and the president of the church after the Savior was resurrected and taken up into heaven. Perhaps Peter's example here can be a lesson to us. We think we are strong in the gospel and claim to be willing to live it at all costs. Yet, sometimes we falter and give in to temptation which disappoints us and makes us all the more determined to be stronger in the faith.

31 But he [*Peter*] spake the more vehemently [*strongly, emphatically*], If I should die with thee, **I will not deny thee in any wise** [*in any way*]. Likewise also said they all [*all the other apostles said the same thing Peter said*].

The Savior's Suffering in Gethsemane

32 And **they came to** a place which was named **Gethsemane** [*the Garden of Gethsemane*]: and he saith to his disciples, Sit ye here, while I shall pray.

"Gethsemane" means "oil press." There is significant symbolism here. The Jews put olives into bags made of mesh fabric and placed them in a press to squeeze olive oil out of them. The first pressings yielded pure olive oil which was prized for many uses, including healing and giving light in lanterns. In fact, we consecrate it and use it to administer to the sick. The last pressing of the olives, under the tremendous pressure of additional weights added to the press, yielded a bitter, red liquid which can remind us of the "bitter cup" which the Savior partook of. Symbolically, the Savior is going into the "oil press" (Gethsemane) to submit to the "pressure" of all our sins which will "squeeze" His blood out in order that we might have the healing "oil" of the Atonement to heal us from our sins.

33 And **he taketh with him Peter and James and John** [*the "First Presidency"*], and began to be sore amazed [*astonished*], and to be very heavy [*with depression and anguish—see Mark 14:33, footnote b*];

34 And saith unto them, **My soul is exceeding sorrowful unto death**: tarry ye here, and watch.

GETHSEMANE, by Liz Lemon Swindle

The JST gives verses 32–34 as follows:

JST Mark 14:36–38

36 And they came to a place which was named Gethsemane, which was a garden; and **the disciples began to be sore amazed**, and to be very heavy, and to complain in their hearts, wondering if this be the Messiah.

37 And Jesus knowing their hearts, said to his disciples, Sit ye here, while I shall pray.

38 And he taketh with him, Peter, and James, and John, and rebuked them [*perhaps because of their doubts expressed in JST verse 36, quoted above*], and said unto them, My soul is exceeding sorrowful, even unto death; tarry ye here and watch.

35 And he went forward a little, and fell on the ground, and **prayed that, if it were possible, the hour might pass from him.**

36 And he said, **Abba** [*an intimate, personal, tender term; "Daddy" in the Aramaic language of New Testament times—see Bible Dictionary, under "Abba"*], **Father, all things are possible unto thee; take away this cup from me: nevertheless not what I will, but what thou wilt.**

Apostle James E. Talmage describes the suffering of the Savior in Gethsemane as follows:

"Christ's agony in the garden is unfathomable by the finite mind, both as to intensity and cause. The thought that He suffered through fear of death is untenable. Death to Him was preliminary to resurrection and triumphal return to the Father from whom He had come, and to a state of glory even beyond what He had before possessed; and, moreover, it was within His power to lay down His life voluntarily. He struggled and groaned under a burden such as no other being who has lived on earth might even conceive as possible. It was not physical pain, nor mental anguish alone, that caused Him to suffer such torture as to produce an extrusion of blood from every pore; but a spiritual agony of soul such as only God was capable of experiencing. No other man, however great his powers of physical or mental endurance, could have suffered so; for his human organism would have succumbed, and syncope would have produced unconsciousness and welcome oblivion. In that hour of anguish Christ met and overcame all the horrors that Satan, 'the prince of this world' could inflict. The frightful struggle incident to the temptations immediately following the Lord's baptism was surpassed and overshadowed by this supreme contest with the powers of evil.

"In some manner, actual and terribly real though to man incomprehensible, the Savior took upon Himself the burden of the sins of mankind from Adam to the end of the world." (*Jesus the Christ*, page 613)

37 And **he** cometh, and **findeth them sleeping**, and saith unto Peter, Simon, sleepest thou? couldest not thou watch one hour?

38 Watch ye and pray, lest ye enter into temptation. **The spirit truly is ready, but the flesh is weak.**

39 And **again he** went away, and **prayed**, and spake **the same words.**

40 And when he returned, he found them **asleep again**, (for their eyes were heavy,) neither wist [*knew*] they what to answer him.

No doubt these humble apostles were very tired by this time of the week (Thursday night). It had been a difficult week for them, worrying about the Savior's safety and the plots to kill Him. No doubt they had had little sleep. Thus, in verse 40, "their eyes were heavy." In other words, they were very sleepy.

41 And he cometh **the third time**, and saith unto them, **Sleep on** now, and take your rest: it is enough, **the hour is come** [*the time for my arrest, trial, and crucifixion is here*]; behold, **the Son of man** [*Christ*] **is betrayed** into the hands of sinners.

42 Rise up, let us go; lo, he [*Judas Iscariot*] that betrayeth me is at hand [*is coming*].

43 And immediately, while he yet spake, cometh **Judas**, one of the twelve, and with him a great multitude with swords and staves [*sticks*], from [*sent by*] the chief priests and the scribes and the elders [*the Jewish religious leaders*].

44 And he [*Judas*] that betrayed him **had given them** [*the soldiers*] **a token** [*sign*], saying, **Whomsoever I shall kiss, that same is he** [*the person I kiss is Jesus*]; take him [*arrest him*], and lead him away safely [*don't let anyone take him away from you*].

45 And as soon as **he** [*Judas*] was come [*arrived*], he goeth straightway [*immediately*] to him [*Jesus*], and **saith, Master, master; and kissed him.**

46 And they laid their hands on him [*grabbed Him; arrested Him*], and took him.

Peter Cuts Off the Ear of a Relative of the High Priest

47 And **one of them** [*Peter*] that stood by drew a sword, and **smote** [*struck*] **a servant of the high priest** [*one of the high priest's relatives—see John 18:10 and 26*]**, and cut off his ear.** [*Jesus healed this man's ear; see Luke 22:51.*]

48 And **Jesus answered** [*responded*] and said unto them, **Are ye come out, as against a thief, with swords and with staves to take me?**

49 I was daily with you in the temple teaching, and ye took me not [*why didn't you arrest me during the daytime?*]: but the scriptures must be fulfilled.

50 And **they** [*the Apostles*] **all forsook him, and fled** [*as Jesus said they would in verse 27*].

51 And there followed him [*Jesus*] a certain young man, having a linen cloth cast about his naked body; and the young men [*soldiers or members of the mob*] laid hold on him [*grabbed the young man*]:

52 And he left the linen cloth, and fled from them [*the soldiers*] naked.

JST Mark 14:57

57 And there followed him a certain young man, **a disciple**, having a linen cloth cast about his naked body; and the young men laid hold on him, and he left the linen cloth and fled from them naked, **and saved himself out of their hands**.

The Trial before Caiaphas

53 And **they led Jesus away to the high priest**: and with him [*Caiaphas, the high priest*] were assembled all the chief priests and the elders and the scribes.

54 And **Peter followed** him [*Jesus*] afar off, even into the palace of the high priest: and he sat with the servants, and warmed himself at the fire.

55 And **the chief priests and all the council sought for witness against Jesus** to put him to death; and found none.

56 For many bare false witness against him, but their witness agreed not together [*the false witnesses they did get contradicted each other*].

57 And there arose certain, and bare false witness against him, saying,

58 We heard him say, I will destroy this temple that is made with hands, and within three days I will build another made without hands.

59 But neither so did their witness agree together [*they contradicted each other also*].

60 And **the high priest** stood up in the midst, and **asked Jesus**, saying, **Answerest thou nothing** [*aren't You going to say anything*]? what is it which these witness against thee?

61 **But he** [*Jesus*] **held his peace, and answered nothing**. Again the high priest asked him, and said unto him, **Art thou the Christ**, the Son of the Blessed [*the Son of God*]?

62 And Jesus said**, I am**: and ye shall see the Son of man [*Jesus; the Son of Man, meaning the Son of Man of Holiness (the Father; see Moses 6:57)*] sitting on the right hand of power, and coming in the clouds of heaven [*the Second Coming*].

63 **Then the high priest rent** [*tore*] **his clothes**, and saith, What need we any further witnesses [*haven't we heard enough*]?

Tearing your clothing was a cultural way of expressing strongest emotion among the Jews.

64 **Ye have heard the blasphemy** [*this man claims to be the Son of God, the Messiah; he is*

mocking God!]: what think ye? And **they all condemned him to be guilty of death.**

Blasphemy, showing blatant disrespect for God, mocking God, and so forth, was a crime punishable by death according to Jewish law.

65 And some began to **spit on him**, and to cover his face [*blindfolded him*], and to **buffet** [*hit*] **him**, and to say unto him, Prophesy [*tell us which one of us is hitting you; see Luke 22:64*]: and the servants did strike him with the palms of their hands.

Peter Denies Knowing Jesus Three Times

66 And as **Peter was beneath** [*in a lower room*] in the palace [*where the trial was taking place*], **there cometh one of the maids** [*servants*] of the high priest:

67 And when **she saw Peter** warming himself, she looked upon him, **and said, And thou also wast with Jesus of Nazareth** [*you are one of Jesus' followers*].

68 But **he denied**, saying, I know not, neither understand I what thou sayest. And he went out into the porch; and the cock [*rooster*] crew [*crowed*].

69 **And a maid saw him** [*Peter*] again, and began to say to them that stood by [*the bystanders*], **This is one of them** [*Christ's followers*].

70 And **he denied it again**. And a little after [*a while later*], they that stood by said again to Peter, **Surely thou art one of them** [*followers of Jesus*]: for thou art a Galilæan, and thy speech agreeth thereto [*we can tell by your Galilean accent*].

71 But he began to curse and to swear, saying, **I know not this man** of whom ye speak.

72 And the second time **the cock crew** [*a rooster crowed again*]. And Peter called to mind [*remembered*] the word that Jesus said unto him [*in verse 30*], Before the cock crow twice, thou shalt deny me thrice [*three times*]. And when he thought thereon, **he wept.** [*See note following verse 30.*]

MARK 15

THIS IS FRIDAY morning, the day on which they crucified the Savior. After conducting an illegal trial during the night at Caiaphas' palace (nighttime trials were illegal according to the Jew's own laws), the Jewish religious leaders now take the Master to Pilate, the Roman governor over that part of the Holy Land. Remember, as mentioned previously, the Romans at this time had not given the Jews the authority to inflict capital punishment (the death penalty). Therefore, the chief priests were very anxious to get Pilate to give the order that Christ be crucified.

1 AND **straightway** [*first thing*] **in the morning the chief priests held a consultation** [*a meeting*] with the elders and scribes and **the whole council**, and **bound Jesus** [*had Jesus tied up*], and carried him away, and **delivered him** [*turned him over*] **to Pilate** [*the Roman governor of that area*].

The Trial before Pilate

2 And Pilate asked him, **Art thou the King of the Jews?** And he answering said unto him, **Thou sayest it** [*in other words, "Yes I am"; see JST, below, and John 18:37*].

JST Mark 15:4
4 And Jesus answering, said unto him, **I am, even as thou sayest.**

Jesus Refuses to Answer the Chief Priests

3 And **the chief priests accused** him of many things: **but he answered nothing.**

4 And **Pilate asked** him again, saying, **Answerest thou nothing** [*aren't You going to speak in Your own defense*]? behold [*look*] how many things they witness [*testify*] against thee.

5 But **Jesus yet answered nothing**; so that Pilate marvelled [*was surprised*].

The Release of Barabbas

6 Now **at that feast he released unto them one prisoner, whomsoever they desired.** [*It was customary for Pilate to release a prisoner of the people's choosing each year at this time.*]

7 And there was one [*criminal*] named **Barabbas**, which lay bound [*in prison*] with them that had made insurrection with him [*with those who had rebelled against the government with him*], who had committed murder in the insurrection.

The name "Barabbas" means "son of the father" (see Bible Dictionary, under "Barabbas"). This may be symbolic in that the "imposter," Satan, stirred up the multitude to demand the release of an "imposter," Barabbas, while the true "Son of the Father" is punished for crimes which He did not commit.

8 And the multitude crying aloud began to desire him to do as he had ever done unto them [*release a prisoner*].

9 But **Pilate** answered them, saying, **Will ye that I release unto you the King of the Jews** [*mocking Jesus*]?

10 For he knew that the chief priests had delivered him for envy [*had had Jesus arrested because they were jealous of His power and popularity among the people*].

11 But **the chief priests moved** [*influenced*] **the people**, that he should rather [*instead*] **release Barabbas** unto them.

12 And **Pilate** answered [*responded*] and said again unto them, **What will ye then that I shall do unto him** [*Jesus*] whom ye call the King of the Jews?

13 And they cried out again, **Crucify him**.

14 Then Pilate said unto them, **Why**, what evil hath he done? And they cried out the more exceedingly [*more loudly*], Crucify him.

15 And so **Pilate**, willing to content [*please*] the people, **released Barabbas** unto them, and **delivered Jesus**, when he had **scourged him** [*had him beaten, whipped, flogged*], **to be crucified**.

"Scourging" was a very severe punishment, and many prisoners did not live through it. It consisted of being whipped with a whip which was composed of leather thongs with bits of metal, bone, etc., secured to the ends of the thongs.

The Soldiers Mock Jesus

16 And the **soldiers led him away** into the hall, called Prætorium [*a room in the governor's house*]; and they call together the whole band [*about six hundred Roman soldiers with a leader over them; see McConkie,* Doctrinal New Testament Commentary, *Vol. 1, p. 781*].

17 And they **clothed him with purple** [*in mockery of His claim to be "King of the Jews"*], and platted [*made, wove*] a **crown of thorns**, and put it about his head,

18 And **began to salute him** [*saying*], Hail, King of the Jews!

19 And they **smote** [*hit*] **him** on the head with a reed [*stick, mock scepter of kingly authority*], and did **spit upon him**, and bowing their knees **worshipped him** [*pretended to worship him*].

20 And when they had **mocked him**, they took off the purple from him, and put his own clothes on him, and **led him out to crucify him**.

21 And **they compel** [*forced*] one **Simon** a Cyrenian, who passed by, coming out of the country [*probably a foreigner [perhaps a Jew who had come for Passover]* who came from Cyrene, a city in northern Africa], the father of Alexander and Rufus, **to bear** [*carry*] **his cross**. [*After the suffering in the Garden of Gethsemane, the whipping, mocking, and so forth, Jesus was too weak to carry His own cross, which was a part of the legally required punishment and torture which went along with crucifixion.*]

The Crucifixion

22 And they bring *[brought]* him unto the place **Golgotha**, which is, being interpreted, The place of a skull.

23 And **they gave him** to drink **wine mingled with myrrh**: but **he received it not** *[refused it]*.

This mixture of wine and myrrh was designed to drug the victim of crucifixion to lessen the pain somewhat. See *Jesus the Christ*, pp. 654–655.

24 And when they had crucified him *[hung him on the cross]*, they parted his garments *[divided up his clothes]*, casting lots upon them, what every man should take *[gambling to see who got what item of clothing]*.

MARK

25 And it was **the third hour** *[about 9 A.M.]*, and **they crucified him.**

26 And the **superscription** *[writing]* of his accusation *[what He was accused of]* was written over *[above Him on the cross]*, **THE KING OF THE JEWS.**

The JST informs us that some of the Jewish chief priests were very frustrated about the sign above the Savior's head, as mentioned in verse 26, above. They wanted Pilate to modify it to read that Jesus "claimed" to be the king of the Jews.

JST MARK 15:29–31

29 And **Pilate wrote** his accusation and put it upon the cross, THE KING OF THE JEWS.

30 There were certain of the **chief priests** who stood by, that said unto Pilate, **Write, that he said**, I am the King of the Jews.

31 **But Pilate said** unto them, **What I have written, I have written.**

The Two Thieves

27 And **with him they crucify two thieves**; the one on his right hand, and the other on his left.

28 And the **scripture** was **fulfilled** *[Isaiah 53:12]*, which saith, And **he was numbered with the transgressors** *[killed with criminals]*.

29 And **they that passed by railed on him** *[shouted, mocked him]*, wagging *[shaking]* their heads, and saying, Ah, thou that destroyest the temple, and buildest it in three days,

These people obviously misunderstood what Jesus said regarding the temple. What He said is in John 2:19–21. He said that if they destroyed His body (the "temple of his body"), He would raise it up in three days (be resurrected in three days). By the time Jesus is on the cross, His statement has been misquoted and spread so that the mockers claim that He said He would destroy their massive temple in Jerusalem and rebuild it in three days.

30 **Save thyself**, and come down from the cross.

31 Likewise also **the chief priests mocking** said among themselves with the scribes, **He saved others; himself he cannot save.**

32 **Let Christ the King of Israel descend** *[come down]* **now from the cross, that we may see and believe.** And they that were crucified with him reviled him *[mocked him]*.

One of the thieves seems to have softened his attitude a bit later. The Savior said to him, "Today shalt thou be with me in paradise." We will do more with this in Luke 23:43.

33 And when **the sixth hour** *[about noon]* was come, there was **darkness** over the whole land until the ninth hour *[about 3 P.M.]*.

34 And at the **ninth hour** *[about three in the afternoon]* Jesus cried with a loud voice, saying, Eloi, Eloi, lama sabachthani? which is, being interpreted, **My God, my God, why hast thou forsaken me?**

This had to have been a most difficult time for the Savior. Apparently, as part of the Atonement, Jesus had to experience what sinners do when they sin so much that the Spirit leaves them. At this point on the cross, we understand that all available help from the Father withdrew in order that the Savior might experience all things, including

the withdrawal of the Spirit which sinners experience.

And some of them that stood by, when they heard it, said, Behold, he calleth Elias [*Elijah*].

36 And one ran and filled a spunge full of vinegar, and put it on a reed, and gave him to drink, saying, Let alone; let us see whether Elias will come to take him down.

37 And **Jesus cried with a loud voice, and gave up the ghost** [*left his body, died*].

38 And the **veil of the temple** was **rent** in twain [*torn in two*] from the top to the bottom.

39 And when the **centurion** [*Roman soldier*], which stood over against him [*across from Jesus*], saw that he so cried out [*had so much strength when he cried out*], and gave up the ghost, he said, **Truly this man was the Son of God.**

> It was common for victims of crucifixion to live two or three days before dying. The soldier was startled because he was experienced in crucifying people and it appeared to him that Jesus, who was still relatively strong, and after only six hours on the cross, had decided to leave His body and did so. That is exactly what happened and the Roman soldier apparently received a witness of Christ at that moment.

40 There were also women looking on afar off: among whom was **Mary Magdalene, and Mary** [*possibly the Savior's mother; see Mark 6:3*] the mother of James the less and of Joses, and Salome;

41 [*Who also, when he was in Galilee, followed him, and ministered unto him;*] **and many other women** which came up with him unto Jerusalem.

The Savior's Body Is Taken Off the Cross

42 And now **when the even** [*evening*] **was come,** because it was the preparation, that is, the day before the sabbath,

43 **Joseph of Arimathaea,** an honourable counsellor, which also waited for the kingdom of God [*who also was a believer*], came, and **went in boldly unto Pilate, and craved** [*requested*] **the body of Jesus.**

44 And **Pilate marvelled if he were already dead** [*was surprised that Jesus was already dead*]: and calling unto him the centurion, he asked him whether he [*Jesus*] had been any while dead [*had been dead very long*].

45 And when he knew it of the centurion [*when the Roman soldier verified that Jesus was indeed dead*], **he gave the body to Joseph.**

46 And he [*Joseph of Arimathaea*] bought fine linen, and took him down [*from the cross*], and wrapped him in the linen, and laid him in a sepulchre [*tomb*] which was hewn [*carved*] out of a rock, and rolled a stone unto the door of the sepulchre.

47 And **Mary Magdalene and Mary the mother of Joses beheld** [*watched to see*] where he was laid.

MARK 16

THIS CHAPTER CONTAINS Mark's account of the resurrection of the Savior. It is a glorious Sunday morning. The faithful women who had watched from a distance as Joseph of Arimathaea hurriedly took the Lord's body down from the cross and laid it in his own new tomb (Mark 15:42–47) have come very early Sunday morning to tenderly finish the customary final preparation of the Savior's body for burial.

The Savior's Resurrection

1 AND when the sabbath [*Saturday for the Jews*] was past, **Mary Magdalene,** and **Mary** the mother of James, **and Salome,** had **bought sweet spices,** that they might come and anoint him [*finish preparing Jesus' body for burial*].

2 And **very early in the morning** the first day of the week [*Sunday*], **they came unto the sepulchre** [*tomb*] at the rising of the sun.

The Stone Was Already Rolled Away

3 And they said among themselves, **Who shall roll** us **away the stone** from the door of the sepulchre *[so we can get into the tomb]*?

4 And when they looked, they saw that **the stone was rolled away**: for it was very great *[large]*.

5 And **entering into the sepulchre** *[the tomb]*, they saw a young man *[two angels—see JST quoted below]* sitting on the right side, clothed in a long white garment; and they were affrighted *[afraid]*.

6 And he *[they]* saith unto them, Be not affrighted: Ye seek Jesus of Nazareth, which was crucified: **he is risen** *[resurrected]*; **he is not here**: behold *[look at]* the place where they laid him.

7 But **go** your way, **tell his disciples** and Peter **that he** *[Jesus]* **goeth** before you *[ahead of you]* **into Galilee**: there shall ye see him, as he said unto you *[in Mark 14:28]*.

JST Mark 16:3–6

3 But when they looked, they saw that the stone was rolled away, (for it was very great,) and **two angels** sitting thereon, clothed in long white garments; and they were affrighted.

4 But **the angels** said unto them, Be not affrighted; ye seek Jesus of Nazareth, who was crucified; he is risen; he is not here; behold the place where they laid him;

5 And go your way, tell his disciples and Peter, that he goeth before you into Galilee; there shall ye see him as he said unto you.

6 And they, entering into the sepulcher, saw the place where they laid Jesus *[this verse is missing from Mark's account in the Bible]*.

8 And **they went out quickly**, and fled from the sepulchre; for they trembled and were amazed: neither said they any thing to any man; for they were afraid.

Jesus Appears to Mary Magdalene

9 Now when Jesus was risen *[resurrected]* early the first day of the week, **he appeared first to Mary Magdalene**, out of whom he had cast seven devils *[Luke 8:2]*.

10 **And she went and told them that had been with him** *[His disciples]*, as they mourned and wept.

11 And **they**, when they had heard that he was alive, and had been seen of *[by]* her, **believed not**.

Jesus Appears to Two on the Road to Emmaus

12 **After that he appeared** in another form **unto two of them** *[two other disciples]*, as they walked *[on the road to Emmaus; see Luke 24:13–35]*, and went into the country.

13 **And they went and told it unto the residue** *[rest of the group]*: neither believed they them.

Jesus Appears to Eleven Apostles

14 Afterward **he appeared unto the eleven** *[Apostles]* as they sat at meat *[as they were eating]*, **and upbraided** *[scolded]* **them** with their unbelief and hardness of heart, **because they believed not them which had seen him after he was risen.**

The Charge to Preach the Gospel to All the World

15 And he said unto them *[the Apostles]*, **Go ye into all the world, and preach the gospel to every creature** *[person]*.

Next, in verse 16, we are taught the vital importance of baptism (for those over age eight—see D&C 137:10).

Baptism Is Essential

16 **He that believeth and is baptized shall be saved; but he that believeth not shall be damned** *[will be stopped in their progress]*.

17 And **these signs shall follow them that believe;** In my name shall they cast out devils *[evil spirits]*; they shall speak with new tongues *[foreign languages]*;

18 They shall take up serpents *[the Apostle Paul had an experience with this in Acts 28:3–6]*; and if they drink any deadly thing, it shall not hurt them: they shall lay hands on the sick, and they shall recover. *[In other words, the Apostles will have divine protection as they carry out the work of the Lord.]*

The Ascension of Christ

19 So then **after the Lord had spoken unto them, he was received up into heaven, and sat on the right hand of God.**

20 **And they went forth, and preached** every where, the Lord working with them, and confirming the word with signs following. Amen.

SHE BROUGHT FORTH HER FIRSTBORN SON, AND WRAPPED HIM IN SWADDLING CLOTHES, AND LAID HIM IN A MANGER.

LUKE 2:7

THE GOSPEL ACCORDING TO ST LUKE

LUKE WAS A physician according to Colossians 4:14 and was a missionary companion to Paul. Most Bible scholars believe that he was of Gentile birth. He is also the author of Acts. His sensitivity to people and their needs shows in his writing. He gives emphasis to the role women played in the life and ministry of the Savior. Perhaps, because he is a physician, he alone of the gospel writers tells of Christ's bleeding during his agony in the Garden of Gethsemane. Luke was not an eyewitness to the Savior's ministry, rather learned from Paul and others about Jesus. It appears that he was writing to the Gentiles, especially the Greeks, to teach them of Jesus and His divine mission as our Savior and Redeemer.

A Note about bolding

In both Matthew and Mark, in this study guide, we used **bold** for teaching emphasis and to suggest things you may wish to underline or otherwise mark in your own scriptures. In Luke and John, we will not use bold, with the idea that you are ready to mark and underline on your own. One of the purposes of marking scriptures (for those who choose to do so) is to personalize your scriptures according to your own needs and circumstances, as directed by the Spirit.

Also, you can underline just a few key words in a particular verse which will then stand out, and, at a glance, give you a review of the content of that verse. For example, in verses 26–27 of Luke, chapter one, you might underline "Gabriel was sent . . . to a virgin . . . Mary" which would then become a quick review for you as to the content of those verses.

LUKE 1

IN CHAPTER ONE, you will see an angel named Gabriel announce to Zacharias that he and his elderly wife, Elizabeth, will have a son (John the Baptist). About six months later, Gabriel (who is the prophet Noah—see Bible Dictionary, under "Gabriel") will also have the privilege of announcing to Mary that she will be the mother of the Son of God. Mary will visit Elizabeth (a relative) who is six months along and the child in her womb will respond to Mary as she enters Elizabeth's home.

You will see beautiful examples of revelation to these humble and righteous people in this first chapter of Luke. In a tender scene, Elizabeth will prophesy (verses 42–45) about Mary; then Mary will also prophesy (verses 46–55). After about three more months, John the Baptist will be born and his father, Zacharias, will prophesy (verses 67–79).

1 FORASMUCH as [*since*] many have taken in hand [*have undertaken*] to set forth in order a declaration of [*to write about*] those things which are most surely believed among us,

> JST LUKE 1:1
> As I am a messenger of Jesus Christ, and knowing that many have taken in hand to set forth in order a declaration of those things which are most surely believed among us;

2 Even as they delivered them unto us, which from the beginning were eyewitnesses [*not all were eyewitnesses of Christ, but were eyewitnesses to the gospel and the growth of the Church*], and ministers of the word;

3 It seemed good to me [*Luke*] also, having had perfect understanding of all things from the

very first [*I have been taught and understand all things from the birth of John the Baptist and from the birth of Jesus up to and including the crucifixion and resurrection of the Savior*], to write unto thee in order, most excellent Theophilus [*"friend of God," probably a Greek official of high rank*],

4 That thou mightest know the certainty [*that you might have a testimony*] of those things, wherein thou hast been instructed.

Having introduced the purpose of his letter to Theophilus, Luke now begins his account of the birth and life of Christ.

5 THERE was in the days of Herod, the king of Judæa, a certain priest [*in the Aaronic Priesthood*] named Zacharias, of the course of Abia [*a descendant of Aaron through Abijah*]: and his wife was of the daughters of Aaron [*was a descendant of Aaron*], and her name was Elisabeth.

The priests who served in the temple at the time of Christ were members of the Aaronic Priesthood. Zacharias was a righteous holder of this priesthood. Those men who fulfilled priestly duties at the temple at Jerusalem were divided into 24 groups or "courses", each group assigned to serve for one week at a time. Zacharias was a member of the eighth "course" or group. Each group had upwards of 1400 men, so the privilege of officiating at the burning of incense in the temple might come once or never in the lifetime of a priest. (See *Jesus the Christ*, pp. 75-76.)

6 And they were both righteous before God, walking in all the commandments and ordinances of the Lord blameless.

7 And they had no child, because that Elisabeth was barren [*had not been able to have children*], and they both were now well stricken in years [*were quite old and had given up on having children*].

8 And it came to pass, that while he [*Zacharias*] executed the priest's office [*carried out his duties in the temple*] before God in the order of his course,

JST Luke 1:8

And while he executed the priest's office before God, in the order of his priesthood,

9 According to the custom of the priest's office, his lot was [*he had been selected*] to burn incense when he went into the temple of the Lord.

Since it was generally a once-in-a-lifetime opportunity for an Aaronic Priesthood priest to have the privilege of burning incense in the temple, as mentioned in the note above, this would have been a very humbling and important day for Zacharias.

10 And the whole multitude of the people were praying without [*outside of the temple, watching for the cloud of smoke from the incense to rise from the temple, and waiting for Zacharias to come back out in a few minutes*] at the time of incense.

Gabriel Announces the Coming Birth of John the Baptist

11 And there appeared unto him [*Zacharias*] an angel of the Lord standing on the right side of the altar of incense.

This angel was Gabriel. He will also appear to Mary in a few months to tell her that she will be the mother of the Son of God. As mentioned previously, we are told that Gabriel is Noah. See Bible Dictionary, under "Gabriel."

12 And when Zacharias saw him, he was troubled, and fear fell upon him.

13 But the angel said unto him, Fear not, Zacharias: for thy prayer is heard; and thy wife Elisabeth shall bear thee a son, and thou shalt call his name John.

One of the important lessons we gain from verse 13, above, is that we should not give up praying for righteous desires of our hearts.

The instruction by the angel to call their son "John" was very definite. Otherwise, they would very likely have named him Zacharias, after his father.

14 And thou shalt have joy and gladness; and many shall rejoice at his birth.

Next, the angel prophecies to Zacharias about the wonderful son he and Elizabeth will have, after having waited all these years.

15 For he shall be great in the sight of the Lord, and shall drink neither wine nor strong drink [*a sign that he was dedicated to a special calling*]; and he shall be filled with the Holy Ghost [*see D&C 84:27*], even from his mother's womb [*before he is born*].

Elder Bruce R. McConkie teaches us more about John the Baptist, as quoted in the *Doctrine and Covenants Student Manual*, pp. 183:

"What concerns us above all else as to the coming of John, however, is that he came with power and authority. He first received his errand from the Lord. His was no ordinary message, and he was no unauthorized witness. He was called of God and sent by him, and he represented Deity in the words that he spoke and the baptisms he performed. He was a legal administrator whose words and acts were binding on earth and in heaven, and his hearers were bound, at the peril of their salvation, to believe his words and heed his counsels.

"Luke says: 'The word of God came unto John the son of Zacharias in the wilderness.' Later John is to say: 'He that sent me to baptize with water, the same said unto me,' such and such things (John 1:33). Who sent him we do not know. We do know that 'he was baptized while he was yet in his childhood [meaning, when he was eight years of age], and was ordained by the angel of God at the time he was eight days old unto this power [note it well, not to the Aaronic Priesthood, but] to overthrow the kingdom of the Jews, and to make straight the way of the Lord before the face of his people, to prepare them for the coming of the Lord, in whose hand is given all power' (D&C 84:24). We do not know when he received the Aaronic Priesthood, but obviously it came to him after his baptism, at whatever age was proper, and before he was sent by one whom he does not name to preach and baptize with water." (*Mortal Messiah*, pp. 384–85).

16 And many of the children of Israel shall he turn to the Lord their God.

17 And he [*John the Baptist*] shall go before him [*go ahead of Christ*] in the spirit and power of Elias [*one who prepares the way for even more important things; see Teachings of the Prophet Joseph Smith, pages 335-336; also see Bible Dictionary, under "Elias"*], to turn the hearts of the fathers to the children, and the disobedient to the wisdom of the just [*righteous*]; to make ready a people prepared for the Lord [*Jesus*].

Zacharias is humbly puzzled by the announcement of the angel, since he and Elizabeth are old, and she is well-beyond the years when she could bear a child.

18 And Zacharias said unto the angel, Whereby [*how*] shall I know this? for I am an old man, and my wife well stricken in years [*we are beyond the years when we can have children*].

19 And the angel answering said unto him, I am Gabriel [*Noah; see note after verse 11 above*], that stand in the presence of God; and am sent to speak unto thee, and to shew thee these glad tidings.

While the limitation placed upon Zacharias, in verse 20, next, as a result of his hesitation to believe the words of the angel, might be viewed as a punishment, it might also be viewed as a kindness, as an assurance that he had indeed seen Gabriel and thus, that he and Elisabeth would surely have the promised son.

20 And, behold, thou shalt be dumb [*unable to talk*], and not able to speak, until the day that these things shall be performed [*until John is born*], because thou believest not my words, which shall be fulfilled in their season.

21 And the people waited for Zacharias, and marvelled that he tarried so long in the temple [*were wondering what was taking him so long*].

22 And when he came out, he could not speak unto them: and they perceived [*understood*] that he had seen a vision in the temple: for he beckoned unto them [*described with his hands that he had seen a vision*], and remained speechless.

23 And it came to pass, that, as soon as the days of his ministration were accomplished [*after his week of temple duties was over; see note after verse five above*], he departed to his own house.

Luke leaves it to our own imaginations to envision the scene that took place in the home of Zacharias and Elizabeth as he returned from his temple service and broke the good news to her.

ANNUNCIATION TO MARY, by Joseph F. Brickey

24 And after those days his wife Elisabeth conceived, and hid herself five months, saying,

25 Thus hath the Lord dealt with me in the days wherein he looked on me, to take away my reproach among men [*to take away the social stigma of being childless*].

Six months after Elizabeth conceived, Gabriel appeared to Mary to tell her that she would be the mother of Jesus Christ. Imagine what a joy it was to Gabriel, or Noah, who preached the gospel and built the Ark in preparation for the Flood, to come back as the angel who had the privilege of announcing the coming birth of the Savior.

Gabriel Announces the Coming Birth of the Son of God

26 And in the sixth month the angel Gabriel [*Noah; see note after verse 11 above*] was sent from God unto a city of Galilee, named Nazareth,

27 To a virgin espoused [*engaged, promised*] to a man whose name was Joseph, of the house of David [*who was a descendant of David*]; and the virgin's name was Mary.

Being "espoused" (verse 27) was a much stronger commitment than engagement is in our day. An espoused couple was bound by covenants to each other even before their marriage and the espousal could not be broken off except through formal action similar to divorce.

28 And the angel came in unto her, and said, Hail, thou that art highly favoured, the Lord is with thee: blessed art thou among women.

29 And when she saw him, she was troubled at his saying, and cast in her mind what manner of salutation this should be [*wondered what kind of a greeting this was*].

30 And the angel said unto her, Fear not, Mary: for thou hast found favour with God.

His Name Is to be Jesus

31 And, behold, thou shalt conceive in thy womb, and bring forth a son, and shalt call his name JESUS.

Next, Gabriel gives Mary a brief description of her special Son. Mary would no doubt have recognized some of the ancient prophecies quoted by the angel, which would help her comprehend the significance of this announcement to her.

32 He shall be great, and shall be called the Son of the Highest [*the son of Heavenly Father*]: and the Lord God [*Heavenly Father*] shall give unto him the throne of his father [*ancestor*] David:

33 And he shall reign over the house of Jacob [*house of Israel; descendants of Jacob*] for ever; and of his kingdom there shall be no end.

34 Then said Mary unto the angel, How shall this be, seeing I know not a man [*I am a virgin*]?

35 And the angel answered and said unto her, The Holy Ghost shall come upon thee, and the power of the Highest [*the highest member of the Godhead, in other words, the Father*] shall overshadow thee: therefore also that holy thing [*holy child*] which shall be born of thee shall be called the Son of God.

JST LUKE 1:35

35 And the angel answered and said unto her, Of the Holy Ghost, and the power of the Highest. Therefore also, that holy child that shall be born of thee shall be called the Son of God.

Some people use verse 35, above, to suggest that the Holy Ghost is the father of Jesus. That is a completely false doctrine. Apostle James E. Talmage teaches the following:

"That Child to be born of Mary was begotten of Elohim, the Eternal Father, not in violation of natural law but in accordance with a higher manifestation thereof; and, the offspring from that association of supreme sanctity, celestial Sireship, and pure though mortal maternity, was of right to be called the 'Son of the Highest.' In His nature would be combined the powers of Godhood with the capacity and possibilities of mortality; and this through the ordinary operation of the fundamental law of heredity declared of God, demonstrated by science, and admitted by philosophy, that living beings shall propagate—after their kind. The Child Jesus was to inherit the physical, mental and spiritual traits, tendencies, and powers that characterized His parents—one immortal and glorified—God, the other human—woman." (*Jesus the Christ*, p. 81)

Next, Gabriel tells Mary that her elderly cousin Elizabeth (actually a relative, not necessarily a cousin—see Luke 1:36, footnote a, in your Bible), is expecting a son.

36 And, behold, thy cousin Elisabeth, she hath also conceived a son in her old age: and this is the sixth month with her, who was called barren [*childless; Elizabeth is six months pregnant*].

37 For with God nothing shall be impossible.

Mary's Humble Response

There is probably not a greater example anywhere in scripture of humble faith and submission to the will of the Lord than the response given by Mary to the angel's announcement.

38 And Mary said, Behold the handmaid of the Lord; be it unto me according to thy word. And the angel departed from her.

Next, Mary will visit Elizabeth.

39 And Mary arose in those days, and went into the hill country with haste [*hurried*], into a city of Juda;

40 And entered into the house of Zacharias, and saluted [*greeted*] Elisabeth.

41 And it came to pass, that, when Elisabeth heard the salutation [*greeting*] of Mary, the babe leaped in her womb [*little John the Baptist jumped inside of Elizabeth*]; and Elisabeth was filled with the Holy Ghost:

Apostle Bruce R. McConkie teaches some comforting doctrine regarding stillborn children based on verse 41 above. It is as follows:

"(The babe leaped in her womb). In this miraculous event the pattern is seen which a spirit follows in passing from his pre-existent first estate into mortality. The spirit enters the body at the time of quickening, months prior to the actual normal birth. The value and comfort attending a knowledge of this eternal truth is seen in connection with stillborn children. Since the spirit entered the body before birth, stillborn children will be resurrected and righteous parents shall enjoy their association in immortal glory." (*Doctrinal New Testament Commentary*, Vol. 1, pp. 84–85)

Elizabeth Prophesies

42 And she [*Elizabeth*] spake out with a loud voice, and said [*note that Elizabeth will now exercise the gift of prophesy; see D&C 46:22*], Blessed art thou [*Mary*] among women, and blessed is the fruit of thy womb [*the child who will be born to you*].

43 And whence is this to me, that the mother of my Lord should come to me [*how do I rate the privilege of having the mother of the Son of God come visit me*]?

44 For, lo, as soon as the voice of thy salutation [*greeting*] sounded in mine ears, the babe [*John*] leaped in my womb for joy.

45 And blessed is she that believed: for there shall be a performance of those things which were told her from the Lord [*everything promised to you will be fulfilled*].

Just as Elizabeth was filled with the Spirit of prophecy, now Mary is given the gift of prophecy (one of the gifts of the Spirit—see D&C 46:22) also. Her beautiful prophecies are recorded in verses 46-55.

Mary Prophesies

46 And Mary said, My soul doth magnify [*praise*] the Lord,

47 And my spirit hath rejoiced in God my Saviour.

JST LUKE 1:46

46 And my spirit rejoiceth in God my Savior.

It is touching to realize that Mary's baby would be her Savior as well as her child. From the verses we are reading here, it seems clear that she was well versed in the scriptures and understood that these prophecies pertained to the son whom she would now bear.

48 For he hath regarded [*seen, considered*] the low estate [*humble condition*] of his handmaiden [*servant*]: for, behold, from henceforth all generations shall call me blessed [*from now on, all people will know me and know how blessed I am*].

49 For he that is mighty [*God*] hath done to me great things; and holy is his name.

JST Luke 1:48

48 For he who is mighty hath done to me great things; and I will magnify his holy name,

50 And his mercy is on them that fear [*respect and obey*] him from generation to generation.

In verses 51–55, we continue gaining marvelous insights into the depth of Mary's understanding concerning the coming Messiah.

51 He hath shewed [*demonstrated*] strength with his arm [*has shown His power*]; he hath scattered [*punished*] the proud in the imagination of their hearts [*because of their pride*].

52 He hath put down [*humbled*] the mighty from their seats [*positions of power*], and exalted them of low degree [*blessed and lifted up the humble*].

53 He hath filled the hungry [*those who "hunger and thirst after righteousness"; see Matthew 5:6*] with good things; and the rich [*the rich who are prideful*] he hath sent empty away.

54 He hath holpen [*helped*] his servant Israel [*the covenant people*], in remembrance of his mercy;

55 As he spake to our fathers [*ancestors*], to Abraham, and to his seed [*posterity*] for ever.

56 And Mary abode with her [*stayed with Elizabeth*] about three months, and returned to her own house.

John the Baptist Is Born

57 Now Elisabeth's full time came that she should be delivered [*the time came for her to have her baby*]; and she brought forth a son.

58 And her neighbours and her cousins heard how the Lord had shewed [*showed*] great mercy upon her; and they rejoiced with her.

As you can see, in verse 59, next, the friends and neighbors of Zacharias and Elizabeth automatically assumed that their miraculous son would be named after his father. Remember, Zacharias has not been able to talk since the visit of Gabriel about nine months ago. Remember also that in verse 13, above, the angel instructed him to name his son "John." Based on what we see in verse 60, he had told Elizabeth about the name and she held firm to that instruction from the angel, even when well-meaning people tried to talk her out of it.

59 And it came to pass, that on the eighth day they came to circumcise the child [*John*]; and they called him Zacharias, after the name of his father.

60 And his mother answered [*responded*] and said, Not so; but he shall be called John [*his name is not Zacharias; it is John!*].

61 And they said unto her, There is none of thy kindred that is called by this name. [*Why name him John? You have no relatives named John.*]

62 And they made signs to his father, how he would have him called [*asked Zacharias what the baby's name should be*].

Next, Zacharias confirms what Elizabeth had told them, and he is immediately able to speak again.

63 And he asked for a writing table [*because he was still unable to speak*], and wrote, saying, His name is John. And they marvelled all [*were all surprised*].

64 And his [*Zacharias'*] mouth was opened immediately, and his tongue loosed, and he spake, and praised God.

65 And fear [*awe*] came on all that dwelt round about them: and all these sayings were noised abroad [*were spread*] throughout all the hill country of Judæa.

66 And all they that heard them laid them up in their hearts, saying, What manner of child shall this be [*what kind of special child is John*]! And the hand of the Lord was with him.

Zacharias Prophecies About John

67 And his father Zacharias was filled with the Holy Ghost, and prophesied, saying,

68 Blessed be the Lord God of Israel [*we are grateful to God*]; for he hath visited [*come; helped*] and redeemed his people,

Zacharias is prophesying about the future as if it had already taken place. This is a common form of prophecy in the Bible.

69 And hath raised up an horn [*"horn" was symbolic of safety, strength, and protection in Jewish culture*] of salvation for us in the house of his servant David [*among us descendants of David*];

70 As he spake by the mouth of his holy prophets, which have been since the world began:

71 That we should be saved from our enemies, and from the hand of all that hate us;

72 To perform the mercy promised to our fathers [*ancestors*], and to remember [*fulfill*] his holy covenant;

73 The oath [*promise*] which he sware [*promised*] to our father [*ancestor*] Abraham,

74 That he would grant unto us, that we being delivered out of the hand of our enemies might serve him without fear [*without fear of being persecuted*],

75 In holiness and righteousness before him, all the days of our life.

76 And thou, child [*little John the Baptist*], shalt be called the prophet of the Highest [*God*]: for thou shalt go before the face of [*ahead of*] the Lord [*Jesus*] to prepare his ways;

77 To give knowledge of salvation unto his people by the remission of their sins,

78 Through the tender mercy of our God; whereby the dayspring [*rising sun, dawn*] from on high hath visited us [*this is the dawn of a new day for us*],

79 To give light to them that sit in darkness [*spiritual darkness*] and in the shadow of death, to guide our feet into the way of peace.

Next, Luke gives a very brief summary of John the Baptist's life from birth to the beginning of his mission to formally prepare the way for the Savior. He does something similar with respect to the life of Jesus, in Luke 2:40 and 52.

80 And the child [*John*] grew, and waxed strong [*gained strength*] in spirit, and was in [*lived in*] the deserts till the day of his shewing [*beginning of his mission*] unto Israel.

LUKE 2

THIS CHAPTER IS probably one of the best known in the Bible. It has the "Christmas Story" about the birth of the Christ Child and the shepherds who came in from the fields to see baby Jesus. It also contains the account of twelve-year-old Jesus teaching in the temple.

1 AND it came to pass in those days, that there went out a decree from Caesar Augustus [*the ruler over the Roman Empire from 31 B.C. to A.D. 14*], that all the world [*everyone in the Roman Empire*] should be taxed.

2 [*And this taxing was first made when Cyrenius was governor of Syria.*]

3 And all went to be taxed, every one into his own city.

This was actually a process of registration or taking a census of all the people who were subject to the Roman government. Based on this census and registration, taxes were later assessed and then collected. The Roman government allowed people to register in the towns where they currently lived, but Jewish custom required that the Jews go to their hometowns to register and be counted. Thus, Joseph and Mary had to travel from Nazareth to Bethlehem, a distance of some one hundred plus miles. See *Jesus the Christ*, pp. 91–92.]

4 And Joseph also went up from Galilee, out of the city of Nazareth, into Judæa, unto the city of David, which is called Bethlehem [*thus fulfilling the prophecy in Micah 5:2 that Christ would be born in Bethlehem*]; (because he was of the house and lineage of David:)
5 To be taxed with Mary his espoused [*married; see Matthew 1:24*] wife, being great with child.

Note: Mary was indeed "great with child", for the Savior was born while she and Joseph were in Bethlehem. It is highly likely that Mary was in labor during the long journey from Nazareth to Bethlehem.

6 And so it was, that, while they were there, the days were accomplished that she should be delivered [*the time came for her to have her baby*].

Jesus Is Born

7 And she brought forth her firstborn son, and wrapped him in swaddling clothes, and laid him in a manger; because there was no room for them in the inn [*JST "inns"*].

"Swaddling clothes" were bands of cloth in which a newborn baby was wrapped. The baby was placed diagonally upon a square piece of cloth. The bottom corner of the square cloth was folded up to cover the baby's feet, and the side corners were folded in to cover the baby's sides. Then bands of cloth were wound around the baby to make a warm, comfortable bundle.

The Birth of Christ Is Announced to the Shepherds

8 And there were in the same country [*in the Bethlehem area*] shepherds abiding [*staying*] in the field, keeping watch over their flock by night.

9 And, lo, the angel of the Lord came upon them, and the glory of the Lord shone round about them: and they were sore [*very*] afraid.

10 And the angel said unto them, Fear not: for, behold, I bring you good tidings of great joy, which shall be to all people.

11 For unto you is born this day in the city of David [*Bethlehem*] a Saviour, which is Christ the Lord.

12 And this shall be a sign unto you; Ye shall find the babe wrapped in swaddling clothes, lying in a manger.

Heavenly Choirs

13 And suddenly there was with the angel a multitude of the heavenly host praising God, and saying,

14 Glory to God in the highest, and on earth peace, good will toward men.

15 And it came to pass, as the angels were gone away from them into heaven, the shepherds said one to another, Let us now go even unto Bethlehem, and see this thing which is come to pass [*which has happened*], which the Lord hath made known unto us.

The Shepherds Find Him

16 And they came with haste [*they hurried*], and found Mary, and Joseph, and the babe lying in a manger.

17 And when they had seen it, they made known abroad the saying which was told them concerning this child [*they told many others what the angel had told them about the birth of the Christ child*].

18 And all they that heard it wondered [*marveled and rejoiced*] at those things which were told them by the shepherds.

19 But Mary kept all these things, and pondered them in her heart.

It is hard to imagine the flood of tender feelings which must have been in Mary's heart, as she looked at her newborn baby, realizing that this was the Son of God, the Promised Messiah, the Savior of the world. Yet, for the moment, it was her tiny, helpless baby boy, to hold and snuggle, to comfort and take care of, for her and Joseph to rear.

20 And the shepherds returned, glorifying and praising God for all the things that they had heard and seen, as it was told unto them.

21 And when eight days were accomplished [*were up*] for the circumcising [*see Bible Dictionary, under "Circumcision"*] of the child, his name was called JESUS, which [*who*] was so named of [*by*] the angel [*see Matthew 1:21 and Luke 1:31*] before he was conceived in the womb.

Both Joseph (Matthew 1:21) and Mary (Luke 1:31) were told by the angel to name the baby "Jesus." Jesus is the Greek form of Joshua or Jeshua, which means "God is help" or "savior." See Bible Dictionary, under "Jesus."

22 And when the days of her purification [*forty days; see Leviticus 12:1–4*] according to the law of Moses were accomplished [*finished*], they brought him [*Jesus*] to Jerusalem, to present him to the Lord [*at the temple*];

23 (As it is written in the law of the Lord [*Exodus 13:2*], Every male that openeth the womb [*firstborn male child*] shall be called holy [*shall be dedicated*] to the Lord;)

24 And to offer a sacrifice according to that which is said in the law of the Lord [*Leviticus 12:6–8, a pair of turtledoves, or two young pigeons.*

Next, a righteous, elderly man named Simeon, who had been promised that he would not die until he had seen the Christ, sees the Christ Child in the temple.

25 And, behold, there was a man in Jerusalem, whose name was Simeon; and the same man was just [*very exact in living the gospel*] and devout [*very faithful*], waiting for the consolation [*redemption; see verse 38*] of Israel: and the Holy Ghost was upon him.

26 And it was revealed unto him by the Holy Ghost, that he should not see death [*die*], before he had seen the Lord's Christ.

27 And he came by the Spirit [*was prompted by the Holy Ghost to come*] into the temple: and when the parents brought in the child Jesus, to do for him after the custom of the law [*to present Him in the temple as required*],

28 Then took he him up in his arms [*Simeon picked Jesus up*], and blessed [*praised*] God, and said,

29 Lord, now lettest thou thy servant depart in peace, according to thy word [*let me die in peace now, as You promised*]:

30 For mine eyes have seen thy salvation [*I have seen the Savior who will bring salvation to us*],

31 Which thou hast prepared before the face of all people [*for everyone*];

32 A light to lighten the Gentiles [*non-Israelites*], and the glory of thy people Israel.

33 And Joseph and his mother marvelled at those things which were spoken of him [*Jesus*].

34 And Simeon blessed them, and said unto Mary his mother, Behold, this child is set [*appointed*] for the fall and rising again of many in Israel; and for a sign which shall be spoken against [*He will run into much opposition*];

35 (Yea, a sword shall pierce through thy own soul also,) that the thoughts of many hearts may be revealed.

JST LUKE 2:35

35 Yea, a spear shall pierce through him to the wounding of thine own soul also; that the thoughts of many hearts may be revealed.

Next, Luke reports that an elderly lady named Anna, who saw the child, Jesus, in the temple, likewise bore witness of Him as the Savior of the world.

36 And there was one Anna, a prophetess, the daughter of Phanuel, of the tribe of Aser [*Asher, one of the twelve tribes*]: she was of a great age, and had lived with an husband seven years from her virginity [*for seven years, then he died*];

37 And she was a widow of about fourscore and four years [*was now about 84 years old*], which departed not from the temple, but served God with fastings and prayers night and day.

38 And she coming in that instant [*seeing Joseph and Mary with baby Jesus*] gave thanks likewise unto the Lord, and spake of him [*bore witness of Christ*] to all them that looked for redemption in Jerusalem.

Have you noticed so far in Luke that both men and women bear witness of the Savior, and that both have been given the gift of prophecy? Luke seems to have a special sensitivity to the role of righteous women as well as faithful men in teaching and bearing witness in the work of the Lord.

39 And when they had performed all things according to the law of the Lord [*when they had performed all the required rituals in the temple, in conjunction with the birth of Jesus*], they returned into Galilee, to their own city Nazareth.

Luke briefly summarizes the youth of Jesus, up until age twelve, in verse 40, next.

40 And the child grew, and waxed strong in spirit, filled with wisdom: and the grace of God was upon him.

In the JST (the Joseph Smith Translation of the Bible) we are given additional insights into the Savior's youth as follows:

JST MATTHEW 3:24–26

24 And it came to pass that Jesus grew up with his brethren, and waxed strong, and waited upon the Lord for the time of his ministry to come.

25 And he served under his father, and he spake not as other men, neither could he be taught; for he needed not that any man should teach him.

26 And after many years, the hour of his ministry drew nigh.

Jesus Teaches in the Temple at Age Twelve

41 Now his parents went to Jerusalem every year at the feast of the passover. [*The Feast of the Passover is celebrated each year by the Jews in March or April, to commemorate the "passing over" of the angel of death over the Israelite homes in Egypt, when the firstborn of the Egyptians were killed. See Bible Dictionary, under "Feasts."*]

42 And when he was twelve years old, they went up to Jerusalem after the custom of the feast [*as was the custom, to celebrate the Passover feast*].

43 And when they had fulfilled the days [*when they were finished*], as they returned [*to their home*], the child Jesus tarried [*stayed*] behind in Jerusalem; and Joseph and his mother knew not of it.

44 But they, supposing him to have been in the company [*they thought he was with friends or relatives in their traveling group*], went a day's journey; and they sought [*looked for*] him among their kinsfolk [*relatives*] and acquaintance.

45 And when they found him not, they turned back again to Jerusalem, seeking him.

46 And it came to pass, that after three days they found him in the temple, sitting in the midst of the doctors [*teachers, men of high education*], both hearing them, and asking them questions.

As you will see, as you read the JST for verse 46, above, it makes a significant change. Jesus was teaching them, rather than they teaching Him.

JST LUKE 2:46

46 And it came to pass, that after three days they

found him in the temple, sitting in the midst of the doctors, and they were hearing him, and asking him questions.

47 And all that heard him were astonished at his understanding and answers.

48 And when they *[Joseph and Mary]* saw him, they were amazed: and his mother said unto him, Son, why hast thou thus dealt with us *[why did you give us such a scare]*? behold, thy father and I have sought thee sorrowing *[we have been looking for You, very worried!]*.

49 And he said unto them, How is it that ye sought me *[why were you looking for me]*? wist ye not *[didn't you know]* that I must be about *[be doing]* my Father's *[Heavenly Father's]* business?

50 And they understood not the saying which he spake unto them. *[Joseph and Mary didn't understand His explanation.]*

51 And he went down *[home]* with them, and came to Nazareth, and was subject *[obedient]* unto them: but *[JST "and"]* his mother kept all these sayings in her heart.

52 And Jesus increased in wisdom and stature, and in favour with God and man.

When he was born, Jesus had the veil over his memory of the premortal life, just as all do. Elder James E. Talmage taught:

"He came among men to experience all the natural conditions of mortality; He was born as truly a dependent, helpless babe as is any other child; His infancy was in all common features as the infancy of others; His boyhood was actual boyhood, His development was as necessary and as real as that of all children. Over His mind had fallen the veil of forgetfulness common to all who are born to earth, by which the remembrance of primeval existence is shut off. The Child grew, and with growth there came to Him expansion of mind, development of faculties, and progression in power and understanding." (*Jesus the Christ*, page 111)

President Joseph F. Smith said that Jesus did not know who He was as He lay in the cradle. See April 1901 General Conference. As stated in verse 52, above, He gained wisdom as He grew. No doubt the veil was gone before He reached age twelve, for He knew who He was and felt the urgency of being about His Heavenly Father's business, as expressed to Joseph and Mary in verse 49 above.

LUKE 3

IN THIS CHAPTER, Luke tells us that John the Baptist has come into the country, preaching and baptizing, and gives us an account of the baptism of the Savior. He informs us that Jesus began His formal mortal ministry at age 30 (verse 23) and then gives the Savior's mortal genealogy back to Adam.

1 NOW in the fifteenth year of the reign of Tiberius Cæsar *[about 29 AD]*, Pontius Pilate being governor of Judæa, and Herod *[Herod Antipas, son of Herod the Great]* being tetrarch *[ruler]* of Galilee, and his brother Philip *[another son of Herod the Great]* tetrarch of Ituræa and of the region of Trachonitis, and Lysanias the tetrarch of Abilene,

John the Baptist Comes Teaching and Baptizing

2 Annas and Caiaphas being the high priests *[the highest Jewish religious leaders]*, the word of God came unto John *[the Baptist]* the son of Zacharias in the wilderness *[where he had been living since he was a small child]*.

3 And he came into all the country about *[around]* Jordan, preaching the baptism of repentance for the remission of sins;

4 As it is written *[in Isaiah 40:3–5]* in the book of the words of Esaias *[Isaiah]* the prophet, saying, The voice of one crying in the wilderness, Prepare ye the way of the Lord, make his paths straight.

The JST adds a little over five verses here, which are left out of the Bible. They are as follows:

JST LUKE 3:5–10

5 For behold, and lo, he shall come, as it is written in the book of the prophets, to take away the sins of the world, and to bring salvation unto the heathen nations, to gather together those who are lost, who are of the sheepfold of Israel;

6 Yea, even the dispersed and afflicted; and also to prepare the way, and make possible the preaching of the gospel unto the Gentiles;

7 And to be a light unto all who sit in darkness, unto the uttermost parts of the earth; to bring to pass the resurrection from the dead, and to ascend up on high, to dwell on the right hand of the Father,

8 Until the fullness of time, and the law and the testimony shall be sealed, and the keys of the kingdom shall be delivered up again unto the Father;

9 To administer justice unto all; to come down in judgment upon all, and to convince all the ungodly of their ungodly deeds, which they have committed; and all this in the day that he shall come;

10 For it is a day of power;

5 Every valley shall be filled, and every mountain and hill shall be brought low; and the crooked shall be made straight, and the rough ways shall be made smooth; [*These things will literally happen at the Second Coming. See Isaiah 40:4, D&C 109:74. Symbolically, the pure gospel of Jesus Christ straightens out our spiritual lives and makes rough obstacles to salvation become smooth, through the Atonement.*]

6 And all flesh shall see the salvation of God.

7 Then said he [*John the Baptist*] to the multitude that came forth to be baptized of him, O generation of vipers [*offspring of poisonous snakes, in other words, "you wicked people"*], who hath warned you to flee from the wrath to come [*the punishments of God*]?

It can be puzzling why John scolds everyone in the crowd. But Matthew indicates that John's scolding was not directed at everyone, rather to some wicked Jewish religious leaders among the crowd. Matthew 3:7 tells us that John was speaking to the Pharisees and Sadducees among the people who had come out to listen to him. They were hypocritical religious leaders and insincere and deserved his scathing rebuke in verse 7 above. See note in this study guide, after Matthew 3:7.

An Invitation to Repent

8 Bring forth therefore fruits [*lives, deeds*] worthy of repentance, and begin not to say within yourselves, We have Abraham to our father [*we are related to Abraham, so we are automatically saved*]: for I say unto you, That God is able of these stones to raise up children unto Abraham. [*God could turn these rocks into descendants of Abraham. The message: You have to earn salvation yourselves. You will not get into heaven because Abraham was righteous and you descend from him.*]

JST LUKE 3:13

13 Bring forth therefore fruits worthy of repentance, and begin not to say within yourselves, Abraham is our father; we have kept the commandments of God, and none can inherit the promises but the children of Abraham; for I say unto you, That God is able of these stones to raise up children unto Abraham.

As mentioned above, it was strongly believed and taught among the Jews at this time that, because they were descendants of Abraham, they were automatically favored by God above all other people. In fact, they felt that they would be in the highest position in heaven, above any Gentile, even if the Gentile converted to God and lived a righteous life.

9 And now also the axe [*symbolic of the punishments from God*] is laid unto the root of the trees [*symbolic of wicked people*]: every tree [*person*] therefore which bringeth not forth good fruit [*does not live righteously*] is hewn [*cut*] down, and cast into the fire [*destroyed*].

10 And the people asked him, saying, What shall we do then?

As you can see, in the next verses, John teaches these people the very essence of living the gospel, in answer to their questions.

11 He answereth and saith unto them, He that hath two coats, let him impart [*give*] to him that hath none; and he that hath meat [*food*], let him do likewise.

12 Then came also publicans [*tax collectors*] to be baptized, and said unto him, Master, what shall we do?

13 And he said unto them, Exact no more [*collect no more taxes*] than that which is appointed you [*than is legal; in other words, be honest with people*].

JST LUKE 3:19–20

19 For it is well known unto you, Theophilus, that after the manner of the Jews, and according to the custom of their law in receiving money into the treasury, that out of the abundance which was received, was appointed unto the poor, every man his portion;

20 And after this manner did the publicans also, wherefore John said unto them, Exact no more than that which is appointed you.

14 And the soldiers likewise demanded of [*asked*] him, saying, And what shall we do? And he said unto them, Do violence to no man [*don't make anyone bribe you to keep you from hurting them*], neither accuse any falsely [*if they won't pay you "protection money"*]; and be content with your wages.

The explanations in parentheses in verse 14 above are taken from several other versions of the Bible which agree that John is telling the soldiers to be satisfied with their wages and not to go around intimidating people and making them pay money to keep the soldiers from hurting them.

15 And as the people were in expectation [*suspense*], and all men mused in their hearts of John [*were wondering about John*], whether he were the Christ, or not;

John the Baptist Teaches That He Is Not the Christ but That Christ Is Coming

16 John answered, saying unto them all, I indeed baptize you with water; but one mightier than I cometh [*Christ*], the latchet of whose shoes I am not worthy to unloose: he shall baptize you with the Holy Ghost and with fire:

Just a note about the symbolism associated with the word "fire," at the end of verse 16, above. In the scriptures, the Holy Ghost is often compared to fire. The symbolism comes from the use of fire to purify gold. The gold ore is put in a container and fire is used to heat the container. The ore melts, the impurities float to the top, and the pure gold settles to the bottom. The impurities are then discarded and pure gold remains. Thus, the gold is purified by fire. Similarly the Holy Ghost purifies us, if we allow it. Example: We commit sin. The Holy Ghost points it out and causes our conscience to burn within us. We respond by repenting. Thus we are purified, bit by bit.

17 Whose fan is in his hand [*who is getting ready to harvest the earth*], and he will throughly purge [*cleanse*] his floor [*the threshing floor, symbolic of the earth*], and will gather the wheat [*the righteous*] into his garner [*barn, symbolic of heaven*]; but the chaff [*the wicked*] he will burn with fire unquenchable [*and they won't be able to put the fire (punishment) out*].

18 And many other things in his exhortation [*warnings and teachings*] preached he unto the people.

John the Baptist Is Put in Prison

19 But Herod the tetrarch [*Roman ruler for that part of Palestine*], being reproved by him [*scolded by John*] for [*because of*] Herodias his brother Philip's wife, and for all the evils which Herod had done,

20 Added yet this above all [*added another huge sin to his collection*], that he shut up [*put*] John in prison.

Jesus Is Baptized

21 Now when all the people were baptized, it came to pass, that Jesus also being baptized [*Matthew 3:13–17*], and praying, the heaven was opened,

22 And the Holy Ghost descended in a bodily shape like a dove upon him *[Jesus; John the Baptist saw the Holy Ghost come upon Christ—see Matthew 3:16 in this study guide]*, and a voice *[the Father's voice]* came from heaven, which said, Thou art my beloved Son; in thee I am well pleased.

Next, in verses 23–38, Luke tells us that the Savior began His mortal mission at age thirty, and then gives His genealogy. Matthew also gives a genealogy of Jesus, in Matthew 1:1–17. Some people, who read these carefully, are confused because the two genealogies don't seem to agree completely. Matthew's account seems to be the royal lineage which would make Joseph, Mary's husband, the legal successor to the throne. He would have been king in Jerusalem if the Romans had not been in power. Thus, Jesus would be in line to be king of the Jews literally. According to Apostle James E. Talmage, Luke's genealogy of Christ seems to be the pedigree of Mary. For more on this, see *Jesus the Christ*, pp. 83–90.

Note that in verse 23, Luke tells us that those who did not realize that Jesus was the Son of God assumed that He was the son of Joseph.

23 And Jesus himself began to be about thirty years of age, being (as was supposed) the son of Joseph, which was the son of Heli,

24 Which was the son of Matthat, which was the son of Levi, which was the son of Melchi, which was the son of Janna, which was the son of Joseph,

25 Which was the son of Mattathias, which was the son of Amos, which was the son of Naum, which was the son of Esli, which was the son of Nagge,

26 Which was the son of Maath, which was the son of Mattathias, which was the son of Semei, which was the son of Joseph, which was the son of Juda,

27 Which was the son of Joanna, which was the son of Rhesa, which was the son of Zorobabel, which was the son of Salathiel, which was the son of Neri,

28 Which was the son of Melchi, which was the son of Addi, which was the son of Cosam, which was the son of Elmodam, which was the son of Er,

29 Which was the son of Jose, which was the son of Eliezer, which was the son of Jorim, which was the son of Matthat, which was the son of Levi,

30 Which was the son of Simeon, which was the son of Juda, which was the son of Joseph, which was the son of Jonan, which was the son of Eliakim,

31 Which was the son of Melea, which was the son of Menan, which was the son of Mattatha, which was the son of Nathan, which was the son of David,

32 Which was the son of Jesse, which was the son of Obed, which was the son of Booz *[Boaz]*, which was the son of Salmon, which was the son of Naasson,

33 Which was the son of Aminadab, which was the son of Aram, which was the son of Esrom, which was the son of Phares, which was the son of Juda,

34 Which was the son of Jacob, which was the son of Isaac, which was the son of Abraham, which was the son of Thara, which was the son of Nachor,

35 Which was the son of Saruch, which was the son of Ragau, which was the son of Phalec, which was the son of Heber, which was the son of Sala,

36 Which was the son of Cainan, which was the son of Arphaxad, which was the son of Sem, which was the son of Noe *[Noah]*, which was the son of Lamech,

37 Which was the son of Mathusala, which was the son of Enoch, which was the son of Jared, which was the son of Maleleel, which was the son of Cainan,

38 Which was the son of Enos, which was the son of Seth, which was the son of Adam, which was the son of God.

JST LUKE 3:45
45 And of Enos, and of Seth, and of Adam, who was formed of God, and the first man upon the earth.

Some people have used the last part of verse 38, as it stands in the Bible, to teach that Adam was literally born to Heavenly Father and that is how he got his mortal body. The JST, quoted above, corrects this.

LUKE 4

IN THIS CHAPTER you will see that Jesus went into the wilderness to commune with His Father as He began His formal mortal ministry. Satan will tempt Him. He will visit His hometown of Nazareth and be rejected. Many will be healed and the fame of the Master will spread rapidly.

As we begin, you will see that a doctrinal question is answered in verse 1. Sometimes the question is asked as to whether or not the Holy Ghost was functioning during the time of the Savior's mortal mission. Based on Luke 4:1, next, the answer is definitely yes. For more on this subject, see Bible Dictionary, under "Holy Ghost." See also Acts 10:38.

1 AND Jesus being full of the Holy Ghost [*after His baptism; see Matthew 3:13-17*] returned from Jordan [*the Jordan River, east of Jerusalem*], and was led by the Spirit into the wilderness,

The Eighth Article of Faith states: "We believe the Bible to be the word of God as far as it is translated correctly . . ." Verse 2, next, is an example of a place where the Bible is not translated correctly. Jesus did not go into the wilderness to be tempted by Satan for forty days; rather He went into the wilderness, after His baptism, "to be with God" (JST–Matthew 4:1).

We will quote a number of JST (Joseph Smith Translation of the Bible) corrections and additions as we go along here. You will see that there are many significant doctrinal changes in the JST. Also, remember that not all of these JST corrections are given in footnotes in your LDS Bible, because there is not enough room to include all the changes and additions the Prophet Joseph Smith made in the translation of the Bible. You may wish to obtain a copy of the complete JST from an LDS bookstore.

2 Being forty days tempted of the devil. And in those days he did eat nothing: and when they [*the forty days of fasting*] were ended, he afterward hungered [*was hungry*].

JST LUKE 4:2
2 And after forty days, the devil came unto him, to tempt him. And in those days, he did eat nothing; and when they were ended, he afterwards hungered.

Jesus Is Tempted by the Devil

As we continue, we will see that the devil tempted the Savior in three major categories in which he likewise tempts us.

1. Physical appetites (verse 3).
2. Materialism and power (verse 7).
3. Vanity and pride (verse 9).

But, as mentioned also in the note following Matthew 4:2, in this study guide, you will see another form of temptation associated with the above temptations. It is the word "if" in verses 3, 7 and 9. The devil challenged Jesus to prove that He was indeed the Son of God. This "if" challenge can be a very effective tool for Satan as he likewise challenges us to "prove it." People often find themselves committing sin or taking foolish chances in order to respond to someone who is challenging their courage or status, or whatever.

3 And the devil said unto him, If thou be the Son of God, command this stone that it be made bread. [*In other words, show me a miracle to prove you are Christ.*]

4 And Jesus answered [*responded to*] him, saying, It is written [*in Deuteronomy 8:3*], That man shall not live by bread alone, but by every word of God.

5 And the devil, taking him up into an high mountain, shewed [*showed*] unto him all the kingdoms of the world in a moment of time.

Verse 5, above, is another place where the Bible translation is incorrect. There is a big difference between the devil taking Jesus to a high mountain and the Spirit taking Him. If the devil were taking Him, it would indicate that the devil is in charge, which he is not! The JST reads:

JST LUKE 4:5
5 And the Spirit taketh him up into a high mountain, and he beheld all the kingdoms of the world, in a moment of time.

6 And the devil said unto, All this power will I give thee, and the glory of them [*the kingdoms of the world*]: for that is delivered unto me [*they are mine; see Revelation 13 heading*]; and to whomsoever I will I give it.

JST LUKE 4:6
6 And the devil came unto him, and said unto him, All this power will I give unto thee, and the glory of them; for they are delivered unto me, and to whomsoever I will, I give them.

7 If thou therefore wilt worship me, all shall be thine.

8 And Jesus answered and said unto him, Get thee behind me, Satan: for it is written [*in Deuteronomy 6:13–14*], Thou shalt worship the Lord thy God, and him only shalt thou serve.

Have you noticed that the Savior is quoting scriptures to thwart the temptations the devil is attempting to use against Him? There is a major message for us in this. It is that there is great strength and safety against temptation for us in the scriptures.

9 And he brought him to Jerusalem, and set him on a pinnacle of the temple, and said unto him, If thou be the Son of God, cast thyself down from hence [*here*]:

JST LUKE 4:9
9 And the Spirit brought him to Jerusalem, and set him on a pinnacle of the temple. And the devil came unto him, and said unto him, If thou be the Son of God, cast thyself down from hence;

10 For it is written [*in Psalm 91:11–12*], He shall give his angels charge [*responsibility*] over thee, to keep thee:

11 And in their hands they shall bear thee up, lest at any time thou dash [*strike*] thy foot against a stone.

12 And Jesus answering [*responding*] said unto him, It is said, Thou shalt not tempt the Lord thy God.

13 And when the devil had ended all the temptation, he departed from him for a season.

By way of review, we see three major forms of temptations plus a fourth in the verses above. First, temptation to gratify physical appetites as tempted by Satan. Second, the temptation for worldly power and glory. Third, the temptation to challenge God to make good on His promises, as if there were some doubt about how good His word is. Fourth, the phrase "If thou are the Son of God." This, for some of us, could be the most difficult temptation of all. Giving in to the challenge to inappropriately attempt to defend our own ego or position would be giving in to pride.

As Luke continues now, he will tell us that the Savior now returned to His home country of Galilee to preach and minister.

14 And Jesus returned in the power of the Spirit into Galilee [*an area in northern Israel*]: and there went out a fame of him [*He became famous*] through all the region round about.

15 And he taught in their synagogues [*Jewish church buildings*], being glorified of all [*everybody said He was great!*].

Jesus Tells the People of Nazareth that He Is the Promised Messiah

16 And he came to Nazareth, where he had been brought up [*His home town*]: and, as his custom was, he went into the synagogue on the sabbath day, and stood up for to read.

Watch now as the Master reads two verses of scripture from Isaiah in the synagogue of His hometown, and then tells the people gathered there that the verses apply to Him.

17 And there was delivered unto him [*brought to Him at His request*] the book of the prophet Esaias [*Isaiah*]. And when he had opened the book, he found the place where it was written [*Isaiah 61:1–2*],

AND HE TAUGHT
IN THEIR
SYNAGOGUES
BEING GLORIFIED
OF ALL.

LUKE 4:15

CHRIST TEACHING, by Robert T. Barrett

18 The Spirit of the Lord is upon me [*Christ*], because he hath anointed [*called*] me to preach the gospel to the poor; he hath sent me to heal the brokenhearted, to preach deliverance [*remission of sins*] to the captives [*those under the bondage of sin*], and recovering of sight to the blind [*spiritually as well as physically*], to set at liberty [*redeem*] them that are bruised [*by sins*],

19 To preach the acceptable year of the Lord [*the time designated by the Father for Jesus to perform His mission on earth, as a mortal; see* Doctrinal New Testament Commentary, *Vol. 1, page 161*].

20 And he closed the book, and he gave it again to the minister, and sat down. And the eyes of all them that were in the synagogue were fastened on him.

21 And he began to say unto them, This day is this scripture fulfilled in your ears. [*In other words, I am the fulfillment of this prophecy of Isaiah.*]

22 And all bare him witness [*spoke well of him (for a few minutes)*], and wondered [*marveled*] at the gracious words which proceeded out of his mouth. And they said [*to each other*], Is not this Joseph's son?

The men of the synagogue, who heard Jesus claim to be the Messiah, after reading the passage from Isaiah, now begin to have doubts. They have heard of the many miracles and things a man named Jesus has been doing throughout the country. Now, when they see that He is the Jesus who grew up in their town, they say, in effect, "Now wait a minute. Isn't this Jesus who is Joseph the carpenter's son? We know His family. He grew up here. He is just a common man, one of us. How can He possibly think He is the Messiah?"

23 And he said unto them, Ye will surely say unto me this proverb [*old saying*], Physician, heal thyself: whatsoever we have heard done in Capernaum, do also here in thy country. [*Prove that You are something special by doing the same miracles You have done elsewhere.*]

You have probably heard the last phrase of verse 24, next, many times. It is often quoted to mean that a person who is famous among people elsewhere is criticized and put down among people he or she grew up with.

24 And he said, Verily I say unto you, No prophet is accepted in his own country.

25 But I tell you of a truth, many widows were in Israel in the days of Elias [*Elijah*], when the heaven was shut up three years and six months, when great famine was throughout all the land;

26 But unto none of them was Elias [*Elijah*] sent, save [*except*] unto Sarepta, a city of Sidon, unto a woman that was a widow.

27 And many lepers [*people with leprosy*] were in Israel in the time of Eliseus [*Elisha*] the prophet; and none of them was cleansed, saving [*except*] Naaman the Syrian [*2 Kings 5:14*].

The point Jesus is making to these men of His hometown seems to be that it wasn't necessary for prophets such as Elijah and Elisha to heal every person in the land or perform the same miracles for everyone in order to be accepted as a prophet sent from God. So why should it be different with Jesus? Why should He be required to perform the same miracles for the people of Nazareth as for others, in order to be accepted by them. Couldn't they exercise faith in what had been done elsewhere?

28 And all they in the synagogue, when they heard these things, were filled with wrath [*were very angry*],

29 And rose up, and thrust him out of the city, and led him unto the brow [*cliff*] of the hill whereon their city was built, that they might cast him down headlong [*headfirst*].

30 But he passing through the midst of them went his way,

It will be interesting to get the rest of the details as to what happened here. This was a great miracle, if these wicked and hardhearted men would pay attention to it.

31 And came down to Capernaum, a city of Galilee, and taught them on the sabbath days.

32 And they were astonished at his doctrine: for his word was with power [*He taught with power and authority*].

A Man Possessed by Evil Spirits Is Healed

33 And in the synagogue there was a man, which had a spirit of an unclean devil [*was possessed by evil spirits*], and cried out with a loud voice,

34 Saying, Let us alone; what have we to do with thee, thou Jesus of Nazareth? art thou come to destroy us? I know thee who thou art; the Holy One of God. [*One of the evil spirits bears witness of Christ.*]

35 And Jesus rebuked [*sharply scolded*] him, saying, Hold thy peace [*be quiet*], and come out of him. And when the devil had thrown him [*tossed Him around*] in the midst, he came out of him, and hurt him not [*no more*].

36 And they were all amazed, and spake [*spoke*] among themselves, saying, What a word is this! for with authority and power he commandeth the unclean spirits, and they come out.

37 And the fame of him went out into every place of the country round about.

The Master Heals Peter's Mother-in-Law

38 And he arose out of [*left*] the synagogue, and entered into Simon's [*Peter's*] house. And Simon's wife's mother [*Peter's mother-in-law*] was taken [*sick*] with a great fever; and they besought him for her [*asked Jesus to heal her*].

39 And he stood over her, and rebuked the fever [*commanded the fever to leave*]; and it left her: and immediately she arose and ministered unto them.

The fact that Peter was married is significant. Some religions believe that celibacy (intentionally not getting married) is the highest form of dedication to God. This is not true. Living worthily of exaltation in a family unit forever is the highest form of dedication to God.

40 Now when the sun was setting, all they that had any sick with divers [*various*] diseases brought them unto him; and he laid his hands on every one of them, and healed them.

41 And devils [*evil spirits*] also came out of many, crying out, and saying, Thou art Christ the Son of God. And he rebuking them suffered them not to speak [*commanded them not to bear witness of Him*]: for they knew that he was Christ.

From verse 41, above, we learn that the veil, which erases our memory of our premortal life, is not upon Satan and the one third of premortal spirits who were cast out of heaven (Revelation 12:4) and down to the earth with him. They knew Christ in premortality and still recognize him here.

42 And when it was day [*the next day*], he departed and went into a desert place: and the people sought [*found*] him, and came unto him, and stayed him [*stopped him*], that he should not depart from them.

43 And he said unto them, I must preach the kingdom of God [*the gospel*] to other cities also: for therefore [*that is the reason*] am I sent.

44 And he preached in the synagogues [*Jewish church buildings*] of Galilee.

LUKE 5

IN THIS CHAPTER, Luke starts out by telling us about the calling of Peter, James, and John to be disciples. Later, they will be called and ordained as Apostles. Watch for the symbolism involved in fishing and the "gospel net."

1 AND it came to pass, that, as the people pressed upon him [*crowded and pushed against Him*] to hear the word of God, he stood by the lake of Gennesaret [*the Sea of Galilee*],

The Calling of Peter, James, and John

2 And saw two ships standing by the lake: but the fishermen were gone out of them, and were washing their nets.

3 And he entered into one of the ships, which was Simon's [*which belonged to Peter*], and prayed [*asked*] him that he would thrust out a little from the land. And he sat down, and taught the people out of the ship.

4 Now when he had left speaking, he said unto Simon [*Peter*], Launch out into the deep, and let down your nets for a draught [*a catch of fish*].

5 And Simon answering [*in response*] said unto him, Master, we have toiled [*worked hard fishing*] all the night, and have taken nothing: nevertheless at thy word I will let down the net.

By way of information, it was the practice at this time for those who fished for a living on the Sea of Galilee to fish during the night.

6 And when they had this done, they inclosed a great multitude of fishes: and their net brake [*started to break; see Luke 5:6, footnote 6a*].

7 And they beckoned [*waved*] unto their partners, which were in the other ship, that they should come and help them. And they came, and filled both the ships, so that they began to sink.

There is beautiful symbolism here. As Peter and others follow the Savior's instructions in faith, they have great success in catching fish. Symbolically, as Peter and the others follow Christ, He will make them "fishers of men," and they will have a large "catch" of converts. See end of verse 10 below.

8 When Simon Peter saw it, he fell down at Jesus' knees [*very humble*], saying, Depart from me; for I am a sinful man, O Lord. [*I am not worthy to be in Thy presence.*]

9 For he was astonished, and all that were with him, at the draught [*catch*] of the fishes which they had taken:

10 And so was [*were*] also James, and John, the sons of Zebedee, which were partners with Simon [*Peter*]. And Jesus said unto Simon, Fear not; from henceforth [*from now on*] thou shalt catch men.

11 And when they had brought their ships to land, they forsook all [*left everything behind*], and followed him.

The Healing of a Leper

12 And it came to pass, when he was in a certain city, behold a man full of leprosy: who seeing Jesus fell on his face [*a cultural way of showing great humility*], and besought [*begged*] him, saying, Lord, if thou wilt [*if you are willing*], thou canst make me clean. [*This sick man has great faith in Christ.*]

Leprosy was one of the most dreaded diseases of the time. It was greatly feared by others, and a person who had the disease was required by law to warn others to stay clear so they would not accidentally touch the leper and risk catching the disease. Lepers were social outcasts. See "Leper" and "Leprosy" in Bible Dictionary.

13 And he [*Jesus*] put forth his hand, and touched him, saying, I will: be thou clean. And immediately the leprosy departed from him.

14 And he charged [*instructed*] him to tell no man: but go, and shew thyself to the priest [*as commanded in Leviticus 14:2*], and offer for thy cleansing, according as Moses commanded, for a testimony unto them.

15 But so much the more went there a fame abroad of him [*this healing caused Jesus to become even more famous*]: and great multitudes came together to hear, and to be healed by him of their infirmities [*sicknesses*].

16 And he withdrew himself into the wilderness, and prayed.

17 And it came to pass on a certain day, as he was teaching, that there were Pharisees [*religious leaders of the Jews*] and doctors of the law [*scribes—see verse 21; religious leaders who interpreted how to live the religious laws of the Jews*] sitting by [*watching*], which were come out of every town of Galilee, and Judæa, and Jerusalem [*who had come from all over, worried about Jesus and His growing popularity*]: and the power of the Lord was present to heal them [*the people from the area who had come to be healed or brought their sick to be healed*].

Jesus Heals a Man with Palsy

18 And, behold, men brought in a bed a man [*carried a man on a bed*] which was taken [*sick*] with a palsy: and they sought means to [*tried to figure out how to*] bring him in, and to lay him before [*in front of*] him [*Jesus*].

19 And when they could not find by what way they might bring him in [*when they couldn't figure out a way*] because of the multitude [*the crowd*], they went upon the housetop, and let him [*the sick man in the bed*] down through the tiling [*roof*] with his couch into the midst before [*in front of*] Jesus.

The Master Forgives Sins, Which Infuriates the Jewish Religious Leaders

20 And when he [*Jesus*] saw their faith, he said unto him, Man, thy sins are forgiven thee.

21 And the scribes and the Pharisees [*religious leaders who were trying to trap Jesus*] began to reason [*discuss among themselves*], saying, Who is this which speaketh blasphemies? Who can forgive sins, but God alone?

"Blasphemy," showing disrespect for God, mocking God, was a violation of law among the Jews which was punishable by death.

22 But when Jesus perceived [*read*] their thoughts, he answering said [*responded, saying*] unto them, What reason ye in your hearts [*why are such thoughts in your hearts*]?

23 Whether [*which*] is easier, to say, Thy sins be forgiven thee; or to say, Rise up and walk?

JST Luke 5:23

23 Does it require more power to forgive sins than to make the sick rise up and walk?

The Savior is saying, in effect, "If I am a fraud, and imposter, as you say I am, which would be safer for me to say, 'Your sins are forgiven.' or 'Rise up and walk.'? Which would be less likely to expose me as a fake?" The obvious answer is "Your sins are forgiven," since there is no immediate way of telling whether or not that happens to the sick man. But as Jesus says "Rise up and walk," there will be immediate evidence as to whether or not He is an imposter. This creates a very tense situation. The JST adds to verse 23 as follows: "Does it require more power to forgive sins than to make the sick rise up and walk?"

24 But that ye may know that the Son of man [*I, the Son of Man, the Son of God; the Son of Man of Holiness (the Father—see* Moses 6:57)] hath power upon earth to forgive sins, [*He said unto the sick of the palsy,*] I say unto thee, Arise, and take up thy couch [*bed*], and go into thine house.

25 And immediately he rose up before them, and took up that whereon he lay [*his bed*], and departed to his own house, glorifying [*praising*] God.

26 And they were all amazed, and they glorified God, and were filled with fear, saying, We have seen strange things to day.

Matthew Is Called to Follow Christ

27 And after these things he [*Jesus*] went forth, and saw a publican [*tax collector*], named Levi [*Matthew*], sitting at the receipt of custom [*where they collected taxes*]: and he [*Jesus*] said unto him, Follow me.

28 And he left all, rose up, and followed him.

29 And Levi [*Matthew*] made him [*Jesus*] a great feast in his own house: and there was a great company of publicans [*tax collectors*] and of others that sat down with them.

30 But their scribes and Pharisees [*the Jewish religious leaders who are trying to trap Jesus*] murmured [*grumbled*] against his disciples [*didn't come directly to Jesus*], saying, Why do ye eat and drink with publicans and sinners?

These hypocritical Jewish religious leaders had strict rules for themselves to avoid associating with publicans and sinners. They considered it a matter of personal righteousness not to do so, and considered that Jesus and His disciples were exposing their sinful natures by eating and associating with such people.

31 And Jesus answering [*responding*] said unto them [*the Pharisees and scribes*], They that are whole [*well*] need not a physician; but they that are sick. [*If I am going to help people, I must associate with them.*]

32 I [*the Son of God*] came not to call the righteous, but sinners to repentance.

Above, Jesus claims very openly to be the Son of God, with power to call sinners to repentance and to forgive sins. This had to be very frustrating to the Pharisees and scribes!

33 And they [*the Pharisees and scribes*]said unto him [*Jesus*], Why do the disciples of John [*followers of John the Baptist*] fast often, and make prayers, and likewise the disciples of the Pharisees; but thine eat and drink? [*In other words, why don't you and your disciples follow the rules we do?*]

John the Baptist is in prison at this time and is soon to be beheaded at Herod's command.

34 And he said unto them, Can ye make the children of the bridechamber fast, while the bridegroom is with them?

35 But the days will come, when the bridegroom shall be taken away from them, and then shall they fast in those days.

Understanding a bit of Jewish culture will help with verses 34-35, above. Wedding imagery is involved. Jesus is the bridegroom, or groom, as we would say it. Faithful followers are the bride. "Bridechamber" would be the place where the wedding feast is held and, symbolically, would be the land of Israel where the Savior was performing His mortal mission. While the groom and the bride are together, much celebrating and feasting-hearing and understanding the Savior's teachings-would take place. It would not make sense to mourn and fast at this time. But, when the Savior is crucified and taken from them, the "children of the bridechamber," the faithful Saints, will mourn and fast.

Next, Jesus will teach that people who are set in their ways do not usually accept new ideas, in this case, the true gospel.

36 And he spake also a parable unto them; No man putteth [*attaches*] a piece of a new garment [*cloth*] upon an old [*symbolic of putting the true gospel into old lifestyles*]; if otherwise, then both the new maketh a rent [*tear*], and the piece that was taken out of the new agreeth not with the old [*is not compatible with the old piece*].

New Wine in Old Bottles

37 And no man putteth new wine [*new gospel*] into old bottles [*scribes and Pharisees, who are set in their evil ways*]; else the new wine will burst the bottles, and be spilled, and the bottles shall perish.

38 But new wine must be put into new bottles; and both are preserved.

Leather bottles were used to store wine. Over time, the leather became hard and inflexible. If new wine were put in old leather bottles, the bottles would break because they could not stretch with the pressure generated by fermentation processes in the new wine.

39 No man also having drunk old wine straightway [*immediately*] desireth new: for he saith, The old is better. [*People who are set in their ways, don't like new ideas, in this case, the true gospel.*]

LUKE 6

IN THIS CHAPTER Luke focuses on the Savior's activities on several Sabbaths, pointing out how the leaders of the Jews attempted to discredit Him by using their traditions against Him. This is ironic because He, as the premortal Christ, was the God of the Old Testament, Jehovah Himself, the one who gave the commandment in the Old Testament to keep the Sabbath day Holy. Additionally in this chapter, Jesus will choose the Twelve Apostles, and continue preaching, pointing out the blessings of living the gospel and the problems that come upon those who don't live it.

1 AND it came to pass on the second sabbath after the first, that he went through the corn *[grain]* fields; and his disciples plucked the ears of corn *[grain]*, and did eat, rubbing them in their hands.

The Jews had developed thousands of laws over the years for observing the Sabbath, which were not in harmony with the laws for Sabbath observance given by the Lord to Moses. One of these laws was that it was forbidden to rub heads of wheat, barley or whatever grain together on the Sabbath because it was considered to be threshing grain (separating the grain kernels from the chaff) which violated the Sabbath.

Watch now as the Pharisees attempt to discredit Jesus regarding the Sabbath. And then watch in verse 5, below, as He tells them that He is the one who gave the commandments concerning the Sabbath.

2 And certain of the Pharisees *[religious leaders of the Jews]* said unto them, Why do ye that which is not lawful *[legal]* to do on the sabbath days?

3 And Jesus answering them said, Have ye not read so much as this, what David did, when himself was an hungred *[hungry]*, and they *[his soldiers]* which were with him;

4 How he went into the house of God, and did take and eat the shewbread *[sacred bread used in the tabernacle and temple]*, and gave also to them that were with him; which it is not lawful to eat but for the priests alone? *[Only the priests were allowed to eat the shewbread.]*

5 And he *[Jesus]* said unto them *[the Pharisees]*, That the Son of man *[a short way of saying "Son of Man of Holiness" (the Father)—see Moses 6:57]* is Lord also of the sabbath. *[in other words, I am the God of the Sabbath.]*

Jesus Heals the Man with the Withered Hand

6 And it came to pass also on another sabbath, that he entered into the synagogue *[Jewish church building]* and taught: and there was a man whose right hand was withered *[crippled]*.

7 And the scribes and Pharisees *[religious leaders]* watched him, whether *[to see if]* he would heal on the sabbath day; that they might find an accusation against him *[that they might get him arrested]*.

8 But he knew their thoughts, and said to the man which had the withered hand, Rise up, and stand forth in the midst *[of the synagogue]*. And he arose and stood forth.

9 Then said Jesus unto them *[the scribes and Pharisees in verse 7]*, I will ask you one thing; Is it lawful *[legal]* on the sabbath days to do good, or to do evil? to save life, or to destroy it?

10 And looking round about upon them all, he said unto the man, Stretch forth thy hand. And he did so: and his hand was restored whole as the other.

This must have been an intense scene. Just imagine how quiet it must have become, as Jesus slowly looked around at all of these wicked religious leaders and hypocrites who had gathered to trap Him, then said to the man with the crippled hand, "Stretch forth thy hand." And then the hand was healed.

11 And they *[the scribes and Pharisees]* were filled with madness *[anger]*; and communed *[discussed]* one with another what they might do to Jesus.

Jesus Calls the Twelve

12 And it came to pass in those days, that he went out into a mountain to pray, and continued all night in prayer to God.

13 And when it was day, he called unto him his disciples: and of them he chose twelve, whom also he named apostles;

14 Simon, [*whom he also named Peter,*] and Andrew his brother, James and John, Philip and Bartholomew,

15 Matthew and Thomas, James the son of Alphæus, and Simon called Zelotes,

16 And Judas the brother of James, and Judas Iscariot, which also was the traitor [*who would betray Jesus*].

17 And he came down [*from the mountain*] with them, and stood in the plain, and the company of his disciples, and a great multitude of people out of all Judæa and Jerusalem, and from the sea coast of Tyre and Sidon, which came to hear him, and to be healed of their diseases;

18 And they that were vexed [*troubled, possessed*] with unclean spirits: and they were healed.

19 And the whole multitude sought to [*tried to*] touch him: for there went virtue [*power*] out of him, and healed them all.

The Sermon on the Plain

Luke next records what is often referred to as "the Sermon on the Plain." Scholars do not agree as to whether or not the Sermon on the Plain is the same as the Sermon on the Mount (Matthew 5, 6, and 7). Either way, we are given much help in understanding these teachings of the Savior by reading 3 Nephi, chapters 12–14. In 3 Nephi 12:1–2, it is clear that the Sermon on the Mount was given to members of the Church and was designed to help them obtain the kingdom of heaven; in other words, celestial glory. The notes in brackets in the next few verses demonstrate one possible way in which this sermon teaches members how to obtain celestial glory.

20 And he lifted up his eyes on his disciples, and said, Blessed be ye poor [*you poor in spirituality, who repent*]: for yours is [*you will obtain*] the kingdom of God [*celestial glory*].

21 Blessed are ye that hunger [*for personal righteousness*] now: for ye shall be filled [*with the Holy Ghost*]. Blessed are ye that weep now [*for your sins, then repent*]: for ye shall laugh [*rejoice*].

22 Blessed are ye, when men shall hate you [*because you are doing what is right*], and when they shall separate you [*reject you*] from their company, and shall reproach [*insult, criticize*] you, and cast out your name as evil [*ruin your reputation*], for the Son of man's [*the Savior's*] sake.

23 Rejoice ye [*be happy*] in that day [*when such things happen to you*], and leap for joy: for, behold, your reward is great in heaven [*it will all be worth it when you get to celestial glory*]: for in the like manner [*in the same way*] did their fathers unto the prophets [*their ancestors persecuted the prophets*].

24 But woe unto you that are rich [*the wicked who are rich*]! for ye have received your consolation [*your reward is your money here on earth, but it won't get you to celestial glory*].

25 Woe unto you that are full [*think you don't need the gospel*]! for ye shall hunger [*wish you had repented*]. Woe unto you that laugh now [*at righteous people, and at the gospel*]! for ye shall mourn and weep [*later in this life or in the next life*].

26 Woe unto you [*the wicked in verses 24–25*], when all [*wicked*] men shall speak well of you [*because you fit right in with them and their wicked lifestyle*]! for so did their fathers [*their ancestors*] to the false prophets.

27 But I say unto you which hear [*pay attention to my teachings*], Love your enemies, do good to them which hate you,

28 Bless them that curse you, and pray for them which despitefully use [*abuse*] you.

29 And unto him that smiteth thee [*hits you*] on the one cheek offer also the other; and him that taketh away thy cloke forbid not to take thy coat also.

30 Give to every man that asketh of thee; and of him that taketh away thy goods ask them not again.

The JST adds to and makes changes to verses 29–30, above.

JST LUKE 6:29-31

29 And unto him who smiteth thee on the cheek, offer also the other; or, in other words, it is better to offer the other, than to revile again. And him who taketh away thy cloak, forbid not to take thy coat also.

30 For it is better that thou suffer thine enemy to take these things, than to contend with him. Verily I say unto you, Your heavenly Father who seeth in secret, shall bring that wicked one into judgment.

31 Therefore give to every man who asketh of thee; and of him who taketh away thy goods, ask them not again.

A major message taught in verses 27–30, above, is that we must develop self-control, character strength, etc., to the point that our personalities and dispositions are not dependent upon how others are treating us.

The "Golden Rule"

31 And as ye would that men should do to you, do ye also to them likewise. [*In other words, treat others the way you would like them to treat you. This is known as "the Golden Rule."*]

32 For if ye love them which love you, what thank have ye? for sinners also love those that love them.

JST LUKE 6:33

33 For if ye love them only who love you, what reward have you? For sinners also do even the same.

33 And if ye do good to them which do good to you, what thank have ye? for sinners also do even the same.

One important message we can get from verses 32–33 above is that if we love "only" (see JST verse 33) people who love us, and we are mean to everyone else, and if we only do good to people who are nice to us, that makes us like most everybody else and does not build Christlike qualities in us.

34 And if ye lend to them of whom ye hope to receive, what thank have ye? for sinners also lend to sinners, to receive as much again. [*In other words, you are not truly generous if you only lend things to people in situations where you will profit by it.*]

JST LUKE 6:34

34 And if ye lend to them of whom ye hope to receive, what reward have you? for sinners also lend to sinners, to receive as much again.

Love Your Enemies

35 But love ye your enemies, and do good, and lend, hoping for nothing again; and your reward shall be great [*because you are then truly loving and truly generous*], and ye shall be the children of the Highest [*you will obtain celestial glory and live in the presence of the Father*]: for he is kind unto the unthankful and to the evil.

The next verses contain more teachings about how to become Christlike and obtain celestial glory.

36 Be ye therefore merciful, as your Father also is merciful.

37 Judge not [*JST Matthew 7:2 "judge not unrighteously"*], and ye shall not be judged: condemn not [*judge someone worthy of being damned by God and hoping they don't get a second chance*], and ye shall not be condemned: forgive, and ye shall be forgiven:

38 Give [*be generous, kind, and forgiving*], and it [*your reward*] shall be given unto you; good measure, pressed down, and shaken together, and

running over [*overflowing*], shall men give into your bosom. For with the same measure that ye mete [*give out*] withal [*how you treat others*] it shall be measured to you again [*given back to you by God*].

The phrase "pressed down, and shaken together, and running over" in verse 38, above, calls to mind someone cooking a delicious meal, who takes ingredients and packs them tightly in the measuring cup, shakes it to make sure there is no dead space, and then adds more ingredients until the cup runs over. Symbolically, the Lord will pack all kinds of rewards in the "cup" of the righteous so that their "cup runneth over" (Psalm 23:5) with blessings and eternal rewards.

39 And he spake a parable [*a story designed to teach a specific point*] unto them, Can the blind lead the blind? shall they not both fall into the ditch? [*Can the spiritually blind lead other spiritually blind people successfully?*]

40 The disciple [*follower; student*] is not above [*better than*] his master [*teacher*]: but every one that is perfect [*has been perfectly prepared*] shall be [*become*] as his master.

The Mote and the Beam

41 And why beholdest thou [*why do you look at*] the mote [*speck; symbolical of a little imperfection*] that is in thy brother's eye, but perceivest not [*don't notice*] the beam [*huge roof beam*] that is in thine own eye? [*Why are you so critical of little imperfections in others but can't see your own huge imperfections?*]

42 Either [*or else*] how canst thou say to thy brother, Brother, let me pull out the mote that is in thine eye [*let me fix your imperfections*], when thou thyself beholdest not the beam that is in thine own eye [*when you are so imperfect yourself*]? Thou hypocrite, cast out first the beam out of thine own eye [*straighten out your own life first*], and then shalt thou see clearly to pull out the mote that is in thy brother's eye [*then you will be able to help others effectively*].

The imagery of a small chip of wood and a huge beam of wood, in verse 42, above, is intentional exaggeration by the Master Teacher to help us see the importance of not criticizing others when we are so imperfect ourselves.

43 For a good tree [*symbolic of good people*] bringeth not forth corrupt fruit [*a wicked life*]; neither doth a corrupt tree [*a wicked person*] bring forth good fruit [*a good life*].

44 For every tree [*person*] is known by his own fruit [*the kind of life he or she leads*]. For of thorns [*from thorn bushes*] men do not gather [*harvest*] figs, nor of a bramble bush gather they [*harvest*] grapes. [*In other words, you can't expect a righteous reward on Judgment Day if you have lived a wicked life, including the hypocrisy of continuously judging others harshly.*]

45 A good man out of the good treasure of his heart bringeth forth that which is good; and an evil man out of the evil treasure of his heart bringeth forth that which is evil: for of the abundance of the heart his mouth speaketh. [*The true feelings and attitudes of our heart show up in the things we say about others.*]

46 And why call ye me, Lord, Lord, and do not the things which I say? [*Why do you pretend to follow me when you don't do what I say?*]

47 Whosoever cometh to me, and heareth my sayings, and doeth them, I will shew [*show*] you to whom he is like:

House Built on a Rock

48 He is like a man which built an house, and digged deep, and laid the foundation on a rock: and when the flood arose, the stream beat vehemently [*fiercely*] upon that house, and could not shake it: for it was founded upon a rock. [*Symbolic of a life built upon Christ and His teachings, which cannot be destroyed by life's troubles.*]

House Not Built on a Rock

49 But he that heareth [*the Savior's teachings*], and doeth not [*does not obey them*], is like a man that without a foundation built an house upon the earth; against which the stream did beat vehemently [*violently*], and immediately it fell; and the ruin of that house was great. [*Much spiritual destruction came upon that person.*]

LUKE 7

IN THIS CHAPTER you will see the Savior heal a Roman soldier's son, and raise the dead son of a widow living in Nain. You will learn more about John the Baptist, and will see Jesus forgive sins.

1 NOW when he had ended all his sayings in the audience of the people, he entered into Capernaum [*on the northwest coast of the Sea of Galilee*].

Healing of the Centurion's Son

2 And a certain centurion's servant, who was dear unto him, was sick, and ready to die. [*A centurion was a Roman soldier in charge of one hundred soldiers.*]

3 And when he heard of Jesus, he sent unto him the elders of the Jews, beseeching [*asking*] him that he would come and heal his servant.

4 And when they came to Jesus, they besought him instantly [*asked Jesus right away to heal the centurion's servant*], saying, That he [*the Roman centurion*] was worthy for whom he [*Jesus*] should do this:

5 For he [*the centurion*] loveth our nation, and he hath built us a synagogue [*a church*].

As Luke continues, you will see that this Roman centurion was a very humble man with pure faith.

6 Then Jesus went with them. And when he was now not far from the house, the centurion sent friends to him, saying unto him, Lord, trouble not thyself: for I am not worthy that thou shouldest enter under my roof [*enter into my house*]:

7 Wherefore neither thought I myself worthy to come unto thee [*I didn't consider myself worthy to come to You so I sent friends*]: but say in a word [*give the word*], and my servant shall be healed.

8 For I also [*like you*] am a man set under authority [*who has authority*], having under me soldiers, and I say unto one, Go, and he goeth; and to another, Come, and he cometh; and to my servant, Do this, and he doeth it.

9 When Jesus heard these things, he marvelled at him, and turned him about [*turned around*], and said unto the people that followed him, I say unto you, I have not found so great faith, no, not in Israel.

10 And they [*the centurion's friends*] that were sent [*to Jesus*], returning to the house, found the servant whole [*healed*] that had been sick.

Widow's Son Is Raised from the Dead

11 And it came to pass the day after, that he [*Jesus*] went into a city called Nain [*a city in Galilee*]; and many of his disciples went with him, and much people [*large crowds of people*].

12 Now when he came nigh [*near*] to the gate of the city, behold, there was a dead man carried out, the only son of his mother, and she was a widow: and much people of the city was with her.

13 And when the Lord saw her, he had compassion on her, and said unto her, Weep not.

14 And he came and touched the bier [*the board being used to carry the dead man*]: and they [*the pallbearers*] that bare [*carried*] him stood still. And he said, Young man, I say unto thee, Arise.

15 And he that was dead sat up, and began to speak. And he delivered him [*turned him over*] to his mother.

16 And there came a fear on all: and they glorified [*praised*] God, saying, That a great prophet [*Jesus*] is risen up among us; and, That God hath visited [*blessed*] his people.

17 And this rumour [*news*] of him [*Jesus*] went forth throughout all Judæa [*the southern region of the Holy Land*], and throughout all the region round about.

18 And the disciples of John [*John the Baptist*] shewed [*showed*] him [*told him*] of all these things [*about Jesus*].

19 And John [*the Baptist*] calling unto him two of his disciples sent them to Jesus, saying, Art thou he that should come [*are you the Messiah*]? or look we for another?

20 When the men [*John the Baptist's disciples*] were come unto him [*Jesus*], they said, John Baptist hath sent us unto thee, saying, Art thou he that should come? or look we for another?

21 And in that same hour he cured many of their [*the people around Jesus at the time*] infirmities and plagues [*diseases*], and of evil spirits; and unto many that were blind he gave sight.

22 Then Jesus answering [*answering the question John the Baptist's disciples asked in verse 20 above*] said unto them, Go your way, and tell John what things ye have seen and heard; how that the blind see, the lame walk, the lepers are cleansed, the deaf hear, the dead are raised, to the poor the gospel is preached.

Every time you read of the miraculous healings performed by the Savior, you may wish to consider them symbolic of his ability to heal all our spiritual "diseases," including spiritual blindness, failure to walk forward into the light of the gospel, grievous sins, spiritual deafness, spiritual death, etc.

23 And blessed is he, whosoever shall not be offended in me [*ashamed to accept Christ and His teachings*].

Jesus Praises John the Baptist

24 And when the messengers of John were departed [*to report back to John the Baptist*], he [*Christ*] began to speak unto the people concerning John [*the Baptist*], What went ye out into the wilderness for to see? A reed shaken with the wind [*a timid fellow, worried about what people think*]?

25 But what went ye out for to see? A man clothed in soft raiment [*high fashion clothing*]? Behold, they which are gorgeously apparelled [*are dressed in expensive clothes*], and live delicately [*an easy life*], are in kings' courts.

26 But what went ye out for to see? A prophet? Yea, I say unto you, and much more than a prophet.

27 This is he, of whom it is written [*prophesied, in Malachi 3:1*], Behold, I send my messenger before thy face, which shall prepare thy way before thee [*Christ*].

28 For I say unto you, Among those that are born of women there is not a greater prophet than John the Baptist: but he [*Christ*] that is least in the kingdom of God is greater than he [*John the Baptist*].

Verse 28, above, can be a bit confusing, but the Prophet Joseph Smith explains it to us. He tells us that John the Baptist is the greatest prophet born of woman, but that He, Christ, who is considered by the Jews to be the least in the kingdom, is above John the Baptist. See *Teachings of the Prophet Joseph Smith*, pp. 275–276.

29 And all the people that heard him, and the publicans [*even the tax collectors*], justified God [*said that God's way is right*], being baptized with the baptism of John [*having been baptized by John*].

30 But the Pharisees and lawyers [*religious leaders among the Jews*] rejected the counsel of God against [*for*] themselves, being not baptized of him [*refused to be baptized by John*].

31 And the Lord [*Jesus*] said, Whereunto then shall I liken the men of this generation? and to what are they like? [*To what shall I compare the wicked of this day?*]

32 They are like unto children sitting in the marketplace, and calling one to another, and saying, We have piped unto you [*played the flute for you*], and ye have not danced; we have mourned [*sung a sad song*] to you, and ye have not wept.

33 For John the Baptist came neither eating bread nor drinking wine; and ye say, He hath a devil.

34 The Son of man [*Jesus*] is come eating and drinking; and ye say, Behold a gluttonous man, and a winebibber [*one who drinks too much wine*], a friend of publicans and sinners!

The main point of verses 31–34 is this: Jesus is telling them (the Pharisees and lawyers in verse 30) that they are like children who are never satisfied. Just as the children who wouldn't dance to happy flute music, neither would they be affected by a sad song, so also are the Pharisees and lawyers. They criticize John the Baptist and won't be affected by his teachings. They criticize Jesus and won't go along with His teachings. They are never satisfied. The righteous can never win, in the eyes of the wicked. No matter what the righteous do, the wicked still criticize them.

35 But wisdom is justified of all her children. [*All things will work out the way they should, whether you like it or not.*]

A Woman Anoints Christ's Feet with Ointment—Her Sins Are Forgiven

36 And one of the Pharisees desired him that he [*Jesus*] would eat with him. And he went into the Pharisee's house, and sat down to meat [*to eat*].

37 And, behold, a woman in the city, which was a sinner [*was a known sinner*], when she knew [*found out*] that Jesus sat at meat [*was eating a meal*] in the Pharisee's house, brought an alabaster box [*an expensive flask—see Luke 7:37 footnote b, in your LDS Bible*] of ointment,

38 And stood at his feet behind him weeping, and began to wash his feet with tears, and did wipe them with the hairs of her head, and kissed his feet, and anointed them with the ointment [*put the ointment on Christ's feet*].

39 Now when the Pharisee which had bidden him [*invited Jesus to eat with him*] saw it, he spake within himself, saying [*he said to himself*], This man, if he were a prophet, would have known who and what manner of woman this is that toucheth him: for she is a sinner.

The Pharisees were very strict about not even touching a known sinner. They considered it a matter of personal righteousness to avoid contact with sinners.

40 And Jesus answering [*responding*] said unto him, Simon [*the Pharisee's name*], I have somewhat to say unto thee. And he saith, Master, say on [*go ahead*].

41 There was a certain creditor [*banker*] which had two debtors [*two people who owed him money*]: the one owed five hundred pence, and the other fifty.

A pence would be about a day's wages. See Luke 7:41, footnote a in your Bible.

42 And when they had nothing to pay [*couldn't pay*], he frankly forgave them both. Tell me therefore, which of them will love him most?

43 Simon answered and said, I suppose that he, to whom he forgave most. And he said unto him, Thou hast rightly judged.

44 And he turned to the woman, and said unto Simon, Seest thou this woman? I entered into thine house, thou gavest me no water for my feet [*you didn't wash my feet (a proper Jewish custom*

when entertaining guests)]: but she hath washed my feet with tears, and wiped them with the hairs of her head.

45 Thou gavest me no kiss: but this woman since the time I came in hath not ceased to kiss my feet.

46 My head with oil thou didst not anoint: but this woman hath anointed my feet with ointment.

47 Wherefore [*therefore*] I say unto thee, Her sins, which are many, are forgiven; for she loved much [*she showed much love and service to me because she has much to be forgiven of and she knows it*]: but to whom little is forgiven, the same loveth little.

48 And he said unto her, Thy sins are forgiven.

49 And they that sat at meat [*dinner*] with him began to say within themselves, Who is this that forgiveth sins also?

50 And he said to the woman, Thy faith hath saved thee; go in peace.

It is logical to assume that this woman had heard Christ's teachings earlier and had already repented deeply. Her humble service to the Master, serving Him to demonstrate her love for Him because of His ability to cleanse and save her from her sins, can be symbolic of our serving the Savior in appreciation for the effects of His Atonement in our lives. Her willingness to appear in public, in spite of the embarrassment of having others gossip about her because of her reputation as a sinner, shows humility and resolve to serve the Savior at all costs.

LUKE 8

AS THE SECOND year of the Savior's formal three-year mortal mission continues, Luke tells us in verse 1, next, that Jesus made another tour of Galilee, preaching and healing throughout the region. You will see that He is now making considerable use of parables in His teaching.

1 AND it came to pass afterward, that he went throughout every city and village, preaching and shewing [*showing*] the glad tidings of the kingdom of God: and the twelve [*Apostles*] were with him,

2 And certain women, which had been healed of evil spirits and infirmities, Mary called Magdalene, out of whom went seven devils,

The Savior had apparently cast seven evil spirits out of Mary Magdalene on an earlier occasion which is not recorded in the Bible.

3 And Joanna the wife of Chuza Herod's steward [*manager of his household*], and Susanna, and many others, which ministered unto him of their substance [*helped to support Jesus, using their own supplies*].

4 And when much people were gathered together, and were come to him out of every city, he spake by a parable [*a story told to teach a specific lesson*]:

The Parable of the Sower

5 A sower [*farmer*] went out to sow [*plant*] his seed: and as he sowed [*planted*], some fell by the way side [*the pathway*]; and it was trodden down [*walked on*], and the fowls of the air [*birds*] devoured [*ate*] it.

6 And some fell upon a rock; and as soon as it was sprung up [*started growing*], it withered away [*dried up and died*], because it lacked moisture.

7 And some fell among thorns; and the thorns sprang [*grew*] up with it, and choked it.

8 And other fell on good ground, and sprang up [*grew*], and bare fruit [*produced a crop*] an hundredfold. And when he had said these things, he cried, He that hath ears to hear, let him hear [*he that is spiritually in tune will understand what I am saying*].

Jesus will explain this parable to his disciples, beginning in verse 11.

9 And his disciples asked him, saying, What might this parable be *[what does this story mean]*?

10 And he said, Unto you it is given to know the mysteries *[the basic teachings, principles, etc.]* of the kingdom of God: but to others *[I teach]* in parables; that seeing they might not see, and hearing they might not understand. *[The spiritually deaf and blind don't want to understand the basics of the gospel.]*

11 Now the parable is this *[I will now explain the parable]*: The seed is the word of God.

12 Those by the way side *[the seeds that fell on the pathway in the field]* are they *[people]* that hear; then cometh the devil, and taketh away the word out of their hearts, lest they should believe and be saved.

Missionaries see application of verse 12 often in their teaching. For instance, they are invited into a home. The people listen to the gospel message and are excited. They make an appointment with the missionaries to return. But when the missionaries return for the next appointment, the family is cold and asks them to leave and not return. Satan has quickly quenched the flame of desire to hear the gospel.

13 They on the rock are they *[people]*, which, when they hear, receive the word with joy; and these have no root, which for a while believe *[stay active for a little while]*, and in time of temptation fall away.

14 And that *[the seeds]* which fell among thorns are they *[people]*, which, when they have heard *[the gospel]*, go forth, and are choked with cares and riches and pleasures of this life, and bring no fruit *[fruit is symbolic of their lives]* to perfection.

15 But that *[seed]* on the good ground are they *[people]*, which in an honest and good heart, having heard the word, keep it, and bring forth fruit with patience *[patiently remain faithful and produce righteous lives]*.

Prophet Joseph Smith gave additional insights into the Parable of the Sower, above. See note following Matthew 13:23 in this study guide.

16 No man, when he hath lighted a candle, covereth it with a vessel *[container]*, or putteth it under a bed; but setteth it on a candlestick, that they which enter in may see the light. *[In other words, let your good example of living the gospel be seen by others so that they can come unto Christ also.]*

17 For nothing is secret, that shall not be made manifest; neither any thing hid, that shall not be known and come abroad. *[God knows all things and all wickedness will eventually be exposed.]*

18 Take heed therefore how ye hear *[how you respond to the gospel when you hear it]*: for whosoever hath *[whoever lives the gospel]*, to him shall be given *[more knowledge, testimony, etc.]*; and whosoever hath not *[does not remain faithful]*, from him shall be taken even that which he seemeth to have *[see D&C 1:33]*.

19 Then came to him his mother and his brethren *[his family; see Luke 8:19, footnote a]*, and could not come at him for the press *[couldn't get through the crowd to talk to Jesus]*.

20 And it was told him by certain *[people]* which said, Thy mother and thy brethren stand without *[outside]*, desiring to see thee.

21 And he answered and said unto them, My mother and my brethren *[in other words, my "family"]* are these which hear the word of God, and do it *[see Mosiah 5:7]*.

JST Matthew 12:44 adds important information to this situation. It says, "And he gave them charge concerning her *[asked them to take good care of His mother while He continued on His mission]*, saying, I go my way, for my Father hath sent me. And whosoever shall do the will of my Father which is in heaven, the same is my brother, and sister, and mother."

22 Now it came to pass on a certain day, that he went into a ship with his disciples: and he said unto them, Let us go over unto the other side of the lake *[Sea of Galilee]*. And they launched forth.

"Master, the Tempest Is Raging"

23 But as they sailed he fell asleep: and there came down a storm of wind on the lake; and they were filled with water, and were in jeopardy *[in danger of sinking]*.

JST LUKE 8:23

23 But as they sailed he fell asleep; and there came down a storm of wind on the lake; and they were filled with fear, and were in danger.

24 And they *[the disciples]* came to him *[Jesus]*, and awoke him, saying, Master, master, we perish. Then he arose, and rebuked *[commanded]* the wind and the raging of the water: and they ceased, and there was a calm.

25 And he said unto them, Where is your faith? And they being afraid wondered, saying one to another, What manner of *[what kind of]* man is this! for he commandeth even the winds and water, and they obey him.

Jesus Heals a Man Possessed by Evil Spirits

26 And they arrived at the country of the Gadarenes, which is over against Galilee *[southeast of the Sea of Galilee]*.

27 And when he went forth to land, there met him out of the city a certain man, which had devils long time *[had been possessed by evil spirits for a long time]*, and ware *[wore]* no clothes, neither abode *[lived]* in any house, but in the tombs *[lived among the graves]*.

28 When he saw Jesus, he cried out, and fell down before *[in front of]* him, and with a loud voice said, What have I to do with thee, Jesus, thou Son of God most high? I beseech *[beg]* thee, torment me not.

The evil spirit seems to be speaking through the man who is possessed here, and is speaking for several evil spirits who posses the man.

29 For he *[Christ]* had commanded the unclean spirit to come out of the man. For oftentimes it *[the evil spirit]* had caught *[seized]* him: and he was kept bound with chains and in fetters *[leg irons]*; and he brake *[broke]* the bands, and was driven of *[by]* the devil *[evil spirit]* into the wilderness.

30 And Jesus asked him *[the evil spirit]*, saying, What is thy name? And he said, Legion: because many devils were entered into him *[many evil spirits were in the man]*.

31 And they *[the evil spirits]* besought *[pleaded with]* him that he would not command them to go out into the deep.

Evil Spirits Enter into a Herd of Swine

32 And there was there an herd of many swine *[pigs]* feeding on the mountain: and they besought *[begged]* him that he would suffer *[allow]* them to enter into them *[the pigs]*. And he suffered them *[allowed them to do so]*.

33 Then went the devils out of the man, and entered into the swine: and the herd ran violently down a steep place into the lake, and were choked *[drowned]*.

34 When they that fed them *[the people whose job it was to take care of the pigs]* saw what was done, they fled *[ran]*, and went and told it *[spread the news]* in the city and in the country.

35 Then they *[the city officials and owners of the pigs]* went out to see what was done; and came to Jesus, and found the man, out of whom the devils were departed *[had been cast out]*, sitting at the feet of Jesus, clothed, and in his right mind: and they were afraid.

36 They also which saw it *[eyewitnesses]* told them by what means he that was possessed of the devils was healed.

37 Then the whole multitude of the country of the Gadarenes round about besought [*asked*] him [*Jesus*] to depart from them [*to leave their part of the country*]; for they were taken with great fear: and he went up into the ship, and returned back again.

It is sad that these men, rather than asking the Savior to stay and teach them, after having performed such a beautiful healing for the man (symbolic of the fact that Christ can heal us from the effects of Satan's influence), instead asked Him to leave their city and go elsewhere. It was no doubt a major economic disaster to lose about 2000 pigs (Mark 5:13). But being materialistic, worrying more about wealth and possessions than spiritual, eternal things, can blind us to the value of the Savior and His Atonement.

38 Now the man out of whom the devils were departed besought him [*asked Jesus*] that he might be with him [*if he could stay with Jesus*]: but Jesus sent him away, saying,

39 Return to thine own house, and shew how great things God hath done unto thee [*stay here and be a witness of the fact that God healed you*]. And he went his way, and published throughout the whole city how great things Jesus had done unto him.

40 And it came to pass, that, when Jesus was returned, the people gladly received him: for they were all waiting for him.

Jairus' Daughter Is Raised from the Dead

41 And, behold, there came a man named Jairus, and he was a ruler of the synagogue: and he fell down at Jesus' feet, and besought him that he would [*asked him to*] come into his house:

42 For he had one only daughter, about twelve years of age, and she lay a dying. But as he went the people thronged him [*crowded and bumped against him*].

A Woman with an Issue of Blood Is Healed

43 And a woman having an issue of blood twelve years [*who had been bleeding for twelve years*], which had spent all her living upon physicians [*she had spent all her money to pay doctors*], neither could be healed of any [*no doctors had successfully treated her illness*],

44 Came behind him, and touched the border of his garment [*robe, cloak*]: and immediately her issue of blood stanched [*the bleeding stopped*].

45 And Jesus said, Who touched me? When all denied [*nobody admitted touching him*], Peter and they that were with him said, Master, the multitude throng thee and press thee [*people in this crowd are bumping You and pressing against You constantly*], and sayest thou, Who touched me [*what do You mean, "Who touched me"*]?

46 And Jesus said, Somebody hath touched me: for I perceive that virtue [*power; strength*] is gone out of me.

47 And when the woman saw that she was not hid [*that she had been discovered*], she came trembling, and falling down before him, she declared unto him before [*in front of*] all the people for what cause [*the reason why*] she had touched him and how she was healed immediately.

48 And he said unto her, Daughter, be of good comfort: thy faith hath made thee whole [*healed*]; go in peace.

49 While he yet spake, there cometh one from the ruler of the synagogue's house [*Jairus' house; see verse 41*], saying to him, Thy daughter is dead; trouble not the Master [*it is too late; don't bother Jesus*].

50 But when Jesus heard it, he answered [*responded to*] him, saying, Fear not: believe only [*just have faith*], and she shall be made whole [*will be healed*].

51 And when he came into the house, he suffered [*allowed*] no man to go in, save [*except*] Peter, and James, and John, and the father and the mother of the maiden [*the dead girl*].

52 And all wept, and bewailed her: but he said, Weep not; she is not dead, but sleepeth.

53 And they [*the mourners*] laughed him to scorn [*mocked and ridiculed Jesus*], knowing that she was dead.

54 And he put them all out [*sent the mourners out of the room*], and took her by the hand, and called, saying, Maid, arise.

55 And her spirit came again, and she arose straightway [*immediately*]: and he commanded to give her meat [*food*].

In the language of our Bible, "meat" means any type of food. "Flesh" means meat, as in beef, lamb, chicken, etc.

56 And her parents were astonished: but he charged [*instructed*] them that they should tell no man what was done.

Some experiences with God are very private and personal and are to be kept to ourselves. Perhaps this is the reason the parents were so instructed by Jesus.

LUKE 9

AS LUKE, WHO was not an Apostle himself, continues, he reports some details to us concerning the training of the twelve Apostles by the Savior. As you can well imagine, this was an intense time of learning and training for these humble men, and the "learning curve" remained steep.

The Twelve Are Sent on Missions

1 THEN he called his twelve disciples together, and gave them power and authority over all devils, and to cure diseases.

2 And he sent them to preach the kingdom of God, and to heal the sick.

This is an important part of the Apostles' ongoing training, and will raise several questions in their minds for which they will seek answers as they return to the Master Teacher for more instruction. They will be ready to hear the answers.

3 And he said unto them, Take nothing for your journey, neither staves [*staffs*], nor scrip [*a bag in which to carry food; see Bible Dictionary, under "Scrip"*], neither bread, neither money; neither have two coats apiece.

4 And whatsoever house ye enter into, there abide, and thence depart.

5 And whosoever will not receive you, when ye go out of that city, shake off the very dust from your feet for a testimony against them [*as a witness that you tried to teach them the gospel; see D&C 60:15*].

6 And they departed, and went through the towns, preaching the gospel, and healing every where.

Just a reminder that the symbol, "¶" at the beginning of verse 7 and many other places in our Bible, means the beginning of a new topic.

7 ¶ Now Herod the tetrarch [*Roman ruler*] heard of all that was done by him [*by Jesus*]: and he was perplexed [*worried*], because that it was said of some, that John was risen from the dead; [*Some people were saying that Jesus was John the Baptist, come back to life, whom Herod had had beheaded.*]

8 And of some, that Elias had appeared [*some said that Jesus was Elijah the Prophet*]; and of others, that one of the old prophets was risen again [*had come back to life*].

9 And Herod said, John [*the Baptist*] have I beheaded: but who is this, of whom I hear such things? And he desired to see him [*wanted to see Jesus*].

The Twelve Report Back from Their Missions

10 And the apostles, when they were returned [*from their missions as mentioned in verses 2–6*], told him all that they had done [*reported back to Him*]. And he took them, and went aside privately into a desert place [*JST "a solitary place"*] belonging to the city called Bethsaida. [*Jesus wanted to have some private time with His Apostles.*]

11 And the people, when they knew it [*when they found out where Jesus was*], followed him: and he received them, and spake unto them of the kingdom of God, and healed them that had need of healing.

Jesus demonstrated His compassion and kindness time and time again, putting aside His needs for rest and privacy, as in verse 11 above, to minister to the people.

The Feeding of the 5,000

12 And when the day began to wear away [*was about gone*], then came the twelve, and said unto him, Send the multitude away, that they may go into the towns and country round about, and lodge, and get victuals [*food*]: for we are here in a desert place. [*There is nowhere here to buy food.*]

13 But he said unto them, Give ye them to eat. [*This must have startled the Apostles!*] And they said, We have no more but five loaves and two fishes; except we should go and buy meat [*food*] for all this people.

14 For they were about five thousand men. [*Matthew 14:21 says there were about 5,000 men plus women and children.*] And he said to his disciples, Make them sit down by fifties in a company [*in groups of fifty*].

15 And they did so, and made them all sit down.

16 Then he [*Jesus*] took the five loaves and the two fishes, and looking up to heaven, he blessed them, and brake, and gave to the disciples to set before the multitude.

17 And they [*all the people*] did eat, and were all filled: and there was taken up of fragments that remained to them twelve baskets [*they gathered up twelve basketfuls of leftovers*].

Peter Bears Testimony That Jesus Is the Christ

18 And it came to pass, as he was alone praying, his disciples were with him: and he asked them, saying, Whom say the people that I am?

19 They answering said, John the Baptist; but some say, Elias [*Elijah*]; and others say, that one of the old prophets is risen again [*has come back to life*].

20 He said unto them, But whom say ye that I am? Peter answering said, The Christ of God.

21 And he straitly [*strictly*] charged [*told*] them, and commanded them to tell no man that thing;

JST LUKE 9:21
21 And he straitly charged them, and commanded them to tell no man of him,

It would seem that this instruction (in verse 21, above) to the Apostles was temporary and for that particular time and circumstance. Perhaps they needed a bit of quiet time together for the Master to teach His disciples about His upcoming death (in about six months) and resurrection. Some manuscripts say, "Don't go and tell anyone in the village."

22 Saying, The Son of man [*Jesus*] must suffer many things, and be rejected of [*by*] the elders and chief priests and scribes [*religious leaders of the Jews*], and be slain, and be raised [*resurrected*] the third day.

23 And he said to them all, If any man will come after me, let him deny himself [*put aside his own needs*], and take up his cross [*sacrifice whatever is necessary*] daily, and follow me.

24 For whosoever will save his life [*preserve his own worldly lifestyle rather than following the Savior*] shall lose it [*will ultimately lose that way of life*]: but whosoever will lose his life for my sake [*will change his lifestyle and follow the Savior*], the same shall save it [*will keep the rich blessings of a righteous life forever*].

25 For what is a man advantaged, if he gain the whole world, and lose himself [*lose his soul*], or be cast away [*be cast away from heaven on Judgment Day*]?

JST LUKE 9:24–25

24 For whosoever will save his life, must be willing to lose it for my sake; and whosoever will be willing to lose his life for my sake, the same shall save it.

25 For what doth it profit a man if he gain the whole world, and yet he receive him not whom God hath ordained, and he lose his own soul, and he himself be a castaway?

26 For whosoever shall be ashamed of me [*will reject me*] and of my words, of him shall the Son of man be ashamed [*he will be rejected by Jesus*], when he shall come in his own glory [*at the Second Coming*], and in his Father's, and of the holy angels.

JST LUKE 9:26

26 For whosoever shall be ashamed of me, and of my words, of him shall the Son of Man [*Son of the Father, who is "Man of Holiness" in Moses 6:57*] be ashamed, when he shall come in his own kingdom, clothed in the glory of his Father, with the holy angels.

27 But I tell you of a truth, there be some standing here, which shall not taste of death, till they see the kingdom of God.

JST LUKE 9:27

27 Verily, I tell you of a truth, there are some standing here who shall not taste of death, until they see the kingdom of God coming in power.

We know that John, the Apostle, was one in this group around the Savior who would "not taste of death" (has not yet died). He was translated and allowed to stay on earth to minister to people until the Second Coming. See D&C 7:3. We don't know who any of the others are, standing by the Savior at this moment in verse 27, who would be translated. We do know that the Three Nephites were translated as described in 3 Nephi 28.

The Mount of Transfiguration

28 And it came to pass about an eight days after these sayings, he took Peter and John and James, and went up into a mountain to pray.

It is now near October, and the Savior will be crucified the following April, thus ending His mortal ministry. Three of his Apostles, Peter, James, and John are already taking on the role of First Presidency. They will experience tremendous additional training now as the Master takes them with Him up on the mountain which is referred to as the Mount of Transfiguration. There, they will see Christ transfigured (shine with brilliant heavenly light) before their eyes, will hear the Father's voice, and will see the great prophets Moses and Elijah, who will minister to Jesus, and from whom they will receive additional priesthood keys. From JST Mark 9:3, we learn that John the Baptist was also there.

29 And as he prayed, the fashion of his countenance was altered, and his raiment [*clothing*] was white and glistering [*shining*].

30 And, behold, there talked with him two men, which were Moses and Elias [*Elijah*]:

31 Who appeared in glory, and spake of his decease [*death*] which he [*Jesus*] should accomplish at Jerusalem.

JST LUKE 9:31

31 Who appeared in glory, and spake of his death, and also his resurrection, which he should accomplish at Jerusalem.

32 But Peter and they that were with him [*James and John*] were heavy with sleep: and when they were awake, they saw his glory, and the two men that stood with him.

33 And it came to pass, as they [*Moses and Elijah*] departed from him [*Christ*], Peter said unto Jesus, Master, it is good for us to be here: and let us make three tabernacles [*small booths, typically used among the Jews for private worship*

during the annual Feast of Tabernacles]; one for thee, and one for Moses, and one for Elias [*Elijah*]: not knowing what he said [*not understanding the situation*].

34 While he thus spake, there came a cloud, and overshadowed them: and they feared as they entered into the cloud.

The Father Bears Witness of the Son

35 And there came a voice [*the Father's voice*] out of the cloud, saying, This is my beloved Son: hear him.

36 And when the voice was past, Jesus was found alone. And they kept it close, and told no man in those days any of those things which they had seen.

For additional information about what took place on the Mount of Transfiguration, see the note after Matthew 17:8 in this study guide.

37 And it came to pass, that on the next day, when they were come down from the hill [*from the Mount of Transfiguration*], much [*many*] people met him.

An Evil Spirit Is Cast Out

38 And, behold, a man of the company [*in the crowd*] cried out, saying, Master, I beseech [*beg of*] thee, look upon my son: for he is mine only child.

39 And, lo, a spirit [*an evil spirit*] taketh [*possesses*] him, and he suddenly crieth out; and it teareth him that he foameth again [*it throws him around and makes him foam at the mouth*], and bruising him [*causes him to get bruised as he tosses around on the ground*] hardly departeth from him [*it hardly ever leaves him so he can have peace*].

40 And I besought [*begged*] thy disciples to cast him out; and they could not.

41 And Jesus answering said, O faithless and perverse [*wicked*] generation [*people*], how long shall I be with you, and suffer you [*put up with your lack of righteousness and faith*]? Bring thy son hither [*here*].

42 And as he [*the man's son*] was yet a coming, the devil [*evil spirit*] threw him down, and tare him [*threw him around some more*]. And Jesus rebuked the unclean spirit [*commanded the evil spirit to leave*], and healed the child, and delivered him again to his father.

43 And they were all amazed at the mighty power of God. But while they wondered every one at all things which Jesus did, he said unto his disciples,

Jesus Prophecies His Arrest

44 Let these sayings sink down into your ears: for the Son of man [*Jesus*] shall be delivered into the hands of men [*arrested and turned over to wicked men*].

45 But they understood not this saying [*didn't understand what He was saying*], and it was hid from them, that they perceived [*understood*] it not: and they feared to ask him of that saying [*were afraid to ask Him to explain what He meant*].

Who Is Greatest among You?

46 Then there arose a reasoning [*a debate*] among them, which of them should be greatest.

47 And Jesus, perceiving the thought of their heart, took a child, and set him by him,

48 And said unto them, Whosoever shall receive this child in my name receiveth [*accepts*] me: and whosoever shall receive me receiveth him [*the Father*] that sent me: for he that is least [*humbly considers himself to be the least*] among you all, the same shall be great.

49 And John answered and said, Master, we saw one *[a person]* casting out devils in thy name; and we forbad him *[told him not to]*, because he followeth not with us *[he is not one of us]*.

50 And Jesus said unto him, Forbid him not *[don't tell him not to]*: for he that is not against us is for us.

51 And it came to pass, when the time was come that he should be received up *[perform the Atonement, be crucified, resurrected and taken up into heaven]*, he stedfastly *[with determination]* set his face to go to Jerusalem,

Jesus and his Apostles have been serving in the Galilee area, in northern Israel. Now, Jesus has told them that they must go south to Jerusalem. Normally, the Jews avoided going straight south from Galilee, because that would require traveling through the province of Samaria. The Jews despised the Samaritans (people of Samaria) and the Samaritans despised the Jews. Thus, the Jews normally traveled around Samaria, to the east, and then south to Jerusalem. But this time, Jesus is heading straight south, right through Samaria, which would no doubt cause his Apostles some extra anxiety.

52 And sent messengers before his face *[ahead of Him]*: and they *[the messengers]* went, and entered into a village of the Samaritans, to make ready for him *[to prepare things for Him to rest, eat, etc.]*.

53 And they *[the Samaritans in the village]* did not receive him *[were rude to Jesus and would not allow him and his followers to buy provisions]*, because his face was as though he would go to Jerusalem *[because they knew He was a Jew and was heading toward Jerusalem]*.

May We Destroy Them With Fire?

54 And when his disciples James and John saw this, they said, Lord, wilt thou that we command fire to come down from heaven, and consume them *[these Samaritans]*, even as Elias did *[is it OK with You if we command fire to come down from heaven and destroy them like Elijah did to the fifty soldiers and their captain who were rude to him; see 2 Kings 1:10]*?

55 But he turned, and rebuked *[scolded]* them, and said, Ye know not what manner of spirit ye are of *[you don't realize how awful your attitude is]*.

56 For the Son of man *[Jesus]* is not come to destroy men's lives, but to save them. And they went to another village.

Next, Luke will use examples for his account that emphasize that one must commit one hundred percent in order to successfully follow Christ.

57 And it came to pass, that, as they went in the way *[along the road]*, a certain man said unto him, Lord, I will follow thee whithersoever thou goest.

58 And Jesus said unto him, Foxes have holes, and birds of the air have nests; but the Son of man *[Christ]* hath not where *[anywhere]* to lay his head.

59 And he said unto another, Follow me. But he said, Lord, suffer *[allow]* me first to go and bury my father.

60 Jesus said unto him, Let the dead bury their dead: but go thou and preach the kingdom of God.

There is probably more to the story than is recorded here. Perhaps "let the dead bury their dead" includes a message that following the Savior requires real commitment and sometimes requires one to leave the comforts of home and family and follow Jesus at all costs.

61 And another also said, Lord, I will follow thee; but let me first go bid them farewell, which are at home at my house.

62 And Jesus said unto him, No man, having put his hand to the plough *[plow]*, and looking back, is fit for the kingdom of God. *[Ultimately, we have to be committed to follow the Savior at all costs. If we achieve this level of commitment, all other things of eternal value, including family, will be ours forever.]*

LUKE 10

IN THIS CHAPTER, Jesus continues to organize the priesthood officers of His church by calling the Seventy and sending them out two by two.

The Seventy Are Called and Sent Out

1 AFTER these things the Lord appointed other seventy also, and sent them two and two before his face *[in advance of Him]* into every city and place, whither he himself would come.

2 Therefore said he unto them, The harvest truly is great *[the potential for converts is large]*, but the labourers are few *[there are relatively few members, missionaries, etc., to spread the gospel]*: pray ye therefore the Lord of the harvest, that he would send forth labourers into his harvest.

3 Go your ways: behold, I send you forth as lambs among wolves *[you will be in danger at times]*.

4 Carry neither purse *[money]*, nor scrip *[food; see Bible Dictionary, under "Scrip"]*, nor shoes *[wear sandals instead]*: and salute no man by the way *[don't stop to visit or delay the work you are assigned; see Doctrinal New Testament Commentary, Vol. 1, p. 433]*.

5 And into whatsoever house ye enter, first say, Peace be to this house.

6 And if the son of peace *[a peaceful person]* be there, your peace shall rest upon it: if not, it shall turn to you again.

7 And in the same house remain, eating and drinking such things as they give: for the labourer is worthy of his hire *[it is worthwhile for people to support you]*. Go not from house to house. *[Don't go methodically from house to house. Go where the Spirit directs.]*

8 And into whatsoever city ye enter, and they receive you, eat such things as are set before you:

9 And heal the sick that are therein, and say unto them, The kingdom of God is come nigh unto you *[the true gospel is now available to you]*.

10 But into whatsoever city ye enter, and they receive you not, go your ways out into the streets of the same, and say,

11 Even the very dust of your city, which cleaveth on *[sticks to]* us, we do wipe off against you *[as a witness that we tried to teach you; see D&C 60:15]*: notwithstanding *[even though you have rejected us]* be ye sure of this, that the kingdom of God is come nigh unto you *[the true gospel of Christ is here for you]*.

12 But I say unto you, that it shall be more tolerable in that day *[Judgment Day]* for Sodom, than for that city *[it is a very serious thing to reject the gospel, knowingly]*.

The JST adds a verse after verse 12, above.

JST LUKE 10:13
13 Then began he to upbraid the people in every city wherein his mighty works were done, who received him not, saying,

13 Woe unto thee, Chorazin! woe unto thee, Bethsaida *[cities where Jesus had preached and done many miracles]*! for if the mighty works had been done in Tyre and Sidon *[non-Jewish cities]*, which have been done in you, they had *[would have]* a great while ago repented, sitting in sackcloth and ashes *[would have humbled themselves]*.

14 But it shall be more tolerable for Tyre and Sidon at the judgment, than for you *[because you have had great opportunities to know the gospel and they haven't]*.

15 And thou, Capernaum, which art exalted to heaven *[whose inhabitants are prideful, cocky]*, shalt be thrust down to hell.

16 He that heareth you *[pays attention to you]* heareth me; and he that despiseth you despiseth me; and he that despiseth me despiseth him that sent me *[the Father]*.

CARRY NEITHER PURSE, NOR SCRIP, NOR SHOES: AND SALUTE NO MAN BY THE WAY.

LUKE 10:4

WITHOUT PURSE OR SCRIP, by Liz Lemon Swindle

JST LUKE 10:17

17 And he said unto his disciples, He that heareth you, heareth me; and he that despiseth you, despiseth me; and he that despiseth me, despiseth him who sent me.

The Seventy Return

The Seventy, who were sent out on missions by the Lord in verse 1, above, now return and report their missions to Him.

17 And the seventy returned again with joy, saying, Lord, even the devils are subject unto us through thy name [*when we do it in the name of Jesus Christ*].

Next, Jesus tells the Seventy that He was there when Lucifer was cast out as a result of his rebellion—see Isaiah 14-12, Revelation 12:7-9, D&C 76:25-27, etc. Among other things, the Savior is instructing these men in the fact that He has power and authority over Satan.

18 And he said unto them, I beheld [*saw*] Satan as lightning fall from heaven.

19 Behold, I give unto you power to tread on serpents and scorpions, and over all the power of the enemy [*Satan and all who work with him in opposing the work of the Lord*]: and nothing shall by any means hurt you.

20 Notwithstanding [*nevertheless*] in this rejoice not [*don't get cocky or boastful*], that the spirits are subject unto you; but rather rejoice, because your names are written in heaven [*you will go to celestial glory*].

21 In that hour Jesus rejoiced in spirit, and said, I thank thee, O Father, Lord of heaven and earth, that thou hast hid these things from the wise and prudent, and hast revealed them unto babes [*humble people who have childlike faith*]: even so, Father; for so it seemed good in thy sight.

Here again we see the powerful contribution of the Prophet Joseph Smith's translation of the Bible, changing just one phrase that makes a world of difference in our understanding (from "the wise and prudent" in verse 21, above, to "them who think they are wise and prudent" in the JST, as given next).

JST LUKE 10:22

22 In that hour Jesus rejoiced in spirit, and said, I thank thee, O Father, Lord of heaven and earth, that thou hast hid these things from them who think they are wise and prudent, and hast revealed them unto babes; even so, Father; for so it seemed good in thy sight.

22 All things are delivered to me of my Father: and no man knoweth who the Son is, but the Father; and who the Father is, but the Son, and he to whom the Son will reveal him.

JST LUKE 10:23

23 All things are delivered to me of my Father; and no man knoweth that the Son is the Father [*Jesus is the "father" of our salvation*], and the Father is the Son [*the "father of our salvation" is the Son of God*], but him to whom the Son will reveal it.

We will pause a moment and explain JST verse 23, above. As you know, some of our Christian brothers and sisters believe that the Godhead consists of three in one and one in three, the three being actually only one personage. Without understanding Bible language and imagery it could be claimed that JST Luke 10:23, quoted above, supports that false concept.

The word "Father" is often used to mean the "creator of" or the "provider of." Even in modern English, we often use "father" in a similar way. For example, George Washington is the "father" of our country. Thomas Edison is the "father" of the electric light bulb. Eli Whitney is the "father" of, or inventor of, the cotton gin. Similarly, Jesus is the "father" of the Atonement, the one who provided the gift of forgiveness and resurrection to us. He is the "father" or creator of the earth, the "father" of our salvation, because He provided the way for us to return to our Heavenly Father.

Thus, in the Biblical language and imagery used in JST Luke 10:23, the "Son" (Jesus Christ) is the "Father" of our salvation, and the "Son" (the only Begotten Son of the Father) which gave Him the power to carry out the Atonement. You will see the same concept and doctrine taught in Mosiah 15:1–5.

Next, the Savior turns to His disciples and reminds them of the blessing they enjoy in knowing what they know about Him and in having seen what they have already seen.

23 And he turned him unto his disciples, and said privately, Blessed are the eyes which see the things that ye see:

24 For I tell you, that many prophets and kings have desired to see those things which ye see, and have not seen them; and to hear those things which ye hear, and have not heard them.

25 And, behold, a certain lawyer stood up, and tempted him [*tried to trick Jesus*], saying, Master, what shall I do to inherit eternal life [*to get to heaven*]?

26 He said unto him, What is written in the law [*to the Jews at the time, "the law" meant the books of Moses, namely, Genesis, Exodus, Leviticus, Numbers, and Deuteronomy*]? how readest thou [*what do you understand the scriptures to say on this matter*]?

27 And he answering said, Thou shalt love the Lord thy God with all thy heart, and with all thy soul, and with all thy strength, and with all thy mind; and thy neighbour as thyself.

28 And he [*Jesus*] said unto him [*the lawyer*], Thou hast answered right: this do, and thou shalt live [*get to heaven*].

The Parable of the Good Samaritan

29 But he, willing to justify himself [*wanting to make himself look good in front of the people who were standing around; see Luke 10:29, footnote a, which sends you to Luke 16:15 for a similar situation*], said unto Jesus, And who is my neighbour?

Jesus will now give the Parable of the Good Samaritan. It is helpful to know that the Jews despised the Samaritans and the Samaritans generally despised and made fun of the Jews. Samaria (the land of the Samaritans) was between Judea (in southern Israel) and Galilee (in northern Israel). When the ten tribes of Israel (who lived in Samaria) were taken into captivity (about 721 b.c.) by the Assyrians, some Israelites were left behind and intermarried with the Assyrian soldiers who occupied Samaria. This intermarrying over the years led the Jews to despise the Samaritans for breaking the Law of Moses in which marrying outside of covenant Israel was forbidden.

30 And Jesus answering said, A certain man went down from Jerusalem to Jericho, and fell among thieves [*was attacked by robbers*], which stripped him of his raiment [*clothing*], and wounded him, and departed, leaving him half dead.

31 And by chance there came down a certain priest [*Jewish priest*] that way: and when he saw him, he passed by on the other side.

32 And likewise a Levite [*another Jewish priest*], when he was at the place, came and looked on him, and passed by on the other side.

JST Luke 10:33

33 And likewise a Levite, when he was at the place, came and looked upon him, and passed by on the other side of the way; for they desired in their hearts that it might not be known that they had seen him.

Just a reminder. As mentioned a number of times already in this study guide, all of the JST corrections and additions are not contained in our LDS Bible. There is not enough room for them, consequently there were some difficult decisions made by the Brethren as to what to include and what to leave out. The JST verse given above, which contains some more information about the priest and the Levite, is not in our Bible. In order to see all of the JST changes, you would need to purchase a copy of the complete JST from an LDS bookstore or find it online.

33 But a certain Samaritan [*a man from Samaria; as mentioned above, Samaritans were despised by the Jews*], as he journeyed, came where he was: and when he saw him, he had compassion on him,

34 And went to him, and bound up his wounds, pouring in oil and wine [*gave him first aid*], and set him on his own beast, and brought him to an inn, and took care of him.

35 And on the morrow when he departed, he took out two pence [*money representing two days' wages*], and gave them to the host [*the innkeeper*], and said unto him, Take care of him; and whatsoever thou spendest more [*beyond what I have paid you*], when I come again, I will repay thee.

THE GOOD SAMARITAN, by Joseph F. Brickey

Did you notice that it costs to be a "good Samaritan"? Certainly, that is one of the important messages for us in this parable.

36 Which now of these three, thinkest thou, was neighbour unto him that fell among the thieves?

37 And he [*the lawyer*] said, He that shewed [*showed*] mercy on him. Then said Jesus unto him, Go, and do thou likewise.

Mary and Martha

38 Now it came to pass, as they went, that he entered into a certain village [*Bethany, near the Mount of Olives, just outside Jerusalem*]: and a certain woman named Martha received him into her house.

What happens next is a rather well-known situation, in which Martha complains to Jesus that her sister Mary, is not helping with the chores associated with preparing a meal for Him. What follows is a lesson by the Savior on priorities and individual needs and personalities.

39 And she had a sister called Mary, which also sat at Jesus' feet, and heard his word.

40 But Martha was cumbered about much serving [*very busy with all the details that needed attention in order to feed the Savior*], and came to him, and said [*complained*], Lord, dost thou not care that my sister hath left me to serve alone [*doesn't it bother you that Mary is not helping me*]? bid her therefore that she help me [*tell her to help me*].

41 And Jesus answered and said unto her, Martha, Martha, thou art careful and troubled about many things [*you are meticulous and always fuss over the tiniest details*]:

42 But one thing is needful: and Mary hath chosen that good part [*has chosen to listen to me and my teachings*], which shall not be taken away from her [*which is a wise thing for her to be doing with her agency*].

Elder James E. Talmage, a member of the Quorum of the Twelve Apostles from 1911-1933, spoke of Mary and Martha as follows:

"There was no reproof of Martha's desire to provide well; nor any sanction of possible neglect on Mary's part. We must suppose that Mary had been a willing helper before the Master's arrival; but now that He had come, she chose to remain with Him. Had she been culpably neglectful of her duty, Jesus would not have commended her course. He desired not well-served meals and material comforts only, but the company of the sisters, and above all their receptive attention to what He had to say. He had more to give them than they could possibly provide for Him. Jesus loved the two sisters and their brother as well. Both these women were devoted to Jesus, and each expressed herself in her own way. Martha was of a practical turn, concerned in material service; she was by nature hospitable and self-denying. Mary, contemplative and more spiritually inclined, showed her devotion through the service of companionship and appreciation." (*Jesus the Christ*, p. 433)

LUKE 11

WE ARE NOW into the last months of the Savior's mortal life. As Luke continues, we will see "the Lord's Prayer" and will feel the beauty of the gospel of love in contrast to the hypocritical attacks upon the Savior and His mission by the Jewish religious leaders.

1 AND it came to pass, that, as he was praying in a certain place, when he ceased, one of his disciples said unto him, Lord, teach us to pray, as John [*the Baptist*] also taught his disciples.

Jesus now gives what is commonly known as "The Lord's Prayer." It is an example of how to pray and of things which can be included in our prayers.

The Lord's Prayer

2 And he said unto them, When ye pray, say, Our Father which art in heaven, Hallowed be [*holy is*] thy name. Thy kingdom come. Thy will be done, as in heaven, so in earth.

3 Give us day by day our daily bread.

AND MARTHA SERVED, by Elspeth Young

4 And forgive us our sins; for we also forgive every one that is indebted to us. And lead us not into temptation; but deliver us from evil.

JST LUKE 11:4

4 And forgive us our sins; for we also forgive every one who is indebted to us. And let us not be led unto temptation; but deliver us from evil; for thine is the kingdom and power. Amen.

Next, Jesus will encourage his disciples to ask Heavenly Father for whatever they need. He reminds them that Heavenly Father is a Father with tender feelings toward His children and who likes to bless and help them. He also encourages them to continue praying for things they need, even if at first they don't get them.

5 And he said unto them [*His disciples*], Which of you shall have a friend, and shall go unto him at midnight, and say unto him, Friend, lend me three loaves [*of bread*];

JST LUKE 11:5–6

5 And he said unto them, Your heavenly Father will not fail to give unto you whatsoever ye ask of him. And he spake a parable, saying,

6 Which of you shall have a friend, and shall go unto him at midnight, and say unto him, Friend, lend me three loaves;

6 For a friend of mine in his journey is come to me, and I have nothing to set before him [*nothing to feed him*]?

7 And he [*the friend in verse 5*] from within [*inside his house*] shall answer and say, Trouble me not: the door is now shut, and my children are with me in bed; I cannot rise and give thee.

8 I say unto you, Though he will not rise and give him, because he is his friend, yet because of his importunity [*because he stays there and keeps knocking at the door and asking for help*] he [*the friend who has bread*] will rise and give him as many as he needeth.

Ask, Seek, Knock

9 And I say unto you, Ask, and it shall be given you; seek, and ye shall find; knock, and it shall be opened unto you.

10 For every one that asketh receiveth; and he that seeketh findeth; and to him that knocketh it shall be opened.

11 If a son shall ask bread of any of you that is a father, will he give him a stone? or if he ask a fish, will he for a fish give him a serpent?

12 Or if he shall ask an egg, will he offer him a scorpion?

13 If ye then, being evil [*being human, imperfect*], know how to give good gifts unto your children: how much more shall your heavenly Father give the Holy Spirit to them that ask him?

JST LUKE 11:14

14 If ye then, being evil, know how to give good gifts unto your children, how much more shall your heavenly Father give good gifts, through the Holy Spirit, to them who ask him.

LUKE

An Evil Spirit Is Cast Out

14 And he was casting out a devil [*an evil spirit*], and it [*the man*] was dumb [*couldn't talk*]. And it came to pass, when the devil was gone out, the dumb spake [*the man who had been possessed by the evil spirit was able to talk*]; and the people wondered [*the crowd was amazed*]

JST LUKE 11:15

15 And he was casting a devil out of a man, and he was dumb. And it came to pass, when the devil was gone out, the dumb spake; and the people wondered.

15 But some of them said, He casteth out devils through Beelzebub the chief of the devils [*Jesus is using Satan's power to cast out evil spirits*].

16 And others, tempting [*testing Him*] him, sought of him a sign from heaven.

17 But he, knowing their thoughts, said unto them, Every kingdom divided against itself is brought to desolation [*is eventually destroyed*]; and a house divided against a house falleth.

18 If Satan also be divided against himself [*if Satan is casting out his own evil spirits*], how shall his kingdom stand [*survive*]? because ye say that I cast out devils through Beelzebub [*Satan*].

19 And if I by Beelzebub [*by the power of Satan*] cast out devils, by whom do your sons cast them out? therefore shall they be your judges.

From JST Matthew 12:22–23, we learn the correct interpretation of verse 19 above:

JST Matthew 12:22–23

22 And if I by Beelzebub cast out devils, by whom do your children cast our devils? Therefore they shall be your judges.

23 But if I cast out devils by the Spirit of God, then the kingdom of God is come unto you [*in effect saying that He is the promised Messiah*]. For they [*some righteous Jews*] also cast out devils by the Spirit of God, for unto them is given power over devils, that they may cast them out.

From the words in the JST, above, we find that there were righteous Jews, obviously baptized and faithful, who were enabled by the Spirit of God to cast out evil spirits. See *Doctrinal New Testament Commentary*, Vol. 1, p. 269.

20 But if I with the finger [*power*] of God cast out devils, no doubt the kingdom of God is come upon you [*you are seeing the true kingdom of God in action and you had better pay attention*].

21 When a strong man armed keepeth his palace [*guards his palace*], his goods are in peace [*his possessions are safe*]:

22 But when a stronger than he shall come upon him, and overcome him, he taketh from him all his armour [*protection*] wherein he trusted, and divideth his spoils [*takes his possessions*].

23 He that is not with me is against me: and he that gathereth not with me scattereth.

24 When the unclean spirit is gone out of a man, he walketh through dry places, seeking rest; and finding none, he saith, I will return unto my house whence I came out.

JST Luke 11:25

25 When the unclean spirit is gone out of a man, it walketh through dry places, seeking rest; and finding none, it saith, I will return unto my house whence I came out.

25 And when he cometh, he findeth it swept and garnished.

26 Then goeth he, and taketh to him seven other spirits more wicked than himself; and they enter in, and dwell there: and the last state of that man is worse than the first.

JST Luke 11:26–27

26 And when it cometh, it findeth the house swept and garnished.

27 Then goeth the evil spirit, and taketh seven other spirits more wicked than himself, and they enter in, and dwell there; and the last end of that man is worse than the first.

Verses 24–26 above are especially difficult to understand without help. Matthew 12:43–45 is similar to Luke 11:24–26, and there is a note following Matthew 12:45 in this study guide which explains these verses.

27 And it came to pass, as he spake these things, a certain woman of the company lifted up her voice, and said unto him, Blessed is the womb that bare thee, and the paps which thou hast sucked [*blessed is the woman to whom you were born and nursed you; praising Mary, the mother of Jesus; this is one of the fulfillments of Mary's prophecy in Luke 1:48*].

28 But he said, Yea rather [*that is true, but even more important*], blessed are they that hear the word of God, and keep [*obey*] it.

29 And when the people were gathered thick [*in a tight crowd*] together, he began to say, This is an evil generation: they seek a sign [*always are wanting proof that I am the Messiah*]; and there shall no sign be given it [*them*], but the sign of Jonas [*Jonah*] the prophet [*the signs they get will be miserable for them, like being swallowed by a whale was for Jonah, when he tried to reject God's call*].

30 For as Jonas was a sign unto the Ninevites [*the people to whom Jonah preached*], so shall also the Son of man [*Jesus*] be to this generation.

31 The queen of the south [*the queen of Sheba*] shall rise up in the judgment with the men of this generation, and condemn them: for she came from the utmost parts of the earth to hear the wisdom of Solomon; and, behold, a greater than Solomon [*in other words, the Son of God*] is here.

The point in verse 31 above seems to be that the Jews will be condemned (damned) by the good example of the Queen of Sheba, who came from far away to learn about God from Solomon, whereas the Jews have the Son of God in their midst, teaching them, and they ignore Him.

32 The men of Nineve [*Nineveh*] shall rise up in the judgment with this generation [*the Jews*], and shall condemn it [*by their good example*]: for they repented at the preaching of Jonas [*Jonah*]; and, behold, a greater than Jonas is here.

33 No man, when he hath lighted a candle, putteth it in a secret place, neither under a bushel, but on a candlestick, that they which come in may see the light.

34 The light of the body is the eye [*the eye takes in light so you can see where you are going*]: therefore when thine eye [*your spiritual eye*] is single [*focused on God's light*] thy whole body also is full of light; but when thine eye is evil [*you look for evil, to participate in*], thy body also is full of darkness.

35 Take heed therefore that the light which is in thee be not darkness.

36 If thy whole body therefore be full of light [*full of gospel light*], having no part dark [*avoiding evil*], the whole [*your whole life*] shall be full of light, as when the bright shining of a candle doth give thee light.

37 And as he spake, a certain Pharisee besought [*requested*] him to dine with him: and he went in, and sat down to meat [*to the meal*].

38 And when the Pharisee saw it, he marvelled [*was surprised*] that he had not first washed before dinner.

The Pharisees were very strict about washing before eating and had made it a very exact part of their religious rituals which made them look righteous in the eyes of others.

39 And the Lord said unto him, Now do ye Pharisees make clean [*wash*] the outside of the cup and the platter [*plate*]; but your inward part is full of ravening [*greed, seeking to rob and plunder the people*] and wickedness.

40 Ye fools, did not he [*God*] that made that which is without [*outside*] make that which is within [*inside*] also? [*God knows that you try to look clean on the outside but that you are filthy with wickedness on the inside.*]

41 But rather give alms of such things as ye have; and, behold, all things are clean unto you. [*In other words, if you would keep my commandments, you could be just as clean on the inside as you are on the outside.*]

JST LUKE 11:42

42 But if ye would rather give alms of such things as ye have; and observe to do all things which I have commanded you, then would your inward parts be clean also.

Although tithing is not the main issue in verse 42, next, (hypocrisy is the issue) it is obvious that it was a common practice among the Jews in New Testament times. This can be helpful to us if non-LDS acquaintances question why the Church requires tithing of its faithful members. We can show them this verse and tell them that tithe paying was commonly practiced in New Testament times.

Tithing

42 But woe unto you [*you are in much trouble*], Pharisees! for ye tithe [*pay exact tithing on*] mint and rue [*herbs*] and all manner of herbs, and pass over [*ignore*] judgment [*being fair to others*] and the love of God: these [*Christlike things*] ought ye to have done, and not to leave the other [*paying tithing exactly*] undone. [*In other words, you go through the motions of being religious but you are not!*]

43 Woe unto you, Pharisees! for ye love the uppermost seats [*the highest, most respected and prestigious seats*] in the synagogues [*Jewish meeting houses*], and greetings in the markets. [*You love to have people notice how important you are.*]

44 Woe unto you, scribes and Pharisees, hypocrites [*people who want to appear to others to be righteous, but in their hearts, they love to be wicked*]! for ye are as graves which appear not [*don't look like graves*], and the men that walk over them are not aware of them [*don't realize that there is rot and corruption just under the surface*].

45 Then answered one of the lawyers, and said unto him, Master, thus saying thou reproachest us also. [*By speaking so disrespectfully to the scribes and Pharisees, you are insulting us lawyers also!*]

46 And he said, Woe unto you also, ye lawyers! for ye lade men [*load people down*] with burdens grievous to be borne [*difficult to carry*], and ye yourselves touch not the burdens with one of your fingers [*you won't lift a finger to help*].

47 Woe unto you! for ye build the sepulchres of the prophets [*build big monuments to dead prophets*], and your fathers [*ancestors*] killed them. [*You pretend to be righteous and honor past prophets, but if you had lived back then, you would have joined your ancestors in killing them!*]

48 Truly ye bear witness [*through your wicked lives*] that ye allow [*agree with*] the deeds of your fathers: for they indeed killed them [*past prophets*], and ye build their sepulchres [*you build big monuments upon past prophets' grave sites to honor them*].

49 Therefore also said the wisdom of God [*God, in his wisdom, said*], I will send them [*the Jews*] prophets and apostles, and some of them they shall slay and persecute:

50 That the blood of all the prophets, which was shed from the foundation [*the earliest days*] of the world, may be required of this generation; [*Since you have murder in your hearts for the prophets and Apostles now, you are as good as guilty of participating in killing all the prophets whose blood has been spilt by the wicked since the beginning of time.*]

51 From the blood of Abel unto the blood of Zacharias [*John the Baptist's father*], which perished [*whom you had executed*] between the altar and the temple: verily I say unto you, It shall be required of this generation. [*You wicked people will answer for all this.*]

52 Woe unto you, lawyers! for ye have taken away the key of knowledge: ye entered not in yourselves, and them that were entering in ye hindered [*stopped*]. [*In other words, you won't get to heaven yourselves and you prevent others from going there too!*]

JST LUKE 11:53

53 Woe unto you, lawyers! For ye have taken away the key of knowledge, the fullness of the scriptures; ye enter not in yourselves into the kingdom; and those who were entering in, ye hindered.

53 And as he said these things unto them, the scribes and the Pharisees [*Jewish religious leaders*] began to urge him vehemently [*strongly and angrily opposed Him*], and to provoke him to speak of many things [*and bombarded Him with many angry questions*]:

54 Laying wait for him [*trying to trap Him*], and seeking to catch something out of his mouth, that they might accuse him [*hoping Jesus would say something for which they could have Him arrested*].

LUKE 12

AS THIS CHAPTER begins, we see a warning to avoid hypocrisy. Some misinterpret "hypocrisy" to mean anyone who belongs to a church and still has faults and imperfections. Such is not the case. Hypocrisy means to actively attempt to appear righteous to others while secretly desiring to be involved in evil, and thus privately and intentionally participating in wickedness. Perhaps you have noticed that the Savior came down hard on hypocrites but was gentle and encouraging to those caught up in other types of sin. Thus, hypocrisy must be considered as one of the most damaging kinds of sin.

1 IN the mean time, when there were gathered together an innumerable multitude [*a huge group*] of people, insomuch that they trode [*were stepping*] one upon another, he began to say unto his disciples first of all, Beware ye of [*watch out for*] the leaven [*yeast*] of the Pharisees, which is hypocrisy.

Here the Master Teacher warns His disciples against the evil doctrines of the Pharisees (Jewish religious leaders). He compares these doctrines to leaven (yeast) which is put in bread dough to make it rise. As the leaven works its way through the entire lump of dough, it influences everything. So also with these hypocritical Jewish leaders, who are influencing everything in Jewish society. (See also Matthew 16:6.)

2 For there is nothing covered, that shall not be revealed; neither hid, that shall not be known. [*God knows all things and all unrepented-of evil deeds will eventually be exposed.*]

3 Therefore whatsoever ye have spoken in darkness shall be heard in the light; and that which ye have spoken in the ear in closets [*spoken secretly*] shall be proclaimed upon the housetops [*broadcast to everyone*].

4 And I say unto you my friends, Be not afraid of them that kill the body, and after that have no more that they can do [*that is all they can do to you*].

5 But I will forewarn you whom ye shall fear: Fear him, which after he hath killed hath power to cast into hell; yea, I say unto you, Fear him [*fear Satan and spiritual death*].

6 Are not five sparrows sold for two farthings, and not one of them is forgotten before God? [*God knows the little birds, so you can be assured that he knows and cares about you.*]

7 But even the very hairs of your head are all numbered. Fear not therefore: ye are of more value than many sparrows.

8 Also I say unto you, Whosoever [*whoever*] shall confess [*be faithful to*] me before men [*in the presence of others*], him shall the Son of man [*Christ*] also confess [*accept*] before the angels of God: [*In other words, he will be invited to live in heaven.*]

9 But he that denieth [*rejects*] me before men shall be denied [*rejected*] before the angels of God.

The JST adds two verses here. They are as follows:

JST LUKE 12:10–11

10 Now his disciples knew that he said this, because they had spoken evil against him before the people; for they were afraid to confess him before men.

11 And they reasoned among themselves, saying, He knoweth our hearts, and he speaketh to our condemnation, and we shall not be forgiven. But he answered them, and said unto them,

10 And whosoever shall speak a word against the Son of man [*Jesus*], it shall be forgiven him: but unto him that blasphemeth against the Holy Ghost [*denies the Holy Ghost*] it shall not be forgiven.

JST LUKE 12:12

12 Whosoever shall speak a word against the Son of man, and repenteth, it shall be forgiven him; but unto him who blasphemeth against the Holy Ghost, it shall not be forgiven him.

11 And when they [*arrest you, and*] bring you unto the synagogues, and unto magistrates [*public officials*], and powers [*the courts, etc.*], take ye no thought how or what thing ye shall answer, or what ye shall say:

12 For the Holy Ghost shall teach you in the same hour what ye ought to say.

13 And one of the company [*a person in the crowd*] said unto him, Master, speak to my brother, that he divide the inheritance with me [*tell my brother to share his inheritance with me*].

14 And he [*Jesus*] said unto him, Man, who made me a judge or a divider [*arbitrator*] over you?

15 And he said unto them, Take heed, and beware of covetousness [*greed*]: for a man's life consisteth not in the abundance of the things which he possesseth [*worldly possessions are not what makes life worthwhile*].

Next, Jesus will give what is known as "The Parable of the Foolish Rich Man." It is given in Perea during the winter of a.d. 31. The main message is "You can't take it with you." The point is that we must avoid allowing our worldly possessions take the place of God in our lives.

The Parable of the Foolish Rich Man

16 And he spake a parable [*a story which teaches a certain lesson*] unto them, saying, The ground of a certain rich man brought forth plentifully [*grew very good crops*]:

17 And he thought within himself, saying, What shall I do, because I have no room where to bestow [*store*] my fruits [*crops*]?

18 And he said, This will I do: I will pull down [*tear down*] my barns, and build greater [*bigger ones*]; and there will I bestow [*store*] all my fruits and my goods.

19 And I will say to my soul [*to myself*], Soul [*self*], thou hast much goods laid up for many years [*you have enough to last for several years*]; take thine ease [*relax, take it easy*], eat, drink, and be merry.

20 But God said unto him, Thou fool, this night thy soul shall be required of thee [*tonight you will die*]: then whose shall those things be, which thou hast provided [*then who will all your stuff belong to*]?

21 So is he that layeth up treasure for himself, and is not rich toward God. [*So it is with people who allow their possessions to take the place of God in their lives.*]

22 And he said unto his disciples, Therefore I say unto you, Take no thought for your life, what ye shall eat; neither for the body, what ye shall put on.

This counsel applies to the Apostles and those involved in full-time service of God, such as missionaries. JST Matthew 6:25–27 makes this very clear as follows:

JST Matthew 6:25–27

25 And, again, I say unto you, Go ye into the world, and care not for the world; for the world will hate you, and will persecute you, and will turn you out of their synagogues.

26 Nevertheless, ye shall go forth from house to house, teaching the people; and I will go before you.

27 And your heavenly Father will provide for you, whatsoever things ye need for food, what ye shall eat; and for raiment, what ye shall wear or put on.

These verses do not apply to everyone. Occasionally, individuals or groups take this literally as applying to them and the results are tragic and disastrous. The Savior continues this counsel to His Apostles in verses 23–33, next.

23 The life is more than meat [*food*], and the body is more than raiment [*clothing*].

24 Consider the ravens: for they neither sow [*plant*] nor reap [*harvest*]; which neither have storehouse nor barn; and God feedeth them: how much more are ye better than the fowls? [*God takes good care of birds and you are much more important than they are.*]

25 And which of you with taking thought can add to his stature one cubit? [*Which of you could think and thus add inches to your height?*]

26 If ye then be not able to do that thing which is least, why take ye thought for the rest? [*Since you can't do such an unimportant thing, why worry about the rest of your needs?*]

27 Consider the lilies [*flowers*] how they grow: they toil not [*they don't work*], they spin not [*they don't weave cloth for clothing*]; and yet I say unto you, that Solomon in all his glory was not arrayed [*dressed*] like one of these.

28 If then God so clothe the grass [*makes the grass beautiful*], which is to day in the field, and

to morrow is cast into the oven [*is gone*]; how much more will he clothe you, O ye of little faith?

JST LUKE 12:30

30 If then God so clothe the grass, which is today in the field, and tomorrow is cast in the oven; how much more will he provide for you, if ye are not of little faith?

29 And seek not ye what ye shall eat, or what ye shall drink, neither be ye of doubtful mind [*don't doubt that the Lord will do this for you*].

30 For all these things [*the things you need daily to take care of your physical needs*] do the nations of the world seek after: and your Father knoweth that ye have need of these things.

The JST adds an entire verse after verse 30, above.

JST LUKE 12:33

33 And ye are sent unto them to be their ministers, and the laborer is worthy of his hire; for the law saith, That a man shall not muzzle the ox that treadeth out the corn.

31 But rather seek ye the kingdom of God; and all these things shall be added unto you.

JST LUKE 12:34

34 Therefore seek ye to bring forth the kingdom of God, and all these things shall be added unto you.

32 Fear not, little flock; for it is your Father's good pleasure to give you the kingdom.

33 Sell that [*what*] ye have, and give alms [*pay your offerings to God*]; provide yourselves bags which wax not old [*leather bags to carry food in*], a treasure in the heavens that faileth not [*doesn't ever run out*], where no thief approacheth, neither moth corrupteth [*ruins*].

The JST makes very significant changes to verse 33, above. Among other things, notice that it says "provide not for yourselves bags."

JST LUKE 12:36

36 This he spake unto his disciples, saying, Sell that ye have and give alms; provide not for yourselves bags which wax old, but rather provide a treasure in the heavens, that faileth not; where no thief approacheth, neither moth corrupteth.

34 For where your treasure is, there will your heart be also.

35 Let your loins be girded about [*be dressed and ready*], and your lights burning [*have your lamps burning, as in the parable of the ten virgins, in Matthew 25:1–13*];

36 And ye yourselves like unto men that wait [*are prepared*] for their lord, when he will return from the wedding; that when he cometh and knocketh, they may open unto him immediately.

The counsel and imagery here deal with our being prepared for the Second Coming. When the Savior actually does come, there will be no time for further preparation to meet Him. As indicated at the end of verse 36, above, we must be prepared to "immediately" open the door for Him, so to speak, when He comes. In other words, those who are prepared and worthy will "immediately" be taken up to meet him at his coming. See D&C 88:96.

37 Blessed are those servants, whom the lord when he cometh shall find watching: verily I say unto you, that he [*Christ*] shall gird [*prepare*] himself, and make them to sit down to meat [*eat, symbolic of partaking of the blessings of the gospel*], and will come forth and serve them.

The Joseph Smith Translation (the JST) adds much for verses 38–48 here. As we continue, we will put a few notes in these verses as they stand in Luke. Then, at the end of verse 48, we will include JST Luke 12:41–57 in its entirety, which covers Luke 12:38–48.

38 And if he shall come in the second watch [*in the middle of the night*], or come in the third watch [*the early morning hours before sunrise; see Bible Dictionary, under "Watches"*], and find them so [*watching and prepared*], blessed are those servants.

The scriptures are very clear that no one knows the exact timing of the Second Coming. See Matthew 24:36 and Mark 13:32.

39 And this know, that if the goodman [*owner*] of the house had known what hour the thief would come, he would have watched [*would not have been caught off guard*], and not have suffered [*allowed*] his house to be broken through [*into*].

40 Be ye therefore ready also: for the Son of man [*Christ*] cometh at an hour when ye think not.

Next, in verse 41, Peter asks Jesus if the advice on preparing for the Second Coming, given in the above verses, applies only to the Twelve, or to all people.

41 Then Peter said unto him, Lord, speakest thou this parable unto us, or even to all?

42 And the Lord said, [*I speak to those who are faithful—see JST, verse 49, quoted below*] Who then is that faithful and wise steward, whom his lord shall make ruler over his household [*who will attain exaltation*], to give them their portion of meat [*their reward*] in due season [*when it is time*]?

43 Blessed is that servant, whom his lord when he cometh shall find so doing [*living righteously*].

44 Of a truth I say unto you, that he will make him ruler over all that he hath [*exaltation; see D&C 84:37–38*].

45 But and if that servant say in his heart, My lord delayeth his coming; and shall begin to beat the menservants and maidens, and to eat and drink, and to be drunken; [*In other words, if people live wickedly because they either don't believe the Lord will come, or think that they have plenty of time to repent after they have "enjoyed" wickedness.*]

46 The lord [*Christ*] of that servant will come in a day when he looketh not for him [*when he is not prepared*], and at an hour when he is not aware, and will cut him in sunder [*he will be destroyed at the Second Coming*], and will appoint him his portion [*punishment*] with the unbelievers.

47 And that servant, which knew his lord's will [*was accountable*], and prepared not himself [*those who knew the gospel but didn't live it*], neither did according to his will, shall be beaten with many stripes [*will be severely punished; in ancient times, each time a person was hit with a whip, it was called a "stripe"*].

This may sound harsh, but we are governed by eternal laws. The Savior has taught us over and over again in the scriptures, that mercy cannot rob justice, "Nay; not one whit" (Alma 42:25). He constantly extends His mercy to us (Jacob 6:4), and through His Atonement allows us to repent, be healed of the aftermath of sin, and become righteous, clean, new people. However, if we ignore the gospel and do not live as we know we should, then the Law of Justice must take over, and we have to suffer for our own sins, which suffering is beyond our ability to comprehend. (See D&C 19:15–19.)

48 But he that knew not [*did not know the gospel, therefore was not as accountable*], and did commit things worthy of stripes, shall be beaten with few stripes. [*All people are born with a conscience, and therefore have some degree of accountability, whether they know the gospel or not.*] For unto whomsoever much is given, of him shall be much required [*see D&C 82:3*]: and to whom men have committed much, of him they will ask the more. [*More is expected of them.*]

As stated in the note at the end of verse 37 above, JST 12:41–57, which covers verses 38–48, is included here and reads as follows:

JST 12:41–57

41 For, behold, he cometh in the first watch of the night, and he shall also come in the second watch, and again he shall come in the third watch.

42 And verily I say unto you, He hath already come, as it is written of him; and again when he shall come in the second watch, or come in the third watch, blessed are those servants when he cometh, that he shall find so doing;

43 For the Lord of those servants shall gird himself, and make them to sit down to meat, and will come forth and serve them.

44 And now, verily I say these things unto you, that ye may know this, that the coming of the Lord is as a thief in the night.

45 And it is like unto a man who is an householder, who, if he watcheth not his goods, the thief cometh in an hour of which he is not aware, and taketh his goods, and divideth them among his fellows.

46 And they said among themselves, If the good man of the house had known what hour the thief would come, he would have watched, and not have suffered his house to be broken through and the loss of his goods.

47 And he said unto them, Verily I say unto you, be ye therefore ready also; for the Son of man cometh at an hour when ye think not.

48 Then Peter said unto him, Lord, speakest thou this parable unto us, or unto all?

49 And the Lord said, I speak unto those whom the Lord shall make rulers over his household, to give his children their portion of meat in due season.

50 And they said, Who then is that faithful and wise servant?

51 And the Lord said unto them, It is that servant who watcheth, to impart his portion of meat in due season.

52 Blessed be that servant whom his Lord shall find, when he cometh, so doing.

53 Of a truth I say unto you, that he will make him ruler over all that he hath.

54 But the evil servant is he who is not found watching. And if that servant is not found watching, he will say in his heart, My Lord delayeth his coming; and shall begin to beat the menservants, and the maidens, and to eat, and drink, and to be drunken.

55 The Lord of that servant will come in a day he looketh not for, and at an hour when he is not aware, and will cut him down, and will appoint him his portion with the unbelievers.

56 And that servant who knew his Lord's will, and prepared not for his Lord's coming, neither did according to his will, shall be beaten with many stripes.

57 But he that knew not his Lord's will, and did commit things worthy of stripes, shall be beaten with few. For unto whomsoever much is given, of him shall much be required; and to whom the Lord has committed much, of him will men ask the more. [*End of JST quote.*]

We will now continue with Luke, chapter 12, as it stands in the Bible.

49 I am come to send fire on the earth [*because people do not keep the commandments, they will be burned at his coming*]; and what will I, if it be already kindled?

JST LUKE 12:58

58 For they are not well pleased with the Lord's doings; therefore I am come to send fire on the earth; and what is it to you, if I will that it be already kindled?

50 But I have a baptism to be baptized with [*I have a "baptism of fire," a most difficult task of my own, namely, to perform the Atonement.*]; and how am I [*JST "I am"*] straitened [*confined, can't go on to other things*] till it be accomplished [*I must not deviate at all from my assigned course, until I have accomplished it*]!

51 Suppose ye [*do you suppose*] that I am come [*have come*] to give peace on earth? I tell you, Nay; but rather division [*to divide the righteous from the wicked*]:

52 For from henceforth [*from now on*] there shall be five in one house divided, three against two, and two against three. [*In other words, some members of a family will accept the gospel and others will not. As a result, they will be divided against each other.*]

53 The father shall be divided against the son, and the son against the father; the mother against the daughter, and the daughter against the mother; the mother in law against her daughter in law, and the daughter in law against her mother in law.

54 And he said also to the people, When ye see a cloud rise out of the west, straightway [*right away*] ye say, There cometh a shower; and so it is. [*You predict the weather by looking at the signs in the sky.*]

55 And when ye see the south wind blow, ye say, There will be heat [*it will be hot*]; and it cometh to pass [*it happens*].

56 Ye hypocrites, ye can discern the face of the sky [*you can predict the weather by looking at the signs in the sky*] and of the earth; but how is it that ye do not discern this time [*why are you so blind to the signs about the coming of Christ, which are all around you*]?

57 Yea, and why even of yourselves judge ye not what is right? [*These signs are so obvious that you should be able to tell what's going on without help!*]

Next, the Savior gives counsel for us to be peacemakers. (Notice in your King James Bible that there is a paragraph mark at the beginning of verse 58. That indicates that there is a change to a new topic here.) He counsels us to work things out quickly with those with whom we have a disagreement, rather than letting it fester and drag on. If we have bad feelings, bitterness, hatred, or whatever toward others, and do not quickly work it out, it is like being thrown into prison. The longer it drags on, the more difficult it is to work through. We pay a much heavier price by allowing such things to go unresolved than if we would quickly and humbly work things out.

58 When thou goest with thine adversary to the magistrate [*when someone takes you to court; symbolic of when you have a disagreement with someone*], as thou art in the way [*as you are on your way to the courthouse*], give diligence [*try hard*] that thou mayest be delivered from him [*to make peace and work things out with him before you go to court*]; lest he hale thee to the judge [*for fear that he will take you in front of the judge*], and the judge deliver thee [*turns you over*] to the officer, and the officer cast thee [*puts you*] into prison.

59 I tell thee, thou shalt not depart thence [*you will not get out of the prison you allowed yourself to be put in*], till thou hast paid the very last mite [*until you have paid dearly every last bit of the punishment*].

LUKE 13

AS WE BEGIN this chapter, we are taught an important lesson to the effect that people who suffer tragedy are not necessarily more wicked than others.

1 THERE were present at that season [*JST "at that time"*] some that told him [*Jesus*] of the Galilæans, whose blood Pilate had mingled with their sacrifices [*who had been killed by Pontius Pilate, the Roman governor*].

2 And Jesus answering [*responding*] said unto them, Suppose ye that these Galilæans were sinners above all the Galilæans, because they suffered such things? [*Do you suppose that they were more wicked than other Galileans, and that's why they were killed?*]

3 I tell you, Nay: but, except ye repent, ye shall all likewise perish.

The reference to the fall of a tower in Siloam, in verse 4, next, is apparently referring to a tragedy that happened in the Jerusalem area.

4 Or those eighteen, upon whom the tower in Siloam fell, and slew them, think ye that they were sinners above all men that dwelt in Jerusalem [*worse sinners than anyone else in Jerusalem*]?

5 I tell you, Nay: but, except ye repent, ye shall all likewise perish.

This next parable is known as "The Parable of the Barren Fig Tree." The main point is that it is what you actually do that counts, not what you say you will do. If you claim to be spiritual and righteous, but your deeds are evil, you will end up being destroyed by your enemies (symbolic of Satan and his evil hosts). It was given in the winter of a.d. 32. The notes in brackets give one possible interpretation out of many possibilities.

The Parable of the Barren Fig Tree

6 He spake also this parable [*a story that teaches a particular point*]; A certain man [*the Father*] had a fig tree [*the Jews*] planted in his vineyard [*on earth*]; and he came and sought fruit [*looked for righteous lives*] thereon [*among the Jews*], and found none.

7 Then said he unto the dresser of his vineyard [*symbolic of Christ; see Talmage,* Jesus the Christ, *p. 443*], Behold, these three years [*the three years of Christ's mission*] I come seeking fruit [*righteousness*] on this fig tree [*among the Jews*], and find none: cut it down [*John the Baptist said, "Now . . . the axe is laid unto the root of the trees"; Luke 3:9; in other words, destruction is almost here for the wicked Jews*]; why cumbereth it the ground [*why let it keep cluttering the earth*]?

8 And he [*Jesus*] answering said unto him, Lord, let it alone this year also, till I shall dig about it [*cultivate it*], and dung it [*nourish it; in other words, let's give the Jews one more chance to repent*]:

9 And if it bear fruit, well [*if they do, wonderful!*]: and if not, then after that [*this one more chance*] thou shalt cut it down [*destroy their nation*].

The Jews did not take advantage of this last opportunity, at that time, to repent. They crucified Christ and persecuted His followers. The Romans completed the destruction of Jerusalem and the Jews about a.d. 70–73.

Christ Heals a Crippled Woman on the Sabbath

10 And he was teaching in one of the synagogues on the sabbath.

11 And, behold, there was a woman which had a spirit of infirmity [*had been weak and sickly*] eighteen years, and was bowed together [*was bent over*], and could in no wise lift up herself [*could not straighten herself out at all*].

12 And when Jesus saw her, he called her to him, and said unto her, Woman, thou art loosed from thine infirmity [*you are set free from being crippled*].

13 And he laid his hands on her: and immediately she was made straight, and glorified [*praised*] God.

14 And the ruler of the synagogue answered [*responded*] with indignation [*anger*], because that Jesus had healed on the sabbath day, and said unto the people, There are six days in which men ought to work: in them therefore come and be healed, and not on the sabbath day. [*In other words, if you want to be healed in my synagogue, come on any of the six days of the week when work is permitted. But don't come to be healed on the Sabbath.*]

15 The Lord then answered him, and said, Thou hypocrite, doth not each one of you on the sabbath loose [*untie*] his ox or his ass from the stall, and lead him away to watering?

16 And ought not this woman, being a daughter of Abraham, whom Satan hath bound, lo, these eighteen years, be loosed [*freed*] from this bond [*the bondage of being crippled*] on the sabbath day? [*You treat your beasts of burden better that you treat this woman.*]

17 And when he had said these things, all his adversaries [*opponents*] were ashamed: and all the people rejoiced for all the glorious things that were done by him.

The Parable of the Grain of Mustard Seed

18 Then said he, Unto what is the kingdom of God like? and whereunto shall I resemble it [*unto what shall I compare it*]?

19 It is like a grain of mustard seed [*a very tiny seed; symbolic of very small beginnings for the Church*], which a man [*God*] took, and cast into his garden [*the earth*]; and it grew, and waxed a great tree [*became a large tree*]; and the fowls of the air lodged in the branches of it.

Joseph Smith explained this parable:

"And again, another parable put He forth unto them, having an allusion to the Kingdom that should be set up, just previous to or at the time of the harvest, which reads as follows—'The Kingdom of Heaven is like a grain of mustard seed, which a man took and sowed in his field: which indeed is the least of all seeds: but, when it is grown, it is the greatest among herbs, and becometh a tree, so that the birds of the air come and lodge in the branches thereof.' Now we can discover plainly that this figure is given to represent the Church as it shall come forth in the last days." (For more of the Prophet's explanation, see *Teachings of the Prophet Joseph Smith*, pp. 98–99 and p. 159.)

The Parable of the Leaven

20 And again he said, Whereunto shall I liken the kingdom of God?

21 It is like leaven [*yeast*], which a woman took and hid in three measures of meal, till the whole was leavened. [*The Church will start out small but*

will expand into the whole world; see Teachings of the Prophet Joseph Smith, *pp. 100 and 102.*]

22 And he went through the cities and villages, teaching, and journeying toward Jerusalem.

23 Then said one unto him, Lord, are there few that be saved [*will just a few be saved*]? And he said unto them,

The Strait Gate

24 Strive to enter in at the strait [*narrow*] gate: for many, I say unto you, will seek to enter in [*into heaven*], and shall not be able.

JST LUKE 13:24
24 Strive to enter in at the strait gate; for I say unto you Many shall seek to enter in, and shall not be able; for the Lord shall not always strive with man.

25 When once the master of the house [*the Lord*] is risen up, and hath shut to the door [*once your opportunities to repent and join Christ are over*], and ye begin to stand without [*outside*], and to knock at the door, saying, Lord, Lord, open unto us; and he shall answer and say unto you, I know you not whence ye are [*you don't belong to Me; you haven't made covenants with Me*]:

JST LUKE 13:25
25 Therefore, when once the Lord of the kingdom is risen up, and hath shut the door of the kingdom, then ye shall stand without, and knock at the door, saying, Lord, Lord, open unto us, But the Lord shall answer and say unto you, I will not receive you, for ye know not from whence ye are.

26 Then shall ye begin to say, We have eaten and drunk in thy presence, and thou hast taught in our streets.

27 But he shall say, I tell you, I know you not whence ye are; depart from me, all ye workers of iniquity [*wickedness*].

28 There shall be weeping and gnashing of teeth [*grinding teeth together in agony*], when ye shall see Abraham, and Isaac, and Jacob, and all the prophets, in the kingdom of God, and you yourselves thrust out.

29 And they [*righteous people who have made and kept covenants with the Lord*] shall come from the east, and from the west, and from the north, and from the south [*in other words, from all nations of the world*], and shall sit down in the kingdom of God.

The Last Shall Be First and the First Shall Be Last

30 And, behold, there are last [*the humble, righteous who are considered by the wicked to be the lowest*] which shall be first [*exalted*], and there are first [*the wicked who considered themselves to be superior to the righteous*] which shall be last [*will receive the lowest rewards on Judgment Day*].

31 The same day there came certain of the Pharisees [*Jewish religious leaders*], saying unto him [*Jesus*], Get thee out, and depart hence [*leave!*]: for Herod will [*desires to*] kill thee.

32 And he said unto them, Go ye, and tell that fox [*King Herod*], Behold, I cast out devils, and I do cures to day and to morrow, and the third day [*the day I am resurrected*] I shall be perfected.

33 Nevertheless I must walk to day, and to morrow, and the day following [*I will not leave; my work requires that I stay here to complete it*]: for it cannot be that a prophet perish out of Jerusalem. [*It is prophesied that I will be killed in Jerusalem, and so it must be.*]

The JST adds a verse here:

JST LUKE 13:34
34 This he spake, signifying of his death. And in this very hour he began to weep over Jerusalem.

34 [*JST "Saying"*] O Jerusalem, Jerusalem, which killest the prophets, and stonest them that are sent unto thee; how often would I have gathered thy children [*your people*] together, as a hen doth

gather her brood [*chicks*] under her wings, and ye would not [*you would not come*]!

There is beautiful symbolism here. The Savior compares Himself to a mother hen, with warm, soft feathers under her wings, where her chicks can be gathered to comfortable safety when danger comes. His invitation to the Jews has been to come to the warm, pleasant peace and safety of the gospel, but they have rejected His offer. As a result, He prophecies their fate, in verse 35, next.

35 Behold, your house is left unto you desolate: and verily I say unto you, Ye shall not see me, until the time come when ye shall say, Blessed is he that cometh in the name of the Lord.

JST LUKE 13:36

36 Behold your house is left unto you desolate. And verily I say unto you, Ye shall not know me, until ye have received from the hand of the Lord a just recompense for all your sins; until the time come when ye shall say, Blessed is he that cometh in the name of the Lord.

LUKE 14

IN THIS CHAPTER we will see the Savior heal again on the Sabbath, which has infuriated the religious leaders of the Jews on many occasions before this. In this case, you will see Jesus directly confront the lawyers and Pharisees on the issue, asking them if it is permissible to heal on the Sabbath, before He heals the man. Their response to His question shows their extreme frustration and fear of public ridicule.

1 AND it came to pass, as he [*Jesus*] went into the house of one of the chief Pharisees [*a man very high up in religious leadership*] to eat bread on the sabbath day, that they [*the Jewish religious leaders who are trying desperately to find a way to get rid of Him*] watched him.

2 And, behold, there was a certain man before him [*in front of Him*] which had the dropsy [*probably edema accompanied by severe swelling*].

3 And Jesus answering [*responding*] spake unto the lawyers and Pharisees, saying, Is it lawful [*legal*] to heal on the sabbath day?

4 And they held their peace [*didn't reply*]. And he took him [*the man with dropsy*], and healed him, and let him go;

5 And answered them [*asked the lawyers and Pharisees*], saying, Which of you shall have an ass or an ox fallen into a pit, and will not straightway [*immediately*] pull him out on the sabbath day?

6 And they could not answer him again to these things [*they couldn't come up with a good answer*].

The Parable of the Chief Seats

7 And he put forth a parable to those which were bidden [*to the guests at the dinner*], when he marked [*noticed*] how they chose out the chief [*most prestigious*] rooms; saying unto them,

JST LUKE 14:7

7 And he put forth a parable unto them concerning those who were bidden to a wedding; for he knew how they chose out the chief rooms, and exalted themselves one above another; wherefore he spake unto them, saying,

As you will see in the verses which follow, the Master is teaching a lesson in being humble.

8 When thou art bidden of [*invited by*] any man to a wedding, sit not down in the highest room [*the room reserved for the guests who were highest in authority in the community*]; lest a more honourable man than thou [*one higher in authority than you*] be bidden of [*invited by*] him;

9 And he that bade thee [*the host*] and him [*the man higher in authority than you*] come and say to thee, Give this man place [*let this guest sit where you are sitting*]; and thou begin with shame [*with embarrassment*] to take the lowest room.

10 But when thou art bidden [*invited*], go and sit down in the lowest room; that when he that bade thee [*the host*] cometh, he may say unto thee, Friend, go up higher: then shalt thou have worship [*respect*] in the presence of them that sit at meat [*at dinner*] with thee.

The main point of the lesson is found in verse 11, next.

11 For whosoever exalteth himself [*pridefully presents himself to others as being important*] shall be abased [*put down, humbled*]; and he that humbleth himself shall be exalted.

The JST makes a subtle clarification to verse 12, next.

12 Then said he [*Jesus*] also to him that bade him, When thou makest a dinner or a supper, call not [*don't invite*] thy friends, nor thy brethren [*family members*], neither thy kinsmen [*relatives*], nor thy rich neighbours; lest they also bid thee again [*return the favor by inviting you to their place*], and a recompence be made thee [*you are thus repaid*].

JST LUKE 14:12

12 Then said he also concerning him who bade **to the wedding**, When thou makest a dinner, or a supper, call not thy friends, nor thy brethren, neither thy kinsmen, nor rich neighbors; lest they also bid thee again, and a recompense be made thee.

Jesus is teaching here that true charity and generosity are demonstrated when you do kind things for others with no thought or chance for reward.

13 But when thou makest a feast, call the poor, the maimed [*crippled*], the lame, the blind:

14 And thou shalt be blessed [*by God*]; for they cannot recompense thee [*pay you back*]: for thou shalt be recompensed at the resurrection of the just [*your payment will be that you are resurrected with the righteous and enter celestial glory*].

15 And when one of them that sat at meat [*dinner*] with him heard these things, he said unto him, Blessed is he that shall eat bread in the kingdom of God [*is with God in heaven*].

This next parable given by the Master is known as the Parable of the Great Supper. The main point is that people who are indifferent to the invitation to participate in the Church and Kingdom of God will lose out and eventually suffer the consequences. The notes in brackets represent one possible interpretation. See Talmage, *Jesus the Christ*, pp. 450–452 for additional information. We understand that this parable was given in Perea (northeast of Jerusalem, and east of the Jordan River) in the winter of a.d. 33.

The Parable of the Great Supper

16 Then said he unto him, A certain man [God] made a great supper [*a great feast of gospel, covenants, etc.*], and bade [*invited*] many [*the people of covenant Israel, including the Jews*]:

17 And sent his servant [*Jesus, the prophets, missionaries, etc.*] at supper time to say to them that were bidden [*invited*], Come; for all things are now ready [*the full gospel is here for you*].

18 And they all with one consent began to make excuse. The first said unto him, I have bought a piece of ground, and I must needs go and see it: I pray thee have me excused [*please excuse me*].

19 And another said, I have bought five yoke of oxen, and I go to prove them [*see how they perform*]: I pray thee have me excused.

20 And another said, I have married a wife, and therefore I cannot come.

21 So that servant came, and shewed [*showed*] his lord these things [*the excuses*]. Then the master of the house [God] being angry said to his servant, Go out quickly into the streets and lanes of the city, and bring in hither the poor, and the maimed [*crippled*], and the halt [*lame*], and the blind [*since the covenant people will not come, go into all the world and invite the Gentiles, who are looked upon by the covenant people as spiritually poor, maimed, halt and blind*].

22 And the servant said, Lord, it is done as thou hast commanded, and yet there is room [*we still have more room, symbolic of the fact that there is plenty of room in the celestial kingdom for everyone who wants to qualify to come*].

23 And the lord [*the Father*] said unto the servant [*Christ*], Go out into the highways and

hedges, and compel [*urge, encourage*] them to come in, that my house may be filled.

The symbolism in the above verses is that the Savior, in His mercy, keeps trying to bring us to the feast of rich blessings prepared by the Father.

24 For I say unto you, That none of those men which were bidden [*invited*] shall taste of my supper. [*None of those of covenant Israel, who refuse to come unto Christ, will partake of the "feast" of gospel blessings.*]

25 And there went great multitudes [*large crowds*] with him: and he turned, and said unto them,

26 If any man come to me, and hate not his father, and mother, and wife, and children, and brethren, and sisters, yea, and his own life also, he cannot be my disciple.

JST LUKE 14:26

26 If any man come to me, and hate not his father, and mother, and wife, and children, and brethren, and sisters, or husband, yea and his own life also; or in other words, is afraid to lay down his life for my sake, he cannot be my disciple.

27 And whosoever doth not bear his cross, and come after me [*whoever is not willing to sacrifice whatever is necessary to follow me*], cannot be my disciple.

The JST adds a verse here, as follows:

JST LUKE 14:28

28 Wherefore, settle this in your hearts, that ye will do the things which I shall teach, and command you.

The whole point here is that if you are half-hearted about following the Savior, you will be unsuccessful.

Next, beginning with verse 28, the Master emphasizes again that one must plan and accept the cost in order to successfully follow Him.

28 For which of you, intending to build a tower, sitteth not down first, and counteth the cost, whether [*to see if*] he have sufficient [*enough money*] to finish it?

29 Lest haply [*JST "unhappily"*], after he hath laid the foundation, and is not able to finish it, all that behold it begin to mock him,

30 Saying, This man began to build, and was not able to finish.

JST LUKE 14:31

31 Saying, This man began to build, and was not able to finish. And this he said, signifying there should not any man follow him, unless he was able to continue; saying,

31 Or what king, going to make war against another king, sitteth not down first, and consulteth [*looks the situation over*] whether [*to see if*] he be able with ten thousand to meet him [*the enemy*] that cometh against him with twenty thousand?

32 Or else, while the other is yet a great way off, he sendeth an ambassage [*ambassador, negotiator*], and desireth conditions of peace.

33 So likewise, whosoever he be of you that forsaketh not all that he hath [*is not willing to sacrifice everything for the gospel*], he cannot be my disciple.

The JST adds the following after verse 33 and overlapping verse 34:

JST LUKE 14:35–37

35 Then certain of them came to him, saying, Good Master, we have Moses and the prophets, and whosoever shall live by them, shall he not have life?

36 And Jesus answered, saying, Ye know not Moses, neither the prophets; for if ye had known them, ye would have believed on me; for to this intent they were written. For I am sent that ye might have life. Therefore I will liken it unto salt which is good;

37 But if the salt has lost its savor, wherewith shall it be seasoned?

34 Salt is good: but if the salt have lost his savour, wherewith shall it be seasoned?

35 It is neither fit for the land, nor yet for the dunghill; but men cast it out. He that hath ears to hear, let him hear.

JST LUKE 14:38

38 It is neither fit for the land, nor yet for the dunghill; men cast it out. He who hath ears to hear, let him hear. These things he said, signifying that which was written, verily must all be fulfilled.

LUKE 15

IN THIS CHAPTER, you will see one of the most famous of the Savior's parables. It is the parable of the lost sheep, in which the shepherd leaves the ninety and nine to find the one that is lost.

1 THEN drew near unto him all the publicans [*tax collectors*] and sinners for to hear him.

2 And the Pharisees and scribes murmured [*grumbled*], saying, This man receiveth [*accepts*] sinners, and eateth with them.

The Pharisees and scribes were very strict about not associating with sinners, as a matter of religion. The following parable which the Savior gives is generally known as the Parable of the Lost Sheep. Joseph Smith tells us that it is directed to the Pharisees and scribes in verse 2 who are complaining that Jesus is associating with sinners. See *Teachings of the Prophet Joseph Smith*, p. 277.

The Parable of the Lost Sheep

3 And he spake this parable unto them [*the grumbling Pharisees and scribes in verse 2*], saying,

4 What man of you, having an hundred sheep, if he lose one of them, doth not leave the ninety and nine in the wilderness, and go after that which is lost, until he find it?

JST LUKE 15:4

4 What man of you having a hundred sheep, if he lose one of them, doth not leave the ninety and nine, and go into the wilderness after that which is lost, until he find it?

5 And when he hath found it, he layeth it on his shoulders, rejoicing.

6 And when he cometh home, he calleth together his friends and neighbours, saying unto them, Rejoice with me; for I have found my sheep which was lost.

7 I say unto you, that likewise joy shall be in heaven over one sinner that repenteth, more than over ninety and nine just persons, which need no repentance.

This parable can remind us of the quote from the Doctrine and Covenants dealing with the worth of souls. We will quote two verses:

D&C 18:10 AND 15

10 Remember the worth of souls is great in the sight of God;

15 And if it so be that you should labor all your days in crying repentance unto this people, and bring, save it be one soul unto me, how great shall be your joy with him in the kingdom of my Father!

Reading verse 7 of Luke 15, above, could make a person feel bad that a repentant sinner makes heaven happier than a righteous person. One could almost be tempted to commit an occasional sin so as to bring more joy to heaven when he or she repents. But wait! That is not at all what verse 7 is saying. Using the Prophet Joseph Smith's explanation that the ninety nine "just persons" represent the Sadducees and Pharisees "that are so righteous; they will be damned anyhow" (*Teachings of the Prophet Joseph Smith*, p. 277–78). We can then understand verse 7 as follows: "There is more joy in heaven over one humble sinner who repents, than over ninety nine self-righteous hypocrites like you Pharisees and Sadducees who claim to be just men who need no repentance!" This verse, then, is actually a scathing rebuke of these evil religious leaders of the Jews, whom the Savior called "whited sepulchres" (Matthew 23:27); in other words, whitewashed coffins which look clean on the outside, but inside are full of rot and filth.

This next parable is usually referred to as the Parable of the Lost Coin. Again, it is in response to the criticism of the Pharisees and scribes in verse 2, and reminds us that it is worth whatever effort is necessary to save one lost soul.

The Parable of the Lost Coin

8 Either [*here is another example:*] what woman having ten pieces of silver [*equal to ten days' wages for a workman—see Luke 15, footnote 8a in your Bible*] if she lose one piece, doth not light a candle, and sweep the house, and seek diligently till she find it?

9 And when she hath found it, she calleth her friends and her neighbours together, saying, Rejoice with me; for I have found the piece which I had lost.

10 Likewise, I say unto you, there is joy in the presence of the angels of God over one sinner that repenteth.

The Parable of the Prodigal Son

We will suggest some possible symbolism in this parable. No doubt you will be able to come up with other symbolism which would also fit in terms of gospel applications in our lives.

11 And he said, A certain man [*symbolic of God*] had two sons [*symbolic of different types of people*]:

12 And the younger of them said to his father, Father, give me the portion of goods that falleth to me [*give me my inheritance now, instead of waiting until you die; symbolism: I am not interested in future exaltation, but rather want to enjoy the ways of the world now*]. And he [*the father*] divided unto them his living [*divided up his property between his two sons; symbolism: our Father in Heaven respects our agency*].

13 And not many days after the younger son gathered all together [*put all his financial resources together*], and took his journey into a far country [*symbolism: he fell away from the Church and participated in the ways of the world*], and there wasted his substance [*financial resources; symbolism: his gospel heritage*] with riotous [*wild*] living [*symbolism: he wasted his potential for joy and happiness in the gospel for temporary worldly, sinful pleasures*].

14 And when he had spent all [*symbolism: when he was wasted away by his wicked lifestyle*], there arose a mighty famine in that land [*symbolism: Satan left him with no support, as taught in Alma 30:60*]; and he began to be in want [*in need, poverty, desperation*].

15 And he went and joined himself to [*got a job with*] a citizen of that country [*symbolism: he didn't yet turn to God for help*]; and he sent him into his fields to feed swine. [*Feeding pigs was about the lowest, most humiliating job a person from Jewish culture could have; symbolism: he was totally humbled.*]

16 And he would fain have filled his belly with the husks that the swine did eat [*he got so hungry that even the carob tree pods he was feeding the pigs started to look good to him*]: and no man gave unto him [*no one gave him anything to help him in his poverty; symbolism: there was no worldly source of effective help for him*].

17 And when he came to himself [*came to his senses; symbolism: he started repenting*], he said, How many hired servants of my father's have bread enough and to spare, and I perish with hunger [*I am starving*]!

18 I will arise and go to my father, and will say unto him, Father, I have sinned against heaven, and before thee [*I have been wicked; symbolic of sincere confession*],

19 And am no more worthy to be called thy son [*symbolism: I am not worthy of exaltation*]: make me as [*let me be*] one of thy hired servants [*symbolism: let me go into one of the other degrees of glory*].

20 And he arose, and came to his father. But when he was yet a great way off [*still a long distance off*], his father saw him [*had been watching for him*], and had compassion, and ran, and fell on his neck [*hugged him*], and kissed him [*symbolism: the Father is merciful and kind and is anxious to "run" to us to help us return to Him*].

21 And the son said unto him, Father, I have sinned against heaven, and in thy sight, and am no more worthy to be called thy son [*symbolism: the son, thoroughly humbled by his wickedness, acknowledges his unworthiness to live with the Father in celestial exaltation*].

22 But the father said to his servants, Bring forth the best robe, and put it on him; and put a ring on his hand, and shoes on his feet:

23 And bring hither the fatted calf, and kill it; and let us eat, and be merry [*symbolic of joy and rejoicing on earth and in heaven when a sinner repents and returns*]:

24 For this my son was dead [*symbolic of being spiritually dead*], and is alive again [*symbolic of rebirth, through the Atonement*]; he was lost, and is found. And they began to be merry [*to celebrate*].

A question sometimes arises among members of the Church as to whether or not the returning prodigal son could ever repent sufficiently to gain exaltation, especially in view of his intentional wickedness. There is much symbolism in verse 22, above, which can help answer that question:

The "robe" is symbolic of royalty and status. It is also symbolic of acceptance by God, as in 2 Nephi 4:33 where Nephi says "O Lord, wilt thou encircle me around in the robe of thy righteousness! O Lord, wilt thou make a way for mine escape before mine enemies!" See also Isaiah 61:10. In Revelation 7:9, white robes are given to those who live in the presence of God (celestial glory). The "best robe" would be symbolic of potential for highest status, in other words, exaltation.

The "ring" is symbolic of authority to rule. Example: a signet ring which a king would use to stamp official documents and make them legal and binding.

"Shoes on his feet": Shoes were very expensive in the days of the Savior's ministry and were only worn by the wealthy and the rulers. Thus, shoes would be symbolic of wealth, power, and authority to rule.

Summary: The cultural symbolism in this verse would lead us to believe that the father was not only welcoming his wayward son back with open arms, but also that he was inviting him to repent and reestablish himself as a ruler in his household, symbolic of potential for exaltation. President David O McKay, in April Conference, 1956, speaking of the prodigal son, said, "The Spirit of forgiveness will be operative" when the prodigal son comes to himself and repents. Elder Richard G. Scott, in October Conference 2002, speaking of Alma the Younger and the four sons of Mosiah, who he said "were tragically wicked," said that there are no "second-class" citizens after true repentance. Said he, "If you have repented from serious transgression and mistakenly believe that you will always be a second-class citizen in the kingdom of God, learn that is not true."

Thus, the prodigal son does not have to remain a "second-class citizen" in the Father's kingdom. However, the older brother may have to change his attitude if he plans to retain his status in the Father's kingdom.

25 Now his elder son [*symbolic of a member who has been active all his life*] was in the field: and as he came and drew nigh [*near*] to the house, he heard musick and dancing.

26 And he called one of the servants, and asked what these things meant [*what is going on?*].

27 And he said unto him, Thy brother is come; and thy father hath killed the fatted calf, because he hath received him safe and sound.

28 And he was angry, and would not go in: [*This is hardly appropriate behavior for one who is supposed to be a faithful son.*] therefore came his father out, and intreated [*pleaded with*] him.

29 And he answering said to his father, Lo [*now see here!*], these many years do I serve thee, neither transgressed I at any time thy commandment: and yet thou never gavest me a kid, that I might make merry with my friends: [*you never killed even so much as a young goat for me to have a party with my friends!*]

30 But as soon as this thy son [*implies "thy son," not my brother anymore*] was come [*came home*], which hath devoured thy living with harlots [*wasted his inheritance with prostitutes*], thou hast killed for him the fatted calf.

31 And he said unto him, Son, thou art ever with me, and all that I have is thine. [*This presupposes that the older son rethinks his attitude about his returning younger brother, repents, and helps him to get reestablished in his father's household.*]

32 It was meet [*needful, good*] that we should make merry [*celebrate*], and be glad: for this thy brother [*emphasizing that he is "your brother," not just "my son"*] was dead [*spiritually*], and is alive

THE PRODIGAL SON, by Liz Lemon Swindle

again [*has repented, is a new person*]; and was lost, and is found.

LUKE 16

THE SAVIOR CONTINUES teaching in parables. This next parable is known as the Parable of the Unjust Steward. This parable probably shouldn't be scrutinized for lots of details or various specific applications in our daily lives, but rather is probably best seen as a general message that people often are more resourceful in dealing with worldly situations than they are in working out their salvation. If we strain at finding detailed applications, we will probably come up with some that don't fit or that don't teach correct doctrine and lessons.

At this point in Luke, the Savior is in Perea (east of the Jordan River and north of Jerusalem), and it is now the winter of a.d. 33.

The Parable of the Unjust Steward

1 AND he said also unto his disciples, There was a certain rich man, which had a steward [*a man in charge of all his business dealings*]; and the same was accused unto him [*someone complained to the rich man*] that he [*the steward*] had wasted his goods [*was mismanaging the business*].

2 And he called him, and said unto him, How is it that I hear this of thee [*what's this I hear about you*]? give an account of thy stewardship [*give me a report on how the business is doing*]; for thou mayest be no longer steward [*I am going to fire you*].

3 Then the steward said within himself, What shall I do? for my lord taketh away from me the stewardship: I cannot dig [*I can't do manual labor*]; to beg I am ashamed [*I would be embarrassed to be a beggar*].

4 I am resolved what to do, that, when I am put out of the stewardship, they may receive me into their houses [*I have a plan, so that, after I am fired, I will have friends who will take care of me*].

5 So he called every one of his lord's debtors [*people who owed the owner money*] unto him, and said unto the first, How much owest thou unto my lord?

6 And he said, An hundred measures of oil. And he said unto him, Take thy bill, and sit down quickly, and write fifty [*if you pay now, I will settle for half of what you owe*].

7 Then said he to another, And how much owest thou? And he said, An hundred measures of wheat. And he said unto him, Take thy bill, and write fourscore [*eighty*].

8 And the lord commended [*congratulated*] the unjust steward, because he had done wisely: for the children of this world are in their generation wiser than the children of light [*often, people in business worry more about their future security on earth than members of the Church worry about their future security in heaven; see Jesus the Christ, p. 463*].

9 And I say unto you, Make to yourselves friends of the mammon of unrighteousness; that, when ye fail [*when your life is over*], they may receive you into everlasting habitations.

Elder Talmage (see reference above in verse 8) suggests that verse 9 basically means that we should make "friends" in heaven by using money wisely and honestly, so that you can enter heaven. Money is often used dishonestly by others, and is thus referred to as "the mammon of unrighteousness."

10 He that is faithful in that which is least [*in small responsibilities*] is faithful also in much: and he that is unjust [*dishonest*] in the least is unjust also in much.

11 If therefore ye have not been faithful in the unrighteous mammon [*if you are not honest in your dealings with people*], who will commit to your trust the true riches [*how can you be trusted with the true riches of eternity, the gospel, covenants, etc.*]?

12 And if ye have not been faithful in that which is another man's [*in the daily world of business*], who shall give you that which is your own [*how do you expect to earn a place in heaven*]?

No One Can Serve Two Masters

13 No servant can serve two masters: for either he will hate the one, and love the other; or else he will hold to the one, and despise the other. Ye cannot serve God and mammon [*you cannot be righteous and worldly at the same time*].

Next, Luke records the Master's response as the Pharisees make fun of Him in public for the things He taught in the verses above.

14 And the Pharisees also, who were covetous [*greedy*], heard all these things: and they derided [*mocked*] him.

15 And he said unto them, Ye are they which justify yourselves before men [*make yourselves look righteous in public*]; but God knoweth your hearts: for that which is highly esteemed among men is abomination in the sight of God [*even though people respect you and think you are righteous, God knows that you are full of evil and wickedness*].

16 The law and the prophets [*the "law" means Genesis, Exodus, Leviticus, Numbers, and Deuteronomy (all written by Moses) and "the prophets" refers to the writings of prophets such as Isaiah, Jeremiah, Daniel, and so forth in the Old Testament at the time of Christ*] were until John [*the Baptist*]: since that time the kingdom of God is preached, and every man presseth [*strives to get*] into it [*JST "every man who seeketh truth presseth into it"*].

17 And it is easier for heaven and earth to pass, than one tittle of the law to fail.

Verses 16 and 17, above, are very fragmentary. Much was left out of the Bible here. The JST adds the following:

JST Luke 16:16–23

16 And they said unto him, We have the law, and the prophets [*we have our scriptures*]; but as for this man [*Jesus*] we will not receive him to be our ruler; for he maketh himself to be a judge over us.

17 Then said Jesus unto them, The law and the prophets testify of me; yea, and all the prophets who have written, even until John [*up to and including John the Baptist*], have foretold of these days.

18 Since that time, the kingdom of God is preached, and every man who seeketh truth presseth [*seeks to get*] into it.

19 And it is easier for heaven and earth to pass, than for one tittle [*tiny bit*] of the law [*the words of God in the Old Testament*] to fail [*not be fulfilled*].

20 And why teach ye the law [*the Old Testament*], and deny that which is written [*that which is prophesied about Me; see verse 17*]; and condemn him [*Jesus*] whom the Father hath sent to fulfill the law [*to fulfill the prophecies about Him given in the Old Testament*], that ye might all be redeemed?

21 O fools! for you have said in your hearts, There is no God [*you secretly believe that there is no God*]. And you pervert [*pollute*] the right way; and the kingdom of heaven suffereth violence of you [*the kingdom of God is badly damaged by you*]; and you persecute the meek; and in your violence you seek to destroy the kingdom; and ye take the children of the kingdom [*righteous Saints*] by force [*you use force to stop righteous people from living their religion*]. Woe unto you [*you are in deep trouble!*], ye adulterers!

22 And they reviled [*angrily responded to*] him again, being angry for the saying [*what Jesus had just said*], that they were adulterers.

23 But he continued, saying, Whosoever putteth away his wife, and marrieth another, committeth adultery; and whosoever marrieth her who is put away from her husband, committeth adultery. Verily I say unto you, I will liken you unto the rich man.

We will now continue with the Bible version as it stands, paying close attention to verse 18 and noting some JST additions to it.

18 [*JST "But he continued, saying,"—in other words, He continued scolding the Pharisees who had attempted to ridicule him in verse 14*] Whosoever putteth away his wife, and marrieth another, committeth adultery: and whosoever marrieth her that is put away from her husband committeth adultery. [*JST adds "Verily I say unto you, I will liken you unto the rich man.*]

The JST additions in verses 17–23, above, provide very important background for verse 18. When taken alone, as it stands in Luke 16:18, and applied to everyone, it becomes a real problem. It would then mean that anyone who is divorced and remarries is guilty of adultery. Divorce is a very serious problem today and in most cases is not justified. Yet, when things are in proper order in the lives of divorcees, and the individuals involved are worthy, the Lord through our prophets today allows people who have been divorced to remarry and be sealed in a temple. Certainly this would not be the case if the very ordinance of marrying immediately made them adulterers. The JST verses quoted above show us that Jesus was addressing the hypocritical Pharisees, who verbally attacked him in verse 14. Thus, we understand that, among other evil practices, the Pharisees were secretly involved in marrying and divorcing to make their sexual conquests seem legal. The Savior said they were adulterers and strongly condemned them for this evil at the end of JST Luke 12:21, which unfortunately was left out of the Bible.

Lazarus and the Rich Man

19 There was a certain rich man [*remember that the Savior is comparing the Pharisees with this rich man; see JST addition to verse 18, above*], which was clothed in purple and fine linen, and fared sumptuously [*lived in luxury*] every day:

20 And there was a certain beggar named Lazarus, which [*who*] was laid at his gate, full of [*covered with*] sores,

21 And desiring to be fed with the crumbs which fell from the rich man's table: moreover the dogs came and licked his sores. [*Symbolizing that dogs take better care of beggars and people in need than the Pharisees do.*]

22 And it came to pass, that the beggar died, and was carried by the angels into Abraham's bosom [*was taken to paradise*]: the rich man also died, and was buried;

23 And in hell he lift up his eyes, being in torments, and seeth Abraham afar off, and Lazarus in his bosom [*with Abraham in paradise*].

24 And he cried and said, Father Abraham, have mercy on me, and send Lazarus, that he may dip the tip of his finger in water, and cool my tongue; for I am tormented in this flame [*it is miserable here in hell*].

25 But Abraham said, Son, remember that thou in thy lifetime receivedst thy good things, and likewise Lazarus evil things: but now he is comforted, and thou art tormented.

26 And beside all this, between us and you there is a great gulf fixed: so that they which would pass from hence to you cannot; neither can they pass to us, that would come from thence.

This "gulf" or barrier between spirit prison and paradise was bridged by the Savior during the time that His body lay in the tomb and His spirit visited the righteous in paradise. There, in paradise, He set up and organized missionary work and authorized the righteous spirits in paradise to go to spirit prison and teach the gospel there. See D&C, Section 138, 1 Peter 3:18 and 4:6.

27 Then he said, I pray thee therefore, father [*Abraham*], that thou wouldest send him to my father's house [*to warn them about what has happened to me*]:

28 For I have five brethren [*brothers*]; that he [*Lazarus*] may testify unto them, lest they also come into this place of torment [*hell, spirit prison*].

29 Abraham saith unto him, They have Moses and the prophets; let them hear them. [*They have already been given that message through the writings of the prophets in the scriptures.*]

30 And he said, Nay, father Abraham [*they don't pay much attention to the scriptures*]: but if one went unto them from the dead, they will repent. [*That would scare them enough to repent.*]

31 And he said unto him, If they hear not [*pay no attention to*] Moses and the prophets, neither will they be persuaded [*converted*], though one rose from the dead [*even if one came back from the dead to them*].

LUKE 17

IN THIS CHAPTER you will see the Savior begin His final journey to Jerusalem from Perea (starting with verse 11), traveling into Galilee and Samaria as He goes. He will heal ten lepers (probably in Samaria) and will teach about His Second Coming.

In verses 1–10, as the chapter begins, Luke records the Master's teachings concerning things that cause people to commit sin, and then tells us of His teachings about forgiveness and faith.

1 THEN said he unto the disciples, It is impossible but [*unavoidable, inevitable*] that offences will come [*things will come along that cause people to sin*]: but woe unto him, through whom they come!

2 It were better for him that a millstone were hanged about his neck, and he cast into the sea, than that he should offend [*cause to commit sin; cause to stumble in the gospel; see Matthew 17:6, footnote a*] one of these little ones [*children or righteous adult members who are childlike in their faith*].

3 Take heed to yourselves [*be careful*]: If thy brother trespass [*sins*] against thee, rebuke [*tell*] him; and if he repent, forgive him.

4 And if he trespass against thee seven times in a day, and seven times in a day turn again to thee, saying, I repent; thou shalt forgive him. [*Be forgiving.*]

5 And the apostles said unto the Lord, Increase our faith.

Verses 6–10, next, seem to be instruction from the Lord on strengthening our faith. First He tells them the power of faith. Then He explains that they must avoid thinking that God owes them because they keep the commandments (see Mosiah 2:22–24). This counsel appears to be designed to keep them humble to enable them to better exercise faith.

6 And the Lord said, If ye had faith as a grain of mustard seed, ye might say unto this sycamine tree [*mulberry tree*], Be thou plucked up by the root, and be thou planted in the sea; and it should obey you.

7 But which of you, having a servant plowing or feeding cattle, will say unto him by and by [*immediately; see Luke 17:7, footnote b*], when he is come from the field, Go and sit down to meat [*sit down and eat your dinner*]?

8 And will not rather [*instead*] say unto him, Make ready wherewith I may sup [*prepare my dinner*], and gird thyself [*clean up*], and serve me, till I have eaten and drunken; and afterward thou shalt eat and drink?

9 Doth he thank that servant because he did the things that were commanded him? I trow [*think*] not.

10 So likewise ye, when ye shall have done all those things which are commanded you, say, We are unprofitable servants: we have done that which was our duty to do.

11 And it came to pass, as he went to Jerusalem, that he passed through the midst of Samaria and Galilee.

Healing of Ten Lepers

12 And as he entered into a certain village, there met him ten men that were lepers [*had leprosy*], which stood afar off [*by law they were not allowed to be near people who did not have leprosy*]:

13 And they lifted up their voices [*spoke loudly*], and said, Jesus, Master, have mercy on us.

14 And when he saw them, he said unto them, Go shew yourselves unto the priests [*as required by the Law of Moses; see Leviticus 14:2*]. And it came to pass, that, as they went, they were cleansed [*healed*].

15 And one of them, when he saw that he was healed, turned back, and with a loud voice glorified [*praised*] God,

16 And fell down on his face at his feet [*humbly laid down at Jesus' feet—a sign of deep humility in Jewish culture*], giving him thanks: and he was a Samaritan.

Samaritans were despised by Jews and Jews were despised by Samaritans (inhabitants of Samaria). Originally, about 700 years before Christ, the ancestors of the Samaritans were members of the tribes of Israel, especially Ephraim. When the Assyrians conquered the ten tribes and took them away into captivity, about 722 b.c., Israelites who were permitted to remain ended up intermarrying with the occupational armies. This led to their being shunned by the Jews and developed into the long-standing ethnic dislike and hatred prevalent at the time of Christ's mortal ministry.

17 And Jesus answering said, Were there not ten cleansed [*healed*]? but where are the nine?

18 There are not found that returned to give glory to God, save this stranger [*foreigner, non Israelite; this may imply that the other nine lepers were Jews*].

19 And he said unto him, Arise, go thy way: thy faith hath made thee whole.

Instruction Regarding the Second Coming

20 And when he was demanded of [*asked by*] the Pharisees, when the kingdom of God should come [*when the Second Coming will be*], he answered them and said, The kingdom of God cometh not with observation [*perhaps meaning you can't tell exactly when it will be through careful calculations and watching of the signs of the times*]:

21 Neither shall they say, Lo here! or, lo there! for, behold, the kingdom of God is within you.

JST Luke 17:21

21 Neither shall they say, Lo, here! or, Lo, there! For, behold, the kingdom of God has already come unto you [*has already been restored among you by the Savior's mortal mission*].

22 And he said unto the disciples, The days will come, when ye shall desire to see one of the days of the Son of man [*Jesus*], and ye shall not see it. [*Perhaps meaning that there will be days when the disciples will long for a day with the Savior, or perhaps meaning that they will long for his Second Coming.*]

23 And they [*people*] shall say to you, See here [*Christ is here*]; or, see there [*Christ is there*]: go not after them, nor follow them [*don't believe them*].

24 For as the lightning, that lighteneth out of the one part under heaven, shineth unto the other part under heaven; so shall also the Son of man be in his day [*at the Second Coming*]. [*In other words, when the Savior comes again, it won't be a low-key event, with His appearing to a small group here or a little group there. Rather, when He comes, everyone will see Him at once, just like everyone, from horizon to horizon, sees a large lightning strike.*]

25 But first [*before His Second Coming*] must he suffer many things, and be rejected of this generation [*he must suffer, be rejected and crucified*].

26 And as it was in the days of Noe [*Noah*], so shall it be also in the days of the Son of man [*at the time of the Second Coming*]. [*At the time of the Second Coming, people will be ignoring the gospel just like they did in the days of Noah.*]

27 They did eat, they drank, they married wives, they were given in marriage, until the day that Noe [*Noah*] entered into the ark, and the flood came, and destroyed them all.

28 Likewise also as it was in the days of Lot [*Abraham's nephew, who chose to live in Sodom; see Genesis 19:1*]; they did eat, they drank, they bought, they sold, they planted, they builded;

29 But the same day that Lot went out of Sodom it rained fire and brimstone from heaven, and destroyed them all. [*All the wicked in Sodom and Gomorrah were destroyed (Genesis 19:24), just like the wicked will be at the Second Coming.*]

30 Even thus shall it be in the day when the Son of man is revealed [*at the Second Coming*].

31 In that day, he which shall be upon the housetop, and his stuff in the house, let him not come down to take it away: and he that is in the field, let him likewise not return back.

32 Remember Lot's wife [*who looked back, in disobedience to very simple instructions from God; see Genesis 19:17 and 26*].

33 Whosoever shall seek to save his life [*by making his own rules*] shall lose it [*will lose salvation*]; and whosoever shall lose his life [*follow God's laws*] shall preserve it [*will gain salvation*].

34 I tell you, in that night [*when the Savior actually comes*] there shall be two men in one bed; the one shall be taken [*taken up to meet Him; see D&C 88:96*], and the other shall be left [*to be burned*].

35 Two women shall be grinding together; the one shall be taken, and the other left.

36 Two men shall be in the field; the one shall be taken, and the other left.

37 And they answered and said unto him, Where, Lord? And he said unto them, Wheresoever the body is, thither will the eagles be gathered together.

The JST clarifies the verses above. We will quote, beginning with JST verse 36, which offers clarification for verse 37, above. JST verses 38–40 are verses that were completely left out of the Bible.

JST LUKE 17:36–40

36 And they answered and said unto him, Where, Lord, shall they be taken?

37 And he said unto them, Wheresoever the body is gathered; or, in other words, whithersoever the Saints are gathered, thither [*to that place*] will the eagles [*the Saints—see verse 38, next*] be gathered together; or, thither will the remainder be gathered together.

38 This he spake, signifying the gathering of his saints; and of angels descending and gathering the remainder unto them; the one from the bed, the other from the grinding, and the other from the field, whithersoever he listeth [*chooses*].

39 For verily there shall be new heavens, and a new earth, wherein dwelleth righteousness [*the Millennium*].

40 And there shall be no unclean thing [*remaining on earth*]; for the earth becoming old, even as a garment, having waxed in corruption [*grown in wickedness*], wherefore it [*the wickedness*] vanisheth away, and the footstool [*earth*] remaineth sanctified [*made holy*], cleansed from all sin [*prepared for the Millennium*].

LUKE 18

THIS NEXT PARABLE is usually known as the Parable of the Unjust Judge. The main point as given in verse 1 seems to be that some situations in life require that we continue to pray for desired blessings over a long period of time, and we shouldn't give up.

The Parable of the Unjust Judge

1 AND he spake a parable unto them to this end [*with this purpose in mind*], that men ought always to pray, and not to faint [*give up*];

2 Saying, There was in a city a judge, which feared not God, neither regarded man:

3 And there was a widow in that city; and she came unto him, saying, Avenge me of mine adversary [*I have been wronged; please render judgment against my enemy*].

4 And he would not for a while: but afterward he said within himself, Though I fear not God, nor regard man [*even though I'm not afraid of God or man*];

5 Yet because this widow troubleth me [*keeps asking me for help*], I will avenge her [*grant her request*], lest [*for fear that*] by her continual coming she weary me.

6 And the Lord [*Jesus*] said, Hear [*pay attention to*] what the unjust judge saith.

7 And shall not God avenge his own elect [*will God not answer the prayers of His Saints for*

justice], which cry [*pray*] day and night unto him, though he bear long with them [*even if it takes a long time before He grants their request*]?

8 I tell you that he will avenge them speedily. Nevertheless when the Son of man [*Jesus*] cometh, shall he find faith on the earth?

JST LUKE 18:8

8 I tell you that he will come, and when he does come, he will avenge his saints speedily. Nevertheless, when the Son of man cometh, shall he find faith on the earth?

This next parable is known as the Parable of the Pharisee and the Publican. Remember that the Pharisees claim to be important religious leaders of the Jews, live in luxury, are secretly wicked and love to look righteous to others. On the other hand, the publicans are tax collectors and are despised by the Pharisees. This parable warns us against thinking that we are better than others and thus despising people.

The Parable of the Pharisee and the Publican

9 And he spake this parable unto certain which trusted in themselves that they were righteous, and despised others:

You will find the main point of this parable given in verse 14.

10 Two men went up into the temple to pray; the one a Pharisee, and the other a publican.

11 The Pharisee stood and prayed thus with himself [*like this, bragging about himself to God*], God, I thank thee, that I am not as other men are, extortioners [*thieves*], unjust [*unrighteous*], adulterers, or even as this publican [*this tax collector*].

12 I fast twice in the week, I give tithes of all that I possess [*I pay tithing on all I have*].

13 And the publican, standing afar off, would not lift up so much as his eyes unto heaven, but smote upon his breast [*a cultural sign of deep sorrow*], saying, God be merciful to me a sinner.

14 I tell you, this man [*the publican*] went down to his house justified [*in harmony with God*] rather than the other [*the Pharisee*]: for every one that exalteth himself [*is lifted up in pride*] shall be abased [*brought down, humbled*]; and he that humbleth himself shall be exalted.

"Suffer Little Children to Come unto Me"

15 And they [*the people*] brought unto him also infants, that he would touch them: but when his disciples saw it, they rebuked them [*scolded those people*].

16 But Jesus called them [*His disciples*] unto him, and said, Suffer [*allow*] little children to come unto me, and forbid them not: for of such is the kingdom of God.

17 Verily I say unto you, Whosoever shall not receive the kingdom of God as a little child shall in no wise [*shall not*] enter therein.

18 And a certain ruler asked him, saying, Good Master, what shall I do to inherit eternal life?

19 And Jesus said unto him, Why callest thou me good? none is good, save [*except*] one, that is, God.

There is no agreement among scholars as to the reason Jesus scolded the ruler for calling Him "good." Perhaps there was a root word for "good" that, among the Jews, was reserved only for the Father. We will have to leave this alone until we are taught more.

20 Thou knowest the commandments, Do not commit adultery, Do not kill, Do not steal, Do not bear false witness, Honour thy father and thy mother.

21 And he said, All these have I kept from my youth up.

22 Now when Jesus heard these things, he said unto him, Yet lackest thou one thing [*there is one thing missing in your life*]: sell all that thou hast,

and distribute unto the poor, and thou shalt have treasure in heaven: and come, follow me.

23 And when he heard this, he was very sorrowful: for he was very rich.

24 And when Jesus saw that he was very sorrowful, he said, How hardly shall they that have riches enter into the kingdom of God [*how hard it is for the rich to enter heaven*]!

Camel and an Eye of a Needle

25 For it is easier for a camel to go through a needle's eye, than for a rich man to enter into the kingdom of God.

> There is a rumor circulating that the "eye of a needle" was a small gate in the walls of Jerusalem, used for entry into the city by night, after the main gates were closed. The rumor states that it was very difficult for a camel to get down and scrunch through the gate. Scholars indicate that this rumor has no truth to it. They indicate that the word "needle," as used in verse 25, refers to an ordinary sewing needle in the original Bible languages. Thus, the message is that it is impossible for those who value wealth above all else to enter heaven—see JST version after verse 27.

26 And they that heard it said, Who then can be saved?

27 And he said, The things which are impossible with men are possible with God.

> JST LUKE 18:27
>
> 27 And he said unto them, It is impossible for them who trust in riches, to enter into the kingdom of God; but he who forsaketh the things which are of this world, it is possible with God, that he should enter in.
>
> Next, you will see Peter catch the significance of what Jesus has just said and ask if he and his fellow Apostles will make it to heaven, since they left everything in order to follow Him.

28 Then Peter said, Lo, we have left all, and followed thee. [*This implies, "We have forsaken all to follow you, so, are we going to get into heaven?"*]

29 And he said unto them, Verily I say unto you, There is no man that hath left house, or parents, or brethren, or wife, or children, for the kingdom of God's sake,

30 Who shall not receive manifold [*much*] more in this present time, and in the world to come life everlasting [*exaltation*].

Jesus Prophecies His Death and Resurrection

31 Then he took unto him the twelve, and said unto them, Behold, we go up to Jerusalem, and all things that are written by the prophets concerning the Son of man [*Christ*] shall be accomplished.

32 For he shall be delivered unto [*turned over to*] the Gentiles [*the Romans*], and shall be mocked, and spitefully entreated [*insulted*], and spitted on:

33 And they shall scourge [*whip, flog*] him, and put him to death: and the third day he shall rise again [*shall be resurrected*].

34 And they understood none of these things: and this saying was hid from them, neither knew they the things which were spoken. [*They could not comprehend what Jesus was saying.*]

A Blind Man Is Healed

35 And it came to pass, that as he was come nigh [*near*] unto Jericho, a certain blind man sat by the way side [*side of the road*] begging:

36 And hearing the multitude pass by, he asked what it meant [*what was happening*].

37 And they told him, that Jesus of Nazareth passeth by.

38 And he cried, saying, Jesus, thou Son of David [*thou descendant of King David, in other words, thou Promised Messiah*], have mercy on me.

39 And they which went before [*ahead of Jesus*] rebuked [*scolded*] him, that he should hold his peace [*told him to keep quiet*]: but he cried so much the more [*even louder*], Thou Son of David, have mercy on me.

40 And Jesus stood [*stopped*], and commanded him to be brought unto him: and when he was come near, he asked him,

41 Saying, What wilt thou that I shall do unto thee? And he said, Lord, that I may receive my sight.

42 And Jesus said unto him, Receive thy sight: thy faith hath saved thee.

43 And immediately he received his sight, and followed him, glorifying [*praising, thanking*] God: and all the people, when they saw it, gave praise unto God.

LUKE 19

AS WE BEGIN this chapter, Jesus is on His way to Jerusalem for the last time and will be crucified in about ten days. We meet a delightful little man (small in physical size) named Zacchaeus who is despised by all (in fact he would have been excommunicated from the Jewish church because he worked for the Romans as a tax collector) but who is deeply good. Watch how the Master honors him.

1 AND Jesus entered and passed through Jericho.

2 And, behold, there was a man named Zacchæus, which was the chief among the publicans [*the chief of the tax collectors*], and he was rich.

3 And he sought to see Jesus who he was [*tried to get where he could get a view of Jesus*]; and could not for the press [*because of the crowd*], because he was little of stature [*he was a little, short man*].

4 And he ran before [*so he ran ahead*], and climbed up into a sycomore tree to see him: for he [*Jesus*] was to pass that way.

5 And when Jesus came to the place, he looked up, and saw him, and said unto him, Zacchæus, make haste [*hurry*], and come down; for to day I must abide [*stay*] at thy house.

This is a rather tender scene. As mentioned in the note at the beginning of this chapter, the people hated tax collectors, considering them to be sinners, and Zacchaeus was the head tax collector. Jesus says, "I must stay at your house," implying that He himself, the Creator of heaven and earth, had a very strong desire to stay with this humble man and reassure him of his worth to God. "I must stay at your house" can also convey the message that this action on the part of the Redeemer was essential for the well-being of Zacchaeus.

6 And he made haste, and came down [*out of the tree*], and received him [*Christ*] joyfully.

7 And when they saw it, they all murmured [*criticized*], saying, That he was gone to be guest with a man that is a sinner.

From the JST of verse 7, quoted next, we see that the disciples still had not finished learning the lesson that the Master judges by what is in the heart, rather than what others think.

JST Luke 19:7

7 And when the disciples saw it, they all murmured, saying, That he was gone to be a guest with a man who is a sinner.

8 And Zacchæus stood, and said unto the Lord [*Jesus*]; Behold, Lord, the half of my goods I give to the poor; and if I have taken any thing from any man by false accusation [*if I have mistakenly collected more taxes than I should from anyone*], I restore him fourfold [*I pay him back four times what I took*].

JST Luke 19:8

And Zaccheus stood, and said unto the Lord, Behold, Lord, the half of my goods I give to the poor; and if I have taken any thing from any man by unjust means, I restore fourfold.

9 And Jesus said unto him, This day is salvation come to this house [*I have come to this house*], forsomuch as [*because*] he also is a son of [*descendant of*] Abraham [*can also mean that Zacchaeus is righteous and honest like Abraham was, and thus will be saved*].

10 For the Son of man [*I, Christ*] is [*has*] come to seek and to save that which was lost [*those who are lost*].

You will no doubt notice some similarities between the parable of the pounds, which the Savior gives next, and the parable of the talents (Matthew 25:14–30) which Jesus will give a few days later on the Mount of Olives.

The Parable of the Pounds

11 And as they heard these things, he added and spake a parable, because he was nigh [*near*] to Jerusalem, and because they thought that the kingdom of God should immediately appear.

The JST clarifies who "they" refers to, as used in the last phrase of verse 11, above.

JST LUKE 19:11

11 And as they heard these things, he added and spake a parable, because he was nigh to Jerusalem, and because the Jews taught that the kingdom of God should immediately appear.

As indicated after verse 10, above, this next parable is known as the Parable of the Pounds. In addition to explaining to the disciples that the Second Coming is still a long way off, which is opposite of what some of the Jewish religious leaders have been teaching the people, this parable seems to have a major message to the effect that each of us is given an equal opportunity to labor diligently in the work of the Lord, and ultimately become gods. Even though we have this equal opportunity, the results of our efforts will vary because of differences in our talents and abilities. Nevertheless, each of us who tries and produces according to our abilities will be given a stewardship to rule over others; in other words, will become gods. On the other hand, those of us who do nothing to further the work of God with our talents and abilities will not become gods.

12 He said therefore, A certain nobleman [*symbolic of Christ*] went into a far country [*symbolic of heaven*] to receive for himself a kingdom, and to return.

13 And he called his ten servants [*symbolic of all people*], and delivered them ten pounds [*each got the same amount of money, one pound—see verses 16, 18, and 20—symbolic of the fact that each of us will ultimately have an equal opportunity to live the gospel and become gods*], and said unto them, Occupy till I come [*put your pound to good use until I return*].

14 But his citizens [*symbolic of rebellious people on earth*] hated him, and sent a message after him, saying, We will not have this man [*Christ*] to reign over us.

15 And it came to pass, that when he was returned [*symbolic of the Second Coming*], having received the kingdom, then he commanded these servants to be called unto him, to whom he had given the money, that he might know how much every man had gained by trading [*symbolic of Judgment Day*].

16 Then came the first [*the first man*], saying, Lord, thy pound hath gained ten pounds.

17 And he said unto him, Well, thou good servant: because thou hast been faithful in a very little, have thou authority over ten cities [*you can be a god*].

18 And the second came, saying, Lord, thy pound hath gained five pounds.

19 And he said likewise to him, Be thou also over five cities [*you can be a god*].

20 And another came, saying, Lord, behold, here is thy pound, which I have kept laid up in a napkin:

21 For I feared thee, because thou art an austere [*very strict*] man: thou takest up that thou layedst not down, and reapest that thou didst not sow. [*In other words, You don't miss a thing!*]

22 And he saith unto him, Out of thine own mouth will I judge thee, thou wicked servant. Thou knewest that I was an austere man, taking up that I laid not down, and reaping that I did not sow:

23 Wherefore then gavest not thou my money into the bank [*why didn't you invest my money;*

symbolically, why didn't you use the talents and abilities I gave you, to do good?], that at my coming I might have required mine own with usury [*interest*]?

24 And he said unto them that stood by, Take from him the pound [*the opportunity to become a god*], and give it to him that hath ten pounds.

25 (And they said unto him, Lord, he hath ten pounds.) [*He has ten pounds already. He doesn't need more.*]

26 For I say unto you, That unto every one which hath shall be given; and from him that hath not, even that he hath shall be taken away from him. [*Those who become gods will continue to increase in the number of worlds they have, whereas, those who prove unworthy of exaltation will lose the blessings reserved for the faithful.*]

JST LUKE 19:25

25 For I say unto you, That unto every one who occupieth, shall be given; and from him who occupieth not, even that he hath received shall be taken away from him.

The word "occupieth," as used in JST verse 25, above, seems to refer back to that same word as used in verse 13.

27 But those mine enemies, which would not that I should reign over them [*who didn't want me to be their ruler; see verse 14*], bring hither [*here*], and slay them before me [*symbolic of the wicked who will be destroyed at the Second Coming*].

28 And when he had thus spoken, he went before [*ahead*], ascending [*climbing*] up to Jerusalem.

Jerusalem was about twenty-five miles up the mountains from Jericho. Luke now gives us his account of the triumphal entry of the Savior into Jerusalem. First, he tells us of the instructions to the disciples for arranging for the donkey upon which the Master will ride. This is itself a rather under-discussed miracle.

29 And it came to pass, when he was come nigh [*near*] to Bethphage and Bethany, at the mount called the mount of Olives [*just outside Jerusalem*], he sent two of his disciples,

30 Saying, Go ye into the village over against you [*across from you*]; in the which at your entering ye shall find a colt [*a young, male donkey*] tied, whereon yet never man sat [*which has not been broken to ride*]: loose [*untie*] him, and bring him hither.

31 And if any man ask you, Why do ye loose him? thus shall ye say unto him, Because the Lord hath need of him.

32 And they [*the two disciples*] that were sent went their way, and found even as he had said unto them [*just as Jesus had prophesied*].

33 And as they were loosing the colt [*untying the donkey*], the owners thereof said unto them, Why loose ye the colt?

34 And they said, The Lord hath need of him.

35 And they brought him [*the donkey*] to Jesus: and they cast their garments upon the colt, and they set Jesus thereon.

This is what is referred to as the "Triumphal Entry," when Jesus rode into Jerusalem to the cheers and praises of multitudes who welcomed Him as the promised One who would free them from their enemies. It is early spring, Passover time, a.d. 34, when Jews from all over throng into Jerusalem to celebrate and worship. As Christ rides into Jerusalem, they spread their clothing and palm leaves (John 12:13) on the path in front of Him, "thus carpeting the way as for the passing of a king" (Talmage, *Jesus the Christ*, p. 514). Many scholars believe that the Triumphal Entry took place on Sunday. This is the first day of the last week of the Savior's mortal life. He will be crucified on Friday.

The Triumphal Entry

36 And as he went, they spread their clothes in the way [*on the path in front of Him*].

37 And when he was come nigh [*near Jerusalem*], even now at the descent of the mount of Olives, the whole multitude of the disciples began to rejoice and praise God with a loud voice for all the mighty works that they had seen;

38 Saying, Blessed be the King that cometh in the name of the Lord: peace in heaven, and glory in the highest.

39 And some of the Pharisees from among the multitude [*in the crowd*] said unto him, Master, rebuke thy disciples [*tell your disciples not to say such things about You*].

40 And he answered and said unto them, I tell you that, if these should hold their peace, the stones would immediately cry out.

41 And when he was come near, he beheld the city [*Jerusalem*], and wept over it,

42 Saying, If thou hadst known, even thou, at least in this thy day, the things which belong unto thy peace [*if only your inhabitants had been righteous and had done things which would have brought you peace*]! but now they are hid from thine eyes [*peace is no longer available*].

43 For the days shall come upon thee, that thine enemies shall cast a trench about thee, and compass thee round, and keep thee in on every side [*you will be attacked by enemy armies who will lay siege against you, dig trenches around you, and surround you*],

44 And shall lay thee [*Jerusalem*] even with the ground [*will tear you down to the ground*], and thy children [*inhabitants*] within thee; and they [*enemy armies*] shall not leave in thee one stone upon another; because thou knewest not the time of thy visitation [*because you would not acknowledge that your day of punishment would come*].

Next, Jesus cleanses the temple again. Brother Talmage suggests that this takes place on Monday. See *Jesus the Christ*, pp. 524–529. John tells us (John 2:14–17) that Jesus cleansed the temple at the beginning of His ministry. Now, three years later, He cleanses it again. This is the second time, and the money changers obviously hadn't learned their lesson the first time. This cleansing of the temple would involve clearing the outer courtyard of the temple grounds of those involved in making these sacred grounds a "den of thieves." Money changers, who exchanged temple coins for foreign currency, and merchants who sold animals for sacrifices had reduced the temple grounds to anything but a sacred place.

Jesus Cleanses the Temple

45 And he [*Jesus*] went into the temple, and began to cast out them that sold therein, and them that bought;

46 Saying unto them, It is written [*in the scriptures; see Jeremiah 7:11*], My house is the house of prayer: but ye have made it a den of thieves.

47 And he taught daily in the temple. [*This must have been very frustrating to the religious leaders of the Jews, especially after Jesus had cleansed the temple.*] But the chief priests and the scribes and the chief of the people sought to destroy him,

48 And could not find what they might do: for all the people were very attentive to hear him. [*They couldn't figure out a way to destroy Jesus without causing a riot among the people.*]

LUKE 20

THIS IS THE last week of the Savior's life. The religious rulers of the Jews are getting desperate. Jesus' popularity is increasing. The huge crowds, including Jewish pilgrims from many countries, are very excited about Jesus, and are no doubt talking enthusiastically about His cleansing of the temple yesterday. These hypocritical religious leaders have lost every public debate with Jesus in the past. They are still losing face with the people. Three groups of Jewish religious leaders, the chief priests, the scribes, and the elders now have joined together to confront the Master.

1 AND it came to pass, that on one of those days [*probably Tuesday; see Talmage,* Jesus the Christ, *p. 530*], as he taught the people in the temple, and preached the gospel, the chief priests and the scribes came upon him with the elders,

Watch as their first point of attack centers on where He claims to get His authority.

2 And spake unto him, saying, Tell us, by what authority doest thou these things [*including cleansing the temple yesterday*]? or who is he that gave thee this authority?

3 And he answered and said unto them, I will also ask you one thing; and answer me: [*I will ask you one question. If you answer Mine, I will answer yours; see Matthew 21:24.*]

It is helpful to remember that John the Baptist had been very popular among the common people. Thus, these Jewish leaders could cause a riot against themselves if they say anything against him.

4 The baptism of John, was it from heaven, or of men [*did John the Baptist have authority from heaven, or was he just an ordinary man*]?

5 And they reasoned with themselves [*talked it over among themselves*], saying, If we shall say, From heaven; he will say, Why then believed ye him not?

6 But and if we say, Of men; all the people will stone us: for they be persuaded [*the people believe*] that John was a prophet.

7 And they answered, that they could not tell whence it was [*they could not answer his question*].

8 And Jesus said unto them, Neither tell I you by what authority I do these things.

In this next parable, known as the Parable of the Wicked Husbandmen, the Savior clearly compares the wicked Jewish religious leaders to the wicked husbandmen who kill the owner's son in an attempt to take the kingdom from him. The notes in brackets in the parable represent one possible interpretation.

The Parable of the Wicked Husbandmen

9 Then began he to speak to the people this parable; A certain man [*symbolic of Heavenly Father*] planted a vineyard [*planted grape vines; symbolic of establishing Israel, especially the Jews (see Isaiah 5:7) in the Holy Land*], and let it forth [*turned Israel over*] to husbandmen [*farmers in charge of the vineyard; symbolic of the religious leaders of the Jews*], and went into a far country [*heaven*] for a long time.

10 And at the season [*at harvest time*] he sent a servant [*symbolic of prophets*] to the husbandmen, that they should give him of the fruit of the vineyard [*the harvest; symbolizing that the leaders were to have taught righteousness and brought people unto God*]: but the husbandmen beat him, and sent him away empty [*rejected the prophets*].

11 And again he sent another servant [*more prophets*]: and they beat him also, and entreated [*treated*] him shamefully, and sent him away empty [*rejected them too*].

12 And again he sent a third: and they wounded him also, and cast him out.

13 Then said the lord of the vineyard [*the owner; symbolic of the Father*], What shall I do? I will send my beloved son [*symbolic of Christ*]: it may be they will reverence him [*respect and honor Him*] when they see him.

14 But when the husbandmen [*symbolic of the religious leaders of the Jews*] saw him, they reasoned among themselves, saying, This is the heir [*everything will belong to Him*]: come, let us kill him, that the inheritance may be ours [*let's kill Jesus so we can keep our power, authority and position over the people*].

15 So they cast him [*the son of the owner; symbolic of the Savior*] out of the vineyard, and killed him. What therefore shall the lord of the vineyard [*in this case, symbolic of Christ*] do unto them?

16 He shall come [*Second Coming*] and destroy these husbandmen, and shall give the vineyard to others [*righteous religious leaders; symbolic of the restoration of the gospel through Joseph Smith*]. And when they heard it, they said, God forbid.

17 And he beheld them [*looked at them*], and said, What is this then that is written [*in the scriptures; see Psalm 118:22*], The stone [*symbolic of Christ, the "Rock of our salvation"*] which the builders [*the Jews*] rejected, the same is become the head of the corner [*cornerstone; capstone*]?

"Capstone" could symbolize "the finisher of our salvation." Strong's *Concordance*, numbers 1137 and 1119, suggest a possible association of words to imply "kneeling." This could tie in with the fact that "all shall bow the knee, and every tongue shall confess" that Jesus is the Christ. (See D&C 76:110 and Philippians 2:10–11.)

18 Whosoever shall fall upon that stone [*Christ*] shall be broken; but on whomsoever it shall fall [*the wicked*], it will grind him to powder.

One of the important messages in verse 18, above, is that Christ and His gospel will ultimately triumph over the devil and his kingdom (see Moses 4:21). A religious movie producer once said, in effect, that we cannot break the commandments of God. We can only break ourselves against them.

19 And the chief priests and the scribes the same hour sought to lay hands on him; and they feared the people [*they tried to figure out a safe way to arrest Him immediately, without causing a riot*]: for they perceived [*they understood*] that he had spoken this parable against them. [*In other words, they understood full well that they were the "wicked husbandmen" in the parable Jesus had just told them in verses 9–16 above.*]

20 And they [*the scribes, Pharisees, and elders*] watched him, and sent forth spies, which should feign [*pretend*] themselves just [*righteous, sincere*] men, that they might take hold of his words [*catch Jesus saying something for which He could be arrested*], that so they might deliver him unto the power and authority of the governor [*the Roman governor, Pontius Pilate*].

21 And they [*the spies in verse 20*] asked him, saying, Master, we know that thou sayest and teachest rightly, neither acceptest thou the person of any [*You don't change Your teachings because of peer pressure*], but teachest the way of God truly: [*They were indeed pretending to be "just men," as instructed by their evil bosses in verse 20.*]

Watch now as these cunning men attempt to get the Master in trouble with the Roman government.

22 Is it lawful [*legal*] for us to give tribute [*pay taxes*] unto Cæsar [*the Roman emperor*], or no?

23 But he perceived their craftiness [*Jesus understood their sly intentions*], and said unto them, Why tempt ye me [*why are you trying to trick Me*]?

24 Shew [*show, pronounced "show"*] me a penny [*a Roman penny representing about a day's wage*]. Whose image [*picture*] and superscription [*writing on the coin*] hath it? They answered and said, Cæsar's.

25 And he said unto them, Render [*pay*] therefore unto Cæsar the things which be Cæsar's, and unto God the things which be God's.

26 And they could not take hold of his words before the people [*their plot didn't work*]: and they marvelled [*were stunned*] at his answer, and held their peace [*kept quiet*].

The three groups of Jewish religious leaders mentioned in verse one are now joined by yet another prominent group, the Sadducees, in their attempts to discredit Jesus and get Him arrested. Since the others have failed miserably, they will now try their hand.

27 Then came to him certain of the Sadducees [*another influential group of Jewish religious leaders*], which deny that there is any resurrection [*who did not believe in the doctrine of resurrection*]; and they asked him,

Seven Brothers, One Wife

28 Saying, Master, Moses wrote unto us [*taught us in the scriptures—Deuteronomy 25:5*], If any man's brother die, having a wife, and he die without children, that his brother should take [*marry*] his wife, and raise up seed unto his brother [*produce children for his dead brother*].

29 There were therefore seven brethren [*brothers*]: and the first took a wife, and died without children.

30 And the second took her to wife [*married her*], and he died childless.

31 And the third took her; and in like manner the seven also: and they left no children, and

died. [*Ultimately, all seven brothers married her in turn, had no children with her, and died.*]

32 Last of all the woman died also.

33 Therefore in the resurrection whose wife of them is she? for seven had her to wife.

Celestial Marriage

Here is a major doctrinal point. Many religions use these next three verses to prove that there is no such thing as eternal marriage and family in the next life. On the contrary, the simple fact that the Sadducees asked the Savior whose wife she would be when they are all resurrected (verse 33 above), is strong evidence that the Savior had indeed preached marriage in the resurrection; in other words, eternal marriage. Otherwise, their question would not make any sense at all!

34 And Jesus answering said unto them, The children of this world marry, and are given in marriage:

35 But they which shall be accounted worthy to obtain that world, and the resurrection from the dead, neither marry, nor are given in marriage:

JST LUKE 20:35

35 But they who shall be accounted worthy to obtain that world, through resurrection from the dead, neither marry nor are given in marriage.

36 Neither can they die any more: for they are equal unto the angels; and are the children of God, being the children of the resurrection.

The above three verses can be confusing. Perhaps these verses are not translated correctly. Perhaps there are some things left out. Whatever the case, we have been given correct doctrine regarding eternal marriage (D&C 132:19–20). We have also been taught that, after everyone from this earth is resurrected, there will be no more eternal marriages performed for former residents of this earth, because such marriages have to be done by mortals for themselves, or by mortals who serve as proxies for those who have died—see D&C 128:15 & 18. Brigham Young said: "And when the Millennium is over, . . . all the sons and daughters of Adam and Eve, down to the last of their posterity, who come within the reach of the clemency of the Gospel, [will] have been redeemed in hundreds of temples through the administration of their children as proxies for them" (Discourses of Brigham Young, p. 395). Since there will be no mortals left on earth after the resurrection is completed, there would be no one left to serve as proxies for eternal marriages.

37 Now that the dead are raised [*the fact that the dead are resurrected; remember that Jesus is talking here to Sadducees, who do not believe in resurrection—see verse 27*], even Moses shewed [*showed; proved*] at the bush [*when he talked to God at the burning bush*], when he calleth the Lord the God of Abraham, and the God of Isaac, and the God of Jacob.

38 For he is not a God of the dead, but of the living: for all live unto him [*everyone will be resurrected*].

39 Then certain of the scribes answering said, Master, thou hast well said.

40 And after that they [*the spies, mentioned in verse 20 above, and perhaps others also in the crowd*] durst not [*didn't dare*] ask him any question at all.

41 And he said unto them, How say they that Christ is David's son [*what do people mean when they say Christ is King David's son*]?

42 And David himself saith in the book of Psalms [*Psalm 110:1*], The LORD [*the Father; see* Doctrinal New Testament Commentary, *Vol. 1, p. 612*] said unto my Lord [*Christ*], Sit thou on my right hand,

43 Till I make thine enemies thy footstool [*until all your enemies have been subdued under your feet*].

44 David therefore calleth him Lord [*God*], how is he then his son [*how can He be David's son*]?

45 Then in the audience [*within hearing*] of all the people he said unto his disciples,

46 Beware of [*watch out for*] the scribes [*religious rulers among the Jews*], which [*who*] desire to walk in long robes, and love greetings in the markets,

and the highest seats in the synagogues, and the chief rooms at feasts [*they love to appear very important in public*];

47 Which devour widows' houses [*take widow's houses from them*], and for a shew [*for show*] make long prayers: the same [*the scribes*] shall receive greater damnation.

LUKE 21

IN THIS CHAPTER, the Savior prophecies the destruction of the temple in Jerusalem and of the city of Jerusalem. He will give a number of the signs of the times which will be fulfilled before His Second Coming. You may wish to review Matthew, chapter 24, which contains more of these signs of the times.

1 AND he looked up, and saw the rich men casting their gifts into the treasury [*depositing their donations in the public donation container at the temple in Jerusalem*].

The Widow's Mite

2 And he saw also a certain poor widow casting in thither two mites [*one mite was about one sixty-fourth of a day's pay; see Bible Dictionary, under "Money"*].

3 And he said, Of a truth [*certainly*] I say unto you, that this poor widow hath cast in more than they all:

4 For all these [*rich men*] have of their abundance cast in unto the offerings of God [*have taken just a bit, relatively speaking, from their wealth*]: but she of her penury [*poverty*] hath cast in all the living that she had. [*She has given everything she has to live on.*]

5 And as some spake of the temple, how it was adorned [*decorated*] with goodly [*beautiful*] stones and gifts, he said,

6 As for these things [*the huge stones used to build the temple*] which ye behold [*see*], the days will come, in the which there shall not be left one stone upon another, that shall not be thrown down [*the temple in Jerusalem will be destroyed*].

Signs of the Times

7 And they asked him, saying, Master, but when shall these things be? and what sign will there be when these things shall come to pass?

The Savior has just told His disciples about the coming destruction of Jerusalem by the Romans, which will be essentially complete by a.d. 73. Next, He will teach them many of the "signs of the times," meaning prophecies which will be fulfilled before the Second Coming. For more complete notes, see Matthew 24 in this study guide.

8 And he said, Take heed [*be careful*] that ye be not deceived: for many shall come in my name, saying, I am Christ; and the time draweth near: go ye not therefore after them. [*There will be many false Christs in the last days. Don't follow them.*]

9 But when ye shall hear of wars and commotions, be not terrified [*don't panic when you see the signs of the times being fulfilled*]: for these things must first come to pass [*must happen before the Second Coming*]; but the end is not by and by [*right away*].

10 Then said he unto them, Nation shall rise against nation, and kingdom against kingdom [*in the last days*]:

11 And great earthquakes shall be in divers [*various*] places, and famines, and pestilences; and fearful sights and great signs shall there be from heaven.

12 But before all these [*things which will happen in the last days*], they shall lay their hands on you [*the disciples*], and persecute you, delivering you up to the synagogues [*arresting you*], and into prisons, being brought before kings and rulers for my name's sake [*because of your service to Me*].

13 And it shall turn to you for a testimony [*it will work out so that you can bear testimony of Me*].

14 Settle it therefore [*determine*] in your hearts, not to meditate before [*think in advance*] what ye shall answer:

15 For I will give you a mouth and wisdom, which all your adversaries shall not be able to gainsay [*oppose, put down*] nor resist.

16 And ye shall be betrayed both by parents, and brethren, and kinsfolks [*relatives*], and friends; and some of you shall they cause to be put to death [*they will kill some of you*].

17 And ye shall be hated of all men for my name's sake [*because of your loyalty to Me*].

18 But there shall not an hair of your head perish [*without the Father noticing it—compare with Matthew 10:29-31; in other words, ultimately, you will be fine in the celestial kingdom*].

19 In your patience [*loyal service at all costs*] possess ye your souls [*you will earn exaltation; the highest degree of glory in the celestial kingdom*].

20 And when ye shall see Jerusalem compassed [*surrounded*] with armies, then know that the desolation thereof is nigh [*the "desolation of abomination" spoken of by Daniel; see notes for Matthew 24:15 in this study guide*].

21 Then let them which are in Judæa flee to the mountains; and let them which are in the midst of it depart out; and let not them that are in the countries enter thereinto.

JST LUKE 21:20

20 Then let them who are in Judea flee to the mountains; and let them who are in the midst of it, depart out; and let not them who are in the countries, return to enter into the city.

Many faithful Saints at the time of the Roman attacks followed the prophetic counsel in verse 21 above. They fled to Pella, east of Samaria, and thus escaped the Romans.

22 For these be the days of vengeance, that all things [*all the prophecies*] which are written may be fulfilled.

23 But woe unto them that are with child [*are pregnant, so they can't run fast*], and to them that give suck [*are nursing, thus have small children and can't run away fast with them in tow*], in those days! for there shall be great distress in the land, and wrath upon this people [*the Jews*].

24 And they [*the Jews*] shall fall [*be killed*] by the edge of the sword, and shall be led away captive into all nations: and Jerusalem shall be trodden down of [*by*] the Gentiles, until the times of the Gentiles be fulfilled.

The JST adds a verse after verse 24, above. It helps us understand that many of the signs of the times given here by the Savior related to the times of the Apostles and early members of the Church immediately following the crucifixion and resurrection of Christ. And others of the signs relate to the last days, in other words, our day.

JST LUKE 21:24

24 Now these things he spake unto them, concerning the destruction of Jerusalem. And then his disciples asked him, saying, Master, tell us concerning thy coming?

25 And there shall be signs [*in the last days*] in the sun, and in the moon, and in the stars; and upon the earth distress of nations [*much trouble between nations*], with perplexity; the sea and the waves roaring [*much trouble upon the oceans and waters*];

JST LUKE 21:25

25 And he answered them, and said, In the generation in which the times of the Gentiles shall be fulfilled, there shall be signs in the sun, and in the moon, and in the stars; and upon the earth distress of nations with perplexity, like the sea and the waves roaring. The earth also shall be troubled, and the waters of the great deep;

26 Men's hearts failing them for fear [*people will be depressed, giving up hope*], and for looking after those things [*because of seeing the terrible things*] which are coming on the earth: for the powers of heaven shall be shaken.

27 And then shall they see the Son of man [*Jesus*] coming in a cloud with power and great glory [*the Second Coming*].

Everyone will see the Savior, when He comes in glory at the time of His Second Coming, including those who caused His crucifixion. See Revelation 1:7.

28 And when these things [*prophecies*] begin to come to pass [*begin to happen*], then look up, and lift up your heads; for your redemption draweth nigh. [*The righteous can rejoice at the Second Coming, because their troubles, persecutions, etc., are over.*]

Next, Jesus gives the Parable of the Fig Tree. The main point is that, just as a farmer can tell when a fruit tree is about to start growing leaves, so also wise Saints will be familiar with the signs of the times so that they will recognize that the Second Coming is near.

The Parable of the Fig Tree

29 And he spake to them a parable; Behold the fig tree, and all the trees;

30 When they now shoot forth [*start putting on leaves and blossoms*], ye see and know of your own selves that summer is now nigh at hand [*close at hand*].

31 So likewise ye, when ye see these things come to pass [*the signs of the times*], know ye that the kingdom of God [*Second Coming*] is nigh at hand [*is getting close*].

32 Verily I say unto you, This generation shall not pass away, till all be fulfilled [*until all the signs of the times have been fulfilled*].

JST Luke 21:32

32 Verily I say unto you, this generation, the generation when the times of the Gentiles be fulfilled, shall not pass away till all be fulfilled.

The "times of the Gentiles" refers to the period of time in the last days when the gospel is being taken to everyone but the Jews. In the days of the Savior's mortal ministry, He and His Apostles took the gospel message only to the Jews. Then, after His resurrection, He instructed them to go into all the world (Mark 16:15.) Thus, the Jews were the "first" to get the gospel in the days of the Savior, and the Gentiles (everyone else) was "last." In the last days it will be just the opposite. First, the gospel will be taken to the Gentiles, then it will go to the Jews. Thus, the "last" (Gentiles) will be first (in the last days) and the "first" (Jews) will be last to get it in the last days. The happy news is that all will ultimately get a chance to understand it and accept it.

33 Heaven and earth shall pass away: but my words shall not pass away [*what I say is absolutely reliable*].

34 And take heed to yourselves [*watch out*], lest at any time your hearts be overcharged with surfeiting [*wicked, lustful living*], and drunkenness, and cares of this life, and so that day [*the Second Coming*] come upon you unawares [*catches you off guard*].

JST Luke 21:34

34 Let my disciples therefore take heed to themselves, lest at any time their hearts be overcharged with surfeiting, and drunkenness, and cares of this life, and that day come upon them unawares.

35 For as a snare [*a trap which catches an unsuspecting animal totally by surprise*] shall it come on all them [*the wicked or foolish*] that dwell on the face of the whole earth.

D&C 106:4–5 differentiates be-tween the "world" and the "children of light" as far as being caught off guard at the Savior's coming is concerned. The "world," meaning the wicked, will be caught off guard, similar to one who is caught unexpectedly by a "thief in the night" (D&C 106:4.) On the other hand, the "children of light" (D&C 106:5), meaning the Saints who are familiar with the signs of the times, are not caught off guard.

36 Watch ye therefore, and pray always, that ye may be accounted worthy to escape all these things that shall come to pass, and to stand [*worthily*] before the Son of man [*Christ*].

JST Luke 21:36

36 And what I say unto one, I say unto all, Watch ye therefore, and pray always, and keep my commandments, that ye may be counted worthy

to escape all these things which shall come to pass, and to stand before the Son of man when he shall come clothed in the glory of his Father.

We understand that, at this point, it is most likely Tuesday evening of the last week of the Savior's life. See Talmage, Jesus the Christ, pp. 563 and 586.

37 And in the day time he was teaching in the temple; and at night he went out, and abode *[spent time teaching]* in the mount that is called the mount of Olives.

38 And all the people came early in the morning to him in the temple, for to hear him.

LUKE 22

IN THIS CHAPTER, Judas Iscariot will make arrangements to betray the Savior. Jesus will institute the sacrament, will suffer in the Garden of Gethsemane, will be betrayed, arrested, subjected to illegal trial, and will be brutally mocked. During the trial at night, Peter will deny knowing Jesus three times.

1 NOW the feast of unleavened bread drew nigh *[near]*, which is called the Passover.

The Feast of the Passover was celebrated in the springtime at about the same time as we celebrate Easter. It commemorated the destroying angel's passing over the houses of the children of Israel in Egypt, when the firstborn of the Egyptians were killed. The Israelites in Egypt at the time were instructed by Moses to sacrifice a lamb without blemish and to put blood from the lamb which was sacrificed on the doorposts of their houses. See Bible Dictionary, under "Feasts." Thus, through the blood of a lamb, the Israelites were protected from the anguish and punishment brought to the Egyptians by the destroying angel.

The symbolism is clear. It is by the "blood of the Lamb" (the sacrifice of the Savior) that we are saved, after all we can do (2 Nephi 25:23). Now, at the time of Passover in Jerusalem, the "Lamb of God," Christ, will present Himself to be sacrificed, that we might be saved. The Feast of the Passover brought large numbers of Jews from near and far to Jerusalem to join in the worship and celebration.

2 And the chief priests and scribes sought how they might kill him; for they feared the people *[were afraid of causing a riot by arresting Jesus]*.

3 Then entered Satan into Judas surnamed Iscariot, being of the number of the twelve *[who was one of the Twelve Apostles]*.

4 And he *[Judas]* went his way, and communed *[plotted]* with the chief priests and captains, how he might betray him *[Jesus]* unto them.

5 And they were glad, and covenanted to give him money *[thirty pieces of silver]*.

Thirty pieces of silver was the current price for an average slave. Thus, it was an insult to Judas and demeaning to the Master to offer him only the going price for a common slave for the Savior.

6 And he *[Judas]* promised *[agreed to the terms]*, and sought opportunity to betray him *[Jesus]* unto them in the absence of the multitude. *[Judas looked for opportunities to betray Jesus quietly, out of sight of the public. We understand this to be taking place at the end of the third day of the last week of the Savior's life, probably Tuesday.]*

7 Then came the day of unleavened bread, when the passover must be killed. *[This is Thursday, the fifth day of the last week of the Savior's mortal life, when the actual feast of the Passover was eaten.]*

8 And he *[Jesus]* sent Peter and John, saying, Go and prepare us the passover, that we may eat *[find a place for us to eat the Passover meal]*.

9 And they said unto him, Where wilt thou that we prepare?

Pay attention to the prophetic details which the Savior now provides as He directs Peter and John to prepare a place for them to eat the Passover meal.

10 And he said unto them, Behold, when ye are entered into the city, there shall a man meet you, bearing a pitcher of water; follow him into the house where he entereth in.

11 And ye shall say unto the goodman [*owner*] of the house, The Master saith unto thee, Where is the guestchamber [*room*], where I shall eat the passover with my disciples?

12 And he shall shew [*show*] you a large upper room furnished: there make ready.

13 And they went, and found as he had said unto them: and they made ready the passover.

The Last Supper

14 And when the hour was come, he sat down, and the twelve apostles with him.

15 And he said unto them, With desire [*deep emotion*] I have desired to eat this passover with you before I suffer:

16 For I say unto you, I will not any more eat thereof, until it be fulfilled in the kingdom of God.

JST LUKE 22:16

16 For I say unto you, I will not any more eat thereof, until it be fulfilled which is written in the prophets concerning me. Then I will partake with you, in the kingdom of God.

Jesus now introduces the sacrament to His Apostles. This final Passover meal, partaken of with them, is known as the "Last Supper."

17 And he took the cup, and gave thanks, and said, Take this, and divide it among yourselves:

18 For I say unto you, I will not drink of the fruit of the vine, until the kingdom of God shall come [*this is the last time I will eat with you during my mortal life; see Matthew 26:29*].

The Sacrament

19 And he took bread, and gave thanks, and brake it, and gave unto them, saying, This is my body [*this represents my body*] which is given for you: this do in remembrance of me.

20 Likewise also the cup after supper, saying, This cup is the new testament [*the new covenant*] in my blood [*represents my blood*], which is shed for you.

21 But, behold, the hand of him [*Judas Iscariot*] that betrayeth me is with me on the table.

22 And truly the Son of man [*Christ*] goeth [*dies*], as it was determined [*planned*]: but woe unto that man by whom he is betrayed!

23 And they began to enquire among themselves, which of them it was that should do this thing [*betray the Savior*].

Who Is Greatest?

24 And there was also a strife [*an argument*] among them, which of them should be accounted the greatest [*which of them was the most important*].

25 And he said unto them, The kings of the Gentiles exercise lordship [*power, authority*] over them; and they that exercise authority upon them are called benefactors.

Those Who Serve Are Greatest

26 But ye shall not be so: but he that is greatest among you, let him be as the younger; and he that is chief, as he that doth serve. [*If you want to be the greatest, you must consider yourself to be the lowest and serve others.*]

27 For whether is greater [*who is commonly considered to be the most important*], he that sitteth at meat [*is eating the meal*], or he that serveth [*who serves the meal*]? is not he that sitteth at meat [*answer: the person eating the meal*]? but I am among you as he that serveth [*I am among you as your servant*].

28 Ye are they which have continued with me in my temptations [*you are my loyal followers*].

29 And I appoint unto you a kingdom [*you will be exalted*], as my Father hath appointed unto me;

30 That ye may eat and drink at my table in my kingdom, and sit on thrones judging the twelve tribes of Israel.

We understand from JST Mark 14:30 that Judas Iscariot has already left the scene to betray the Master. Thus, Christ's statement to the Apostles that they are appointed a kingdom, verses 29–30 above, would apply to the eleven remaining Apostles, not to Judas.

31 And the Lord said, Simon [*Peter*], Simon, behold, Satan hath desired to have you, that he may sift you as wheat:

JST LUKE 22:31

31 And the Lord said, Simon, Simon, behold Satan hath desired you, that he may sift the children of the kingdom as wheat. [*Satan would like to destroy Peter's effectiveness, so that the members of the Church would be without his leadership.*]

32 But I have prayed for thee, that thy faith fail not [*so that Satan will not be successful*]: and when thou art converted, strengthen thy brethren.

It is significant that the Savior says to Peter, "When thou art converted, strengthen thy brethren." Peter feels that he is already completely converted and strong in the faith. Yet, this will be a most difficult night for him, as he denies knowing the Savior on three different occasions. Afterwards, he will be much stronger as we see in Acts, chapter 4 and elsewhere.

33 And he said unto him, Lord, I am ready to go with thee, both into prison, and to death.

34 And he said, I tell thee, Peter, the cock [*rooster*] shall not crow this day, before that thou shalt thrice deny that thou knowest me.

Denying knowing the Savior is not the same as denying the Holy Ghost. Denying the Holy Ghost, as described in D&C 76:31–35, is an unforgivable sin. Peter's denying that he knows the Savior and has been one of His followers for three years is not unforgivable, though so doing brought Peter deep anguish and tears.

35 And he said unto them, When I sent you [*on your first missions; see Matthew 10:9-10*] without purse [*money*], and scrip [*a bag to carry food in; see Bible Dictionary, under "Scrip"*], and shoes [*a sign of wealth and power in the culture of the day*], lacked ye any thing [*were any of your needs not taken care of*]? And they said, Nothing.

36 Then said he unto them, But now, he that hath a purse, let him take it, and likewise his scrip: and he that hath no sword, let him sell his garment, and buy one. [*Things have changed, so from now on, equip yourselves as well as you can.*]

37 For I say unto you, that this that is written [*in Isaiah 53:12*] must yet be accomplished in me [*the prophecies about His atoning sacrifice must now take place*], And he was reckoned among the transgressors [*including the prophecy that he would be killed with transgressors (Isaiah 53:12), which was fulfilled by the two thieves on crosses*]: for the things concerning me have an end. [*The things that are going to happen to me have a purpose, namely, they will lead up to my accomplishing the Atonement.*]

38 And they said, Lord, behold, here are two swords. And he said unto them, It is enough. [*The Apostles still don't seem to grasp the significance of what Jesus just told them, that He must go through with the Atonement. Otherwise, they would not have mentioned the swords for defending Him against the coming dangers.*]

39 And he came out, and went, as he was wont [*as was His custom*], to the mount of Olives; and his disciples also followed him.

The Garden of Gethsemane

40 And when he was at the place [*the Garden of Gethsemane—see Matthew 26:36*], he said unto them, Pray that ye enter not into temptation.

"Gethsemane" means "oil press." There is significant symbolism here. The Jews put olives into bags made of mesh fabric and placed them in a press to squeeze olive oil out of them. The first pressings yielded pure olive oil which was prized for many uses, including healing and giving light in lanterns. In fact, we consecrate it and use it to administer to the sick. The last pressing of the olives, under the tremendous pressure of additional weights added to the press, yielded a bitter, red liquid which can remind us of the "bitter cup" which the Savior partook of. Symbolically, the Savior is going into the "oil press" (Gethsemane) to submit to the "pressure" of all our sins which will "squeeze" His blood out in order that we might have the healing "oil" of the Atonement to heal us from our sins.

41 And he was withdrawn from them about a stone's cast, and kneeled down, and prayed,

42 Saying, Father, if thou be willing, remove this cup from me: nevertheless not my will, but thine, be done.

43 And there appeared an angel unto him from heaven, strengthening him. [*Apostle Bruce R. McConkie suggested that this angel might be Michael (Adam); see April 1985 General Conference*].

44 And being in an agony he prayed more earnestly: and his sweat was as it were great drops of blood falling down to the ground.

JST LUKE 22:44

44 And being in an agony, he prayed more earnestly; and he sweat as it were great drops of blood falling down to the ground.

Some Christians wonder whether or not Jesus actually did sweat drops of blood, or if it was figurative, because of the wording in Luke. Mosiah 3:7 and D&C 19:18 clear up any doubt. He did bleed from every pore.

45 And when he rose up from prayer, and was come to [*returned to*] his disciples, he found them sleeping for sorrow [*exhausted by their worrying about Jesus and His safety*],

JST LUKE 22:45

45 And when he rose up from prayer, and was come to his disciples, he found them sleeping; for they were filled with sorrow;

46 And said unto them, Why sleep ye? rise and pray, lest ye enter into temptation.

The Betrayal

47 And while he yet spake, behold a multitude [*a group of soldiers and others, with swords and sticks, sent by and accompanied by the chief priests and elders; see Matthew 26:47, Luke 22:52*], and he that was called Judas, one of the twelve, went before them [*Judas led them*], and drew near unto Jesus to kiss him.

48 But Jesus said unto him, Judas, betrayest thou the Son of man [*Son of God*] with a kiss?

49 When they which were about him [*Jesus' Apostles*] saw what would follow [*what was about to happen*], they said unto him, Lord, shall we smite with the sword?

50 And one of them [*Peter*] smote [*struck*] the servant of the high priest, and cut off his right ear.

51 And Jesus answered and said, Suffer ye thus far [*let them arrest me*]. And he touched his ear [*the servant's ear*], and healed him.

52 Then Jesus said unto the chief priests, and captains of the temple, and the elders, which were come to him, Be ye come out, as against a thief [*as if I were a thief, trying to hide from you*], with swords and staves?

53 When I was daily with you in the temple, ye stretched forth no hands against me [*Why didn't you arrest me in broad daylight, when I was in the temple?*]: but this is your hour, and the power of darkness [*this is the evil hour you've planned, so go ahead with your plot*].

54 Then took they him [*they arrested Him*], and led him, and brought him into the high priest's house [*palace*]. And Peter followed afar off [*at a distance*].

Peter Denies Knowing Jesus

55 And when they [*the rowdy crowd who had come to help arrest Jesus*] had kindled a fire in the

midst of the hall [*courtyard*], and were set down together, Peter sat down among them.

56 But a certain maid [*young lady*] beheld [*saw*] him as he sat by the fire, and earnestly looked upon him [*and stared at him*], and said, This man was also with him [*Jesus*].

57 And he denied him [*denied knowing Jesus*], saying, Woman, I know him not.

58 And after a little while another saw him, and said, Thou art also of them [*you are one of Jesus' followers*]. And Peter said, Man, I am not.

59 And about the space of one hour after another [*person in the crowd*] confidently affirmed [*spoke with confidence*], saying, Of a truth [*for sure*] this fellow also was with him: for he is a Galilæan.

60 And Peter said, Man, I know not what thou sayest. And immediately, while he yet spake [*while he was speaking*], the cock crew [*the rooster crowed*].

61 And the Lord [*Jesus*] turned, and looked upon Peter. And Peter remembered the word of the Lord, how he had said unto him, Before the cock crow, thou shalt deny me thrice [*three times*].

62 And Peter went out, and wept bitterly.

The Mocking and Trial

63 And the men that held Jesus mocked him, and smote [*hit*] him.

64 And when they had blindfolded him, they struck him on the face, and asked him, saying, Prophesy, who is it that smote thee? [*Use Your power to tell us who hits You.*]

65 And many other things blasphemously [*mockingly*] spake they against him.

The Trial before Caiaphas

66 And as soon as it was day, the elders of the people and the chief priests and the scribes came together, and led him into their council [*this council was known as the Sanhedrin and was the highest court run by the Jewish religious leaders; see Bible Dictionary, under "Sanhedrin"*], saying,

67 Art thou the Christ? tell us. And he said unto them, If I tell you [*if I say "Yes."*], ye will not believe:

68 And if I also ask you, ye will not answer me, nor let me go.

69 Hereafter shall the Son of man sit on the right hand of the power of God [*after you are finished with Me, I will sit on the right side of the Father up in heaven*].

70 Then said they all, Art thou then the Son of God? And he said unto them, Ye say that I am [*"I am."—see Mark 14:62*].

71 And they said, What need we any further witness [*why do we need any more evidence*]? for we ourselves have heard of his own mouth [*we heard from His own mouth that He claims to be the Son of God*].

LUKE 23

IN THIS CHAPTER, Luke reports that Jesus was taken to Pilate, then to Herod, and back to Pilate again. Pilate releases a criminal named Barabbas in place of Jesus. He tells us of the crucifixion of the Savior and the burial in the garden tomb of Joseph of Arimathaea.

The Trial before Pilate

1 AND the whole multitude of them [*the Sanhedrin, Luke 22:66 above*] arose, and led him unto Pilate [*the Roman governor*].

Next, you will see that the Jewish leaders attempted to get Jesus convicted of high treason against the Romans.

2 And they began to accuse him, saying, We found this fellow perverting [*undermining*] the nation [*the Roman Empire*], and forbidding to

give tribute to Cæsar, saying that he himself is Christ a King.

In saying that Jesus told people not to pay taxes (tribute) to Caesar, these religious leaders show their true colors as liars. Christ had specifically taught "Render therefore unto Caesar the things which be Caesar's" (Luke 20:25).

3 And Pilate asked him, saying, Art thou the King of the Jews? And he answered him and said, Thou sayest it. [*John 18:37 records the Master's response as "To this end was I born, and for this cause came I into the world;" in other words, "Yes, I am."*]

4 Then said Pilate to the chief priests and to the people, I find no fault in this man.

5 And they were the more fierce, saying, He stirreth up the people, teaching throughout all Jewry, beginning from Galilee to this place [*from Galilee in the north to Jerusalem in the south*].

6 When Pilate heard of Galilee, he asked whether the man were a Galilæan [*whether or not Jesus was a citizen of Galilee*].

What Pontius Pilate is trying to do here is avoid the responsibility of handling the case of Jesus by sending Him to the Roman governor of Galilee, who at that time was Herod, and who happened to be visiting Jerusalem.

The Trial before Herod

7 And as soon as he knew that he belonged unto Herod's jurisdiction, he sent him to Herod, who himself also was at Jerusalem at that time.

8 And when Herod saw Jesus, he was exceeding [*very*] glad: for he was desirous to see him of a long season [*he had wanted to meet Jesus for a long time*], because he had heard many things of him; and he hoped to have seen some miracle done by him.

9 Then he questioned with him in many words; but he answered him nothing [*Jesus refused to answer Herod at all*].

10 And the chief priests and scribes stood and vehemently [*angrily*] accused him [*presented their case against Jesus to Herod*].

Second Hearing before Pilate

11 And Herod with his men of war set him at nought [*ridiculed him*], and mocked him, and arrayed [*dressed*] him in a gorgeous robe, and sent him again to Pilate.

12 And the same day Pilate and Herod were made friends together: for before they were at enmity between themselves [*they were enemies before this*].

13 And Pilate, when he had called together the chief priests and the rulers and the people,

14 Said unto them, Ye have brought this man unto me, as one that perverteth the people [*undermines the nation*]: and, behold, I, having examined him before you [*in front of you*], have found no fault in this man touching those things whereof ye accuse him [*I find no truth in the things you accuse Jesus of*]:

15 No, nor yet Herod [*neither did Herod find Him guilty*]: for I sent you to him; and, lo, nothing worthy of death is done unto him [*"by him"—see Luke 23, footnote 15a, in your LDS Bible; in other words, Jesus has done nothing worthy of death*].

16 I will therefore chastise [*lightly punish*] him, and release him.

17 (For of necessity [*according to custom; see Matthew 27:15 in this study guide*] he must release one [*a prisoner*] unto them at the feast.)

18 And they cried out all at once, saying, Away with this man, and release unto us Barabbas:

19 (Who for a certain sedition [*undermining the government*] made in the city, and for murder, was cast into prison.)

The name "Barabbas" means "son of the father" (see Bible Dictionary, under "Barabbas"). This may be symbolic in that the "imposter," Satan, stirred up the multitude to demand the release of an "imposter," Barabbas, while the true "Son of the Father" is punished for crimes which He did not commit.

20 Pilate therefore, willing to release Jesus, spake again to them.

21 But they cried, saying, Crucify him, crucify him.

22 And he said unto them the third time, Why, what evil hath he done? I have found no cause of death in him: I will therefore chastise him, and let him go.

23 And they were instant [*insistent*] with loud voices, requiring [*demanding*] that he might be crucified. And the voices of them and of the chief priests prevailed [*won out, meaning that Pilate gave in*].

24 And Pilate gave [*passed*] sentence that it should be as they required [*demanded*].

Pilate was a weak leader, an embarrassment to the Roman Empire. About three years after this public show of weakness on his part, he was removed from office by the Roman Empire, and tradition has it that he was banished and later committed suicide. See Smith's Bible Dictionary, pp. 519–520.

25 And he released unto them him [*Barabbas*] that for sedition and murder was cast into prison, whom they had desired; but he [*Pilate*] delivered Jesus to their will [*turned him over to the people, as they had requested*].

26 And as they led him away, they laid hold upon [*siezed*] one Simon, a Cyrenian, coming out of the country [*a foreigner; probably a Jew from the city of Cyrene, in northern Africa, likely in Jerusalem for the Passover*], and on him they laid the cross [*made him carry Jesus' cross*], that he might bear it after [*carry it behind*] Jesus.

The Savior would have been very weak, physically, by now, having suffered in Gethsemane, having been mocked and hit by the soldiers, Luke 22:64, and scourged (whipped), Matthew 27:26. Thus, He was too weak physically to carry His own cross, which was a normal part of the punishment of crucifixion without resorting to His divine powers.

27 And there followed him a great company of people, and of women, which also bewailed [*cried*] and lamented [*mourned for*] him.

28 But Jesus turning unto them said, Daughters of Jerusalem, weep not for me, but weep for yourselves, and for your children.

29 For, behold, the days are coming, in the which they shall say, Blessed are the barren, and the wombs that never bare, and the paps which never gave suck. [*In other words, women who never had children are the fortunate ones. This would be exactly opposite of Jewish culture of the day, in which women who had no children were considered to be the unfortunate ones and were looked down upon.*]

30 Then shall they begin to say to the mountains, Fall on us; and to the hills, Cover us. [*Conditions will get so bad in Jerusalem that people will desire death rather than face the persecutions and difficulties which will come.*]

31 For if they do these things in a green tree, what shall be done in the dry? [*If they do such wicked things in good times, what will they do when bad times come?*]

The JST adds another verse here.

JST LUKE 23:32
This he spake, signifying the scattering of Israel, and the desolation of the heathen, or in other words, the Gentiles.

The Two Thieves

32 And there were also two other, malefactors [*criminals*], led with him to be put to death.

The Crucifixion

33 And when they were come to the place, which is called Calvary, there they crucified him, and the malefactors *[thieves]*, one on the right hand, and the other on the left.

34 Then said Jesus, Father, forgive them; for they know not what they do. And they parted his raiment, and cast lots.

> The JST makes a very important doctrinal clarification to verse 34, above.
>
> JST LUKE 23:35
>
> 35 Then said Jesus, Father, forgive them; for they know not what they do. (Meaning the soldiers who crucified him,) and they parted his raiment and cast lots.
>
> (Remember, as noted several times already in this study guide, that the JST verses often have different numbers than the equivalent verses in the King James Bible—the one we use in English-speaking areas of the Church—because Joseph Smith's additions and corrections often involved adding additional verses.)
>
> The statement, verse 34 (JST verse 35) above, which Jesus uttered from the cross, shows His compassion for those who were crucifying Him. As noted in the JST, Joseph Smith taught that it applied to the Roman soldiers, rather than to the Jewish religious leaders who arranged His crucifixion and did know what they were doing.
>
> The Savior's Statements from the Cross
>
> Jesus uttered a total of seven recorded statements from the cross. These statements and the references for them are given next and are in chronological order:
>
> 1. **"Father, forgive them; for they know not what they do."** Luke 23:34.
> 2. **"Today shalt thou be with me in paradise."** Luke 23:43.
> 3. **"Woman, behold thy son!" Behold thy mother!"** John 19:26-27.
> 4. **"My God, my God, why hast thou forsaken me?"** Matthew 27:46.
> 5. **"I thirst."** John 19:28.
> 6. **"It is finished."** John 19:30.
> 7. **"Father, into thy hands I commend my spirit."** Luke 23:46.

35 And the people stood beholding *[staring]*. And the rulers *[religious leaders of the Jews]* also with them derided *[mocked]* him, saying, He saved others; let him save himself, if he be Christ, the chosen of God *[the Messiah]*.

36 And the soldiers also mocked him, coming to him, and offering him vinegar,

37 And saying, If thou be the king of the Jews, save thyself.

38 And a superscription also was written over him *[a sign was put above Him on the cross]* in letters of Greek, and Latin, and Hebrew, THIS IS THE KING OF THE JEWS.

39 And one of the malefactors *[thieves]* which were hanged *[being crucified]* railed on him *[angrily yelled insults at Him]*, saying, If thou be Christ, save thyself and us.

40 But the other *[thief]* answering *[responding]* rebuked him *[scolded the other thief]*, saying, Dost not thou fear God, seeing thou art in the same condemnation?

41 And we indeed justly; for we receive the due reward of our deeds *[we are getting what we deserve]*: but this man hath done nothing amiss *[wrong]*.

42 And he said unto Jesus, Lord, remember me when thou comest into thy kingdom.

43 And Jesus said unto him, Verily I say unto thee, To day shalt thou be with me in paradise.

> It is a common belief that the thief on the cross went to paradise. This is not the case. Our Bible Dictionary explains this. It says: "The Bible rendering is incorrect. The statement would more accurately read, 'Today shalt thou be with me in the world of spirits' since the thief was not ready for paradise." See Bible Dictionary, under "Paradise." No doubt, with his humble attitude, this thief accepted the gospel as taught by missionaries in Spirit Prison.

44 And it was about the sixth hour *[about noon]*, and there was a darkness over all the earth until the ninth hour *[about 3 P.M.]*.

> In the Jewish time system, the "sixth hour" would be about noon, the "ninth hour" would be

about 3 p.m. in our time system. We understand that Jesus was nailed onto the cross at the "third hour" which would be about 9 a.m.

45 And the sun was darkened, and the veil of the temple was rent in the midst [*torn in two*].

46 And when Jesus had cried with a loud voice, he said, Father, into thy hands I commend my spirit: and having said thus, he gave up the ghost [*left His body*].

47 Now when the centurion [*Roman soldier in command of one hundred soldiers*] saw what was done, he glorified God, saying, Certainly this was a righteous man.

It apparently startled the Centurion that Jesus had so much strength that He could speak so loudly. Usually it took two to three days for victims of crucifixion to die, and near the end they were so exhausted they would not be able to speak loudly at all. To this soldier, experienced at crucifying people, it was as if Jesus had voluntarily left His body when He so chose, which indeed he did—see John 10:18!

48 And all the people that came together to that sight, beholding the things which were done, smote their breasts, and returned.

Pounding on one's chest, "smote their breasts" in verse 48 above, was a cultural way of expressing deep fear and a feeling of impending doom, destruction, etc. It had gotten extremely dark and foreboding over the last three hours. And that, plus Christ's loud voice when He left His body must have terrified them. Thus they beat their chests, with a feeling of doom hanging over them as they left for home.

49 And all his acquaintance, and the women that followed him from Galilee, stood afar off, beholding these things [*watching these things*].

Joseph of Aramathaea Donates the Tomb

50 And, behold, there was a man named Joseph, a counsellor [*a member of the council of the Jews*]; and he was a good man, and a just:

Luke 23, footnote 50a in your Bible, indicates that Joseph of Aramathaea was, in effect, a senator in the leading governing council of the Jews. He was a good man. This is a pleasant reminder that there were good men also among the leaders of the Jews at the time of Christ.

51 (The same had not consented to the counsel and deed of them;) [*Joseph had opposed the decision of the Jewish religious leaders to execute Jesus*] he was of Arimathæa, a city of the Jews: who also himself waited for the kingdom of God [*was a faithful, righteous man*].

52 This man went unto Pilate, and begged [*requested*] the body of Jesus.

53 And he took it down [*from the cross*], and wrapped it in linen, and laid it in a sepulchre [*a tomb*] that was hewn [*cut*] in stone, wherein never man before was laid.

54 And that day was the preparation, and the sabbath drew on. [*It was getting very late on Friday and the Sabbath was about to begin. The Jewish Sabbath was held on Saturday.*]

55 And the women also, which came with him [*Jesus*] from Galilee, followed after [*followed Joseph of Arimathaea*], and beheld [*saw*] the sepulchre, and how his body was laid.

56 And they returned, and prepared spices and ointments; and rested the sabbath day according to the commandment. [*It was too late for them to anoint Jesus' body with spices and ointments, as was customary, because such work was forbidden on the Sabbath. So they went home and kept the Sabbath holy, and planned on coming back to the tomb early Sunday morning to finish final preparations for the Savior's proper burial.*]

LUKE 24

THIS CHAPTER IS the account of the Savior's resurrection. Luke gives us quite a few details, which are not included in the accounts of Matthew and Mark. It is Sunday morning, and one of the most glorious days on earth ever recorded.

The Resurrection

1 NOW upon the first day of the week [*Sunday*], very early in the morning, they [*the women named in verse 10, below*] came unto the sepulchre [*tomb*], bringing the spices which they had prepared, and certain others with them.

2 And they found the stone rolled away from the sepulchre.

3 And they entered in, and found not the body of the Lord Jesus.

4 And it came to pass, as they were much perplexed thereabout [*they were very concerned about this*], behold, two men [*angels*] stood by them in shining garments:

5 And as they [*the women*] were afraid, and bowed down their faces to the earth, they [*the angels*] said unto them, Why seek ye the living among the dead?

JST LUKE 24:2–4

2 And they found the stone rolled away from the sepulcher, and two angels standing by it in shining garments.

3 And they entered into the sepulcher, and not finding the body of the Lord Jesus, they were much perplexed thereabout;

4 And were affrighted, and bowed down their faces to the earth. But behold the angels said unto them, Why seek ye the living among the dead?

Watch now as the two angels gently remind these faithful women about the Savior's prophecies of His crucifixion and resurrection to them. Imagine the look on these women's faces as they remembered and realization dawned that the Master was alive!

6 He is not here, but is risen [*has been resurrected*]: remember how he spake unto you when he was yet in Galilee,

7 Saying, The Son of man [*The Son of God*] must be delivered into the hands of sinful men, and be crucified, and the third day rise again.

8 And they remembered his words,

9 And returned from the sepulchre, and told all these things unto the eleven [*the eleven Apostles—Judas was no longer among them*], and to all the rest.

10 It was Mary Magdalene, and Joanna, and Mary the mother of James, and other women that were with them, which told these things unto the apostles.

11 And their words seemed to them [*the Apostles*] as idle tales [*nonsense*], and they believed them not.

12 Then arose Peter, and ran unto the sepulchre; and stooping down, he beheld the linen clothes [*Jesus' burial clothing*] laid by themselves, and departed, wondering in himself at that which was come to pass [*wondering what had happened*].

Two Traveling on the Road to Emmaus

13 And, behold, two of them [*two of Christ's disciples, not Apostles*] went that same day to a village called Emmaus, which was from Jerusalem about threescore furlongs [*about 7 miles from Jerusalem*].

14 And they talked together of all these things which had happened.

15 And it came to pass, that, while they communed together and reasoned, Jesus himself drew near, and went [*started walking*] with them.

16 But their eyes were holden that they should not know him. [*Jesus kept them from recognizing Him yet.*]

17 And he said unto them, What manner of communications are these that ye have one to another, as ye walk, and are sad [*what are you talking about that makes you so sad*]?

18 And the one of them, whose name was Cleopas, answering said unto him, Art thou only a stranger in Jerusalem, and hast not known

the things which are come to pass therein these days? *[You must have just arrived or You would know the tragic things which have happened here in recent days.]*

19 And he said unto them, What things? And they said unto him, Concerning Jesus of Nazareth, which *[who]* was a prophet mighty in deed and word *[powerful in actions and teaching]* before God and all the people:

20 And how the chief priests and our rulers delivered him *[turned Him over]* to be condemned to death, and have crucified him.

As these two disciples of the Master continue chatting with this Stranger who has joined them, you can feel their disappointment as they express to Him their dashed hopes.

21 But we trusted that it had been he which should have redeemed Israel *[we were hoping that He would turn out to be the promised Messiah who would free us from our enemies]*: and beside all this, to day is the third day since these things were done *[and besides that, it has been three days now since He was crucified]*.

We see from verses 22–24, next, that these two disciples were among "all the rest" in verse 9, above, when the breathless women excitedly told the eleven Apostles what the angels had told them.

22 Yea, and certain women also of our company *[of our group of followers of Jesus]* made us astonished *[told us an amazing story]*, which were early at the sepulchre *[who went to the tomb early this morning]*;

23 And when they found not his body, they came, saying, that they had also seen a vision of angels, which *[who]* said that he was alive.

24 And certain of them *[Peter and John—see John 20:2–8]* which were with us went to the sepulchre, and found it even so as the women had said *[found the tomb empty, just like the women said]*: but him they saw not *[but Peter and John didn't see Christ]*.

The implication here is that since Peter and John didn't see Jesus, and the women's account couldn't be trusted, because of the emotional state they were in, the whole thing about Jesus has turned out to be a big disappointment for these two disciples on the road to Emmaus.

Watch now as the resurrected Christ teaches a firm lesson on faith, reminding these disappointed disciples of the numerous prophecies in the Old Testament which fit what has just happened.

25 Then he said unto them, O fools, and slow of heart to believe all that the prophets *[such as Isaiah and Jeremiah]* have spoken:

26 Ought not Christ to have suffered these things, and to enter into his glory? *[In other words, why is it so hard to believe that Jesus was the Christ, that He suffered, died, was resurrected, and has entered into His glory in heaven?]*

27 And beginning at Moses and all the prophets *[starting with the writings of Moses (Genesis, Exodus, Leviticus, Numbers, and Deuteronomy) and continuing with the other Old Testament prophets]*, he expounded unto them *[taught them]* in all the scriptures the things concerning himself *[prophesying of Him]*.

28 And they drew nigh *[near]* unto the village *[Emmaus]*, whither they went *[which was their destination]*: and he made as though he would have gone further *[indicated that He was going to go farther]*.

29 But they constrained him *[begged Him]*, saying, Abide *[stay]* with us: for it is toward evening, and the day is far spent. And he went in to tarry *[stay]* with them.

30 And it came to pass, as he sat at meat *[supper]* with them, he took bread, and blessed it, and brake, and gave to them.

31 And their eyes were opened, and they knew him; and he vanished out of their sight.

32 And they said one to another, Did not our heart burn within us, while he talked with us by the way *[along the way]*, and while he opened *[explained]* to us the scriptures?

AND THEY FOUND
THE STONE ROLLED
AWAY FROM THE
SEPULCHRE.

LUKE 24:2

33 And they rose up the same hour, and returned to Jerusalem, and found the eleven gathered together, and them [*other members*] that were with them,

34 Saying, The Lord is risen indeed, and hath appeared to Simon [*Peter*].

35 And they [*the two disciples to whom Jesus had appeared on the way to Emmaus*] told what things were done in the way [*as they walked along the road*], and how he was known of them in breaking of bread [*how they finally recognized Jesus when He served them supper*].

The Resurrected Christ Appears to the Eleven and Others in the Room

36 And as they thus spake, Jesus himself stood in the midst of them, and saith unto them, Peace be unto you.

37 But they were terrified and affrighted [*frightened*], and supposed that they had seen a spirit [*thought they were seeing a ghost*].

38 And he said unto them, Why are ye troubled? and why do thoughts arise in your hearts?

39 Behold [*look at*] my hands and my feet, that it is I myself: handle [*feel*] me, and see; for a spirit hath not flesh and bones, as ye see me have.

40 And when he had thus spoken, he shewed [*showed*] them his hands and his feet.

A major doctrine is taught in verses 39–40, above, namely that the Savior now has a resurrected body of flesh and bone. The same is true of the Father. The Doctrine and Covenants confirms this.

D&C 130:22

22 The Father has a body of flesh and bones as tangible as man's; the Son also; but the Holy Ghost has not a body of flesh and bones, but is a personage of Spirit. Were it not so, the Holy Ghost could not dwell in us.

41 And while they yet believed not for joy [*they were so happy they could hardly believe what was happening*], and wondered [*marvelled*], he said unto them, Have ye here any meat [*do you have any food*]?

42 And they gave him a piece of a broiled fish, and of an honeycomb.

43 And he took it, and did eat before them [*before their eyes*].

44 And he said unto them, These are [*this is what I meant by*] the words which I spake unto you, while I was yet with you, that all things must be fulfilled, which were written in the law of Moses, and in the prophets, and in the psalms [*in other words, the Old Testament*], concerning me.

The Savior now teaches a vital summary of His mission and Atonement.

45 Then opened he their understanding, that they might understand the scriptures, [*then He taught them.*]

46 And said unto them, Thus it is written, and thus it behoved Christ to suffer [*Christ had to suffer*], and to rise from the dead the third day:

47 And that repentance and remission of sins should be preached in his name among all nations, beginning at Jerusalem. [*The Atonement had to be accomplished in order for repentance and remission of sins to be made available to all people, beginning at Jerusalem.*]

48 And ye are witnesses of these things.

49 And, behold, I send the promise of my Father upon you: but tarry ye [*wait*] in the city of Jerusalem, until ye be endued with [*clothed with, endowed with*] power from on high.

50 And he led them out as far as to Bethany [*about one to two miles from Jerusalem*], and he lifted up his hands, and blessed them.

The Savior's Ascension into Heaven

51 And it came to pass, while he blessed them, he was parted [*separated*] from them, and carried up into heaven.

52 And they worshipped him, and returned to Jerusalem with great joy:

53 And were continually in the temple, praising and blessing God [*expressing gratitude to God*]. Amen.

WOMAN AT THE WELL, by Robert T. Barrett

THE GOSPEL ACCORDING TO ST JOHN

JOHN WAS ONE of the original twelve Apostles. Before that, he was a disciple of John the Baptist, along with Peter, James, and Andrew. He was a fisherman by trade, in partnership with Peter, Andrew (Peter's brother) and James (John's brother).

Whereas the gospels of Matthew, Mark, and Luke cover essentially the same material, presenting a narrative of the Savior's mortal life and teachings, the Gospel of John emphasizes the Savior's role in the overall plan of salvation and presents many more doctrines taught by Him. Matthew, Mark, and Luke are sometimes referred to as "the Synoptic Gospels," meaning that they are "from the same view," in other words, they are similar.

According to D&C 7:3, John was translated (has not died yet) and will continue to preach the gospel on earth and help with the gathering of Israel until the Second Coming. In 1831, the Prophet Joseph Smith said that, at that time, John was working with the lost ten tribes, preparing them for their return. See *History of the Church*, Vol. 1, p. 176. John is the author of four other books in the Bible, 1 John, 2 John, 3 John and the book of Revelation.

JOHN 1

THIS CHAPTER CONTAINS John's introduction to the Savior's mortal life and mission. He introduces Him as the Creator of the world and gives many details about His work. He then tells us about the baptism of Jesus by John the Baptist and the calling of several men who would later become Apostles.

Joseph Smith made many additions and clarifications in verses 1–34. The JST (Joseph Smith Translation of the Bible) contains these changes. You can read JST John 1:1–34, in its entirety, in the back of your LDS Bible in the section titled, "Joseph Smith translation." We will include many of these JST changes as we study chapter 1.

By the way, just by glancing at the large number of footnotes included in your LDS Bible for John, chapter 1, you can tell that John's account contains a large number of doctrines.

1 IN the beginning was the Word, and the Word was with God, and the Word was God.

JST JOHN 1:1

1 In the beginning was the gospel preached through the Son. And the gospel was the word, and the word was with the Son, and the Son was with God, and the Son was of God.

2 The same [*Christ*] was in the beginning with God [*the Father*].

3 All things were made by him; and without him was not any thing made that was made. [*Christ is the Creator.*]

4 In him was life; and the life was the light of men.

JST JOHN 1:4

4 In him was the gospel, and the gospel was the life, and the life was the light of men;

5 And the light shineth in darkness [*in the spiritually dark world*]; and the darkness comprehended it not.

JST JOHN 1:5

5 And the light shineth in the world, and the world perceiveth it not.

6 There was a man sent from God, whose name was John [*John the Baptist*].

7 The same came for a witness, to bear witness of the Light, that all men through him might believe.

JST JOHN 1:7

7 The same came into the world for a witness, to bear witness of the light, to bear record of the gospel through the Son, unto all, that through him men might believe.

8 He [*John the Baptist*] was not that Light, but was sent to bear witness of that Light.

9 That was the true Light [*Christ*], which lighteth every man that cometh into the world [*see D&C 93:2*].

The "Light of Christ" is often referred to as the "conscience" which is given to every person born into this world. This is true, and as a result, all people have a basic God-given ability to tell right from wrong, and thus are accountable to God for their behaviors. But the Light of Christ is much more than a conscience. A major purpose of it is to lead people to the true gospel, where they can be baptized and receive the Holy Ghost, which is a far more powerful "light."

10 He was in the world, and the world was made by him, and the world knew him not.

JST JOHN 1:10

10 Even the Son of God. He who was in the world, and the world was made by him, and the world knew him not.

11 He came unto his own, and his own received him not [*His own people rejected Him*].

12 But as many as received him, to them gave he power to become the sons of God [*power to become exalted; see D&C 76:24*], even to them that believe on his name:

JST JOHN 1:12

12 But as many as received him, to them gave he power to become the sons of God; only to them who believe on his name.

13 Which were born, not of blood, nor of the will of the flesh, nor of the will of man, but of God. [*In other words, Jesus was literally the Son of God, not just a highly successful man born to mortal parents.*]

JST JOHN 1:13

13 He was born, not of blood, nor of the will of the flesh, nor of the will of man, but of God.

14 And the Word [*Christ*] was made flesh [*received a mortal body*], and dwelt among us, (and we beheld his glory, the glory as of the only begotten of the Father,) full of grace [*ability to help us*] and truth.

Sometimes confusion arises between Christ's being the "Only Begotten of the Father" and our being spirit sons and daughters of God. In other words, we are also begotten of the Father. So, how can we be begotten of the Father if Christ is the "Only Begotten" of the Father? The answer is simple. In premortality, all of us, including Jesus, were begotten and born as spirit children of our heavenly parents (see Proclamation on the Family, September 23, 1995, second paragraph). But Jesus was the only mortal whose father was Heavenly Father. Thus, Jesus is the "Only Begotten of the Father (as a mortal), and that is what the phrase "Only Begotten" means, wherever we find it in the scriptures and in the teachings of the leaders of the Church.

15 John [*the Baptist*] bare [*bore*] witness of him [*Christ*], and cried [*preached*], saying, This was he of whom I spake, He that cometh after me is preferred before me [*is higher in authority than I am*]: for he was before me.

JST JOHN 1:15

15 John bear witness of him, and cried, saying, This is he of whom I spake; He who cometh after me, is preferred before me; for he was before me.

16 And of his fulness have all we received, and grace for grace. [*We have been taught the fulness or the complete gospel by Christ, thus are in a position to proceed step by step until we gain exaltation.*]

JST JOHN 1:16

16 For in the beginning was the Word, even the Son, who is made flesh, and sent unto us by the will of the Father. And as many as believe on his name shall receive of his fullness. And of his fullness have all we received, even immortality and eternal life, through his grace.

17 For the law was given by Moses, but grace and truth came by Jesus Christ.

JST JOHN 1:17-18

17 For the law was given through Moses, but life and truth came through Jesus Christ.

18 For the law was after a carnal commandment, to the administration of death; but the gospel was after the power of an endless life, through Jesus Christ, the Only Begotten Son, who is in the bosom of the Father.

Verse 17 and JST verse 18, above, are basically saying that the Law of Moses was a schoolmaster law to help prepare the Israelites for the higher law which the Savior restored to earth. No one could be saved in celestial exaltation through the Law of Moses. It is only through the full gospel, with all covenants and ordinances, that we can be exalted. By the way, this would not be a particularly popular thing for John the Baptist to say, because people of his day would look upon it as a "put down" for Moses, whom they considered to be their most important prophet.

18 No man hath seen God at any time; the only begotten Son, which is in the bosom of the Father, he hath declared him.

JST JOHN 1:19

19 And no man hath seen God at any time, except he hath borne record of the Son; for except it is through him no man can be saved.

Many Christians use verse 18 above, as it stands in the Bible, to argue that Joseph Smith could not have seen Heavenly Father. Most of them won't accept the JST change, which clears up the matter. Therefore, it is sometimes helpful to invite them to turn to Acts 7:55-56, and show them that Stephen saw both the Father and the Son.

19 And this is the record of John [*the Baptist*], when the Jews sent priests and Levites [*religious leaders of the Jews*] from Jerusalem to ask him, Who art thou?

20 And he [*John the Baptist*] confessed, and denied not; but confessed, I am not the Christ.

JST JOHN 1:21

21 And he confessed, and denied not that he was Elias; but confessed, saying; I am not the Christ.

The word "Elias," among other definitions, means "one who prepares the way." See Bible Dictionary, under "Elias." Obviously, the Jewish religious leaders were familiar with prophecies that said that an Elias would prepare the way before the Messiah (example: Isaiah 40:3), and thus, when they heard all the talk about John the Baptist, they sent some of their men to ask him some questions.

21 And they asked him, What then? Art thou Elias? And he saith, I am not. Art thou that prophet? And he answered, No.

JST JOHN 1:22

22 And they asked him, saying; How then art thou Elias? And he said, I am not that Elias who was to restore all things. And they asked him, saying, Art thou that prophet? And he answered, No.

Verse 21 above may need a bit of clarification. First of all, as you can see in the JST, Joseph Smith added "I am not that Elias who was to restore all things." This is very helpful, because it lets us know that we are dealing with two different definitions of "Elias" in these verses. One Elias is a "preparer." The other "Elias" is a "restorer." John the Baptist is the "preparer" while Jesus is the "restorer." See Bible Dictionary, under "Elias." So, what John the Baptist is emphatically saying to the questioners in verse 21 is "No, I am not the Messiah! Rather, I am the Elias who is preparing the way for Him."

22 Then said they [*the messengers sent from the Jewish religious leaders in verse 19 above*] unto him, Who art thou? that we may give an answer to them that sent us. What sayest thou of thyself [*tell us about you*]?

23 He said, I am the voice of one crying in the wilderness, Make straight the way of the Lord, as said the prophet Esaias [*Isaiah; see Isaiah 40:3*].

24 And they which were sent were of the Pharisees. [*Pharisees were another group of religious leaders among the Jews.*]

25 And they asked him, and said unto him, Why baptizest thou then, if thou be not that Christ, nor Elias neither that prophet? [*In other words, why are you baptizing if you are not the prophesied Messiah?*]

JST John 1:26

26 And they asked him, and said unto him, Why baptizest thou then, if thou be not the Christ, nor Elias who was to restore all things, neither that prophet?

26 John answered them, saying, I baptize with water: but there standeth one among you, whom ye know not; [*referring to Jesus, who is just preparing to begin His mortal ministry.*]

27 He it is, who coming after me is preferred before me [*is higher in authority than I*], whose shoe's latchet [*sandal buckle*] I am not worthy to unloose.

JST John 1:28

28 He it is of whom I bear record. He is that prophet, even Elias, who, coming after me, is preferred before me, whose shoe's latchet I am not worthy to unloose, or whose place I am not able to fill; for he shall baptize, not only with water, but with fire, and with the Holy Ghost.

28 These things were done in Bethabara beyond Jordan, where John was baptizing.

Jesus Is Baptized

29 The next day John seeth Jesus coming unto him, and saith, Behold the Lamb of God, which taketh away the sin of the world. [*John the Baptist bears witness of Jesus to the crowd around him.*]

30 This is he of whom I said, After me cometh a man which is preferred before me: for he was before me.

31 And I knew him not: but that he should be made manifest to Israel, therefore [*this is the reason, in answer to the question in verse 25*] am I come baptizing with water.

JST John 1:30

30 And John bare record of him unto the people, saying, This is he of whom I said; After me cometh a man who is preferred before me; for he was before me, and I knew him, and that he should be made manifest to Israel; therefore am I come baptizing with water.

Look carefully at JST John 1:30, quoted above and compare it with John 1:31, above. Did you see the difference? It is a very important change. The Bible says, "I knew him not," which would indicate that John the Baptist did not recognize Jesus. However, the JST gives the true account and says, "I knew him," indicating that John the Baptist did know and recognize Jesus. See also verse 33 and compare with JST, verse 32. (Remember, as explained previously many times in this study guide, the JST verse numbers are sometimes different than the equivalent verses in the Bible because of corrections to the Bible text.)

32 And John bare record, saying, I saw the Spirit descending from heaven like a dove, and it abode upon him.

JST John 1:31

31 And John bare record, saying; When he was baptized of me, I saw the Spirit descending from heaven like a dove, and it abode upon him.

Sometimes people ask whether or not the Holy Ghost, on occasions, changes into a dove. The answer is "No." The Prophet Joseph Smith taught:

"The Holy Ghost is a personage, and is in the form of a personage. It does not confine itself to the *form* of the dove, but in *sign* of the dove. The Holy Ghost cannot be transformed into a dove; but the sign of a dove was given to John to signify the truth of the deed, as the dove is an emblem or token of truth and innocence." (*Teachings of the Prophet Joseph Smith*, 1976, pp. 275–276.)

33 And I knew him not: but he that sent me to baptize with water, the same said unto me, Upon whom thou shalt see the Spirit descending, and remaining on him, the same is he which baptizeth with the Holy Ghost.

JST John 1:32

32 And I knew him; for he who sent me to baptize with water, the same said unto me; Upon whom thou shalt see the Spirit descending, and remaining on him, the same is he who baptizeth with the Holy Ghost.

34 And I saw, and bare record that this is the Son of God.

Although John already was acquainted with Jesus (see JST in verses 31 and 32 above), the Holy Ghost bore strong witness of the Savior to John at the time he baptized Christ.

35 Again the next day after John stood, and two of his disciples [*the day after he baptized Jesus, John the Baptist was standing with two of his own followers*];

36 And looking upon Jesus as he walked [*and seeing Jesus as He walked by*], he [*John*] saith, Behold [*look!*] the Lamb of God!

37 And the two disciples [*John's followers*] heard him [*John the Baptist*] speak, and they followed Jesus.

38 Then Jesus turned, and saw them following, and saith unto them, What seek ye [*what can I do for you*]? They said unto him, Rabbi, (which is to say, being interpreted, Master,) where dwellest thou [*where do you live*]?

It may be that the two disciples of John the Baptist who left John and began following Jesus were caught a bit off guard when the Master turned and asked what He could do for them (verse 38 above). Perhaps, at a loss for something to say, they quickly stammered, "Uh, where do You live?" Of course we don't know if this was the case, but it brings a bit of a smile to our faces when we consider this as a possibility.

Whatever the case, He was very kind to them and invited them to "Come and see" (verse 39, next).

39 He saith unto them, Come and see. They came and saw where he dwelt [*lived*], and abode [*stayed*] with him that day: for it was about the tenth hour [*about 4 P.M.*].

40 One of the two which heard John speak, and followed him, was Andrew, Simon Peter's brother. [*Andrew will become one of the Savior's original twelve Apostles, as will Peter.*]

JST JOHN 1:40

40 One of the two who heard John, and followed Jesus, was Andrew, Simon Peter's brother.

41 He first findeth his own brother Simon [*Peter*], and saith unto him, We have found the Messias [*the promised Messiah*], which is, being interpreted, the Christ [*"the Anointed One"*].

Anointing is a very significant thing in the Bible. It means "being prepared for" a future event or blessing. David was "anointed" to become king some years before he became king. When we administer to the sick, we "anoint" him or her first, in preparation for the actual blessing. Christ was the "Anointed One," meaning he was prepared in advance to actually perform the Atonement when the time was right for his mortal mission.

42 And he [*Andrew*] brought him [*Peter*] to Jesus. And when Jesus beheld [*saw*] him, he said, Thou art Simon the son of Jona: thou shalt be called Cephas, which is by interpretation, A stone.

JST JOHN 1:42

42 And he brought him to Jesus. And when Jesus beheld him, he said, Thou art Simon, the son of Jona, thou shalt be called Cephas, which is, by interpretation, a seer, or a stone. And they were fishermen. And they straightway left all, and followed Jesus.

It is interesting to watch the Master at work, building Peter's self-image and confidence. Ima-gine Peter saying to himself afterward, "Wow! He called me a rock. That means He thinks I am a 'rock solid' person. Well, I'll just make sure I am!"

43 The day following Jesus would [*decided to*] go forth into Galilee, and findeth Philip, and saith unto him, Follow me.

JOHN

44 Now Philip was of Bethsaida, the city of Andrew and Peter [*the same city where Andrew and Peter lived*].

JST JOHN 1:44

44 Now Philip was at Bethsaida, the city of Andrew and Peter.

45 Philip findeth Nathanael, and saith unto him, We have found him [*the Messiah*], of whom Moses in the law [*the first five books of the Old Testament*], and the prophets [*Old Testament prophets such as Isaiah and Jeremiah*], did write, Jesus of Nazareth, the son of Joseph [*the carpenter of Nazareth*].

When Nathanael asks his question, in verse 46, he gets a very important answer which can apply to all of us.

46 And Nathanael said unto him, Can there any good thing come out of Nazareth? Philip saith unto him, Come and see.

47 Jesus saw Nathanael coming to him, and saith of him, Behold an Israelite indeed, in whom is no guile!

48 Nathanael saith unto him, Whence knowest thou me [*how do You know me*]? Jesus answered and said unto him, Before that Philip called thee, when thou wast under the fig tree, I saw thee [*I saw you sitting under a fig tree before Philip talked to you*].

49 Nathanael answered and saith unto him, Rabbi, thou art the Son of God; thou art the King of Israel.

50 Jesus answered and said unto him, Because I said unto thee, I saw thee under the fig tree, believest thou? thou shalt see greater things than these.

51 And he saith unto him, Verily, verily, I say unto you, Hereafter ye shall see heaven open, and the angels of God ascending and descending upon the Son of man [*Christ; the JST corrects this to read "Son of Man"*].

Note: Jesus is often referred to as "the Son of man" in the New Testament. Moses 6:57 in the Pearl of Great Price teaches us what it means and how it should be written. It says, "For, in the language of Adam, Man of Holiness is his name [Heavenly Father's name], and the name of his Only Begotten is the Son of Man, even Jesus Christ." Therefore, the full name of the Savior, in the language of Adam, would be "Son of Man of Holiness." For whatever reason, the printers of the King James Bible neglected to capitalize "Man" and thus printed it "Son of man."

JOHN 2

NEXT COMES ONE of the most famous miracles performed by the Master. It is the turning of water into wine. After telling us of this miracle, John will speak of the cleansing of the temple in Jerusalem, as Jesus begins His three-year ministry. He will cleanse the temple again during the last week of His mortal life (see Matthew 21:12–16 and Luke 19:45–46) after His triumphal entry into Jerusalem. In this chapter the Savior will prophesy His death and resurrection.

The JST will add very important items to the account of this first recorded miracle of the Savior (see verse 11), as He turns water to wine. Pay special attention to the difference in meaning between verse 4 and JST verse 4.

The First Recorded Miracle

1 AND the third day there was a marriage in Cana of Galilee; and the mother of Jesus was there:

JST JOHN 2:1

1 And on the third day of the week, there was a marriage in Cana of Galilee; and the mother of Jesus was there.

2 And both Jesus was called [*invited*], and his disciples, to the marriage.

Some have wondered if this could be Jesus' marriage. Several factors combine to suggest that this would not be the case. For one thing, in the culture of the day, the marriage would be held at the groom's home town. If it were Jesus' wedding, it would have been held in Nazareth. Another thing against this notion is that Jesus and His disciples were invited to attend (verse 2). This would be a bit strange if He were the groom. Yet another factor is that the master of ceremonies of the festivities called the groom over to talk to him (verse 9), and there is no indication that this was Jesus. And finally, if it were Christ's wedding, one would expect the Gospel writers to mention it.

It does appear from the next verses that Mary, Jesus' mother, had a role in helping to host the guests at this wedding celebration. Perhaps she was a good friend of the family. Whatever the case, she knew who her Son was, and when they ran out of wine, she requested His help.

3 And when they wanted wine [*when they ran out of wine*], the mother of Jesus saith unto him, They have no wine.

4 Jesus saith unto her, Woman, what have I to do with thee? mine hour is not yet come [*I have time to help*].

JST JOHN 2:4

4 Jesus said unto her, Woman, what wilt thou have me to do for thee? that will I do; for mine hour is not yet come.

We understand that the phrase, "mine hour is not yet come," in verse 4, above, is a way of saying, in effect, that Jesus had not yet begun His formal mission. Verse 13 marks the beginning of His formal three-year mortal mission. It is also helpful to note that the word "woman" was a term of high respect in the days of Jesus.

5 His mother saith unto the servants, Whatsoever he saith unto you, do it [*do whatever He says*].

6 And there were set there six waterpots of stone, after the manner of the purifying of the Jews, containing two or three firkins apiece.

When we do the math, we see that this was apparently a rather large wedding celebration. Wedding feasts customarily lasted the better part of a week and there were apparently more guests than expected at this one. A "firkin" was a little more than 8 gallons. See Bible Dictionary, under "Weights and Measures," then under "bath" and "firkin." So, there were six containers, with a capacity of 16 to 24 gallons each. This would make a total of about 96 to 144 gallons of water which Jesus turned into wine. Thus, we sense that this was a rather unexpectedly large group, which apparently caught the host off guard when it came to having sufficient wine for the festivities.

Imagine the looks on the servants' faces as they carried out the Master's instructions, next.

7 Jesus saith unto them [*the servants*], Fill the waterpots with water. And they filled them up to the brim.

8 And he saith unto them, Draw out now, and bear unto the governor of the feast [*take wine out of the containers and take some to the master of ceremonies*]. And they bare it.

JST John 2:8

8 And he said, Draw out now, and bear unto the governor of the feast. And they bare unto him.

9 When the ruler [*host, master of ceremonies*] of the feast had tasted the water that was made wine, and knew not whence it was [*didn't know where it came from*]: (but the servants which drew the water knew;) the governor of the feast called the bridegroom [*the groom*],

10 And saith unto him, Every man at the beginning [*of the celebration*] doth set forth good wine; and when men have well drunk, then that which is worse: but thou hast kept the good wine until now.

Since wine was expensive, the common practice was to set good wine out at the beginning of the feast, then when the guests had drunk enough to become less discriminating, less expensive wine was served to save on expenses. The master of ceremonies was surprised that the groom was serving the best wine at this point of the feast.

11 This beginning of miracles [*the first miracle*] did Jesus in Cana of Galilee, and manifested forth his glory; and his disciples believed on him. [*This was a faith-promoting miracle for His disciples.*]

JST John 2:11

11 This beginning of miracles did Jesus in Cana of Galilee, and manifested forth his glory; and the faith of his disciples was strengthened in him.

12 After this he went down to Capernaum, he, and his mother, and his brethren [*probably His half-brothers, children of Joseph and Mary; see John 2:12, footnote a in your LDS Bible*], and his disciples: and they continued [*stayed*] there not many days.

The Beginning of the Savior's Formal Three-Year Public Mortal Mission

13 And the Jews' passover was at hand, and Jesus went up to Jerusalem,

This marks the beginning of the Savior's formal three-year public ministry. The Feast of the Passover was celebrated in the springtime at about the same time as we celebrate Easter. It brought large numbers of Jews from near and far to Jerusalem to join in the worship and celebration. It commemorated the destroying angel's passing over the houses of the children of Israel in Egypt, when the firstborn of the Egyptians were killed. The Israelites in Egypt at the time were instructed by Moses to sacrifice a lamb without blemish and to put blood from the lamb which was sacrificed on the doorposts of their houses. See Bible Dictionary, under "Feasts."

Thus, through the blood of a lamb, the Israelites were protected from the anguish and punishment brought to the Egyptians by the destroying angel. The symbolism is clear. It is by the "blood of the Lamb" (the sacrifice of the Savior) that we are saved, after all we can do (2 Nephi 25:23). This is the first Passover attended by Jesus after he began His three-year ministry. Three years from now, at the time of Passover in Jerusalem, the "Lamb of God," Christ, will present Himself to be sacrificed that we might be saved.

The First Cleansing of the Temple

14 And found in the temple [*the outer courtyard or "temple grounds"*] those that sold oxen and sheep and doves, and the changers of money sitting:

Because Jews came from all over, including many other countries to worship at the temple in Jerusalem, it had become big business for merchants to sell sacrificial animals and to exchange foreign money for temple coin. It was a wild, boisterous scene of animal sounds, merchants yelling at patrons to buy from them, etc., anything but reverent and worshipful, which met the Savior's eyes as He approached the temple. He will cleanse the temple again in three years during the last week of His life.

15 And when he had made a scourge [*whip*] of small cords, he drove them all out of the temple, and the sheep, and the oxen; and poured out the changers' money, and overthrew the tables;

16 And said unto them that sold doves, Take these things hence [*get these things out of here*]; make not my Father's house an house of merchandise [*a common market place*].

17 And his disciples remembered that it was written [*in the scriptures*], The zeal of thine house hath eaten me up [*Psalm 69:9*].

18 Then answered the Jews [*the Jewish religious leaders respond-ed*] and said unto him, What sign shewest thou unto us, seeing that thou doest these things [*where did You get authority to cleanse the temple*]?

19 Jesus answered and said unto them, Destroy this temple, and in three days I will raise it up. [*In other words, Jesus is telling them that He is the Messiah. That is where He gets His authority. When they kill Him, as prophesied, He will resurrect in three days.*]

20 Then said the Jews [*who missed the point completely*], Forty and six years was this temple in building [*it took forty six years to build this temple*], and wilt thou rear it up [*rebuild it*] in three days?

21 But he spake of the temple of his body.

John indicates in verse 22, next, that when the disciples first heard this prophecy from Him that He would be resurrected three days after His death, it did not sink in. But when He was actually resurrected, they remembered back upon this prophecy and that He had told them it would take place.

22 When therefore he was risen from the dead [*resurrected*], his disciples remembered [*recalled*] that he had said this unto them; and they believed the scripture, and the word which Jesus had said.

23 Now when he was in Jerusalem at the passover, in the feast day [*on Thursday, the day of the actual Passover feast*], many believed in his name, when they saw the miracles which he did.

24 But Jesus did not commit himself unto them [*did not let down His guard*], because he knew all men,

JST JOHN 2:24

24 But Jesus did not commit himself unto them, because he knew all things,

25 And needed not that any should testify of man: for he knew what was in man [*He knew their thoughts*].

JOHN 3

MANY MEMBERS OF the Church are extra familiar with this chapter because of verse 3, which is much quoted in teaching the necessity of baptism.

1 THERE was a man of the Pharisees [*who was a Pharisee*], named Nicodemus, a ruler [*leader*] of the Jews:

The Pharisees were prominent religious leaders among the Jews. Jesus' popularity has begun to threaten their position of power and control over the Jews. They will play a prominent role in getting Him crucified. However, Nicodemus is a good man and will oppose the majority of the Pharisees. He now sincerely seeks Jesus out to ask Him questions. He is probably many years older than Jesus. In about three years, he will help Joseph of Arimathea take Christ's crucified body, prepare it for burial and gently place it in the tomb. See John 19:38–42.

2 The same [*Nicodemus*] came to Jesus by night, and said unto him, Rabbi [*"my master," a humble, respectful term for "my teacher"*], we know that thou art a teacher come from God: for no man can do these miracles that thou doest, except God be with him.

3 Jesus answered and said unto him, Verily, verily, I say unto thee, Except a man be born again, he cannot see the kingdom of God.

Simply put, being "born again" means to be baptized and then to be directed by the Holy Ghost to become a new person, cleansed from sin and worthy to comfortably enter into the celestial kingdom.

In effect, Jesus is saying to Nicodemus, "I want you to be my child, spiritually, to be born again spiritually, and then let the Holy Ghost teach you in the ways of righteousness so that you can live with me in celestial glory." (Compare with Mosiah 5:7)

Obviously, Nicodemus does not understand the symbolism at first, and so asks a good question, seeking clarification.

4 Nicodemus saith unto him, How can a man be born when he is old? can he enter the second time into his mother's womb, and be born?

Baptism and the Gift of the Holy Ghost Are Essential

5 Jesus answered, Verily, verily [*this is the main point; listen carefully*], I say unto thee, Except a man be born of water [*baptized*] and of the Spirit [*receive the gift of the Holy Ghost*], he cannot enter into the kingdom of God [*he cannot be taught the things he must do to become celestial*].

6 That which is born of the flesh is flesh; and that which is born of the Spirit is spirit [*there is a difference between being a common person and being a spiritual person*].

7 Marvel not that I said unto thee, Ye must be born again.

8 The wind bloweth where it listeth [*where it will*], and thou hearest the sound thereof, but canst not tell whence it cometh [*where it comes from*], and whither it goeth [*where it is going*]: so is every one that is born of the Spirit. [*Perhaps meaning that that is how it is with one who has the gift of the Holy Ghost. Promptings come and inspiration is given. We don't demand it or control it any more than we can control the wind, but it does come and it comes according to the will of the Lord.*]

9 Nicodemus answered and said unto him, How can these things be?

10 Jesus answered and said unto him, Art thou a master [*religious ruler*] of Israel, and knowest not these things? [*Nicodemus was a member of the Sanhedrin, the chief ruling body of religious leaders over the Jews; see Bible Dictionary, under "Sanhedrin."*]

11 Verily, verily, I say unto thee, We speak that [*what*] we do know, and testify that we have seen; and ye [*the people of the world*] receive not our witness [*do not accept our testimony*].

Verses 11–21 seem to be a direct quote which would be familiar to Nicodemus. See John 3:11, footnote b. We don't know where it comes from, but the Savior used it to teach this good man.

12 If I have told you earthly things [*simple basics such as faith, repentance, and baptism*], and ye believe not, how shall ye believe, if I tell you of heavenly things?

13 And no man hath ascended up to heaven, but

he that came down from heaven, even the Son of man which is in heaven. [*Christ bears witness that He is the Son of God.*]

14 And as Moses lifted up the serpent in the wilderness [*Numbers 21:8–9*], even so must the Son of man [*Christ*] be lifted up: [*Christ will be crucified as part of His Atonement.*]

15 That whosoever believeth in him should not perish [*spiritually*], but have eternal life [*exaltation*].

By the way, "eternal life," as used in the scriptures, always means exaltation in the highest degree of glory in the celestial kingdom. "Immortality" is the term that is used for "living forever" after being resurrected. All people who have ever been born into mortality will eventually be resurrected and will thus have immortality, regardless of whether they go to a degree of glory or even to outer darkness. (See D&C 88:28–32.)

Keep in mind that the Savior is continuing to answer Nicodemus' question in verse 9, above. As mentioned after verse 11, verses 11–21 appear to be a direct quote from scriptures that Nicodemus would recognize. Verse 16, next, is beautiful and is often quoted in our day. If you are marking verses in your own Bible, you may wish to mark this one now.

16 For God so loved the world, that he gave his only begotten Son, that whosoever believeth in him should not perish, but have everlasting life [*exaltation*].

17 For God sent not his Son into the world to condemn the world; but that the world through him might be saved.

18 He that believeth on him is not condemned [*stopped in progress*]: but he that believeth not is condemned already, because he hath not believed in the name of the only begotten Son of God.

JST JOHN 3:18

18 He who believeth on him is not condemned; but he who believeth not is condemned already, because he hath not believed on the name of the Only Begotten Son of God, which before was preached by the mouth of the holy prophets; for they testified of me.

The JST addition, "testified of me" is a most significant addition, because it tells us that Jesus was telling Nicodemus clearly that He, Jesus, is the Son of God.

19 And this is the condemnation [*this is the reason people get condemned, in other words, stopped in their spiritual progress*], that light is come into the world [*because the gospel is presented to them*], and men loved darkness rather than light [*and people choose wickedness rather than the gospel*], because their deeds were evil.

20 For every one that doeth evil hateth the light [*wickedness, by its very nature, makes you hate light and truth*], neither cometh to the light, lest his deeds should be reproved. [*People involved in wickedness won't come to the light because they don't want to face the consequences of their sins.*]

21 But he that doeth truth [*lives righteously*] cometh to the light, that his deeds may be made manifest [*made known*], that they are wrought in God [*accomplished through God's help*].

JST JOHN 3:21–22

21 But he who loveth truth, cometh to the light, that his deeds may be made manifest.

22 And he who obeyeth the truth, the works which he doeth they are of God.

The Savior's personal teaching session with Nicodemus ends with verse 21 (JST 21–22), above. We are left not knowing the outcome, but we do know that he defended Jesus to the Pharisees (John 7:50) and that he assisted with the Savior's burial (John 19:39).

22 After these things came Jesus and his disciples into the land of Judæa [*the southern province of the Holy Land in which Jerusalem was located*]; and there he tarried [*remained*] with them, and baptized.

For a short period of time here, the missions of John the Baptist and Jesus overlapped.

John the Baptist

23 And John [*the Baptist*] also was baptizing in

Aenon near to Salim [*in the Jordan River, about half way between the Sea of Galilee and the Dead Sea*], because there was much water there: and they came, and were baptized.

The fact that John the Baptist was baptizing in a place where there was "much water" is another reminder that he was baptizing by immersion. In fact, the word "baptize" means to immerse. See Bible Dictionary, under "Baptism."

24 For John was not yet cast into prison [*the Baptist hadn't yet been put in prison*].

25 Then there arose a question between some of John's disciples [*John the Baptist's followers*] and the Jews about purifying. [*In other words, a debate as to whether or not direct descendants of Abraham, such as the Jews, even needed baptism in order to be "purified."*]

The "purifying," mentioned in verse 25 above, refers to the purifying power of baptism. A long-standing apostate Jewish tradition taught that only Gentile converts needed to be baptized, and that direct descendants of Abraham, such as the Jews, were exempted from baptism. In fact, they had substituted other washing and cleansing rites for themselves. See Mark 7:1–8. See *Doctrinal New Testament Commentary*, Vol. 1, p. 146.

26 And they [*John's disciples*] came unto John, and said unto him, Rabbi [*"my master;" see Bible Dictionary, under "Rabbi"*], he [*Jesus*] that was with thee beyond Jordan, to whom thou barest witness [*of whom you bore testimony*], behold, the same baptizeth, and all men come to him.

JST John 3:27

27 And they came unto John, and said unto him, Rabbi, he who was with thee beyond Jordan, to whom thou bearest witness, behold, the same baptizeth, and he receiveth of all people who come unto him.

Perhaps John's followers are a bit jealous or concerned that "all men come to him." In other words, they are saying, "Everybody is coming to Jesus." Perhaps they are worried that Jesus is taking away from John's popularity.

27 John answered and said, A man can receive nothing, except it be given him from heaven [*each of us only does the work assigned to us by God*].

28 Ye yourselves bear me witness [*you are my witnesses*], that I said, I am not the Christ, but that I am sent before him. [*In effect, saying that Jesus' mission is to be the Messiah. My mission is to prepare the way for Him.*]

29 He that hath the bride [*He to whom the Church belongs*] is the bridegroom [*Jesus*]: but the friend [*John the Baptist*] of the bridegroom, which standeth and heareth him, rejoiceth greatly because of the bridegroom's voice: this my joy therefore is fulfilled. [*In effect, John is saying that he is very happy just to be a friend of Jesus and to hear Him preaching.*]

Verse 30, next, is one of the sweetest, most humble statements ever uttered. Among other things, John the Baptist is saying that his own mission and popularity are drawing to a close, and he humbly accepts that fact.

30 He must increase, but I must decrease.

31 He [*Jesus*] that cometh from above [*from heaven*] is above all [*is in charge of all things here*]: he that is of the earth is earthly [*I am just an ordinary man*], and speaketh of the earth: he that cometh from heaven is above all.

32 And what he hath seen and heard, that he testifieth; and no man receiveth his testimony [*people will reject Christ*].

JST John 3:32

32 He who cometh from above is above all; he who is of the earth is earthly, and speaketh of the earth; he who cometh from heaven is above all. And what he hath seen and heard, that he testifieth; and but few men receive his testimony.

Did you notice that JST verse 32, above, changes "no man receiveth his testimony" to "but few men receive his testimony"? This is a significant doctrinal change.

33 He that hath received his testimony hath set to his seal that God is true. [*Those who accept Christ's testimony certify that this is God's work.*]

34 For he [*Christ*] whom God [*the Father*] hath

sent speaketh the words of God: for God giveth not the Spirit by measure unto him. [*Jesus is not limited like we are in how much of the Spirit of God He has.*]

JST JOHN 3:34
34 For he whom God hath sent, speaketh the words of God; for God giveth him not the Spirit by measure, for he dwelleth in him, even the fullness.

35 The Father loveth the Son, and hath given all things into his hand [*has given Jesus full authority to accomplish his mission*].

36 He that believeth on the Son hath everlasting life [*will receive exaltation*]: and he that believeth not the Son shall not see life [*will not be exalted*]; but the wrath [*punishment*] of God abideth on him [*will come upon him*].

JST JOHN 3:36
36 And he who believeth on the Son hath everlasting life; and shall receive of his fullness. But he who believeth not the Son, shall not receive of his fullness; for the wrath of God is upon him.

JOHN 4

IN THIS CHAPTER, among other things, John gives us the account of the woman at the well. It is a well-known, delightful, and deeply moving story. We will watch as the Master teaches her about "living water." Perhaps you are already noticing that John gives much about the Savior's ministry that is not contained elsewhere in the New Testament.

As the chapter opens, we see that opposition to Jesus is mounting in Judea, and, as a result, He determines to go north to the province of Galilee. In so doing, He chooses to go through Samaria, rather than skirting it as is normally the practice among the Jews at the time. Once again, the JST will be very significant to our correct understanding of what John writes.

1 WHEN therefore the Lord knew how the Pharisees had heard that Jesus made and baptized more disciples than John,

2 (Though Jesus himself baptized not, but his disciples,)

Verse 2 above is a mistranslation in the Bible. The JST corrects this as follows (note that JST verses 2 and 4 have been left out of the Bible):

JST JOHN 4:1-4
1 When therefore the Pharisees had heard that Jesus made and baptized more disciples than John,

2 They sought more diligently some means that they might put him to death; for many received John as a prophet, but they believed not on Jesus.

3 Now the Lord knew this, though he himself baptized not so many as his disciples;

4 For he suffered them for an example [*Jesus set the example for them*], preferring one another.

3 He left Judæa, and departed again into Galilee.

4 And he must needs go through Samaria.

JST JOHN 4:6
6 And said unto his disciples, I must needs go through Samaria.

Normally, the Jews avoided going through Samaria. The Jews despised the Samaritans (people of Samaria) and the Samaritans despised the Jews. Thus, the Jews normally traveled around Samaria in order to get to Galilee. But this time Jesus is heading straight north, right through Samaria, which would no doubt cause His Apostles some extra anxiety.

5 Then cometh he to a city of Samaria, which is called Sychar, near to the parcel of ground that Jacob gave to his son Joseph [*who was sold into Egypt*].

The fact that the Master is weary as they arrive at Jacob's well is a reminder that He suffered "hunger, thirst, and fatigue" (Mosiah 3:7) during His mortal sojourn, and thus understands our physical trials through His own personal experience. As He sits down on the side of the well, the stage is set for each of us to drink deeply from the well of "living water" offered us by the Savior.

The Woman at the Well

6 Now Jacob's well was there. Jesus therefore, being wearied with his journey, sat thus on the well: and it was about the sixth hour [*about noon*].

7 There cometh a woman of Samaria to draw water [*to get water from the well*]: Jesus saith unto her, Give me to drink [*please give me a drink*].

8 (For his disciples were [*had*] gone away unto the city to buy meat [*food, provisions*].)

The following account of the Savior and the Samaritan woman is both delightful and profoundly moving. For our purposes, we will imagine her to be somewhat feisty and a bit sharp-tongued. We might imagine also a bit of a twinkle in the eyes of the Savior as He begins this conversation.

9 Then saith the woman of Samaria unto him, How is it that thou, being a Jew, askest drink of me, which am a woman of Samaria? for the Jews have no dealings with the Samaritans. [*In other words, why would a Jew like You ask a Samaritan woman like me for a drink? Don't You know that Jews don't have anything to do with us?*]

JST John 4:11

11 Wherefore he being alone, the woman of Samaria said unto him, How is it that thou being a Jew, askest drink of me, who am a woman of Samaria? The Jews have no dealings with the Samaritans.

Watch, now, as the Savior gets her curiosity up.

10 Jesus answered and said unto her, If thou knewest the gift of God, and who it is that saith to thee, Give me to drink; thou wouldest have asked of him, and he would have given thee living water. [*In effect, if you knew about the gift Father in Heaven has for you, and who I am, you would have asked me for a drink, and I would have given you "living water."*]

The phrase "living water" was a familiar Old Testament phrase, having been used by Old Testament prophets to describe the blessings which flow from Jehovah to His faithful people. We will quote Jeremiah as an example:

Jeremiah 2:13

13 For my people have committed two evils; they have forsaken me the fountain of living waters, *and* hewed them out cisterns, broken cisterns, that can hold no water.

We will quote from the Institute of Religion New Testament student manual regarding the term "living water."

"Israel's prophets had repeatedly declared that the Lord was as a fountain of living water that Israel had rejected. (See Jeremiah 2:13; Isaiah 8:6.)

"Jesus himself, as Jehovah, had pled with ancient Israel to repent and return to him so that he could nourish and sustain them. And in his pleading, Jehovah had used the word water as a figure of speech. (See Isaiah 58:11.)" (*Life and Teachings of Jesus and His Apostles*, p. 38)

Bruce R. McConkie taught about "living water." He said:

"His solemn invitation, 'If any man thirst, let him come unto me, and drink,' was a plain and open claim of Messiahship. In making it he identified himself as the very Jehovah who had promised drink to the thirsty through an out pouring of the Spirit. After such a pronouncement his hearers were faced with two choices: Either he was a blasphemer worthy of death, or he was in fact the God of Israel" (*DNTC*, 1:445–46).

You can find other references in the Topical Guide under "Living Water." As you know, we use the phrase often today in referring to the gospel of Jesus Christ which brings blessings that flow from heaven into our lives, providing refreshment, cleansing, and eternal life to the faithful.

11 The woman saith unto him, Sir, thou hast nothing to draw with, and the well is deep: from whence then hast thou that living water? [*Sir, You don't even have anything to get water out of the well. It is way too deep. So, from where do You think you are going to get me some of Your so-called "living water"?*]

12 Art thou greater than our father Jacob, which gave us the well, and drank thereof himself, and his children, and his cattle? [*In effect, do You think your "living water" is better than the water Jacob provided us here in this well? It was good enough for Jacob and his family and his animals. In other words, what makes You think Your water is better than the Prophet Jacob's?*]

Watch as the Master Teacher takes her from being curious to a state of deep desire to partake of what He has to offer. She is still thinking of literal water, but the transition from the literal to the symbolic is about to take place in her mind.

13 Jesus answered and said unto her, Whosoever [*whoever*] drinketh of this water shall thirst again [*will just get thirsty again*]:

14 But whosoever drinketh of the water that I shall give him shall never thirst [*will never be thirsty again*]; but the water that I shall give him shall be in him a well of water springing up into everlasting life [*eternal life*].

15 The woman saith unto him, Sir, give me this water, that I thirst not, neither come hither to draw.

As you can see, the woman still doesn't get it. She thinks Jesus is talking about some kind of magical water that, when someone drinks it, he or she will never get thirsty again. She wants some so that she doesn't ever have to come to the well again and do the hard work of getting water. Watch how the Savior really gets her attention by the next things He says to her. A wonderful teaching moment has been quickly generated by the Master Teacher! She is about to learn that He truly is "a prophet."

16 Jesus saith unto her, Go, call thy husband, and come hither [*go get your husband and bring him back here*].

17 The woman answered and said, I have no husband. Jesus said unto her, Thou hast well said, I have no husband [*you were certainly right when you said that you have no husband*]:

18 For thou hast had five husbands; and he whom thou now hast is not thy husband [*you are not married to the man you are living with now*]: in that saidst thou truly [*you were certainly telling the truth when you said you have no husband*].

19 The woman saith unto him, Sir, I perceive that thou art a prophet. [*Sir, it just dawned on me that you are a prophet.*]

20 Our fathers [*ancestors*] worshipped in this mountain [*worshipped here in Samaria, rather than in Jerusalem*]; and ye [*you Jews*] say, that in Jerusalem is the place where men ought to worship.

A little review of history is helpful here. After King Solomon died, the twelve tribes split into two nations, Israel (ten of the tribes) in the north, with headquarters in Samaria, and Judah (the tribe of Judah and part of Benjamin) in the south, with headquarters in Jerusalem. There was much animosity between the two nations. Consequently, the people of the northern kingdom, Israel, even refused to come to Jerusalem to worship. Instead, they set up an apostate temple and apostate priests in their own country of Samaria and worshipped there.

21 Jesus saith unto her, Woman, believe me, the hour cometh, when ye shall neither in this mountain [*here in Samaria*], nor yet at Jerusalem, worship the Father. [*In other words, there will be a complete apostasy such that no one will have correct knowledge of God, thus, no one can worship correctly.*]

22 Ye worship ye know not what: [*because of apostasy and ignorance, you Samaritans don't really know who or what you worship*] we [*Jews*] know what we worship: for salvation is of the Jews [*salvation comes from the Jews, through Christ*].

23 But the hour cometh, and now is, when the true worshippers shall worship the Father in spirit and in truth [*the time has arrived when Jesus will restore the true gospel, so that sincere people can worship the Father by the power of the Holy Ghost with true doctrines*]: for the Father seeketh such to worship him.

The next verse has often been used to discredit Joseph Smith's testimony that "the Father has a body of flesh and bones" (D&C 130:22). This is another place where the Bible was not translated correctly (8th Article of Faith). JST verse 26 straightens this out.

24 God is a Spirit: and they that worship him must worship him in spirit and in truth.

JST John 4:26

26 For unto such hath God promised his Spirit. And they who worship him, must worship in spirit and in truth.

25 The woman saith unto him, I know that Messias [*Messiah*] cometh, which is called Christ: when he is come, he will tell us all things. [*This woman is familiar with the prophecies about the coming of the Messiah, who will be known as Christ.*]

26 Jesus saith unto her, I that speak unto thee am he [*the Messiah, Christ; the Jehovah of the Old Testament; see John 4:26, footnote a, in your LDS Bible*].

JST JOHN 4:28

28 Jesus said unto her, I who speak unto thee am the Messias.

27 And upon this [*just as Jesus finished saying this to the woman*] came his disciples, and marvelled [*were surprised*] that he talked with the woman [*that He would talk with a Samaritan woman*]: yet no man said, What seekest thou? or, Why talkest thou with her? [*But none of the disciples dared scold Him for so doing.*]

Watch now as this rather surprised and amazed Samaritan woman hurries back into the city and tells the men that she has met a prophet at Jacob's Well who is no doubt the Messiah spoken of in the scriptures.

28 The woman then left her waterpot [*left it at the well*], and went her way into the city, and saith to the men,

29 Come, see a man, which told me all things that ever I did [*who knows everything about me*]: is not this the Christ?

30 Then they went out of the city, and came unto him [*Jesus*].

31 In the mean while his disciples prayed him, saying, Master, eat [*urged Him to eat the food they had bought*].

32 But he said unto them, I have meat [*food*] to eat that ye know not of.

Here, the Master Teacher creates a teaching moment to help His disciples understand more about Him and His mission, as well as their mission. At first, they miss the point completely, thus are "off balance" and in a state of readiness to learn.

33 Therefore said the disciples one to another, Hath any man brought him ought [*anything*] to eat? [*The Savior said He has food (verse 32), so the disciples assume someone else must have brought Him something to eat while they were gone buying food.*]

34 Jesus saith unto them, My meat [*that which the Savior must partake of*] is to do the will of him that sent me, and to finish his work.

The implication here is that the "meat," which the Savior has been given, is to partake of all the work and suffering necessary, as assigned Him by the Father, to accomplish the Atonement.

35 Say not ye, There are yet four months, and then cometh harvest? behold, I say unto you, Lift up your eyes, and look on the fields; for they are white already to harvest. [*In effect, you say that harvest is four months away. I say that harvest time is now. In other words, it is time to start "harvesting souls," gathering converts into my Church now.*]

36 And he that reapeth [*he who helps the Savior gather converts*] receiveth wages [*receives a reward*], and gathereth fruit unto life eternal [*stores up blessings for himself in heaven, namely exaltation*]: that both he that soweth [*the prophets of old, who laid the foundation by planting the gospel seeds—see JST verse 40, at the end of verse 38 below*] and he that reapeth [*he who harvests*] may rejoice together.

The main message in verse 36, above, seems to be that those who plant the gospel seed, but don't get to be around long enough to see it grow to maturity in the people, will rejoice together with the missionaries and others who actually bring the people into the Church.

37 And herein is that saying true, One soweth, and another reapeth [*one person plants and another person harvests*].

38 I sent you to reap that whereon ye bestowed no labour [*I sent you to harvest where you did not do any of the work to plant and nourish the crop*]: other men laboured [*prophets of old laid the foundation*], and ye are entered into their labours [*you finish what they started*].

JST JOHN 4:40

40 I have sent you to reap that whereon ye bestowed no labor; the prophets have labored, and ye have entered into their labors.

Having listened in as Jesus taught His disciples some important lessons, in the verses above, we now watch as Samaritans from the city arrive and meet the Savior themselves.

JESUS SAITH UNTO HIM, RISE, TAKE UP THY BED, AND WALK.

JOHN 5:8

39 And many of the Samaritans of that city believed on him for [*because of*] the saying of the woman, which testified, He told me all that ever I did.

40 So when the Samaritans were come unto him, they besought him that he would tarry with them [*they asked Him to stay with them*]: and he abode [*remained*] there two days.

41 And many more believed because of his own word;

42 And said unto the woman, Now we believe, not because of thy saying: for we have heard him ourselves, and know that this is indeed the Christ, the Saviour of the world.

Certainly one of the major messages we learn from the example of the Samaritan woman is the great power of personal testimony shared with others, which invites them to come and learn for themselves from the Master.

43 Now after two days he departed thence [*He left there*], and went into Galilee.

44 For Jesus himself testified, that a prophet hath no honour [*is rejected*] in his own country.

Jesus' "own country" was His home town of Nazareth. Indeed, the people there rejected Him. (See Luke 4:16-30.)

45 Then when he was come into Galilee, the Galilæans received him, having seen all the things that he did at Jerusalem at the feast [*at the Passover feast*]: for they also went unto the feast.

The Healing of the Nobleman's Son

46 So Jesus came again into Cana of Galilee, where he made the water wine [*see John 2:1–11*]. And there was a certain nobleman, whose son was sick at Capernaum.

47 When he heard that Jesus was come out of Judæa into Galilee, he went unto him, and besought [*begged*] him that he would come down, and heal his son: for he was at the point of death.

48 Then said Jesus unto him, Except ye see signs and wonders, ye will not believe.

49 The nobleman saith unto him, Sir, come down ere my child die [*please come before my child dies*].

50 Jesus saith unto him, Go thy way; thy son liveth [*has been healed*]. And the man believed the word that Jesus had spoken unto him, and he went his way [*headed home*].

51 And as he was now going down, his servants met him, and told him, saying, Thy son liveth.

52 Then enquired he of them the hour when he began to amend [*the nobleman asked his servants when his son began to get better*]. And they said unto him, Yesterday at the seventh hour [*about 1 p.m.*] the fever left him.

53 So the father knew that it was at the same hour, in the which Jesus said unto him, Thy son liveth: and himself believed, and his whole house [*he and his household were converted to Christ*].

54 This is again the second miracle [*the first one, according to John, was turning water into wine; see John 2:11*] that Jesus did, when he was come out of Judæa into Galilee.

JOHN 5

THIS IS THE beginning of the second year of the Savior's mortal mission. He begins this year by traveling to Jerusalem for the feast of the Passover. As you have probably learned already from Matthew, Mark, and Luke, the leaders of the Jews were extremely opposed to the healings which Jesus performed on the Sabbath. They felt that such activity violated the Lord's holy day. Little did they know that Jesus was the God of the Old Testament, Jehovah Himself, who gave the commandment to keep the Sabbath Day holy. They were caught up in what they considered to be the letter of the law and completely missed the spirit of the law. We will see this now as the Savior heals a man on the Sabbath.

1 AFTER this there was a feast [*Passover*] of the Jews; and Jesus went up to Jerusalem.

Healing a Crippled Man on the Sabbath

2 Now there is at Jerusalem by the sheep market a pool, which is called in the Hebrew tongue Bethesda, having five porches.

3 In these [*porches*] lay a great multitude of impotent [*crippled*] folk, of blind, halt [*lame*], withered, waiting for the moving of the water.

4 For an angel went down at a certain season into the pool, and troubled the water: whosoever then first after the troubling of the water stepped in was made whole [*healed*] of whatsoever disease he had.

> Apparently there was a false belief which gave sick and crippled people hope that they would be healed if they were the first to get into the water after the water started being moved by an unseen angel. This is superstition and is not the way God works.

5 And a certain man was there, which had an infirmity thirty and eight years [*had been an invalid for thirty-eight years*].

6 When Jesus saw him lie [*lying there*], and knew that he had been now a long time in that case [*in that situation*], he saith unto him, Wilt thou be made whole [*would you like to be healed*]?

7 The impotent [*crippled*] man answered him, Sir, I have no man, when the water is troubled, to put me into the pool: but while I am coming, another steppeth down before me [*when I try to get into the water first, someone else always beats me to it*].

8 Jesus saith unto him, Rise, take up thy bed, and walk.

9 And immediately the man was made whole [*was healed*], and took up his bed, and walked: and on the same day was the sabbath [*this all happened on the Sabbath*].

10 The Jews [*religious leaders of the Jews, Pharisees—see Matthew 12:2 and 10*] therefore said unto him that was cured [*the man who had been healed*], It is the sabbath day: it is not lawful [*legal*] for thee to carry thy bed.

11 He answered them, He that made me whole [*the man who healed me*], the same said unto me, Take up thy bed, and walk.

12 Then asked they him, What man is that which said unto thee, Take up thy bed, and walk?

13 And he that was healed wist not who it was [*didn't know the name of the man who had healed him*]: for Jesus had conveyed himself away, a multitude being in that place [*Jesus had left right after healing him and was quickly lost in the crowd by the pool*].

14 Afterward Jesus findeth him [*the man He had healed*] in the temple [*in the temple courtyard*], and said unto him, Behold, thou art made whole [*you have been healed*]: sin no more, lest a worse thing come unto thee.

> This had to be a specific case in which future sinning on the part of the man who had been healed would cause physical punishment. We must avoid generalizing this situation to apply to all people. Otherwise, we would come to believe, as did the Jews at the time, that all illness is caused by sin. Imagine the gossip which would go around about anyone who was sick if we believed this false notion!

15 The man departed, and told the Jews that it was Jesus, which had made him whole. [*Now that the healed man had met Jesus on the grounds of the Temple, and thus knew His name, he apparently found the Pharisees and told them the name of the man who had healed him.*]

16 And therefore did the Jews persecute Jesus, and sought to slay him, because he had done these things on the sabbath day.

> The Tradition of the Elders and the Sabbath Day
>
> Over the centuries, the Jewish religious leaders had imposed upon the Jews literally thousands of rules and laws concerning Sabbath behavior. These became known as the "tradition of the elders." See Matthew 15:2, Mark 7:5. They were caught up in the "letter of the law" as opposed

to the "spirit of the law" regarding the Sabbath. As evidenced in verse 16 above, it was against the law to heal on the Sabbath. A few additional examples of these "traditions of the elders" follow:

Things a faithful Jew was not allowed to do on the Sabbath (according to the Tradition of the Elders):

1. Scatter two seeds (it was considered to be planting).

2. Sweep or break a single clod of dirt (it was considered to be plowing).

3. Pluck one blade of grass.

4. Water fruit or remove a dead leaf.

5. Pick fruit or even lift it from the ground.

6. Cut a mushroom (it was a double sin, one of both harvesting and of planting, because a new one would grow in place of the old one).

7. Roll wheat together to take away the husks (guilty of sifting with a sieve).

8. Rub the ends of wheat stalks (guilty of threshing).

9. Throw wheat stalks up in the air (guilty of winnowing).

10. Dip a radish in salt for too long a time (could be dipped into salt as long as it was not left too long which would make one guilty of pickling).

11. Rub mud off a dress (mud on a dress might be crushed in the hand and shaken off, but the dress must not be rubbed for fear of bruising the fabric).

12. Spit on the ground then rub it into the soil with the foot (it was considered irrigating because something might grow where you spit; however, it was legal to spit into a handkerchief, or spit upon rocks because nothing would grow).

13. Put a plaster on a sore.

14. Write a big letter, leaving room for two small ones (but it was okay to write one big letter occupying the space of two small letters).

15. Carry a burden that was heavier than a fig.

16. Carry a piece of food larger than the size of an olive.

17. Carry objects that could be put to practical use, for instance, two horse hairs (because they could be made into a bird trap), a scrap of clean paper (because it could be written on), a small piece of paper already written upon (because it could be made into a wrapper).

18. Carry enough ink to write two letters.

19. Carry enough wax to fill up a small hole.

20. Carry a pebble (because you might aim it at a little bird).

21. Carry a small piece of broken pottery (because you could stir coals of a fire with it).

22. Write two letters, either with the right or left hand (but you could write letters in sand, because they would not remain). It was also permitted to write letters with the hand turned upside down, or with the foot, or with the mouth or the elbow.

23. Save a house or its contents from fire (however, you could rescue the scriptures and phylacteries (tiny leather boxes with scripture scrolls in them which the Jews tied to their foreheads or left arms) and the cases that contained them, plus food and drink needed for the Sabbath. Also, if food were in a basket, the whole basket could legally be carried out with everything in it. Only absolutely necessary clothing could be saved, however, a person might put on a dress, bring it out, take it off, go back in and put on another, save it and so on.

24. Carry a legal burden more than a Sabbath day's journey, which was 2,000 cubits (about 3,000 feet). (However, on Friday, a person could deposit food for two meals 2,000 cubits from his house. Then, on the Sabbath, he could go the 2,000 cubits, sit down and eat, and then that would be considered to be his residence and so he could go another 2,000 cubits from that point).

25. Provide first aid, unless the person's life was in danger.

26. Set broken bones.

27. Perform a surgical operation.

28. Wear a plaster on a wound or sore (unless the purpose was to prevent the wound from getting worse rather than an attempt to heal it).

29. Wear false teeth or wear a gold plug in a tooth.

30. Replace wadding if it fell out of the ear.

31. Light a fire.

32. Keep an oven warm.

33. Eat an egg that had been laid on the Sabbath (unless the hen had been kept for eating rather than laying eggs, in which case the egg could be eaten because it was considered to be a part of the hen that had fallen off).

(Adapted from *The Mortal Messiah*, pp. 199–212)

17 But Jesus answered them [*in answer to the Jewish religious leaders' criticism of His healing*

on the Sabbath, verse 16], My Father worketh hitherto, and I work [*in effect, my Father has done much of His work on the Sabbath, and I will continue to do so too*].

18 Therefore [*because of Jesus' reply*] the Jews sought the more [*even more*] to kill him, because he not only had broken the sabbath, but said also that God was his Father [*claims to be the Son of God*], making himself equal with God.

In the next verses, Jesus humbly gives credit and honor to His Father and explains Their relationship as They work together in complete harmony for the salvation of our souls.

19 Then answered Jesus and said unto them, Verily, verily, I say unto you, The Son can do nothing of himself, but what he seeth the Father do: for what things soever he [*the Father*] doeth, these also doeth the Son likewise. [*In other words, the Son does nothing that is not in complete harmony with the Father's will. See* Doctrinal New Testament Commentary, *Vol. 1, p. 192.*]

Occasionally, members of the Church use verse 19 above to suggest that Heavenly Father was the Savior of the world upon which He grew up. Their reasoning is: Since Jesus said that He does nothing but what He sees the Father do, and since Jesus is our Savior, the Father had to have been the Savior on the world upon which He grew up as a mortal. Of course it is possible that the Father was the Savior on His world, but to use this verse to "prove" it is not sound thinking. Brigham Young said, "The Savior told his disciples as he saw the Father do, so does he, and as Joseph Smith saw Jesus do, so did Joseph do, and as I saw Joseph do, so do I also." (Taken from remarks which appear to have been given at the dedication of the Seventies Hall in Nauvoo, late December, 1844. See *BYU Studies*, Winter 1978, Volume 18, No. 2, pp. 177–78.) Joseph Smith was not crucified. Brigham Young was not martyred in Carthage Jail. From that same volume of *BYU Studies*, p. 176, Joseph Smith says, "For the Savior says, the work that my Father did, do I also, . . . He took himself . . . a body and then laid down his life that he might take it up again, . . . We then also took bodies to lay them down, to take them up again."

The point of verse 19, above, is that Jesus was, in all things, in perfect harmony with the Father's will.

20 For the Father loveth the Son, and sheweth [*shows*] him all things that himself doeth [*that He Himself does*]: and he will shew him greater [*more*] works than these, that ye may marvel.

21 For as the Father raiseth up the dead [*resurrects people*], and quickeneth them [*causes them to become alive spiritually*]; even so the Son [*Christ*] quickeneth [*gives eternal life to*] whom he will.

Since every person who has ever been born on earth will be resurrected (1 Corinthians 15:22), in other words, will be "quickened," the last phrase in verse 21 above cannot mean that Jesus will be selective as to whom He resurrects. Another scriptural use of the word "quicken" is "to be made alive spiritually," which, in turn, leads to eternal life (exaltation). Jesus will be our final judge, and as such will give exaltation to "whom he will,' according to the laws of justice and mercy.

22 For the Father judgeth no man, but hath committed all judgment unto the Son: [*The Father has given all the responsibility for final judgment to Jesus.*]

23 That all men should honour the Son, even as they honour the Father. He that honoureth not the Son honoureth not the Father which hath sent him.

24 Verily, verily, I say unto you, He that heareth my word, and believeth on him that sent me [*Heavenly Father*], hath everlasting life [*exaltation in the highest degree of glory in the celestial kingdom*], and shall not come into condemnation [*will not be stopped from eternal progress*]; but is passed from death unto life.

Gospel to Be Preached in Spirit Prison

25 Verily, verily, I say unto you, The hour is coming, and now is, when the dead [*in spirit prison; 1 Peter 3:18–21, D&C 138*] shall hear the voice of the Son of God: and they that hear [*obey*] shall live.

26 For as the Father hath life in himself [*is "an immortal, resurrected, exalted being"* (Doctrinal New Testament Commentary, *Vol. 1, p. 194*)];

so hath he given to the Son to have life in himself [Jesus has power over death];

27 And hath given him authority to execute judgment also, because he is the Son of man [*the Son of God*]. [*See Moses 6:57 for an explanation of why Jesus is called the Son of Man.*]

Resurrection for All

28 Marvel not at this: for the hour is coming, in the which all that are in the graves shall hear his voice,

29 And shall come forth [*everyone will be resurrected*]; they that have done good, unto the resurrection of life [*eternal life, exaltation*]; and they that have done evil, unto the resurrection of damnation [*those who will have limits placed on their progression; see D&C 76:112*].

30 I can of mine own self do nothing [*Jesus follows the Father's commands exactly*]: as I hear, I judge: and my judgment is just [*completely fair*]; because I seek not mine own will, but the will of the Father which hath sent me.

31 If I bear witness of myself, my witness is not true [*valid*]. [*The law of witnesses requires that there be at least two witnesses.*]

32 There is another [*the Father*] that beareth witness of me; and I know that the witness which he witnesseth of me is true.

33 Ye sent unto John [*the Baptist*], and he bare witness unto the truth.

34 But I receive not testimony from man: but these things I say, that ye might be saved.

JST JOHN 5:35

35 And he received not his testimony of [*from*] man, but of God, and ye yourselves say that he is a prophet, therefore ye ought to receive his testimony. These things I say that ye might be saved.

35 He [*John the Baptist*] was a burning and a shining light: and ye were willing for a season to rejoice in his light.

36 But I have greater witness than that of John [*than that which John the Baptist gave of Me*]: for the works [*restoring the gospel, performing the Atonement, and such.*] which the Father hath given me to finish, the same works that I do, bear witness of me, that the Father hath sent me.

JST JOHN 5:37

37 But I have a greater witness than the testimony of John; for the works which the Father hath given me to finish, the same works that I do, bear witness of me, that the Father hath sent me.

37 And the Father himself, which hath sent me, hath borne witness of me. Ye [*the Jews*] have neither heard his voice at any time, nor seen his shape [*meaning that the Father has "shape," a resurrected, physical body; see D&C 130:22*].

JST JOHN 5:38

38 And the Father himself who sent me, hath borne witness of me. And verily I testify unto you, that ye have never heard his voice at any time, nor seen his shape;

38 And ye [*the Jews*] have not his word abiding in you [*do not have the Father's gospel in your hearts*]: for whom he [*the Father*] hath sent, him ye believe not [*you refuse to believe what I am teaching you*].

Verse 39, next, needs to be read carefully, in order to understand what is actually being said. Remember that the Master is addressing the hypocritical religious leaders of the Jews who are proud of their knowledge of the scriptures but who violate the gospel constantly in daily living.

39 Search the scriptures; for in them ye think ye have eternal life [*since you won't listen to Me, go ahead and keep studying your scriptures, the Law of Moses, and so forth, without help, thus perpetuating your spiritual blindness; you think you can be saved that way; it won't work*]: and they are they which testify of me. [*If you understood the scriptures correctly, you would see that they testify of Me.*]

40 And ye will not [*refuse to*] come to me, that ye might have life [*eternal life*].

41 I receive not honour from men. [*I am not honored by men like you.*]

42 But I know you [*the Jews who are angry because Jesus healed the invalid on the Sabbath, and now want to kill Him; see verse 16 above*], that ye have not the love of God in you [*I know the evil which is in your hearts.*]

43 I am come [*have come*] in my Father's name, and ye receive me not [*you reject Me*]: if another shall come in his own name, him ye will receive. [*You accept false leaders and false prophets who build themselves up in the eyes of the people for personal gain, who practice priestcraft; see Alma 1:12 and 16.*]

44 How can ye believe, which receive honour one of another, and seek not the honour that cometh from God only? [*How can you believe and trust those who join together to build themselves up, rather than seeking God?*]

45 Do not think that I will accuse you [*I will not even need to bear witness against you*] to the Father: there is one that accuseth you, even Moses, in whom ye trust [*because the teachings of Moses about Me, which you blatantly misinterpret and refuse to believe, will bear witness against you*].

46 For had ye believed Moses [*if you believed Moses, who clearly taught about Me*], ye would have believed me: for he wrote of me.

47 But if ye believe not his writings, how shall ye believe my words? [*If you won't believe Moses, how can you possibly believe Me?*]

Moses was the most important prophet in Jewish culture. In fact, the Jews were constantly angered by the fact that Jesus did not do things the way Moses taught, forgetting that many of the things Moses gave them were "schoolmaster" laws (Galatians 3:24), specifically designed to prepare them for the higher laws the Messiah would give them.

JOHN 6

THIS IS THE beginning of the third year of the Savior's mortal ministry. As you can see, John's account deals mostly with the final year of the Master's mortal ministry (John 5 dealt with the second year of His formal mortal mission). In this chapter, you will see the feeding of the 5,000 and the Savior's walking on the water. The Bread of Life sermon will be given and Peter will testify that Jesus is the Christ. The JST will continue to be a great blessing to us as we study the life of Christ. By this stage of His mortal mission, large crowds of people are constantly following Him.

1 AFTER these things Jesus went over the sea of Galilee, which is the sea of Tiberias.

2 And a great multitude followed him, because they saw his miracles which he did on them that were diseased [*sick*].

3 And Jesus went up into a mountain, and there he sat with his disciples.

4 And the passover, a feast of the Jews, was nigh [*near*].

Feeding of the 5,000

5 When Jesus then lifted up his eyes, and saw a great company [*huge crowd*] come unto him, he saith unto Philip, Whence [*where*] shall we buy bread, that these may eat [*to feed all these people*]?

In verse 6, next, John points out to us the Master Teacher's technique as He provides learning opportunities for His Apostles. They are, in effect, involved in a three year "MTC" training.

6 And this he said to prove [*test*] him: for he himself knew what he would do.

7 Philip answered him, Two hundred pennyworth of bread is not sufficient for them, that every one of them may take a little. [*Two hundred days' wages would not buy enough for everyone to have more than a little—see Mark 6:37, footnote a.*]

8 One of his disciples, Andrew, Simon Peter's brother, saith unto him,

9 There is a lad here, which hath five barley loaves, and two small fishes: but what are they among so many?

10 And Jesus said, Make the men sit down. Now there was much grass in the place. So the men sat down, in number about five thousand [*plus women and children; see Matthew 14:21*].

11 And Jesus took the loaves; and when he had given thanks, he distributed to the disciples, and the disciples to them that were set down; and likewise of the fishes as much as they would [*everyone ate as much as they wanted*].

12 When they were filled [*when the people in the crowd were full*], he said unto his disciples, Gather up the fragments that remain, that nothing be lost [*wasted*].

13 Therefore they gathered them together, and filled twelve baskets with the fragments [*leftovers*] of the five barley loaves, which remained over and above unto them that had eaten.

14 Then those men, when they had seen the miracle that Jesus did, said, This is of a truth that prophet that should come into the world [*this is definitely the Messiah*].

Unfortunately, as you will see in verse 15, next, most of the multitude failed to see the spiritual symbolism involved in the Savior's feeding all of them until they were full. Their minds and hearts were so focused on immediate physical needs and desires that they missed the spiritual implications.

15 When Jesus therefore perceived that they [*the members of the multitude who had just been fed*] would come and take him by force, to make him a king, he departed again into a mountain himself alone.

Apparently, the multitude felt that if they could have Jesus for their king, He would feed them every day and take care of all their needs so they wouldn't have to work. Therefore, they tried to force Him to be their king. They missed the symbolism that Christ can indeed take care of all our spiritual needs by giving us the "bread of life" on a daily basis.

16 And when even [*evening*] was now come, his disciples went down unto the sea,

17 And entered into a ship, and went over the sea toward Capernaum [*on the northwest side of the Sea of Galilee*]. And it was now dark, and Jesus was not come to them [*had not joined them*].

The Tempest Rages

18 And the sea arose by reason of a great wind that blew [*a terrible storm came up*].

Jesus Walks on the Water

19 So when they had rowed about five and twenty or thirty furlongs [*about three to four miles from shore*], they see Jesus walking on the sea, and drawing nigh [*getting close*] unto the ship: and they were afraid.

20 But he saith unto them, It is I; be not afraid.

21 Then they willingly received him into the ship: and immediately the ship was at the land whither they went [*the ship was suddenly at its destination, a miracle recorded only by John*].

22 The day following [*the day following the feeding of the 5,000*], when the people which stood on the other side of the sea [*near where they had been fed by the Master the day before*] saw that [*realized that*] there was none other boat there, save [*except*] that one whereinto his disciples were entered, and that Jesus went not with his disciples into the boat, but that his disciples were gone away alone; [*In other words, the next day the crowd came to see if Jesus was still there, so they could get Him to feed them again. They knew that the disciples had taken the only boat available the night before and had headed toward Capernaum without Jesus. At any rate, they saw that neither Jesus nor His disciples were there, so they determined to try to find them.*]

23 (Howbeit [*however*] there came other boats from Tiberias nigh unto the place where they did eat bread [*some boats from Tiberias came that morning and came to shore near the site of the feeding of the 5,000*], after that the Lord had given thanks:)

24 When the people therefore saw that Jesus was not there, neither his disciples, they also took shipping [*got aboard the boats from Tiberias*], and came to Capernaum, seeking for Jesus.

25 And when they had found him on the other side of the sea, they said unto him, Rabbi, when camest thou hither [*when did You come here*]?

26 Jesus answered them and said, Verily, verily [*this is very important; listen carefully!*], I say unto you, Ye seek me, not because ye saw the miracles, but because ye did eat of the loaves, and were filled. [*You are not looking for me because you want to obey my gospel, but rather just to be fed again. In*

other words, you are looking for me for the wrong reasons.]

JST John 6:26

26 Jesus answered them and said, Verily, verily, I say unto you, Ye seek me, not because ye desire to keep my sayings, neither because ye saw the miracles, but because ye did eat of the loaves and were filled.

27 Labour not for the meat which perisheth [*don't spend all your effort working for worldly things which do not last*], but for that meat [*food, symbolic of spiritual priorities*] which endureth unto everlasting life [*which brings exaltation*], which the Son of man [*Christ*] shall give unto you: for him hath God the Father sealed [*sent*].

Now begins a brief series of interesting questions and answers between the spiritually blind and insensitive crowd and the Master Teacher.

Question

28 Then said they unto him, What shall we do, that we might work the works of God? [*What would it take to teach us how to multiply loaves and fishes?*]

Answer

29 Jesus answered and said unto them, This is the work of God, that ye believe on him whom he hath sent. [*You must develop faith in Jesus Christ.*]

Question

30 They said therefore unto him, What sign shewest thou then, that we may see, and believe thee? what dost thou work? [*They are getting a bit irritated that He is stalling and not teaching them how to multiply loaves and fishes. They challenge Him to show them a sign to prove to them that He has not lost the power which He had yesterday when He fed them.*]

31 Our fathers did eat manna in the desert; as it is written, He gave them bread from heaven to eat. [*In other words they seem to be taunting Jesus, saying in effect, "Hint, hint. Moses gave our ancestors bread (manna) every day when he was their leader. What's the matter? Aren't You as capable as Moses?"*]

What follows in verses 32–58 is known as the "Bread of Life" sermon. It is famous and contains tremendous symbolism. Have you noticed that the Savior masterfully uses familiar objects and everyday settings as background for teaching gospel doctrines and principles? We see this method throughout His teaching.

Answer

The Bread of Life Sermon

32 Then Jesus said unto them, [*Answer:*] Verily, verily, I say unto you, Moses gave you not that bread from heaven [*Moses didn't give you that manna*]; but [*furthermore*] my Father giveth you the true bread [*symbolic of Christ*] from heaven.

33 For the bread of [*from*] God is he [*Christ*] which cometh down from heaven, and giveth life [*resurrection and the possibility of eternal life*] unto the world.

34 Then said they unto him, Lord, evermore give us this bread [*give us bread so we will never get hungry again*].

As you can see from verse 34, above, they still don't get the point (see also verse 52). They don't understand the symbolism that Christ and His gospel will nourish them spiritually forever in celestial glory.

Next, Jesus explains His role as the Redeemer, and that He has been sent to earth by the Father to enable us to return to Him. In effect, He is giving them a short course in the Plan of Salvation.

35 And Jesus said unto them, I am the bread of life: he that cometh to me shall never hunger [*spiritually*]; and he that believeth on me shall

never thirst [*spiritually*]. [*In other words, those who hunger and thirst after righteousness and eternal life and come unto Christ will be nourished eternally.*]

36 But I said unto you, That ye also have seen me, and believe not.

37 All [*all the righteous people*] that the Father giveth me shall come to me; and him that cometh to me I will in no wise [*never*] cast out [*of my kingdom*].

38 For I came down from heaven, not to do mine own will, but the will of him [*the Father*] that sent me.

39 And this is the Father's will which hath sent me, that of all which he hath given me [*all the righteous Saints*] I should lose nothing [*none of them*], but should raise it up again at the last day [*resurrect them in the resurrection of the righteous*].

40 And this is the will of him that sent me, that every one which seeth the Son, and believeth on him, may have everlasting life: and I will raise him up at the last day.

> **JST John 6:40**
> 40 And this is the will of him that sent me, that every one which seeth the Son, and believeth on him, may have everlasting life; and I will raise him up in the resurrection of the just at the last day.

> The "resurrection of the just" as used in JST verse 40, above, is a term which means those who will attain exaltation, which is the highest degree of glory in the celestial kingdom.

> Sadly, as you can see from verses 41–42, next, these people still don't get it. They are typical of people who are so focused on material things that they can't see the spiritual.

41 The Jews then murmured [*grumbled*] at him, because he said, I am the bread which came down from heaven.

42 And they said, Is not this Jesus, the son of Joseph, whose father and mother we know? how is it then that he saith, I came down from heaven? [*How can Jesus have come down from heaven? We know His parents. We've known Him all His life.*]

43 Jesus therefore answered and said unto them, Murmur not among yourselves [*don't criticize me among yourselves for saying what I've said*].

44 No man can come to me, except the Father which hath sent me draw him: and I will raise him up at the last day.

> The JST makes major changes to verse 44, above:

> **JST John 6:44**
> 44 No man can come unto me, except he doeth the will of my Father who hath sent me. And this is the will of him who hath sent me, that ye receive the Son; for the Father beareth record of him; and he who receiveth the testimony, and doeth the will of him who sent me, I will raise up in the resurrection of the just.

45 It is written in the prophets [*in the Old Testament; Isaiah 54:13*], And they shall be all taught of God. Every man therefore that hath heard, and hath learned of the Father, cometh unto me. [*Everyone who has properly understood Old Testament prophets will be motivated to come unto Me.*]

46 Not that any man hath seen the Father, save he which is of God [*except he who is worthy, such as Stephen in Acts 7:55–56*], he hath seen the Father.

47 Verily, verily, I say unto you, He that believeth on me [*Christ*] hath everlasting life [*will be exalted, will be placed into the highest degree of glory in the celestial kingdom and will become a god—see D&C 132:20*].

48 I am that bread of life. [*Symbolism: Jesus is the spiritual "bread" sent to us by the Father, that, when we eat it, that is, when we internalize it and make it part of our lives, we are exalted.*]

49 Your fathers [*ancestors, mentioned in verse 31*] did eat manna in the wilderness, and are dead [*and still died spiritually*].

50 This is the bread [*symbolic of Christ's gospel and His Atonement*] which cometh down from heaven, that a man may eat thereof [*internalize*

it], and not die [*not die spiritually*].

51 I am the living bread which came down from heaven: if any man eat of this bread, he shall live for ever [*shall have eternal life*]: and the bread that I will give is my flesh, which I will give for the life of the world. [*Jesus will sacrifice His body through suffering in the Garden of Gethsemane and crucifixion in order to accomplish the Atonement and provide eternal life for those who qualify.*]

52 The Jews therefore strove [*argued*] among themselves, saying, How can this man give us his flesh to eat? [*They still don't get the point!*]

Just as the Savior repeated the message time and time again in the previous verses, so He will repeat it several times in the next verses. He is giving these spiritually insensitive people every chance to understand that they must accept His Atonement and His gospel in order to be saved. They must symbolically eat Him ("he that eateth me," verse 57), that is, eat or internalize everything He is and offers them and make it a part of their lives, in order to receive eternal life. Sadly, many of them will still not get the point, even after so much repetition, and will leave Him (verse 66).

53 Then Jesus said unto them, Verily, verily, I say unto you, Except [*unless*] ye eat the flesh of the Son of man [*Christ*], and drink his blood, ye have no life in you. [*Unless you take advantage of the Atonement and make it part of your lives, you will not have the life and light of the gospel here in mortality or in the world to come.*]

54 Whoso eateth my flesh, and drinketh my blood, hath eternal life; and I will raise him up at the last day.

JST JOHN 6:54

54 Whoso eateth my flesh, and drinketh my blood, hath eternal life; and I will raise him up in the resurrection of the just at the last day.

55 For my flesh is meat [*symbolic of spiritual food*] indeed, and my blood is drink [*symbolic of spiritual drink*] indeed. [*This is sacrament symbolism.*]

56 He that eateth my flesh, and drinketh my blood, dwelleth in me, and I in him. [*He becomes one with me, united with me in the gospel.*]

57 As the living Father hath sent me, and I live by the Father: so he that eateth me [*internalizes my gospel*], even he shall live by me [*will be saved through living in accordance with my gospel*].

58 This is that bread which came down from heaven [*this is the Savior who was sent to earth from heaven*]: not as your fathers did eat manna [*physical nourishment*], and are dead: he that eateth of this bread [*spiritual nourishment*] shall live for ever [*will have eternal life, exaltation*].

59 These things said he in the synagogue [*Jewish church building*], as he taught in Capernaum.

60 Many therefore of his disciples [*followers*], when they had heard this [*the Bread of Life Sermon*], said, This is an hard saying; who can hear it? [*This is too deep for us. Nobody can understand what He is saying.*]

61 When Jesus knew in himself that his disciples murmured at it, he said unto them, Doth this offend you [*are you bothered, offended by what I have taught about the Bread of Life*]?

62 What and if ye shall see the Son of man ascend up where he was before? [*Would it offend you if you saw me go back up into heaven where I came from? Jesus will do exactly that after His resurrection.*]

Next, we are taught the necessity of having the help of the Holy Ghost in order to understand the message of salvation that the Savior is giving these people. This is an important reminder of the vital role the gift of the Holy Ghost plays in our lives. Those who do not have it cannot understand the depth and beauty of these things.

63 It is the spirit that quickeneth [*it is the Holy Ghost that gives you understanding*]; the flesh profiteth nothing [*you can't possibly understand what Jesus just said from an intellectual, academic basis*]: the words that I speak unto you, they are spirit [*spiritual*], and they are life [*they bring eternal life*].

64 But there are some of you that believe not. For Jesus knew from the beginning who they were that believed not, and who should betray him.

65 And he said, Therefore said I *[this is the reason I said]* unto you, that no man can come unto me, except it were given unto him of my Father.

JST JOHN 6:65
65 And he said, Therefore said I unto you, that no man can come unto me, except he doeth the will of my Father who hath sent me.

As you can see from verse 66, next, many people deserted Jesus after He gave the Bread of Life sermon, above.

66 From that time many of his disciples went back *[left him]*, and walked no more with him.

67 Then said Jesus unto the twelve, Will ye also go away? *[Is this doctrine of the Bread of Life so hard to accept that you, too, will leave Me?]*

Peter's Testimony

68 Then Simon Peter answered him, Lord, to whom shall we go? thou hast the words of eternal life. *[This is the right answer!]*

69 And we believe and are sure that thou art that Christ, the Son of the living God.

Next, Jesus prophesied that one of the Twelve would betray Him. In verse 71, John explains who it was to whom the Master was referring.

70 Jesus answered them, Have not I chosen you twelve, and one of you is a devil?

71 He spake of Judas Iscariot the son of Simon *[not Peter, the Apostle, rather, a different Simon]*: for he it was that should *[would]* betray him, being one of the twelve.

JOHN 7

IT IS FALL now and Jesus will be crucified and resurrected in the spring. He is traveling and teaching in Galilee, but will go to Jerusalem for the Feast of Tabernacles. As John begins this chapter, he informs us that many of the Savior's own close relatives do not believe that He is the Messiah.

1 AFTER these things Jesus walked in Galilee: for he would not walk in Jewry *[in Judea, in the Jerusalem area]*, because the Jews sought to kill him.

2 Now the Jews' feast of tabernacles was at hand.

The Feast of Tabernacles was held in the fall at harvest time in Jerusalem. See Bible Dictionary, under "Feasts." It drew large crowds and was a week-long celebration of thanksgiving which included daily animal sacrifices, and a ceremony where people waved palm, myrtle, willow, and citrus branches toward the cardinal points of the compass (north, south, east and west), symbolizing the presence of God throughout the universe.

Next, in verses 3–5, there may be a hint of criticism on the part of Jesus' close relatives, likely including His own half-brothers, who do not believe in Him (verse 5), as they tell Him, in effect, that He really ought to go to Jerusalem for the Feast of Tabernacles so He can parade Himself in front of His disciples as well as huge numbers of people. There is a hint that these family members and close relatives were embarrassed that Jesus was part of their family.

3 His brethren *[close relatives, probably including his own brothers; see McConkie,* Doctrinal New Testament Commentary, *Vol. 1, p. 437]* therefore said unto him, Depart hence *[leave]*, and go into Judæa, that thy disciples also may see the works that thou doest.

JST JOHN 7:3
3 His brethren therefore said unto him, Depart hence, and go into Judea, that thy disciples there also may see the works that thou doest.

4 For there is no man that doeth any thing in secret, and he himself seeketh to be known openly *[no man keeps to himself who wants everybody to know who he is]*. If thou do these things, shew thyself to the world *[get out in public and let them see you]*.

5 For neither did his brethren *[His half-brothers, the sons of Joseph and Mary]* believe in him.

6 Then Jesus said unto them, My time is not yet come *[perhaps meaning that the time for His atoning sacrifice in Jerusalem has not yet arrived—compare with Matthew 26:18]*: but your time is alway ready *[you can go to Jerusalem any time, so you go ahead and go for the Feast of Tabernacles]*.

7 The world cannot hate you [*the people of the world don't hate you because you are just normal people and most of them don't even know you*]; but me it hateth, because I testify of it, that the works thereof are evil [*but they hate me because I tell them they are wicked*].

8 Go ye up unto this feast [*the Feast of Tabernacles in Jerusalem*]: I go not up yet unto this feast; for my time is not yet full come [*it is not time for me to go*].

9 When he had said these words unto them, he abode still [*still remained*] in Galilee.

10 But when his brethren were gone [*had gone*] up, then went he also up unto the feast, not openly, but as it were in secret. [*The religious leaders of the Jews had already indicated that they wanted to kill Him; see verse 1.*]

11 Then the Jews sought him [*looked for him*] at the feast, and said, Where is he?

12 And there was much murmuring [*much talk*] among the people concerning him: for some said, He is a good man: others said, Nay; but he deceiveth the people [*He is a fraud*].

13 Howbeit [*however*] no man spake openly of him for fear of the Jews.

14 Now about the midst of the feast [*the middle of the week-long festivities*] Jesus went up into the temple, and taught.

15 And the Jews marvelled, saying, How knoweth this man letters, having never learned [*how does Jesus know so much; He hasn't had the formal training that our religious leaders have*]?

16 Jesus answered them, and said, My doctrine is not mine, but his that sent me. [*My Father is my teacher.*]

Verse 17, next, is a simple formula for gaining a testimony of the gospel.

17 If any man will do his will, he shall know of the doctrine, whether it be of God, or whether I speak of myself. [*If any one will live the gospel, he will find out that it is true.*]

18 He that speaketh of himself [*teaches his own, man-made doctrines*] seeketh his own glory: but he [*Christ*] that seeketh his glory that sent him [*the glory of the Father*], the same is true [*He is a true messenger, one you can trust*], and no unrighteousness is in him.

19 Did not Moses give you the law [*the first five books of the Old Testament*], and yet none of you keepeth the law [*none of you obey it*]? Why go ye about to kill me?

20 The people answered and said, Thou hast a devil [*you are crazy*]: who goeth about to kill thee [*what makes You think anybody is out to kill You*]?

Next, the Master points out the hypocrisy of the Jews who are accusing Him of breaking the Sabbath.

21 Jesus answered and said unto them, I have done one work [*I healed the crippled man on the Sabbath*], and ye all marvel.

22 Moses therefore gave unto you circumcision; (not because it is of Moses, but of the fathers;) [*in other words, not because it originated with Moses, rather with Abraham*] and ye on the sabbath day circumcise a man.

23 If a man on the sabbath day receive circumcision, that the law of Moses should not be broken; are ye angry at me, because I have made a man every whit whole on the sabbath day? [*You have your priorities mixed up. You allow a man to be circumcised on the Sabbath, but you get angry at me for healing a man on the Sabbath.*]

24 Judge not according to the appearance, but judge righteous judgment.

JST John 7:24

24 Judge not according to your traditions, but judge righteous judgment.

25 Then said some of them of Jerusalem [*who were from Jerusalem*], Is not this he, whom they seek to kill?

26 But, lo, he speaketh boldly [*look, He is speaking out boldly in public*], and they [*the Pharisees, etc.*] say nothing unto him. Do the rulers know indeed that this is the very Christ? [*Maybe they think He actually is Christ and are afraid of Him.*]

27 Howbeit [*regardless of what they think*] we know this man whence he is [*we know where Jesus comes from, namely Nazareth*]: but when Christ [*the promised Messiah*] cometh, no man knoweth whence he is [*no one will know where he comes from*].

It was a false tradition among the Jews that no one would know where the true Christ came from.

28 Then cried Jesus in the temple [*Jesus spoke loudly so everyone could hear*] as he taught, saying, Ye both know me, and ye know whence I am: and I am not come of myself [*I have not come on my own*], but he that sent me is true, whom ye know not [*rather, I have been sent by the Father, whom you do not know because of your wickedness*].

29 But I know him: for I am from him, and he hath sent me.

30 Then they sought to take him [*wanted to arrest him*]: but no man laid hands on him, because his hour was not yet come. [*No one was able to seize him because it was not time yet for His trial and crucifixion.*]

31 And many of the people believed on him, and said, When Christ cometh, will he do more miracles than these which this man hath done? [*In other words, this has to be the Christ.*]

32 The Pharisees heard that the people murmured [*were saying*] such things concerning him; and the Pharisees and the chief priests sent officers to take him [*to arrest Him*].

33 Then said Jesus unto them, Yet a little while am I with you, and then I go unto him that sent me [*then I will return to my Father in Heaven*].

34 Ye shall seek me, and shall not find me: and where I am, thither [*there*] ye cannot come.

Here again, as in so many other places, John is pointing out to us that we are watching a group of people who are very learned in the letter of the law and the scriptures but haven't a clue what it is really about because they don't understand anything about the simple Plan of Salvation. Watch now, as they again stumble over details because they do not understand or accept the "big picture."

35 Then said the Jews among themselves, Whither [*where*] will he go, that we shall not find him? will he go unto the dispersed among the Gentiles, and teach the Gentiles [*will He go to the Greeks and teach them; see John 7:35, footnote a*]?

36 What manner of saying is this that he said [*what does He mean by saying*], Ye shall seek me, and shall not find me: and where I am, thither ye cannot come?

37 In the last day [*the eighth and final day of the Feast of Tabernacles, the climactic finale to the celebrating—see Bible Dictionary under "Feasts"*], that great day [*the culmination*] of the feast, Jesus stood and cried, saying, If any man thirst, let him come unto me, and drink.

38 He that believeth on me, as the scripture [*Isaiah 44:3, 55:1*] hath said, out of his belly shall flow rivers of living water.

Picture if you will, throngs of Jews crowding the grounds around the temple, watching in rapt attention as water from the stream of Siloam (symbolic of water drawn from the wells of salvation—see Isaiah 12:3) was carried to the altar and then poured upon it, flowing down off it onto the ground, in a great ritual show symbolic of the living waters, including the Holy Ghost, which flow from the altar of God onto the earth to quench the spiritual thirst of the faithful—see Isaiah 44:3, 55:1. Perhaps, at that very moment, Jesus stood, and, with a loud voice, spoke to the onlookers saying, "If any man thirst, let him come unto me, and drink (verse 37, above)." There could not have been a more dramatic setting. Jesus was openly claiming to be the Messiah and to be the Jehovah of the Old Testament who had promised to give "living waters" to the faithful.

39 (But this spake he of the Spirit, which they that believe on him should receive: for the Holy Ghost was not yet given; because that Jesus was not yet glorified.)

JST JOHN 7:39

39 (But this spake he of the Spirit, which they that believe on him should receive; for the Holy Ghost was promised unto them who believe, after that

Jesus was glorified.)

The phrase "the Holy Ghost was not yet given," in verse 39 above, causes some to believe that the Holy Ghost was not here at all during the time Jesus was here. This is not the case. The Holy Ghost was obviously functioning and active on earth during the Savior's mortal ministry. He attended the Savior's baptism (Matthew 3:13–17). The Savior was "full of the Holy Ghost" in Luke 4:1. Thus, our understanding is that, while the Holy Ghost did function during Christ's mortal ministry, the full power of the Gift of the Holy Ghost was not here. See Bible Dictionary, under "Holy Ghost."

In the next verses, we watch a debate among the people as to who this Jesus really is.

40 Many of the people therefore, when they heard this saying [*what Jesus said in verses 37 and 38 above*], said, Of a truth this is the Prophet [*some prophet who was to come before Christ; see* Doctrinal New Testament Commentary, *Vol. 1, p. 448*].

41 Others said, This is the Christ. But some said, Shall Christ come out of Galilee?

42 Hath not the scripture said, That Christ cometh of the seed of David [*would be a descendant of David*], and out of the town of Bethlehem, where David was? [*Referring no doubt to the prophecy in Micah 5:2 that Christ was to be born in Bethlehem, and thus, they thought, should come from Bethlehem, not Nazareth in Galilee.*]

43 So there was a division among the people because of him.

44 And some of them [*the officers in verse 45*] would have taken him [*arrested him*]; but no man laid hands on him.

45 Then came the officers [*soldiers*] to the chief priests and Pharisees [*Jewish religious leaders*]; and they said unto them, Why have ye not brought him [*why didn't you arrest Jesus*]?

46 The officers answered, Never man spake like this man [*nobody ever taught like He does*].

47 Then answered them the Pharisees [*then the Pharisees and chief priests said to the soldiers*], Are ye also deceived [*has Jesus got you fooled also*]?

48 Have any of the rulers or of the Pharisees believed on him [*have any of us rulers been deceived by him*]?

49 But this people who knoweth not the law are cursed. [*The people don't understand the teachings of Moses. That's why they are subject to being deceived by Jesus.*]

Nicodemus Defends Jesus

Next, Nicodemus will defend Jesus, which is a very risky thing to do under the circumstances. Perhaps you remember that Nicodemus was the Pharisee who came to Jesus by night and was taught the necessity of baptism and the gift of the Holy Ghost (see John 3:1–21). He will also help Joseph from Aramathea prepare the body of the crucified Lord for burial (see John 19:39).

50 Nicodemus saith unto them, (he that came to Jesus by night, being one of them [*Nicodemus was a member of the Pharisees*],)

51 Doth our law judge any man, before it hear him, and know what he doeth? [*Why are we violating our own laws? We haven't even given Jesus a fair trial and already we are judging Him.*]

52 They answered and said unto him, Art thou also of Galilee [*has He converted you too*]? Search, and look: for out of Galilee ariseth no prophet. [*Check the scriptures. There is no mention of a Prophet who comes from Galilee.*]

53 And every man went unto his own house.

JOHN 8

IT IS THE day after the Feast of Tabernacles and large crowds of people gather to listen to Jesus as He teaches in the courtyard of the temple in Jerusalem. The scribes and Pharisees are very frustrated because, despite repeated attempts to discredit Jesus and get Him arrested, they continue to fail to reach their goal. John now reports yet another attempt to trap Him in His words, as these Jewish leaders drag a woman taken in adultery to Jesus, in front of the crowd, and ask what He recommends be done to her. Their hope is that they can get Him to say something in opposition to the Law of

Moses concerning punishment for adultery, in order that they can have Him arrested. Watch and see what happens.

1 JESUS went unto the mount of Olives [*just a few minutes' walk east of Jerusalem*].

2 And early in the morning he came again into the temple [*the courtyard of the temple*], and all the people came unto him; and he sat down, and taught them.

The Woman Taken in Adultery

3 And the scribes and Pharisees [*hypocritical religious leaders of the Jews*] brought unto him a woman taken in adultery; and when they had set her in the midst,

JST JOHN 8:3
3 And the scribes and Pharisees brought unto him a woman taken in adultery; and when they had set her in the midst of the people,

4 They say unto him, Master, this woman was taken in adultery, in the very act [*we caught her right while she was doing it*].

One has to wonder why these Jewish leaders didn't also bring the man who was involved with this woman to the Savior. Perhaps he was one of their own. In JST Luke 16:21, Jesus called these leaders "adulterers." We don't know if the man was a fellow Pharisee, but it is pure hypocrisy to single out the woman for embarrassment and humiliation, and let the man escape.

Next, they remind Him of what the Law of Moses said regarding the matter, and then ask a question.

5 Now Moses in the law commanded us, that such should be stoned: but what sayest thou?

These evil men are still trying to trap Jesus by getting Him to say something against Moses and his laws. Imagine how quiet it was as the crowd hushed in an attempt to watch and hear the Master's response. Imagine also how frightened the woman was.

6 This they said, tempting him [*trying to lure Him into a trap*], that they might have to accuse him [*in order for them to build a legal case against Him*]. But Jesus stooped down, and with his finger wrote on the ground, as though he heard them not.

"He That is Without Sin… First Cast a Stone"

7 So when they continued [*kept*] asking him, he lifted up himself [*stood up*], and said unto them, He that is without sin among you [*perhaps implying whoever has not committed the same sin; see* Doctrinal New Testament Commentary, *Vol. 1, p. 451*], let him first cast a stone at her.

8 And again he stooped down, and wrote on the ground.

9 And they which heard it, being convicted by their own conscience, went out [*left*] one by one, beginning at the eldest, even unto the last: and Jesus was left alone, and the woman standing in the midst.

JST JOHN 8:9
And they which heard it, being convicted by their own conscience, went out one by one, beginning at the eldest, even unto the last; and Jesus was left alone, and the woman standing in the midst of the temple.

10 When Jesus had lifted up himself [*had stood up*], and saw none but the woman, he said unto her, Woman, where are those thine accusers? hath no man condemned thee? [*Where did the men go who wanted to stone you? Didn't any of them condemn you to death?*]

11 She said, No man, Lord. And Jesus said unto her, Neither do I condemn thee: go, and sin no more.

JST JOHN 8:11
11 She said, No man, Lord. And Jesus said unto her, Neither do I condemn thee; go, and sin no more. And the woman glorified God from that hour, and believed on his name.

Jesus did not forgive the woman at this point. Obviously, she has some serious repenting to do. But He did not condemn her, meaning that she

HE THAT IS
WITHOUT SIN
AMONG YOU, LET
HIM FIRST CAST A
STONE.

JOHN 8:7

HE THAT IS WITHOUT SIN,

by Liz Lemon Swindle

still had time and opportunity to repent. The Joseph Smith Translation, cited above at the end of verse 11, confirms that she began repenting.

Next, Jesus teaches that He is the light of the world.

The Light of the World

12 Then spake Jesus again unto them, saying, I am the light of the world: he that followeth me shall not walk in darkness [*spiritual darkness*], but shall have the light of life [*eternal life*].

13 The Pharisees therefore said unto him, Thou bearest record of thyself; thy record is not true. [*You are not following the law of witnesses.*]

14 Jesus answered and said unto them, Though I bear record of myself, yet my record is true: for I know whence I came [*where I am from*], and whither I go [*and where I am going*]; but ye cannot tell whence I come, and whither I go.

15 Ye judge after the flesh [*you are judging me by worldly standards*]; I judge no man [*perhaps meaning that the day of final judgment has not yet arrived and the opportunity to repent and change their ways is still available*].

16 And yet if I judge, my judgment is true [*valid*]: for I am not alone, but I and the Father that sent me. [*Jesus has another witness of Himself and His mission, namely, the Father.*]

17 It is also written in your law, that the testimony of two men is true. [*This is the law of witnesses the Jews were referring to in verse 13.*]

18 I am one that bear witness of myself, and the Father that sent me beareth witness of me.

19 Then said they unto him, Where is thy Father? Jesus answered, Ye neither know me, nor my Father: if ye had known me, ye should have [*would have*] known my Father also.

20 These words spake Jesus in the treasury [*one of the temple buildings*], as he taught in the temple: and no man laid hands on him; for his hour was not yet come [*John is reminding us that the time for the Savior's arrest, trial, crucifixion, and resurrection was not yet here at this time*].

21 Then said Jesus again unto them, I go my way, and ye shall seek me [*to kill me*], and shall die in your sins: whither I go, ye cannot come. [*You can't come to heaven because you refuse to repent.*]

22 Then said the Jews, Will he kill himself? because he saith, Whither I go, ye cannot come. [*Does He mean that He is going to commit suicide, and that is how He will get away from us so that we can't follow Him around?*]

23 And he said unto them, Ye are from beneath; I am from above: ye are of this world; I am not of this world. [*In effect, we are worlds apart.*]

24 I said therefore unto you, that ye shall die in your sins: for if ye believe not that I am he [*the Messiah*], ye shall die in your sins.

25 Then said they unto him, Who art thou? And Jesus saith unto them, Even the same that I said unto you from the beginning. [*I already told you.*]

26 I have many things to say and to judge of you: but he [*the Father*] that sent me is true; and I speak to the world those things which I have heard of him.

27 They understood not that he spake to them of the Father.

Have you noticed that John places great emphasis on the Savior honoring His Father and bearing witness of Him? 3 Nephi, chapter 15, likewise teaches of this.

28 Then said Jesus unto them, When ye have lifted up [*crucified*] the Son of man [*me*], then shall ye know that I am he [*the Messiah*], and that I do nothing of myself; but as my Father hath taught me, I speak these things. [*In effect, you will know that I am God's Son and that I bring you His word.*]

29 And he that sent me is with me: the Father hath not left me alone; for I do always those things that please him.

30 As he spake these words, many believed on him.

31 Then said Jesus to those Jews which believed on him, If ye continue in my word, then are ye my disciples indeed;

The Truth Sets Us Free

32 And ye shall know the truth, and the truth shall make you free.

Verse 32 is one of the most profound verses in all the scriptures. It is a simple and powerful fact. The truth sets us free. For example, if people believe that a baby who dies without baptism is forever damned from returning to heaven, D&C 137:10 sets them free from the anguish and lingering guilt of having neglected this rite for the child.

If one has lived a life of serious sin, and upon repenting and changing lifestyle, still believes that he or she will forever be a "second-class" citizen in the Church, Isaiah 1:18 will set him or her free from feelings of being permanently limited by past lifestyle. So will Elder Richard G. Scott's talk in October Conference, 2000, set such persons "free," in which he taught: "If you have repented from serious transgression and mistakenly believe that you will always be a second-class citizen in the kingdom of God, learn that is not true."

As we move on to verse 33, next, a little background is helpful. The Jews at the time of Christ had a very strong tradition that they were privileged above others because they were direct descendants of Abraham. Watch now as they put this false notion into action, and watch the Savior's response to them.

33 They answered him, We be Abraham's seed [*we are descendants of Abraham*], and were never in bondage [*slavery*] to any man [*we don't need to be set free*]: how sayest thou [*what do You mean when You say*], Ye shall be made free?

34 Jesus answered them, Verily, verily, I say unto you, Whosoever committeth sin is the servant of sin [*is a slave to sin*].

35 And the servant abideth not in the house for ever [*slaves don't live in the master's house*]: but the Son abideth ever [*but the Son lives in the Father's house*].

36 If the Son therefore shall make you free, ye shall be free indeed. [*If I make you free from sin, you are free indeed!*]

37 I know that ye are Abraham's seed [*descendants*]; but ye seek to kill me, because my word hath no place in you [*because you have rejected Me*].

38 I speak that which I have seen with my Father: and ye do that which ye have seen with your father [*the devil; see verse 44*].

39 They answered and said unto him, Abraham is our father [*we are direct descendants of Abraham, implying that that fact gives them special privilege*]. Jesus saith unto them, If ye were Abraham's children [*true followers*], ye would do the works of Abraham.

40 But now ye seek to kill me, a man that hath told you the truth, which I have heard of God [*from the Father*]: this did not Abraham [*Abraham would not try to kill me*].

41 Ye do the deeds of your father [*the devil; see verse 44*]. Then said they to him, We be not born of fornication [*we have not "stepped out" on God; in other words, we are not apostates*]; we have one Father, even God. [*We are completely loyal to God.*]

Just a brief note about the word "fornication," as used in verse 41, above. It is obvious that these Jews knew the symbolic use of the term as often found in the scriptures. The words "fornication" and "adultery" are often used in the Bible to refer, symbolically, to complete disloyalty to God. Example: Revelation 14:8, Jeremiah 3:8-9. See Bible Dictionary, under "Adultery."

42 Jesus said unto them, If God were your Father [*if you were true followers of God*], ye would love me: for I proceeded forth and came from God; neither came I of myself, but he sent me.

Next, Jesus poses a question to these people, and then answers His own question. The JST makes an important one-word change to verse 43. It teaches us that there are some people who, because of their beliefs or lifestyle, simply can't stand the truth.

43 Why do ye not understand my speech? even because ye cannot hear my word.

JST JOHN 8:43

43 Why do ye not understand my speech? even because ye cannot bear my word.

Next, in verse 44, the Savior gives us a rather brief but concentrated description of the devil.

44 Ye are of your father the devil, and the lusts of your father ye will do [*you live the wicked lifestyle sponsored by your "father," the devil*]. He was a murderer from the beginning, and abode not in the truth, because there is no truth in him. When he speaketh a lie, he speaketh of his own: for he is a liar, and the father of it. [*The devil is the father of lies.*]

45 And because I tell you the truth, ye believe me not.

46 Which of you convinceth [*convicts—see John 8:46, footnote a, in your Bible*] me of sin? And if I say the truth, why do ye not believe me?

47 He that is of God [*the righteous*] heareth God's words: ye therefore hear them not, because ye are not of God.

JST JOHN 8:47

47 He that is of God receiveth God's words; ye therefore receive them not, because ye are not of God.

The change from "hear" to "receive" by the Prophet Joseph Smith in verse 47, above, is a major message for us. As learners, we have the obligation to actively receive the gospel when we hear it, rather than simply hearing it.

48 Then answered the Jews, and said unto him, Say we not well that thou art a Samaritan [*You are an apostate Yourself—see verse 41*], and hast a devil?

The phrase "thou art a Samaritan" in verse 48 above is saying, in effect, that Jesus is "illegitimate," and God is not his father. The Samaritans came from remnants of the ten northern tribes of Israel, who intermarried with non-covenant people, mainly Assyrian occupational armies, beginning in about 722 B.C., and apostatized. Thus, Samaritans were considered by the Jews to be former members of the House of Israel who had "stepped out on God" by marrying nonmembers and thereby had polluted the race. They were "illegitimate" children, therefore, were despised by the Jews.

49 Jesus answered, I have not a devil; but I honour my Father, and ye do dishonour me.

50 And I seek not mine own glory: there is one that seeketh and judgeth.

51 Verily, verily, I say unto you, If a man keep my saying, he shall never see death [*spiritual death*].

52 Then said the Jews unto him, Now we know that thou hast a devil [*now we know that You are possessed by a demon*]. Abraham is dead, and the prophets; and thou sayest, If a man keep my saying, he shall never taste of death [*will never die*].

Next, these people who are completely missing the point about spiritual death retort back to Jesus that Abraham was righteous and he died, so what He is saying about death can't be true.

53 Art thou greater than our father Abraham, which is dead? and the prophets are dead: whom makest thou thyself [*who do You think You are*]?

54 Jesus answered, If I honour myself, my honour is nothing: it is my Father that honoureth me; of whom ye say, that he is your God:

55 Yet ye have not known him [*you don't follow Him, you don't know Him*]; but I know him: and if I should say, I know him not, I shall be a liar like unto you: but I know him, and keep his saying [*follow His instructions*].

56 Your father [*ancestor*] Abraham rejoiced to see my day [*saw my day in vision*]: and he saw it, and was glad.

57 Then said the Jews unto him, Thou art not yet fifty years old, and hast thou seen Abraham?

58 Jesus said unto them, Verily, verily, I say unto you, Before Abraham was, I am [*in effect, I am the God who appeared to Abraham*].

"I am" in verse 58 above is usually written "I AM," and is another name for Jehovah, the God of the Old Testament. See John 8:58, footnote b, in your Bible. See also Exodus 3:14. Jesus has just told the Jews, in terms they understand, that He is Jehovah, the God of the Old Testament, and that the reason He has seen Abraham (verse 57 above) is that he is the God of Abraham and appeared to him. Because the Jews finally understand clearly who Jesus is claiming to be, they are furious with Him, as shown in verse 59, next.

59 Then took they up stones to cast at him: but Jesus hid himself, and went out of the temple, going through the midst of them, and so passed by.

JOHN 9

YET AGAIN JESUS will heal on the Sabbath, and the Jews will accuse Him of violating the Sabbath as a result. You will find the dialogue between the Jewish leaders and the blind man who was healed fascinating. They will interrogate him and attempt to get him to discredit Jesus, but he will refuse. Finally, since he refuses to go along with them, they will excommunicate him from their church (verse 34).

It may be that verse 1, next, is a connection back to chapter 8, verse 59. If so, then it is saying that as Jesus was escaping from the angry Jews who were trying to stone Him at the end of chapter 8, He saw a blind man and stopped.

1 AND as Jesus passed by, he saw a man which was blind from his birth.

Some people have come to believe the false notion that physical illness in general is caused by sin. This was a common belief among the Jews in New Testament times. We see this reflected in verse 2, next.

2 And his disciples asked him, saying, Master, who did sin, this man, or his parents, that he was born blind?

The Savior straightens out this mistaken idea in the case of the blind man, and then bears witness that the Father sent Him to be the light of the world.

3 Jesus answered, Neither hath this man sinned, nor his parents: but that the works of God should be made manifest [*be shown*] in him.

4 I must work the works of him that sent me, while it is day: the night cometh, when no man can work.

JST JOHN 9:4

4 I must work the works of him that sent me, while I am with you; the time cometh when I shall have finished my work, then I go unto the Father.

5 As long as I am in the world, I am the light of the world.

A Blind Man Is Healed

6 When he had thus spoken, he spat on the ground, and made clay of the spittle, and he anointed the eyes of the blind man with the clay,

There is perhaps symbolism in the use of "clay", in verse 6 above. "Clay" is symbolic of this earth as well as of our mortal bodies. Touching the blind man's eyes with the clay so he could see can symbolize the fact that those who are faithful in this mortal experience will eventually be enabled to "see" as God sees as they enter into exaltation.

7 And said unto him, Go, wash in the pool of Siloam, (which is by interpretation, Sent.) He went his way therefore, and washed, and came seeing [*could see*].

Did you notice that the word "sent," in verse 7, above, is capitalized? It is capitalized because it refers to Christ. Thus, we see symbolism here. Among the possible symbolism is: If we "wash" our spiritual eyes in the "living water" from Christ, we will be able to see the things of eternity clearly.

Watch now as people take the focus from a simple and beautiful miracle and ruin it by interrogating the once-blind man to the point of excommunicating him because of his simple, honest answers.

8 The neighbours therefore, and they which before had seen him that he was blind, said, Is not this he that sat and begged [*isn't this the blind man who used to be a beggar*]?

9 Some said, This is he: others said, He is like him [*he just looks like that blind man*]: but he [*the blind man*] said, I am he [*I am the one who was healed*].

10 Therefore said they unto him, How were thine eyes opened?

11 He answered and said, A man that is called Jesus made clay, and anointed mine eyes, and said unto me, Go to the pool of Siloam, and wash: and I went and washed, and I received sight.

LORD I BELIEVE, by Liz Lemon Swindle

AND HE SAID, LORD, I BELIEVE. AND HE WORSHIPPED HIM.

JOHN 9:38

12 Then said they unto him, Where is he? He said, I know not.

13 They brought to the Pharisees him that aforetime was blind. [*Some Jews brought the formerly blind man to the Pharisees.*]

14 And it was the sabbath day when Jesus made the clay, and opened his eyes. [*Jesus had healed the blind man on the Sabbath.*]

15 Then again the Pharisees also asked him how he had received his sight. He said unto them, He [*Jesus*] put clay upon mine eyes, and I washed, and do see [*and I can see*].

16 Therefore said some of the Pharisees, This man is not of God, because he keepeth not the sabbath day [*Jesus can't be sent by God, because He breaks the Sabbath by healing people on it*]. Others said, How can a man that is a sinner do such miracles? And there was a division among them.

17 They say unto the blind man again, What sayest thou of him, that he hath opened thine eyes [*what's your opinion of Jesus*]? He said, He is a prophet.

The Jewish religious leaders are trying desperately to discredit Jesus in the eyes of the people and it is not working. They now try to discredit the blind man's parents by suggesting that they don't really know for sure that their son was born blind.

19 And they asked them, saying, Is this your son, who ye say [*claim*] was born blind? how then doth he now see [*if he was really blind, how could he see now*]?

20 His parents answered them and said, We know that this is our son, and that he was born blind:

21 But by what means he now seeth, we know not [*we don't understand what happened so that he can now see*]; or who hath opened his eyes, we know not: he is of age; ask him: he shall speak for himself. [*Ask him. He is old enough to speak for himself.*]

22 These words spake his parents, because they feared the Jews [*the religious rulers of the Jews*]: for the Jews had agreed [*plotted*] already, that if any man did confess that he was Christ, he should be put out of the synagogue. [*Anyone who says Jesus is the prophesied Messiah will be excommunicated.*]

23 Therefore said his parents, He is of age; ask him. [*The parents were afraid of getting excommunicated, so they told the Pharisees to ask their son what happened.*]

By now it must have become very bothersome to the blind man who was healed to have such a negative fuss made over a beautiful and straightforward miracle through which his sight was restored. You can sense his frustration in the next verses and perhaps some disgust with these distracters. Surely we can admire the boldness in his replies as he steadfastly maintains his position that Jesus healed him, thus risking his membership in the Jewish church.

24 Then again called they [*the Pharisees*] the man that was blind, and said unto him, Give God the praise: we know that this man [*Jesus*] is a sinner. [*Give God the praise for your being healed, but don't give this imposter, Jesus, any credit.*]

25 He answered and said, Whether he be a sinner or no, I know not [*whether or not Jesus is a sinner, I don't know*]: one thing I know, that, whereas I was blind, now I see [*but one thing I do know: I was blind and now I can see*]. [*This formerly blind man is not intimidated by the Jewish rulers, which must have been frustrating for them.*]

26 Then said they to him again, What did he [*Jesus*] to thee? how opened he thine eyes?

27 He answered them, I have told you already, and ye did not hear [*what's the matter, are you dense?*]: wherefore would ye hear it again [*why do you want me to tell you again*]? will ye also be his disciples [*are you being converted to Him too*]?

28 Then they reviled him [*insulted him*], and said, Thou art his disciple [*you have become a follower of Jesus*]; but we are Moses' disciples.

29 We know that God spake unto Moses: as for this fellow, we know not from whence he is [*we don't know where He comes from*].

We sense that this blind man might well have been one of the "noble and great ones" (Abraham 3:22) from our premortal existence as we watch him now boldly take on these Jewish religious leaders who have been battering him constantly to try to get him to renounce Jesus.

30 The man answered and said unto them, Why herein is a marvellous thing [*well, this is getting more interesting all the time*], that ye [*the big religious leaders who are supposed to know these things*] know not from whence he is, and yet he hath opened mine eyes.

31 Now we know that God heareth not sinners: but if any man be a worshipper of God, and doeth his will, him he heareth. [*If Jesus were a sinner, God would not support Him in such miracles.*]

32 Since the world began was it not heard that any man opened the eyes of one that was born blind.

JST JOHN 9:32

32 Since the world began was it not heard that any man opened the eyes of one that was born blind, except he be of God.

33 If this man [*Jesus*] were not of God, he could do nothing.

34 They answered and said unto him, Thou wast altogether born in sins, and dost thou teach us [*you, a complete sinner, have the gall to pretend to teach us*]? And they cast him out. [*They excommunicated him.*]

Watch now as the Savior seeks out the formerly blind man who humbly receives the Master's message of salvation.

35 Jesus heard that they had cast him out; and when he had found him, he said unto him, Dost thou believe on the Son of God?

36 He answered and said, Who is he, Lord, that I might believe on him?

37 And Jesus said unto him, Thou hast both seen him [*NIV "thou hast now seen him"*], and it is he that talketh with thee. [*You are talking with Him now.*]

38 And he said, Lord, I believe. And he worshipped him.

39 And Jesus said, For judgement I am come into this world [*I have come to the world so that all people can receive a fair judgment*], that [*so that*] they which see not might see [*so that the spiritually blind, who repent, can see spiritual things*]; and that they which see [*who claim to see, but are in spiritual darkness*] might be made blind [*can use their agency to remain spiritually blind*].

Watch now as some of these Pharisees, having caught on to what the Savior said in verse 39, above, openly ask if they fit into the category of those who are spiritually blind.

40 And some of the Pharisees which were with him heard these words, and said unto him, Are we blind also?

41 Jesus said unto them, If ye were blind, ye should have no sin: but now ye say, We see; therefore your sin remaineth. [*If you were ignorant of the truth, you would not be accountable, but it is as you say; you are sinning against light, therefore you remain accountable.*]

JOHN 10

NEXT, THE MASTER uses the imagery of a shepherd leading his sheep to illustrate that He is the Good Shepherd, and other, unauthorized shepherds (Pharisees, etc.) try to sneak in and lead the sheep astray. In the days of Jesus, it was a common practice for several shepherds to keep their sheep overnight in the same enclosure, so that only one guard would have to be on duty through the night. The next morning, each shepherd would come to the enclosure, identify himself to the guard, and then literally call his own sheep to come out of the herd to him, often calling each of his sheep by its own name. His sheep recognized his voice and came out of the herd and followed him throughout the day as he led them to pasture and water. It is a fascinating sight in the Holy Land, even today, to see sheep following a shepherd who is leading his sheep, rather than herding them from behind.

In this chapter you will find the reference to the Nephites in the Americas (verse 16).

The Parable of the Good Shepherd

1 VERILY, verily, I say unto you, He that entereth not by the door into the sheepfold, but climbeth up some other way, the same is a thief and a robber [*is not authorized by God to lead the sheep; symbolic of Satan, apostates, and others, who try to lead us astray*].

2 But he [*Christ*] that entereth in by the door [*is authorized by God*] is the shepherd of the sheep.

3 To him the porter [*guard*] openeth; and the sheep hear his voice: and he calleth his own sheep by name, and leadeth them out.

4 And when he putteth forth his own sheep, he goeth before them [*leads them, rather than herding them*], and the sheep follow him: for they know his voice.

5 And a stranger will they not follow, but will flee from him: for they know not the voice of strangers.

6 This parable spake Jesus unto them: but they understood not what things they were which he spake unto them.

Next, Jesus explains the parable of the good shepherd.

7 Then said Jesus unto them again, Verily, verily, I say unto you, I am the door of the sheep [*symbolic of the door to heaven*].

8 All that ever came before me are thieves and robbers [*any others who have come before me and claim to be the doorway to heaven are false shepherds*]: but the sheep did not hear them [*my true followers don't come to them when they call*].

9 I am the door: by me if any man enter in, he shall be saved, and shall go in and out, and find pasture [*will be nourished by God*].

10 The thief [*symbolic of Satan, the wicked, and so forth*] cometh not, but for to steal, and to kill, and to destroy: I am come that they might have life [*to bring the faithful eternal life*], and that they might have it more abundantly.

11 I am the good shepherd: the good shepherd giveth his life for the sheep [*Jesus will give His life for us*].

12 But he that is an hireling [*a hired servant*], and not the shepherd, whose own the sheep are not [*who does not own the sheep*], seeth the wolf coming, and leaveth the sheep, and fleeth: and the wolf catcheth them, and scattereth the sheep.

13 The hireling fleeth [*runs away when danger comes*], because he is an hireling, and careth not for the sheep [*he doesn't love the sheep like the owner does*].

14 I am the good shepherd, and know my sheep, and am known of mine [*the Savior's true followers know His voice and come when He calls*].

15 As the Father knoweth me, even so know I the Father: and I lay down my life for the sheep [*Jesus will give His life for His people as He performs the Atonement*].

Other Sheep

16 And other sheep I have, which are not of this fold [*are not on this continent*]: them also I must bring, and they shall hear my voice; and there shall be one fold, and one shepherd [*all of my righteous followers will ultimately come together with me in celestial glory*].

We know from 3 Nephi 15:21 that Jesus was referring to the Nephites on the American continent when He said, "Other sheep I have, which are not of this fold; them also I must bring, and they shall hear my voice;" (verse 16 above). We know also that there were yet other sheep besides the Nephites. To the Nephites, Jesus said, "I say unto you that I have other sheep, which are not of this land, neither of the land of Jerusalem" (3 Nephi 16:1). As we read 3 Nephi 17:4, we are told that Jesus was referring to the lost ten tribes.

17 Therefore [*for this reason*] doth my Father love me, because I lay down my life, that I might take it again.

Verse 18, next, is significant doctrinally. In the strictest sense, no one killed Jesus or took His life. No one could. He gave it as a free-will offering for our sins.

18 No man taketh it from me, but I lay it down of myself. I have power to lay it down [*to leave my body*], and I have power to take it again [*I have power to resurrect*]. This commandment have I received of my Father. [*This is what my Father asked me to do.*]

19 There was a division therefore again among the Jews for [*because of*] these sayings [*because Jesus said that no one could kill Him, rather, He would give His life willingly, then resurrect Himself*].

20 And many of them said, He hath a devil [*He is possessed by an evil spirit*], and is mad [*has lost His mind*]; why hear ye him [*why do you even listen to Him*]?

21 Others said, These are not the words of him that hath a devil. Can a devil open the eyes of the blind?

Verse 22, next, begins a new topic. In your LDS King James Version of the Bible (English), you will see a paragraph mark at the beginning of the verse signaling a new subject to you, the reader.

It is the winter before the crucifixion and the Savior is in Jerusalem at the time of the Feast of Dedication. It was eight days of festivities celebrating the dedication of a new altar of burnt offering in 165 B.C. after the old one had been desecrated by Antiochus Epiphanes, the king of Syria in 168 B.C. No fasting or mourning for any calamity of the past was allowed, which would mar the great gladness and rejoicing accompanying the celebration. Huge torches illuminated the streets and public gathering places in the city, and thus it became known as the Feast of Lights. (See Bible Dictionary, under "Feasts.")

Watch now as Jesus attends the Feast of Dedication.

22 And it was at Jerusalem the feast of the dedication, and it was winter.

23 And Jesus walked in the temple in Solomon's porch.

24 Then came the Jews round about him, and said unto him, How long dost thou make us to doubt [*how long are You going to keep us wondering about who You really are*]? If thou be the Christ, tell us plainly.

25 Jesus answered them, I told you, and ye believed not [*in effect, I have told you many times and in many ways that I am Christ, but you won't believe Me*]: the works [*miracles and teaching*] that I do in my Father's name, they bear witness of me [*they tell you who I am*].

26 But ye believe not, because ye are not of my sheep, as I said unto you. [*You have been in apostasy so long that you no longer even recognize the voice of the Good Shepherd when He calls.*]

27 My sheep hear my voice, and I know them, and they follow me:

28 And I give unto them eternal life; and they shall never perish [*they will never suffer spiritual death*], neither shall any man pluck them out of my hand [*no one can take them away from Me*].

29 My Father, which gave them me, is greater than all; and no man is able to pluck them out of my Father's hand.

30 I and my Father are one. [*The Father and Son are completely united in all things.*]

Next, the Jews accuse the Savior of blasphemy (mocking God) which, under their law, was a crime punishable by death.

31 Then the Jews took up stones again to stone him [*to throw rocks at Him and kill Him*].

32 Jesus answered them, Many good works have I shewed [*shown*] you from my Father; for which of those works do ye stone me? [*In effect, I have done many wonderful miracles and much good; for which of these things are you going to stone Me?*]

33 The Jews answered him, saying, For a good work we stone thee not; but for blasphemy; and because that thou, being a man, makest thyself God. [*We are not stoning You for those things, rather because You have mocked God and claim that You are God.*]

34 Jesus answered them, Is it not written in your law [*Psalm 82:6*], I said, Ye are gods [*you can become gods*]?

This is a very important doctrinal point. Many Christians are very offended by our teaching that we can become gods (D&C 132:20). Here in the Bible itself is a statement, confirmed by the Savior Himself, that we can become gods. He reaffirms what had already been given in Psalm 82:6.

35 If he called them gods, unto whom the word of God came, and the scripture cannot be broken; [*If your scriptures teach that you can become gods, why is it blasphemy* (*mocking God*) for me to say I am a God?]

As mentioned previously, blasphemy, according to Jewish law, was a sin which could get a person executed.

36 Say ye of him [*me*], whom the Father hath sanctified [*prepared*], and sent into the world, Thou blasphemest; because I said, I am the Son of God [*are you saying that I mock God by claiming to be His Son*]?

37 If I do not the works of my Father [*if what I do doesn't remind you of the Father*], believe me not [*then don't believe me*].

38 But if I do [*remind you of the Father*], though ye believe not me, believe the works: that ye may know, and believe, that the Father is in me, and I in him.

39 Therefore [*because of what He said*] they sought [*attempted*] again to take [*arrest*] him: but he escaped out of their hand,

40 And went away again beyond Jordan into the place where John at first baptized; and there he abode [*stayed*].

41 And many resorted [*went*] unto him, and said, John did no miracle [*John the Baptist didn't do miracles*]: but all things that John spake of this man [*Jesus*] were true [*everything he said about Jesus turned out to be true*].

42 And many believed on him there.

JOHN 11

AS THIS CHAPTER begins, Jesus and His disciples are staying in Perea (across the Jordan River, east of Jericho—see John 10:40, roughly 30 miles from Jerusalem), where there is relative safety from the Jews in Jerusalem who had recently attempted to stone Him. It is the Master's last winter during His mortal ministry.

John, chapter 11, is a chapter that especially touches the heart. You will see the Savior's love for Mary, Martha, and Lazarus as He weeps with tender emotion (verse 35) and then watch His power over death as He raises Lazarus from the dead. Lazarus had become very ill, and his sisters, Mary and Martha, had sent for the Master to come heal him. Jesus did not come immediately, as they hoped He would, and Lazarus died. Watch now as a great lesson unfolds concerning the Savior's tender mercy and His power to bring resurrection to all.

Lazarus Is Sick

1 NOW a certain man was sick, named Lazarus, of Bethany [*about two miles outside of Jerusalem on the far side of the Mount of Olives, on the road to Jericho*], the town of Mary and her sister Martha [*the town where Mary and Martha lived*].

2 (It was that Mary which anointed the Lord with ointment, and wiped his feet with her hair [*Matthew 26:7, John 12:2-3*], whose brother Lazarus was sick.)

JST JOHN 11:2

2 And Mary, his sister, who anointed the Lord with ointment and wiped his feet with her hair, lived with her sister Martha, in whose house her brother Lazarus was sick.

3 Therefore his sisters sent unto him [*Jesus*], saying, Lord, behold, he [*Lazarus*] whom thou lovest is sick.

4 When Jesus heard that, he said, This sickness is not unto death, but for the glory of God, that the Son of God might be glorified thereby. [*In effect, He won't be dead very long. He will die, verses 13–14, and this situation will help many to believe in God and to have a chance to be much more aware of who I am.*]

5 Now Jesus loved Martha, and her sister, and Lazarus.

6 When he had heard therefore that he was sick, he abode [*stayed*] two days still in the same place [*Perea*] where he was.

7 Then after that saith he to his disciples, Let us go into Judæa [*to the Jerusalem area*] again.

8 His disciples say unto him, Master, the Jews of late [*just recently*] sought to [*attempted to*] stone thee; and goest thou thither [*there*] again?

His disciples are very worried about His safety and don't want Him going to Mary and Martha's house in Bethany, because it is only two miles from Jerusalem where the Jews are who have already tried to kill Him.

9 Jesus answered, Are there not twelve hours in the day? If any man walk in the day, he stumbleth not, because he seeth the light of this world. [*In effect, I must keep right on going with my work.*]

10 But if a man walk in the night, he stumbleth, because there is no light in him.

11 These things said he: and after that he saith unto them, Our friend Lazarus sleepeth; but I go, that I may awake him out of sleep.

12 Then said his disciples, Lord, if he sleep, he shall do well [*if he is just sleeping, he will be ok, implying again that they don't want Him going near Jerusalem*].

13 Howbeit [*however*] Jesus spake of his death: but they thought that he had spoken of taking of rest in sleep.

Lazarus Is Dead

14 Then said Jesus unto them plainly, Lazarus is dead.

15 And I am glad for your sakes that I was not there, to the intent ye may believe [*in effect, I am glad he is dead, because what is going to happen will strengthen your testimonies*]; nevertheless let us go unto him.

16 Then said Thomas, which is called Didymus [*the twin*], unto his fellow disciples, Let us also go, that we may die with him.

JST JOHN 11:16

16 Then said Thomas, which is called Didymus, unto his fellow disciples, Let us also go, that we may die with him; for they feared lest the Jews should take Jesus and put him to death, for as yet they did not understand the power of God.

This Apostle of Christ, Thomas, is usually known mainly as "doubting Thomas," because he refused to believe that Jesus had been resurrected unless he could see Him personally and feel the wounds in His hands and side. (See John 20:25–28.) Here we see Thomas in a much different light. He is a man of courage and conviction, and encourages the other disciples to join him in going to Jerusalem with Jesus so that they could all die with Him.

17 Then when Jesus came [*arrived in Bethany at Martha's house*], he found that he [*Lazarus*] had lain in the grave four days already.

JST JOHN 11:17

17 And when Jesus came to Bethany, to Martha's house, Lazarus had already been in the grave four days.

Four days is very significant because of Jewish beliefs about death. They had a false belief that the spirit must remain by a dead person's body for three days. After that, the person is for sure dead. The fact that Lazarus had been dead for four days, and in fact, had already begun to stink (verse 39) left no doubt in the minds of the mourners that he was dead.

18 Now Bethany was nigh [*near*] unto Jerusalem, about fifteen furlongs off [*two miles away*]:

A "furlong," as used in verse 18, above, is about 607 English feet (see John 11, footnote 18a, in your Bible). Thus, 15 times 607 is 9,105 feet, or about 1.7 miles.

19 And many of the Jews came to Martha and Mary, to comfort them concerning their brother.

20 Then Martha, as soon as she heard that Jesus was coming, went and met him: but Mary sat still in the house.

21 Then said Martha unto Jesus, Lord, if thou hadst been here, my brother had not died [*if You had come quickly, when I first sent word to You of Lazarus' illness, he would not have died*].

Next, Martha expresses her great faith in Jesus. We see that she has been taught the doctrine of resurrection as she responds to the Master's assurance that Lazarus will be resurrected.

22 But I know, that even now, whatsoever thou wilt ask of God, God will give it thee. [*Martha has great faith, and hints that she believes that even now, Lazarus could be brought back to life.*]

23 Jesus saith unto her, Thy brother shall rise again.

24 Martha saith unto him, I know that he shall rise again in the resurrection at the last day.

Verse 25, next, is a very well-known verse in the Bible. You may wish to mark it in your own scriptures. In a significant way, it is a very brief summary of the Savior's purpose and mission. Through His Atonement, all will be resurrected and eternal life (exaltation) is made available to all, contingent on repenting and living the gospel.

"I Am the Resurrection and the Life"

25 Jesus said unto her, I am the resurrection, and the life [*in effect, I have power over death and can give eternal life*]: he that believeth in me, though he were dead, yet shall he live:

26 And whosoever liveth [*is spiritually alive*] and believeth in me shall never die [*spiritually*]. Believest thou this?

Martha's Testimony of Christ

27 She saith unto him, Yea, Lord: I believe that thou art the Christ, the Son of God, which should come into the world. [*I believe that You are the promised Messiah.*]

28 And when she had so said, she went her way, and called Mary her sister secretly, saying, The Master is come, and calleth for thee.

29 As soon as she heard that, she arose quickly, and came unto him [*Jesus*].

JST JOHN 11:29

29 As soon as Mary heard that Jesus was come, she arose quickly, and came unto him.

30 Now Jesus was not yet [*had not yet*] come into the town, but was in that place where Martha met him.

31 The Jews then which were with her in the house, and comforted her, when they saw Mary, that she rose up hastily and went out, followed her, saying, She goeth unto the grave [*to Lazarus' tomb*] to weep there.

32 Then when Mary was come where Jesus was, and saw him, she fell down at his feet, saying unto him, Lord, if thou hadst been here, my brother had not [*would not have*] died.

33 When Jesus therefore saw her weeping, and the Jews also weeping which came with her, he groaned in the spirit, and was troubled [*This was a very emotional time for Jesus.*],

34 And said, Where have ye laid him [*where have you buried him*]? They said unto him, Lord, come and see.

35 Jesus wept.

Verse 35 is the shortest verse in the Bible. It is a reminder of the great kindness and compassion the Master has for us.

36 Then said the Jews, Behold how he loved him!

37 And some of them said, Could not this man, which opened the eyes of the blind, have caused that even this man should not have died [*couldn't Jesus have prevented Lazarus from dying if He had been here*]?

Lazarus Is Raised from the Dead

38 Jesus therefore again groaning in himself cometh to the grave. It was a cave [*tomb*], and a stone lay upon it.

39 Jesus said, Take ye away the stone [*open the tomb*]. Martha, the sister of him that was dead, saith unto him, Lord, by this time he stinketh:

for he hath been dead four days.

40 Jesus saith unto her, Said I not unto thee, that, if thou wouldest believe, thou shouldest see the glory of God [*you would see the power of God in action*]?

Imagine the hush and the looks on people's faces as they watch with rapt attention as the stone is rolled away!

41 Then they took away the stone from the place where the dead was laid. And Jesus lifted up his eyes, and said, Father, I thank thee that thou hast heard me.

As you have no doubt noticed, the Son humbly gives credit to the Father in all things, pointing our minds past Him and to the Father. Here we are seeing it again.

42 And I knew that thou hearest me always: but because of the people which stand by I said it [*I said it out loud for the benefit of the people who have gathered around*], that they may believe that thou hast sent me.

43 And when he thus had spoken, he cried with a loud voice, Lazarus, come forth.

44 And he that was dead came forth, bound hand and foot with graveclothes: and his face was bound about with a napkin. Jesus saith unto them, Loose him [*unwrap him*], and let him go.

45 Then many of the Jews which came to Mary, and had seen the things which Jesus did, believed on him.

46 But some of them went their ways to the Pharisees, and told them what things Jesus had done.

The Pharisees are beside themselves with frustration and anger. All their attempts to stop Jesus have failed. And now He has raised a man from the dead, and many people saw it happen.

47 Then gathered the chief priests and the Pharisees a council [*the chief religious leaders of the Jews called an emergency meeting*], and said, What do we [*what can we do about Jesus*]? for this man doeth many miracles.

48 If we let him thus alone [*if we don't do something*], all men will believe on him: and the Romans shall come and take away both our place [*our positions of authority*] and nation. [*They are concerned about their own power and prestige. They are an example of the fact that wickedness does not promote rational thought.*]

49 And one of them, named Caiaphas [*the highest religious leader among the Jews at that time*], being the high priest that same year, said unto them, Ye know nothing at all [*You are a pack of idiots!*],

50 Nor consider that it is expedient for us, that one man should die for the people, and that the whole nation perish not. [*The solution is clear. It is better that Jesus die, than our whole nation be disrupted and destroyed by the Romans.*]

51 And this spake he not of himself: but being high priest that year, he prophesied that Jesus should die for that nation;

52 And not for that nation only, but that also he should gather together in one the children of God that were scattered abroad.

Verses 51–52, above, present a problem. The way it is written, it sounds like the wicked high priest, Caiaphas, is actually prophesying that it is necessary for Jesus to die in order to gather the righteous from all the world and save them, which is true. In verse 51, John says that Caiaphas spoke "not of himself," implying perhaps that, by virtue of his office, the Spirit came upon him and caused him to prophesy truth. Apostle James E. Talmage helps us understand this matter. He taught:

"The chief priests, who were mostly Sadducees, and the Pharisees with them assembled in council to consider the situation created by this latest of our Lord's great works. The question they discussed was: "What do we? for this man doeth many miracles. If we let him thus alone, all men will believe on him: and the Romans shall come and take away both our place and nation." As stated by themselves, there was no denying the fact of the many miracles wrought by Jesus; but instead of earnestly and prayerfully investigating as to whether these mighty works were

JOHN

not among the predicted characteristics of the Messiah, they thought only of the possible effect of Christ's influence in alienating the people from the established theocracy, and of the fear that the Romans, taking advantage of the situation, would deprive the hierarchs of their "place" and take from the nation what little semblance of distinct autonomy it still possessed. Caiaphas, the high priest, cut short the discussion by saying: "Ye know nothing at all." This sweeping assertion of ignorance was most likely addressed to the Pharisees of the Sanhedrin; Caiaphas was a Sadducee. His next utterance was of greater significance than he realized: "Nor consider that it is expedient for us, that one man should die for the people, and that the whole nation perish not." John solemnly avers that Caiaphas spake not of himself, but by the spirit of prophecy, which, in spite of his implied unworthiness, came upon him by virtue of his office, and that thus: "He prophesied that Jesus should die for that nation; and not for that nation only, but that also he should gather together in one the children of God that were scattered abroad." But a few years after Christ had been put to death, for the salvation of the Jews and of all other nations, the very calamities which Caiaphas and the Sanhedrin had hoped to avert befell in full measure; the hierarchy was overthrown, the temple destroyed, Jerusalem demolished and the nation disrupted. From the day of that memorable session of the Sanhedrin, the rulers increased their efforts to bring about the death of Jesus, by whatever means they might find available. They issued a mandate that whosoever knew of His whereabouts should give the information to the officials, that they might promptly take Him into custody (*Jesus the Christ*, 1982 edition, p. 498).

53 Then from that day forth they [*the council of the Pharisees, known as the Sanhedrin; see Bible Dictionary, under "Sanhedrin"*] took counsel together for to put him to death.

54 Jesus therefore walked no more openly among the Jews; but went thence [*from there*] unto a country near to the wilderness, into a city called Ephraim [*about 15 miles north of Jerusalem*], and there continued [*stayed*] with his disciples.

55 And the Jews' passover was nigh [*close*] at hand: and many went out of the country up to Jerusalem before the passover, to purify themselves [*to prepare themselves to properly observe Passover week*].

This is the final Passover for the Savior during His mortal life. He will spend the final week of His life teaching the people during the Passover week festivities and worship in Jerusalem. He will be crucified on Friday of that week. The religious rulers of the Jews will be watching for Jesus to see if He will come to Passover this year.

56 Then sought they [*they watched*] for Jesus, and spake [*spoke*] among themselves, as they stood in the temple, What think ye, that he will not come to the feast? [*They were wondering whether or not Jesus would show up in Jerusalem, because of the danger to Him.*]

JST John 11:56

56 Then sought they for Jesus, and spake among themselves, as they stood in the temple, What think ye of Jesus? Will he not come to the feast?

57 Now both the chief priests and the Pharisees had given a commandment, that, if any man knew where he were [*if any one spotted Jesus*], he should shew it [*report it*], that they might take [*arrest*] him.

JOHN 12

THIS CHAPTER BEGINS the last week of the Savior's mortal life. It is Passover time in Jerusalem and Jews from many countries have joined the huge crowds in Jerusalem in preparation for the festivities and worship. The Passover meal itself will be held on Thursday. It is eaten in celebration of the passing of the destroying angel over the homes of the children of Israel in Egypt when the firstborn sons of all the families of the Egyptians were slain in order to persuade Pharaoh to let the Israelite slaves go free.

There is much symbolism associated with the Passover. The children of Israel were held in bondage (slavery) by the Egyptians, symbolizing the bondage of Satan and the accompanying abuse of agency. After repeated attempts by Moses to get Pharaoh to let the Israelite slaves go free, the children of Israel were instructed by Moses (Exodus 12:5) to select and sacrifice a male lamb (symbolizing Christ), without blemish (symbolizing that Christ was perfect), of the first year (symbolizing that Christ was in the prime of life when He accomplished the Atonement). They were to take hyssop (Exodus 12:22), a sponge-like plant (associated with Christ on the cross, see John 19:29), dip it in the blood of the lamb, and then put the blood on the lintel (top of the door frame) and on the door posts of the front door of their dwelling (Exodus 12:7 and 22). This blood of the lamb provided protection for their household.

The ensuing death of the firstborn of Pharaoh and all other Egyptian families caused the Israelite slaves to be set free. The death of the "firstborn" is symbolic of the death of the Savior, the "Firstborn" of the Father in the spirit world (Colossians 1:15). The Savior is referred to as "the Lamb of God." It is through the blood of the Lamb of God that we are set free from the bondage of sin. During the Passover, at the very time the Jews are celebrating being set free from Egyptian bondage by the blood of lambs, the Lamb (Christ) will present Himself to be sacrificed in order that all of us might be set free from physical death and from the bondage of sin.

John begins this chapter by informing us that Mary, Martha's sister, anointed the Savior's feet with very expensive ointment, and Judas Iscariot was irritated because he considered such use of expensive ointment to be a waste of money.

1 THEN Jesus six days before the passover [*this would probably be on Saturday, since Passover was on Thursday*] came to Bethany, where Lazarus was [*lived*] which had been dead, whom he raised from the dead.

2 There they made him a supper; and Martha served: but Lazarus was one of them that sat at the table with him.

3 Then took Mary [*the sister of Martha and Lazarus*] a pound of ointment of spikenard, very costly [*very expensive; see note in verse 5*], and anointed [*poured it on*] the feet of Jesus, and wiped his feet with her hair: and the house was filled with the odour of the ointment.

4 Then saith one of his disciples, Judas Iscariot, Simon's son, which should betray him [*the one who would betray Christ*],

5 Why was not this ointment sold for three hundred pence [*about 300 days' wages*], and given to the poor?

6 This he said, not that he cared for the poor; but because he was a thief, and had the bag [*the money purse*], and bare what was put therein. [*Judas Iscariot was apparently the treasurer of the Twelve.*]

7 Then said Jesus, Let her alone: against the day of my burying hath she kept this. [*She has anointed my body in preparation for my death and burial.*]

JST John 12:7

7 Then said Jesus, Let her alone; for she hath preserved this ointment until now, that she might anoint me in token of my burial.

It would appear here that Mary is more sensitive and aware of what is going to happen to Jesus than most of the others are at this time.

8 For the poor always ye have with you; but me ye have not always.

9 Much [*many*] people of the Jews therefore knew that he was there: and they came not for Jesus' sake only, but that they might see Lazarus also, whom he had raised from the dead. [*People didn't come just to see Jesus, but they were also curious to see Lazarus who had been brought back to life after having been dead for four days.*]

Having Lazarus around, healthy and very much alive, after he had been dead for four days, did not help the cause of the Jewish religious leaders at all. Therefore, as you will see in verse 10, next, they make plans for him.

10 But the chief priests consulted [*plotted*] that they might put Lazarus also to death;

11 Because that by reason of him many of the Jews went away, and believed on Jesus. [*They wanted to get rid of Lazarus due to the fact that many Jews were being converted to Jesus because of His raising Lazarus from the dead.*]

Next comes what is known as the "Triumphal Entry" of Jesus into Jerusalem. Excitement about Jesus was making its way through the large crowds in Jerusalem, and when word came that Jesus was even now approaching the city, large numbers of people lined the streets and threw pieces of clothing along the way in front of the Master. They took palm branches and laid them in the path also. Symbolically, in Jewish culture, palm branches represent triumph and victory over enemies. In effect, the people were excitedly welcoming Jesus as a king.

The Triumphal Entry

12 On the next day [*probably Sunday*] much people that were come to the feast [*of Passover*], when they heard that Jesus was coming to Jerusalem,

13 Took branches of palm trees, and went forth to meet him, and cried, Hosanna: Blessed is the King of Israel that cometh in the name of the Lord.

The Hosanna Shout

In conjunction with the dedication of our temples, we participate in what is known as the Hosanna Shout. See *Mormon Doctrine*, p. 368. "Hosanna" means "Lord, save us now." See Bible Dictionary, under "Hosanna." Another translation of Hosanna is "O, please, Jehovah, save (us) now, please!"

During the dedication of the Kirtland Temple on March 27, 1836, Joseph Smith gave a dedicatory prayer. In the prayer (D&C 109), the Prophet pled with the Lord "that we may be clothed upon with robes of righteousness, with palms in our hands, and crowns of glory upon our heads, and reap eternal joy for all our sufferings" (D&C 109:76). The prayer was followed by the Saints standing and participating in the Hosanna Shout. Afterward, they sang "The Spirit of God," which includes the phrase, "Hosanna, Hosanna to God and the Lamb!" (See *Mormon Doctrine*, p. 368, for more about the Hosanna Shout.)

Today, worthy members are invited to bring clean, white handkerchiefs with them to temple dedications. These handkerchiefs are symbolic of palm branches, and represent victory and triumph over our enemies of sin and weakness through the Atonement of Christ.

14 And Jesus, when he had found a young ass [*a young, male donkey, which had never been ridden; see Luke 19:30*], sat thereon; as it is written [*in Zechariah 9:9*],

JST JOHN 12:14

14 And Jesus, when he had sent two of his disciples and got a young ass, sat thereon; as it is written,

15 Fear not, daughter of Sion: behold, thy King cometh, sitting on an ass's colt.

Next, in verse 16, John indicates that when this was actually happening, he and the other disciples did not realize that they were watching prophecy being fulfilled.

16 These things understood not his disciples at the first: but when Jesus was glorified [*had been resurrected*], then remembered they that these things were written of him, and that they had done these things unto him.

17 The people therefore that was with him when he called Lazarus out of his grave, and raised him from the dead, bare record. [*The people who were with Jesus when he raised Lazarus from the dead, spread the word among the Passover crowds that Jesus was coming into Jerusalem.*]

18 For this cause the people also met him [*this is why the crowds came to meet Him as He arrived*], for that they heard that he had done this miracle [*because they heard that He had raised a man from the dead*].

19 The Pharisees therefore said among themselves, Perceive ye how ye prevail nothing [*we can't seem to do anything about Jesus*]? behold, the world is gone after him [*everybody is starting to follow Him*].

20 And there were certain Greeks among them that came up to worship at the feast:

21 The same came therefore to Philip [*an Apostle; see John 1:44*], which was of Bethsaida of Galilee, and desired him, saying, Sir, we would see Jesus [*we would like to see Jesus*].

22 Philip cometh and telleth Andrew [*an Apostle*]: and again Andrew and Philip tell [*told*] Jesus.

23 And Jesus answered them, saying, The hour

is come, that the Son of man [*Christ*] should be glorified [*the time has come for Jesus to finish His mortal mission*].

Next, the Master Teacher explains why He must die and be buried.

24 Verily, verily, I say unto you, Except a corn [*kernel*] of wheat fall into the ground and die, it abideth [*remains*] alone: but if it die, it bringeth forth much fruit [*if it dies and is buried, it grows and produces much wheat*].

25 He that loveth his life [*selfishly lives according only to worldly desires*] shall lose it; and he that hateth his life in this world [*prioritizes on spiritual, eternal values*] shall keep it unto life eternal.

26 If any man serve me, let him follow me; and where I am, there shall also my servant be [*if we follow Jesus, we will be with Him in heaven*]: if any man serve me, him will my Father honour [*with celestial glory and exaltation*].

Next, Jesus gets quite personal as He shares His thoughts with His close followers.

27 Now is my soul troubled [*this is getting very difficult; see D&C 19:18*]; and what shall I say? Father, save me from this hour [*in effect, should I ask my Father to save me from what I am now going to have to go suffer*]: but for this cause [*the Atonement*] came I unto this hour [*to this point in my mortal life*].

The Father's Voice Is Heard

28 Father, glorify thy name. Then came there a voice [*the Father's voice*] from heaven, saying, I have both glorified it, and will glorify it again.

29 The people therefore, that stood by, and heard it, said that it thundered: others said, An angel spake [*spoke*] to him.

30 Jesus answered and said, This voice came not because of me, but for your sakes. [*In other words, you were allowed to hear my Father's voice to strengthen you.*]

31 Now is the judgment of this world [*the Savior's accomplishing of the Atonement now will finish qualifying Him to judge the world*]: now shall the prince of this world [*Satan; see John 12:31, footnote a*] be cast out. [*In other words, the Savior's Atonement will pave the way for righteous people to overcome Satan and cast him out of their lives through repentance.*]

32 And I, if I be lifted up from the earth [*crucified; see verse 33*], will draw all men unto me. [*Through His Atonement, He will have power to bring all people to Himself, then on to the Father, if they will repent.*]

33 This he said, signifying what death he should die [*indicating that He would die by crucifixion*].

Next, some of the people challenge Him, quoting an Old Testament verse that says that Christ will remain forever. That they don't understand the context of that verse is clear. What they are saying, in effect, is that if He were the Christ, He would remain with them forever, and would not be killed and thus leave them. Therefore, He cannot be the prophesied Messiah.

34 The people answered him [*responded to what He had just said and then asked*], We have heard out of the law [*the Old Testament, 2 Samuel 7:16*] that Christ abideth [*will remain*] for ever: and how sayest thou [*so, why are You saying that*], The Son of man must be lifted up? who is this Son of man?

35 Then Jesus said unto them, Yet a little while is the light with you [*He will be with you for just a little bit longer*]. Walk while ye have the light [*take advantage of this time*], lest [*for fear that*] darkness come upon you: for he that walketh in darkness knoweth not whither he goeth.

36 While ye have light, believe in the light [*believe in Him*], that ye may be the children of light [*in order that you might become His righteous followers; compare with Mosiah 5:7*]. These things spake Jesus, and departed, and did hide himself from them.

37 But though he had done so many miracles before them, yet they [*the majority*] believed not on him:

38 That the saying of Esaias [*Isaiah*] the prophet might be fulfilled, which he spake [*Isaiah 53:1*],

Lord, who hath believed our report [*who believes us prophets*]? and to whom hath the arm of the Lord been revealed [*who recognizes the hand of the Lord in things*]?

39 Therefore they could not [*did not*] believe, because that Esaias [*Isaiah*] said again [*in Isaiah 6:10*],

40 He hath blinded their eyes, and hardened their heart; that they should not see with their eyes, nor understand with their heart, and be converted, and I should heal them [*it is just as Isaiah was told by the Lord when he received his call to preach to hard-hearted Israel*].

Referring to verse 40 above, it is important to understand that God does not make people spiritually blind nor harden their hearts. They are given agency and can become that way by ignoring the gospel.

41 These things said Esaias [*Isaiah*], when he saw his [*Christ's*] glory [*Isaiah 6:1–5*], and spake of him [*spoke of Christ*].

42 Nevertheless among the chief rulers also many believed on him; but because of the Pharisees they did not confess him, lest they should be put out of the synagogue: [*By now, many of the chief religious rulers of the Jews had come to believe that Jesus was the Messiah, but they would not admit it for fear of being excommunicated.*]

43 For they loved the praise of men more than the praise of God.

44 Jesus cried [*spoke loudly*] and said, He that believeth on me, believeth not on me, but on him that sent me. [*If you believe in Jesus, you believe in the Father.*]

45 And he that seeth me seeth him that sent me [*if you see Jesus, it is as if you were seeing the Father*].

While the message above is clear, namely, that if you believe in the Savior and follow Him, you are, in effect, believing in the Father and following Him, there is a literal aspect also to verse 45. We are told by the Apostle Paul, in Hebrews 1:3, that Jesus is "the express image" of the Father. In other words, the Savior and His Father are exact look-a-likes. See *Doctrinal New Testament Commentary*, Vol. 3, p. 138.

46 I am come a light into the world, that whosoever believeth on me should not abide in darkness [*will not live in spiritual darkness*].

47 And if any man hear my words, and believe not, I judge him not [*it is not yet time for final judgment; such people may still rethink and repent*]: for I came not to judge the world [*at this time*], but to save the world.

Jesus will be our final Judge. See John 5:22.

48 He that rejecteth me, and receiveth not [*does not accept*] my words, hath one that judgeth him: the word that I have spoken, the same shall judge him in the last day. [*People are made accountable when they hear and understand the gospel. Therefore, the words of the Savior will be a witness against them on final Judgment Day, if they have not responded and come unto Christ.*]

49 For I have not spoken of myself [*on my own*]; but the Father which sent me, he gave me a commandment, what I should say, and what I should speak.

50 And I know that his commandment is life everlasting [*leads to eternal life*]: whatsoever I speak therefore, even as the Father said unto me, so I speak.

JOHN 13

JOHN NOW TELLS us what happened after the Passover meal had been eaten by the Savior and His Apostles. It is later Thursday evening, and, as soon as Judas Iscariot leaves (verse 30), Jesus will expound many of the doctrines of the gospel to the remaining eleven Apostles, comprising the rest of chapter 13 through chapter 17. This will be a culminating time of learning for them and for us, as the Lord's mortal ministry draws to a close.

First, before Judas leaves, the Redeemer, the great Jehovah, the Creator and Savior of worlds without number (D&C 76:24), will humbly wash the Apostles' feet. Notice Peter's response at first, and then see how quickly he changes his mind as he is taught a true principle. He is a wonderful example to all of us of immediate change upon learning a gospel truth.

1 NOW before the feast of the passover, when

Jesus knew that his hour was come that he should depart out of this world unto the Father, having loved his own which were in the world, he loved them unto the end.

2 And supper being ended [*they had finished eating the Passover meal*], the devil having now put into the heart of Judas Iscariot, Simon's son, to betray him;

3 Jesus knowing that the Father had given all things into his hands, and that he was come from God, and went to God [*and would return to God*];

Jesus Washes the Apostles' Feet

4 He riseth [*arose*] from supper, and laid aside his garments; and took a towel, and girded himself.

5 After that he poureth water into a bason [*basin*], and began to wash the disciples' feet, and to wipe them with the towel wherewith he was girded.

This must have been an especially tender time, when the Master of all demonstrated that He was the servant of all. The washing of the dusty, tired feet of guests was a gesture of hospitality and service in the culture of the Jews. Among other things, the Savior was demonstrating by His actions that He was a humble servant to His Apostles.

6 Then cometh he to Simon Peter: and Peter saith unto him, Lord, dost thou wash my feet [*are You going to wash my feet too*]?

7 Jesus answered and said unto him, What I do thou knowest not now [*you don't understand now*]; but thou shalt know hereafter [*but later you will understand*].

8 Peter saith unto him, Thou shalt never wash my feet. [*Peter apparently felt that it was not necessary for Jesus to wash his feet—see JST below.*] Jesus answered him, If I wash thee not, thou hast no part with me. [*Symbolically, if he is not cleansed by the Savior, he will not be with Him in eternity.*]

JST JOHN 13:8

8 Peter saith unto him, Thou needest not to wash my feet. Jesus answered him, If I wash thee not, thou hast no part with me.

9 Simon Peter saith unto him, Lord, not my feet only, but also my hands and my head. [*In that case, please wash me completely.*]

10 Jesus saith to him [*Peter*], He that is washed [*is clean spiritually*] needeth not [*needs no more*] save [*except*] to wash his feet, but is clean every whit [*every bit. In other words, Peter, you are spiritually clean, and all I need to do is wash your tired dusty feet here this evening as a token of my being your servant; more is not necessary*]: and ye are clean, but not all [*you Apostles are "clean," except for Judas Iscariot—see verse 11*].

JST JOHN 13:10

10 Jesus saith to him, He that has washed his hands and his head, needeth not save to wash his feet, but is clean every whit; and ye are clean, but not all. Now this was the custom of the Jews under their law; wherefore, Jesus did this that the law might be fulfilled.

11 For he knew who should [*would*] betray him; therefore said he, Ye are not all clean.

12 So after he had washed their feet, and had taken his garments, and was set down again, he said unto them, Know ye what I have done to you?

13 Ye call me Master and Lord: and ye say well; for so I am. [*They are correct in calling Him Master and Lord, because that is who He is.*]

Serve One Another

14 If I then, your Lord and Master, have washed your feet; ye also ought to wash one another's feet. [*You ought to serve one another.*]

15 For I have given you an example, that ye should do as I have done to you.

16 Verily, verily, I say unto you, The servant is not greater than his lord [*no servant is greater than his master*]; neither he that is sent greater

than he that sent him [*the messenger is not greater than the one who sent him*].

17 If ye know these things, happy are ye if ye do them.

18 I speak not of you all: I know whom I have chosen: but that the scripture [*Psalm 41:9*] may be fulfilled, He [*Judas Iscariot*] that eateth bread with me hath lifted up his heel against me [*has become my enemy*].

19 Now I tell you before it come [*Jesus is prophesying this before it happens*], that [*so that*], when it is come to pass [*has happened*], ye may believe that I am he.

JST JOHN 13:19
19 Now I tell you before it come, that, when it is come to pass, ye may believe that I am the Christ.

20 Verily, verily, I say unto you, He that receiveth whomsoever I send [*His servants, missionaries, Apostles, etc.*] receiveth me; and he that receiveth me receiveth him that sent me [*the Father*].

One of Them Will Betray Him

21 When Jesus had thus said, he was troubled in spirit [*was sad*], and testified, and said, Verily, verily, I say unto you, that one of you shall betray me.

22 Then the disciples looked one on another [*at one another*], doubting of whom he spake [*trying to figure out which one of them He meant*].

23 Now there was leaning on Jesus' bosom [*laying his head on Jesus' chest*] one of his disciples, whom Jesus loved [*John*].

From verse 23, above, you can see an interesting aspect of John's writings. He is so humble that he never directly gives his name, rather always refers to himself indirectly.

24 Simon Peter therefore beckoned to him [*motioned to John*], that he should ask who it should be of whom he spake. [*Peter signaled to John, who was leaning his head on the Savior at the moment, to quietly ask Him who it was that would betray Him.*]

25 He then lying on Jesus' breast [*had his head on Jesus' chest or on the front of his shoulder*] saith unto him, Lord, who is it [*which one of us is it*]?

26 Jesus answered, He it is, to whom I shall give a sop [*a small chunk of bread, used to dip into gravy, juice, or whatever*], when I have dipped it. And when he had dipped the sop, he gave it to Judas Iscariot, the son of Simon.

Jesus must have whispered the answer to John, because none of the others at the table seemed to have heard his answer—see verse 28, below.

27 And after the sop [*after Judas had taken the sop*] Satan entered into him [*Satan's influence came upon him strongly*]. Then said Jesus unto him, That thou doest, do quickly [*what you have in mind to do, do quickly*].

28 Now no man at the table [*none of the others*] knew for what intent he spake this unto him.

29 For some of them thought, because Judas had the bag [*the money purse; apparently Judas handled the finances for the Twelve*], that Jesus had said unto him, Buy those things that we have need of against [*for*] the feast; or, that he should give something to the poor.

Judas Leaves to Betray Jesus

30 He [*Judas*] then having received the sop [*accepted the sop from Jesus*] went immediately out: and it was night.

As stated in the introductory notes to this chapter in this study guide, the Lord will now proceed to teach these brethren many important doctrines. It is, in effect, their final major classroom instruction in their three-year "MTC" training before they go on their missions after the Savior departs.

31 Therefore, when he was gone out [*when Judas had left*], Jesus said, Now is the Son of man [*the Son of God; Son of Man of Holiness; see Moses 6:57*] glorified, and God is glorified in him. [*The time has arrived for His Atonement, in which He*

will be glorified, and in which He will bring glory to His Father.]

32 If God be glorified in him, God shall also glorify him in himself, and shall straightway [*right away*] glorify him.

33 Little children [*in effect, my dear Apostles, who still have much to learn*], yet a little while I am with you. Ye shall seek me: and as I said unto the Jews, Whither [*where*] I go, ye cannot come [*they cannot come to heaven with Him now*]; so now I say to you.

Love One Another

34 A new commandment I give unto you [*He renews a very old commandment*], That ye love one another; as I have loved you, that ye also love one another.

35 By this shall all men know that ye are my disciples, if ye have love one to another.

Did you catch how important it is to show love one to another, as taught in verse 35, above? The simple fact is that if we don't, we are not followers of Christ.

36 Simon Peter said unto him, Lord, whither goest thou? Jesus answered him, Whither I go [*where I am going*], thou canst not follow me now [*in other words, Peter can't follow Jesus to heaven now*]; but thou shalt follow me afterwards [*after he has finished his mission, he can come to heaven*].

We see Peter's basic boldness and courage in verse 37, next.

37 Peter said unto him, Lord, why cannot I follow thee now? I will lay down my life for thy sake. [*Peter apparently thinks Jesus is telling him that He, Jesus, must go it alone in Jerusalem, and Peter wants to stay close to Him and defend Him with his life if necessary.*]

Before the Cock Crows

38 Jesus answered him, Wilt thou lay down thy life for my sake? Verily, verily, I say unto thee, The cock [*rooster*] shall not crow, till thou hast denied me thrice [*three times*].

Denying knowing the Savior is not the same as denying the Holy Ghost. Denying the Holy Ghost, as described in D&C 76:31–35, is an unforgivable sin. Peter's denying that he knows the Savior and has been one of His followers for three years is not unforgivable, though so doing brought Peter deep anguish and tears.

JOHN 14

YOU MAY FIND many of the Savior's teachings in this chapter quite familiar. Many of these verses are quoted often in talks and lessons in the Church. As mentioned earlier, the Master is teaching His remaining eleven Apostles many things now, before He goes to Gethsemane and then is betrayed and arrested.

1 LET not your heart be troubled [*don't worry*]: ye believe in God [*the Father*], believe [*have faith*] also in me.

2 In my Father's house are many mansions: if it were not so, I would have told you. I go to prepare a place for you.

Joseph Smith explained the meaning of verse 2 above, wherein it says "In my Father's house are many mansions." He said it should be, "In my Father's kingdom are many kingdoms." Also, "There are mansions for those who obey a celestial law, and there are other mansions for those who come short" (Teachings of the Prophet Joseph Smith, p. 366). We know from D&C 76 that there are three degrees of glory, each of which has some degree of reward and glory. Even the telestial kingdom is so glorious that it "surpasses all understanding" (D&C 76:89). We know from D&C 131:1 that even the celestial kingdom has three "mansions" or degrees. Thus, the Father's "house," or kingdom, does indeed have "many mansions" or categories. Obviously, Jesus will prepare a place for His faithful Apostles, whom He will leave shortly, in the highest mansion (exaltation) of His Father (see verse 3 below).

3 And if I go and prepare a place for you, I will come again, and receive you unto myself; that where I am, there ye may be also.

JST JOHN 14:3

3 And when I go, I will prepare a place for you,

and come again and receive you unto myself; that where I am, ye may be also.

4 And whither I go ye know, and the way ye know. [*They have been taught where He is going, and how to get there themselves.*]

These wonderful Apostles are still undergoing intensive training by the Savior. To those of us who are familiar with the concepts in these verses because we have been taught them most of our lives or since we joined the church, there may be a temptation to wonder why it is taking so much time and repetition for these brethren to catch on. We must remember that they grew up in an environment of apostate Judaism very foreign to these simple truths.

5 Thomas [*one of the Apostles*] saith unto him, Lord, we know not whither thou goest; and how can we know the way? [*We don't know where You are going, so how can we know the way to get there?*]

6 Jesus saith unto him, I am the way, the truth, and the life [*Christ has everything we need*]: no man cometh unto the Father, but by me [*except through Him*].

7 If ye had known me [*in effect, if you had truly known me and understood me and what I have been teaching you*], ye should have [*would have*] known my Father also: and from henceforth [*from now on*] ye know him, and have seen him [*because you have seen me*].

8 Philip [*one of the Apostles*] saith unto him, Lord, shew us the Father, and it sufficeth us [*and that will be sufficient for us*].

9 Jesus saith unto him, Have I been so long time with you, and yet hast thou not known me [*and you still don't understand*], Philip? he that hath seen me hath seen the Father; and how sayest thou then [*so why do you say*], Shew [*show*] us the Father?

10 Believest thou not that I am in the Father, and the Father in me? the words that I speak unto you I speak not of myself: but the Father that dwelleth in me, he doeth the works. [*In effect, Don't you understand that the Father and I are a team and we work together in perfect unity? Everything I do is, in effect, what the Father is doing for you.*]

11 Believe me that I am in the Father, and the Father in me: or else believe me for the very works' sake. [*In effect, if you can't believe that I and my Father are perfectly unified in the work we do, at least believe me because of the works you have seen and heard me do, which could come from no one but the Father.*]

12 Verily, verily, I say unto you, He that believeth on me, the works that I do shall he do also; and greater [*additional*] works than these shall he do; because I go unto my Father.

The word "greater" in verse 12 above can have at least two meanings. In addition to meaning more significant or more spectacular or more powerful, higher, etc., it can also mean additional or on-going, continued, etc. It is used this way in D&C 7:5 where the Savior tells Peter that John the Beloved will stay on the earth until the Second Coming, and thus "do more, or a greater work" than he has done up to now.

For more on this, see Strong's *Exhaustive Concordance of the Bible*, word #3187, where "greater" is also defined as "more."

There is also another aspect of the word "greater" as used by the Master in this promise to His Apostles. When they are exalted, and have become gods, they will indeed do greater works, in the common sense of the word. They will have spirit offspring, will create worlds, and as gods, will do even greater, more magnificent and higher things than they ever saw Christ do while He was among them. See Joseph Smith's teachings on this in Lectures on Faith, pp. 64–66.

13 And whatsoever ye shall ask in my name, that will I do, that the Father may be glorified in the Son.

14 If ye shall ask any thing in my name, I will do it.

Verses 15–26, below, will speak of two different "Comforters." One of these Comforters is the Holy Ghost. The other is the Savior Himself and includes the Father on occasions.

Verses 16, 17, and 26 speak of the Holy Ghost.

Verses 18, 21, 23, and 28 speak of the Savior.

For more on this, see *Teachings of the Prophet Joseph Smith*, pp. 149 to 151.

15 If ye love me, keep my commandments.

16 And I will pray the Father, and he shall give you another Comforter [*the Holy Ghost—see*

LET NOT YOUR
HEART BE
TROUBLED: YE
BELIEVE IN GOD,
BELIEVE ALSO
IN ME.

JOHN 14:1

Doctrinal New Testament Commentary, *Vol. 1, p. 737*], that he may abide [*be*] with you for ever;

17 Even the Spirit of truth; whom the world cannot receive [*the world, meaning those who are not members of the Church, cannot receive the Gift of the Holy Ghost*], because it seeth him not, neither knoweth him: but ye know him; for he dwelleth with you, and shall be in you.

18 I will not leave you comfortless: I [*Jesus*] will come to you. [*This is spoken of as the "Second Comforter." See* Doctrinal New Testament Commentary, *Vol. 1, p. 738.*]

19 Yet a little while, and the world seeth me no more [*in effect, I will be crucified and gone, as far as most people are concerned*]; but ye see me [*you will see me after I am resurrected*]: because I live [*resurrect*], ye shall live also. [*Because of the Atonement, they will resurrect also and have eternal life.*]

20 At that day ye shall know that I am in my Father, and ye in me, and I in you. [*Jesus is still responding to Thomas's question in verse 5 and to Philip's request in verse 8.*]

JOHN

21 He that hath my commandments, and keepeth them, he it is that loveth me: and he that loveth me shall be loved of my Father, and I will love him, and will manifest myself to him [*as the "Second Comforter"*].

22 Judas [*one of the faithful Apostles*] saith unto him, not Iscariot [*not Judas Iscariot who has already left to betray Jesus*], Lord, how is it that thou wilt manifest thyself unto us, and not unto the world?

JST JOHN 14:22

22 Judas saith unto him, (not Iscariot,) Lord, how is it thou wilt manifest thyself unto us, and not unto the world?

23 Jesus answered and said unto him, If a man love me, he will keep my words: and my Father will love him, and we will come unto him [*the "Second Comforter," and make our abode with him*].

24 He that loveth me not keepeth not my sayings [*does not keep my commandments*]: and the word [*gospel*] which ye hear is not mine [*did not originate with me*], but the Father's which sent me [*originated with the Father who sent me*].

25 These things have I spoken unto you, being yet present with you [*while He is still with them*].

What the Holy Ghost Does for Us

26 But the Comforter, which is the Holy Ghost, whom the Father will send in my name, he shall teach you all things, and bring all things to your remembrance, whatsoever I have said unto you. [*This is a description of some of the things the Gift of the Holy Ghost can do for us.*]

27 Peace I leave with you, my peace I give unto you: not as the world giveth, give I unto you. Let not your heart be troubled, neither let it be afraid.

28 Ye have heard how I said unto you, I go away, and come again unto you. [*The Apostles had the "Second Comforter" for forty days, after Christ's resurrection; see Acts 1:3, as the Savior ministered personally to them and taught them.*] If ye loved me, ye would rejoice, because I said, I go unto the Father: for my Father is greater than I.

29 And now I have told you before it come to pass [*I have told you ahead of time that I will be arrested, tried, crucified, and resurrected*], that [*so that*], when it is come to pass [*after it has all happened*], ye might believe.

30 Hereafter I will not talk much with you [*we can't keep talking much longer*]: for [*because*] the prince of this world cometh, and hath nothing in me. [*In effect, the Savior is saying, "We can't talk much longer because Satan is bringing Judas Iscariot and the high priests with their soldiers to arrest Me. Satan has no power over Me, but you are still vulnerable to his temptations."*]

JST JOHN 14:30

30 Hereafter I will not talk much with you; for the prince of darkness, who is of this world, cometh, but hath no power over me, but he hath power over you.

31 But that the world may know that I love the Father; and as the Father gave me commandment,

IF YE LOVE
ME, KEEP MY
COMMANDMENTS.

JOHN 14:15

even so I do [*Jesus is completely obedient to the Father*]. Arise, let us go hence [*let us go to the Garden of Gethsemane*].

JST John 14:31

31 And I tell you these things, that ye may know that I love the Father; and as the Father gave me commandment, even so I do. Arise, let us go hence.

Mark 14:26 tells us that they sang a hymn at this point. Luke 22:39 tells us that Jesus then led his eleven remaining Apostles to the Mount of Olives. Matthew 26:36 informs us that they went to Gethsemane, a garden with olive trees, near the foot of the Mount of Olives. The time is getting short, because, as Jesus knows, Judas Iscariot and the high priests and their soldiers will be coming shortly.

JOHN 15

THE SAVIOR CONTINUES teaching His Apostles in this, His last major discourse of His mortal mission. The time of His betrayal through Judas is now even closer. As chapter 15 begins, we see an allegory in which the Lord illustrates the absolutely essential relationship between His Apostles and Himself and between Himself and His Father. In this, we are also taught that without the Savior, we would be like green branches cut off from the tree which provides nourishment to us. Without it, we would dry up and shrivel away. Apostle James E. Talmage discussed this allegory. He taught:

"In superb allegory the Lord thus proceeded to illustrate the vital relationship between the apostles and Himself, and between Himself and the Father, by the figure of a vinegrower, a vine, and its branches: 'I am the true vine, and my Father is the husbandman. Every branch in me that beareth not fruit he taketh away: and every branch that beareth fruit, he purgeth it, that it may bring forth more fruit.' A grander analogy is not to be found in the world's literature. Those ordained servants of the Lord were as helpless and useless without Him as is a bough severed from the tree. As the branch is made fruitful only by virtue of the nourishing sap it receives from the rooted trunk, and if cut away or broken off withers, dries, and becomes utterly worthless except as fuel for the burning, so those men, though ordained to the Holy Apostleship, would find themselves strong and fruitful in good works, only as they remained in steadfast communion with the Lord. Without Christ what were they, but unschooled Galileans, some of them fishermen, one a publican, the rest of undistinguished attainments, and all of them weak mortals? As branches of the Vine they were at that hour clean and healthful, through the instructions and authoritative ordinances with which they had been blessed, and by the reverent obedience they had manifested.

"'Abide in me,' was the Lord's forceful admonition, else they would become but withered boughs. 'I am the vine,' He added in explication of the allegory; 'ye are the branches: He that abideth in me, and I in him, the same bringeth forth much fruit: for without me ye can do nothing. If a man abide not in me, he is cast forth as a branch, and is withered; and men gather them, and cast them into the fire, and they are burned. If ye abide in me, and my words abide in you, ye shall ask what ye will, and it shall be done unto you. Herein is my Father glorified, that ye bear much fruit: so shall ye be my disciples.' Their love for one another was again specified as an essential to their continued love for Christ. In that love would they find joy. Christ had been to them an exemplar of righteous love from the day of their first meeting; and He was about to give the supreme proof of His affection, as foreshadowed in His words, 'Greater love hath no man than this, that a man lay down his life for his friends.' And that those men were the Lord's friends was thus graciously affirmed; 'Ye are my friends, if ye do whatsoever I command you. Henceforth I call you not servants; for the servant knoweth not what his lord doeth: but I have called you friends; for all things that I have heard of my Father I have made known unto you.' This intimate relationship in no sense modified the position of Christ as their Lord and Master, for by Him they had been chosen and ordained; and it was His will that they should so live that whatever they asked in the name of the holy friendship which He acknowledged should be granted them of the Father." (*Jesus the Christ*, 1982, pp. 604–605)

We will now proceed with our study of this chapter, adding notes giving some possible symbolism for the elements of the allegory. There are no JST changes for chapter 15.

Jesus Is the True Vine

1 I AM the true vine [*grape vine; symbolic of the fact that the true gospel comes from Christ*], and my Father is the husbandman [*farmer, owner; symbolic of the fact that the Father owns the earth*].

2 Every branch [*branch growing from the vine; symbolic of people*] in me that beareth not fruit [*people*

who live wickedly] he taketh away [*the wicked will be destroyed*]: and every branch [*every person*] that beareth fruit [*who lives righteously*], he purgeth it [*prunes it, cuts out inappropriate behaviors and sin, nourishes it, shapes it, and so forth*], that it may bring forth more fruit [*symbolic of continuing progress in the lives of the Saints*].

3 Now ye are clean [*you have become clean*] through the word [*through the gospel with the Atonement*] which I have spoken [*taught*] unto you.

4 Abide in me, and I in you [*stay connected with the True Vine and He will continue to nourish you*]. As the branch cannot bear fruit of itself, except it abide in [*stay attached to*] the vine; no more can ye, except ye abide in me. [*Just as a branch of a vine cannot live without remaining attached to the vine, so we cannot live righteous lives unless we stay connected to Him.*]

The beautiful symbolism in verse 4 above is vitally important for us. How do we attach ourselves to the "vine" so that we can remain securely fastened to Christ? Answer: "Ye shall bind yourselves to act in all holiness before me—" (D&C 43:9). How do we "bind" ourselves to the true vine (Christ, verse 1, above)? Answer: We make and keep covenants. Thus, by making covenants, we bind ourselves securely to the True Vine, receive constant nourishment from His roots, and are privileged to be pruned, shaped, and strengthened by the Husbandman so that we can return to live with Him forever.

Jesus continues this explanation in the next verses.

5 I am the vine, ye are the branches: He that abideth in me, and I in him, the same bringeth forth much fruit [*produces much good*]: for without me ye can do nothing.

6 If a man abide not in me, he is cast forth as a branch [*is cut off and thrown away*], and is withered [*and dries up*]; and men gather them, and cast them into the fire, and they are burned [*symbolic of the destruction of the wicked*].

7 If ye abide in me [*if we stay faithful to Him*], and my words abide in you [*and we are faithful to His gospel*], ye shall ask what ye will [*want*], and it shall be done unto you.

8 Herein is my Father glorified [*this is how His Father is glorified*], that ye bear much fruit; so shall ye be my disciples. [*This reminds us of Moses 1:39 which says: "For behold, this is my work and my glory—to bring to pass the immortality and eternal life of man."*]

9 As the Father hath loved me, so have I loved you: continue ye in my love [*remain faithful to Him*].

10 If ye keep my commandments, ye shall abide in my love; even as I have kept my Father's commandments, and abide in his love.

11 These things have I spoken unto you, that my joy might remain in you, and that your joy might be full.

Love One Another

12 This is my commandment, That ye love one another, as I have loved you.

13 Greater love hath no man than this, that a man lay down his life for his friends. [*This is exactly what Jesus will do in a few hours.*]

14 Ye are my friends, if ye do whatsoever I command you.

As you read verse 15, next, notice what is happening in terms of the relationship between Christ and His eleven Apostles. In a very real way, this is a "graduation."

15 Henceforth [*from now on*] I call you not servants; for the servant knoweth not what his lord doeth: but I have called you friends; for all things that I have heard of my Father I have made known unto you [*in effect, I have taught you everything*].

This is a significant change in status, from servants to friends. The Savior said the same thing to early members of the Church in our day in D&C 84:77.

16 Ye have not chosen me, but I have chosen you, and ordained you, that ye should go and bring

forth fruit [*bring converts into the Church, help members to come unto Christ*], and that your fruit should remain: that whatsoever ye shall ask of the Father in my name, he may give it you.

"Ye have not chosen me, but I have chosen you, and ordained you" in verse 16 above is a most important matter for people to understand. We do not set up our own church and then choose the Savior to be our leader. It is the other way around. He is the leader, and invites us to join Him for our salvation. Unfortunately, all other churches have been built up by people. The authority of the priesthood flows from Christ to us, not from us to Christ.

Love One Another

17 These things I command you, that ye love one another.

Next, the Master explains why so many people hate righteous people.

18 If the world hate you, ye know that it hated me before it hated you. [*If they were not doing what is right, the world would not hate them.*]

19 If ye were of the world [*if you were worldly and wicked*], the world would love his own [*the world would love you because you would be just like they are*]: but because ye are not of the world, but I have chosen you out of the world, therefore [*that is why*] the world hateth you.

20 Remember the word that I said unto you [*remember when I taught you*], The servant is not greater than his lord [*Matthew 10:24*]. If they have persecuted me, they will also persecute you; if they have kept my saying [*obeyed my teachings*], they will keep yours also.

21 But all these things will they do unto you for my name's sake, because they know not him [*the Father*] that sent me.

22 If I had not come and spoken unto them, they had not had sin [*they would not have been accountable*]: but now they have no cloke [*cover or excuse*] for their sin.

23 He that hateth me hateth my Father also.

24 If I had not done among them the works which none other man did, they had not had sin [*they would not have become accountable*]: but now have they both seen and hated both me and my Father.

25 But this cometh to pass, that the word might be fulfilled that is written in their law [*this is a fulfillment of the prophecy in Psalm 35:19*], They hated me without a cause.

More about the Function of the Holy Ghost

26 But when the Comforter [*the Holy Ghost*] is come, whom I will send unto you from the Father, even the Spirit of truth, which proceedeth from the Father, he shall testify of me:

As you saw in verse 26, above, another function of the Holy Ghost is to testify to us of Christ. John 14:26 and 16:13 explain additional functions. You may wish to cross-reference them to verse 26, here.

Because of the wording in verse 26, some students of the gospel wonder if the Holy Ghost was functioning on earth while the Savior was here in mortality. The Holy Ghost was functioning on earth during the Savior's ministry as exemplified by the Holy Ghost descending like a dove at the Savior's baptism. See Matthew 3:16. See also Luke 4:1 which informs us that the Holy Ghost was upon the Savior. Apparently, though, the full power of the Gift of the Holy Ghost was not present until after Jesus was taken up. (See Bible Dictionary, under "Holy Ghost.")

27 And ye also shall bear witness, because ye have been with me from the beginning.

JOHN 16

AS JESUS CONTINUES His discourse before they arrive at the Garden of Gethsemane, He cautions the Eleven to avoid falling away because of the coming persecution upon them, and teaches more about the mission of the Holy Ghost, which will be a major source of strength for them.

1 THESE things have I spoken unto you, that ye should not be offended [*fall away; stumble, crumble under the coming pressure and persecution*].

The word "offended", as used in verse 1 above, means to stumble, to crumble under pressure, to fall away, to apostatize. It is used the same way as in Matthew 11:6, where the Savior says "And blessed is he, whosoever shall not be offended in me." Footnote a, for Matthew 11:6, sends the reader to Isaiah 8:14 and Matthew 24:10 where the above definitions are verified.

2 They shall put you out of the synagogues [*Jewish church buildings and centers of learning*]: yea, the time cometh, that whosoever killeth you will think that he doeth God service.

3 And these things will they do unto you, because they have not known the Father, nor me.

4 But these things [*these warnings of coming persecutions*] have I told you, that when the time shall come, ye may remember that I told you of them. And these things I said not unto you at the beginning [*of His mission*], because I was with you.

5 But now I go my way to him that sent me [*to the Father*]; and none of you asketh me, Whither goest thou?

6 But because I have said these things unto you, sorrow hath filled your heart.

7 Nevertheless I tell you the truth; It is expedient [*necessary*] for you that I go away: for if I go not away, the Comforter [*the Holy Ghost*] will not come unto you; but if I depart, I will send him unto you. [*See note following John 7:39 about whether or not the Holy Ghost functioned on earth during Christ's mortal ministry.*]

8 And when he is come, he will reprove [*convict*] the world of [*with respect to*] sin, and of [*with respect to*] righteousness, and of [*with respect to*] judgment: [*in effect, after the full Gift and power of the Holy Ghost has come upon you, it will inspire and direct you and bear witness through you such that your teachings and deeds will stand as a witness against the wicked of the world for rejecting righteousness and refusing to believe that the day of judgment will come.*]

9 Of sin, because they believe not on me; [*They will be accountable, convicted, of their sins because the Holy Ghost will bear witness to them as you preach.*]

10 Of [*with respect to*] righteousness [*your teaching of me and my gospel*], because I go to my Father, and ye see me no more; [*They will be held accountable for your testimonies and teachings, because I am no longer here to teach them.*]

JST John 16:10

10 Of righteousness, because I go to my Father, and they see me no more;

11 Of [*with respect to*] judgment, because the prince of this world [*Satan, see John 12:31, footnote a*] is judged. [*They will reject the witness of the Holy Ghost which will accompany your testimonies and will thus be judged for their sins, like Satan, whom they choose to follow, is judged for his sins.*]

Apostle Bruce R. McConkie suggested some possibilities for interpreting verses 9–11, above. He said:

"These are difficult verses which have come to us in such a condensed and abridged form as to make interpretation difficult. The seeming meaning is: 'When you receive the companionship of the Spirit, so that you speak forth what he reveals to you, then your teachings will convict the world of sin, and of righteousness, and of judgment. The world will be convicted of sin for rejecting me, for not believing your Spirit-inspired testimony that I am the Son of God through whom salvation comes. They will be convicted for rejecting your testimony of my righteousness—for supposing I am a blasphemer, a deceiver, and an imposter—when in fact I have gone to my Father, a thing I could not do unless my works were true and righteous altogether. They will be convicted of false judgment for rejecting your testimony against the religions of the day, and for choosing instead to follow Satan, the prince of this world, who himself, with all his religious philosophies, will be judged and found wanting'" (*Doctrinal New Testament Commentary*, Vol. 1, p. 754).

12 I have yet many things to say unto you, but ye cannot bear them now [*you are not ready for them now*].

More about the Function of the Holy Ghost

13 Howbeit [*however*] when he [*the Holy Ghost*], the Spirit of truth, is come [*when the gift of the Holy Ghost has come upon you in full power*], he will guide you into all truth: for he shall not speak of himself; but whatsoever he shall hear [*from Heavenly Father and Jesus*], that shall he speak: and he will shew [*show*] you things to come.

14 He shall glorify me [*bear witness of Christ*]: for he shall receive of mine [*He gets His instructions from me and my Father, see verse 15*], and shall shew it unto you.

15 All things that the Father hath are mine: therefore said I [*that is why I said*], that he shall take of mine, and shall shew it unto you.

16 A little while, and ye shall not see me: and again, a little while, and ye shall see me, because I go to the Father.

Verse 16, above, is a short verse but is saying a lot. Among other things, it says that in just a short while He will be crucified and will thus be separated from them while He goes as a spirit to the spirit world and visits the spirits in paradise (1 Peter 3:18-21; D&C 138:18-30). Then, when He is resurrected, He will come and they will see Him again. Verse 17, next, informs us however, that the Eleven did not understand what He meant.

17 Then said some of his disciples among themselves, What is this that he saith unto us, A little while, and ye shall not see me: and again, a little while, and ye shall see me: and, Because I go to the Father?

18 They said therefore [*they continued to wonder, among themselves*], What is this that he saith, A little while? we cannot tell [*understand*] what he saith.

Next, John lets us feel the kindness of the Master, as He, knowing that His Apostles were reluctant to ask, explains what He meant to them.

19 Now Jesus knew that they were desirous to ask him, and said unto them, Do ye enquire among yourselves of that I said [*about what I just said*], A little while, and ye shall not see me: and again, a little while, and ye shall see me?

20 Verily, verily, I say unto you, That ye shall weep and lament [*when the Savior is crucified*], but the world shall rejoice: and ye shall be sorrowful, but your sorrow shall be turned into joy [*when He is resurrected and they see Him again*].

21 A woman when she is in travail [*is in labor*] hath sorrow, because her hour is come [*because the time for her baby to be born has arrived*]: but as soon as she is delivered of the child [*as soon as her baby is born*], she remembereth no more the anguish, for [*because of*] joy that a man is born into the world.

22 And ye now therefore have sorrow [*you will indeed have sorrow because of what will happen in the next few hours*]: but I will see you again, and your heart shall rejoice, and your joy no man taketh from you.

23 And in that day ye shall ask me nothing. Verily, verily, I say unto you, Whatsoever ye shall ask the Father in my name, he will give it you.

JST JOHN 16:23

23 And in that day ye shall ask me nothing but it shall be done unto you. Verily, verily, I say unto you, Whatsoever ye shall ask the Father in my name, he will give it you.

24 Hitherto have ye asked nothing in my name [*up to now, you have not had to ask Father for things in my name, because I have been here with you*]: ask, and ye shall receive, that your joy may be full.

25 These things have I spoken unto you in proverbs [*with examples and illustrations*]: but the time cometh, when I shall no more speak unto you in proverbs, but I shall shew you plainly of the Father.

26 At that day ye shall ask in my name: and I say not unto you, that I will pray the Father for you: *[Then, you will pray directly to the Father, in the name of Jesus Christ, rather than having Him pray to the Father for you.]*

27 For the Father himself loveth you, because ye have loved me, and have believed that I came out from God.

28 I came forth from the Father [*I am the Father's Son*], and am come [*have come*] into the world: again, I leave the world, and go to [*return to*] the Father.

29 His disciples said unto him, Lo, now speakest thou plainly, and speakest no proverb. [*Yes! Now you are speaking clearly without relating it to other things we understand.*]

30 Now are we sure that thou knowest all things, and needest not that any man should ask thee: by this we believe that thou camest forth from God.

31 Jesus answered them, Do ye now believe?

32 Behold, the hour cometh [*the time is coming*], yea, is now come [*in fact, has now arrived*], that ye shall be scattered, every man to his own, and shall leave me alone: and yet I am not alone, because the Father is with me.

33 These things I have spoken unto you, that in me ye might have peace. In the world ye shall have tribulation [*many troubles*]: but be of good cheer [*be happy, optimistic*]; I have overcome the world.

JOHN 17

IT IS STILL Thursday evening (see Talmage, *Jesus the Christ*, 1982, p. 593). By way of review, the Passover meal, known as the Last Supper, was eaten by Jesus and the twelve Apostles. During the evening, Jesus introduced the sacrament and tenderly washed the Apostles' feet. Sometime during the evening, Judas Iscariot left to betray Jesus to the Jewish high priests and their soldiers. After Judas had left (John 13:30-31), Jesus began teaching the remaining eleven Apostles great doctrines which stretched their minds and strengthened their understandings. These teachings are recorded, beginning with John 13:31 and continuing to the end of John, chapter 16. Sometime, during or after this discourse, the Savior led the Eleven to the Mount of Olives, just outside of Jerusalem, where He "lifted up his eyes to heaven" and gave what is known as "The Great Intercessory Prayer." It is recorded in John 17:1-26. In the first three verses, Jesus formally offers Himself as the great sacrifice for our sins, in order that we might have eternal life. He is the one who intercedes for us, allowing the law of mercy to act on our behalf. Thus, it is called the "intercessory" prayer.

After finishing this prayer, the Master will lead His little band of faithful Apostles back down the Mount of Olives to a garden which was named Gethsemane, where He will suffer and bleed at every pore. Shortly thereafter, the Master will be arrested and taken to the ruling high Priest's palace for trial.

The JST has no changes for this chapter.

The Great Intercessory Prayer

1 THESE words spake Jesus, and lifted up his eyes to heaven, and said, Father, the hour is come [*the time to begin the Atonement has arrived*]; glorify thy Son, that thy Son also may glorify thee:

2 As thou hast given him [*Christ*] power over all flesh [*over all people*], that he should give eternal life [*exaltation*] to as many as thou hast given him.

Just a reminder. The term "eternal life," as used in verse 2, above, always means exaltation when it is used in the scriptures. Exaltation is the highest degree of glory in the celestial kingdom (see D&C 132:19-20). Those who attain it will be gods and will live in the family unit forever.

Verse 3, next, is a famous verse. You may wish to mark it in your own scriptures if you have not already done so.

3 And this is life eternal, that they might know thee the only true God, and Jesus Christ, whom thou hast sent.

In D&C 132:24, the phrase "this is life eternal" is rendered with a bit different wording. It is "this is eternal lives," which emphasizes the fact that the faithful Saints who earn "eternal life" will have "eternal lives," meaning there will be no end to the spirit children they will have in eternity. See last two lines of D&C 132:19.

4 I have glorified thee on the earth: I have finished the work which thou gavest me to do.

5 And now, O Father, glorify thou me with thine own self with the glory which I had with thee before the world was.

6 I have manifested thy name unto the men [*the Apostles*] which thou gavest me out of the world: thine they were, and thou gavest them me; and they have kept thy word [*the Eleven have remained faithful*].

Next, the Savior emphasizes that the Eleven now have firm testimonies.

7 Now they have known that all things whatsoever thou hast given me are of thee.

8 For I have given unto them the words which thou gavest me; and they have received [*accepted*] them, and have known surely that I came out from thee, and they have believed that thou didst send me.

9 I pray for them: I pray not for the world [*He is not referring to the world at this point of His prayer*], but for them which thou hast given me; for they are thine.

10 And all mine are thine, and thine are mine; and I am glorified in them.

11 And now I am no more in the world [*I am leaving*], but these are in the world [*My Apostles have to stay here*], and I come to thee. Holy Father, keep through thine own name those whom thou hast given me, that they may be one, as we are.

It is obvious that the Savior is speaking so that the Apostles can hear Him. You may wish to imagine, in your mind's eye, the faces of these humble Eleven as they listen to this powerful prayer, given in their behalf.

12 While I was with them in the world, I kept them in thy name: those that thou gavest me I have kept, and none of them is lost, but [*except*] the son of perdition [*Judas Iscariot*]; that the scripture might be fulfilled.

13 And now come I to thee; and these things I speak in the world [*within hearing of my Apostles while I am still here on earth*], that they might have my joy fulfilled in themselves.

14 I have given them thy word; and the world hath hated them, because they are not of the world [*they are not worldly*], even as I am not of the world.

15 I pray not that thou shouldest take them out of the world, but that thou shouldest keep [*protect*] them from the evil.

16 They are not of the world, even as I am not of the world.

17 Sanctify them [*make them holy, pure, and fit to be in Thy presence*] through thy truth: thy word is truth.

18 As thou hast sent me into the world, even so have I also sent them into the world.

In verse 18, above, we see the Savior saying, in effect, that just as the Father sent Him into the world on a mission, so also has He sent His Apostles into the world on a mission.

19 And for their sakes I sanctify myself, that they also might be sanctified through the truth.

20 Neither pray I for these alone, but for them also [*everyone*] which shall believe on me through their word [*through their teachings*];

21 That they all [*all the righteous*] may be one [*united in purpose*]; as thou, Father, art in me, and I in thee, that they also may be one in us [*so that all of them can be united in purpose with us*]: that the world may believe that thou hast sent me.

22 And the glory which thou gavest me I have given them; that they may be one [*united*], even as we are one:

The Prophet Joseph Smith taught that the word "one," as used in these verses, means "agreed as one." (See *Teachings of the Prophet Joseph Smith*, p. 372.)

23 I in them, and thou in me, that they may be made perfect in one [*agreed, in unity, harmony*]; and that the world may know that thou hast sent

me, and hast loved them, as thou hast loved me.

24 Father, I will [*desire*] that they also, whom thou hast given me, be with me where I am [*live with me in celestial glory*]; that they may behold my glory, which thou hast given me: for thou lovedst me before the foundation of the world [*in the premortal life*].

25 O righteous Father, the world hath not known thee: but I have known thee, and these [*Apostles*] have known that thou hast sent me.

26 And I have declared unto them thy name, and will declare it: that the love wherewith thou hast loved me may be in them, and I in them.

We will quote from the New Testament student manual used by the Institutes of Religion of the Church for a brief summary of the Savior's prayer in verses 1–26, above.

"With a perfect understanding of his mission and that the time of his atonement was 'at hand,' Jesus concluded the teaching portion of his ministry with a prayer that has sometimes been referred to as the high-priestly or great intercessory prayer. (See John 17.) These designations are not inappropriate, for, as we shall see, Jesus, our Great High Priest, first offered himself as an offering; then, as Mediator, he interceded on behalf of worthy members of his kingdom. The pattern for this had been established in ancient Israel.

"Once each year, the presiding high priest in ancient Israel entered into the holy of holies, the most sacred place within the tabernacle. There he would perform certain rites in connection with the Day of Atonement, a day set aside for national humiliation and contrition. Having bathed himself and dressed in white linen, he would present before the Lord a young bullock and two young goats as sin offerings, and a ram as a burnt offering in behalf of his sins and those of the people. The high priest's role was that of a mediator, or one who interceded with the Lord in behalf of the people. His role, of course, was but a type of the great mediating role of the Savior in our behalf. Thus, when Jesus pleaded to the Father for all those who believed on him, he did so as our Intercessor, or Great High Priest.

"The prayer he offered on this occasion had three distinct parts:

"In the first part (see John 17:1–3), Jesus offered himself as the great sacrifice. His hour had come.

"The next part of the prayer (see John 17:4–19) was a reverent report to the Father of his mortal mission.

"In the last part (see John 17:20–26) of his prayer, Jesus interceded not only for the eleven apostles present, but for all who shall believe on Jesus 'through their word,' in order that all would come to a perfect unity, which unity invested Christ in them as Christ is in the Father. Thus all would be perfect in unity, and the world would believe that the Father had sent his Son." (*Life and Teachings of Jesus and His Apostles*, p. 171–172)

JOHN 18

AFTER OFFERING THE "Great Intercessory Prayer," recorded in chapter 17, above, the Savior led His weary Apostles to the Garden of Gethsemane. John does not give any detail here of what transpired in the Garden, rather gives considerable information about the arrest, the trials, and Peter's denial of knowing Jesus. For the details of the Savior's suffering in Gethsemane, you may wish to read Matthew 26:36–46, Mark 14:32–42, and Luke 22:39–46.

The Garden of Gethsemane

1 WHEN Jesus had spoken these words, he went forth with his disciples over the brook Cedron, where was a garden [*the Garden of Gethsemane*], into the which he entered, and his disciples.

"Gethsemane" means "oil press." There is significant symbolism here. The Jews put olives into bags made of mesh fabric and placed them in a press to squeeze olive oil out of them. The first pressings yielded pure olive oil which was prized for many uses, including healing and giving light in lanterns. In fact, we consecrate it and use it to administer to the sick. The last pressing of the olives, under the tremendous pressure of additional weights added to the press, yielded a bitter, red liquid which can remind us of the "bitter cup" which the Savior partook of. Symbolically, the Savior is going into the "oil press" (Gethsemane) to submit to the "pressure" of all our sins which will "squeeze" his blood out in order that we might have the healing "oil" of the Atonement to heal us from our sins.

2 And Judas also, which betrayed him, knew the

place: for Jesus ofttimes resorted thither [*went there*] with his disciples.

The Betrayal by Judas

3 Judas then, having received a band of men [*soldiers*] and officers from the chief priests and Pharisees, cometh thither [*there*] with lanterns and torches and weapons.

4 Jesus therefore, knowing all things that should come upon him, went forth, and said unto them, Whom seek ye?

5 They answered him, Jesus of Nazareth. Jesus saith unto them, I am he. And Judas also, which betrayed him, stood with them [*the soldiers and officers*].

In verse 6, next, it is interesting to see the immediate reaction of the soldiers and those with Judas as the Master announces to them that He is the one they are looking for.

6 As soon then as he [*Christ*] had said unto them, I am he, they went backward, and fell to the ground.

7 Then asked he them again, Whom seek ye? And they said, Jesus of Nazareth.

8 Jesus answered, I have told you that I am he: if therefore ye seek me, let these go their way [*let my Apostles go free*]:

9 That the saying might be fulfilled, which he spake, Of them which thou gavest me have I lost none.

Next, we see Peter's courage and concern for Jesus' safety as he boldly draws his sword and strikes at one of the officers, cutting off his right ear.

10 Then Simon Peter having a sword drew it, and smote [*struck*] the high priest's servant, and cut off his right ear. The servant's name was Malchus. [*Malchus was a relative of the high priest. See John 18:26.*]

11 Then said Jesus unto Peter, Put up thy sword into the sheath: the cup which my Father hath given me, shall I not drink it? [*Should I not go ahead with the Atonement?*]

Luke reports that Jesus healed the servant's ear at that point—see Luke 22:51. One would think that seeing such a miracle would have encouraged the soldiers and officers to leave Him alone and desire to follow Him rather than arresting Him. But verse 12, next, indicates that they went ahead and arrested Him.

12 Then the band and the captain and officers of the Jews took Jesus, and bound him,

Jesus was taken first to Annas, the former Jewish high priest, then across the courtyard to Caiaphas, the current high priest (the chief religious officer among the Jews at the time), then to Pilate (the Roman governor), to Herod (the Roman governor of Galilee who happened to be in Jerusalem), and then back to Pilate, who turned Him over to be scourged and crucified. These details come from a combination of information taken from Matthew, Mark, Luke, and John.

In the next verses, John tells us about the trials before Annas, Caiaphas, and Pilate. He intermixes this account with the account of Peter and the troubles he faced as he waited elsewhere as Jesus went through the trials before Annas and Caiaphas. Thus, it is a bit difficult to decide which of the next verses deal with the trial before Annas and which relate to the trial before Caiaphas. We will simply note that there was an illegal night trial before Annas and then He was sent to Caiaphas for another illegal trial at night. (It was against the Jew's laws to hold trials at night.) And we will feel sympathy for Peter as he goes through the miserable experiences leading up to the early morning when the cock crows, after he has denied knowing Jesus three times.

Tried before Annas

13 And led him away to Annas first; for he was father in law to Caiaphas, which was the high priest that same year.

Annas had served as high priest, which was the chief religious office among the Jews, for several years, before being taken out of office by the Romans. Even though his son-in-law, Caiaphas, was now the chief officer, Annas still had tremendous influence. (See Bible Dictionary, under "Annas.")

Tried before Caiaphas

14 Now Caiaphas was he, which gave counsel to the Jews, that it was expedient [*necessary*] that one man should die for the people.

Peter Denies Knowing Jesus

15 And Simon Peter followed Jesus, and so did another disciple: that disciple was known unto the high priest, and went in with Jesus into the palace of the high priest.

16 But Peter stood at the door without [*outside*]. Then went out that other disciple, which was known unto the high priest, and spake unto her that kept the door [*guarded the door*], and brought in Peter.

Peter Denies Once

17 Then saith the damsel [*young lady*] that kept the door unto Peter, Art not thou also one of this man's [*Jesus'*] disciples? He saith, I am not.

18 And the servants and officers stood there [*in the courtyard*], who had made a fire of coals; for it was cold: and they warmed themselves: and Peter stood with them, and warmed himself.

19 The high priest then asked Jesus of [*about*] his disciples, and of [*about*] his doctrine. [*The illegal trial by night begins.*]

To read a full account of the illegal aspects of Christ's trial, see *Jesus the Christ*, pp. 644–648.

20 Jesus answered him, I spake [*spoke*] openly to the world; I ever [*constantly*] taught in the synagogue [*in the Jewish churches*], and in the temple, whither [*where*] the Jews always resort [*go*]; and in secret have I said nothing.

21 Why askest thou me [*why ask me about my doctrine*]? ask them which heard me [*ask the people*], what I have said unto them: behold, they know what I said.

22 And when he had thus spoken, one of the officers which stood by struck Jesus with the palm of his hand, saying, Answerest thou the high priest so [*how dare You talk like that to the high priest!*]?

23 Jesus answered him, If I have spoken evil, bear witness of the evil [*tell me what I said that was not correct*]: but if well, why smitest thou me [*if what I said was true, why did you slap me*]?

24 Now Annas had sent him bound [*still tied up to make sure he could not escape*] unto Caiaphas the high priest.

Peter Denies the Second Time

25 And Simon Peter stood and warmed himself. They said therefore unto him, Art not thou also one of his disciples? He denied it, and said, I am not.

26 One of the servants of the high priest, being his kinsman whose ear Peter cut off, saith, Did not I see thee in the garden with him? [*This man had good reason to recognize Peter!*]

Peter Denies the Third Time

27 Peter then denied again: and immediately the cock crew [*the rooster crowed*].

28 Then led they Jesus from Caiaphas unto the hall of judgment [*to the Roman governor's place*]: and it was early [*in the morning; the two previous trials before Annas and Caiaphas had taken place during the night*]; and they themselves went not into the judgment hall, lest they should be defiled [*be made unclean*]; but that they might eat the passover.

It is ironic and sad to think that, even while they were turning the "Lamb of God" over to be executed, they themselves were being very careful not to become unclean in any way that might prevent them from finishing Passover worship, in which they showed gratitude for blessings received by the shedding of the blood of sacrificial lambs, representing Christ.

Tried before Pilate

29 Pilate then went out unto them, and said, What accusation bring ye against this man [*what are you accusing Jesus of*]?

30 They answered and said unto him, If he were not a malefactor [*criminal*], we would not have delivered him up [*turned Him over*] unto thee.

31 Then said Pilate unto them, Take ye him, and judge him according to your law [*you handle it*]. The Jews therefore said unto him, It is not lawful for us to put any man to death [*under Roman law, we Jews cannot execute anyone*]:

32 That the saying of Jesus might be fulfilled, which he spake, signifying what death he should die.

Watch now as Pilate asks Jesus specifically if He is the King of the Jews. Jesus will ask him a question in return.

33 Then Pilate entered into the judgment hall again, and called Jesus, and said unto him, Art thou the King of the Jews?

34 Jesus answered him, Sayest thou this thing of thyself, or did others tell it thee of me [*are you asking because you, yourself, want to know, or because others have told you I am*]?

35 Pilate answered, Am I a Jew [*how should I know what is going on; I am not a Jew*]? Thine own nation and the chief priests have delivered thee unto me: what hast thou done?

36 Jesus answered, My kingdom is not of this world: if my kingdom were of this world [*if this were my time to be king on earth*], then would my servants fight, that I should not be delivered to the Jews: but now is my kingdom not from hence [*here on earth*]. [*The time will come, during the Millennium, when Christ becomes everyone's King here on earth, literally. But that time has not yet come at the time Pilate is questioning the Master.*]

The answer Jesus gives to Pilate, in verse 37, next, is a brief and beautiful summary statement of the Savior's mortal mission.

37 Pilate therefore said unto him, Art thou a king then? Jesus answered, Thou sayest that I am a king. To this end was I born [*for this purpose I was born*], and for this cause came I into the world, that I should bear witness unto the truth. Every one that is of the truth heareth [*hears and obeys*] my voice.

38 Pilate saith unto him, What is truth? And when he had said this, he went out again unto the Jews, and saith unto them, I find in him no fault at all [*I do not find Jesus guilty of anything*].

39 But ye have a custom [*you have a tradition*], that I should release unto you one at the passover [*every year, at Passover time, I release a criminal of your choosing*]: will ye therefore that I [*would you like me to*] release unto you the King of the Jews?

Next, the Jews, who have crowded the courtyard of the Roman governor, and who have been incited by their religious leaders to demand the crucifixion of Jesus, respond loudly to Pilate's question.

40 Then cried they all again, saying, Not this man, but Barabbas. Now Barabbas was a robber.

Ironically, the name "Barabbas" means "son of the father" (see Bible Dictionary, under "Barabbas"). This may be symbolic in that the "imposter," Satan, stirred up the multitude to demand the release of an "imposter," Barabbas, while the true "Son of the Father" is punished for crimes which He did not commit.

JOHN 19

THIS CHAPTER IS John's account of the crucifixion of the Savior. While all four of the Gospels writers (Matthew, Mark, Luke, and John) give an account of the Crucifixion, John adds much that is not mentioned by the other three. The following is a list of verses from this chapter of John which contain unique information or significant additions to what the other recorded:

Unique Contributions of John

Verses in John 19 which contain unique information about the Crucifixion: 1–5, 8–14, 16–17, 20–27, 31–37, 39.

Scourging

1 THEN Pilate therefore took Jesus, and scourged him [*had Him whipped*].

Scourging involved tying the victim to a frame or column, with the arms pulled tightly upward to put tension on the back muscles, and then whipping him with a whip which was made of leather strips with sharp bits of metal and bone fastened to them. Often, a victim of scourging did not survive to continue on to be crucified.

The Crown of Thorns and Mocking

2 And the soldiers platted [*wove*] a crown of thorns, and put it on his head, and they put on him a purple robe [*mockingly symbolic of His being "King of the Jews"*],

3 And said, Hail, King of the Jews! and they smote [*hit*] him with their hands.

4 Pilate therefore went forth again, and saith unto them, Behold, I bring him forth to you, that ye may know that I find no fault in him [*I do not find Him guilty of any crime*].

5 Then came Jesus forth [*where the crowd could see Him*], wearing the crown of thorns, and the purple robe. And Pilate saith unto them, Behold the man [*just look at this pitiful man*]!

"Crucify Him!"

6 When the chief priests therefore and officers saw him, they cried out, saying, Crucify him, crucify him. Pilate saith unto them, Take ye him, and crucify him: for I find no fault in him.

7 The Jews answered him, We have a law [*a law against blasphemy (mocking God) making it punishable by death*], and by our law he ought to die, because he made himself [*claimed to be*] the Son of God.

Pilate Is Afraid

8 When Pilate therefore heard that saying, he was the more afraid;

9 And went again into the judgment hall, and saith [*said*] unto Jesus, Whence art thou [*where do You come from*]? But Jesus gave him no answer.

10 Then saith Pilate unto him, Speakest thou not unto me? knowest thou not that I have power to crucify thee, and have power to release thee? [*Don't You think You ought to answer me. Don't You realize I have power to have You crucified or to set You free?*]

11 Jesus answered, Thou couldest have no power at all against me, except it were given thee from above: therefore he that delivered me unto thee hath the greater sin [*referring to Caiaphas; see McConkie,* Doctrinal New Testament Commentary, *Vol. 1, p. 809*]

12 And from thenceforth [*from then on*] Pilate sought [*tried*] to release him: but the Jews cried out, saying, If thou let this man go, thou art not Cæsar's friend: whosoever maketh himself a king speaketh against Cæsar. [*If you release Him, you are not loyal to Caesar, because Jesus claims to be the king, instead of Caesar.*]

13 When Pilate therefore heard that saying [*that it could appear that Jesus was undermining the Roman government*], he brought Jesus forth, and sat down in the judgment seat in a place that is called the Pavement, but in the Hebrew, Gabbatha.

14 And it was the preparation of the passover, and about the sixth hour: and he saith unto the Jews, Behold [*look*] your King!

15 But they cried out, Away with him, away with him, crucify him. Pilate saith unto them, Shall I crucify your King? The chief priest [*Caiaphas*] answered, We have no king but Cæsar.

The Crucifixion

16 Then delivered he [*Pilate*] him [*Jesus*] therefore

unto them to be crucified. And they took Jesus, and led him away.

17 And he bearing his cross went forth into a place called the place of a skull, which is called in the Hebrew Golgotha:

JST JOHN 19:17

17 And he bearing his cross went forth into a place called the place of a burial; which is called in the Hebrew Golgotha;

18 Where they crucified him, and two other [*the two thieves*] with him, on either side one, and Jesus in the midst [*middle*].

Next, Pilate frustrates and angers the chief priests by instructing that a sign be placed on the cross. They ask him to rework the wording on the sign, but he refuses.

19 And Pilate wrote a title, and put it on the cross. And the writing was, JESUS OF NAZARETH THE KING OF THE JEWS.

20 This title then read many of the Jews: for the place where Jesus was crucified was nigh [*near*] to the city: and it was written in Hebrew, and Greek, and Latin.

21 Then said the chief priests of the Jews to Pilate, Write not, The King of the Jews; but that he said, I am King of the Jews. [*Don't write "King of the Jews," rather, write "He claimed to be King of the Jews."*]

22 Pilate answered, What I have written I have written [*I will not change it*].

23 Then the soldiers, when they had crucified Jesus, took his garments [*clothes*], and made four parts [*and divided them into four piles*], to every soldier a part; and also his coat: now the coat was without seam, woven from the top throughout [*was woven as one continuous piece of fabric*].

24 They said therefore among themselves, Let us not rend it [*tear the coat into four pieces*], but cast lots [*gamble*] for it, whose it shall be: that the scripture [*Psalm 22:18*] might be fulfilled, which saith, They parted my raiment [*clothing*] among them, and for my vesture [*clothing*] they did cast lots. These things therefore [*to fulfill prophecy*] the soldiers did.

Next, Jesus, despite His extreme pain, focuses on His mother, Mary, and asks John to take care of her after He is gone. This implies that Joseph had already passed away and that Mary was a widow.

25 Now there stood by the cross of Jesus his mother [*Mary*], and his mother's sister, Mary the wife of Cleophas, and Mary Magdalene. [*Mary was a very beautiful and common name among the Jews.*]

26 When Jesus therefore saw his mother, and the disciple [*John the Beloved Apostle*] standing by, whom he loved, he saith unto his mother, Woman [*a term of great respect in Jewish culture*], behold thy son!

27 Then saith he to the disciple [*John*], Behold thy mother! And from that hour that disciple took her unto his own home. [*The Savior asked John to take care of His mother from then on, and he did.*]

The Savior's Mortal Mission Is Finished

28 After this, Jesus knowing that all things were now accomplished [*knowing that He had now finished everything which the Atonement required of Him as a mortal*], that the scripture might be fulfilled, saith, I thirst.

29 Now there was a vessel full of vinegar, mingled with gall, and they filled a sponge with it, and put upon hyssop, and put to his mouth.

30 When Jesus therefore had received the vinegar, he said, It is finished: and he bowed his head, and gave up the ghost [*and left his body*].

Elder James E. Talmage points out that Jesus accepted the vinegar mixture (verse 30) only after "all things were . . . accomplished" (verse 28). In other words, He refused to accept anything that would provide any relief from His suffering, until all the mortal requirements of the Atonement were satisfied. See *Jesus the Christ*, 1982 edition, p. 661.

Seven Statements from the Cross

Jesus uttered a total of seven recorded statements from the cross. The references for these statements and the statements themselves follow, and are in chronological order:

1. Luke 23:34: "Father, forgive them; for they know not what they do."
2. Luke 23:43: "Today shalt thou be with me in paradise."
3. John 19:26-27: "Woman, behold thy son!"; "Behold thy mother!"
4. Matthew 27:46: "My God, my God, why hast thou forsaken me?"
5. John 19:28: "I thirst."
6. John 19:30: "It is finished."
7. Luke 23:46: "Father, into thy hands I commend my spirit."

31 The Jews therefore, because it was the preparation [*time to make preparations for the Sabbath*], that the bodies should not remain upon the cross on the sabbath day, (for that sabbath day was an high day,) besought Pilate that their legs might be broken, and that they might be taken away.

Among the Jews at this time in history, the days of the week, Monday, Tuesday, etc., went from about sundown to about sundown of the next day, rather than from midnight to midnight as is the case with our calendar system. Therefore, the Jewish religious leaders were very concerned about violating one of their laws which said people should not be crucified on the Sabbath. Their Sabbath (held on Saturday) would start at about six Friday evening. Jesus and the two thieves had been crucified at about nine that morning (Friday). Persons being crucified often lived two or three days. Therefore, these religious rulers of the Jews asked Pilate to have soldiers break the legs of the three "criminals" who were being crucified to kill them with additional pain and shock, so that their bodies could be taken off their crosses in order to avoid violating the Sabbath. Pilate agreed and sent soldiers to do the deed.

32 Then came the soldiers, and brake [*broke*] the legs of the first [*one of the thieves*], and of the other [*thief*] which was crucified with him.

33 But when they came to Jesus, and saw that he was dead already, they brake not his legs:

34 But one of the soldiers with a spear pierced his side, and forthwith came there out blood and water.

35 And he [*John; see John 19:25, footnote 35a*] that saw it bare record, and his record [*the Gospel of John*] is true: and he knoweth that he saith true, that ye might believe.

Remember that we mentioned previously that John always refers to himself indirectly in his writing, as is the case in verse 35, above.

Next, John points out two prophecies which were fulfilled by what he just recorded in verses 33–34.

36 For these things were done, that the scripture [*Psalm 34:20, Numbers 9:12*] should be fulfilled [*in order to fulfill the prophecy which says*], A bone of him shall not be broken.

37 And again another scripture [*Zechariah 12:10*] saith, They shall look on him whom they pierced.

JOHN

Joseph of Arimathaea Requests Permission to Remove the Body of Jesus from the Cross

38 And after this Joseph of Arimathæa [*from Ramah; a member of the Sanhedrin, see Bible Dictionary, under "Joseph"*], being a disciple of Jesus, but secretly for fear of the Jews, besought [*asked*] Pilate that he might take away the body of Jesus: and Pilate gave him leave [*permission*]. He came therefore, and took the body of Jesus.

Nicodemus Helps

39 And there came also Nicodemus [*one of the Jewish religious rulers, see Bible Dictionary, under "Nicodemus"*], which at the first came to Jesus by night [*John 3:2*], and brought a mixture of myrrh and aloes [*costly spices with which to prepare Christ's body for burial*], about an hundred pound weight.

40 Then took they [*Joseph and Nicodemus*] the body of Jesus, and wound it in linen clothes with the spices, as the manner [*custom*] of the Jews is to bury.

Jesus' Body Is Placed in a New Tomb

41 Now in the place where he was crucified there was a garden; and in the garden a new sepulchre [*tomb*], wherein was never man yet laid [*which had never been used*].

42 There laid they Jesus therefore because of the Jews' preparation day; for the sepulchre was nigh [*near*] at hand. [*There was an urgency to get Jesus' body into a tomb, in order not to violate the approaching Sabbath, and this tomb was close by.*]

Imagine the Savior's feelings, having left His pain-ridden mortal body, as He now enters spirit world paradise where "an innumerable company of the spirits of the just, who had been faithful" (D&C 138:12) await Him. From rejection, mocking, and crucifixion He now enters the realm where faithful Saints welcome Him and anxiously await His message to them. Among other things, He will inform them that their long wait for resurrection is over and that they will be resurrected with Him in a short three days. He will organize them into a great missionary force through which His gospel will be preached to the spirits in spirit prison (D&C 138:30–34).

JOHN 20

IT IS EARLY Sunday morning, and the Savior, having come from a joyful reception for Him in spirit world paradise (D&C 138:11-19), has been resurrected and is preparing to appear to His faithful disciples who still don't grasp the fact that He will literally return to them as a resurrected personage (as John explained in John 12:16).

Imagine John's feelings as he records this part of his account. He was one of the first of the brethren to come to the empty tomb after being told by the women (who had already been to the tomb) that the Master had been resurrected. While John only mentions Mary Magdalene here, Luke informs us that other women were with her (Luke 24:10), and Mark tells us that Mary, the mother of James, and Salome accompanied Mary Magdalene (Mark 16:1).

In John's account, he tells us of Mary Magdalene seeing the open tomb first, and then running and telling Peter and John. Then he modestly informs us that he outran Peter to the empty tomb but waited until Peter arrived and then went into the tomb after Peter entered it.

Next, he shows us that the resurrected Lord appeared to Mary Magdalene and then to the disciples. Thomas is not there for that appearance and declares that he will not believe it unless he sees for himself. Eight days later, he will see, and will believe.

We will now get more details from John's record in this chapter.

Mary Magdalene Comes to the Tomb

1 THE first day of the week [*Sunday*] cometh Mary Magdalene early, when it was yet dark, unto the sepulchre [*Christ's tomb*], and seeth the stone taken away from the sepulchre.

JST JOHN 20:1
1 The first day of the week cometh Mary Magdalene early, when it was yet dark, unto the sepulcher, and seeth the stone taken away from the sepulcher, and two angels sitting thereon.

2 Then she runneth, and cometh to Simon Peter, and to the other disciple [*John*], whom Jesus loved, and saith unto them, They have taken away the Lord out of the sepulchre, and we [*the ladies mentioned above*] know not where they have laid him.

Peter and John Run to the Tomb

3 Peter therefore went forth, and that other disciple [*John*], and came to the sepulchre.

4 So they ran both together: and the other disciple did outrun Peter [*John outran Peter*], and came first to the sepulchre.

5 And he stooping down, and looking in, saw the linen clothes lying; yet went he not in. [*John waited for Peter to arrive.*]

6 Then cometh Simon Peter following him, and went into the sepulchre [*tomb*], and seeth the linen clothes lie [*saw the strips of linen which Joseph and Nicodemus had used to wrap the Savior's body in*],

7 And the napkin [*burial cloth*], that was about [*was wrapped around*] his head, not lying with the linen clothes, but wrapped together [*folded*] in a place by itself.

8 Then went in also that other disciple [*John*], which came first to the sepulchre, and he saw, and believed.

9 For as yet they knew not [*did not understand*] the scripture, that he must rise again from the dead [*as John explained in John 12:16*].

10 Then the disciples went away again unto their own home.

JST JOHN 20:10
10 Then the disciples went away again unto their own homes.

Jesus Appears to Mary Magdalene

11 But Mary [*Mary Magdalene; see verse 1*] stood without [*outside*] at the sepulchre weeping: and as she wept, she stooped down, and looked into the sepulchre,

12 And seeth two angels in white sitting, the one at the head, and the other at the feet, where the body of Jesus had lain.

13 And they say [*said*] unto her, Woman, why weepest thou? She saith unto them, Because they have taken away my Lord, and I know not where they have laid him. [*Someone has taken Jesus' body away, and I don't know where they put it.*]

14 And when she had thus said, she turned herself back [*away from the angels*], and saw Jesus standing, and knew not that it was Jesus.

15 Jesus saith unto her, Woman, why weepest thou? whom seekest thou? She, supposing him to be the gardener, saith unto him, Sir, if thou have borne him hence [*if you have taken His body somewhere*], tell me where thou hast laid him, and I will take him away.

16 Jesus saith unto her, Mary. She turned herself, and saith unto him, Rabboni; which is to say, Master.

This is a very tender moment. Mary is very concerned about where the Savior's body has been taken. After turning away from the tomb and the two angels therein, she sees a man whom she assumes is the caretaker. The question comes up as to why she did not immediately recognize Jesus. Several possibilities exist. One is that she had been crying and was so distraught that she didn't even take a good look at Jesus at first. Another possibility is that she hadn't turned all the way around from the tomb. She "turned herself back" from the tomb and the angels in verse 14, yet she "turned herself" in verse 16, implying that she had not turned completely toward where Jesus was standing when she first turned from the tomb. Whatever the explanation, when Jesus said "Mary," she recognized His voice, apparently looked again, and her sorrow was over.

17 Jesus saith unto her, Touch me not; for I am not yet ascended to my Father: but go to my brethren, and say unto them, I ascend unto my Father, and your Father; and to my God, and your God.

JST JOHN 20:17
17 Jesus saith unto her, Hold me not; for I am not yet ascended to my Father; but go to my brethren, and say unto them, I ascend unto my Father, and your Father; and to my God, and your God.

The Joseph Smith Translation change in verse 17, above, may solve a bit of a problem otherwise encountered when reading Matthew and then reading John. The common understanding of verse 17 is that the resurrected Lord told Mary not to touch Him. Yet, Matthew 28:8–9 informs us that some women were met by Jesus as they ran from the empty tomb to tell the disciples that the Master's body was gone. They were allowed to hold Him by the feet and worship him. So why was Mary Magdalene not allowed to touch Him (John 20:17)? The answer may be, that she was. The JST changes "touch me not" to "hold me not." The Greek, which was translated as "touch me not" in our New Testament, is often translated as "do not hold me" or "do not hold on to me." The Greek word itself is "harpazo," which is the continuous action of holding. Strong's *Exhaustive Concordance* #0680, defines it as "to fasten one's self to, adhere to, cling to." Thus, it is possible, using the JST as a reference, that Jesus was, in effect, telling Mary "Don't keep holding Me. I must leave." Whatever the case, we will certainly get clarification on it some day.

18 Mary Magdalene came and told the disciples that she had seen the Lord, and that he had spoken these things unto her.

Jesus Appears to the Disciples

19 Then the same day at evening, being the first day of the week [*Sunday*], when the doors were shut where the disciples were assembled for fear of the Jews [*the disciples were afraid that the Jews would arrest them too*], came Jesus and stood in the midst, and saith unto them, Peace be unto you.

20 And when he had so said, he shewed [*showed*] unto them his hands and his side. Then were the disciples glad, when they saw the Lord.

21 Then said Jesus to them again, Peace be unto you: as my Father hath sent me, even so send I you.

22 And when he had said this, he breathed on them, and saith unto them, Receive ye the Holy Ghost:

In the Jewish culture, "breathed on them" is very significant. The same word is used in Genesis 2:7, where God breathed on Adam and he became a living soul. The symbolism in verse 17, above, seems to be that of "breathing" additional life or "power" into the Apostles. In April Conference, 1955, Apostle Harold B. Lee suggested that it was at this time, after the Savior's death, that He confirmed them and gave them the Gift of the Holy Ghost. This would certainly fit in with Christ's promise to His Apostles that, after He had gone, He would send them "another Comforter" (the Holy Ghost). See John 14:16.

23 Whose soever sins ye remit [*forgive*], they are remitted unto them; and whose soever sins ye retain, they are retained.

Thomas Doubts

24 But Thomas, one of the twelve, called Didymus [*meaning "twin"*], was not with them when Jesus came.

25 The other disciples therefore said unto him, We have seen the Lord. But he said unto them, Except I shall see in his hands the print of the nails, and put my finger into the print of the nails, and thrust my hand into his side, I will not believe. [*This is how Thomas came to be known as "Doubting Thomas."*]

Thomas Sees the Resurrected Christ

26 And after eight days again his disciples were within [*inside the house*], and Thomas with them: then came Jesus, the doors being shut, and stood in the midst, and said, Peace be unto you.

27 Then saith he to Thomas, Reach hither [*here*] thy finger, and behold [*look at*] my hands; and reach hither thy hand, and thrust it into my side: and be not faithless, but believing.

28 And Thomas answered and said unto him, My Lord and my God.

29 Jesus saith unto him, Thomas, because thou hast seen me, thou hast believed: blessed are they that have not seen, and yet have believed.

30 And many other signs truly did Jesus in the presence of his disciples, which are not written in this book:

John, having born his testimony to us in verse 30, above, now finishes this chapter by explaining why he has selected the things he has written for us.

31 But these are written, that ye might believe that Jesus is the Christ, the Son of God; and that believing ye might have life [*eternal life, exaltation*] through his name.

RECEIVE YE THE HOLY GHOST.

JOHN 20:22

JOHN 21

IN MATTHEW 26:32, Jesus told His Apostles that He would meet them in Galilee after His resurrection. Matthew 28:9–10 informs us that He told the women to tell the brethren to go to Galilee and there they would see Him. And Matthew 28:16 records that before Jesus' crucifixion, He had "appointed them" to meet Him in Galilee after His death.

In this beautiful chapter, John tells us that they followed those instructions and he gives us details about what took place. There are no JST additions or corrections for this chapter.

1 AFTER these things [*after everything John has told us so far*] Jesus shewed [*showed*] himself again to the disciples at the sea of Tiberias [*the Sea of Galilee*]; and on this wise shewed he himself [*and this is how He showed himself to them*].

As we get to verse 2, next, several of the disciples have already journeyed to Galilee in anticipation of meeting the Savior there. While waiting there, they have decided to go fishing.

2 There were together Simon Peter, and Thomas called Didymus, and Nathanael of Cana in Galilee, and the sons of Zebedee [*James and John*], and two other of his disciples.

3 Simon Peter saith unto them, I go a fishing. They say unto him, We also go with thee. They went forth, and entered into a ship immediately; and that night they caught nothing.

In the days of Jesus, it was common for fishermen to fish at night on the Sea of Galilee, when the fishing was best. Peter, having been a professional fisherman on that lake before the Savior said "Come follow me," now takes his fellow disciples and they fish all night, with absolutely no success. The "sons of Zebedee," verse 2 above, were James and John, and they, too, had been professional fishermen, before being called by Jesus to follow Him. It must have been extra frustrating for these professionals to have zero success fishing. Watch now as the Savior gets their attention. Perhaps it is appropriate to imagine a bit of a smile on His face and a twinkle in His eye.

4 But when the morning was now come, Jesus stood on the shore: but the disciples knew not that it was Jesus. [*He was apparently far enough away that they didn't recognize Him.*]

Something quite wonderful is now going to happen. The tired disciples have had absolutely no success fishing throughout the night. In the morning, this stranger on the shore asks them if they have had any luck. He then tells them to simply cast their net overboard on the other side of the ship. Perhaps there are few things worse than a stranger telling professionals how to do their work. Nevertheless, they do what He says and suddenly the net fills with so many fish (153 big fish, see verse 11) that they could hardly pull it in.

This rings a bell. An almost identical thing had happened three years ago when He first called Peter, Andrew, James, and John (see Luke 5:1–11). Jesus had come by, and because of the crowd, had requested that Peter take Him a little way out from the shore in his ship. When He was through speaking to the crowd, He told Peter to go out farther into the lake and let down his nets. Peter replied that they had fished all night with no success, but, since Jesus said to do it, he did. Their net filled with so many fish that the net began to break. James and John quickly brought their ship out to help, and the large number of fish almost sank both ships.

Now, the same thing is happening again. Could it be the Master who is on the shore now?

5 Then Jesus saith unto them, Children, have ye any meat [*have you caught any fish*]? They answered him, No.

6 And he said unto them, Cast the net on the right side of the ship, and ye shall find. They cast therefore, and now they were not able to draw it [*bring it in*] for the multitude [*because of the large number*] of fishes.

7 Therefore that disciple whom Jesus loved [*in other words, John, the Beloved Apostle*] saith unto Peter, It is the Lord. Now when Simon Peter heard that it was the Lord, he girt his fisher's coat unto him, (for he was naked [*stripped to the waist*],) and did cast himself into the sea [*Peter jumped in and swam to shore, a distance of about 300 feet—see verse 8*].

8 And the other disciples came in a little ship; (for they were not far from land, but as it were two hundred cubits [*about a hundred yards*],) dragging the net with fishes.

9 As soon then as they were come to land, they saw a fire of coals there, and fish laid thereon, and bread.

This is a very touching scene. No one in the universe could be busier than the Savior. Yet He had taken the time to cook breakfast for His weary, discouraged disciples who had fished all night with no success.

10 Jesus saith unto them, Bring of the fish which ye have now caught.

11 Simon Peter went up, and drew the net to land full of great [*large*] fishes, an hundred and fifty and three: and for all there were so many, yet was not the net broken.

There is symbolism here. Jesus told the Apostles, when He called them, that He would make them "fishers of men" (Matthew 4:19). The fact that the Savior helped them have such success with actual fish is symbolic of the fact that He will help them have great success in bringing souls into the gospel net and unto the Father.

12 Jesus saith unto them, Come and dine. And none of the disciples durst ask him, Who art thou? knowing that it was the Lord.

13 Jesus then cometh, and taketh bread, and giveth them, and fish likewise.

14 This is now the third time that Jesus shewed himself to his disciples, after that he was risen from the dead.

Next, the Master Teacher creates a teaching moment and uses it to teach Peter, who will become the President of the Church. He repeats the main point of the lesson three times, in verses 15, 16, and 17.

Feed My Sheep

15 So when they had dined, Jesus saith to Simon Peter, Simon, son of Jonas, lovest thou me more than these [*do you love me more than these fish*]? He saith unto him, Yea, Lord; thou knowest that I love thee. He saith unto him, Feed my lambs.

16 He saith to him again the second time, Simon, son of Jonas, lovest thou me? He saith unto him, Yea, Lord; thou knowest that I love thee. He saith unto him, Feed my sheep.

17 He saith unto him the third time, Simon, son of Jonas, lovest thou me? Peter was grieved because he said unto him the third time, Lovest thou me? And he said unto him, Lord, thou knowest all things; thou knowest that I love thee. Jesus saith unto him, Feed my sheep.

Next, in verses 18–19, Jesus tells Peter that he will be crucified when his mission is over.

Jesus Foretells Peter's Martyrdom

18 Verily, verily, I say unto thee, When thou wast young, thou girdedst thyself [*dressed yourself*], and walkedst whither thou wouldest [*and went wherever you wanted to*]: but when thou shalt be old, thou shalt stretch forth thy hands [*you will be crucified*], and another shall gird thee, and carry thee whither thou wouldest not [*where you don't want to go*].

19 This spake he, signifying by what death he should glorify God. [*Jesus thus indicated to Peter how he would die when his mortal mission was over*.] And when he had spoken this, he saith unto him, Follow me.

Bruce R. McConkie explained verses 18–19, above. He taught

"'Thou shalt follow me,' our Lord said to Peter on that recent day when the chief apostle pledged, 'I will lay down my life for thy sake' (John 13:36–38). How literally the Master then spoke, and how fully Peter is to do as he offered, he now learns. He is to be crucified, a thing which John in this passage assumes to be known to his readers. Peter's arms are to be stretched forth upon the cross, the executioner shall gird him with the loin-cloth which criminals wear when crucified, and he shall be carried where he would not, that is to his execution (2 Pet. 1:14–15; *Doctrinal New Testament Commentary*, Vol. 1, p. 863).

20 Then Peter, turning about, seeth the disciple whom Jesus loved [*John*] following; which also leaned on his breast at supper [*at the last supper—see John 13:23*], and said [*asked the question*], Lord, which is he that betrayeth thee?

21 Peter seeing him [*John*] saith to Jesus, Lord, and what shall this man do [*what will happen to John*]?

John Will Be Translated

22 Jesus saith unto him, If I will that he tarry till I come *[if I want him to remain alive until my second coming]*, what is that to thee? follow thou me.

23 Then went this saying abroad among the brethren, that that disciple *[John]* should *[would]* not die: yet Jesus said not unto him, He shall not die; but, If I will that he tarry till I come, what is that to thee?

Because of the wording of verses 22 and 23 above, it is not clear from the Bible whether or not John was allowed to remain on earth until the Second Coming. However, through modern revelation, in D&C 7:3, we know that John was allowed to remain. He was translated and will not die until the Lord's coming. Joseph Smith gave us more information about John in *History of the Church*, volume 1, p. 176. He said that at that time, 1831, John was working with the lost ten tribes, preparing them for their return. More information about translated beings can be found in 3 Nephi 28, where details about the Three Nephites are given.

Finally, strong testimony is born to us that the things written by John are true.

24 This is the disciple which testifieth of these things, and wrote these things: and we know that his testimony is true.

25 And there are also many other things which Jesus did, the which, if they should be written every one, I suppose that even the world itself could not contain the books that should be written. Amen.

This concludes Part 1 of The New Testament Made Easier (Family Deluxe Edition). Part II of The New Testament Made Easier (Family Deluxe Edition) covers the remainder of The New Testament from Acts through Revelation.

ARTWORK

ROBERT T. BARRETT

The Baptism of Christ

Christ and Peter

Christ Teaching

Woman at the Well

LIZ LEMON SWINDLE

No Man Knoweth the Hour

The Sower

Gethsemane

Without Purse or Scrip

The Prodigal Son

He That Is Without Sin

Lord, I Believe

ARTWORK

ELSPETH YOUNG

Go Forth to Meet the Bridegroom

And Martha Served

JOSEPH F. BRICKEY

Annunciation to Mary

The Good Samaritan

SOURCES

Martin Luther edition of the German Bible, which Joseph Smith said was the most correct of any then available.

McConkie, Bruce R. *Doctrinal New Testament Commentary (DNTC)*. 3 vols. Salt Lake City: Bookcraft, 1965–73.

McConkie, Bruce R. *Mormon Doctrine*. 2d ed. Salt Lake City: Bookcraft, 1966.

McConkie, Bruce R. *The Mortal Messiah*. Salt Lake City: Deseret Book, 1979.

New International Version of the Holy Bible (NIV). Grand Rapids, Michigan: Zondervan Publishing House, 1984.

Smith, Joseph. *History of The Church of Jesus Christ of Latter-day Saints (HC)*. Edited by B. H. Roberts. 2d ed. rev., 7 vols., Salt Lake City: The Church of Jesus Christ of Latter-day Saints, 1932–51.

Smith, Joseph. *Joseph Smith's "New Translation" of the Bible* (JST). Independence, Missouri: Herald Publishing House, 1970.

Smith, Joseph. *Teachings of the Prophet Joseph Smith (TPJS)*. Selected by Joseph Fielding Smith. Salt Lake City: Deseret Book, 1976.

Strong, James. *The Exhaustive Concordance of the Bible*. Nashville: Abingdon, 1890.

Talmage, James E. *Jesus the Christ*. Salt Lake City: Deseret Book, 1962.

The Life and Teachings of Jesus and His Apostles, The New Testament Student Manual, Religion 211. Salt Lake City: The Church of Jesus Christ of Latter-day Saints, 1979.

About the Author

DAVID J. RIDGES taught for the Church Educational System for thirty-five years and taught for several years at BYU Campus Education Week. He taught adult religion classes and Know Your Religion classes for BYU Continuing Education for many years. He has also served as a curriculum writer for Sunday School, seminary, and institute of religion manuals.

He has served in many callings in the Church, including Gospel Doctrine teacher, bishop, stake president, and patriarch. He and Sister Ridges have served two full-time CES missions together. They are the parents of six children and grandparents of eleven grandchildren so far. They make their home in Springville, Utah.

CFI CEDAR FORT
Publishing & Media
AN IMPRINT OF CEDAR FORT, INC.

ISBN 978-1-4621-1474-0 USA $49.99 CAN $56.99

WWW.DAVIDJRIDGES.COM
WWW.CEDARFORT.COM